THE MACMILLAN COMPANY
NEW YORK • CHICAGO
DALLAS • ATLANTA • SAN FRANCISCO
LONDON • MANILA
BRETT-MACMILLAN LTD.
TORONTO

ALEXANDER HAMILTON

Youth to Maturity

1755-1788

ALEXANDER HAMILTON

Youth to Maturity

1755-1788

by

Broadus Mitchell

★

New York

The Macmillan Company

1957

© Broadus Mitchell 1957

First Printing

Gen'l,

Printed in the United States of America

Library of Congress catalog card number: 57–5506

o   7-23-57

To
Louise Pearson Mitchell

Contents

[vii]

Foreword

FEW IN American history have been so creative as Alexander Hamilton. His passion was the construction of a well knit, prosperous nation. He furnished not only purposes, but means for carrying these into effect. He was in many ways foremost in fashioning in this new country a firm, representative republic. His economic insight and skill are not to be separated from his political and legal objects, for each was the vehicle of the other. He was quick to understand that national wealth and well-being consist not merely in material resources, but in social organization.

Hamilton has been typed in the minds of too many as the brilliant strategist of a privileged class and, in the same behalf, as the deft technician of the Treasury. Both estimates diminish his true greatness. The first notion makes him the foil of Thomas Jefferson, taken as the evangel of democracy. In this view Hamilton, the advocate of partisan policy, has been put in opposition to a more generous and enduring philosophy. These talented leaders were surely hostile to each other in the formation of the United States, but they emerge, in a just rehearsal of their lives, as complementary protagonists. Hamilton's preachment was so blended with his practice that his contribution to the American achievement does not stand out with the purity of Jefferson's signal idea. Actually, each partook of the other, and succeeding generations may be thankful to both. If a contrast we must have, then Jefferson stood for rights, Hamilton for responsibility.

As to the second contracted conception of Hamilton, his distinction among finance ministers rests upon more than fiscal competence, for his Treasury measures were but instruments in an imaginative national program. The particulars of funding and taxes with which he dealt in office, unfamiliar to most then and since, have tended to put him beyond ready understanding, and to make him, accordingly, the object of undiscriminating enthu-

[ix]

siasm or suspicion, depending upon the observer. The basis of his Treasury policy was philosophical and moral, and, given his principles, another could have translated them into practical devices. Not the least of his premises, giving wide limits to his plans and reports, was his confidence in the future growth of the economy of the country. Seeking to promote this varied development, he rejected *laissez faire* as announced by Adam Smith in Britain. Instead, in a young nation, rich in potential resources, but immature, with a sparse population, he invoked the power of central government to promote and correct economic forces. Thus it came that, so far from individualist, he was collectivist. He owed much to the mercantilist statesmen who had passed from the scene in Europe, but who offered, in modern terms, an early example of national economic planning.

If Hamilton was in contrast personally and politically to Jefferson, he coincided with the purposes of Washington. From the time they met, in spite of and because of differences in gifts, they developed a remarkable partnership. It is impossible to portray the one without appreciation of the other. Washington's steadier judgment was supplemented by Hamilton's more fertile contrivance; Hamilton's successes, as public minister and party leader, could not have been registered without Washington's sponsorship. The association of these two is one of the delights in setting forth Hamilton's history.

Hamilton's life was intense, as though he foresaw it would be relatively short. His ambition and industry as a youth led at once to the championing and establishment of American independence. His restless zeal gave no interval for relaxation. All was grist to his mill; what he experienced immediately prompted proposal for remedy or extension, and no sooner did he urge a policy than he commenced devising means of realization. This tight sequence of object lesson, advocacy, and successful result has persuaded admirers and foes alike that Hamilton's achievement was semimiraculous. Inspection shows, of course, that he had models, in literature and in institutions, for his recommendations and administrative methods. But when these are discovered they yet remain a mechanical assemblage of aids. To swift selection, combination, and inference he added elements more readily praised than traced to any source except the capacity of genius.

Hamilton's precocity, or apparent precognition, is accounted for in some degree if we accept the tolerable evidence that he was in fact two years older than has generally been supposed.

Acquaint yourself with his thoughts and doings in pressing times as you will, you are constantly surprised by his inventiveness and facility. One of the keen pleasures in following his story is the verve and taste of his language. As others have remarked, paraphrase of Hamilton, though necessary for condensation, is impious, for he chose the right words to put his points.

This first of two volumes carries Hamilton's career through his triumph in ratification of the Constitution by New York in 1788. It falls roughly into three parts: (1) West Indian birth and boyhood, and apprenticeship in the counting house of Nicholas Cruger in Christiansted, St. Croix; (2) arrival on the mainland, youth and early manhood as aide-de-camp to General Washington in the Revolution; (3) vain attempts to bolster the frail Confederation, strengthening his resolve that it must be replaced by a competent central government; the Annapolis and Philadelphia conventions, the *Federalist* papers, and the culminating scene at Poughkeepsie. Hamilton's policies by this time were perfectly formed. It remained for him to embody them in a legislative and administrative program, focused in the Treasury but reaching into every department of governmental responsibility. Later, resumption of his busy law practice meant anything but retirement from public life. He continued as advisor of President Washington; as Federalist party leader, during much of John Adams' administration he governed out of office, often gratuitously. As inspector general of the army he prepared the country for a war with France that was fortunately averted. The advent of Jefferson's Republicans placed him in persevering opposition. This led to his last act of patriot honor, which established his political enemies and pulled the trigger of Burr's pistol by which he fell at Weehawken in 1804.

Alexander Hamilton, of fixed purpose as an architect of the new nation, yet had his human flaws. In an instance which he himself confessed for a praiseworthy reason, he offended against marital morals. He was guilty on a few occasions of political lapses unworthy of his high standard of public conduct. These may not be dismissed as amiable foibles; they were defects which,

however, reduce the paragon to the living person, and as such
are grateful features of the portrait. Numerous portrayers of
Hamilton and his contemporaries, unconcerned with minor demerits, have distorted the picture in a major respect. Lavishing
pains on the economic background, they have presented Hamilton
as a lay figure, the spokesman of property against the people. His
very virtues are given a sly, sinister cast. This plausible interpretation, cautious or crude in different hands, recommends itself as
revisionist realism. It professes itself historically profound.
While certain lights upon the subject are revealing, the pose is not
to the life.

At whatever danger of being called romantic, I reject this description of Hamilton's rôle. By trade an economist, with leanings to the popular side, I may escape the charge of naïve infatu-
ation. Hamilton was not a special pleader for the rich, constructing American institutions for the salvage and advancement of their
claims. His only client was the whole country. In a crisis of
confusion at home and abroad he sought stability and system in
which a young nation could mature. He availed himself of those
with a property stake in present and future. While others were
distracted, this group was compact, at once influential and man-
ageable. Here was a coalesced company whose demands coincided with the indispensable object of restored national credit.
Hamilton used them for a noble purpose, was not used by them.

This profile has its shadings. Hamilton's tastes and associations
were aristocratic. While his connections, marital and political,
were with families of wealth, and during the last decade he
earned an excellent income as a lawyer, he was never possessed
of capital, and declined proffers of funds that would have allowed
him to speculate. His attachment to the enterprising and the
fortunate was intellectual and personal rather than material.
Further, redolent democracy, as we have known it since, was then
in its beginnings. The ambition of American independence had
bulked larger than that of individual liberty. The feasibility of
popular government had not been demonstrated; manhood suffrage lay in the future. Slavery had been guaranteed twenty
years of imports of fresh Africans. The French Revolution was
notorious for violence, whatever promise it held of virtue. In
Britain the Industrial Revolution which a generation later was to

produce demands for reform of Parliament was only commencing. The Federalists had a name before their opponents were known as anything but Antis. The members of the constitutional convention, chosen by the legislatures, were all but unanimous in the plan of a central government which manifestly would not be agrarian in solicitude. The opponents of the Constitution, when it was submitted for adoption, were advocates of state autonomy rather than of democracy, and not always for admirable reasons. So that Hamilton, now thought of as protagonist of a cunning minority, really fell in with the majority position. Much of the censure visited upon him was because he admired the British constitution, not because he translated ours into action.

At the planting of the American nation, two modes of tending presented themselves. One was to cultivate for a vigorous root structure, nipping back some green shoots for that purpose. This preparatory method, involving an amount of national self-denial, was advocated by Hamilton. The other was to invite upper growth and quick blossoms, though the digging was shallow. This was the preference of the Anti-Federalists until, as more experienced National Republicans, they learned better, and adopted some of the practices of their opponents. The two courses have persisted in American public life, with changing party designations and with altering emphasis. Central authority or state volition? The wisdom of control or the philosophy of let-alone? More government or less? It is artificial to generalize about their relative values, for in the event each has amended the other, as was foreseen by the most prudent advocates on both sides. However favor fluctuates, Hamilton will always stand as patron of government guidance, while Jefferson remains the champion of local, even individual, free will. It is idle to speculate concerning Hamilton's allegiance were he able to return to the American scene. Such have been the mutations in times and terms that, with his penchant for employing organized direction, he might now be called not a conservative, but a liberal. Specifically, the collectivist developments during the depression of the 1930's might have hailed him as progenitor. He was fitted to approve much of the fiscal counsel of Lord Keynes.

It is possible, by selecting quotations, to represent that Hamilton had a trust in the people besides a constant concern for their welfare. However, the weight of testimony, over the years and in a variety of circumstances, indicates clearly more of paternalism than of fraternity.

Hamilton, as developer of national resources, has meaning for the modern world in which powerful rival governments contend for the loyalty of backward peoples. He knew how to replace anarchy by organization. But he did not suppose that this could be accomplished through material betterment alone, especially if conferred from the outside. The precious ingredient of improvement was political self-respect. While material sufficiency supported this, independence was the spring of the machine. Under present conditions of superior communication and transport which have contracted the globe, his penchant for consolidation of contiguous units into a larger jurisdiction would doubtless operate, though with preservation of autonomy in the new grouping. A parliament of man was hardly in his lexicon.

Some have divined that Hamilton's motive force was love of power, and that he imaged his personal ambition in an abstraction, the nation. But the American nation could not be conceived of, much less fashioned, except in terms of serviceable constitution, restored credit, lively commerce, and balanced production. Promotion of these means, with Hamilton, was in no sense narrow nor interested, but was an office of generous patriotism.

The reader exploring Alexander Hamilton's thoughts and actions is helped by a detail of his appearance and manner. He was below middle height, about five feet seven inches,[1] and slight of frame. All evidence agrees with Sullivan's testimony that he was "remarkably erect and dignified in his deportment."[2] Portraits from life[3] show features regular and well proportioned—a good forehead, nose longish and deeply indented at the bridge, mouth "moderately large," and firm chin.

"His complexion," said Sullivan, "was exceedingly fair, and varying from this only by the almost feminine rosiness of the cheeks. His might be considered, as to figure and color, an uncommonly handsome face."[4] His hair, of which we have several locks,[5] was of fine texture, brown with a hint of red; he wore it "turned back from his forehead, powdered and collected in a club behind."[6] His eyes were dark blue and deep set.

These are externals. His face in repose had a thoughtful, even "rather . . . severe" expression, which readily broke into smiling animation in conversation. "He united with dignity and feeling, and much force and decision, delightful manners, great sweetness, and was infinitely agreeable."[7] There was a gaiety about him, the other side of his intent disposition. The lilt seldom appears in his writings, but is plain in the record of certain of his friendships, as with John Laurens and his sister-in-law, Angelica Church.[8] His charm consisted not only of easy display of lively intellect. He was emotionally sympathetic, another name for his perception. His eloquence sprang from understanding and solicitude.

A word as to method of this book. A biographer who undertakes to rehearse the story must be often in doubt how far, and how frequently, to supplement recital with reflection on the meaning of an incident. Some interpretation is proper, as the materials exhibited are necessarily partial. Generally, within the limits of the author's industry (and, hopefully, the reader's patience), the facts have been allowed to speak for themselves, as the best means of avoiding bias.

Mere mention of their names gives no notion of my obligation to archivists and librarians whose ingenious kindness I received over long periods. They include especially Robert W. Hill, Edward Morrison, Jean McNiece, Sylvester Vigilante, Ivor Avellino, Lewis M. Stark, and Maud D. Cole, of the New York Public Library; Wayne Andrews and Wilmer R. Leech, of the New-York Historical Society; C. P. Powell and Elizabeth G. McPherson, of the Library of Congress; Thompson R. Harlow, of the Connecticut Historical Society; Stephen T. Riley, of the Massachusetts Historical Society; Milton Halsey Thomas, of the Columbia University Library; Clarence S. Brigham, of the American Antiquarian Society; Guy S. Klett, of the Presbyterian Historical Society; Joseph L. Andrews, of the Bar Association of New York; Landon M. Townsend and Polly Beaton, of the Bank of New York; W. Neil Franklin and Margareth Jorgensen, of the United States Archives. Without the unfailing help of Miss Jorgensen, I could never have located, much less explored, the rich materials in the Danish records of St. Croix now lodged in the United States Archives. As historian, archivist, and—beyond the call of duty—translator, she opened to me ledgers and lists that otherwise would have remained mute. Edgar Challenger and D. S. Brookes, of St. Christopher; Flavilla W. Losch, Harry E. Taylor, and C. R. Conrad, of St. Croix, gave me eager aid in the documents and local associations of the islands of Hamilton's youth. Axel Linvald, director of the Rigsarkivet, Copenhagen, kindly answered numerous inquiries, and arranged for me to have the help of J. O. Bro-Jørgensen, who verified references to materials in Copenhagen. Generalinde Julie Ramsing, of that city, aided me with reprints and cast additional light on the contribution of her late husband to Mrs. Atherton's work.

Rutgers University has been most generous in grants by the Research Council for travel and leave from teaching duties. Donald F. Cameron and Ellen C. Kelley of the library have a particular share of my gratitude. Joseph F. Talarico, Donald Tailby, and Philip Marcus each reviewed parts of the manuscript and saved me from slips. Ethel Baier deciphered before she could type. Many others, not named, have offered friendly suggestions, or have answered my questions, from specialized knowledge. My wife has exhorted me to precision without pedantry, and has been loyally patient when my project in authorship tested the marriage tie.

B. M.

New York City
February 1957

I

Angels Sat on His
Tarnished Cradle

Two achievements of Alexander Hamilton are impressed on public memory. The chief is his conduct—we may say creation—of the Treasury of the United States. Less distinct are his efforts, earlier, for a new constitution conferring effective national powers; here figures his principal part in *The Federalist*. These combine to describe his contribution to America's greatness. Aside from the moment when he fell in a duel with Aaron Burr, the remainder of his career blends in a record of firm patriotism marked by notable competence.

In the awareness of most, his story begins with his youthful arrival on this continent shortly before the Revolution. Naturally, his birth and boyhood in the West Indies comprise a preface brief and vague. Because his parentage and early years are removed and shadowy in present recollection, it is desirable to set down, with particularity, what is known of this first third of his life.[1]

Alexander Hamilton was born in the British Virgin Islands in the Leeward group of the West Indies, probably on January 11, 1755. He was the younger son of James Hamilton and Rachael (Fawcett) Lavien. His father was the fourth son of Alexander Hamilton, Laird of Grange, Stevenston parish, Ayrshire, Scotland, and his wife, Elizabeth Pollock, married in 1711. His mother was the second daughter of John Fawcett and his wife, Mary Uppington, married on the island of Nevis, on August 21, 1718. Charlestown, Nevis, is generally taken to be Hamilton's birthplace.[2]

[1]

On the principal street is shown the double flight of stone entrance steps, all that remains of the house locally reputed to have
been that of Hamilton's birth.   From the location, overlooking the
sea, and the size of the walled garden, about a third of an acre, with
its great entrance gate, this must have been an imposing dwelling—
indeed, too fine to have been occupied entire by Hamilton's parents
at any stage in their known history.   Several families named Hamilton, in better circumstances, lived on Nevis at the time (see below),
and this perhaps was the home of one of them.   Supposing Hamilton to have been born at Charlestown, the aspect of the place cannot have changed much since his childhood.   Numbers of solid,
somber houses must be that old, and the same walled lanes run inland from the harbor toward the volcanic cone that is the island's
central feature.[3]

In reciting particulars of names, dates, and locations demanded
by biographical exactitude, something more appealing, and not less
important, is lost.   This is the surpassing beauty of the scenes in
which this boy grew up. It may not be a pathetic fallacy to suppose
that the charm of his early environment lay upon his life.   Of
course sea, sky, mountain, and meadow were not all of it. Sunshine
could turn to murk, trade wind to tropic tornado, combers on the
reef to tidal wave that wrecked the harbor.   Such occasional violence of nature was matched, too, by the systematic violence—and
not all latent—of the slave society.   The paradise had its serpent
of greed and villainy.   In addition, such a clime—turquoise, green,
and gold—was congenial to pirates, cowardly and cruel.   The history of the Antilles is strewn with warfare, often not petty, which
left bones to this day upon the beaches.   But if a child, endowed
for nobility of mind and heart, could choose a birthplace, where
better than Nevis, its fertile slopes rising to a bold height habitually
shrouded in its own special cloud?   Adjacent St. Kitts is similar,
though less spectacular, and St. Croix, where Alexander spent his
early youth, is a milder version of them both.   When he left he
never returned, and his allusions to the island chapter of his life
were chary.   But one may fancy that in a stressful career he did,
now and again, sail back in memory to a picture-place no one of
his sensitivity could ever forget.

Hamilton's mother was born on Nevis, probably in 1729, and
remained there until she was eleven or more likely until sixteen.

Her father is said to have been of French Huguenot extraction, and to have been physician as well as planter.[4]   He may have been the son of John Fawcett, Jr., who was listed in Captain Thomas Butler's militia district on Nevis in 1677–1678.[5]   Thirty years later in a Nevis census is John Fawsett, with two white females, three black males, and four black females.[6]   This second of the name, presumed to have been the maternal grandfather of Alexander Hamilton, may have been the same who received a deed of property on Nevis from Captain Frank Keynall to John and Mary Fawcett in 1714.[7]   Here, then, seem to have been John and Mary Fawcett, with a daughter, on Nevis in 1714.

However, in the parish register of St. George's, Gingerland, Nevis, under marriages, August 21, 1718, we find "Mr. John Faussett and Mrs. Mary Uppington."[8]   The designation "Mrs." did not necessarily mean that Mary Uppington had been married before, being simply the contraction of "Mistress," a term of respect frequently appearing in the register.[9]   John may have married a second time (and another Mary), or the John of 1718 may have been the son or other relative of the John of the deed from Captain Keynall in 1714.[10]   A second marriage seems more likely.   The weight of the evidence is that this John Fawcett had two daughters, Ann, who married James Lytton on Nevis about 1730, and Rachael, who married John Michael Lavien, probably in 1745.   Even if Ann was married at fifteen or sixteen, she was born earlier than John Fawcett's marriage to Mary Uppington in 1718.   It is here assumed that Ann and Rachael were half-sisters, separated in ages by approximately the difference in the dates of their marriages. No birth or baptismal record has been found for either.   That Ann married about 1730 is argued from the fact that she had three or four children by the time the family moved from Nevis to the neighboring Danish island of St. Croix where her husband, James Lytton, bought "Grange" plantation, No. 9 in Kompaniets Kvarter (Company's Quarter), on May 24, 1738.[11]   The children were John Faucett (*sic*), Peter, James, and a daughter of unknown name, born respectively about 1730, 1733, 1735, and 1738.[12]   The Lyttons had four more children, a son and three daughters, born on St. Croix.   Our interest is in Ann (born on August 23, 1743, baptized on December 11),[13] Alexander Hamilton's cousin, twelve years his senior.   She fixes her mother,

Ann (Fawcett) Lytton, as the older half-sister of Hamilton's mother.

The Fawcetts lived in St. George's Parish, Gingerland, and, by tradition, on a plantation which is only a couple of miles from the church. The house, where the island slopes to the south, overlooked the sea. Nothing remains of it except a few stones, and a nearby settlement, called after the family, has likewise disappeared.[14] The Fawcetts' seven children followed in rapid succession. In fact the birth register of St. George's notes, "1718 June 26 John son of Mr. John ffaussett by Mary his Wife,"[15] which would be two months before the couple were married. Peter was born and died within six months in 1720, and the same name, as was common, was given to the third son, born the next year. These names were preserved in the family, for Rachael, Alexander Hamilton's mother, called her first son Peter, and her half-sister Ann Lytton had sons John and Peter. Frances Fawcett was born in 1723, and a son Lillilstone was baptized in 1731.[16]

In the period between these two last, for which the records are missing, must have been born, hardly later than 1729, judging from her marriage about 1745, Rachael, who became the mother of Hamilton. If her father was a medical practitioner, he was unable to save his own children, for the youngest son died under the age of three,[17] and within a few years, in a single month in the autumn of 1736, died, obviously in an epidemic, Frances, Elizabeth (of whose birth no record appears), and Peter.[18]

As St. George's Church was the center of the community in which Rachael Fawcett grew up, a word may be said about its present aspect. The stone structure, Father Dennington explained, has been substantially rebuilt after repeated damage from hurricane and earthquake. It now faces west, but formerly ran the other way and had no transepts. Tombstones of circa 1724 and 1742 which form part of the floor apparently remained in place. Indeed, all of the modest, low, dark gray building presents the appearance of age. Though the island is subtropical (16° north latitude) this portion of it, called Gingerland, has a stark look, more like a heath than like a garden. The fields, once so productive, are now mostly untilled. The impression of loneliness, in spite of the beating sunshine, is due perhaps to the complete silence that wraps the scene. Life as it used to be lived in Rachael Fawcett's youth two centuries ago has lapsed. Abolition of slavery in this and the other English islands two generations after her death was of course right, but it relaxed and then destroyed local organization. Central sugar factories (Nevis cane is carried eleven miles by water from Charlestown to Basseterre, St. Kitts) have gone far to finish the process.

John and Mary Fawcett came to be at odds with each other. On February 5, 1740, William Matthews, Chancellor and Ordinary in Chief for the Leeward Caribee Islands, issued a writ of supplicavit for separate maintenance of Mary; her husband was obliged to divide her property from his, and she agreed to accept from him an annual income of £53 in lieu of any dower claims.[19] We do not know the reasons.[20] Perhaps the loss of five children bore its part. Probably she was years younger than he, and that may have entered. Whether Rachael, now presumably eleven, remained with her father or went with her mother, and if the latter, where, we are ignorant. Our next certain news of Rachael is the will of her father, leaving her all of his estate, as well real property as funds here or elsewhere, of which she is appointed sole executrix. This was recorded on the Danish island of St. Croix, probably shortly before December, 1745.[21] We wonder why Rachael, sixteen in 1745, was made executrix, instead of some older person on Nevis, or James Lytton, Dr. Fawcett's son-in-law, a successful planter and frequently named guardian on St. Croix.[22] Nothing was left to Ann Lytton, perhaps because her husband was well established.[23]

It is likely that John Fawcett died in 1745 and that Mary and her daughter Rachael then left Nevis, or possibly St. Kitts. They were on St. Croix in October, 1745, and Mary Fawcett was godmother at the christening of James and Ann Lytton's child Josia on November 21.[24] From this time forward most of the records of Mary Fawcett and Rachael are of St. Croix, though both of them at intervals lived elsewhere. The anchor on St. Croix was the Lytton family, though other relatives and friends had moved there about the same time, 1737–1738, following a drought on Nevis.[25]

One who made the transfer from Nevis to St. Croix was John (Johan, Johann) Michael Lavien, and thereby hangs a tale. He was either living or trading in St. Croix in 1740,[26] though four years later he was referred to as "Merchant in Neeves." This was when he bought a sugar plantation in Queen's Quarter. James Lytton and Edward Evans were witnesses to the deed, evidence of the

friendly relations between them and Lavien at this time.[27]   This
place was sold at auction before the end of the year to Town Judge
Poul Lindemark,[28] and in the following February, Lavien bought
half a cotton plantation.   This was "Contentment," No. 12, Company's Quarter,[29] and he gave a bond, written in Dutch, to Henry
Stumpius for the purchase price, 550 rigsdaler.

Probably in this year, 1745, Rachael Fawcett was married to
John Michael Lavien.   This date is tolerably fixed because this year
she was not living with her mother,[30] and her son, Peter Lavien, was
born the following year, 1746.[31]

Hamilton's son, though admitting that his father "rarely . . .
dwelt upon his personal history," said that Lavien was a Dane who,
"attracted by [Rachael's] beauty, and recommended to her mother
by his wealth, received her hand against her inclination."[32]   The
remainder of his statement, concerning Rachael's separation from
Lavien and subsequent events, which we can check, is so inaccurate
as to cast doubt on all of it.   Hamilton himself in 1782, writing his
wife of the death of Peter Lavien, said, "You know the circumstances that abate my distress, yet my heart acknowledges the rights
of a brother."[33]   This may be taken as an implied defense of his
mother.   The surname of Rachael's husband occurs in various
forms, as with others in polyglot islands in a day of careless spelling.[34]   This bearer of it was probably German-Jewish.[35]

The marriage seems to have been unhappy from the start. Lavien
must have been considerably older than Rachael.[36]   Lavien's
money troubles may have figured in the domestic disharmony.

In the year of their marriage his debt to the Danish West India
Company had increased to 1,930 rigsdaler, 2 real, twice the cost of
a full sugar plantation such as he had relinquished the year before.
In 1748 he was debited by the company with the large sum of
2,432 rdl.   The whole of his recorded purchases from cargoes of
company ships would not make a mercantile stock.[37]   Nothing we
can trace in his history makes him appear a rich man.   His attempts
as independent planter were marked by vicissitudes, he became
manager or overseer for others (possibly a renter),[38] complained of
the small amount of his earnings from which he must support his
son,[39] and toward the last was superintendent of—in the end a mere
roomer in—the hospital at Fredericksted.[40]   He seems never to
have been named to an office of public honor or trust.   On the

other hand, Rachael's relatives knew him well (James Lytton went surety for him)[41] before the marriage, and continued to have friendly dealings with him after Rachael left him and after he, with opprobrious accusations, secured a divorce.[42]

Ironically, the Laviens' first home was named "Contentment." It is the nearest plantation to Christiansted, southwestward, and adjoins land of the Moravian church. It is just off the main road of the island, along which some of the slave quarters stand. More of these, in half ruinous state, are encountered before one comes to the dwelling, a medium-sized square stone structure with a low wing that contained kitchen and rooms for domestics. The house is in a depression with no outlook; time and tenants have not improved its appearance. Probably it was here that their son Peter was born. After three years they moved to the nearby plantation "Beeston Hill."[43]

It must have been while here that Rachael's behavior became so unwifely, according to Lavien's complaint,[44] that he had her put in jail in the fort in Christiansted. If we may trust the stipulation of the Danish law under which Lavien had his wife imprisoned, he must have alleged that she had "twice been guilty of adultery" and that he was no longer living with her.[45] However, hoping she would mend her ways, he freed her from jail and lawsuit. But instead of living with him she went off to another place (later referred to as "an English island") where she begot several—afterward specified as two—illegitimate children. She had left him permanently about nine years before this complaint; that is, around 1750, after five years of married life, such as it was. Lavien sought a divorce because Rachael had "shown herself to be shameless, rude and ungodly," had "completely forgotten her duty and let husband and child alone, and instead gave herself up to whoring with everyone," which things were "so well known that her own family and friends must hate her for it. . . ." He was specially prompted to sue for divorce because if he died she, as his widow, might claim for her whore-children what belonged to his son.

This petition was received by the Temperret (matrimonial) Court on February 26, 1759, and Rachael and three witnesses named by Lavien[46] were summoned to appear at a hearing on April 18 in Baron von Proeck's house. On March 2 the summons was served on Rachael Lavien "on the plantation owned by the Town

Captain, and also proclaimed . . . in the Fort, where she was in
jail, which were her two last places of residence here in the country. . . ." Parenthetically, though the Town Captain's (Bertram
Pieter de Nully's) plantation ("Catharine's Rest" in Company's
Quarter)[47] was mentioned before the Fort,[48] it may be that Rachael
went there after she was released from jail. Possibly De Nully
interceded for her. Her mother may have been living on De
Nully's plantation at the time.[49]

Rachael did not respond to the summons. The court judged
that Lavien's case against her was proved, and dissolved the marriage with the declaration that "said Rachael Lewin shall have no
rights whatsoever as wife to either John Michael Lewin's person or
means. . . . Also, Rachael Lewin's illegitimate children are denied
all rights or pretensions to the plaintiff's possessions." Lavien was
free to marry again, but "His Majesty is reserved the right to
Rachael. . . ."[50] *£+ 474*

Recital of the divorce decree has taken us ahead of our story.
Doubtless Rachael and her mother left St. Croix together, or her
mother a little later, in 1750. On October 5 of this year Mary
Fawcett gave notice in the usual form that her creditors should present their claims, as she intended to leave the island, and on the 24th
of the month she receipted for the price of a slave she had sold.[51]
Beyond "English islands" mentioned by Lavien, we do not know
where they went or how long they remained together. Rachael's
marital troubles did not alienate her mother or her relatives who
remained on St. Croix, as we shall see. In 1754 it was said that
Mary's debt of 6 rdl. to the estate of John Roach could not be collected, "as she is not here [St. Croix], but in poverty has left the
island."[52] It is most likely that mother and daughter went to St.
Kitts. However, in July, 1755, Mary Fawcett was living on the
nearby Dutch island of St. Eustatius. She described herself as
"late of the Island of Nevis but now of the Island of St. Eustatia [,]
Widow," but she remained a British subject, for she acknowledged
"our Sovereign Lord George the Second."[53]

This much has been preliminary, though needful, to an understanding of Alexander Hamilton's origin. Probably by 1752, perhaps earlier, Rachael Fawcett had begun to live with James Hamilton, a young Scotsman in the islands, ten or eleven years her
senior. It is guessed that they met on St. Kitts, where, much later,

he worked for a firm of merchants.[54]   We know painfully little
about him except that he was the father of a famous son.   He
came of a long Scottish line of Hamiltons, possessed of the same
lands for centuries.   They were not of the ducal branch of the
family, though their seat in Ayrshire had belonged to the Earl of
Glencairne and went back to the twelfth century.   James Hamilton was the fourth of nine sons of Alexander and Elizabeth Hamilton of Cambuskieth or Grange, and was born about 1718.[55]   His
grandson thought he came to the West Indies to seek his fortune
when less than nineteen.[56]

He was never successful.   He proved unequal to his responsibilities to his common-law wife and young sons, throwing them on their
own devices and the assistance of relatives.   For long intervals his
whereabouts were unknown to Alexander, who had reason to believe, however, that his father was in want.   With occasional financial aid from Alexander and, at one point, from a friend in St.
Vincent, he managed, in spite of ill health toward the last, to rub
along to the age of eighty-one.   Alexander hoped that his friend
Robert Troup, in case of his own death, would see that his father's
drafts were paid and should not "return upon him and increase his
distress."   And he added a few words of explanation: "Though as
I am informed, a man of respectable connections in Scotland, he
became, as a merchant, bankrupt at an early day in the West Indies
and is now in indigence."[57]   And to his cousin, head of the family
in Scotland, Alexander confirmed that "my father's affairs at a very
early day went to wreck; so as to have rendered his situation during
the greatest part of his life far from eligible."[58]   In 1783 Alexander
inquired of his brother James, "what has become of our dear
father?   It is an age since I have heard from him. . . . Perhaps
alas! he is no more, and I shall not have the pleasing opportunity of
contributing to render the close of his life more happy than the
progress of it.   My heart bleeds at the recollection of his misfortunes and embarrassments.   Sometimes I flatter myself his brothers
have extended their support to him, and that now he is enjoying
tranquillity and ease; at other times I fear that he is suffering in
indigence."   If his father was living, he was ready to devote himself
and all he had to help him.[59]

That James Hamilton had endearing as well as feckless qualities
is evident in the fact that he did not forfeit his son's affection.[60]

James Hamilton (senior)[61] and Alexander mutually acknowledged their relation of father and son. As will appear below, James Hamilton, Rachael, and their two sons are found transferring (from Nevis or St. Kitts) to St. Croix at the same time in 1765. Alexander took pains to give his father news of his marriage and wrote to his wife of his hope that they would know each other affectionately.[62] He urged that his father come to live with him in New York.[63] Between 1796 and 1799 he remitted to his father and brother several thousand dollars.[64] He wrote intimately of James Hamilton, Sr., as his father to the Hamiltons in Scotland.[65] Finally no other than Edward Stevens (whose natural brother some reputed Hamilton to be) made search in Christiansted for a will supposed to have been left by Alexander's father, James Hamilton.[66] Hamilton's hope that his children might visit their relatives in Scotland was not realized until years after his death, 1837, when his son James was guest of the laird, the same to whom his father had written so long before. The octogenarian laird dispensed family tales, Tory views, and toddy of excellent Highland whisky that had eluded the exciseman in a fashion that would have been condemned by his distinguished American cousin.

Hamilton's son said that Rachael's marriage to Lavien "proving unhappy, she applied for and obtained a divorce, and removing to St. Christopher's, there married" James Hamilton "and had by him several sons, of whom Alexander was the youngest."[67] The mistakes here were probably due to ignorance of contemporary records rather than to filial desire to legitimatize his father's birth. We know that Lavien obtained the divorce, Rachael not even appearing in the proceeding in person or by proxy, and that under Danish law she was forbidden to remarry. We have no record of her marrying James Hamilton, were that possible. As we shall see, six years after she left her husband, her mother in a deed called her Rachael Lavion; at this time she had two sons by James Hamilton. Three years after this, Lavien stigmatized these boys as illegitimate as contrasted with Peter Lavien, whom "the plaintiff in his marriage with her has begotten." Nor did James Lytton, their uncle, at the probate proceedings following Rachael's death, interpose any claim that the Hamilton sons were legitimate. Hamilton's grandson admitted that Rachael and James were not married, but sought to exculpate Rachael.[68]

Given a celebrated man, known to be of illegitimate birth on distant foreign soil, writers, unhampered by scrutiny of documents, were willing to supply him with a variety of fathers and with an imaginary mother. Among imputed parents are Lavien,[69] the planter Thomas Stevens of Antigua and St. Croix,[70] Dr. William Hamilton,[71] "a Miss Hamilton" of Nevis,[72] Governor Walterstorff of St. Croix,[73] and George Washington, who was in Barbados about the time Rachael could have been there![74] The statement sometimes made that Hamilton had Negro blood[75] or at any rate had a child or children by Negro women[76] is without foundation as to the first and not verifiable as to the second. Rachael is always among the whites in the St. Croix tax lists.[77]

While the domestic relationship between Rachael Fawcett and James Hamilton was informal—technically adulterous on her part —such arrangements were frequent in the islands; and in England itself at the time the severity of the marriage laws encouraged their breach.[78] The union of these two endured for fifteen years or more, and must have been commendably distinguished from the casual extramarital connections of the planters, often with slave women.[79] We do not know where they lived, besides on St. Kitts and St. Croix, and, probably, Nevis. We find them, perhaps as visitors, on St. Eustatius in 1758, enjoying esteem and filling an honorable office. On October 1, "James Hamilton and Rachel Hamilton his wife" stood as godfather and godmother at the christening of Alexander, the four-months son of "Alexander Fraser and Elizabeth Thornton his wife."[80]

Our first documentary evidence of the parentage of Alexander Hamilton and his older brother James, aside from incidental evidence, is in the record of the probate court of Christiansted, St. Croix, February 22, 1768.[81] The court met at the house where Rachael had died four days earlier, to appraise her effects for division of the inheritance among her children, "who are 3 sons." After naming "Peter Lewine, born in the deceased person's marriage with John Michael Lewine," the record went on to designate "also two sons, namely James Hamilton and Alexander Hamilton, one 15 and the other one 13 years old, who are the same bastard children born after the deceased person's divorce from said Lewine."[82]

This puts the birth of James in 1753 and of Alexander in 1755.

We can count on these dates because "Present for the two minor children and heirs was Mr. James Lytton on behalf of Peter Lytton, who is a son of the minor children's mother's sister." That is, the Hamilton boys' uncle by marriage attended the appraisal of Rachael's effects to protect their interest pending the appearance of his son Peter Lytton. He would be able and, as one of the most responsible men on the island, who had often been the servant of the court, would have every reason to supply accurate information of the boys' names and ages for the record.

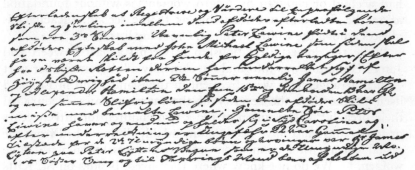

Facsimile of portion of record of probate court, Christiansted, St. Croix, February 22, 1768, in which the age of Alexander Hamilton is given as 13 years. This puts his birth in 1755, two years earlier than has commonly been supposed.

Of course, it is possible that James Lytton was mistaken in giving their ages, or that the clerk did not put down accurately what he said; errors often occur in legal documents. On the other hand, the public records of St. Croix at the time, petty though the matters might be, were kept with almost painful precision. James Lytton, as the head of the family, only four days after Rachael's death would be acutely aware of the plight of her illegitimate children, his relatives; in the absence of their father they were virtually orphans, with questionable claim on anything left by their mother, and they would, in fact, become his charges. Until this document came to light Hamilton's year of birth was universally taken to be 1757 (January 11).[83]

If he was born in 1755, as seems reliable, his precocity remains extraordinary but becomes believable. The difference of two years is more significant for his performances in youth and early manhood, but has its importance all along in his career. He himself, mentioning his age in several connections (each time approximately), in effect assigned different years for his birth.[84] True, the year 1757, for his birth, fits his statement, much later, that he came to this continent "at about sixteen" if we assume that he arrived in 1773. If we accept independent evidence that he transferred to the mainland in 1772, he by his own account was born in 1756. On the other hand, he said he left college for the army (which was certainly in the spring of 1776) "by the age of nineteen." This confirms 1757 as his birth year. However, in a communication to the Christiansted newspaper, April 6, 1771, signed "A.H.," he gave his age as "about seventeen" (that is, born 1754).[85] Several of his closest friends (Fish, Pickering, Mason) thought him younger than he was,[86] while Brissot de Warville was in error the other way.[87]

Our first notice of the Hamilton household on St. Croix is in the spring of 1765 when Alexander was ten. It seems likely that James Hamilton brought Rachael and the boys with him when he came from St. Kitts to collect a debt for Archibald Ingram, whose head clerk he was. Alexander Moir of the firm of Moir & Gordon, of Christiansted, St. Croix, had informed that he intended to leave for Europe, and instructed his creditors to present their claims. We know of the incident only because Moir & Gordon refused to pay Ingram £807. 11s. 11d., and James Hamilton as Ingram's representative was obliged to recover it in the Christiansted Gaesteretsdom (special court in the case of a stranger).[88] When James Hamilton returned to St. Kitts he left his family on St. Croix. This must have been the "separation between him and me, when I was very young," of which Alexander wrote in after life, and which "threw me upon the bounty of my mother's relatives, some of whom were then wealthy. . . ."[89] It may be that James Hamilton never saw Rachael and their two boys again. James Hamilton is never mentioned as a resident of St. Croix, for example in the poll-tax lists.

It seems unlikely that he deliberately abandoned his family. Alexander was writing to him filially almost seven years afterward, and continued to treat him with affection and solicitude, not resentment. On the other hand, we have no evidence that he aided Rachael in the two years that she lived after his departure or that he took any responsibility for his sons after her death. He may have been one of the sufferers in a slave revolt on Tobago in 1771. Thirty slaves of the "Coromatic nation" resolved to destroy the white inhabitants, "attacked Mr. Hamilton's house" and "wounded three white men desperately, two of whom are since dead. Mr. Hamilton was shot through the thigh, but is recovering."[90] It is inferred that he lived on several of the southern islands before he moved to St. Vincents prior to June 1793. He was assisted by a friend in settling his business in that part of the world (which probably meant paying his debts) in anticipation of joining Alexander in Philadelphia. But poor health plus the danger of a voyage during the war between England and France deferred his taking ship.[91] He died and was buried on St. Vincents in 1799.[92]

When Rachael returned to St. Croix in 1765 she had to rely mostly on her own efforts for the support of herself and her sons. The breakup of her sister's family, the Lyttons, of which Alexander wrote years afterward,[93] had already commenced. The eldest daughter married a merchant who needed assistance from James Lytton; he soon died in poverty, and she and her second husband did not long survive. The husband of Ann (Alexander's favorite cousin) went bankrupt and they had left the island, consigning their daughter to the care of Ann's parents. James Lytton, Jr., the younger son, after business losses, with his second wife absconded with slaves belonging to his first wife's estate, and finally settled at the Bay of Honduras. Peter Lytton married an aged widow who died shortly after Rachael reached St. Croix. He sold his plantations, invested to poor purpose in enterprises in Christiansted, was twice absent from the island, and on his second return committed suicide.[94]

James Lytton himself had sold his Grange plantation six months before Rachael's arrival, and with his wife, Ann, and their granddaughter had moved to a rented apartment in Torvegade (Market Street) in Christiansted. In spite of losses because of his children's misfortunes and delinquencies, he was still a rich man.[95] But, borne down by regrets not of his making, and by age, he and his wife soon returned to Nevis late in 1765; she must have died there, for he was alone when he came back two years later.[96]

Nicholas Cruger's
"Young Man"

MISHAPS in the ranks of his relatives had depressing effect on the prospect of Alexander, coming to St. Croix as a boy of ten. Had the Lytton family remained intact and thriving, he might have been absorbed into their numerous undertakings, which included merchandising and banking as well as planting. Had he been sent by the family to the mainland for schooling (like John Hallwood, a grandson of James Lytton)[1] he might have returned to St. Croix for opportunities that awaited him. As it was, the backing needed to overcome his handicap failed him, and he attached himself to the fortunes of the continental colonies.

Rachael did not allow herself to be an embarrassment to her sister and brother-in-law. Whatever her irregularities before, she now took hold and proved a better provider than James Hamilton had been. She rented a house in Christiansted, No. 34 Kompagnietsstraede (Company's Lane) from the merchant Thomas Dipnall for 12 rigsdaler a month. Here she ran a small store, selling provisions and other plantation supplies bought from Dipnall, her landlord, and from Beckman & Cruger for whom Alexander later worked as a clerk.[2] Thus Alexander's acquaintance with business, though of a petty sort, commenced at about the age of ten, some years before he entered Cruger's establishment; he may have helped his mother wait on customers, and made his first trials at keeping accounts for her.[3]

In addition to the store, Rachael had the income from hiring out slaves, at least three of whom, and probably others, came to her from her mother. On May 4, 1756, Mary Fawcett, of St. Christopher, desiring to provide for the future of her three dear female slaves Rebecca, Flora, and Esther, hired them to Archibald Hamm for her lifetime, but after her death the women, with any children they might have, were to go to her beloved daughter Rachael Lavion.[4]

Rachael was taken ill with fever in February, 1768, and her son Alexander had the same complaint. Ann McDonnell took care of Rachael for a week before Dr. Heering[5] was called on February 17. He bled her, gave her fever medicine, and the following day administered an emetic and gave her and her son fever medicine. From Thomas Dipnall was ordered "a chicken for 'Elicks.'" On February 19 Rachael had fever medicine with valerian, alcohol for her head, and in the afternoon a decoction, while her son was bled and given an enema. Rachael died at nine in the evening. Ann McDonnell laid out the body (but later her claim for this service was reduced by the probate court from 25 to 10 rdl.). Dipnall furnished eggs, white bread, and cakes for the funeral; Peter Lytton paid 40 rdl. for eleven yards of black material to cover the coffin; James Towers, town judge, advanced money for a pair of shoes for James and black veils for both the children. Alexander must have recovered sufficiently to attend the funeral. The parish clerk of the English church summoned friends to the ceremony and assembled the pallbearers. Rachael's body was taken in a hearse to the family plot of James Lytton on Grange plantation and was buried there, February 20, by the English minister, the Reverend Cecil Wray Goodchild.[6] Beside the grave stood, surely, James Lytton, who had known all of Rachael's history since her childhood; his son Peter, who was made guardian of the boys; and James, fifteen, and Alexander, thirteen. As Alexander turned away he lifted the veil of his childhood, and ever after looked at his world with the candid eyes of a man.

The little burial ground is now discovered with difficulty in the tangled woods a few hundred yards downhill from the plantation house.[7] Which of the dozen brick-mounded graves is Rachael's we may not say, for identifying slabs, where they existed, have been taken for the uses of the living; they have been built into

copings or serve as door stones. This lost spot is part of America's story. For here lies the original of Alexander Hamilton's peculiar ardor. Under the ancient mahogany trees on the Grange hilltop Mrs. Atherton erected a monument to Rachael with the sufficient encomium "She was the mother of Alexander Hamilton." The dates Mrs. Atherton assigned, taken from the St. John's Church burial register, make Rachael too young; at her death she was thirty-nine, not thirty-two.[8] In a life of mischances, such an error after death is no matter. Her memorial is different.

The probate court found Rachael's property of value to consist of five women slaves, one of whom had a daughter named Rachael, and three Negro boys. The judge was told, doubtless by James Lytton, Sr., that Rachael Lavien had given one of the Negro boys, Ajax, to her son Alexander, and another, called Christian, to her son James. A considerable stock in trade of salt pork, butter, and flour in the storehouses belonged mostly to merchants from whom Rachael had ordered. Her personal effects revealed a scantily furnished household and wardrobe: 6 silver spoons, 7 silver teaspoons, 1 pair of sugar tongs, 2 chests, 1 bed with feather comforter and bolster, and 34 books; her articles of clothing were 4 dresses, 1 red skirt, 1 white skirt, and 1 black silk sun-hat. The slaves were hired to Captain William Egans.[9] No bill presented was earlier than 1767, showing that Rachael had paid promptly in an island where a year's credit was frequent.

At the auction[10] Peter Lytton, guardian of the Hamilton boys, bought the books. One would give a good deal to know their titles, for they probably composed much of Alexander's education to this point, and we may think they were his after his cousin bid them in. From his literary imitations shortly after this it is likely that among the volumes were works of Pope and Machiavelli's *The Prince* (this and perhaps some more in French), together with sermons and other devotional pieces.

When the estate was settled[11] the assets were 1700 rigsdaler, 3 real, 3 styver and charges against it were 1067 rdl. 4 r. 3½ st. But the Hamilton brothers' lot was not to be softened by this small inheritance. John Michael Lavien had appeared and, producing his divorce decree, claimed all for Peter Lavien, Rachael's only legitimate child. James and Alexander, according to the laws, Book 5, Chapter 2, Article 71, could receive nothing from their

mother's estate. Peter Lavien, returned from South Carolina, signed for the net amount, 632 rdl. 6 r. 5½ st.[12]

Nor did the Hamilton orphans have the protection of their elder relatives, for James Lytton and his son Peter died within a month of each other in the summer of 1769.[13] With James Lytton—capable, successful, honorable, and long-suffering—the pillar of the house had fallen. Thereafter deterioration of the family was progressive. Unseemly wrangling over Lytton's estate continued for a generation.[14]

Though Alexander Hamilton was left nothing in James Lytton's will,[15] he had intimate knowledge of the contests between the heirs. He receipted for advances by the executors to his much older cousin Ann (Lytton) Venton,[16] who appears later in the annals as Ann Mitchell. Hamilton's deep gratitude toward her from this time forward must mean that she took his part and probably helped him with this and other money when he was neglected by others.

We do not know at what age Alexander began a clerkship with Beckman & Cruger, merchants in Christiansted. His older brother James was apprenticed to the carpenter Thomas Mc-Nobeny.[17] If Alexander was put to work in 1766, when eleven, this would correspond with commencement of the Beckman & Cruger business,[18] and with his father's final severance from the family. In addition, at this time Alexander was thought old enough to sign a legal document.[19] Both boys were then living with their mother in Company's Lane, Christiansted.[20] It is more likely that he started with Cruger a couple of years later, about the time of the death of his mother, when he was thirteen.[21] Our first proof of his being with Cruger is in his letter of November 11, 1769 (the earliest preserved), to his friend about his own age, Edward Stevens, who was studying either on the continent or on a neighboring island, possibly Antigua.[22]

Alexander is doubtful whether he will be on St. Croix when Edward returns, "for, to confess my weakness, Ned, my ambition is prevalent, so that I contemn the grovelling condition of a clerk or the like, to which my fortune, etc., condemns me, and would willingly risk my life, though not my character, to exalt my station." This shows that Alexander had been already some time in Cruger's employ, for the absent Edward knew of it. In addi-

tion it indicates, not least in the composition of the letter itself, that his work, by this time, was clerical, and not merely running errands. However, we may believe that three years earlier, when only eleven, he was already quite equal to penmanship and figuring.

The choice of callings for the two boys—James to be a carpenter, Alexander a merchant—points to a difference in their aptitudes. Aside from Alexander's own testimony that he "always had a strong propensity to literary pursuits,"[23] and his mental precocity, we are at a loss to explain his early proficiency in writing and accounts. He mentioned his having "been taught to repeat the Decalogue in Hebrew, at the school of a Jewess, when so small that he was placed standing by her side on a table."[24] Apart from this, we do not know whether he went to school before he was sent to the continent at the age of nearly eighteen. His childhood education may have been from his mother[25] and grandmother; if so, it was unusually precise for him to learn to *write* in French as he did when a young man. He may have come under one of the schoolmasters in Christiansted who offered what was beginning to be called an English as opposed to a classical education, that is, mathematics and its applications, geography and perhaps some elements of the natural sciences, but with the omission of Latin and Greek.[26] Whatever was his formal training, it was early supplemented by miscellaneous reading, doubtless in the thirty-four books which his mother possessed. His favorite authors were Pope and Plutarch.[27] Probably after he commenced with Cruger he used such time as he had for study of mathematics and chemistry[28] and for reading on political and ethical subjects.[29] Certainly his knowledge and intellectual tastes at the time of his clerkship extended far beyond the usual equipment of even a studious youth of his years, and had a development, albeit still self-conscious, which must have been the surprise of all who encountered him intimately.

But Alexander Hamilton's education on St. Croix was not confined to formal study, however limited, and to eager private reading. Cruger's countinghouse must have been his real school.[30] This apprenticeship, as it came to entail his sole responsibility for purchase and sale of several cargoes, gave him practice not only in commercial correspondence, but in management. Those who say that Hamilton, twenty years later, entered upon the duties of the United States Treasury with no previous experience should not forget, along with his work as continental receiver of taxes and his legal practice in New York, his first little flier as a man of business in Christiansted. His concerns for Cruger were petty by comparison, of course, but for an alert mind they held their lessons.

One must be aware of Alexander's environment to understand his service with Cruger and the aftereffects of his St. Croix boyhood and youth. The island, with others in the group, had been in Danish possession since 1733 when they were acquired from France. St. Croix is nineteen miles long east and west and of varying breadth up to five miles. Its 50,000 acres were divided into 381 plantations, highly cultivated, mostly in sugar cane, to the tops of the hills. Its population, slightly more than 24,000, was twelve to one slave; the whites, aside from officials and soldiers who were apt to be Danes, were primarily English and Scotch who had come from the neighboring islands. Christiansted on the north coast, the larger of the two towns and the capital, had some 3,500 people, almost three-fourths black; Frederiksted, at the west end, had something over five hundred inhabitants, fewer than two hundred white. On the plantations the slaves outnumbered the whites more than twenty to one. Christiansted, a half-mile square, had six hundred houses in twenty streets, the principal ones running roughly north and south, terminating at the waterfront. The shallow harbor is guarded, like a golf green, by a perilous coral reef three-fourths of a mile out; entrance, except for the smallest coasters, then and now must be with the services of a pilot. Better, but unprotected, anchorage was at Frederiksted, where heavier cargoes were landed.[31]

The commerce of the island was dictated by its staple agriculture. Devoted principally to cane, with some cotton and less coffee, exports, by statute rather than by economic law, went chiefly to Denmark—muscovado sugar, molasses, and rum. Imports of building lumber, staves and hoops for casks, livestock, and foodstuffs were mainly from the continental colonies, though some fish and meat and most manufactured wares came from Denmark. Like all agricultural societies not self-sustaining, but supplying a market with a few products, this was a speculative one. While political allegiance was to Denmark, economic fealty was apt to be to Dutch bankers. The small white aristocracy, at least potentially wealthy, strove to compensate for remoteness, and insularity, by luxury which was often extravagance. If the ease of the planters in their airy mansions with mahogany furniture and imported cheeses, sconces, silks, and laces contributed to Hamilton's love of elegance, so must the degradation of the blacks have made him the persistent foe of slavery. He had in St. Croix enough evidences of the evil in the many macrons (runaways), mulattoes who inherited only the status of the mothers, and punishments which could not quiet the planters' horrid fear of revolts more destructive than hurricanes.[32] The economy and culture of the whites were parasitic and flamboyant, like many of the tropic plants of the island.

Fortunately, the waterfront area of Christiansted, the scene of Alexander Hamilton's youthful career, remains unchanged after almost two centuries. This part of the town was declared a National Historic Site in 1952 and will be protected against desecration in the name of progress or by catchpenny heedlessness. Of course, the beauty of the landscape would not alter—the green hills that cup the harbor, the lapis sea within the reef, the profounder blue beyond. That the fortress-like buildings yet stand in the converging streets compliments the workmen who erected them under the Danes in the eighteenth or, in cases of more elegant structures, under the French in the seventeenth century. The yellow, buff, raspberry, and salmon colonnaded fronts shade the sidewalks, some of these paved with the figured tiles of old. The Custom House where Alexander had many errands is the same. The sloops and schooners that nudge the wharf are identical with the *Thunderbolt* or *Betsey* of Captains Newton and Lightbourne whose cargoes the young clerk supervised.

The business of Beckman & Cruger,[33] established in 1766, which had been taken over by Nicholas Cruger or by Kortright & Cruger in 1769, was in export of island products, especially raw sugar, and import of plantation supplies. It was one of a small number of export-import firms in Christiansted with permanent store and warehouse and stock regularly on hand. Others dealt in similar goods from time to time, but they might be primarily planters, or ship captains turned merchant long enough to dispose of a particular cargo.[34] The Cruger firm during Alexander's employment owned one or more small vessels that traded among the islands and made voyages to the mainland. Cruger also freighted other vessels.

Uncertainty exists about the location of Cruger's store where Hamilton worked. The commodious building at Nos. 56–57 Kongensgade (King's Street), the street floor used for a store as long as anyone can remember, is entrenched in tradition as the place of business of Cruger and his partners. It is in the block next to the main Christiansted wharf; its deep lot runs back to what was formerly a landing for sizable vessels; its yard corresponds to a contemporary advertisement of a sale of slaves; it has an ancient masonry safe intact—all of which favors the belief that this was the scene of Hamilton's clerkship.[35] On the other hand, tax lists and real-estate surveys give unbroken records of Cruger's store having been at Nos. 7–8, on the other side of the street, a block farther from the main wharf. The western portion of this double lot is occupied by a solid large house, recently somewhat changed in outward features, which may be the same that Cruger rented in 1766 from Dr. Robert Mears, later from Counselor Soeboetker and Justice Klingenberg, and bought in 1770.[36]

Nicholas Cruger (born in New York, 1743, died in St. Croix, 1801), Alexander Hamilton's employer and patron, had the closest family and business ties with New York City. It is likely that this connection determined sending Alexander there, which had much to do with subsequent American history. Cruger was of the third generation of merchants. The immigrant, John, established in New York as merchant shipper in 1700, was alderman and later mayor till his death in 1744. He was German, and had lived in England before he came to America and married the eldest daughter of Hendrick Cuyler of Albany, who was Dutch. Their sons Tileman and Henry went as merchants to the Caribbean, and Henry afterward settled in England. The youngest son, John, was mayor of New York, speaker of the Assembly, delegate to the Stamp Act Congress, and a founder and first president, 1768–1770, of the New York Chamber of Commerce.[37]

Nicholas Cruger, Hamilton's friend, was the fourth and youngest son of Henry. He probably inherited business connections of his uncle John on St. Croix.[38] With partners and alone he was a merchant there for twenty years. His brother Tileman was similarly situated in Curaçao. Another brother, Henry (II), was educated at King's College, became a merchant and mayor of Bristol, England, was elected to Parliament with Edmund Burke; he returned to the United States in 1790 and was elected a senator from New York. His eldest brother, John Harris Cruger, married the daughter of Oliver De Lancey and was a fighting loyalist as lieutenant-colonel in "De Lancey's Battalions."

Nicholas Cruger identified himself with two of the chief families of St. Croix by marrying first Anna, daughter of Town Captain Bertram Pieter De Nully and his wife Catharine,[39] and at her death Ann, daughter of Isaac and Elizabeth Markoe, whose connections were not less consequential.[40]

Cordial and honorable, Cruger quickly made a place for himself in the little St. Croix community. He was appointed one of the three chief guardians on the island.[41] At the time of Hamilton's clerkship, say 1768–1772, Cruger's business dealings were with his father, uncle, and brothers in New York, his brother Tileman Cruger in Curaçao, and with other firms in the islands. David Beckman, ten years his senior, who had been his partner for the first three years, seems to have left the firm in 1769,[42] and Cruger was alone except for occasional joint enterprises with Cornelius Kortright, also an offshoot of a powerful New York merchant family,[43] which later performed a special service for Hamilton. In 1771 "Messrs. Kortright & Cruger" advertised for sale "At said Cruger's Yard, Three Hundred Prime Slaves."[44] They were in the same trade the next year when they wrote to Henry Cruger, Jr., "We have a Danish Guinea man Just arriv'd with 250 Gold Coast Slaves they will sell well . . . for half produce and half Cash or bills."[45] Partly in Alexander's hand is a letter from Kortright & Cruger about the slave trade.[46] Cornelius Kortright and Cruger were close friends, as were their families in New York, and Kortright, longer established on St. Croix, stood ready to assist Cruger with advice and credit in the latter's separate operations.[47]

Cruger had excellent backing and correspondents, but was hardly to be described at this stage as an "opulent" merchant.[48] He relied heavily on relatives for financial assistance; but, even so, bills drawn on him by his brother went to protest to the latter's great injury.[49] Shortly before Hamilton left Cruger's employ,

Cruger was in debt and worried, but could not appeal to Mr. Kortright ("my Dependance in a case of this nature") because Kortright, like other of the wealthiest planters, "had been cruelly usd by the Gentlemen in Amsterdam & he realy has it not in his power this year."[50]   Not negligent in his affairs, Cruger was at this time inattentive to them, having the excuse that he was sick, absent, then convalescent, and finally was in love.   However, in a dozen years more of business in St. Croix he prospered.   Unlike two of his brothers, he was an enthusiast for the Revolutionary cause, suffered capture, imprisonment, and condemnation of a cargo on this account in 1779, and was chairman of the committee of New Yorkers that escorted Washington in his triumphant entry into the city in 1783.[51]   On his last return to New York,[52] in 1785, he continued as a merchant, at 16 Duke Street;[53] he must have had varied interests, flowing from his wide family associa- tions.   He continued in America to be the warm friend and sup- porter of Alexander Hamilton.

Our knowledge of Hamilton's commercial apprenticeship is from some seventy letters pertaining to Cruger's business and cov- ering eleven months (August 26, 1771 to July 27, 1772).   All are copies for the firm's own records.   Most are entirely in Hamilton's hand; others are in Cruger's or in that of another copyist.   Spe- cial interest attaches to a score of letters written by Hamilton between early November 1771 and late February 1772 when he was left in charge of Cruger's affairs in St. Croix in his employer's absence.[54]

Nicholas Cruger, "by reason of a very ill state of health," left St. Croix for New York on October 16, 1771.[55]   His "clarke" or "young man"—Alexander Hamilton, lacking three months of seventeen—showed himself already acquainted with every aspect of the business and probably had been deputed before to act for his employer in more important matters than copying outgoing letters.   Once Alexander consulted Cruger's "attorneys"—doubt- less Kortright and another business associate vested with final au- thority.   The prudence and decision he now displayed demon- strated his powers and promise, and probably earned him his chance in life—the opportunity to go to the mainland for an edu- cation.   His letter describing the hurricane the following autumn, published in the local newspaper, may have been the final incident that rallied support and shipped him off. But more substantial evidence of his deserts would have been needed to persuade his benefactors. In Cruger's absence young Hamilton had dealt with ship captains, planters, merchants, and lawyers in a way that must have impressed them. Numbers of these may have subscribed to his maintenance in America.

Alexander immediately picked up loose ends of uncompleted transactions and began with new business. In addition to direct dealings with customers and correspondents, he kept Cruger informed of developments and took care, like a good proxy, to save his principal unnecessary trouble or worry.[56] The youthfulness of the author shows in an exultant eagerness to be the complete little merchant.[57]

In spite of a spell of sickness, Alexander reported that he had "sold about 30 bbls flour more & Collected a little more money from different people."[58] Soon, however, he was obliged to impart: "Your Philadelphia flour is . . . of a most swarthy complexion—& withal very untractable; the Bakers complain that they cannot by any means get it to rise. . . . I have observ'd a kind of worm . . . about the surface—which is an indication of age—it could not have been very new when shipd." As the market was overstocked he had some thought of accepting eight pieces of eight from any buyer of good credit who would take forty or fifty barrels.[59] Within a fortnight he was able to dispatch Captain William Newton in the long-expected *Thunderbolt* to Tileman Cruger at Curaçao. He explained Nicholas Cruger's share in vessel and cargo, took pains to salvage the value of casks and staves on board, and prepared for defense against the "Guarda Costas" (Spanish revenue patrols) when the voyage was continued to the Main (Venezuela?) for mules. "Capt. Newton must arm with you," Alexander informed Tileman Cruger, "as he could not so conveniently do it here. Give me leave to hint . . . that you cannot be too particular in your instructions to him. I think he seems to lack experience in such voyages."[60] Perhaps, however, the patrols were to be discounted as a competitor's trick. When a large sloop with seventy mules from the Main arrived, Alexander noted: "The Captain talks largely of Danger & difficultys upon the Coast—but no doubt exaggerates a good deal by way of Stimulation."[61] By this time horses and mules, especially the latter, had mostly replaced oxen as draft animals on St. Croix.[62]

There was "not a moment of time to spare" in speeding Captain Newton down and back with the mules, for the crops were forward. Alexander wrote three business letters on Sunday.[63] To add to his worry, the new *Thunderbolt,* though "a fine vessel indeed," was "not so swift as she ought to be. . . ."[64]

Waiting for a sailing to New York, he could not write to Cruger for six weeks. Then it was to congratulate him on his improved health, report delivery of plate and stockings to Miss Nancy de Nully, Cruger's fiancée, a cheese to her mother, and acknowledge a present of cheese and apples for himself. He had sold candles, hoops, codfish and alewives; the superfine flour was so much in demand by the hitherto complaining bakers that he was raising the price. "Believe me Sir I Dun as hard as is proper."[65]

Then Captain Newton hove into the harbor in the *Thunderbolt* packed with sick mules. Alexander was equal to the emergency. He dealt swiftly with the ailing cargo, immediately provided a new lading for the vessel, and dispatched her back to Curaçao. He confessed his troubles to Tileman Cruger: "Two days ago Capt. Newton delivered me . . . 41 Mules in such order that I have been obliged to send all of them to pasture—and . . . I expect at least a third will die—the highest offer made me for 20 of the best was 70 ps [pieces of eight]—whereas if they had been in good order I could readily have obtained £40 round. . . ." In spite of this unfortunate first voyage, they must try a second time, and he wished to a good market the codfish, bread, and rum he was sending. Then Captain Newton must take in grass, guns, and go to the Spanish Main for more mules, sixty instead of the forty-eight the captain said was his limit.[66]

Nicholas Cruger returned from New York to St. Croix in a voyage of nineteen days, and beginning on March 11, 1772, resumed correspondence in conduct of his affairs. He confirmed his deputy's actions.[67] The fifty letters that have been preserved betray no hiatus in the business during Cruger's sojourn on the continent.[68] Hamilton's precaution to see the mules of the second voyage of the *Thunderbolt* well fed was rewarded when Captain Newton brought up fifty in such good condition that they sold for £36 each on the average. As it was too late to return for more mules, the vessel was freighted with sugar and cotton for New York.[69]   Cruger was not above a little deception to avoid duties.   What Alexander knew of these practices could not have failed to guide his precautions, twenty years later, for detecting evasions of the United States customs.[70]   Alexander also knew at first hand of the slave trade of Kortright & Cruger.[71] That Alexander was constantly ready to apply himself is visible in the correspondence, for his script appears at almost any point— beginning, end, or in the middle of letters copied mostly by others.[72]

However, his thoughts and pen were not confined to such base topics as smoked fish, whale oil, cooperage, and cordage.   He escaped from "the grovelling condition of a clerk" into realms of fancy and speculation.   In the spring of 1771, with an apology for his youth, he submitted two sets of verses, signed "A.H.," to the editor of the local newspaper.   Of the first, a pastoral, the opening stanza ran:

> "In yonder mead my love I found
>   Beside a murm'ring brook reclin'd;
> Her pretty lambkins dancing round
>   Secure in harmless bliss.
> I bad the waters gently glide
>   And vainly hush'd the heedless wind,
> Then, softly kneeling by her side
>   I stole a silent kiss—"

and the lines continued, once or twice becoming a flute-note franker than the inhibited models he was following.   The second piece described a capricious mistress.[73]   In later life he wrote verses from time to time, as we shall see.   His sentimental ones, while tasteful in a mannered fashion, and true to form (they scanned perfectly), were facile but not original.   In the excitement of New York controversy on the eve of the Revolution we are told that he wrote impromptu doggerel lampoons.   It is a pity that none has survived, for his muse was more political than poetic.   Indeed, in Christiansted, he suddenly quit the bisque images of shepherdess and swain for prose jottings on the theory and practice of government.

The week after his polite courtship in the meadow, there appeared in the same columns "Rules for Statesmen," ostensibly from a correspondent in London, but probably the work of the same young penman. If so, they give Hamilton's earliest—and latest—view of the need for authority. Here again he was imitative, but declared the belief in central responsibility which became his tenet. He praised the British system of setting over all departments "a Prime Minister like a Commander in Chief; . . . I think this wise regulation a wholesome restraint on the people, whole [whose] turbulence, at times, . . . require[s] a Dictator. . . ." From "some years gleaning from Machiavel, Puffendorff, &c" he would endeavor to advise "by what means a Premier may act most to the honour of his Prince, and the enlargement of his own power."[74]

These contributions (and perhaps others, for the best file of the St. Croix newspaper is incomplete) were printed more than a year before Hugh Knox, who encouraged his literary efforts, and inserted Alexander's famous hurricane letter (below), could have known him. His reluctance to allow the latter to be printed is in keeping with his pains not to be identified as the author of earlier productions. His first writings on the mainland, far more thorough and industrious, appeared anonymously. Adolescent shyness was the cause in the beginning, but this blended into the fashion of the time and the political prudence that gave pseudonyms to his most celebrated essays.

3

To Continent
and Career

NICHOLAS CRUGER, after the drought that greeted his return to St. Croix, was able to view the prospect of the island with satisfaction: "We are mak'g good Crops, prais'd be God, & have noble seasons of rain that give us every assurance of great Crops the ensuing season."[1]

This and every other buoyant expectation was destroyed by the hurricane that struck St. Croix and neighboring islands at the end of August, 1772. The tempest was said to be the worst in memory or record. It swept St. Croix at dusk without warning. The Windwards were hit two days earlier, but had no means of notifying the Leewards of the storm's course. It blew, with one lull, for six hours. The sea rose twelve or fourteen feet, parting all vessels in the harbor from their anchors and driving them on shore. Thirty persons were killed, more were dangerously wounded. (In the local newspaper names were given for whites only.) Crops were torn up by the roots. The air during the hurricane had a sulfurous smell, leaving cistern water tasting of niter. Losses on St. Croix, while large, were less than a current estimate of a million sterling. In the emergency, Provision Master Gentzmann at the King's Magazine, Christiansted, would sell, "for the use of the inhabitants," rye flour, butter, pork, and beef at low prices (less by the amount of the duty), but only for cash. A movement was afoot for petitioning the king for permanent "liberties . . . of trade hitherto confined. . . ." Loans were expected to be opened in Copenhagen and Amsterdam, and help might come from "the hither Continent" (North America). American papers carried repeated notices.[2]

The storm, it is said, "blew Hamilton into history." Whether or not his written account of the fury of nature prompted admirers, soon after the disaster benefactors sent him to the continent for an education.[3] His description of the hurricane, with pious reflections, was written within the week as a letter to his father ("Honoured Sir") September 6. It was published almost a month later, October 3, in the *Royal Danish-American Gazette* at Christiansted with this explanation: "The following letter was written . . . by a Youth of this Island, to his Father; the copy of it fell by accident into the hands of a gentleman, who, being pleased with it himself, shewed it to others to whom it gave equal satisfaction, and who all agreed that it might not prove unentertaining to the Publick. The Author's modesty in long refusing to submit it to Publick view, is the reason of its making its appearance as late as it now does."[4]

It is a florid bit, penned in self-conscious emotion, but fitting the hortative taste of the day and calculated to provoke a response in those who had passed through the ordeal. A few lines are sufficient to give the flavor:

"Good God! what horror and destruction. . . . It seemed as if a total dissolution of nature was taking place. The roaring of the sea and wind—fiery meteors flying about in the air—the prodigious glare of almost perpetual lightning . . . the ear-piercing shrieks of the distressed, were sufficient to strike astonishment into Angels. . . . My reflections . . . are set forth in the following self-discourse. 'Where now, oh! vile worm, is all thy boasted fortitude and resolution? what is become of thy arrogance and self-sufficiency? . . . how contemptible you now appear. And for why? the jarring of elements—the discord of clouds? Oh! impotent presumptuous fool! how durst thou offend that Omnipotence, whose nod alone were sufficient to quell the destruction that hovers over thee, or crush thee into atoms?' " He must not exult in his deliverance to the point of forgetting the woes of others: "see tender infancy pinched with hunger and hanging on the mother's knee for food! . . . her poverty denies relief—her

breast heaves with pangs of . . . pity—her heart is bursting—
the tears gush down her cheeks. . . ."

We may readily reconstruct the circumstances under which
Alexander's effusion was produced and brought to public notice.
The hurricane happened Monday night, August 31, 1772. On
the following Sunday Hugh Knox, the Presbyterian minister of
Christiansted, addressed a community meeting with a rehearsal of
the experience and inevitable moral exhortations.[5] While under
the spell of Knox's words Alexander went home and gave his
briefer but not more restrained reflections to his father. The
impress of the sermon is unmistakable.[6] Alexander probably
showed the copy to Knox (the "accident" by which it fell into
his hands despite); Knox with appropriate observations passed it
to others, and, as an occasional assistant in editing the *Gazette*,[7]
persuaded the writer to allow it to be printed there.

Since this perceptive, warmhearted clergyman played a determining part in Hamilton's career, and followed him with encouragement when the protégé had outrun the patron, it is proper
at this point to tell something about him.[8] He was born in 1727
(and thus was almost thirty years Hamilton's senior), in the north
of Ireland, and was of Scotch blood.[9] Arriving in America at the
age of twenty-four with a classical education and "remarkably
prepossessing . . . personal appearance and manners," it is likely
that he applied to his countryman the Reverend Francis Alison
for a position as assistant in the latter's academy at New London,
Pennsylvania.[10] Though he had no place for Knox, it was doubtless Alison who recommended him to the Synod of Philadelphia
for a license to preach. Knox presented himself for examination
by the Presbytery of New Castle, at Elk River, in August 1751,
but seems to have been rejected.[11]

Alison persisted in his good offices, and secured for Knox a small
school at Head of Bohemia, Delaware, under patronage of the
Reverend John Rodgers, minister of churches at St. George's and
Middletown nearby.[12] Knox became a disciple of Rodgers, attended his church regularly, and was popular as schoolmaster.
For more than a year his lack of "real piety," which the elders at
Elk River perhaps suspected, did not discover itself. But then
one Saturday afternoon, in the Middletown tavern, companions
called on the "parson," as they named him for his religious zeal, to

give them a sermon. When two refusals did not put them off, Knox mimicked Mr. Rodgers in his discourse of the Sunday before with such spirit that "his profane hearers were deeply affected." The tavern keeper, in the next room, believed that Rodgers had set up his pulpit in the public house. Knox himself sat down in contrition that became conversion, and the next morning, with no word to anyone, quit that part of the country.[13] Some months later he implored Mr. Rodgers's forgiveness for the mock sermon and begged his recommendation to President Aaron Burr for admission to the College of New Jersey, then at Newark.[14] Knox graduated, A.B., in 1754, remained for a year of theological study with President Burr, and was awarded the A.M. degree.[15]

The Dutch Reformed church in the island of Saba, Netherlands West Indies, applying to the New York Presbytery for a minister (the Calvinist creeds being the same), Knox was ordained in 1755 and dispatched to the call.[16] On this tiny mountainous island (five square miles, 180 dwellings) Knox remained for seventeen years. Though he married Mary, the daughter of Governor Peter Simmons, and lived in perfect harmony in the governor's house,[17] he was intellectually and spiritually lonely[18] in this singularly isolated spot. The island was and is approached only by surfboats, and the settlement, called The Bottom because it nestles in the crater of the extinct volcano, is a thousand feet up, and is reached by tortuous paths through the rocks.[19] It is a tribute that in his confinement he preserved his good sense and charity and, like John on Patmos, could entertain visions of another world. He regularly ordered books, published sermons and moral essays, and conducted an exacting correspondence with at least one fellow clergyman whom he had known in his first years in New Jersey.[20]

Knox visited St. Croix in September and October 1771 "& found a number of Scotch, English, Irish & north American presbyterians there, who gave me a cordial & unanimous invitation to come among them." A first plan of "a coalition with the Dutch & a Colleagueship with the dutch minister," though most of the Dutch had subscribed to it, was abandoned when "the English party thought best to have a place of worship of their own. . . ."[21] His inadequate salary of 800 pieces of eight on Saba, against 1200 pcs. on St. Croix, was assigned as a reason for this removal.[22]   An attack on his character in 1770, notwithstanding he was elaborately exculpated, as attested by official certificates,[23] probably made him restless to leave.   Doubtless the superior size, population, and prosperity of St. Croix, of which he spoke with admiration, had most influence.

It is likely that Knox transferred permanently to Christiansted, St. Croix, where he was "Minister of the Presbyterian Church,"[24] in May 1772.   He may have known young Hamilton from his visit of the previous autumn, but any longer association before Alexander left for the mainland in October 1772 is ruled out.[25] An immediate sympathy sprang up between them.   Both had the taste for study and literature in a community more given to ledgers and litigation.   Alexander's gifts were obviously to be his reliance, and probably from the first Knox was alert to contrive means of fulfilling the boy's ambitions.   In his published sermons we have hints of his sharp lookout for talent that would reward encouragement.   He praised Maecenus, patron of Virgil, Horace, and Livy, for "drawing these incomparable geniuses out of obscurity, and cherishing and developing their parts. . . ."[26] Nor could Knox have forgotten what he himself owed to the early friendship of Alison and Rodgers.   Alexander moreover was an orphan, for his father bade fair to continue absent.   The youth in Cruger's store having attracted his attention, the clergyman doubtless pressed on him his own and others' printed rules of right conduct.[27]   Besides, probably Knox, so far as brief months allowed, directed Hamilton's miscellaneous reading.[28]

We may think that Hugh Knox influenced Alexander to support the cause of the American colonies in his polemics answering the "Westchester Farmer."   Knox was a stout partisan of independence, as we know from his later letters to Hamilton and from the fact that he wrote a formal defense which he intended should be offered to Congress through Hamilton.[29]   Plausibly, a further influence of Knox was on Hamilton's noticeable early piety.[30] Solicitous letters of Knox in later years, when his protégé was playing an active part in securing American independence, showed the same prescience of Hamilton's role which marked his first intervention on the boy's behalf.

While the hurricane leveled crops and buildings, it raised up charity.   The disaster produced a generosity that called forth high praise at the time.³¹   Knox publicly thanked Governor-General Ulrich Wilhelm Van Roepstorff for his attention, official and private, to the distresses of St. Croix,³² and young Hamilton in his letter on the hurricane included the same appreciation of benevolence.   It may be that this mellow mood, directed to Alexander by his description of the calamity, was responsible for the offer of admiring elders to transfer him from island countinghouse to mainland classroom.³³   The evidence points to Hugh Knox as proposer and organizer of the plan to send Alexander to America. He wrote Hamilton a dozen years later, "I have always had a just & secret pride in having advised you to go to America, & in having recommended you to some [of] my old friends there."³⁴   Since the contributions were sizable,³⁵ and promptly pledged, we may suppose that they came from a few individuals of wealth who had knowledge of the young man's ability and promise.   His relatives were in poor state to help;³⁶ if his cousin, Ann Venton, supplemented with remittances, as is probable, these were hard-won advances from her father's estate.   Probably the chief benefactors were Nicholas Cruger,³⁷ Alexander's employer, who was grateful for his service and could muster means, and his partner Cornelius Kortright, who must have observed the youth's management of the business in Cruger's absence.   It is to be noticed that it was Kortright & Company in New York, "to whom West India produce was consigned, to be sold and appropriated to the support of Hamilton."³⁸   David Beckman, though away from the island at the time,³⁹ would be a probable contributor, for he was an old friend of the family, merchant and planter, and later took letters between Knox and Hamilton.⁴⁰   The merchant Thomas Stevens may have helped. He was the father of Alexander's young friend Edward, who had already been sent to school on the continent. Alexander may have been a guest in the Stevens home a few years before.   Town Captain De Nully, on whose plantation Alexander's mother had lived, and who was the father-in-law of Cruger, perhaps assisted.   James Towers, the probate judge, connected with Hamilton in several ways, and Governor Van Roepstorff perhaps were smaller contributors.

Aside from his friends Hugh Knox, the Presbyterian minister, and Nicholas Cruger, his recent employer, of whom we may be certain, we can only speculate about those assembled at the wharf on a day in September or October 1772 when Alexander Hamilton sailed for Boston.[41]   The vessel is not further identified than by the recollection that as she approached the continent a stubborn fire broke out and all were for a time in peril.[42]   No such mishap is noted in the shipping news of Boston or New York, though other accidents and misfortunes of incoming craft are frequently mentioned.[43]   "Waters from St. Croix" reached Boston before October 22 and may have brought Alexander Hamilton;[44] however, some evidence, mentioned below, is that the young West Indian did not come until nine months later, in the early summer of 1773. The fact that he took ship for Boston rather than for New York direct would indicate that his friends, whenever joined in his behalf, used the first opportunity to get him to the continent, even at extra expense in reaching his final destination.

This was Alexander's permanent farewell to his home in the West Indies, for he never returned and, indeed, after he landed at Boston never left the continent.   We may think that as he accepted the good wishes for his future, and saw the town receding, he was excited and hopeful rather than regretful.   Though the pang of his mother's death was four years behind, and pain for his father's absence was older, the daily round in Christiansted could hardly hold for a youth so zestful many charms that competed with the prospect of a real sea voyage and at the end of it wider exploits for which he had yearned.   Past the cay and out through the reef where the surf broke—these were the last confinements of the little lovely world of his boyhood.   Beyond lay a limitless land, where nobody knew his story.

But growing up in a small island 1,300 miles from New York was in several ways advantageous to Alexander Hamilton in the career he was to have on the continent.   He was able to view the mainland, its people and problems, with detachment, as his prior experience had been elsewhere.   Already when he came he had lived under two sovereignties—British on Nevis-St. Kitts, something of which he would remember, and Danish on St. Croix. Denmark's oversight of her American possession was genuinely restrictive in phases, violable in others, but amiable in all. Reaching North America when he did, between youth and manhood, receptive and yet almost ready to form firm judgments, he was presented with colonial contrasts.   Denmark was a petty continental power, ruling Caribbean islands less than one-hundredth her size, while Britain, in insular majesty, was mistress here of vastly more territory and potential resources. St. Croix, with neighbors under British, French, Dutch, and Spanish flags, must be and was content to remain subordinate to a European king, while the English colonies on the mainland, with only Spain at hand, and that in the territorial penumbra, were rising to rebellion.[45]

In another particular Hamilton's boyhood and youth in the miniature society of St. Croix were to serve him in the greater forum to which he came. His responsibilities as Cruger's deputy had thrown him in touch with the principal figures of the island, whether in private or in public life. He had known and dealt with men in authority, at least such as was there wielded. His attitude toward them was deferential but not diffident. He arrived in America with the awe of personages worn off. Moreover, his contacts, though at secondhand, had included distant places, through Cruger's correspondence with merchants in England, North and South America, as well as in the other islands of the Caribbean. In advance of seeing them, Boston, New York, and Philadelphia were for him more than places on a map. Amsterdam loans, long before he contracted them for a needy nation, were known to him through the familiar dealings of island sugar planters. He had been in, and by proxy a part of, one of the world's crossroads of trade.

When Alexander Hamilton arrived at Boston[46] he found that cradle of liberty in lusty cry, with no soothing rocking but instead rude jolts from Lieutenant-Governor Hutchinson and the king and Commons. Five in a taunting crowd had been killed by Captain Preston's guard on a snowy night in King Street more than two years earlier. That this was promptly dubbed the "horrid massacre" was not the earliest evidence of the zeal with which Boston "incendiaries" improved their cause. The next month a merchant of the town summed up much in a brief diary entry, "Capt. Scot Brings an acct of the Repeal of the Duties on Glass, Oyl Paper & painters Colours but the Duty on Tea still Remains."[47] With the tea duty remained the Sons of Liberty, gone on from drinking the king's health to defying his tax, and town meetings that overflowed from Faneuil Hall into Old South Church. James Otis who damned unwarranted searches later got "into a mad Freak"

and broke windows in the Town House and fired from his own, but
still was chosen a committeeman to wait on Hutchinson "ab[ut] the
Judges Salary."[48]   This last was the demand at the time of young
Hamilton's arrival—that the colony, not the crown, should pay the
piper and thereby call the tune from the bench.[49]

Between whiles, "Hallooing in the street" of "a mob of upwards
a thousand people" that had tarred and feathered an informer and
put him in a cart, and burning of contraband at the beacon on the
Common gave way to dutiful displays.   If Alexander lingered in
Boston until October 25 he surely saw "the Hon. Col. Hancock"
at the head of "his Excellency's Company of Cadets," turned out
this time to celebrate the thirteenth anniversary of George III's
accession to the throne.   The resplendent Hancock felt confirmed
in his own regality.   "The Company being under Arms and in
uniform Dress made a very fine and respectable Appearance, they
were exercised on the Common until Noon, and having refreshed
themselves at the Colonel's, they marched into King-Street, where
after firing three Vollies, they performed . . . a Variety of Evolutions. . . ."[50]

However, this was an interlude in Boston's yeasty penchant for
protest.   We may be certain that Alexander read the newspapers,
for all his life he was alert to the press for its effect on public
opinion.   The political editorials and letters in the Boston sheets of
those days jumped out at the beholder, prodding him into partisan-
ship on one side or the other.[51]

"America [n] Solon" commenced an indignant letter in the
Boston Gazette of October 12: "The People of this Country are
much alarmed by the report that the Judges of this Province, have
Salaries appointed them by another Power, contrary to the . . .
meaning of the Charter."   Though the port of Boston was yet to
be "shut up," many of the shops must have been closed as shoppers
immured themselves in meetings that issued remonstrances and
more meetings to receive official replies that in turn brought rejoinders.   Sam Adams, called by a Tory, with eloquent restraint,
"as equal to the task of forwarding a rebellion as most men," was
at his provocative best.   His middling private figure, by the heats
engendered, was cast against the sky in a massive mirage, and already the figment was becoming the fact.

Probably, as a young stranger, Alexander would not attend citizens' meetings, though joining the magnetized crowds was the only ticket of admission required. However, he could not escape what was passing in the center of continental excitement when, on October 28, "the Freeholders and other Inhabitants . . . met at Faneuil Hall to Enquire into . . . a Report . . . that Salaries are annexed to the Offices of the Judges of the Superior Court . . . whereby they are rendered Independent of the Grants of the General Assembly . . . contrary to . . . invariable Usage." The resulting protest to Hutchinson commanded big type, and his reply was subjoined.[52]

"Oliver Cromwell" introduced his exhortation with vehement verse:

> "Our Wives, & our Babes, still protected shall know,
> Those who dare to be free, shall ever be so;
> On these Arms & these Arts they may safely rely,
> For as FREEMEN we'll live, or like HEROES we'll die."[53]

As he had no friend nor introduction in Boston, young Hamilton while there would lodge at one of the taverns. State Street was full of signs inviting strangers. The Exchange, at the northwest corner of Exchange Street, was then kept by Daniel Jones. Joseph Ingersol was licensed at the famous Bunch of Grapes at the southeast corner of Kilby, though this "best punch house in Boston," where royal governors on arrival were entertained at "elegant" dinners, may have been beyond the purse of Alexander. The Marlborough Head was "next the Grapes" and perhaps was a compromise between refinement and economy. The Sign of Oliver Cromwell, Joshua Bracket, host, was in School Street near the home of James Otis.[54]

Since the way had been prepared for Alexander in New York and New Jersey—support and ready-made friends with knowledge and advice—he doubtless did not tarry over the educational advantages of Boston, with Harvard College and a variety of preparatory schools at hand.[55] Perhaps young Hamilton went from Boston to New York by sea, which was cheaper and usually faster than by land. If not, "the first stage coach that ever was improv'd on this Road," that of Nicholas Green, was leaving Boston on its regular run to New York on October 26. If Alexander decided to "depend on his Fidelity and Dispatch" he applied to the proprietor at the Royal Exchange Tavern or "at Mr. John Boardman's, opposite the Three Doves in Marlborough-Street, South-End."[56]

We are principally dependent on the recollections of Hercules Mulligan for our knowledge of Alexander's arrival in New York, his early transfer to Elizabethtown, New Jersey, for schooling, his abortive effort to enter the College of New Jersey at Princeton, and further particulars of his first years in this country.[57] Mulligan knew Alexander "shortly after his arrival in the City of New York. . . ."[58] In these few days the young stranger would present himself at the counting house of Kortright & Company, the firm that was to receive and sell West Indian produce for his benefit. Here in addition to Lawrence Kortright he would meet his partner, Hugh Mulligan. Alexander would also deliver letters of introduction he had brought from Hugh Knox to Dr. John Rodgers and the Reverend John Mason,[59] leading Presbyterian clergymen of the city.

In sending his protégé to Rodgers, Knox, as we have seen, was addressing his own early patron. John Rodgers (1727–1811) was born of Irish parents in Boston but grew up in Philadelphia. There, at the age of twelve, he was so moved, it is said, by the evangelical preaching of George Whitefield that a lantern he held for the speaker at an open-air meeting fell from his hand and broke on the pavement. But Whitefield had shed the "New Light" for the more ardent Presbyterians of America, and in its beams Rodgers walked. At the academy of the Reverend Samuel Blair in Chester County, Pennsylvania, he acquired the classics and the friendship of the Reverend Samuel Davies who was later to succeed Jonathan Edwards as president of Princeton. Rodgers, licensed to preach, went to Virginia as assistant to Davies as roving missionary, and was expelled by the legislature at the urging of the clergy of the established church. Settling in Delaware, he nursed the talents of Hugh Knox. He became pastor of the Wall Street and Brick churches in New York City in 1765, the Reverend James Caldwell of Elizabethtown preaching the installation sermon. He was among the first to welcome John Witherspoon to America, and between them grew an intimate and lasting friendship.[60]

Hugh Mulligan doubtless turned Alexander over to his younger bachelor brother Hercules, who promptly took the youth under his

wing and went with him to meet Drs. Rodgers and Mason.   Hercules Mulligan was born in Coleraine, County Antrim, Ireland, in
1740, and thus was thirty-two, or fifteen years older than Alexander.[61]   He was probably employed by Kortright & Company before
he entered business for himself as tailor and haberdasher prior to
his admission as a freeman of New York in 1765.[62]   In 1772, when
Alexander arrived, his shop and home were in Water Street "next
door to Philip Rhinelander's china store, between Burling's Slip and
the Fly Market."[63]   It was likely that Alexander lodged here before
he moved over to New Jersey; he later "boarded with" Mulligan's
family.[64]

Mulligan cut a figure in the Revolution, at first public and later,
probably through the agency of Alexander Hamilton, exceedingly
private.   He is said to have been one of the "Liberty Boys" who
fought with British soldiers on Golden Hill (now John Street west
of William) in January 1770, six weeks before the Boston massacre.[65]   He was more responsibly a member of the Committee of
One Hundred named in May 1775, and helped haul off the guns
from the Battery in August of that year.   In escaping from New
York after the battle of Long Island he was taken by the British
and held in the city during the war.   After Hamilton was appointed to Washington's staff in 1777, Mulligan became a spy
("confidential correspondent") of the commander in chief.   Desire to acknowledge this service, it is alleged, prompted Washington, on entering New York with the American army after the
British evacuation, to take his first breakfast with Mulligan.[66]   In
1786 Mulligan was a member of the Society for Promoting the
Manumission of Slaves, in which Hamilton was early active, and
their relations continued to be close and affectionate.[67]

Young Hamilton had been sent to the continent for his education.   The choice of New York, dictated by the connections of
Knox, Cruger, and Kortright there,[68] was lucky for his later role in
American public life.   By this accident a mid-colony point became
his locus.   New York was necessary for union, and union was
essential to New York.   Hamilton was in the most fortunate position for national action.   He would have come to prominence and
influence in any case, but, had he been identified with the South or
New England, would have been hampered by sectional commitments.   As it was, he was saved any handicap on this score.

It was intended from the first that he should go through college. We know this from the subjects and speed of his preparatory study, and from his prompt application, as soon as that was accomplished, for college entrance. How and where to make up his lacks in Latin and Greek (of which he could have no knowledge) and in mathematics beyond arithmetic? Only assiduous work for nearly a year filled these deficiencies. If he could have afforded a private tutor, that would have been the best answer to his needs, for, not yet ready for college, he was already older than some students at graduation.[69] He could not be held to the slow pace usual in classes under a schoolmaster; his mental maturity and ability to express himself would embarrass him and others if he had much younger deskmates. He must attend a school where the masters would conform the instruction to his special requirements.

As Elias Boudinot and William Livingston, prominent in the circle of Knox's acquaintance, were established at Elizabethtown, New Jersey, and as that village had an excellent academy under a Princeton Presbyterian headmaster, his friends in New York sent him there.[70] The place had been settled for more than a century, and had early been the capital of the province, but had not grown beyond some fourscore of houses dotted along five roads.[71] An old litigation over land rights, between settlers brought in by Berkeley and Carteret, and the "Elizabethtown Associates" who had bought from the Indians, still rumbled along as a sort of obbligato to the life of the community. This contest between privilege and popular claims exhibited the hardihood in dispute of Quakers, Puritans, and Scotch-Presbyterians. The difference was symbolized in the two churches, St. John's (Anglican) and the Presbyterian. The latter, as became dissenters, was the more assertive, and its leaders, who were Hamilton's patrons, were soon to be conspicuous in the Revolutionary cause.[72]

The Academy, on the grounds and under the auspices of the church, where Alexander became a pupil in the autumn of 1772, had earlier been taught "to universal Acceptance by Mr. T. Reeve."[73] The two-story wooden building with a cupola, "on the upper end of the Burial Yard Lot" (now southwest corner of Broad Street and Caldwell Place) was erected partly from popular subscription, partly from church funds. Elias Boudinot was certainly a leader in the project, and from what we know of his charitable concern for education he proposed that the school accept "a Number of Free Scholars in this Town. . . ."[74]   It is likely, from all the circumstances, that Alexander received tuition aid indirectly through Boudinot or William Livingston or both.

Francis Barber was chosen by the Visitors[75] to take charge of the Academy beginning November 1771. He requires more than passing notice,[76] for he was Alexander's first teacher if we think of systematic education. The youth spent more hours in the company of Barber than that of any other person at Elizabethtown, and master must have been a model for pupil in ideals and conduct. Previously, perhaps since his graduation at Princeton four years earlier, Barber had been teaching a Latin school at Hackensack, and "those of his Pupils who have been sent to the Colleges, were found well fitted for a Reception."[77]   Barber was born at Princeton, New Jersey, November 26, 1750,[78] and thus was only four years Alexander's senior. He was the eldest of four children of Patrick Barber, an Irish immigrant settled at Princeton.[79]   After preparing, probably at the Nassau Hall Grammar School, he graduated in 1767, A.B., from the college,[80] and was awarded the A.M. three years later. It may have been during the year of Alexander's enrollment in Barber's Academy that Barber married Mary Ogden of Elizabethtown; when she died in October, 1773,[81] he was so distressed as to be incapacitated for several months from carrying on the work of his school, which devolved on his ushers.[82]

Barber's continuous, courageous, and varied service through the Revolution proves his steadfast character. That Hamilton, as his pupil, had been impressed by his intelligence and reliability is certain; that Hamilton, as Washington's aide, recommended his former teacher for military assignments demanding resourcefulness and judgment is reasonably assumed. On the outbreak of the Revolution, Barber gave up the Academy and was active in recruiting before he was commissioned major in the Third New Jersey Regiment in January 1776.[83]   As Hamilton was instrumental in inaugurating the work of Steuben as inspector-general, he may have proposed Barber for one of four divisional inspectors, a post requiring tact no less than system.[84]   The old friendship may have figured in Barber's appointment as deputy adjutant general for Sullivan's expedition against the Indians.[85]   He and Hamilton were in the same battles—Trenton, Princeton, Brandywine, Germantown,

Monmouth, and at Yorktown Barber was in Hamilton's command that stormed a British redoubt. Having survived three battle wounds and been promoted colonel of his regiment, he was killed by the falling of a tree near headquarters at Newburgh just as the final peace was about to be proclaimed.[86]

The Elizabethtown Academy, at the time Alexander was galloping through the course in 1772–1773, was the best established and best staffed in the area with the possible exceptions of the preparatory departments of King's College at New York and of the College of New Jersey at Princeton.[87] Besides offering "the languages" (the old staples Latin and Greek), the Academy was conforming to the growing demand for English literature and composition, elocution, mathematics, and geography.[88] The work in Latin and Greek was not described, but taken for granted. The Academy prepared for any college, especially Princeton; the entrance requirements of the latter were, besides the common branches, the ability to write Latin prose, translate Vergil, Cicero, and the Greek gospels, and a commensurate knowledge of Latin and Greek grammar.[89]

4

Elizabethtown and
Quest for College

ELIZABETHTOWN was a good foster home for Alexander in his first year in America.   While adjacent to New York and in the cultural radius of Philadelphia as well, its identity was preserved.   The community felt the currents of discussion that flowed up and down the coast from Boston to Charleston, but had its own position of leadership in New Jersey.   Had Hamilton remained in Boston where he landed, his commitment to the cause of the colonies would have been prompter and by the same sign premature.   He was here to learn, and, so far as public questions were concerned, the informed detachment of Elizabethtown was conducive to calm consideration.   His mentors, among the leading figures in the province, were slow to rebel against the policy of Great Britain toward the colonies.   New Jersey had no prominent personages who early caught the revolutionary fire, much less any who made themselves torches like Otis, Sam Adams, and Hancock of Massachusetts, Richard Henry Lee and Patrick Henry of Virginia, or Christopher Gadsden of South Carolina.   Instead, William Livingston, Elias Boudinot, Elias Dayton, Aaron Ogden, Richard Stockton, and others like them long reposed faith in appeals to king and Parliament.   Reconciliation to the mother country was their wish, armed resistance was their fear, American independence was their worst conjecture.   This was the language of the group even while serving in continental and provincial congresses, and their loyalty was not relinquished until news of the battles of Lexington and Concord.[1]

[44]

The chief of Alexander's older friends in Elizabethtown, to both of whom he brought letters from Hugh Knox,[2] were William Livingston and Elias Boudinot. Men of parts and position, strong Presbyterians both, of comfortable means, they made themselves foster parents of the young West Indian and he became a familiar in their handsome homes. The notion that Alexander was a waif cast up on an alien shore, with his own way to make unaided, is revised by our knowledge of his reception at Elizabethtown. He could hardly have found a warmer welcome or sponsors more likely to furnish him with favorable introduction. Their influence on a gifted youth, in opinions as well as in kindness, is not to be missed. Francis Barber's political principles in 1772–1773 when Alexander was his pupil must be inferred from his later instant enlistment in the military forces of New Jersey and his unfaltering fidelity during the war. We know far more of the ideas and advocacies of his hosts Livingston and Boudinot. Both men were deliberate by training and habit, conservative by economic interest; when young Hamilton was their protégé at Elizabethtown they were watching the rise of the Revolutionary storm but hoping that it might be averted with reason and honor.

William Livingston (1723–1790) was a lanky man with a large long nose, a firm mouth, and dark hair tied behind.[3] His mental integrity and candor combined with a contentiousness almost perverse; vexation at trifles in the family circle corresponded to fractiousness in public controversies. In spite of constant discharge of public trusts, deep down he wished to be let alone. The times and his talents made him a sort of circulating hermit, which in itself was enough to explain his irritability.[4] Born at Albany, a younger son of Philip, second lord of Livingston Manor, and his wife Catherine Van Brugh, Scottish and Dutch traditions made him an assertive Calvinist. He wanted to study painting in Italy but found himself, in obedience to parental prudence, learning instead Latin paradigms and logic at Yale, where he graduated at the head of his class in 1741. He then read law with James Alexander,[5] whose penchant for protest he copied, and left this master for another. He married Susanna French of Albany, whose father's landholdings in New Jersey gave the young man an early connection with that province. His busy law practice in New York did not prevent him from indulging his literary bent. Longest remembered of his verse was "Philosophic Solitude, or the Choice of a Rural Life,"[6] and he contributed his opinions, in regular columns, to New York newspapers. The first of these publications, the "Independent Reflector" (fifty-two numbers, 1752–1753), was a separate paper, or periodical tract for the times, of Livingston and some of his friends; it suspended when the printer refused longer to bring out such telling excoriations of ministerial abuses.[7]   Thereafter he filled and perhaps sometimes subsidized space in other sheets[8] to insist on civil liberties,[9] separation of church and state, and support of representative government.[10]   As spokesman of the Whig, Presbyterian, dissenter party in colonial New York, Livingston opposed the Tory Episcopal faction.   The issue was only incipiently independence; clashes were over specific proposals held to connote undue home-government interference.   Such was Livingston's fight against establishing King's College, funds for which came from public lotteries, as an adjunct of the Church of England.[11]

Having pined for solitude, Livingston prepared for a rural life by winding up his law practice in New York, May 1772,[12] and retiring to Elizabethtown.   He lived in the village during erection of the house on his estate, a mile to the northward, until the fall of 1773.[13] As Alexander left for New York about then, if he was a guest in the Livingston home part of the time while a student in Barber's school it must have been at Elizabethtown and not at Liberty Hall.[14]

The year that Hamilton was in Elizabethtown was one of domesticity for William Livingston.   His one dabble in politics was a lampoon on the royal governor and an opinion favoring the Assembly against him.[15]   Livingston's lively intelligence and acrid wit could not have failed to furnish the young stranger a slant on the passing scene.   At the Livingstons' he surely met public figures and three men with whom, before many years, he was to be more closely identified than any could then guess.   William Alexander, later called Lord Stirling for his claim to a Scottish title, Livingston's brother-in-law, lived at nearby Basking Ridge; Hamilton was to know him better as major general in the Revolution.   William Duer on his way from England had tarried in the West Indies, and was soon to marry the Stirlings' daughter Catherine.   Duer became Hamilton's associate promoter in an ill-starred industrial venture at Passaic Falls and, ere recklessness overtook him, Hamilton's first assistant in the Treasury.   Different from both of these, combining

Stirling's steadfastness and Duer's acuteness, was John Jay, who married Alexander's friend Sarah Livingston at Liberty Hall the following spring. His name was to be linked with Hamilton's in every way that like purposes could suggest. In addition the Livingston and Stirling sons and daughters were Alexander's familiars now and in the years to come; possibly through the Livingston girls he met his wife. It has been said that Hamilton had no boyhood, that he leaped from earning his living as an orphan into man's estate. But his years of school and college show that his overflowing energy and spirits left opportunity for youthful enjoyment. The warm friendships he formed from the first with his elders grew from their approval of his diligence and maturity, but these qualities do not explain his intimacy with those of his own age, such as his companions at Elizabethtown and in King's.

We are tempted, in trying to account for qualities in Alexander Hamilton, to conjecture influences where they did not exist. It is possible that what he got from William Livingston was good dinners and family friendship. But, however impalpable, a good deal of Livingston's polemic skill, straightforward writing style, and zeal for civil liberties must have impressed the sensitive young visitor who was soon to equal and surpass him in these features.[16] Nor should we discount the example Livingston gave of convictions not readily revised, though set aside when events dictated another course of action.[17]

Similar to Livingston in principles, but of more emotional nature, was Elias Boudinot (1740–1821), to whom, as host and patron, Alexander was even more indebted. Alexander and Boudinot had links from the start, besides the recommendation of Hugh Knox. Like Hamilton on his mother's side, Boudinot on his father's side was of French extraction, and the parents of both had lived in the West Indies.[18] Boudinot studied law with Richard Stockton, of "Morven," Princeton, with whom he was doubly connected since each married the other's sister.[19] A recollection of Elias and of Elisha, of a date a little after Hamilton's stay, was of "two brothers, lawyers, elegant men, tall, handsome and every way prepossessing," who "used to attend the court . . . and whenever they spoke, crowds were attracted to hear them. . . ."[20]

Just at the time of Alexander's arrival at Elizabethtown, Boudinot paid "Cash for Purchase of Great House & Lott."[21] This was

Boxwood Hall, now shorn of its wings but otherwise restored, a few minutes' walk across Horse Hollow to the Academy. Here it is believed Alexander was a guest during much of his student year. The Boudinots lived comfortably from his law practice, real-estate dealings, and produce from his farm at Basking Ridge.[22] The two little girls were Susanna Vergereau, eight, and Anna Maria, a baby of seven months when Alexander first knew the family.[23] That the young West Indian was welcomed as a frequent visitor or guest for months at a time is assumed from circumstantial evidence. Alexander's tuition to Barber—£5 a year plus £1 10s for "wood and cost of house cleaning" and another pound for "Entrance light Money"—would have been paid by himself from remittances through Kortright & Company, but entertainment in the homes of his patrons was a major assistance in stretching his income.[24]

Alexander's piety, or at least religious observance, on which a college friend soon remarked, carried over from St. Croix[25] and could not save being intensified in the Presbyterian environment of Elizabethtown and especially by association with Elias Boudinot, who had a theological preoccupation that must either put one on his knees or make him a rebellious blasphemer.[26] At some time in his youth Hamilton assiduously outlined the first two chapters of Genesis and the Book of Revelation.[27] Such zeal bespoke belief. Boudinot, unlike Livingston, was without reserve; his goodheartedness threatened to be overwhelming, even ostentatious, in a fashion that Hamilton, certainly at a later date, would not have admired in another. The prime example, aside from provisions of his remarkable will,[28] was at the funeral service for the Reverend James Caldwell, his pastor who was killed by a British sentry at Elizabethtown Point, and whose wife had earlier been slain by a chance shot through her window in the battle at Springfield. As the coffin rested on Boudinot's broad doorstone he ranged the nine orphan children around it and appealed to the assembled mourners to adopt or otherwise provide for them. The affection of Alexander for the family is preserved in consolatory lines he wrote for Mrs. Boudinot on the death of her younger child, Anna Maria, which occurred in September, 1774. Though in a manner less fulsome than Boudinot's own, they mirror something of the home atmosphere.[29]

Hamilton and Boudinot were to be thrown much together in after years; they bargained with the British for the exchange of prisoners, excoriated a mutinous threat of soldiers to Congress for what it was, and Boudinot at the most critical junctures came forward in Congress to defend with all his weight and skill Hamilton's Treasury policies. Hamilton in turn gratified Boudinot by proposing him as director of the Mint, though the young nation could have used the Jerseyman's powers and prestige in more profitable assignments.

Other friends and preceptors of Alexander at Elizabethtown require mention. Across the road from Boudinot, in a tasteful house that had belonged to Governor Jonathan Belcher,[30] lived William Peartree Smith. He was a New York man, bred to the law, but, having an independent fortune, he never practiced. A classmate of Livingston at Yale, they collaborated in journalistic attacks on Episcopal pretensions and moved to Elizabethtown together. Smith was a leader in many civic enterprises; he was trustee of the Church, visitor to the Academy, and entered the Revolutionary contest as member of the New Jersey Committee of Correspondence, Provincial and Continental congresses. His facile pen was ever at the service of the patriots. Alexander must have been often in his house, for his son Belcher, though a sophomore at Princeton, was about Alexander's age, and "Caty," who was to marry Elisha Boudinot, was slightly younger.

At the center of the community was the Reverend James Caldwell, the Presbyterian pastor whom Alexander heard preach every Sunday and who was the close supervisor of the Academy in the churchyard.[31] A "New Lights" apostle of George Whitefield, who had roused Elizabethtown a generation earlier, Caldwell "was uncommonly eloquent and pathetic, rarely preaching without weeping himself, and at times would melt his whole audience into tears."[32] Always, as he said, "much connected with the public,"[33] with the outbreak of war, as Commissary for New Jersey, he was provider for the troops as well as pulpiteer, and gave his life in the cause.[34]

If all of Caldwell's tendencies were separatist, in politics as in religion, those of Dr. Thomas Bradbury Chandler, rector of St. John's Episcopal Church, were orthodox and loyal. Portly, "of a countenance expressive of high intelligence, though considerably marred by the small pox, of an uncommonly blue eye," he deplored Whitefield's revival, widened the breach between Church and Meeting and soon that between people and Parliament. Though

rarely would Alexander desert Caldwell's sermon for Chandler's
service, the vocal Church of England clergyman must have been
the first of assertive Tory sentiments whom Alexander encountered,
and afterward they were antagonists in the pamphleteering that
preceded the Revolution. Dr. Chandler fled to England with
President Myles Cooper of King's College and lived there on a
royal pension for a decade[35] before returning to this country in his
last years.

We shall meet with many instances of Hamilton's capacity to cut
through a large amount of work at maximum speed, though with
assiduous effort. This facility, or habit, was shown at Elizabethtown, where he made the most of his opportunities in the Academy.
After studying till midnight he was often seen in the cemetery at an
early hour preparing his lessons for the day.[36]

At this pace, in less than a year at the Academy he was prepared
to enter college, and Mulligan (his bursar-guardian) was so informed in a letter from Barber. Alexander "came to N.Y., and
told me he preferred Princeton to King's Colledge because it was
more republican."[37] Every circumstance drew Hamilton toward
the College of New Jersey at Princeton. Hugh Knox, of St. Croix,
and his masters at Elizabethtown were Princeton graduates. Elias
Boudinot had been elected a trustee only the year before; Dr. John
Rodgers, William Livingston, and William Peartree Smith were
trustees, and the two last had sons there at the time. The whole
connection of the Presbyterian community in which Alexander had
been lodged was with Princeton. In addition to these personal
reasons, Alexander had formed a political preference, doubtless
pointed by conversations with Livingston and Smith who had casti-
gated claims of Church of England privilege at the New York
college. He likely heard at first hand from Belcher Smith, Brockholst Livingston, and other Elizabethtown boys who were at Princeton about student debates and other doings there.[38] Mulligan,
when Alexander came over to discuss college plans, probably expected the boy to remain with him in New York and attend
King's.[39] So Alexander wanted to offer him other than casual
grounds for choosing Princeton, that he thought it "more republican."[40]

Aside from subtler intimations of Princeton's democratic claim,
President Witherspoon's open boast of it, and the rejoinders he

provoked, had been much in the newspapers during the previous year. Princeton had among its eighty-five students "many from the *West Indies*,"[41] and Witherspoon had been angling for more from that quarter with an eye to tuition money and collateral gifts. Following his successful canvassing trips in this country, especially to the southward, the trustees early in 1772 urged him to make a tour of the West Indies, which had been represented to the board as holding prospects of pupils and funds.[42] Witherspoon did not make the journey, but he plowed the ground for emissaries in March, 1772, with an *Address* to the Islands.[43] In his zeal to display the peculiar attractions of Princeton, President Witherspoon, unintentionally as he afterward explained, posed comparisons unfavorable to other American colleges, especially King's in New York. This led to a newspaper and pamphlet controversy that explored the relative independence and democracy of the two institutions.[44]

If Hamilton preferred the republicanism of Princeton to the royalist leanings of King's, we may suppose that before he had spent a year in this country he had shed any overseas loyalties brought from the West Indies and was well on the way to embracing the colonies' contentions. In any event he applied at Princeton in person, but, despite his deliberate choice of that College, did not want to be accepted unless on an important condition which he proposed. His New York friend Hercules Mulligan tells the story:

"I went with him to Princeton to the House of Dr. Witherspoon . . . with whom I was well acquainted, and I introduced Mr. Hamilton to him and proposed to him to Examine the young gentleman which the Doctor did to his entire satisfaction. Mr. Hamilton then stated that he wished to enter either of the classes to which his attainments would entitle him but with the understanding that he should be permitted to advance from Class to Class with as much rapidity as his exertions would enable him to do. Dr. Witherspoon listened with great attention to so unusual a proposition from so young a person and replied that . . . he would submit the request to the trustees . . . & in about a fortnight after a letter was received from the President stating that the request could not be complied with because it was contrary to the usage of the College and expressing his regret because he was convinced that the young gentleman would do honor to any seminary at which he should be educated."[45]

Hamilton's application called for special consideration, not only for its novelty but because Dr. Witherspoon was impressed by the young man's answers to his questions and because West Indian students were particularly solicited. The possibility that this promising student, sponsored by Princeton alumni and trustees, would seek and gain entrance to the rival college in New York City on his own terms—which happened—[46] doubtless occurred to Dr. Witherspoon. If there was documentary evidence of the episode in the records of Princeton University it has disappeared.[47]

Had Alexander Hamilton been admitted to the College of New Jersey at Princeton on his plan of acceleration without regard to the formal program, his after-career would probably have been different. Though Princeton, college and village, early caught and sustained the Revolutionary spirit, he would have been fifty miles from the metropolis and would have missed the stirring public events in New York City in which, already as a student, he had his part. At Princeton he would have made lasting, valuable friends, but not the same as those who became a corps of companions in his later life. He might have been drawn, following college, to Philadelphia, where his setting, though propitious, would have been less critical for the country's future than that of New York.

Princeton was founded, reared, and fed by Presbyterians, dissenters.[48] President John Witherspoon, a Scotsman in the John Knox tradition, was no less a political than a pulpit evangel, soon to shock his closest supporters with his enthusiasm for American independence. King's College, by contrast, was early fostered and carried forward by Anglicans firmly attached to the British Crown. They yielded only such share in control of the institution to other sects of New York as they could not avoid. The president, Myles Cooper, bred at Oxford, was by charter stipulation "a member of, and in communion with the Church of England, as by law established."[49] Morning and evening he or his deputy intoned prayers which were all but liturgical, while the students chanted responses.[50] For intercession with his own trustees Cooper looked to Thomas Secker, Archbishop of Canterbury, who had chosen him, "very well affected to the government," to head the College.[51] In a remonstrance of 1774 against the Continental Congress, attributed to

Cooper,[52] Bostonians and other New Englanders were described as "these rebellious Republicans, . . . hair-brained fanaticks, as mad . . . as the ANABAPTISTS OF MUNSTER. . . ."

Though at the time Alexander Hamilton chose King's, President Myles Cooper may not yet have been labeled "a tory and an obnoxious man,"[53] the Episcopal and royalist tendencies of the institution, which Livingston had stigmatized, lingered about it. "A party-college," he had forecast, "in less than half a century, will put a new face upon the religion, and in consequence . . . affect the politics of the country." If the college was managed by one sect, "Would not . . . care be bestowed in tincturing the minds of the students with the . . . sentiments of that sect. Would not the students . . . after . . . their education . . . fill all the offices of the government?"[54]

The fact was that from a student in King's College, Alexander Hamilton, came ringing answers to the Tories to whom President Cooper belonged. The Revolution ended every fear Livingston raised; the land donated by Trinity Church remained the foundation of the institution's prosperity, while its liturgy disappeared.

We cannot understand Hamilton's education at King's, which ran so quickly from gown to town, without a glance at President Myles Cooper. He was another man from Dr. Samuel Johnson, his predecessor. The conscienceful Johnson, from being a Congregationalist, became "dubious of the lawfulness of [his] ordination," and posted to England for priest's orders. But Cooper, bred at Queen's College, Oxford, was born in the Church of England and became deacon and priest in his early twenties. Johnson had got his learning mostly by himself, and it was deeper than that poured over Cooper. Johnson wrestled with his soul, while Cooper enjoyed life. Johnson no sooner lost one wife than he married another to obtain "a careful and disinterested housekeeper."[55] Cooper, in spite of handsome looks and graceful ways, remained all his life a bachelor; at King's he kept a garret well stocked with wine and a table so rich that he suffered the effects. The somber Johnson confined his pen to prose, but Cooper the year he was ordained published *Poems on Several Occasions*,[56] mostly polite love verse to Sylvia, Cynthia, and Delia, but sometimes scornful or close to carnal. Alexander when a student in King's was "greatly attached" to the president who carried himself with an

air.[57]   Though Alexander was eighteen years Cooper's junior, they
had much in common—good looks, gift for expression, love of elegance and, it may be at the beginning of their association, a similar
attachment to the British monarchy under which both had been
born.[58]

Alexander Hamilton's presence at King's in the academic year
1773–1774 rests on the testimony of his intimate friend Robert
Troup, who more than thirty-six years later recorded that "I became acquainted with [him] in the year 1773 at Kings . . . in
New York, where I was a student. . . . When [Hamilton] entered
College, he did it as a private student, and not by annexing himself
to a particular class.   The President, and Professors, instructed him
at their leisure hours."[59]   Hamilton made studious progress in the
languages[60] and other branches and, having "originally destined
himself to the Science of Physic . . . he was regular in attending
the anatomical lectures, then delivered in the College by Dr.
Clossey."[61]   Notices of Dr. Clossy's lectures appeared in the newspapers, and it may be that Hamilton attended them, as any member of the public, on payment of the fee, was privileged to do.[62]   If
he first intended fitting himself for the practice of medicine he may
have been led to it, as previously mentioned, because Hugh Knox,
his clerical patron of St. Croix, was also physician and apothecary;
in addition, his boyhood friend on St. Croix and fellow student
at King's, Edward Stevens, was probably already intending for
Edinburgh to study medicine.

Troup had good means of knowing when Hamilton was first at
King's, in whatever status; Troup graduated A.B. in 1774;[63] consequently 1773–1774 was the only session when he and Hamilton
could have been fellow students.   He roomed with Hamilton in the
college building[64] and named the other "particular associates" of
Hamilton in college—Edward Stevens, Samuel and Henry Nicoll.[65]

The redoubtable Hercules Mulligan, who met Hamilton at the
boat, as it were, remembered differently.   Writing, like Troup, a
full generation after the events, he shifted the dates forward a year,
saying Alexander first came to New York in October 1773, prepared for college at Barber's Academy, and "entered King's . . .
Colledge in the spring of 1775 in the Sophomore Class" but on his
own special plan.   He "boarded with" the Mulligan family.[66]

The fact is that the register of students and faculty of King's

College has in the hand of President Myles Cooper the name of Alexander Hamilton under "Admissions Anno 1774."[67] He was one of seventeen admitted that year, his name occurring next to last.[68] This would seem to be definitive for the date of Hamilton's formal entrance, or matriculation, but several circumstances leave the exact date, or even the year, in some doubt. The list of this class and others, none alphabetical, may have been written in the book at a later time, not when the class entered or graduated, which would make room for error.[69] The official roster was carelessly kept; Hamilton was doubtless at King's "as a private student," as Troup said, in the academic year 1773–1774, and then formally entered, as per the Matricula, in 1774, perhaps "in the Sophomore Class" as Mulligan remembered. He no longer "destined himself to the Science of Physic," because when actually enrolled he was not designated "S.M." (student of medicine).[70]

On his plan of passing the examinations in King's in different subjects as rapidly as possible, Hamilton commenced as a private pupil with Professor Robert Harpur in mathematics on September 20, 1774. He was to pay £4 4s. per quarter. Though others whom Harpur tutored, or their parents, remitted promptly, Hamilton seems not to have met his charge for nine years. Opposite his name in Harpur's account book is the notation: "1783. By Cash rec.^{d} from him, now Col. Hamilton, as a present at the close of the War 5 Guin.^{s} = 9–6–8."[71]

Because Hamilton later was obliged to make many mathematical calculations, and to understand others prepared for him, Robert Harpur holds special interest for us. At the time Alexander became his private pupil Harpur was in his early forties.[72] Scotch-Irish, he studied at Glasgow University, abandoned the idea of entering the Presbyterian ministry, and taught for a few years in Ireland before coming to New York in 1761. Here he was immediately welcomed in King's as professor of mathematics and natural philosophy.[73] Two years later, under Cooper's presidency, Harpur with five others was made M.A. of King's. More exacting than his colleagues, the students frequently met his discipline with individual defiance or collective jeers.[74]

It is not remarkable if Harpur was testy, for he was overworked, turning every way to make a penny. Besides his duties in the college, for which he was receiving £38 10s. a quarter salary, he took anywhere from 9 to 17 private pupils in each of the years 1771–1775, receiving in 1772 "Cash on acc. of private Tuition D.^{r} 16 Pupils. . . . The whole amo.^{t} of this Year £63. 17. 6."[75]

We have an illustration, in a manuscript exercise book, of what Harpur was giving a private pupil, a member of the sophomore class. It belonged to Samuel Bayard, who bought it in 1774.[76] The examples are ingenious and make rapid progress from "the single Rule of Three"[77] and "Simple Interest, 1773,"[78] to commercial applications in discount, partner's shares, and especially the exchange of currencies; the last pages are headed "Surveying 1774."[79] However, Harpur was proficient in much more complicated mathematics, as appears from pages of astronomical calculations in his journal and account book of circa 1780–1785.[80]

Rebellious Town,
Tory Gown

As the "Book of Misdemeanours," covering most of the time Alexander was in King's, does not log him for disobedience to any of the rules, he obeyed them or was not detected in infringements.   The statutes adopted in 1763, when Myles Cooper became president, were more meticulous than those of 1755 in Samuel Johnson's time.[1] Cooper patterned his rules after those of the Oxford colleges, which seemed to cherish discipline for discipline's sake, though this made the president and tutors as much monitors as mentors.

If the regulations were generally observed we may assume that Alexander attended morning prayers (beginning between five and seven o'clock in summer and six and eight in winter), afternoon and evening prayers, and church twice every Sunday.   This was not irksome to him if we may believe his college mate Troup, who said that Alexander "was attentive to public worship . . . and in the habit of praying upon his knees both night and morning." In justifying his own belief, he strengthened Troup's.   He had read polemical writers on religious subjects, of which the library had more than a sprinkling.   His habit of praying, already remarked when a guest in Boudinot's home, was persevered in after he joined the army.   Hamilton in later life was only formal in religious observance, but there is no reason to doubt his conspicuous devotion at this earlier period.   He had been among churchmen, lay and clerical, since he came into the hands of Hugh

Knox. His hymn, "The Soul Entering into Bliss," was written in St. Croix.[2]

He was in his room by nine at night in winter and ten in summer; he did not "convene . . . with persons of bad fame," play cards or dice, or compel the president to break down his door on a random visit. He did not go through the college gates after they were locked by the porter, nor enter or leave "through the fence . . . or over it." To crown this record of compliance, Alexander may have received "in the most honorary manner, and publicly," presentations of books bought with the fines of the wicked. The monetary mulct might be as high as ten shillings, but that was better than the penalty "to translate into Latin 4 Pages of Dr Chandler's Charity Sermon," or "4th Section of the third Chapter of Puffendorf." More than half of those who matriculated with Hamilton ran afoul of the college rules of conduct. The earliest in trouble was the luckless Moncrieffe, who was campused, then further sinned by "breaking through . . . Confinement," for which he was to "make public Acknowledgments, in the Chapel and to translate N°s 255, 256. of the Spectator into Latin." Refusing to be immured at his exercises, he drew double punishment, but friends broke down his door and he loosed himself forever, disappearing from the records. Others "mist [prayers] *both* times," or went into the country for a week without leave, but survived to graduate.[3] To sustain constant study and docility (if the bill of fare had not been changed since 1761) the steward offered for the midday meal "roast beef and pudding" on Sundays, "corned beef . . . and mutton pye" on Thursdays, "leg mutton and soup" on Fridays. Similar substantial dinners on other days (all predetermined) compensated for slender breakfasts of coffee or tea, bread and butter, and suppers better only by the addition of cheese.[4]

Troup said that Hamilton, Stevens, the Nicolls, and himself— "particular associates . . . in College"—formed themselves into a weekly club for improvement in writing and debating, and "the Club was continued until we were separated by the revolution." He remembered Hamilton's performances as "displays of richness of genius, and energy of mind."[5] Persistence of the club explains the presence in it later of Nicholas Fish;[6] he had left his studies at Princeton to read law with John Morin Scott in New York, and was one of the "young gentlemen" of the town who joined the collegians in discussions and soon in military drills. In this small student literary society Hamilton "occasionally & confidentially" read parts of his political pieces before publication.[7]

Hamilton gave evidence of having made industrious use of the college library. He had had few books in St. Croix; the libraries of Boudinot and Livingston at Elizabethtown must have been excellent, but the King's collection was the largest he had met.[8] Most of the books were not selected, but were gifts: "Joseph Murray Esq.[r] bequeathed his Estate & Library"; "The Rev.[d] Dr. Bristow of London bequeathed his Library, ab.[t] 1500 vols."; "Sundry Gentlemen of Oxford gave Books whose names are in them."[9] We have no complete list, but about a hundred of the books survived the Revolution.[10] The rescued volumes are mainly theological treatises, polemical sectarian pamphlets,[11] or reflect the fancy of their donors for fruit culture and equally extraneous subjects. The chief exceptions are Hutchinson's *History of Massachusetts-Bay* (Boston, 1764), and *A New and General Biographical Dictionary* (London, 1761–1762, 11 volumes).[12] However, we are safe in saying that the works referred to by Hamilton in his pamphlets published in 1774–1775 while he was at King's were in the college library, with the possible exception of the letters of "A. W. Farmer" which he was answering and may have bought from a bookseller, Noel or another. By reference or quotation he showed a knowledge of Grotius, Pufendorf, Locke, Montesquieu, Berlamqui, Hobbes,[13] Blackstone, Postlethwayt, Hume, Lex Mercatoria, recent Parliamentary debates and acts, colonial charters, acts of the General Assembly of New York, the Pennsylvania Farmer, Johnson's dictionary, and an account of the wars of Charles XII and Peter the Great.

Hamilton's college studies led early into political polemics. As his bent was for practical idealism, no sooner had he become well acquainted with a problem and settled his conclusions upon it than he wanted to persuade others of his point of view in open discussion. All his life the learning process with him was swift and thorough, and he as speedily wished to turn his labors to account. When most young men of his age were uncertain of themselves, he went at a bound from closet to the court of public opinion. Expression in speech and writing was a pleasure to him, and with the minimum of self-consciousness he entered debate on the issues that were rapidly riving the colonies from Great Britain.

Several of his closest friends spoke of his contributing political pieces to the newspapers on his first arrival at Boston and more credibly after he became a student at King's in New York.

"I hope Mr. Hamilton continues busy," wrote John Jay to Alexander McDougall as early as December 5, 1775. "I have not received Holt's paper these three months, and therefore cannot judge of the progress he makes." Fish, groping back for particulars of Hamilton's career, queried, "When began he to *write* on the question between G.B. & the colonies? Where are his papers to be found? . . . Holt's Gazette?"[14] A return visit of Hamilton to Boston shortly after the Tea Party, said to have launched him as patriot protagonist,[15] is doubtful, but without this he would have been stirred by newspaper reports of the progress of protests from New Hampshire to Georgia.[16]

If Hamilton published "a Defence of the Destruction of the Tea," presumably in Holt's paper, it is not possible to identify it. Pseudonymity of letters to the editor and cards to the public baffle detection. A staccato, impassioned appeal[17] may reflect youthful enthusiasm; a reasoned argument, with citation of authorities, may betray the academic viewer of the scene. The first piece of "Americanus" appeared in Holt's patriot paper on December 16, 1773, the second on February 24, 1774. Influenced by Locke, ". . . the *British* Parliament," he said, "has no more right of legislation here than it has in the empire of the Great Mogul." But "The case as to his Majesty, is widely different; . . . the very charters which confirm our liberty reserve to him a sovereign authority." The British colonies in America were "distinct independent states," and admitted to be so by Charles II. He referred seriatim to acts of Parliament, each "an unwarrantable exercise of . . . arbitrary power unknown to the British constitution" insofar as intended to bind persons "out of the realm." He applauded the proposal of the Virginia Burgesses of "an *union of Counsel*" for opposition, and recommended "an *annual congress,* as tending to a greater intimacy of union. . . ." The congress should meet in the metropolis of the most central colony (New York?). Historical recital preceding inferences, systematic listing of laws, citation of Hutchinson's *His-*

tory of Massachusetts-Bay, and anticipation of arguments used by Hamilton later may all point to his authorship.

"Monitor" in Holt's *New York Journal,* November 9, 1775, and following, reviewed the controversy, upheld the Continental Congress, and stressed economic injuries with hints of Hamilton's hand: "The progressive evolution of this execrable scheme shall be traced in my next paper. In the mean time, suffice it to observe, that one soul animates . . . every successive act of administration—a desire to enslave this country, and eat up the fruits of our industry in the endless train of taxes." "S-P——M," not directed to the current controversy, but straight out of Child and Anderson on commerce, has the ring and references of Hamilton's known productions.[18] But many champions offered,[19] and, beyond the certainty that he was one contributor to the patriotic press following the excitement in Boston, speculation about particular pieces is vain.

The colony of New York at first played a supporting rather than a volunteering role in resistance to measures of the British ministry that led to the Revolution. Among several causes that held her to the rear of Massachusetts, Virginia, and South Carolina in promptness and vehemence of decision, the chief was the close commercial tie of her metropolis with the mother country. Other circumstances were diversity of the population in origin, property, religious tenets, and the vulnerable geographic position of the province, with the Hudson a highway to the hinterland. The region about Albany was Indian frontier to the westward and to the northward was linked to Canada by the fur trade. Local self-government, owing partly to the enormous holdings of the landed aristocracy of the interior, was comparatively undeveloped. New York was a poor conductor for the electric charges that ran through other colonies.

When the ship *Nancy,* Captain Lockyer, arrived with tea at Sandy Hook on April 18, 1774, having lost her mizzen and an anchor, she met another gale of wind from citizens of New York. According to agreement, the vessel was not permitted to come up. The resolve of the committee was accepted by consignees and the captain was sent off by a rally at Murray's wharf and a band that played "God Save the King." Captain Chambers of the *London* did not fare so well. At first denying that he had eighteen boxes of fine tea aboard, he later confessed them as his private venture. His dissemblance had prepared the "Mohawks . . . to do their

Duty at a proper Hour," but before they could arrive some in the crowd "broke the Cases and started their Contents in the River. . . ." and the captain was glad to escape.[20]

But *ad hoc* committee contrivance and mob action in imitation of Boston were easier than formal deputizing of pledged patriots to represent New York in the Continental Congress to assemble at Philadelphia in September. The standing committee, the same as had approved recent dutiful addresses to Governor Tryon on his departure for a visit to England,[21] demanded the right of nomination, with no candidates to be put up by popular voice. Numbers in public positions in those tense times practiced poising themselves as delicately as the touring entertainers Johnston and Brendon, advertised to perform at Hampden-Hall near the upper barracks. Among other feats they "Will lay down on their Back on the Wire, balance a Straw on the Nose, and rise up with the same. . . . Any person that chuses, may blow a Peacock's Feather through a Cane, and they will catch the same in balance on the face."[22]

Not so the Sons of Liberty, whose following, nominally of "mechanics," included Whiggish citizens of all callings and classes in active concert with "true sons" in Boston.[23] Their application to the official Committee of 51 for a hand in the business was denied on Monday, July 4, 1774. Benjamin Booth moved, John De-Lanc(e)y seconded, to put McDougall's motion "referring the nomination of Delegates to the Committee of Mechanics for their concurrence, or whether it should be referred only to the town at large." McDougall's proposition was lost, 24–13.[24] Then Theophilact (*sic*) Bache moved, DeLancey seconding, that the Committee name five persons to attend a general congress, "and that the freeholders and freemen of the city and county of New York be summoned to appear at a convenient place to approve or disapprove of such persons for this salutary purpose. . . ." Captain Sears and Peter Livingston, of the aggressive minority, tried to get in under the majority's guard. They placed in nomination Isaac Low, James Duane, Philip Livingston, John Morin Scott, and Alexander McDougall. But they were disappointed in the vote, in which Scott and McDougall, most vehement, were excluded and John Alsop and John Jay were substituted in their places. Noon on Thursday, July 7, at the City Hall was set for the convening of freeholders to consider these nominees.[25]

However, the spokesmen of the opposition had a card up their sleeve. They immediately issued a handbill[26] declaring it "highly necessary, to convene the good People of this Metropolis, in the Fields . . . where every Friend to the true interest of this distressed Country, is earnestly requested to attend;—when Matters of the utmost Importance to their Reputation and Security, as Freemen, will be communicated." This meeting, called by "a Number of Citizens," was to be at six o'clock in the afternoon, July 6, the day before that planned by the official Committee of 51.

This "great meeting in the Fields," where the liberty pole stood (now City Hall Park), brought New York City into the chorus of opposition, and fetched Alexander Hamilton into American public life. It is related[27] that he often walked under the large trees in Batteau (now Dey) Street, talking to himself in an undertone. Perhaps he was rehearsing his lessons at King's, perhaps the lessons he was offering others in his newspaper essays in the colonies' behalf. In any event one of the neighbors, falling into conversation with him, was struck by his pertinence of thought and aptness of speech and urged him, on the spur of the moment, to mount the platform that afternoon.[28] Alexander demurred, but listened in the large crowd that gathered as McDougall, the chairman—himself a symbol of official intolerance of protest—"fully explained" the purpose of the meeting. McDougall condemned "the dangerous tendency of the numerous vile arts used by the enemies of America, to divide and distress her councils, as well as the misrepresentations of the virtuous intentions of the citizens of this metropolis, in this . . . alarming state of the liberties of America."

Nine resolutions were twice read and "being separately put . . . they were passed without one dissentient." We may believe that the "nem. con." votes owed something to the fervor and reasoning of the young collegian, now emboldened to take the stand. He began falteringly amidst deprecatory murmurs at his boyish appearance, but soon summoned his arguments and held the audience in gratified surprise. He reinforced the resolves that denounced the Boston Port Act under which "our brethren" are "now suffering in the common cause of these Colonies"; asserted the unity of America in resisting unconstitutional parliamentary taxations, and urged an agreement "to stop all importation from, and exportation to, Great-Britain" till the harbor of Boston was unblocked. This expedient "will prove the salvation of North-America and her liberties"; otherwise "fraud, power, and the most odious oppression, will rise triumphant over right, justice, social happiness, and freedom." Deputies for New York in the coming congress were directed to consent for the city in these and "all . . . other measures . . . the congress shall . . . judge advancive of these great objects. . . ." The counties were solicited to follow in choosing delegates, or, that failing, to authorize the city deputies to act for them. A subscription should be set on foot for relief of the poor of Boston, and the resolves were to be given the widest publication.[29] It is not surprising that the newspapers made no mention of young Hamilton's unscheduled speech, and gave only the formal action of the meeting. Editors employed no reporters, could not themselves scout for material for their columns, because they must manage job printing, put inquirers in touch with advertisers of everything from wet nursing to real estate, and often sold medical remedies besides. They were content to "take in" local notices.

However, from this time forward Alexander Hamilton was publicly identified as a champion of the colonies. Only the precocity of his next writings, his pamphlets against the "Westchester Farmer," prevented many of his elders from suspecting him as the anonymous author. His volunteer speech in the Fields[30] gave him the friendship of McDougall, Lamb, Willett, and other spirited leaders with whom he was to be intimately connected thenceforth. The stated Committee of 51 was prompt to rebuke the rump assemblage of the day before, disavowing "all such Proceedings, . . . calculated to throw an Odium on this Committee, and to create groundless Jealousies and Suspicions on their Conduct, as well as Disunion among our Fellow Citizens."[31] But this correction was futile, for the city and soon the colony had been aroused to join the common protest.

Alexander Hamilton from the beginning shared the country-wide outlook and mode of action made tangible in the first Continental Congress. Though born and bred in small islands, his attachment was never provincial. He did his full duty in New York—no one more assiduously—but with the purpose of serving America. Nationalism was his passion. Numerous others of prime abilities, who played creative parts in intercolonial resistance, lapsed into sectional loyalty, destroyed their earlier influence, and positively hampered further efforts at unity. Patrick Henry, George Clinton, and Samuel Adams are instances. Though comparisons be odious, contrast of personalities points the distinction. More, while continuing in the widest councils, were so far identified as local spokesmen as to limit their patriotic services. John Rutledge, Richard Henry Lee, George Mason, Gouverneur Morris, Rufus King, and Fisher Ames, with many differences between them, are examples. Their provincial interests led them into party contests, not only legitimate but serviceable. Hamilton became the foremost of his party, but the springs of his action, however misconceived toward the end, were national, and did not belong to New York or the middle states. His most persevering antagonists, though they thrust at him from every angle, recognized that this was his strength.

This note was sounded in Hamilton's next effort, the earliest of his pamphlets, *A Full Vindication of the Members of Congress.* It is dated December 15, 1774, a month after *Free Thoughts, on the Proceedings of the Continental Congress . . .* By a Farmer," to which he replied. Hamilton's answer drew a rejoinder, *A View of the Controversy,* which in turn led to his more elaborate rebuttal, *The Farmer Refuted* (February 5, 1775). The "Farmer" is generally agreed to have been Samuel Seabury, then Episcopal rector at Westchester, New York, though he may well have had agricultural information, if not assistance in the actual writing, from Isaac Wilkins, who was an undoubted Westchester farmer.[32]

Samuel Seabury (1729–1796) was the most successful of the clerical Tories in New York and New Jersey. Like his father, he was missionary and physician. Graduating at Yale in 1748, he completed medical training at Edinburgh, was ordained priest at Fulham Palace, and filled several assignments before settling at Westchester, where he ministered to souls, minds (he was a teacher, too), and bodies. Early a leader among his brethren, with Inglis, Chandler, and others he campaigned to secure American bishops, colliding with William Livingston in the process. He was kidnaped at his home and illegally imprisoned at New Haven for his loyalist recalcitrance, but soon repaid his persecutors by entering the British lines and serving as guide on Long Island, while he supported himself on military chaplaincies. Though he had been awarded the divinity degree by Oxford, after the war the

Archbishops of Canterbury and York were reluctant to consecrate him for Connecticut. He resorted successfully to the Scottish non-juring bishops. With backswept locks, stout, masterful, vividly oratorical, he rescued his public character and rapidly extended the power of his church in America.[33]

Hamilton, primed for bigger game than he had yet aimed at, perhaps leveled on Seabury's *Free Thoughts*[34] because he knew of its origin in President Myles Cooper's circle of loyalist friends. The outspoken Cooper may have revealed in the King's College community the identity of the author, for Hamilton in his answers showed this knowledge or at least a working suspicion that his opponent was no farmer. Besides, Seabury addressed himself particularly to New York, and essayed to treat the position of the West Indies vis-à-vis the continent. Alexander was undismayed by the genuine gifts of the Farmer, more than twice his age and a practiced polemicist; indeed, the cogency and liveliness of the work was a welcome call to the young patriot's powers.[35]

The subsequent fame of Alexander Hamilton has made his replies to the Westchester Farmer readily available;[36] every account of his career has included at least allusion to these smooth stones picked by David out of the brook. By the same sign, Seabury's pamphlets that called them out have stood only in reflected light. Yet his pieces are deserving of compressed review, and not only to put the points that the college student volunteered to refute. Amidst numerous able loyalist publications,[37] these provoked Hamilton's rejoinder. They show Seabury's conviction, ingenuity, force, and eloquence; unfortunately it is not possible to catch in brief quotation his homely illustrations familiar to farmers, calculated to split counties from city and New York from other colonies, much less the fun he pokes at slips of Congress.

After a clerical invocation, Seabury condemns the members of Congress who "are broken up without . . . attemping . . . one step that tended to peace: they have gone from bad to worse, and have . . . basely betrayed the interests of all the Colonies."[38] He identifies himself with "the Farmers [who] are of the greatest benefit to the state, of any people in it," and who will be injured by the agreements against trade and consumption. It is unfair to boycott Ireland, the West Indies, and the manufacturers of Britain, "to force them all to join their clamours with ours." This attempt at commercial blackmail for the sake of the "abominable scheme" of American republican independence must prove abortive. We could not incite riots in England. She would raise duties against our trade, enforce them with her navy, or crush us in a single military campaign.[39]

Meantime the places deprived of our goods could supply themselves from other quarters; particularly the West Indies "produce now many of the necessaries of life," or Canada, Florida, and Georgia would send to the islands the flour, lumber, and horses they have of us. He skillfully distracts attention from fundamental rights to ridicule the "confounded combustion" caused by resentment of a trifling tax on tea.[40] His jabs at Congress as the enemy of farmers follow rapidly. "You had better trust to the mercy of a Turk" rather than rely on the honor of merchants not to exact unconscionable profits in a restricted market. Farmers have recently had prices of their produce regulated by New York City mayor and aldermen. Committeemen will prosecute offenders against the agreements. "Will you submit to them . . . ? . . . by Him that made me, I will not.—No, if I must be enslaved, let it be by a King at least, and not by a parcel of upstart lawless Committee-men. If I must be devoured, let me be devoured by the jaws of a lion, and not *gnawed* to death by rats and vermin."[41]

He knows enough about sheep to remind Congress that the breed cannot be improved by keeping wethers. He elevates the New York General Assembly above an informal continental gathering sparsely deputed; peace may be restored if farmers will "Renounce all dependence on Congresses, and Committees . . . your *constitutional* representatives . . . are the true, and legal . . . defenders of your rights. . . ."[42]

Hamilton soon responded with his *Full Vindication . . . of Congress,* in which he promised that the Farmer's "*sophistry* is exposed, his *cavils* confuted, his *artifices* detected, and his *wit* ridiculed. . . ." The pamphlet is remarkable beyond his years for calm statement and spirited argument, though, aside from his intimate allusions to disabilities of the West Indies, it contains no information which one of his age (all but twenty) might not have come by. The wit is apt to be lugged in; the banter is heavy-handed.

He began by upholding the competence of Congress. The commotion was not over a tax on tea, raised by turbulent men who wanted to erect America into an independent government, which he nowhere espoused. The argument was whether the colonists could preserve their lives and properties assured by the law of nature, the British Constitution, and the colonial charters. Further petitions, on which his opponent relied, would be fruitless. "The exigency of the times requires vigorous and probable remedies; not weak and improbable" ones. Withholding trade was the only alternative to armed resistance.[43] This was justified in self-protection; besides, the people of Britain, Ireland, and the West Indies were guilty of a political crime if they antagonized the colonies' rightful demands; the British manufacturers were already in a degree confederates in the iniquity of their rulers. Hamilton here begged the question, and went on to urge, irrelevantly, that "we are ready to receive with open arms . . . sufferers by the operation of our measures, and recompense them with every blessing our country affords to honest industry." If, in retaliation, the mother country should put a stop to our whole trade, we had internal resources from which to live. He hinted at his future advocacy: "if, by the necessity of the thing, manufactures should once . . . take root among us, they will pave the way . . . to the . . . grandeur and glory of America; and, by lessening its need of external commerce, will render it . . . securer against the encroachments of tyranny."[44]

Britain would not risk a war which must be calamitous to her. As to the West Indies, he could say from "a pretty general acquaintance" that sugar islands could not be shifted to production of food, and that any prospect of supplying themselves from Canada was illusory. Non-exportation was a precautionary counterpart to non-importation, and he believed the two would prevail on the ministry to abandon malignant schemes.[45]

Hamilton addressed the last part of his argument to the farmers of New York. He made the tax on tea, if allowed to stand, the portent of innumerable ruinous exactions of Parliament. Here he reduced his effectiveness by exaggeration; he pictured the arbitrariness of the Quebec Act in the overwrought fashion then common. He concluded by showing that farmers would suffer less than merchants and others by the agreements, even if non-exportation came into operation. Throughout he upheld obedience to

Congress and the necessity of New York joining in the continental effort.[46]

The Farmer answered Hamilton's tract, specifically, in his *View of the Controversy*. While he began with *argumentum ad hominem* and later attacked the position of the Whigs generally, on the whole he replied to Hamilton's points seriatim, and renewed his plea for orderly petition and definition of concessions asked from Britain. In four areas the Westchester clergyman expressed views which, as it happened, Hamilton was to spend much of his life in vindicating. First, Seabury upheld the right of criticizing public characters, a freedom of speech and press from which Hamilton had sought to screen the Congress.[47] Second, he distinguished local from national legislative authority: "Every thing that relates to the internal . . . government of the province which [the assemblies] represent comes properly before them. . . . But all laws relative to the empire in general, or to all the colonies conjunctively . . . must be left to the parliament."[48] Third, command over economic resources was inherent in political responsibility: ". . . in every government, *legislation* and *taxation* . . . must be conjoined. If you divide them, you weaken and finally destroy the government. . . ."[49] And fourth, to the argument that an omnipotent Parliament could take a pound as logically as a penny, Seabury responded with the reasoning Hamilton often used afterward: ". . . no scheme of human policy can be so contrived and guarded, but that something must be left to the integrity, prudence, and wisdom of those who govern."[50]

Influenced by disdain of the Congress in comfortable, loyalist Westchester,[51] Seabury declared that representatives from New York "were not chosen by a hundredth part of the people."[52] Hamilton was begging the question when he assumed that Britain was executing "a regular plan to enslave America."[53] In advance of experience under the Confederation, Seabury pictured the animosities in trade that would ensue were the regulating power of Parliament withdrawn.[54] He scouted the notion that the colonists could manufacture cotton and wool sufficient for their clothing,[55] and with more certainty showed that Hamilton had overstated the tax burdens borne by landowners and farmers in Britain.[56] Into Hamilton's informed testimony on the West Indies he somehow read a malice against their people.[57]

Hamilton made swift rejoinder with his *Farmer Refuted*.[58] In an admirable introductory note he respected the sincerity of opponents "Because he remembers the time when he had strong prejudices on the side *he* now opposes."[59] This second essay is more precise and documented than his first.   It reminds of his later work in which original sources and weighty authorities are cited, at the expense of iteration, until the point at issue is clinched.   He soon passed from undignified retort to sober, painstaking demonstration; as was natural, the subject opened upon him as he investigated it, and his opponent as such receded in his attention.[60]

He began his serious discourse by amplifying his understanding of natural law, since Seabury said he skimmed too lightly over the subject before.   Here he embraced the free compact origin of civil society, and declared, with Blackstone, that moral obligation was before law rather than, as with Hobbes, proceeding from the dictates of human government.[61]   He founded his claims of colonial rights in "the law of nature, and that *supreme law* of every society—*its own happiness,*" in a way that sounds more like Jefferson than like Hamilton's later reasonings.   However, having established ethical origin, his concern was with legal application of freedom in society. "I am inviolably attached to the essential rights of mankind," he said, "and the true interests of society.   I consider civil liberty . . . as the greatest of terrestrial blessings."[62]   This avowal is brief and general and was made when Hamilton was twenty.   Later in life he continued to found civil law on natural rights; but, having done so, he was content to argue for freedom of press and speech within the Constitution.   His concept of liberty was Roman rather than Saxon.   We shall see that he wanted to restrict the "democratical societies" to prevent them from abetting another Whisky Insurrection, that he thought a Bill of Rights should be appended after the Constitution was ratified, not before, and that he did not oppose the Alien and Sedition Acts with vigor.   These were lapses from his own principles.

Seabury and other loyalist writers lumped king and Parliament as possessing constitutional authority over the colonies.   Hamilton confined colonial sovereignty to the crown.   "The dependence of the colonies on Great Britain," he observed, "is an ambiguous . . . phrase.   It may either mean dependence on the people of Great Britain or on the king.   In the former sense it is absurd and unaccountable; in the latter, it is just and rational. . . . The most valid reasons can be assigned for our allegiance to the king . . . , but not one . . . for our subjection to parliamentary decrees. We hold our lands in America by virtue of charters from British monarchs, and are under no obligations to the Lords and Commons for them."[63] To make valid laws, legislators must be chosen by the people, and the people of Britain could not choose representatives for the colonists.[64] America was a part of the dominions of the king, but was without the realm and so was without the jurisdiction of Parliament.[65] The colonies had conceded to Great Britain, Parliament with the king, the right to regulate their trade. But no legislature outside the colonies could legally raise a revenue from their commerce, tax them internally, or make general statutes for them.[66]

Hamilton neglected a good deal of history in declaring there was no need of "general laws for all the colonies." He forgot, possibly did not know of, the incentives to the abortive Albany Plan of 1754, though that scheme for uniting the colonies for dealings with the Indians and for defense rested, to be sure, upon the king in council rather than upon Parliament. "Let every colony attend to its own internal police," he urged, "and all will be well. How have we managed heretofore? The Parliament has made no general laws for our good, and yet our affairs have been conducted much to our ease and satisfaction."[67] This was directly counter to his own later wisdom.

Yet this final answer to the Farmer contained, in the germ, ideas that became emphatic with Alexander Hamilton as his policies matured. Such was his perception of the extraordinary resources of America and the development they would undergo.[68] He thought that private, selfish interest was the cement of society, but society should be warned against uncontrolled avarice.[69] Adam Smith was soon to embed the motive of self-interest in liberal political economy; what Hamilton added, through his lifetime, was the more deliberate use of this passion, or failing, for public benefit.

In reviewing this debate with the Farmer we are reminded that the enjoinders of his opponent were those to order and legality which we generally associate with Hamilton's bent. At a later stage he was to be assailed for his attraction to the British Constitu-

tion, and for his mistrust of all that flowed from the French Revolution to America.   Why did this young man wade into troubled
waters with a current evidently setting toward revolt?[70]   He had
been bred in insular obedience to a European monarch.[71]   He had
spent his first American year among Elizabethtown friends who
then deplored a break with Britain, and at King's was under the
tutelage of loyalists.   Half of the Crugers and most of the Kort-
rights, who were by way of being his guardians in America, were
true to King George.   He said he changed his strong loyalist
prejudices because of "the superior force of the arguments in favor
of the American claims."   Had he imbibed more from Boudinot,
Livingston, Caldwell, and Barber than they themselves were prepared to admit at the time?   Did his discussions with his fellow
collegians convince him in the colonies' cause?   Did his attention
to newspapers, tracts, and parliamentary debates give this direction
to his reading in standard authors on political philosophy?   The
mechanics of his conversion, however, are of less importance than
the fact of it.   Though Hamilton early joined the military forces,
fought through most of the war, and was as fervid as the next for
independence, he was a radical conservative, not a revolutionary.
Perhaps the radical is courageous where the revolutionary is
venturesome.   The radical chooses his port, steers by a chart, takes
soundings, while the revolutionary believes his craft safer if he
ignores harbor lights and beats to the open sea.   Hamilton, as a
statesman, was for competent correctives, which is not the same
as committing one's cause to the arbitrament of Heaven.

Hamilton was no doctrinaire; instead, after his best exertions for
what he believed to be thorough remedies, he would accept and
work for the practicable.   The division among Americans in the
quarrel with Britain demonstrated, as Hamilton was quick to
recognize, that honest men could prefer compromise and accommodation to rebellion.   Why was he not found in that respectable
company?   Youthful enthusiasm cannot be the answer, for there
were Tories of his years.[72]   Though he early reasoned that Britain
would not have an easy victory, if at all, it is not likely that he made
his decision on military grounds.

One may guess that he became a revolutionist because, paradoxically, of his attachment to law, especially as law defined civil
rights.   Of course, many others were similarly moved.   This may

be called his one dogma, yet he cleaved to it not so much whether-or-no as because he considered maintenance of it necessary to render society happy and effective.   Civil rights were the arduous means to a worthy end.   Procedural reasons blended with principle. He wanted liberty under law, but law, to him, celebrated and did not cramp rights.

Captain of a Spruce
Artillery Company

ALEXANDER HAMILTON's attachment to civil rights brings us to the next episode in his college career—if, indeed, we should not say that stirring events were now his teachers. He has oftenest been regarded as the advocate of law rather than of liberty; the rights he cherished, it has been said, were those of property, not of persons.[1] The fact is that he feared and opposed irresponsibility, especially as expressed in local mobs, regional rebellion (of Daniel Shays or the Whisky Boys) or in the guillotine of the sans-culottes. Repeatedly during his life he vindicated civil rights of individuals; naturally this was always against popular clamor, and several times in defense of persons whose opinions countered his own.

The first instance of which we have record[2] was his protection of President Myles Cooper, of King's College, the night of May 10, 1775, against a mob that menaced him for his conspicuous part in championing Tory tenets.[3] If we wonder how an anonymous pamphleteer was so readily identified for attack, we learn that a "few days previous had been published a letter, dated Philadelphia, April 25, 1775, addressed to Dr. Cooper and four other obnoxious gentlemen of New-York, ascribing . . . to their assurances of the defection of the latter city, all the hostile proceedings of England. . . . They are denounced as parricides, and told that the Americans . . . will no longer satisfy their resentment with the execution of villians [sic] in effigy; and the letter concludes—'Fly for your

[74]

lives, or anticipate your doom by becoming your own executioners (Signed) Three Millions.' "[4]

The mob that made for the college building, where Dr. Cooper lived,[5] late at night, was of size—Troup, an eyewitness, said "in great force,"[6] Cooper himself recorded "Four hundred men, a murderous band."[7] Of course no one knew, in the darkness and excitement, how many there were. Hamilton, accompanied by his friend Troup, saved the sleeping Dr. Cooper from whatever indignity or danger awaited him. "When the mob approached the . . . College, . . . Hamilton took his stand on one of the stoops, and proceeded with great animation . . . to harangue the mob on the . . . disgrace it would bring on the cause of liberty; of which they avowed themselves to be the Champions." This "short delay gave Dr. Cooper an opportunity of escaping from the College without being touched."[8] Troup garnished the tale in a reminiscent letter to Pickering. Hamilton "diverted their attention, until the affrighted clergyman, who, at first imagining he was exciting the mob, exclaimed from an upper window, 'Don't listen to him, gentlemen, he is crazy, he is crazy,' and took refuge in the ship-of-war."[9]

While it is difficult to discredit Troup, narratives nearest the time of the happening[10] make no mention of young Hamilton's harangue to hold the mob at bay. When the menacing intruders were still shaking the "groaning gate" of the college grounds, before they broke it down, according to Dr. Cooper, his pupil ran ahead, woke and hustled him out by the back way just as the "furious throng" forced the doors to his rooms. Hamilton went with Cooper to the bank of the Hudson whence the president reached refuge in the house of a friend.[11]

Foiled in the attempt to seize Dr. Cooper, the mob went after "his Printer, James Rivington,"[12] who lived, presumably, over his shop in Hanover Square nearby. Doubtless advised by the threatening Philadelphia letter, Rivington had tried to exculpate himself in an address to the public.[13] His promise not to offend popular ardor in future was not thought satisfactory, if the mob thought at all. "M.ʳ Rivington the Printer of one of our newspapers was attacked by the same Mob [as had committed the 'most scandalous outrage upon D.ʳ Cooper'] and rescued out of their Hands by the

Resolution of one or two friends [.]   He has since taken refuge on Board of the Man of War and will not yet venture to return to his House.   His Crime is only the liberty of the Press[.]"[14]

Rivington's respite was brief.   Hamilton reprehended a second attack which stopped his paper and expelled him to England. What Captain Isaac Sears, a leader of the Sons of Liberty, found his fellow New Yorkers unwilling to do, he could perpetrate at the head of invaders from Connecticut.   Sears set out from New Haven on November 20, 1775, with companions to arrest Samuel Seabury and other chief Tories of Westchester.[15]   On their way they were joined by eighty horsemen under three captains.[16] Sending their Westchester prisoners back to New Haven, the Connecticut contingent rode into New York at noon of the 23rd and, with fixed bayonets, "drew up in close order before the printing office of the infamous James Rivington."   A detachment rifled it of types.   All "then . . . marched out of town to the tune of Yankee: doodle [*sic*]."   No citizen offered objection on the scene. On the contrary, "The . . . concourse . . . assembled at the Coffee-House bridge . . . gave them three hearty cheers."[17]

Alexander Hamilton, in a long letter to John Jay, then sitting in the Continental Congress in Philadelphia, promptly deplored the incident for its political tendencies, but failed to resent it as an unworthy affront to freedom of the press.   We have no evidence for Mulligan's praise of Hamilton for trying to turn the Connecticut raiders from their purpose.[18]   Jay was known for patriotism prudent as well as firm.   Hamilton begged that he would use his influence in Congress to prevent action of one colony that embarrassed another and endangered the common resistance.   "In times of such commotion as the present," he observed, "while the passions of men are worked up to an uncommon pitch there is . . . danger of fatal extremes.   The same state of the passions which fits the multitude, who have not a sufficient stock of reason and knowledge to guide them, for opposition to tyranny and oppression, . . . naturally leads them to a contempt . . . of all authority."   This was the case with the irruption of horsemen from New England who took away Rivington's types.   "Though I am fully sensible how . . . pernicious Rivington's press has been,[19] . . . yet I cannot help condemning this step."   He had a subtler reason for his remonstrance; namely, that New York loyalty to ministerial measures would be bolstered by fresh excuse for the old antagonism toward New England. Further, New York must appear a weak contender in the American cause if another colony sent in to chastise Tories. If Congress would station troops, "raised in Philadelphia or the Jerseys or any other province except New England," in disaffected parts of New York, "Rivington will be intimidated & the tories will be convinced that the other colonies will not tamely see the general cause betrayed by the Yorkers." He did not object if Tories were repressed and overawed, but this should be done by intercolonial authority.[20]

In the period of uncertainty that preceded actual fighting, Hamilton and his friends prepared against eventualities by military drill. The pamphlet war on the bookstalls defined issues. Acts of civic violence, featuring tar pot and pillow feathers, carried matters further, but were sporadic and could be branded as irresponsible. However, when young Yorkers of spirit began forming themselves into uniformed, armed companies, an element of grim anticipation was introduced.[21] As early as 1774, as Troup remembered it, but perhaps not until the spring of 1775, Hamilton, Fish, and Troup were among volunteers drilling every morning in St. George's churchyard. Their trainer was Maj. Edward Fleming "who lived in New York . . . had been the Adjutant of a British Regiment . . . an excellent disciplinarian—and ardently attached to the American cause." Both Troup and Fish spoke of Hamilton's eager and constant attendance, by which "He became exceedingly expert in the manual exercise."[22]

The designation of the volunteer company in which Alexander enrolled is in doubt. His son thought "They assumed the name of Hearts of Oak."[23] Troup, a member, recalled that his companions were "uniformed in short green coats, and leather caps having the inscription of 'Freedom or death' in front."[24] "The Corsicans" had almost this costume and also Fleming for captain, which prefers them above "The Bold Foresters."[25]

The collegians' drill under Fleming in the chapel grounds was a brief, and in Hamilton's case intensive, introduction to more serious military assignment. Colonel John Lasher's battalion, of which Hamilton's company was one, was raised before the colony militia was organized under the Provincial Congress. The Continental Congress, May 26, 1775, ordered that the New York

militia be armed, trained, and that a number of men be embodied
and kept in the city for its protection against British troops.   The
Provincial Congress made imperfect response, merely recommending in newspapers and handbills that inhabitants furnish themselves
with arms, "to use all Diligence to perfect themselves in the Military
Art, and if necessary to form themselves into Companies. . . ."
Early in June, 1775, Philip Schuyler and Richard Montgomery
were nominated for major general and brigadier of New York
troops in case a Continental army should be raised; later that
month provisions were made for active recruiting.[26]

Hamilton's first time under fire was the night of August 23–4,
1775, when he helped remove a score of cannon from the Battery,
and the *Asia* man-of-war, with grape and ball, tried to prevent
seizure of the king's property.   We have Mulligan's eyewitness
testimony to Hamilton's part, and official and other first-hand
detailed accounts of the affair.

When at length the *Asia* of 74 guns answered his anxious summons, Lt. Gov. Colden, in Tryon's absence, wrote Captain George
Vanderput of his "particular Satisfaction.   You will be surprised
Sir to find how entirely the legal authority of Governm.^t is now
superceded in this place."[27]   Governor Tryon returned to relieve
the apprehensive Colden, but he too was at a distance on Long
Island the night of August 23.[28]   However, Captain Vanderput
had got word that some people intended removing the cannon from
the Battery.   As it was his duty to protect them, he sent a boat to
lie near, watch, and report developments.[29]   The Provincial Congress, meeting in the city, had ordered the guns hauled away from
beneath Fort George.[30]   Consequently some of the light infantry
belonging to Colonel Lasher's battalion and artillerymen under
Captain John Lamb marched to the Battery at eleven o'clock at
night.[31]   They met no interference from the fort, as the few troops
there had been removed to the *Asia* as long ago as June.   Governor
Tryon's civil authority was at an end; he contemplated ruefully
imprisonment as a hostage, or finding refuge on a warship where
salt provisions acting on his "billious Habit of Body" would prove
fatal.[32]

Soon after midnight when the Americans had dragged nine or
ten mounted guns up Broadway, a musket was fired from the *Asia*'s

barge. Captain Vanderput said later this was as a signal to the ship and was not directed at the Battery, but the party on shore thought differently, got together, and discharged their muskets after the barge until it was out of range. One man in the barge was killed. Soon the *Asia* began firing single cannon, followed by a broadside. All shots from the vessel were aimed for the Battery, not against the city at large, though some went high enough to pierce roofs and topple chimneys.[33] Hamilton may have been one of those, militiamen and citizens, who let go with muskets after the receding barge. Following that, he helped drag off a cannon, for he seized the rope from the hands of Mulligan and gave Mulligan his musket to hold. As Hercules Mulligan, appropriately, was a large, powerful man, better able to pull a cannon than the slight youth who insisted on taking his place, Alexander must have been possessed to do his utmost. When he returned, the *Asia* had opened fire, and Hamilton met Mulligan retreating. He asked for his piece, and, told by Mulligan it was left in the battery, "he went for it, notwithstanding the firing continued, with as much unconcern as if the vessel had not been there."[34] Twenty-one ninepounder cannon were successfully got off the Battery and drawn up under the liberty pole on the Common.[35]

Alexander had been studying gunnery,[36] perhaps with the assistance of Robert Harpur in the mathematics necessary. We do not know why he pitched on this, except that it was a preferred branch, requiring special education. When the Provincial Congress, January 6, 1776, ordered that an artillery company be raised for the defense of the colony,[37] Hamilton seized the opportunity to obtain the command. On February 23 the Congress recorded that "Col. McDougall recommended Mr. *Alexander Hamilton* for Capt. of a Company of Artillery. . . ."[38] The Congress was to consider the recommendation next morning, and doubtless discussion occurred, though no note of it appears. McDougall had presided at the meeting in the Fields where Alexander was a surprise speaker, and Alexander probably came in contact with him in the months that followed. Whether the collegian solicited McDougall's support for nomination to the captaincy we do not know, but it seems likely. If so, the favor was returned later when Hamilton was in position to urge McDougall for important posts. Troup said that John Jay, a member of the Provincial Congress, "at . . . Mc-

Dougall's request," obtained Hamilton's commission from the
Congress.[39]   Perhaps this took a little doing because of Hamilton's
youth and lack of experience.   Proof of fitness was required.
This was soon furnished in "A Certificate of *Stephen Badlam,* Capt
of Artillery, . . . that he has examined Alexander Hamilton and
judges him qualified. . . ."   The Congress thereupon, March 14,
1776, *"Ordered,* that . . . *Alexander Hamilton* be and he is
hereby appointed Captain of the Provincial Company of Artillery
of this Colony."[40]

Hamilton's company, as indicated in his commission, at this
stage belonged to the province only, as distinct from units spoken
of as "Continental Troops raising in this Colony."[41]   It was
Mulligan's memory that Hamilton's commission was not granted
until he had fulfilled the condition of raising 30 men for his
company; "I went with him that very afternoon and we engaged
25 men."[42]

Probably after Hamilton was nominated as captain of the New
York Artillery Company, but before his commission was issued, the
ever solicitous Elias Boudinot had sought for him appointment as
aide-de-camp to William Alexander, Lord Stirling, then in command in New York City.   Boudinot obtained Stirling's approval,
but when he visited Hamilton his protégé declined the offer, preferring to take his chances of a field command, even though in a
purely provincial company.[43]   One does not know the fortunes of
war, but this decision was more momentous for him than Hamilton
guessed.   Had he taken the staff position with Stirling he would
not have had his fighting that nourished his ambition to return to
field command in the siege of Yorktown.   More important, he
might not have become aide to Washington with all that that meant
in launching him in his national career.

Recruiting his men without so much as the aid of uniforms
furnished to those in the Continental service, Captain Hamilton
"with his own funds equipped them."[44]   This meant that the
captain used his personal credit and perhaps met some bills until
amounts for clothing were deducted from the men's pay.   Alsop
and Jas. Hunt rendered a bill to Col.^o Andrew (Capt. Alexander)
Hamilton for seventy-five pair of buckskin breeches "Delivered
the Soldiers of the New York Artillery" in batches between March

and July 1776, evidently as recruiting proceeded. As the price of this article rose from 36 s. to 48 s., Hamilton had old breeches repaired, and issued to one of his gunners a pair "half worn." Always attentive to his dress, Hamilton paid 64 s. for his own breeches and for his shoes several times the cost of those for his company. His account with Curtenius, Commissary of Clothing of New York, came to £188.16.9, covering "blue Strouds," "blue Shalloon," "Oznabrigs," 30 gross and 8 dozen buttons, and he promised to send the money "as soon as he was in Cash." Hamilton's men wore blue coats with buff cuffs and facings, after the style specified by Captain John Lamb for his company recruited for the Continental service.[45]

Captain Hamilton's first assignment, probably sought by him, when he had been commissioned less than three weeks, was to detail men from his company to guard the colony records, replacing Continental troops who served at a greater charge.[46] This duty was doubtless welcomed by Hamilton, even before his company was complete, because equipment for artillery drill was not procurable.[47]

Hamilton explained to the Provincial Congress at the end of May 1776 that he had difficulty in bringing his company to strength while he was unable to offer the higher pay of artillerymen allowed by the Continental Congress in revision of the original scale published the year before. His company by their articles were to be subject to the same regulations and have the same pay as the Continental artillery, and the discrimination had lately caused "many marks of discontent" among his men. Captain Beauman enlisted at the higher scale, "and this makes it difficult for me to get a single recruit: for men will naturally go to those who pay them best." Also, could he be allowed the small "actual expenses" of sending recruiting officers into the country? And could his men be furnished the frock given to the other troops as a bounty? "This frock would be extremely serviceable in summer, while the men are on fatigue; and would put it in their power to save their uniform much longer." The Provincial Congress granted each request. Hamilton was to be allowed 10s. for every man enlisted up to 100.[48]

Hamilton's company numbered sixty-eight officers and men in October 1776.[49] Their names were predominantly English, with some Irish,[50] Scotch,[51] and a few Dutch.[52]   Many were illiterate, obliged to make their marks in the pay book.   The few roll calls surviving show all officers present and fit for duty.   They were James Moore, captain-lieutenant; James Gilliland, first lieutenant; John Bane (Bean?), second lieutenant; Thomas Thompson, third lieutenant; the noncommissioned officers were Sergeants Samuel Smith, Richard Taylor, James Deasy, and Corporals Robert Barber, John Stakes (*sic*), Martin Johnson.[53]   On October 4 eleven of the men were sick absent, two had deserted, and two were prisoners. Hamilton's deserters were probably not different from others advertised at the time.   Captain Robert Johnson of the "York Forces" would pay $12 for lodging in jail or delivering "to any committee on the continent" David Babcock, about twenty-five, fair complexion, straight black hair, slow in speech, five feet eight inches high, had on when he went away a brown regimental coat turned up with green, buckskin breeches, and blue yarn stockings. Or one could have the same reward for turning in Thomsin Oddle, from size and gear more conspicuous.   He was six feet, three inches, twenty-six years old, apt to swear and blaspheme ("his common word, damn my wig"), fair complexion, black curled hair; decamped in a light blue regimental coat turned up with green, and "a pair of streaked trowsers."[54]

Two old friends spoke of the zeal and success with which our young captain trained his men; "he proceeded with indefatigable pains, to perfect [his company] in every branch of discipline and duty; and it was not long before it was esteemed the most beautiful model . . . in the whole army."   Steuben's excellent "Instructions for the Captain," published by Congress three years later, were anticipated by Hamilton in his care for the health, discipline, accoutrements, clothes, and record-keeping in his artillery company.[55]   The raw troops hastily gathered for the defense of New York, throwing up crude earthworks, more nearly resembled gangs of laborers than they did soldiers; their lack of subordination, absence from roll calls, and neglect of drill[56] were bound to draw favorable comment for a brisk company like Hamilton's.

Captain Hamilton continued to be jealous for the equal treatment of his provincial artillerymen.   At the end of July he was asking the New York Congress to authorize Mr. Curtenius, the commissary, to give his company the full Continental ration which his contract called for, and not "almost a third less provisions than the whole army besides receives." Characteristically, Hamilton enclosed the standard "rates of rations."[57]

Following complaint in the Provincial Congress that 1,200 militia to be raised in New York City and County, ordered by the Continental Congress, was too heavy a drain, Hamilton's company was counted as part of the quota and August 9 was incorporated into General John Morin Scott's brigade. These troops were encamped in July at Greenwich (Village). From an advertisement in general orders July 5 of a lost pocketbook it seems that "Capt Hamilton's Quarters" were sufficiently known to attract the steps of an honest finder who wanted the reward of £3; incidentally, the sum lost, 10 guineas, was in three currencies.[58]

Hamilton's next letter to the New York Congress carried a suggestion that proved influential. First Lieutenant Johnson had been promoted out of the company, and Hamilton observed that in supplying the vacancy, "It would be productive of much inconvenience should not the inferior officers succeed in course, and . . . I doubt not you will think it proper to advance Mr. Gilleland and Mr. Bean, and fill up the third lieutenancy with some other person." Hamilton's candidate was Thomas Thompson, the first sergeant, who "has discharged his duty in the present station with uncommon fidelity . . . and expertness . . . and his advancement will be a great encouragement . . . to my company in particular, and will be an animating example to all men of merit to whose knowledge it comes."[59]

The proposal to advance from the ranks, on principle, evidently seemed to Congress sufficiently novel to warrant directing Colonel (James?) Livingston to "call on Capt. Hamilton & inquire into this matter & report to this house."[60] Livingston confirming next day Hamilton's facts, Congress in a resolution described the sergeant in Hamilton's words, promoted him to the lieutenancy, and announced the rule: "this Convention will exert themselves in promoting from time to time such privates and non-Commissioned Officers . . . as shall distinguish themselves by their Sobriety, Valour and Subordination . . ." and it was "Ordered, that this Resolution be published in the newspapers of this State."[61] Hamilton's good opinion of Thompson, whom he later urged for promotion over the heads of others to a captain-lieutenancy,[62] was confirmed in the event.   Thompson was killed leading his men in a charge at the battle of Springfield.[63]

This recommendation to promote from the ranks—practically Hamilton's earliest act as a public officer—worked with much besides to make the American army a democratic one as distinguished from those of Europe.   Not to wring too much out of the incident, it would have been easy for the young captain, in his home city that had become the focus of the war, to prefer one of his college friends or another of social pretensions.[64]   But he made worth, not birth, the claim.

7

New Jersey Retreat
and Retaliation

CAPTAIN Alexander Hamilton, after months of drill and supplying members of his artillery company to work on the defenses of Manhattan Island, must have been among the most attentive to the warning of Washington in general orders of August 8, 1776: ". . . the Movements of the enemy, and intelligence by Deserters, give the utmost reason to believe, that the great struggle, in which we are contending for every thing dear to us, and our posterity, is near at hand. . . ." The commanding redoubt which Hamilton's unit had helped to construct would be the first to give the alarm on approach of the British transports. "A Flag in the day time, or a light at Night, in the Fort on Bayard's hill, with three Guns from the same place fired quick, but distinct, is to be . . . a signal for the troops to repair to their . . . posts, and prepare for action. . . ." All drums would beat immediately.[1] Possibly Hamilton would be the very one to run up the flag or light, and order fuses put to the three quick guns. Mounting tension was not relieved when six days later orders announced that the enemy had been embarked for some time and were prevented only by bad weather from attacking. Our troops were to keep two days' victuals ready dressed and canteens filled. Directions for the signal were repeated.[2]

The Bayard's Hill stronghold (at what is now the intersection of Canal and Mulberry streets), had the best elevation of the works designed to protect the little city of New York, then confined to the

[85]

tip of Manhattan below Chambers Street. The town had 4,000 houses and 25,000 population, though many of the people had left when the troops turned the place into an armed camp, and shortly more were to flee. The island jutted sharply into the bay; the Grand Battery below Fort George looked east half a mile to the wooded Columbia Heights on Long Island and west two miles to Powles Hook in New Jersey.[3]

When Lord Stirling took over command at New York from General Charles Lee early in March 1776 he put 4,000 men to work furthering the fortifications on Manhattan and Long Island. A dozen earthworks on lower Manhattan stretched around from the Jersey Battery on the west to Thompson's at Horn's Hook on the east. Spencer's redoubt (Monroe and Rutgers streets) was the southeast anchor of a line of forts extending halfway across the island. The chief of these was on Bayard's Hill, an irregular heptagonal work constructed by Lasher's Independent Companies commencing early in March,[4] and consequently Hamilton was especially connected with it.[5] The men of the Independent Companies were relieved of their fatigue duty on May 16 with Washington's thanks "for their masterly manner of executing the work. . . ."[6] Nicholas Fish, with more enthusiasm than experience, called it "a Fortification superior in Strength to any my Imagination could ever have conceived," though we know that late in March it contained twelve six-pounders and required only two commissioned, 4 noncommissioned officers, and twenty privates to man it.[7]

New York and its dependencies were lost to the Americans in the battle of Long Island, August 27–29, 1776, and remained the advantageous base for the enemy for seven years, to the end of the war. The next actions—at Kip's Bay, Harlem Heights, White Plains, and Fort Washington—were preliminaries to American retreat across the Jerseys. Hamilton's part in this opening scene in the middle states was that of spirited preparation for a defense that collapsed, followed by tenuous resistance until hopes revived at Trenton.

All evidence indicates that he was not in the engagement on Long Island, but was stationed during those days in Bayard's Hill redoubt on Manhattan. The assumption that Hamilton was at Brooklyn[8] is from a careless reading of his friend Mulligan's recollection.

We may believe that our young captain of artillery, with others, was doubtful whether the third of Washington's troops, thrown over to the defense of Brooklyn Heights, could withstand a mass attack. General Charles Lee, when he took command at New York in February, had determined that this overlooking elevation must be fortified if the city was to be held; later Stirling and Washington agreed.[9] But the manning of the Long Island defenses, and the feasibility of holding them, even were a larger force available for that assignment, caused misgivings. Mulligan tells us that before the battle, Hamilton, the Reverend John Mason, perhaps Rhinelander and Troup, dining at his house, "were lamenting the situation on Long Island and suggesting the best plans for its removal when Mr. Mason and Mr. Hamilton determined to write an anonymous letter to Genl. Washington pointing out their ideas of the best means to draw off the Army." Mulligan saw Hamilton draft the plan, heard it read, and gave it to Colonel Webb of Washington's staff. He had no doubt the general attended to it "because my impression at that time was that the mode of drawing off the army which was adopted was nearly the same as that pointed out in the letter."[10] In spite of his circumstantial narration of the incident, Mulligan may have transposed the concern of the time[11] into a concrete scheme for evacuation worked out in his presence.

Washington's management of the escape across the East River the night of August 29–30, entirely without detection, has been pronounced masterly. He was the last to leave the Brooklyn ferry after the Cape Anne boatmen had set over all troops, stores, and guns. This was in spite of a squall in the river the early part of the night but with the help of fog in the morning. His reports, before and after he took command at the scene, indicate that plans had not been made in advance for evacuation. Thus his dispatch to the New York legislature from Long Island on the 28th seems to show that he was not aroused to the defeat of the day before; he was sure he needed all the men he had there for "the defence of these lines. . . ."[12] The decision to abandon the island was not taken until after the enemy advanced late that afternoon to open their first parallel for a siege of our principal works.[13] If Hamilton and his friend Dr. Mason proposed anything to Washington concerning withdrawal from Long Island, some days before the engagement, they must have argued the reasons for it, much as Wash-

ington and the council of war afterward gave them, but did not
detail means of embarking the forces as Mulligan remembered.
Neither of them, certainly not Dr. Mason, could have known the
disposition of troops prior to the event. The exposed position of
the defenses was plain beforehand.[14]

The British dalliance of a fortnight following their victory on
Long Island was taken up by the Americans in headquarters debate
and queries to Congress whether they should give up lower Manhattan to an enemy whose powerful fleet controlled the surrounding
waters. Greene was in the minority in urging "a general and
speedy retreat from this island . . . to oppose the enemy successfully, and secure ourselves from disgrace. I think we have no
object this side of King's Bridge." He would burn the city; two-
thirds of the property in it belonged to Tories, anyhow.[15] The result of a council was "a course . . . between abandoning [the city]
totally and concentring our whole strength for its defence." General Israel Putnam was to garrison the town with 5,000 troops;
9,000 were to go to Kingsbridge, and the remaining 6,000 effectives
were to occupy the intervening space. It was too likely that the
enemy would sever the connecting line at its weakest points, with
danger to portions of the army cut off without support, but the
intention was to defer British possession.[16] Hamilton's company,
assigned to Scott's brigade, but soon transferred with other artillery
to the command of Knox,[17] was under Putnam in the lower Manhattan forts.[18]

Only two days were used for purposeful withdrawal before the
Howes struck the morning of September 15 at the most vulnerable
spot on the East River, Kip's Bay.[19] The inferior earthworks were
manned by militia. As soon as Washington knew of the landing
he galloped down from Harlem Heights, only to meet the defenders
in panic flight. British warships[20] had cannonaded "to scour the
Grounds and cover the landing of their Troops . . . on the appearance of the Enemy, not more than Sixty or Seventy in Number," our men "ran away in the greatest confusion without firing a
single Shot." Washington's furious efforts to rally them were of
no avail. Seeing from "this . . . dastardly conduct" that nothing
could be expected of these frantic cowards, he "sent orders to
secure the Heights. . . ."[21]

General Putnam, from the city, sent aid to Kip's, but it was no use.   He could only join the other brigades in the flight toward Bloomingdale, then rush back "to call off the pickets and guards."[22] Colonel Knox was just quitting his partially dismantled battery for Harlem Heights when he found Silliman's brigade falling back from Corlear's Hook.   With them he entered Fort Bunker Hill nearby, where, supposing escape cut off, he proposed to make a desperate defense.   If Mulligan's memory was correct, Captain Hamilton was there and must have been active in whatever hasty preparations were made.   Major Aaron Burr, Putnam's aide, coming up, rescued the party with his information that the way was open to the Bloomingdale Road.[23]

Hamilton was doubtless with one of the last contingents to reach Harlem Heights, about nightfall.   After the anxious exit by a tramp of seven or eight miles,[24] encumbered by field pieces, and soaked by rain, the men lay in the open on their arms.   Already entrenching had begun on Harlem Heights by troops stationed there,[25] and Washington wrote the next day, "I should hope the Enemy would meet with a defeat in case of an Attack" if his men behaved tolerably.[26]

They immediately behaved very well indeed.   An accidental encounter of reconnoitering parties persuaded Washington to enlarge the action into a little battle in which the Americans retrieved their misconduct of the day before by driving the British in open combat.   We have no reason to suppose that Hamilton shared in this engagement except in the confidence imparted to our forces.[27] It was at Harlem Heights, according to one story, that Hamilton first met Washington.   The commander-in-chief, struck by the diligence of the young captain's company in throwing up an earthwork, invited Hamilton to his marquée.[28]   Certainly in some fashion Hamilton came unmistakably to Washington's notice before he was invited to join the general's staff at Morristown in February or March, 1777.   If Washington fixed Hamilton in his eye independently of General Greene, who is said, four or five months earlier, to have wished to place him near the commander-in-chief, the introduction holds additional compliment.   However, the opportunity for Washington to observe the zeal and proficiency of Hamilton would have been greater in the retreat across New Jersey and in the actions at Trenton and Princeton than in the camp at Harlem.   Hamilton's reputed offer to attempt to retake Fort

Washington, mentioned below, implies some confidence of Washington in him, but that occurrence is doubtful.

Enemy frigates, on October 9, broke through obstructions preparing in the channel of the Hudson, and three days later a fleet landed Howe's troops in force on Throgs Neck in Westchester, thus promising to cut the Americans off behind as before.[29]   Immediately a council of war at Harlem determined that to prevent "a design of Hemming us in . . . our forces must be taken from hence, and extended toward East and West Chester so as to out flank them."[30]

The principal action in this quarter was at White Plains on October 28.   General Howe directed his attack against Chatterton's Hill, a detached ridge to the southwest of the main American lines.   The reason for this choice[31] was a puzzle then and since, for it necessitated crossing the Bronx River (only a few rods wide, it is true) under fire and fighting up steep slopes.   Meanwhile Washton's center, in the flat of the village, was only weakly fortified. However, a thorough cannonade threw the American militia into confused retreat; though partially rallied, the brief defense fell to continental troops.   Fifteen minutes gave the British and Hessians possession; the Americans "moved off the hill in a . . . body, neither running nor observing the best order."[32]

No witness or contemporary writer, so far as found, placed Hamilton in the fight at Chatterton's Hill (battle of White Plains), which calls in question ascription to him, by his son and others, of a valiant and skillful role.   Nor is there evidence that the two field pieces of the Americans were those of Hamilton's company.[33]

We do have a particular, competent account of the artillery on Chatterton's Hill from Colonel John Haslet, who yielded command but gave good advice when McDougall came up.   After the defense had been strengthened by substituting continentals for militiamen, McDougall ordered one of the field pieces forward to bear on the enemy approaching the creek.   The gun was "so poorly appointed, that myself was forced to assist in dragging it along the rear of the regiment.   While so employed, a cannon-ball struck the carriage, and scattered the shot about, a wad of tow blazing in the middle.   The artillerymen fled.   One alone was prevailed upon to tread out the blaze and collect the shot.   The few that returned made not more than two discharges, when they retreated with the field-piece. At this time the Maryland battalion was warmly engaged, and the enemy ascending the hill."[34]

Washington moved his main army to Peekskill November 10–11, preparatory to crossing to New Jersey, and Hamilton and his artillery company were in this contingent.[35] General Charles Lee was left in command at North Castle;[36] General Heath was posted to guard the Highlands;[37] while the commander in chief would, if possible, prevent the enemy from reaching Philadelphia.[38]

The final act on Manhattan Island, until the commander in chief entered New York seven years later, was the unconditional surrender of Fort Washington, designed to dominate passage of the Hudson. The post was doomed in any case, as the enemy moved freely on all sides of it by land and water, but timely evacuation would have saved 2,850 troops, cannon, arms, supplies and, equally important, the spirits of the patriot army and of the country. The fault was Washington's, not only officially, but in fact. The calamity was due to his hesitation to give positive orders for abandonment until, standing on the very ground, he saw that he had delayed too long. From the time that British vessels demonstrated their capacity to pass the obstructions in the river his judgment told him that the place, and also Fort Lee on the palisades nearly opposite, were useless and untenable. He was distracted by his duties at White Plains and above, and was too far dissuaded by the formal council of his officers, by the misplaced confidence of General Greene, and by the demand of Congress that the river be blocked.[39]

These particulars of the fall of Fort Washington are necessary to discredit a fancied offer of derring-do by Alexander Hamilton; namely, that if he could share command of a storming party with Major Ebenezer Stevens, he would engage to retake the works.[40] All circumstances are as much against Hamilton having made the proposal as the rejection of it by Washington, if made, was a foregone conclusion. Hamilton himself was at Hackensack; Fort Lee was hurriedly abandoned on November 20, leaving its armament and large stores to Cornwallis; Washington was pressing his retreat across the Passaic[41] and drawing Lee's force after him to what was evidently the new seat of war.[42] Even had troops been available on the east side of the Hudson they could not have recaptured a fort which Magaw, with his excellent garrison, could not defend.

In the seven weeks of the retreat across New Jersey, the assaults on Trenton and Princeton, and then withdrawal to winter refuge at Morristown, Hamilton won his spurs. His service before this had been zealous but preparatory. Now, like the others of Washington's dwindling, harassed band, he proved that he was no "summer soldier" nor "sunshine patriot." The experience of danger met and surmounted remained with him in the four following years of staff duty and would not let him rest until he had returned to field command. His performance in New Jersey, in endurance and in action, recommended him to Washington for reception into his military family. Hamilton's trials in this short period gave him fitness as an aide which he could not have acquired without the personal knowledge of marching and fighting.

This may be the place to take a summary view of Alexander Hamilton's six years as a soldier in the Revolution. Back in the West Indies, irked as Cruger's copyist, he had professed to his young friend Neddy Stevens: "my ambition is prevalent, so that I contemn the grovelling condition of a clerk . . . and would willingly risk my life . . . to exalt my station. . . . I wish there was a war."[43] Within less than seven years his ambition, more than ever prevalent, found scope in the contest for American independence. Ironically, except for the beginning and end of his service, he had a clerk-like assignment, as aide-de-camp to the commander in chief. But now he was a clerk with a difference. He plied both sword and quill, and it was hard to know with which he wrote and with which he fought. He was emissary of Washington in preparing campaigns, and transmitted and executed orders on the battlefield as staff attendant. He labored at headquarters in correspondence, half military, half diplomatic—with Congress, legislatures, governors, and officers. So far as his station and experience allowed, he was alter-ego of his commander, encouraged to use the force and judgment which Washington would have employed had his time and energies extended to the calls upon him. This was possible because of mutual confidence and attachment the more extraordinary when we consider the difference of age, position and, indeed, of talents of the two. The one divergence between them during the war was Hamilton's fault, a compound of youthful pride and presumption.

The rift was soon closed; Hamilton had his combat exploit that had driven him to his errantry, and a new chapter of profounder collaboration between the two opened.

Hamilton's war training, in his situation and with his bent, was a political even more than a military school. If English statesmen were made on the playing fields of Eton, many in America were taught on the battlefields of the Revolution. Final triumph lent assurance, but more than this, the struggle impressed the requirements of their country if it was to justify their sacrifices and fulfill its promise. Numbers proved apt pupils—Washington himself, Greene who died too soon to put off tunic for toga, Knox, Boudinot, Pickering, and peculiarly Hamilton. It is dangerous to say that others, who served in civil instead of military capacities during the war, profited less from experience of the times or made contributions, then and afterward, in any wise inferior. We think immediately of Madison, Jefferson, Jay, Franklin, the Adamses, Wilson, Gouverneur Morris and so many more. Yet for the military men who continued ministers of state and legislators there remained a claim of parenthood which deepened their commitment.

The emotional deposit from military devotion was less in Hamilton's case than the lessons in statecraft which he could not have received so intimately in any other fashion. The lack of ways and means was lamented in a feckless Congress, but cried louder in an empty commissary. Jarring sectional and state demands were manifest in debate and ballot, and soldiers drew inferences for the future. When political jealousies thinned armies, imperiled the lives of troops, and delayed victory on which all hopes depended, the danger was poignant to men in uniform as it could not be to more distant beholders.

Hamilton's military duties took him to every theater of the war, 1776–1781, save to Champlain, the Carolinas and Georgia, and the Iroquois country of Sullivan's expedition. As a member of Washington's staff—and, as it happened, both before and after this—he moved with the commander in chief everywhere, and went on detached missions besides. He knew well all of the principal officers, many of the subordinates, and maintained a private correspondence with numbers in addition to the headquarters communications in which he had part. With two groups he had particularly close contact, the foreign officers and the civil authorities responsible for finance and supply. His command of the French language, his urbanity and social gifts made him useful and welcome with the first, while his grasp of economic and political problems designed him for the second. He was sent on errands at once military and diplomatic, in the exchange of prisoners and to persuade a reluctant general to comply with Washington's wishes before invoking the commander in chief's positive orders.

In addition he was correspondent, at headquarters, of the New York Assembly and in his private capacity he made recommendations to the superintendent of finance and others. Not only did the exigencies of war acquaint him intimately with chief public vexations and prod him to solutions, but the friendships he formed in the service stood him in stead in afteryears of his career as legislator, secretary of the Treasury, lawyer, and party leader. His first term in the Continental Congress, 1782–1783, when fiscal means to disband the army were as acute as maintenance had been before, was virtually a continuance of his military duties. Of course his much later return to active assignment as inspector general, when he was readying the country for anticipated war with France, benefited directly from his youthful military life.

For these reasons Hamilton's years in the army were not the mere martial interlude or patriotic interruption that belonged to so many. He was at the center of operations, in closest intimacy with the commander in chief, virtually for the duration. He was not only privy to policy throughout, but was an instrument in forming and administering it. This was his early, sudden, and protracted introduction to public life. Indeed, it was so prolonged and varied that his practical education was completed while he was yet in uniform. Precocious anyhow, his political principles were matured and his characteristic expedients were framed in the progress of the war. His headquarters appointment determined his marriage and all that his place in the Schuyler circle was to mean. Most of all, his association with Washington not only commenced but ripened.

Therefore in following Alexander Hamilton from camp to camp, from battle to parley and to battle again we shall not be treating an episode, but a development. What came later is not understandable except for this tutelage. The following seven years, from

Yorktown to the ratification of the Constitution, show the development and application of principles already formed.

But this is not the place for a narrative of the Revolution. In the life of Hamilton the civil aspects of the conflict are superior to military happenings as such. With all of his eagerness and proficiency, his post throughout was a subordinate though confidential one. He was shaped by these trying events more than he could shape them. We shall follow the fortunes of war only as they impinged upon an artillery captain, later a lieutenant colonel at headquarters who was receiving mighty impressions.

We have three glimpses of Captain Hamilton in the anxious, all but hopeless flight across New Jersey and the retaliatory strokes at the end. Only the first, when his battery helped to delay Cornwallis's advance at New Brunswick, rests on contemporary testimony; the others, when he cleared a Trenton street of Hessians, and fired into a college building at Princeton in which a hundred of the enemy had forted themselves, are of later report. Loss of the strongholds on the Hudson had shorn the army in New Jersey of the means of resistance and almost of the ability to survive.[44] The victorious enemy was in pursuit through a flat country offering few obstacles. The Americans kept a jump ahead toward a helpless capital which they could not defend. Washington was unable to hold intact his "not above 3000 Men," for, "much broken and dispirited,"[45] they decamped when enlistments expired or, lacking that excuse, deserted outright.[46] To make the peril worse, Washington's one resource, the army left with General Charles Lee at White Plains, long failed to join him. Lee ignored repeated entreaties until every pretense was exhausted, and then moved at a snail's pace until British horsemen captured him at Basking Ridge on December 13.[47] Jerseymen, in spite of Washington's exhortations through Governor Livingston, took Howe's protections instead of arms in their own defense.[48]

If we ask how far these distresses of command seeped through to Hamilton, responsible for a handful of artillerymen, the answer must be that his ardent solicitude told him much. His worries in these weeks, we may believe, were more than for his shoeless soldiers in blanketless bivouacs in the frosty woods. Hackensack, escape across the Passaic River at Acquackinack, down that stream to Newark, departure just ahead of the advance guards of the enemy,

past Alexander's old school at Elizabethtown, on through Wood-
bridge and so over the Raritan into New Brunswick on November
29. Here Washington wrote two days later that the enemy, twice
his numbers and far more than twice his strength, had pressed on to
Bonum Town. Then in a postscript in the afternoon, "The
Enemy are fast advancing, some of 'em are now in sight."⁴⁹ Six
hours later, from a point halfway to Princeton, he further reported
to Congress that after his last "the enemy appear in several parties
on the Heights opposite Brunswic and were advancing in a large
body towards the crossing place. We had a smart canonade
whilst we were parading out Men but without any or but little loss
on either side. It being impossible to oppose them with our present
force . . . we shall retreat to the West side of Delaware. . . ."⁵⁰

Captain Hamilton's battery of two guns was part of this "smart
canonade."⁵¹ The contemporaries taking particular notice of
Hamilton's role at the Raritan were G. W. P. Custis and James
Wilkinson, though neither was on the scene.⁵² The former said the
commander in chief, "charmed by the brilliant courage and admirable skill" of Hamilton, sent an aide to discover who he was and at
an interview at the first halt "marked him for his own." Inaccuracies otherwise leave this in doubt; Custis had the British pressing on the Americans in their retreat at the ford, though Washington recorded that eighteen hours after he left, the enemy "had not
entered Brunswick . . . but were on the opposite side of the
Raritan."⁵³ Wilkinson followed Washington's terse account, but
singled out Hamilton's service.

Having exchanged shots with the advancing British, Hamilton
posted after his retreating comrades. This may have been when
his absorption struck "a veteran officer," who "noticed a youth, a
mere stripling, small, slender, almost delicate in frame, marching
. . . with a cocked hat pulled down over his eyes, apparently lost
in thought, with his hand resting on a cannon, and every now and
then patting it, as if it were a favorite horse or a pet plaything."⁵⁴

If we leave aside the cannonade across the Raritan, which seems
to have been more diligent than dangerous, it may be that Captain
Hamilton's first time under battle fire was in the surprise descent
upon the Hessians at Trenton the day after Christmas, 1776.
Though Washington confided a fortnight earlier that, failing enlistment of a new army, "I think the game will be pretty well up,"

he had already pondered the venture to rescue military credit and revive the people's hopes.[55] Here was an enterprise which Hamilton's eagerness ran to meet.[56] Yet all of his enthusiasm and discipline must have been needed to sustain his little company of bombardiers and matrosses that night of ice, sleet, and snow. When the column divided at Birmingham, three miles toward Trenton, Hamilton's battery, with those of Forrest and Bauman, took the upper, or Scotch, road under General Greene;[57] the right wing, under General Sullivan, with other batteries, paralleled them on the river road.

Though the Americans did not reach Trenton till broad day, at eight o'clock, it was the pickets, driven in from their posts, that first alarmed the town. American riflemen were already firing from windows, barns, and fences when Hamilton's battery was planted at the head of King Street and Captain Thomas Forrest's on the same high ground commanding Queen Street. Obliged to turn out into the streets to form their regiments, the Hessians were caught like tenpins in a bowling alley. They could not escape the shot and shell that raked the confined space between the houses. By the time those of the enemy who had not been killed, wounded, or made their escape toward Bordentown collected in a semblance of order on the open ground south of the village, they found themselves surrounded and obliged to surrender.

The Revolution held so many instances of anxiety for the Americans that each reader of the history will judge which was most painful to the patriot mind and perilous to the cause. The week between the surprise capture of the Hessians at Trenton and the victory at Princeton was such a desperate interval. Shame threatened to mock success. For hardly had Washington fallen back across the Delaware with his 900 prisoners to Newtown in Bucks County, Pennsylvania, than most of his continentals promised to depart with the expiration of their enlistments December 31. This would leave only Scott's Virginians as a dependable corps on which to rally recently recruited Pennsylvanians, spirited but untried, and Jersey militia, summoned but as yet unseen. Cadwalader, by a fortunate inadvertence, was east of the river, following up the Trenton stroke of the 26th by occupying Burlington and other key positions, and beckoned Washington to join him and clear West Jersey of the enemy.[58]

But the force with Washington, problematic in a matter of hours, was exhausted from lack of sleep and food; ice in the Delaware was too weak for crossing on foot and too thick for prompt passage by boats; the roads were mire; 8,000 king's men under Cornwallis were astir to retrieve their rude reverse. Washington resolved nevertheless to seize the forbidding opportunity to "beat up the rest of the [enemy's] quarters bordering on and near the river. . . ."[59] In spite of—indeed, because of—discouragements, more than the river was crossed December 30–31. A six-week extension of service of the continentals was bought with a bounty of $10 per man who stepped forward in response to the solemn appeal of the commander in chief. Most talented of the orators before the regiments was Quartermaster-General Thomas Mifflin. At Crosswicks his promises were as glowing as his "overcoat made up of a large rose blanket." Booty would be added to bounty. It was distinctly on the commercial side, but the case called for every inducement.[60] At the same time, justifying his emergency action, Congress vested Washington for six months with autocratic power to raise and organize troops and impress matériel. The admission of previous failures of Congress was more important for the future than the authority immediately conferred. However, the confession in this crisis was not needed to convince Hamilton and other thoughtful observers of the incompetence of congressional military management, and must have confirmed his belief that time waited upon a more effective central government.

We may assume that Captain Hamilton was witness to these scenes and helped in the cannonade that delayed the advance of the British from Princeton toward Trenton and then halted the enemy on the north bank of Assunpink Creek at the latter village. He would have known nothing of the council of war in the early evening, January 2, that determined on a bold extrication of the army from the trap in which it lay between creek and river; however, like other young officers, he must have had forebodings of what the morrow would bring.[61] Nor could he have guessed, as they hitched the artillery at one o'clock in the morning of January 3 behind the deceptively blazing camp fires, that the enemy's left was to be detoured in a strike for Princeton.[62]

From that point on we are uncertain of Hamilton's movements. From his known enterprise in pressing into forward action, it is unlikely that his were the "two pieces of . . . cannon . . . left to amuse the enemy" at Trenton.[63]   Probably he was in the "great train of artillery"[64] that skirted Sand Town and followed a new woods road a dozen miles to reach Princeton as the sun rose over hoar-frosted fields.[65]   Here a bloody quarter-hour decided the day. Lieutenant-Colonel Charles Mawhood, leading British regimentals from Princeton by the old road toward Maidenhead (now Lawrenceville), was as astonished at spying the Americans "as if an army had dropped perpendicularly upon them."[66]   Mawhood wheeled his men, recrossed the Stony Brook bridge, and made for an orchard whence they repelled the attack of General Hugh Mercer's column.   Mercer fell, many times wounded, and his troops, flying before the grapeshot, musket balls, and bayonets, threw into disordered retreat Cadwalader's Philadelphia militia that had moved to support him.   "But two pieces of artillery stood their ground and were served with great skill and bravery" until Washington rallied Mercer's and Cadwalader's brigades and put the British to rout.[67]

A body of British hitherto not engaged joined the garrison in the village of Princeton; they advanced briefly against two regiments of Americans in the hollow to the south, but lost heart and threw themselves into the college building, Nassau Hall.   Accounts of what followed conflict, but agree that American cannon were brought to bear on the emergency fortress.   The story that Hamilton's battery opened on the structure, that a ball entered the chapel and passed through a portrait of George II,[68] is not supported by anyone present at the action.   The number in Nassau Hall who surrendered prisoners is variously given as between sixty and two hundred.[69]   The extreme fatigue of Washington's soldiers prevented him from pushing on to New Brunswick as he had planned.   With six or eight hundred fresh troops in a forced march, he believed, he could have "destroyed all their Stores, and Magazines, taken . . . their Military Chest, containing seventy thousand pounds, and put an end to the War."[70]   As it was, the Americans had only time to escape the British arriving in pursuit from Maidenhead, and marched by Kingston, Rocky Hill, Somerset Court House, and Pluckemin to Morristown.

8

Aide-de-camp
to Washington

HAMILTON was continually reading. Any little interval, no
matter how unpropitious his surroundings, turned him to books
which he inwardly digested for future use. Poetry was the one
alleviation to purposeful culling from works on history, statecraft,
and commerce. Special point attaches to notes he took in the
back of his pay book of the New York Artillery Company. These
must have been jotted down in the winter and spring of 1777 at
Morristown. They occupy pages left blank when his command
was terminated;[1] he would not have had opportunity for keeping
a commonplace book while the army was on the move and part
of the time fighting. The chief of the three works he read, or
read in, was Postlethwayt's *Universal Dictionary of Trade and
Commerce* in two thick folio volumes, unwieldy to have been
carried about. The other books represented in these quotations
and memoranda are smaller, Plutarch's *Lives* and Demosthenes'
Orations, but how he came by these and more that he read during
his military service is a guess.

Tracing Hamilton's notes to the passages in Postlethwayt's
formidable repository[2] indicates that he read systematically after
most inquirers would have quit, then skipped to the beginning of
Volume II, in which he did less. Postlethwayt must have been
Hamilton's introduction to areas of national economy in which he
later held influential opinions and which he dealt with in prac-

[100]

tical fashion. His reading for the tracts against the Westchester Farmer had been to support a particular argument; most of it was political and legal, and much concerned events in the controversy itself. Now he was stocking his mind with wider economic information. Obviously he wanted to remember and probably to use it, else he would not have taken the pains to reduce it to writing. His intention was at first satisfied with factual material, pages of his notes being devoted to commercial geography, describing regions of Europe and Asia and giving chief productions and exports country by country. Manufactures came in for particular mention, along with mining, especially of the precious metals, and the numbers of vessels and men engaged in the Dutch fisheries.[3]

However, he tired of this, became selective in his notes, and surely in his reading too, and chose to set down generalizations from both observation and reasoning. Thus: "The Ballance of Trade with the Portuguese not so considerable in favour of the English as is imagined."[4] "Postlethwaite supposes the quantity of Cash necessary to carry on the circulation in a state one third of the rents to the land proprietors or $\frac{1}{9}$ the whole Product of the lands. . . ."[5] And "It has been judged . . . that the labour of 25 persons is nearly sufficient to provide . . . all the necessaries of life for 100 persons."[6] He recorded that the "proportion" of gold and silver as settled by Sir Isaac Newton's proposition was 1 to 14, but generally throughout Europe 1 to 15, and "in China I believe it is 1 to 10."[7] These and other economic aphorisms were stored away to be applied later in debates and reports. As he went on with his reading his attention was attracted to the topics of money, funds, and population. He filled two of his pages with copying "Dr. Halleys Table of Observations exhibiting the probabilities of life. . . ."[8] He gave a "Short Rule to determine the average interest per annum for any sum of money for a given term of years at a given rate, discharging annually an equal proportion of the principle [*sic*]," and in an example used a twenty-year loan at 8 per cent.[9]

Then he began to make deductions of his own which have superior importance for his later polices. Impressed by the utility of the French Council of Commerce "to represent all things relative to trade and manufactures and propose regulations," and by the account of consular reports, he emphasized a question: "Are the limits of the several States & the arts on which they are founded ascertained and are our ministers provided with them? What intelligence has been given to Congress, by our ministers of the designs [,] strength by sea & land, actual interests & views, of the different powers in Europe."[10] This was to reappear six years later when, as a member of the Continental Congress, he presented a plan, not then adopted, for establishing diplomatic and consular services. Sounding as though it might have come from him in the revenue debate in Congress is the "Query? Would it not be adviseable to let all taxes [,] even those imposed by the States [,] be collected by persons of Congressional appointment and would it not be adviseable to pay the collectors so much per Cent on the sums collected?"[11]

If Postlethwayt's *Dictionary* was the first economic work that Hamilton met with, and if he pried in it with curiosity and zeal that led him to take notes, then the recommendations of this author may be assumed to have had a part in forming Hamilton's views and later policies. Postlethwayt explained that he interlarded his collected items with reasoning of his own. This is obvious on examining the encyclopedia in connection with treatises and tracts which appeared under his single authorship.[12] Attempts to attribute opinions readily become speculative. This is particularly true where the tutored was as original as the teachers, acted in a different environment, in response to his own experience and problems, and had advice and assistance from numerous quarters. In Hamilton's case the invitation to comparison is compelling because we soon find him addressing himself to economic solutions with the minimum of obvious preparation. Allowing all room for practical prompting and unusual perspicacity, sources he had, and they ask to be identified and explained. Others will appear as we proceed, but Postlethwayt stands near the beginning.

Malachy Postlethwayt (1707?–1767), English chronicler and interpreter of commercial lore in both private and public domains, was a latter-day mercantilist. He wrote in the period when regulation as the maxim of economic statecraft was yielding to release of individual initiative. In this transition Richard Cantillon and the Physiocrats led by Quesnay were anticipators of Adam Smith's doctrine of liberty. While doubtless influenced by these,[13] Postlethwayt's own pattern of thought conformed more nearly to the mixed, or perplexed, views of Sir James Steuart and David Hume. With Postlethwayt goods rather than gold had become the cynosure. Skillful labor for the sake of ample consumption was brought into the calculation. A favorable balance of trade was still a watchword, but the satisfactory supply of money thus afforded would quicken internal commerce, which ought to be nearly free of controls. Lively competition in production of all sorts at home would stimulate ingenuity and lower costs, especially reducing the rate of interest. This last, with domestic trade according to natural laws, was to be the means of national prosperity. Wise statesmanship, fending off foreign wares, affording security, and nourishing circulation and credit, would further wealth and well-being of the people.[14] From Postlethwayt's *omnium gatherum* spiced with pointed opinion the young Hamilton undoubtedly received first impressions which remained with him, to be pondered and enriched, after he had forgotten where they came from. The similarity of the two in bent for promoting the public economy by a combination of limitation and liberty, or guidance by a loose rein, can scarcely be missed. Expedients such as protection to home industry, sufficient currency, and support of credit through banks and discharge of government debt are items of agreement which confirm the supposition of influence.

Hamilton's extracts from Plutarch's *Lives* conclude his commonplace book. With little effort on our part to read into them, they bear on the rôle he was to have in the American state. "Theseus was the first," he noted, "who out of inclination to popular government parted with the regal power."[15] Hamilton was taken with Romulus as the founder of Rome and with Camillus and his means of rebuilding the city.[16] Romulus, having subdued his enemies abroad, "grew haughty and affected absolute government." And "Whoever gives up his right, or extends his claim too far, is no more a king, but either a slave to the people or a tyrant and so becomes odious . . . to his subjects." Hamilton approved of the senate with which Lycurgus sought to new-model the Spartan state: ". . . the Senate was to the commonwealth what the ballast is to a ship and preserved the whole in a just equilibrium. For they always adhered to the Kings so far as to oppose a democracy and on the other side assisted the people to prevent tyranny."[17]

Of special pertinence is Hamilton's quotation from Demosthenes' Philippic 1: "As a general marches at the head of his troops, so ought wise politicians . . . to march at the head of affairs; . . . they ought not to want the *event,* to know what measures to take; but the measures which they have taken, ought to produce the *event.*"[18]

We do not know how or when Captain Hamilton of the New York Artillery Company first came to Washington's personal notice, or by whose recommendation he was invited to join the commander in chief's military family.   Various occasions were mentioned by contemporaries as leading to this.   The biographer of General Greene, relying on tradition, said that in New York in the summer of 1776, in visiting Washington's headquarters, Greene passed the Park (or Fields) where he was attracted by the competent drill of a company of artillerists and particularly by the precision and bearing of their commander.   He sent to compliment Captain Hamilton, invited him to dinner, and thus began their friendship,[19] which may have resulted later in Hamilton's preferment.   Reports of Washington's approval of Hamilton's work at Harlem Heights and New Brunswick have been noticed above.   Elias Boudinot had suggested Hamilton for Stirling's staff, and when Hamilton declined that appointment, may have interested himself further; Stirling may have done so; or Knox, with Hamilton's exploits at Trenton and Princeton fresh in mind, may have been the instrument.[20]

However it occurred, Washington, shorthanded at headquarters,[21] must have welcomed the assistance of a young field officer well reputed, not only educated but known for his patriotic writings, of cheerful temper and prepossessing appearance and manner. Lieutenant Colonel George Baylor, who had been Washington's "first [i.e., principal] Aid de Camp," had not returned after taking the Hessian colors to Congress, for he received permission to command a cavalry regiment.   Though Baylor was "not in the smallest degree a penman," Robert Hanson Harrison, who possessed that faculty, as recently as the end of January had been detained from camp by illness.   Washington wrote in his own hand, urged him not to come out too soon, and asked that he "forward the Inclosed to Captn. Hamilton. . . ." Quite possibly, this was an invitation to him to join the staff. Alexander Hamilton was announced in general orders of March 1, 1777, as "aide-de-camp to the Commander in Chief, and is to be respected and obeyed as such." His commission as lieutenant-colonel bore that date.[22] Probably he had been serving at headquarters before his formal appointment; Pickering remembered seeing him there in February.[23]

As his aide without interruption for four years, Hamilton was in daily, almost hourly company of Washington—in camp, on marches and journeys, and on the battlefield. He was at the nerve center of the war, where came all intelligence and whence issued all major orders and correspondence with public authorities. The Revolution, like all protracted struggles, especially of a nation aborning, was a medley of contingent forces; the fortunes of the conflict underwent changes inherent in the length of it, such as alteration in recruitment and supply, and occasional improvement but general deterioration of the finances. Hamilton was at the focus of these anxious developments, military, economic, and political. Concerns of moment, requiring surveys, analyses, reports, and recommendations, were mingled with immediate vexations such as jealousies of generals, neglect or obduracy of subordinate officers, and applications of civilians with many pleas, not to speak of the demands of actual fighting. To be an intimate witness to this arduous scene was much, but to act in it with emotion and a measure of responsibility was more. Hamilton's later restless efforts to consolidate national gains may not be understood except by remembering problems of the war. And at headquarters he got to know personalities of the Revolution who were to figure in the sequel. Seeing them tested under stress, he learned their strengths and weaknesses, their merits and foibles, which were dependable and which were marplots. Of course, foremost of these leaders was Washington, who was synonymous with the war and with the country's prospect as long as he lived. It is hard to say whether familiarity with the crisis or with the chief actor in it was more determining in Hamilton's contribution.

In her moving story of Washington's military family, Whiteley[24] gives the impression that the youngsters at headquarters were ardent clerks and couriers, endeared to the commander in chief by their devotion.   But for Hamilton and others this was a fruitful apprenticeship in public affairs.   Of the thirty-two (counting all, from first to last of the war) most were in their twenties, a few in their thirties, as Mifflin, Reed, Tilghman, and Harrison. All were selected for their reliability, alertness, and courage.   It is to be remembered that the entire population was younger then than since; soldiers were of less age than those in other callings. Young officers with qualifications for aides were apt to be precocious; their acceptance of junior staff posts argued a worthy willingness to sacrifice personal military ambitions.   Boys were men, men were called elderly when we would now think them in their prime.   For example, Baron Steuben, forty-eight when he arrived at Valley Forge, was soon spoken of as an old gentleman; Washington was a patriarch while still in full vigor; Franklin, seventy-five when Cornwallis surrendered, was an ancient in the Revolutionary circle.   Generally Washington's aides gave a good account of themselves afterward in stations of private achievement and public trust.   Besides Hamilton, different roles of national prominence were played by Edmund Randolph, Mifflin, Pickering, John Trumbull, McHenry, and Richard Varick.

The members of the floating company at headquarters with whom Hamilton was in closest association throughout his service were Robert Hanson Harrison and Tench Tilghman.   Both were Marylanders.   Harrison, known as the "Old Secretary," had been Washington's neighbor and occasionally his lawyer at Alexandria, and was secretary of the Fairfax Committee (Washington, chairman) which drew the Virginia Resolves of July 1774.   Ten years older than Hamilton, he promptly gave the youngster his friendship, called him the "Little Lion."   The commander in chief, soliciting Joseph Reed's return, wrote of Harrison in 1775 that while "clever, and perfectly confidential," he "has never yet moved upon so large a scale as to comprehend at one view the diversity of matter, which comes before me, so as to afford the ready assistance which every man in my situation must stand more or less in need of."   Time soon supplied the required experience.   He would not join the Board of War in the autumn of 1777 because that body, in its inspiration, was critical of Washington.   He resigned at headquarters in March 1781 to become

Chief Judge of the Maryland General Court. Continued ill health, and his private affairs, prevented him from being a delegate to the Constitutional Convention and from accepting a seat on the Supreme Court, offered by Washington and urged by Hamilton. Later he consented, but sickness compelled him to withdraw.

Loyal is peculiarly the word for Tench Tilghman. He had the longest tenure of any in the military family, from August 1776, when he came as a volunteer, declining rank and pay, until he stood by Washington's side when the general surrendered his commission to Congress, December 1783. Of excellent competence, honorable, modest, notably considerate of others, he had no jealousy of Hamilton's readier part in proposing policy. He was chosen by Washington to take the news of Cornwallis's surrender to Congress. After the war he resumed business as the Baltimore partner of Robert Morris. He died in his early forties, like Harrison, after long ill health.[25]

Whatever was the case with his companions in the saddle and at the writing table, tribulations at headquarters were not lost on Alexander Hamilton. They turned up in all that he wrote, said, and did in remaking a shambling governmental structure and supplying instruments and policies in nearly every department. Not only so; while yet a junior in Washington's military family he analyzed the causes, fiscal and political, of the country's plight, and in volunteer recommendations to Robert Morris and James Duane forecast what he actually achieved a decade later. Further, many of his letters written in camp for Washington's signature were of his own construction not only in form but in ideas.

One is constantly prompted to lay Hamilton's superior grasp and power of statement to inborn gift and let it go at that. Beyond a point this must be the plea, for his best work was of a different order of excellence from the offerings of most of those about him. But we can go far in accounting for the unaccountable. He made eager deductions from object lessons at headquarters because he was committed not only to the cause but to the country in peculiar fashion. Nearly without exception his fellow aides came of families long rooted in America; this had recommended them to Washington in the first place, and after the war they would enter on careers more or less prepared for them, or would resume callings in which they had commenced. Hamilton, by contrast, had no birthright. He was adopted by America because he had already adopted this country. He was the convert who is more zealous than the inheritor of a faith. He had nothing in his earlier life or locus to return to. St. Croix was a memory in which affection and gratitude were mingled with embarrassment if not, in the estimation of outsiders, with shame. His family in that distant island was quondam. Washington's headquarters family, if we leave aside the domestic attentions of Mulligan, Boudinot, and Livingston, was the first the young stranger ever knew. Beyond that comradery was America to be vindicated and established as his future home. If we are to ascribe this to personal ambition we must say in the same breath that he saw his private advantage in terms of public welfare.

Washington several times said what qualities he looked for in an aide—education, sense, good temper. "As to Military knowledge, I do not expect to find Gentlemen much skilled in it. If they can write a good Letter, write quick, are methodical, and diligent, it is all I expect to find in my Aids."[26] Earlier he complained that only Reed and Harrison of his staff could afford him the least assistance in writing. "At present my time is so taken up at my desk, that I am obliged to neglect many other essential parts of my duty; it is absolutely necessary . . . for me to have persons that can think for me, as well as execute orders."[27] At the outset with an aggregation of migrant militia poorly officered; departments of supply, intelligence, and hospitals unorganized and many of their duties falling on the commander in chief; a Congress (not to speak of the states) jealous to preserve authority rather than discharge responsibility, Washington had to be a one-man headquarters. ". . . the Weight of the whole War," said Tilghman, "may . . . be said to lay upon his Shoulders."[28]

Many of the letters and orders issuing from headquarters with Washington's signature show, if only in their variety and number, that Adjutant General Timothy Pickering was correct in saying "I have every reason to believe that not only the composition, the clothing of the ideas, but the ideas themselves, originated generally with the writers. . . . Hamilton and Harrison in particular, were scarcely in any degree his amanuences. . . ."[29] Washington explained to the President of Congress that his letters from headquarters were "first drawn by his secretary and . . . aides de camp."[30]   So unmistakable was Hamilton's constant service to Washington in this respect, during the Revolution and afterward, that in recounting their cooperation one runs out of ways of saying "wrote for Washington," "composed for the General's signature," and so on.   These covering phrases, especially as applied to the reasoned, discretionary pieces, connote much more than faithful transfer to paper of Washington's thought, though not of his wishes.   Washington would have been the last to represent differently their joint authorship.   The point need not be labored. Whatever the originality of the helper in the particular letter or report, the trend and temper of all belonged to the commander in chief.   Undoubtedly with new aides and those less apt in anticipating his wishes in the written word, Washington dictated memoranda of what was to be conveyed in a dispatch.[31]   "I wish to the Lord the General would give me the heads or some idea, of what he would have me write," complained Harrison to Pickering one day at Valley Forge, coming down from Washington's chamber.   Pickering was pertinaciously anxious, in reminiscences committed to his commonplace book in old age, to emphasize Washington's debt to Hamilton, and not always with grace toward the former.   "During a long series of years, in war and in peace, Washington . . . enjoyed the advantages, of Hamilton's eminent talents, integrity & felicity; and these qualities fixed him in his confidence to the last hour of his life. . . . in intellect [Hamilton] was immensely his superiour."   Pickering was not afraid to maintain the heresy, he told Gore, that "in talents of every kind," Hamilton "infinitely surpassed" Washington.   Pickering rested his opinion on "acts certainly *his* [Hamilton's] *own,* and not *imputed* to him as . . . Head of an army, or the civil Chief of a nation."   (But then he added a revision in red ink: "infinitely . . . is too strong a word, while *greatly* or even vastly hardly express Hamilton's superiority.")[32]

The admiring Pickering is here cited, not for unprofitable, and unjustified, comparison of virtues, but to indicate the confidence Washington placed in Hamilton at headquarters.

General Philip Schuyler's appreciation of Hamilton's superior merits as an aide to the commander in chief was formed before Schuyler had any notion that the young man would become his

son-in-law. He had studied the "character . . . of the . . .
gentlemen who composed the general's family. . . . I discovered
in all, an attention to the duties of their station; in some, a considerable degree of ability, but [in Hamilton] only I found those
qualifications so essentially necessary to the man who is to aid
and counsel a commanding general, environed with difficulties
of every kind, and . . . whose correspondence must . . . be
. . . frequently so delicate as to require much judgment and address. . . ."

Later Schuyler remarked Hamilton's special usefulness in dealings with the French officers, particularly after French forces arrived in America. He was proud that "men of genius, observation and judgment" confirmed his estimate.[33]

The Arnold Tavern at Morristown, on the west side of the village green, was the first of many quarters in which Hamilton lived
in personal as well as official intimacy with the commander in
chief.[34] Naturally Washington wanted his aides and secretaries
at instant call at all hours, which meant that wherever possible
they were under the same roof with him. He preferred that they
have few distractions and commitments elsewhere, particularly
that they be not married.[35] Probably here as elsewhere when the
general settled down in winter quarters, the young officers of his
staff had a bedroom together and spent their long working hours
in another room furnished with writing tables. Washington had
a separate office which, in the crowded condition of his places of
temporary abode during the war, was apt to be his only sitting
room, if indeed he had time for sitting.

Aside from an occasional dance or other entertainment and the
brief respite of dinner-table conversation, the acolytes had to find
their pleasure in spirited discharge of their assignments. "Aides-
de-Camp are persons in whom entire confidence must be placed,"
Washington explained, "and it requires men of abilities to execute
the duties with propriety and dispatch. . . . I give in to no kind
of amusement myself, and consequently those about me can have
none, but are confined from morning till eve, hearing and answering the applications and letters. . . . If these gentlemen had the
same relaxation from duty as other officers have in their common
routine, there would not be so much in it. But, to have the mind

always upon the stretch, scarce ever unbent, and no hours for recreation, makes a material odds."[36]

"Winter quarters," said Tilghman to the merchant Robert Morris, "is to us what the stoppage of navigation used to be to you, . . . an increase in business in the way of paper, pens and ink."[37] And he assured his father, ". . . you need be under no Apprehension of my losing [my health] on the Score of Excess in living," for "Vice is banished from . . . the General's Family. . . . We never sup, but go early to bed and are early up."[38] In his letters from headquarters at Morristown, Hamilton frequently referred to "hurry of business" that prevented him from writing at length,[39] or said Washington was so engaged that he had not been able to bring an important matter to his attention.[40] John Laurens's letters to his father furnish glimpses of pressing demands on Washington's aides, particularly while Hamilton was absent on his northern mission (below). Laurens could not ask leave for the briefest visit away from camp. Thus from White Marsh, "Between copying and composing I have inked a great deal of paper and it begins to be time for me to join in the concern of my snoring Companions, who are extended before the fire in the Style which we practiced formerly in the interior parts of So Carolina." Later, inaccuracies should be excused because he wrote "in a hurry . . . in a small noisy crouded Room."[41]

However, Hamilton's duty at this time was not so largely in writing letters as in other assistance to the commander in chief.[42] His correspondence shows that much of his time was devoted to gathering intelligence of the enemy's situation and activities from deserters, prisoners, and persons who had come out from New York.[43] We know that Washington personally and exclusively received the reports of his spies.[44] Of course, all of Hamilton's work in extracting, weighing, and organizing knowledge of the enemy was in closest cooperation with Washington. This gave him from the start a peculiarly confidential relation to the general, and by the same token the best acquaintance with calculations on which American military movements were based.[45]

A connected duty was that of examining disaffected persons, or those believed to be so, brought by the military to headquarters. If sifting the stories of prisoners and deserters required judgment, separating dangerous Tories from minor offenders and innocuous suspects demanded a scrupulous sense of justice. In dividing cases for military punishment from those belonging to civil authority and in recommending severity or leniency of treatment, the aide was reflecting the wisdom of the commander. At the same time much of Hamilton's own habitual jealousy for civil jurisdiction, and for rights of the accused, entered into the explanations he made.[46]

The life of an aide at headquarters was not all grind. The young gentlemen of Washington's military family assisted him by receiving and entertaining all manner of visitors. The amenities were preserved, even though politeness must often take the place of viands. Mrs. Washington's arrival at a winter camp was the signal for wives of higher officers to join their husbands, sometimes bringing daughters. In the vicinity of Morristown were the homes of numbers of congenial families, and others from a few miles southward retreated there to escape British raids. Winter quarters were kept for months; particularly while Sir William Howe was the opponent, war was a seasonal business, except for minor excursions and alarums. Reviews and parades, arranged for visiting diplomats and other distinguished guests, broke the routine. Brother officers were constantly invited to Washington's table, with many of whom, partly by this means, Hamilton became personally intimate.

Alexander Graydon has left us a glimpse of Hamilton this first winter at Morristown. He "presided at the General's table, where we dined; and in a large company in which there were several ladies, among whom I recollect one or two of the Miss Livingstons and a Miss Brown, he acquitted himself with an ease, propriety and vivacity, which gave me the most favourable impression of his talents and accomplishments. . . ." In the evening Graydon went with Hamilton and Tilghman to drink tea with some of the ladies of the village, including those with whom they had dined.[47]

We may guess at Hamilton's outfit as aide by noting what his companion, John Laurens, thought would "contribute to the propriety of the Commander in chiefs family. . . ." Laurens had "but one pair of breeches that are wearable," so wanted white cloth "to reinforce me in that article." If this emergency was supplied, and he was not to disgrace his station, he would beg

"blue and buff Cloth, Lineing, Twist yellow flat double gilt Buttons sufficient to make me a Uniform Suit . . . , besides corded
Dimitty for Waistcoats and Breeches against the opening of the
Campaign. . . ." Gold epaulettes, gloves, hair powder, pomatum,
and a comb would be added touches.[48] Hamilton, ever elegant,
would have approved Laurens's silver spurs, though he doubtless
preferred his own "waiter" assigned from the troops instead of
being followed, like the young South Carolinian, by black "Berry"
in a hunting shirt and "a check'd one" to change to.

Hamilton's grace and sparkle, especially evident in his spirited
conversation, must have been an asset in the general's household
in those years of stern endurance. These qualities the young
West Indian did not have to summon; they were so pronounced
that, even much later, some who did not know him were deceived
into supposing him light-headed or at least superficial. Not that
Washington himself, contrary to the idea of him as a worshipful
graven image, found difficulty in unbending. Martha Dainger-
field (Mrs. Theoderick) Bland wrote from Morristown at this
time to her sister-in-law of *"our* Noble & Agreable Commander
(for he Commands both sexes) . . . we visit [the Washingtons]
twice or three times a week by particular invitation . . . he is Generally busy in the forenoon—but from dinner til night he is free
for all company his Worthy Lady seems to be in perfect felicity
while she is by the side of her *Old Man* as she calls him. we
often make partys on Horse Back the Genl his lady, Miss Living-
stone & his Aid de Camps . . . at which time General Washington throws of [f] the Hero and takes on the chatty agreable Companion—he can be down right impudent some times. . . ." Colonel Hamilton, in "our riding party Generly," was called "a sens-
able Genteel polite young fellow a West indian."[49]

As Timothy Pickering pointed out,[50] and as anyone will notice
from reading letters in Washington's hand, the general improved
in accuracy of writing as months and years of the war gave him
extraordinary practice. The example of his more correct aides
in this department was of benefit to him in a period when the
ordinary rules of spelling and punctuation were neglected by all
but a few. Harrison and Tilghman were practiced writers, and
McHenry added genuine literary taste and animation. Hamilton
had these qualities and, besides, a force of expression not shown

in the same degree in the work of his companions. With him, putting thoughts into words was not a problem or preoccupation, but a familiar means. Having something he was eager to say, setting it down was relatively simple.

Anticipating further mention, it may be noted here that Hamilton's drafts for Washington, written in camp and field, differed little from what was copied and sent. In longer papers, prepared in his own character, especially in afteryears—such as cabinet documents, Treasury reports, newspaper essays—he often made revisions; verbal changes avoided needless offense, while additions, frequently extensive, amplified. He rarely rearranged, showing that he had thought out the argument before commencing its presentation. He never halted for want of figures and dates, but left blanks to be filled later.

The relief which the aide's expertness as a writer offered to the commander in chief speaks in the great budget of military (and often broadly public) correspondence. Custis may have been partial in picturing Hamilton as the regular reliance of the general at times of unusual pressure. In the campaigns of 1777–1778, Custis recorded, "the habit at . . . headquarters was for the General to dismiss his officers at a very late hour of the night to catch a little repose, while he, . . . drawing his cloak around him, and trimming his lamp, would throw himself upon a hard couch, not to sleep, but to think." Close by, in a blanket but "all accoutred," snored the short but active Billy, his body-servant. If an express arrived, the "dispatches being . . . read, there would be heard in the calm deep tones of that voice, so well remembered . . . , the command of the chief to his now watchful attendant, 'Call Colonel Hamilton.' "[51]

Certain it is that these two, for the duration of Washington's official life, composed a partnership of the written word, culminating in the *Farewell Address.* As they habitually worked together the blend of minds and modes of expression was so complete as often to defy particular attribution. All that may be observed— and this from independent evidence—is that Washington's judgment was the more reliable, and that Hamilton's information and choice of words formed the excellent complement. In the nature of the case, however, Washington must often have supplied only the outlines of a report to Congress, plan of campaign, or important letter to a commander, which Hamilton was to draw. The general then approved the draft. In a large number of instances the character of the document was determined more by the actual writer than by the signer. This was true where much material was to be digested and organized, where a communication was in a series all executed by Hamilton, or where the mode of statement was as significant as the substance of what was said. Hamilton so familiarized himself with Washington's wishes that he could proceed in a correspondence all but independently.

It is necessary to read the hundreds of his letters and other papers for the commander in chief to appreciate Hamilton's original contribution. Frequently this is confirmed by what he was writing privately to friends at the same time on the same subjects, though of course these personal views reflected, to an unknown extent, Washington's influence. If it were possible to listen in on their headquarters (and later, cabinet) conversations when an official paper was to be prepared for Washington's signature, the truth of Hamilton's agency would be evident. "A word to the wise" would probably describe these exchanges. What is to be remembered, in estimating relative responsibility for results, is that Washington had in Hamilton not only an assistant, but an associate. The difference of age and position was in great degree neutralized by the mental force and fertility of the younger man. When did a general or chief of state, with multiform demands upon him for decisions, have at his elbow such a resourceful helper? We know of concrete instances in which Washington adopted Hamilton's opinion, once, at least, in correction of his own.[52]

These are general observations. Their pertinence will appear when we come to treat particular joint products of Washington and Hamilton.

However demanding the duties of aide, Alexander Hamilton found time for correspondence from headquarters which was extra-official and nominally, at least, unofficial.[53] This began with letters, intended to be semiweekly, to a standing committee, informing the New York legislature of military prospects. The exchanges (for Hamilton heard from the committee with queries and proposals) were continued, with interruptions, from March 20 to September 1, 1777, when approach of the enemy to Phila-

delphia put an end to them.[54]   This was a delicate undertaking,
lest opinion of the aide be taken for intention of the commander.
Hamilton at the outset explicitly cautioned that the views he advanced were solely his own, indeed "will probably, so far from
being a transcript of those of the General, differ widely from them
in many respects."[55]

While Hamilton was their correspondent, the New York legislature must have been the best informed of any not only on dangers
to that province and means of meeting them,[56] but on the national
outlook military and political.   Advices from patriot headquarters were peculiarly important to New York, the base of enemy
operations.   Because of the strategic location of New York between eastern and southern states, Hamilton seems to have hoped
that some of his observations on policy would be usefully
communicated elsewhere.   Thus he explained persuasively why
"Howe's only hope" of drawing the American army into a general
engagement must be frustrated.   "I know the comments that
some people will make on our Fabian conduct," he forewarned.
"It will be imputed . . . to cowardice, or to weakness.   But the
more discerning . . . will conceive, that it proceeds from the
truest policy.   The liberties of America are an infinite stake.   We
should not . . . put it upon . . . a single cast of the die.   The
loss of one general engagement may effectually ruin us. . . ."
He showed why Howe could not recruit from Britain or the Continent, while the American forces were strengthening in men and
materials.   Meantime, even at the expense of suffering depredations, our wisdom was in "constantly goading their sides in a . . .
teasing way."[57]

Hamilton's eager pen could not stop at the demands of duty.
Not content with posting the legislative committee on headquarters happenings, he volunteered his views on the state constitution
just then adopted.   Since his opinion was *post facto,* he omitted
particulars of his objections and offered only observations on
critical points.   They are noticed here for chronological sequence,
though they concern us for the future because the whole of his
participation in New York politics was under this instrument, and
because he afterward changed his mind on a cardinal feature.[58]
He had looked forward to receiving a copy when printed, and
thanked Gouverneur Morris for it ten days later.[59]   Morris wrote

that he thought it lacked vigor in the executive; this sprang from
"the spirit which now reigns in America, suspiciously cautious."
It was unstable, "from the very nature of popular elective governments." It was dilatory, but the two-branch legislature was
considered less grasping of power than a single house.[60]

Hamilton partly agreed, partly disagreed with these criticisms.
The governor would have more qualifications for vigor if elected
not by "the people at large" (there was in fact a freehold tenure)
but by "the deliberative wisdom of a select assembly." The instability of popular governments was a favorite but he thought
mistaken notion. Pure democracy, with legislative or judicial
powers in the collective body of the people, would lead to convulsions. "But a representative democracy, where the right of
election is well secured and regulated & the exercise of the legislative, executive and judicial authorities is vested in select persons,
chosen *really* and not *nominally* by the people" would be most
likely, he supposed, to be happy and durable. This remained a
tenet with Hamilton, but he had altered his view on the next item
by the time the Constitution of the United States was in the making. Writing to Morris, he looked askance at the senate provided
in the plan of government for New York. Senators must have a
freehold of £100, members of the lower house of £20. Hamilton
feared the senate would tend "to degenerate into a body purely
aristocratical." He believed "a simple legislature" (one house)
would not abuse power in a state with such fullness and equality
of popular representation.[61]

In his letters to the New York legislature in July and August,
1777 Hamilton foretold with prescience the military events of the
next months. The unaccountable Howe would be fool enough
to move southward to the useless seizure of Philadelphia instead of
northward to meet Burgoyne in the latter's march from Canada
down the Hudson. Of course, Hamilton had at his command
the information, most of it partial and much of it contradictory,
that came to headquarters. We may judge of his intelligence
service for Washington by the skill with which he sifted and balanced, and passed on to Gouverneur Morris,[62] reports from many
sources. From numerous calculations he judged, and Washington agreed with him, that Burgoyne could not advance below the
New Hampshire Grants (Vermont) "with more than between five

and six thousand men," exclusive of some Canadians and Indians. He seconded Morris's accurate sketch of the obstacles that Burgoyne would encounter in broken roads and want of transport, provisions, and forage in penetrating a hostile country. For our part, General Schuyler would have 5,000 Continentals to stop the invader's progress, and New England, roused to the danger, would supply him, hopefully, up to twice as many militia.[63]

Hamilton's next bulletin, addressed to R. R. Livingston, sought to dispel the forebodings of his alarmed friend. The peril of New York from the penetration of Burgoyne had his quick sympathy. He had the "warmest regard" for the people of the state which he considered "in a great measure, as my political parent."[64] If Burgoyne was not speedily checked, the threat to the common cause would bring the main army to the rescue of New York. This was the more feasible because Howe seemed to be sailing for Charleston. Two regiments from Peekskill were joining the northern defenders. More particularly, Morgan's picked corps were on their march; "well-used to rifles and to wood-fights," they would help dissipate the "panic dread" of Burgoyne's Indians. For some time Hamilton had been working for the dispatch of these sharpshooters. Their number, about 500, should be exaggerated in popular report. All that the young aide forecast of their bold expertness was to be borne out in the event at Saratoga.[65]

This about closed Hamilton's seriatim reports from headquarters to the New York legislature. By the time he wrote to Gouverneur Morris a fortnight later,[66] Hamilton had moved with Washington's army to Wilmington and was about to be absorbed in the futile effort to prevent the British from taking Philadelphia. Herkimer had turned back St. Leger at Oriskany, Stark had overrun Burgoyne's Germans in their side-attack at Bennington; these trouncings prepared for the enemy's complete defeat at Saratoga. This done, Hamilton was to go to Albany, as Washington's envoy, to draw down victorious troops to replenish the broken ranks at Valley Forge. From this time forward the active fighting shifted away from the New York centers, or the main American army was at hand on the Hudson. Anyway, Colonel Hamilton was too occupied in camp and field to carry on a regular extra-army correspondence.

In military strategy of the Revolution, Hamilton was as Fabian as Washington. A smaller army, poorly equipped and trained, depending in large part on fluctuating militia, would do best to produce the attrition of the enemy rather than risk attack or seek a general engagement. The British force was expeditionary, could establish only limited bases, and was separated by three thousand miles of sea from recruits.[67] Difficult as it often was for the patriots to collect the resources of their country, these were ample and self-renewing season after season. However, Hamilton was keenly aware that support for this worrying warfare hung upon maintaining morale, which was most damaged by depreciation of the currency. Enemy capture of cities and other posts where they must keep garrisons and thus divide their strength was not regretted except as it pulled down public confidence, pushed up prices, and injured our credit, economic and political, with friends abroad.

Hamilton repeatedly assured private correspondents that the loss of Philadelphia, which he expected after Howe was obviously determined on the move, could have only this danger.[68] The prospect was disturbing enough to make the young aide put a premium upon the protection of the capital city, or perhaps he was yielding to the loud demands of the country which Washington felt bound to obey. From the heights of Wilmington, the best of the poor positions that offered, Hamilton wrote with animation to Robert R. Livingston: "The enemy will have Philadelphia if they dare make a bold push for it, unless we fight them a pretty general action. I opine we ought to do it, and that we shall beat them soundly if we do. The Militia seem pretty generally stirring: Our army is in high health & spirits. We shall I hope have twice the enemy's numbers. I would not only fight them, but I would attack them; for I hold it an established maxim, that there is three to one in favour of the party attacking."[69]

His spirits were plucked up by news of American successes at Oriskany and Bennington; as Howe was "now fairly set down to the Southward,"[70] and "his intentions against Philadelphia being reduced to a certainty,"[71] the Eastern states could focus on finishing off Burgoyne. He was encouraged, too, by information of Howe's distress for horses after many starved on the six-week sea trip from New York to Head of Elk.[72]

This confidence was misplaced, as the battle of Brandywine,

September 11, 1777, soon proved.   If either side lacked horses, or rather horsemen, it was the Americans, for General Sullivan, who was directed to picket the crossings upstream, had far too few scouts and couriers for this essential service.   This permitted Sullivan and Washington to remain ignorant of the country above and of the movement of Cornwallis northward in a circuit to take the Americans by surprise in the rear.   It was Howe's trick of Long Island repeated, and no efforts of Sullivan, Conway, Washington, Greene, Stirling, and Wayne could counteract the advantage thus gained.   A promised investigation into Sullivan's omission was never made, and Washington exculpated him in a letter penned by Hamilton.[73]   The fact was that Washington's own headquarters, a mile east of Chad's, were singularly unconcerned during hours in the morning of the battle when enemy movements might have been detected.[74]

American defeat at the Brandywine, followed by equinoctial rains that found the troops separated from the baggage train with the tents, did not wet down the ardor of the army to encounter Howe again before he could press into Philadelphia.   Hamilton, from the halt at Yellow Springs on September 17, wrote Washington's dispatch describing the situation to the apprehensive Congress.[75]   As the enemy closed in on the city the aide was busier on horseback than at his camp desk.   The next day he was directed with a party of horse under Captain Richard Henry Lee to destroy flour stored in mills at Daverser's (or Daviser's) ferry on the Schuylkill (Valley Forge) that lay in Howe's path to the capital.   This proved the occasion of warning Congress to quit the place before the invader.   Hardly had Hamilton and his men accomplished their task when the British were on their heels.   Fire of the vedettes left at the top of the rise overlooking the mill gave the briefest moment for escape.   As the enemy detachment galloped down, Hamilton and four of his dragoons sprang into a flat-bottomed boat that he had drawn to the bank, and pushed off under volleys that killed one of his companions, wounded another, and disabled Hamilton's horse.   Worse would have happened except that Lee, choosing to dash back across the bridge over the millrace, attracted some of the shots.

Instantly on landing Hamilton sent off a hasty note to President Hancock: "If Congress have not yet left Philadelphia, they ought to do it immediately without fail; for the enemy have the means of throwing a party this night into the city." At nine o'clock that night, fearing that his first messenger had been intercepted, he repeated the caution in a second and longer explanation of the danger. The main body of the enemy was only four miles from Swede's ford. By means of a boat left, in the sudden alarm, on their side of the river, the British would get possession of the one he had used, which, in spite of his efforts, had been abandoned afloat. These boats would ferry fifty men at a time, "in a few hours . . . perhaps sufficient to overmatch the militia who may be between them and the city. This renders the situation of Congress extremely precarious . . . my apprehensions for them are great. . . ." His fears, though still vivid in the wake of his own perilous escape, were calmed by hopes that the army might catch up with the enemy before they could pass the Schuylkill.[76]

Congress, thus admonished by Hamilton's eager concern for their safety, at once acted on plans to remove to Lancaster.[77] The speed and extra circumspection with which John Adams obeyed this resolve—he was on his horse and pounding a prudent circuit by way of Trenton and Bethlehem—did not prevent that censorious statesman from blaming Hamilton's "false alarm which occasioned our flight from Philadelphia. Not a soldier of Howe's" he observed in the diary of his elaborate personal retreat, "has crossed the Schuylkill."[78]

Hamilton's warning to Congress, if precipitate at all, left only a few days in which to snatch from Philadelphia supplies for the army before the enemy captured all. Washington, under his emergency powers, dispatched his aide to the city to impress blankets, clothing, especially shoes, and horses from the citizens. Hamilton penned his own instructions from the commander in chief for this unwelcome but imperative errand. He took pains to justify, against all objectors, the forced contributions, and to exhort to patriotic compliance with orders.[79] Though making a special plea to the women of Philadelphia,[80] and sending collecting parties out, "this very active officer could not obtain a supply, in any degree, adequate to the pressing . . . wants of the army."[81] But he moved vessels with military stores up the Delaware "with so much vigilance, that very little public property fell, with the city, into the hands of the British general."[82] Whatever was procured was rescued quickly, for Hamilton was in the city less than two full days.[83]   His exertions did not need to be spurred by a further urgent order from Washington.[84]   In spite of his mighty hurry Hamilton found time to send off express to Congress a report of the posture of the two armies when he left camp.   Washington was moving up the Schuylkill above Valley Forge to counter the effort of the British to gain his right.   Hamilton did what he could to put a good face on the surprise defeat of Wayne at Paoli.[85]

Washington detailed to Congress marches and countermarches since Brandywine.   The Americans were hampered by lack of intelligence in a disaffected region and by the barefoot state of at least a thousand troops, but the sum of it was that Howe had got a head start toward the capital and would enter it before this letter could reach Lancaster.   Washington hoped that defenses on the Delaware below Philadelphia would prevent Howe from getting supplies by water, as they could surely be stopped by land, and so the taking of the city "may, instead of his good fortune, prove his ruin."[86]   This was whistling to keep up courage, for within three days the British were ensconced in Philadelphia.   The river forts were soon battered down,[87] and the enemy had access to supplies by vessels and foraging parties.

Before he failed in this last attempt to seal up the enemy in Philadelphia, Washington resolved to attack Howe where he lay with his main force to the north of the city.   In the battle of Germantown, October 4, 1777, Hamilton opposed a tactic which helped to forfeit American success that day.   The whole engagement was enveloped in fog, military as well as meteorological. The village was strung out for a couple of miles along the Skippack road, a part of that leading from Philadelphia to Reading.   The British were encamped on the Philadelphia side of the principal cross-lane, which formed the center of the settlement.   Washington's plan was for four columns to attack this position simultaneously at dawn.   The columns were to march some sixteen miles by four roads roughly parallel but—those on east and west—at some points six or more miles apart.   The cooperation of these divisions in the surprise assault demanded exact timing and silence in the approach.   But every mischance happened.   The forces fell behind schedule, for day broke as the forward units reached Chestnut Hill, four miles short of the objective.[88]   A thick mist became denser during the morning, hampering commanders following the extreme right and left roads, which they did not know anyhow, so that these columns never reached the action. The British picket at Mount Airy, instead of being driven in silently by the bayonet, put up stiff and noisy resistance that alerted the main force a mile to the rear. Colonel Musgrave came to the rescue with such effect that for a time he occupied not only Sullivan, but Wayne and Conway along the Skippack road. Then instead of falling back farther, Musgrave threw several companies into the stone mansion of Benjamin Chew, where they barricaded themselves and kept up an incessant fire from the second-floor windows.

Washington and his staff came upon this scene when the question was whether to press past or first to subdue this fortress. Several junior officers, notably Hamilton and Pickering, were for driving forward, posting only enough troops to surround and imprison the impromptu garrison within the walls. But "Brigadier Knox opposed the measure with earnestness, denouncing the idea of leaving an armed force in the rear," and he prevailed with Washington. Hamilton and Pickering despairingly pleaded that a summons to surrender would result in the death of Lieutenant (William) Smith, who volunteered to advance with the flag, and that time taken to reduce the house would sacrifice the main battle which lay ahead.[89] Young Smith, assistant to Adjutant General Pickering, was mortally wounded, which pointed the latter's strictures. Hamilton, soon afterward, must have been concerned to see his friend and fellow aide, Lieutenant Colonel John Laurens, shot in the shoulder as he made an attempt with Mauduit du Plessis to fire the house with straw from the stable. Knox took out his chagrin in continuing to batter at the mansion with his six-pounders with no more result than to leave a few scars visible to this day as evidence of his frustration. Stephen, drawn by the uproar, without orders turned aside from his appointed route to the front, joining Woodford's artillery to Knox's. Thus the augmented besiegers lost a full hour.

Not only so, but the halt and bombardment at the Chew House helped turn victory beyond School Lane to defeat. The units under Greene, Sullivan, and Wayne at length drove through the main British line, "soon were in possession of a part of their artillery,—about thirty pieces,—and among their tents."[90] But, said Wayne, when "the Enemy were broke, Dispersed & flying on all Quarters . . . a *Wind Mill* attack was made on a House into which Six Light Companies had thrown themselves to Avoid our Bayonets.   —this gave time to the Enemy to Rally—our Troops . . . fell back to Assist in what they deemed a Serious matter— the Enemy finding themselves no further pursued and believing it to be a Retreat followed—Confusion ensued, and we ran away from the Arms of Victory ready Open to receive us [.]"[91]

The Americans, in confusion, pushed back whence they came, unchecked by Washington's exertions to rally them, in which Hamilton must have joined.   Only fatigue[92] slowed the retreat, which eventually ended twenty-four miles north of Germantown at Perkiomen.   Hamilton drafted Washington's report to Congress, which attributed retreat "at the instant when Victory was declaring herself in our favor" to "the extreme haziness of the weather."[93]

Looking far back on that day at Germantown, Henry Lee rightly remarked that more was amiss than loss of precious time at Chew's, more than fog and the too complicated scheme of approach.   The troops were worn down in body and mind, had not the discipline that could substitute for refreshment, and were led by generals eager but inexperienced.[94]

9

Success of a
Delicate Mission

THE lack of unity—the positive disunity—of the country was sharply illustrated in the military events of the summer and autumn of 1777. Three regions—New England, the Middle States, and the Southern—were distinct in geography, economy, and culture. Each area had its own internal differences, on which we need not dwell except to note that the conflict between New England and New York over the autonomy of the "New Hampshire Grants" that became Vermont bespoke underlying jealousies and endangered the common cause. The Southern states, naturally more distinct both from the Middle States and from New England than either of these regions from each other, did not figure at this stage of the war; they were destined, ironically, to offset other rivalries and become a national bond.

Unhappily, the war, which was the occasion of such concord as existed, was a poor political harmonizer. A fiercer, faster conflict, had such permitted America to be triumphant, would have aided the process. As it was, except for the early winter of 1776, when Washington in desperation made his surprise strokes at Trenton and Princeton, this leisurely war was regularly suspended for half of every year in all but furtive minor actions. Sir William Howe's lethargy as a commander—caution is too polite a word for his sodden strategy—was a military boon to the patriot effort, but by the same sign was a political thwart that served the king better than

Sir William knew. His inactivity and failure to coordinate, even in plan, the movement of his forces, invited the cooling of American ardor and the reduction of the war to a series of local perils.

The next significant episode in Hamilton's career is intimately concerned with the internal contest between New England and the Middle States as represented in their political and military leaders. The incident was Hamilton's mission to Gates in October–November 1777 when he was bidden to draw from that victorious general a sizable proportion of his troops to reinforce Washington, just settling down to a winter watch on Philadelphia, whose investment he had been unable to prevent.

The scene of Hamilton's tribulation and eventual exploit was the Hudson River from Albany to Peekskill, and, by extension, northward to Ticonderoga and southward to Manhattan Island. The Hudson was the chief military highway of the war, inviting the enemy to cut off New England from the Middle States. This river was also a political division between American states that then formed the military theater.

As long as American domination of the Hudson was imperiled, especially from the north, New England was terrified. Those states were fearfully resentful when Ticonderoga was abandoned by St. Clair in July 1777. They visited their wrath on General Schuyler, who had no foreknowledge of St. Clair's evacuation.[1] Schuyler's military sins, in New England eyes, dated from his earlier ill-success in Canada, but dislike was deeper. The dominant figure in northern New York, he had rejected the claims of the Green Mountain Boys in the New Hampshire Grants. Patroonish holder of spreading lands, in the Dutch tradition, and influential with the Indians that supplied the rich fur trade, he was the object of jealous suspicion by small yeomen farmers eastward of the Hudson. Ironically, the failure of New England to support his efforts to protect the whole region against Burgoyne's incursion intensified hostility to Schuyler. Moreover, he was the friend of Washington, who at the beginning of the war had withdrawn from Boston, which he held, for New York which he could not hold. This helped incite against Schuyler the antagonism of the Adamses, whose patriotism at this time made them partisans of Gates. The harassed Schuyler, on his part, though just, was not always soothing to his critics.[2]

Hamilton knew all the parts of this schism from headquarters correspondence, critical portions of which he had helped conduct. For Washington he encouraged Schuyler by pointing out the impediments to Burgoyne's penetration,[3] and prudently ordered to the northern force New England commanders—Glover, Lincoln, and Arnold.[4]   However, at the end of July Congress required an investigation into the forfeit of Ticonderoga, remanded Schuyler to headquarters, and directed Washington to name the officer to replace him.   Samuel Adams in the name of New England delegates urged Gates.   Washington demurred, reminding Congress that as they had taken separate responsibility for the northern department, the portentous choice of a substitute general should be theirs.   Gates was promptly appointed.   Washington's escape from his embarrassment served for the time, but it rose to plague him afterward when he was obliged to deal with the victorious Gates as a semi-independent commander under the special patronage of Congress.   Meanwhile, Hamilton prepared for Washington a reassurance to the New York Council of Safety, sympathizing with the distresses of that state,[5] deploring jealousies harmful to the common cause, and declaring his belief that New England ("capable of powerful efforts") was sure to respond in the crisis.[6]

Had Hamilton, at the time of his errand to Gates, been in the intimate connection with Schuyler which he was soon to form, his slights at the hands of the New England favorite would have been harder to bear.   Indeed, as Schuyler's son-in-law, he could not have been chosen for the mission.

Once Burgoyne surrendered to Gates at Saratoga, and Sir Henry Clinton did not pursue his late penetration up the river, New England settled back in vast relief.   But more, her self-rescue, as she saw it, induced her to survey the military scene and to ask whether her savior, Gates, was not the only savior of America. Barely medium in build, short-sighted and bespectacled, with thin graying hair, Gates looked more like a chief clerk than like a commander, but his physical inferiority to Washington seemed to emphasize his superiority in martial talents.   Already had been building up, to later culmination, the Conway cabal, genuine or supposed, to substitute Gates for Washington as commander in chief.   Conway flattered Gates, to the prejudice of Washington, and Gates listened too eagerly.   Echoes of these exchanges may be caught between the lines of Hamilton's letters while on his errand.

The conversation of the camps at White Marsh and Albany must have informed his suspicions of what was afoot between the principals.   Later Hamilton was accused of bringing a betraying sentence of Conway's to Washington's eye, but the disproved charge recoiled on the maker of it.   The drama of Gates's elevation as the conqueror of Burgoyne, years after played itself out to his precipitate flight as the conquered of Cornwallis at Camden, to Hamilton's unkind glee.[7]

Washington sent Hamilton to Gates not as messenger, but, under the delicate circumstances, as his ambassador.   There was no time in the long confidential association of Washington and Hamilton when the latter was vested with so much discretion, though on other occasions, much later, the younger man had the reputation of the older as truly in his keeping.   In Hamilton's letters and in the correspondence of everybody else concerned in his errand to the Hudson, it is patent that he was acting as Washington's deputy. Gates was to cavil at being obliged to respond to such second-hand authority, little guessing the latitude of Washington's charge to his aide.   Not only so, but this was one of numerous instances in which Hamilton played two parts, executing what were in some sense his own directions, departing from them where he found necessary, but careful to justify his revisions.   Washington had aides and secretaries good and bad, at some periods all of them so unfit in essential respects that he was obliged to do their work with his. The commander in chief's choice of the youngest of his helpers at headquarters to hold parleys with Gates was a special compliment to qualities on which he could rely in the crisis.   No one else in Washington's staff had the combination of fidelity, spirit, prudence, verbal facility, and military knowledge requisite for the assignment. This comparison would seem to be invidious in the instance of Colonel Joseph Reed, older than Hamilton, a man of proved parts, and a volunteer in Washington's family.   He may have been passed over then as too recently and therefore too little informed on the military position, but events were to give proof of his graver defect of personal loyalty—and, one may say in consequence, of judgment.

Our story begins with a council of war called by Washington— five major generals and ten brigadiers—at the temporary camp at Whitpain, October 29, 1777.   This was four days after he had received reliable report of Burgoyne's surrender, though not from Gates, as will appear in course. Hamilton took the minutes of the meeting,[8] and thus was in at the commencement of the negotiation. It was calculated that the enemy had 10,000 fit for duty, the Americans 11,000, but this number soon to be reduced to 9,000 by expiration of militia terms. It was concluded that before Howe could be attacked, twenty regiments must be drawn to the main army from the northern, besides Morgan's riflemen who were already dispatched southward. Washington was advised to send one of his aides to procure the reinforcement from Gates. Congress was notified by Washington, in Hamilton's hand, of the decision of the war council; while Washington would not "frustrate any important plans [Gates] may have formed," he could not "conceive that there is any other object now remaining that demands our . . . most vigorous efforts so much as the destruction of the enemy in this quarter. Should we be able to effect this, we shall have little to fear in future."[9]

Washington wrote to Gates, congratulating him on his victory, and regretting, in monitory phrases, that news of it had not come, however briefly, from Gates himself. He introduced his aide and explained that Hamilton was sent "by the advice of my Gen.[1] Officers . . . to lay before you a full state of our situation, and that of the Enemy in this Quarter. He is well informed . . . and will deliver my Sentiments upon the plan of operations . . . now necessary. . . ." Washington forbore to enter into detail, partly because—a reminder of Gates's neglect—he was not "well advised how matters are circumstanced on the North River. . . ."[10] Gates's failure to notify Washington directly and instantly of the surrender of the enemy in the most critical theater of the war betrayed a disrespect toward the commander in chief which forecast his resistance to the objects of Hamilton's mission.

Washington's instructions to Hamilton[11] charged: ". . . you are chiefly to . . . point out, in the clearest and fullest manner, to General Gates, the absolute necessity . . . for his detaching a very considerable part of the army at present under his command, to the reinforcement of this; a measure that will, in all probability, reduce General Howe to the same situation in which General Burgoyne now is, should he attempt to remain in Philadelphia without being able to remove the obstructions in the Delaware, and open a free communication with his shipping." But later in the instructions this positive injunction was conditionally withdrawn: "If . . . you should find that [General Gates] intends, in consequence of his Success, to employ the troops under his command upon some expeditions, by the prosecution of which the common cause will be more benefited than by their being sent down to reinforce this army, it is not my wish to give interruption to the plan." If Gates's objects were trivial or otherwise ineligible, then Washington's requirement of reinforcement was to stand.

This gave Hamilton the widest discretion. If he found sufficient virtue in Gates's independent intentions he was empowered to approve them in place of the decision of the war council at headquarters. This meant no less than that Hamilton was to decide, in the light of Gates's designs, whether the war was to be prosecuted in the next months in the north or in Pennsylvania—against Sir Henry Clinton or against Sir William Howe. It is true that Washington limited the field of Hamilton's choice by ruling out certain possible proposals of Gates, leaving it difficult to conjecture what better he could have in view. Even so, the trust reposed in a young aide (not quite twenty-three years old) is remarkable testimony to the fitness of the deputy.

Haste was an object. Hamilton was bidden on October 30 to set out for Albany immediately; he was to hurry forward Morgan's corps and other contingents ordered toward the main army.[12] Hamilton reached New Windsor, at a distance of 150 miles, late on November 1;[13] that is, he rode seventy-five miles a day. Albany, by the route used, on the east side of the river, was 254 miles from White Marsh.[14] We do not have the date of Hamilton's arrival at Albany,[15] but it was probably November 5 at noon. He spent some time at Fishkill on November 2 in conversations with General Putnam and other commanders, and was obliged to recross the river; but say he was on the road five days, or accomplished an average of sixty miles a day. Had Washington's emissary not been vested with discretion to settle matters with Gates, a round trip and a return to Albany would have been necessary, which, even if performed by express riders, would have taken some ten days, which was evidently more than the situation allowed.

Moreover, Washington had not only the uncertainty of what to order, but felt he must accomplish the business, if possible, by a request of Gates, by securing his willing cooperation. Schuyler being displaced, Gates, in his northern bailiwick, was "more peculiarly under . . . direction of Congress."[16] Hamilton's mission was a diplomatic one, with deference and persuasion indicated before ultimate authority was resorted to.

From Fishkill, on November 2, Hamilton wrote to Washington[17] of the beginning of his disappointments. Early that morning, near New Windsor on the west side of the river, he had met Colonel Morgan with his corps headed for White Marsh. Morgan gave information that "all the northern army were marching down on both sides the river," would probably arrive at New Windsor and Fishkill by next day, and that Putnam, after a council, had determined to send Washington four thousand men. So Hamilton posted to the east bank "in expectation that matters were in such a train as to enable me to accomplish my errand without going any farther." But at Fishkill he met (Major James M.) Hughes, an aide-de-camp of Gates, who revealed that the true situation at Albany was far different. Glover's and Nixon's brigades, which Washington thought had also been detached by Gates to report to Putnam, together with Patterson's brigades and Warner's mountain boys, were in fact to remain at Albany, where barracks were building for them. However, Hamilton in Washington's name ordered Putnam to dispatch to Washington Poor's and Learned's brigades, Warner's brigade of Massachusetts militia, and seven hundred Jersey militia. The militia were included, though not comprehended in Washington's instructions, because Hamilton had gathered that Howe at Philadelphia was receiving large reinforcements from New York. Lee's and Jackson's regiments and the detachment of McDougall's division, all of which Washington and his council wanted southward, had not marched but were ordered, at Hamilton's insistence, to do so. However, Putnam showed signs of wavering. Hamilton believed he was keeping more troops than were needed in that quarter. So strongly was Hamilton "impressed with the importance of endeavoring to crush Mr. Howe" that he would like to draw off all the Continentals, leaving Putnam 1,600 militia. With fresh horses Hamilton would recross the river, hurry on troops he expected to find there, and make haste to Albany "to get the three brigades there sent forward."

Hamilton met the real check when he opened the business of his mission to Gates and found him "inflexible in the opinion that two brigades at least of Continental troops should remain . . . near this place."[18]   Washington wanted all three brigades to join him. Gates had been quick enough to order reinforcements to his own assistance.[19]   Also, Gates had promised Washington "considerable" reinforcement once Burgoyne was beaten.[20]   Hamilton used all arguments in his power, but the best he could secure was a single brigade.   Gates objected that Sir Henry Clinton might not have gone to join Howe, but could return up the river, despoil "the finest arsenal in America" (at Albany) before stores and artillery could be moved, and ravage New England.   Further, "should this place be left so bare of troops as I proposed," Gates declared he could not "enterprise any thing against Ticonderoga."

The burden resting on Alexander Hamilton, as he pleaded, only to be faced with refusal, was great for one so young and who acted in another's name.   For once in his life he felt that too much was expected of him.   Not that he complained for an instant; instead, his whole concern was for the protection of Washington and for the commander in chief's approval of his actions.   The passage in his letter to his chief is revealing, not only of what passed in his mind at the moment, but of the whole delicate national military and political situation as he saw it:

"I found myself infinitely embarrassed, and was at a loss how to act.   I felt the importance of strengthening you as much as possible, but . . . I found insuperable inconveniences in acting diametrically opposite to the opinion of a gentleman whose successes have raised him to the highest importance.   General Gates has won the entire confidence of the Eastern States; if disposed to do it, by addressing himself to the prejudices of the people he would find no difficulty to render a measure odious which it might be said, with plausibility enough to be believed, was calculated to expose them to unnecessary danger, notwithstanding their exertions during the campaign had given them the fullest title to repose and security. General Gates has influence and interest elsewhere [that is, in Congress]; he might use it if he pleased to discredit the measure there also.   On the whole, it appears to me dangerous to insist on sending more troops from hence while General Gates appears so warmly to oppose it. . . . These considerations . . . determined me not to insist upon sending either of the other brigades remaining here. I am afraid what I have done may not meet with your approbation, . . . but I ventured to do what I thought right. . . ." He comforted himself with the thought that he was sending to Washington some 7,500 troops total, of whom 2,000 were militia not expected.

Having seen the young aide's quandary, we must understand Gates's military position and his state of mind, which were different things. A review of his correspondence (he received and wrote five or six letters a day)[21] for a month prior to Hamilton's visit and a similar period afterward reveals the grounds of his reluctance to comply with Washington's request for reinforcement. Of course, there was no notion of drawing troops from his command until after Burgoyne's surrender on October 17, 1777, except for Morgan's corps of riflemen which Washington wanted earlier but which was not dispatched until later.[22] For a time after Burgoyne's surrender the need for forces in the northern department, at Albany, Fishkill, and other posts may well have seemed to Gates serious, if not pressing. A general more eager than Gates to relinquish most of his victorious army to a distant commander in chief, to be thrown into a winter campaign, may have found reason for not divesting himself suddenly once the main body of the enemy in his quarter had laid down their arms. Dangers from other directions loomed. The intentions of Sir Henry Clinton at New York were not known. Gates remained responsible in his area after the imminent peril from Burgoyne had been removed.

In addition, and equally important, Gates's consequence, genuine enough until his final victory, was blown up in his own mind by the chorus of congratulation that poured in upon him. Not a little of this fulsome praise came from personages close to Washington, and contained unconcealed comparisons to the damage of the commander in chief. The New England states, especially Massachusetts and Connecticut, were at the feet of their deliverer. Henry Laurens, President of Congress, was strong in his expressions of gratitude and confidence, but others in that body were adulatory, even fawning. Besides, though we do not know how far, if at all, Gates gave active encouragement to dissatisfaction with Washington, he shared it. He would have been a wiser and more loyal lieutenant than he was if the prejudicial insinuations that beat upon his ears did not titillate his vanity. Washington, as we shall see, conveyed to his critics his cold resentment.

Gates's self-esteem was stirred, too, because he had his own critic in Benedict Arnold. After the first engagement with Burgoyne, Arnold blamed Gates for not following up his success, and called for swift action while there was yet time.[23] The Massachusetts Assembly provided expresses to bring word of Gates's progress against Burgoyne, and he received cheering private assurance from others in that quarter.[24] Congress approved the prowess of the troops under Gates in the repulse of Burgoyne.[25] James Lovell, Massachusetts member of Congress, after picturing the enemy on the loose on the Delaware, confided that "Your army & the eastern militia are now strongly contrasted with those in the Middle State [s]. . . . It is said Howe would not have passed more than 70 Miles, from the Ships which landed him, in his whole Skin in Y^r neighbourhood, or among Yankee Stone walls. . . . Our [hope?] springs all from the Northward, and about all our Confidence."[26]

General Gates must have been alarmed by the fall of Forts Montgomery and Clinton, and demolition of Fort Constitution by the Americans, as this meant the enemy was behind as well as in front of him.[27] Sir Henry Clinton, at Fort Montgomery, took measures to join General Burgoyne at Albany, crushing Gates between them. News of this was contained in a hollow bullet swallowed by the spy when captured by the Americans.[28]

Accounts Gates received of the battle of Germantown, even allowing for the fog, were calculated to give him the impression that Washington's generalship was feckless.[29] His own skill, as shown in his second defeat of Burgoyne, on October 7, stood in agreeable contrast.[30] Gates's crowning success, in compelling the surrender of Burgoyne with his army of 5,000, was enough to reduce to little the burning of Kingston by the British the afternoon before the formal capitulation took place.[31] In negotiations from October 13 to 16 Burgoyne, after some bluster, acceded to all of the demands of Gates that mattered. It is not possible to tell whether the description of Burgoyne's extremity was composed by Gates or by James Wilkinson, his adjutant general, but it is triumphant in contrast to what were, naturally enough, the British commander's less colored admissions.[32] Gates was afterward criticized for some articles in the convention, but nothing could diminish his signal achievement. He was soon to have official and private gratitude for his victory, but before that he was notified of the burning of mills and houses on the upper Hudson. Responsible observers feared that "their Capital design is to burn . . . Albany and Destroy our Stores there [.]"[33]

Some with the main army were prompt to congratulate Gates on a success that contrasted with Washington's lack of it. Joseph Reed, after a salute to Gates, regretted that "this Army, . . . notwithstanding the Labours . . . of our amiable Chief [,] has yet gathered no Laurels."[34] Anthony Wayne showed disgruntlement at his treatment and added: ". . . whether I shall remain longer in the service than this Campaign depends on Circumstances —there are Certain Generals—as *Lee—Gates—Mifflin* & c.ᵃ who will point out by their Conduct the line which I shall follow. . . ."[35] A few days later Wayne said that Gates's success "Must eventually save this (Otherwise) Devoted Country." Brandywine and Germantown were opportunities bungled, but he did not despair of better results "if our Worthy General will but follow his own good Judgment without listning [*sic*] too much to some Council. . . ."[36] Brigadier General Conway would send Gates his plan for instruction of the army, this with a slur on the main command.[37] Walter Stewart was afraid Mifflin would not continue in the service: "I can assure you we want a few such men as him with us, as Activity, and Enterprize seem to be almost banish'd our Camp."[38] After the surrender of Burgoyne the congratulatory letters to Gates from civilian correspondents, some of them in official posts, were more extravagant than before.[39]

Congress called on the people for a day of thanksgiving that God "hath been pleased . . . to crown our arms with most signel [*sic*] success."[40] Three days later resolutions thanked Gates in the name of the thirteen United States for defeating an army of 10,000 men, and securing the surrender of 6,000; a gold medal was to be struck and presented to General Gates.[41]

As Hamilton left it in his first interview, Gates was to dispatch only one brigade in addition to those already marched, leaving two brigades and some detached regiments in and about Albany. Learning that Patterson's brigade was the one Gates proposed to send, Hamilton made inquiries and was disappointed to find, as he wrote Gates, that it was "by far the weakest of the three now here, and does not consist of more than about six hundred rank and file fit for duty." The militia regiment with it of two hundred could not be counted because its term of service would expire before these troops could reach Washington's camp. Hamilton was resentful because Gates, having received a concession, was not acting in good faith. Hamilton felt "under the necessity of desiring, by virtue of my orders" from General Washington that either Nixon's or Glover's brigade be substituted for Patterson's. He reiterated his belief, supported by the judgment of trustworthy informants at Albany, that Gates could safely part with two brigades. However, one strong brigade Washington must have, and "As it may be conducive to dispatch to send Glover's brigade, if agreeable to you, you will give orders accordingly."[42]

The general return of the army commanded by Gates, the day of Burgoyne's surrender, October 17, just a fortnight earlier, shows 7,716 rank and file of Continentals and 3,382 of militia, a total of 11,098, to which were to be added the complements of commissioned and noncommissioned officers. This army had been reduced by return to General Washington of Morgan's corps of 800, and the number remaining at Albany had been further diminished by detachment of Poor's, Learned's, and Warner's units. This left Gates with three brigades—Nixon's, Glover's, and Patterson's. Nixon's had, at the general return, fit for duty, 854 rank and file, all Continentals; Glover's had 1,362 fit for duty, of whom 444 were militia; Patterson's had 1,070 fit, of whom 338 were militia.[43] Thus Patterson's, eliminating its militia, was the weakest of the three, being 122 fit rank and file below Nixon's, and 630 below Glover's total. Two weeks later, at the time of Hamilton's remonstrance to Gates against the selection of Patterson's brigade, the situation had changed somewhat if Hamilton was correct in describing Patterson's as consisting of "about six hundred rank and file fit for duty" together with "a militia regiment . . . of about two hundred. . . ." Even so, unless proportions of effectives had altered, Patterson's was 85 per cent as strong as Nixon's in Continentals, not "little more than half as large," as Hamilton wrote. Patterson's Continentals did number little more than half the usable troops of Glover's.[44]

Between Hamilton's complaint to Gates of November 5 against accepting Patterson's brigade, and Gates's agreement to the final plan, Hamilton must have talked with Gates at least once more.[45] For we find Gates reporting to Washington that he would send two brigades, not one as he had at first insisted.[46] Gates's unwilling acquiescence is plain in the sentences crossed out in his draft of his reply to the requisition of Washington as pressed by Hamilton. In it we read, better than in Hamilton's own words, the contest between older and younger man, and see how Gates must have belabored Washington over Hamilton's shoulder.[47]

After sending upward of 5,000 men "to the Succour of the Southern Army" he had hoped a further draft from the northern department would have been unnecessary, "but Colonel Hamilton acquaints me that it was the unanimous Opinion of a Council of War that the whole of the Eastern Regits should march from hence & that Troops were only to be Station'd at peeks Kill, & in the Highlands for the defense of the Country this Way. [Crossed out: *I confess I want wisdom to discover the Motives that Influenced the Giving such an Opinion* and *I am astonished*] with the Greatest Defference to The Opinion of this Council of War, I must inform Your Ex^cy that Troops posted at peeks Kill, or in the Highlands, cannot prevent the Enemy from Destroying this City, and Arsenal, whenever they please to make the attempt. . . ." and he gave his reasons.

"Col. Hamilton After presenting me with Your Excellencys Letter Verbally Demanded that almost the whole of the Troops now in this Department should be ordered to proceed directly for New Windsor— I told the Colonel, that [crossed out: *whatever Orders he Gave in Your Excellency's Name in Writing*] Your Excellency's Orders should be obey'd; but that if my Opinion was to be taken . . . I was intirely Averse to more than One Brigade being sent from hence," since that would risk the security of Albany. [Crossed out: *that all hopes of ever*[?] *possessing Canada Vanishes with the Troops taken from hence,*] and of course every good Effect of the ruin of General Burgoyne's Army totaly [*sic*] lost, should The Enemy Succeed in an Attempt to possess this Town."

Gates's chagrin at being compelled, in the end, to go along with the young colonel's use of Washington's authority is plain in a passage that, on second thought, he struck out. It reads: "Although it is Customary & even Absolutely necessary to direct Implicit Obedience to be paid to the Verbal Orders of Aids de Camp in Action, or while upon the Spot—yet I believe it is never practiced to Delegate that Dictatorial power, to One Aid de Camp sent to an Army 300 Miles distant; [.]"[48]

The second draft,[49] more chastened, added only his formal compliance: "Upon mature Consideration of all Circumstances, I have, nevertheless, ordered General Glover's Brigade to be added to General Patterson's, in Reinforcement to your Army, and they will march, immediately. . . ." In the course of their discussions Gates must have talked at large, for he added, "Col. Hamilton . . . will report everything that I wish to have you acquainted with, as well with Respect to the present State, as the future Operations this Way."

Gates, having resigned himself, soon found that the hurt to his pride was more than that to his post. He forthwith reduced danger to the Albany arsenal by sending 30 brass cannon and 3,000 stand of arms inland.[50] Almost immediately he could write to Congress that the enemy had "evacuated every post on this side," would probably evacuate Ticonderoga within the month, and must surely have done so had he been left troops to threaten it.[51]

Having carried his point with Gates at Albany, and turned homeward, Hamilton found new problems awaiting him, farther down the river, in the recalcitrance of troops and the irresponsibility of General Israel Putnam.[52] Patterson's brigade was appearing at New Windsor on the 10th in all the vessels Hamilton had been able to procure, and Glover's was marching down on the other side where the roads were better. But this, for the time being, was all of his accomplishment, for "I am pained beyond expression," he wrote, "to inform your Excellency that on my arrival here I find every thing has been neglected and deranged by General Putnam. . . ." Poor's and Learned's brigades remained at New Windsor and across the river at Fishkill, and Warner's militia had been drawn to Peekskill "to aid in an expedition against New-York, which . . . is at this time the hobby-horse with General Putnam. Not the least attention has been paid to my order in your name for a detachment of one thousand men from the troops hitherto stationed at this post. Every thing is sacrificed to the whim of taking New York."

He described both obstacles, the troops and their commander. The brigades of Poor and Learned would not march for want of pay, six or eight months in arrears, and necessaries. Poor's men had mutinied, a captain killed a man and was himself shot, and "These difficulties, for want of proper management," had stopped the troops from proceeding. Hamilton at once supplied this management. With Governor Clinton's aid in persuasion and in borrowing five or six thousand dollars for the purse, Learned's brigade, under Colonel Bailey, had marched that morning for Goshen and, hopefully, would continue to Washington's headquarters. Hamilton would soon see Poor and try to start him along.[53]

Hamilton's efforts to counteract the caprices of Putnam corroborated others' estimate of the unfitness of the old leader to command on the lower Hudson. The only need for troops in that quarter was to protect against plundering parties and to push work on fortifications. " 'T is only wasting time and misapplying men to employ them in a suicidal parade against New York, for in this it will undoubtedly terminate. New York is no object if it could be taken, and to take it would require more men than could be spared from more substantial purposes. Governor Clinton's ideas coincide with mine."[54] Hamilton took pains to forward to Washington the most reliable news he could get from New York City; he believed the fright of the Tories meant the place had been stripped bare of Sir Henry Clinton's troops to add to the strength of Howe at Philadelphia.[55] Hamilton and Governor Clinton worked together to impress Washington's peril on Gates, "to try if this will not *extort* from him a further reinforcement."[56]

His patience tried by the studied objections of Gates, Hamilton found the blundering and foolishness of Putnam more than he could bear without reporting to Washington that "every part of this gentleman's conduct . . . gives general disgust."[57] He wished "General Putnam was recalled from the command of this post, and Governor Clinton would accept it." He had not been able to see Putnam, who was at White Plains eyeing New York, but had sent him an order "in the most emphatic terms" to send Washington his Continentals and retain the militia. He hoped that Washington would interpose with Putnam to get obedience.[58]

Hamilton had remonstrated with Putnam on November 9 because "all his Excellency's views have been hitherto frustrated, and . . . no single step of those I mentioned to you has been taken to afford him the aid he absolutely stands in need of, and by delaying which the cause of America is put to the utmost conceivable hazard. . . . How the non-compliance can be answered to General Washington you can best determine." Then the aide used language which only General Putnam at this stage could misconstrue or fail to execute: "I now, sir, in the most explicit terms, by his Excellency's authority, give it as a positive order from him, that all the Continental troops under your command may be immediately marched to King's Ferry, there to cross the river and hasten to reinforce the army under him."[59]

To make matters worse, Hamilton was brought down by "fever and violent rheumatic pains" for several days at New Windsor. Imagining he had got the better of his complaint, "and anxious to be . . . attending to the march of the troops," he crossed the ferry to Fishkill "in order to fall in with General Glover's brigade, which was on its march from Poughkeepsie." At Peekskill (Kennedy's house) Hamilton had a relapse and was unable to proceed.[60] Governor Clinton a week later, alarmed by his condition, sent posthaste to Dr. John Jones, at Bellemont, to attend him, but the physician was himself ill and could do no better than return the messenger with directions for Hamilton's treatment.[61] This did not answer, for two days later he "seem'd . . . to be drawing nigh his last. . . ." After a similar interval, "the Coldness came on again, and encreased (he was then cold as high as his knees)," so that the doctor, who had finally reached him, "Thought he could not survive. . . ." However, four hours later the fever abated and he was soon pronounced on the mend.[62]

Thus further frustrated, he must by his manner have irked some of the local commanders. Colonel Hugh Hughes, a partisan of Gates, remarked a week later: "Colonel Hamilton, who has been very ill of a nervous Disorder, at Peekskill, is out of Danger, unless it be from his own sweet Temper."[63] Matters had not been helped when Hamilton was told that Poor's brigade was detained from marching to Washington's relief because "they were under an operation for the itch. . . ."[64]

From Peekskill, on November 15, Hamilton gave Washington

a progress report on his efforts to dispatch the different units south-ward. Poor's brigade had crossed the ferry; Glover's was pre-pared to do so. He hoped to get up Parsons's brigade from White Plains, in spite of Putnam's wish to keep it there. Some regiments not expected were joined to the forces going southward.[65]

In the midst of his troubles Hamilton must have been pleased to receive General Washington's assurance, "I approve entirely of all the steps you have taken; and have only to wish, that the exer-tions of those you have had to deal with, had kept pace with your zeal and good intentions." He hoped his aide would soon be well enough "to push on the rear of the whole reinforcement beyond New Windsor."[66]

The reinforcements drawn down from the Hudson by Hamil-ton's exertions were eagerly awaited by the main army at White Marsh. Within a few days after Washington wrote Hamilton, Fort Mifflin fell, "the Consequence of which will be the loss of all our Other works & Shipping on the River."[67] The British, be-hind a curved line of redoubts from Schuylkill to Delaware, were believed to be numerically superior to the Continentals in the American army, even before Sir Henry Clinton's reinforcements arrived from New York. An officer with Washington wrote to Gates: "We are ill Cloathed, the Winter is on, to Hutt near the Enemy will be as arduous as dangerous, to retire back for Quar-ters & thereby leave the Country Open appears to be intolerable. . . . Our troops express their wishes for another tryal and must be greatly animated by the arrival of yours."[68] And General St. Clair showed his anxiety: "it is certain our Discipline and . . . Numbers . . . are inferior to theirs, but when your victorious Troops arrive, they will make our Scale preponderate but what can delay them so—Morgan has been arrived above a Fortnight."[69]

Washington described for Gates the strong position of Howe in Philadelphia; Howe's reinforcement from New York unluckily arriving before "ours from the northward, it was out of my power to afford adequate relief to Fort Mifflin, which fell after a most gallant defence of seven Weeks." The works on the Jersey shore were lost as a consequence.[70] Perhaps Gates had a twinge or two because he had not hastened assistance to his commander in chief, who was now about withdrawing to the winter camp of Valley Forge.

Meanwhile the opinion of the council of war at White Marsh, of Washington, and of Hamilton that Gates needed few troops at Albany after the surrender of Burgoyne, was borne out. Gates himself informed the President of Congress, November 16, 1777, that the enemy had evacuated and destroyed Ticonderoga, Mount Independence, and had retired to Isle aux Noir and St. John's. They had abandoned all posts on the North River also, even to Kingsbridge.[71]

Soon General Gates, who shortly before had been so insistent on retaining a sizable force to buttress Albany, was drawn from the Hudson to Pennsylvania to become president of the new Board of War. None of the five members was in Congress. Gates was to keep his military rank and return to field command if that was judged more essential. Congress entertained a high sense of his peculiar fitness to discharge the duties of an office upon the right execution of which "the safety & Interest of the United States eminently depend."[72] Placing Gates, in uniform, at the head of the Board of War could be construed as a slight to Washington, for in something more than a titular sense Gates was put in control of military operations. No cabal of jealous officers and suspicious members of Congress—if one existed in an organized way—could have come closer to its ambition of preferring Gates to Washington without substitution of Gates as commander in chief.

Winter of
Our Discontent

HAMILTON busied himself in every way he could conceive to sustain the resistance of America, especially when this was at low ebb in the winter of Valley Forge, 1777–1778. The letters and reports he prepared for Washington he informed with more than usual firmness and foresight. In private pleas to friends in positions of influence he sought to support the frail structure, military and political. Others at headquarters, loyal to commander and cause, executed their duties faithfully. Hamilton exerted constant ingenuity that went beyond obvious obligation. He displayed the difference between excellent discharge of responsibility and the search for opportunities to discountenance internal strife and buttress united resolve. His capacities and zeal to use them could not be confined by minor station or by his youth. He was the man-boy, matching enthusiasm with wisdom, plan, and patience. It was in this that his peculiar helps to Washington consisted. The general had a confidence in the original powers of his aide that spoke in assignment to him of critical errands, negotiations, and correspondence. And well he might, for here was the rare deputy, able to frame his own instructions and then execute them. As far as was possible in any young associate, he relieved his chief of multiple demands by taking tasks, all but nominally, into his own hands. In these extensions of Washington's self Hamilton's skill in expression, oral and written, was a prime facility. This

quality was more than verbal deftness.   Precision and illumination of words sprang from mental grasp and perfected purpose.
While an animated mind was the source of apt sentences, the first
without the second would have been far less serviceable.   One
must follow the collaboration of Washington and Hamilton from
day to day to appreciate the latter's gift in catching and conveying his principal's intentions.   This fidelity became more fruitful
even when Hamilton moved into spheres of independent responsibility.   He could not have become the cabinet minister had he
not, in the interval between war and new government, striven in Congress, constitutional convention, and *Federalist* papers to promote
the objects he shared with Washington.   But this is anticipation.

Offer of amnesty by Britain held little danger of relaxing
America's perseverance, but that of alliance by France might
prove a precious bane.   They were proffered simultaneously when
news of the battles of Saratoga and Germantown prompted the
enemy to forgiveness and the friend to open treaty.   Britain's
pride made her propose too little—peace, pardon, and cancella-
tion of all acts toward the colonies of the previous fifteen years
that had angered the Americans.   Congress countered with a fit resolve of Gouverneur Morris that no parley was possible while
King George's armed forces remained in America, or this country's independence was not acknowledged.

Hamilton was as firm.   The British Colonel (later General)
FitzPatrick, intimate friend of Charles Fox and himself an in-
fluential Whig, being about to return home, sought the views of
Lafayette.   The marquis invited him "to a friendly dinner at
Germantown [lying] between the two armies.   The American
General took with him Colonel hamilton and there much politi-
cal discourse took place between them [*sic*] three where General
FitzPatrick was assured that the mission of the Commissioners
from Great Britain would prove fruitless and that nothing short
of Independency could be accepted by the United States."[1]
Former Governor Tryon, one not apt to conciliate patriot opinion,
was commissioned to broach the proposition.   His request to
Washington to circulate the acts of Parliament in the army was
accurately called by the commander in chief "extraordinary and
impertinent," but Hamilton prevailed on the general to answer
with politer disdain.   Free currency, he replied in Hamilton's

words, had been given to the British overtures, with confidence
in the fidelity of officers and men to the United States. In return
he was sending the rejection by Congress with the expectation
that Tryon would distribute among offending loyalists the recommendation to the states to acquit all who returned to their allegiance.[2]

The promise of a new order of aid from France—troops and
fleets as well as munitions and money—determined the issue of
the war. Years afterward Nicholas Fish thought it his duty to
record that this boon originated with Hamilton. ". . . for some
considerable time previous to the arrival of the French army . . .
Hamilton had conceived the idea," and had weighed it in his own
mind before suggesting to Lafayette the effect a small cooperating
French force would have, especially if under the marquis' command. Lafayette took to it with zeal and promptitude, addressed the French government, and used the influence of his
family to obtain action. Besides Lafayette, Hamilton revealed
this to no one except Fish.[3] Without doubt Hamilton was one
of many who longed for this turn of events, and belonged to the
smaller number in a position to help bring it about. Fish's statement was made to Mrs. Hamilton, in recalling his intimacy with
Hamilton at the siege of Yorktown where the French alliance
proved triumphant. We need not question the integrity of the
narrator. Probably, though, affection and pride led him to call
unique what was rather an early and ardent wish on Hamilton's
part.

Congress in a proclamation to the people rallied resistance, but
as staunch a leader as Nathanael Greene queried Washington on
the extent of our military preparations now that such powerful
outside help was in sight. The day the treaties were ratified
here, May 5, 1778, when the camp was on the eve of celebrating,
Hamilton penned for Washington a reply which was plainly intended to be for more than the quartermaster-general. The favor
of France could not "justify the least relaxation in . . . the provisions you . . . are making in your department. . . ." These
must "be continued in their fullest vigor and extent." Britain,
confronted by a fresh enemy, could muster further resources. Besides, the enemy army here was formidable. It would not be
withdrawn without a further push, "if . . . only to make the

way for a negotiation." Our failure to prepare against British victories "might be fatal" to home sentiment and growing friendships abroad. We might need to take the offensive, which would call for our amplest strength at all points. In any event, our salvation lay in unremitted effort. The letter was characteristic in raising all contingencies and showing how each demanded "a powerful army, well furnished with every apparatus of war."[4]

Students have worked over the tailings of history to discover whether earlier writers, worshipful of Washington, did not overdraw the man in the manifestation of Providence. Was he the knight *sans reproche?* Were those recorded as his enemies, by the same sign, hostile to the salvation of their country? Specifically, was there, in the winter of Valley Forge, a "Conway Cabal," in the sense of a conspiracy of jealous men in army and Congress concerted to depose the commander in chief and put Gates in his place?[5] Such an exercise in revision, taking a second skeptical look, is altogether desirable. It could result in overthrow of accepted doctrine; if it comes up with substantial amendment of received views, or even with minor items of hitherto omitted realism, it is positively serviceable. Or if the review in the end confirms previous conclusions, it has been worth while.

In the present case recrushing and further wash of the ore has recovered some gold dust. Probably there was no formulated plot against Washington, though Hamilton thought differently. He had suspected a faction, but since had "discovered such convincing traits of the monster that I cannot doubt its reality in the most extensive sense. . . . I believe it unmasked its batteries too soon, . . . but . . . will only change the storm to a sap."[6] Room for criticism of Washington's role existed, and not all who seized the occasion were disingenuous in motive. In approving the familiar cast of characters, virtuous and wicked, allowance must be made for particulars which we cannot recapture and which induced to honest confusion, since dissipated in the perspective of time.

This much said, the older findings commend themselves. One need not be rhapsodic in the conviction that Washington possessed qualities superior to the wisdom of his critics. Embracing all was his willingness to endure detraction without rejoinder rather than injure the cause to which he devoted himself. This was not self-love disguised as solicitude for harmony in the army and steadiness in the public. No man, knowing his own strength, was more humble in asserting it. The usual catalogue of Washington's endowments need not be run over—integrity, courage, and the capacity to turn hope into accomplishment. By comparison his competitors, as they thought themselves, were lacking in differing degrees.

"My Enemies take an ungenerous advantage of me," he charged; "they know the delicacy of my situation, and that motives of policy deprive me of the defence I might otherwise make against their insiduous [*sic*] attacks."[7] Washington's rueful reflection was accurate. Not his least claim was the fortitude with which he bore thrusts rather than reveal secrets or invite dissension. Such a needful combination of traits did not belong to others in that protracted crisis of the country. Some of his comrades had several or all of these elements in their makeup, but not in the same fortunate proportions. They were his helpmeets, loyal to him because faithful to their own lights. In another category were actors in the scene, more or less conspicuous, who were fatally limited in moral firmness. At the extreme was Arnold, but scattered along were more who, in this way and that, for their own reasons, would damage a cause that they would not betray. This appraisal, if it is just, introduces us to the circle of compatriots viewing Washington with resentment.

Most of the lapses from discipline and morale at Valley Forge —desertions, wholesale resignation of officers, jealous bickerings, raids on farms, and oversevere punishments—resulted from the hunger, cold, and illness for which that encampment became the byword. Washington's deference to Congress was a glory and a fault. Legislative neglect and mismanagement was the fundamental trouble. The commander in chief remonstrated repeatedly, feelingly, and pointed out the wretched consequences of continuing in such courses. Leading a revolution in the name of popular self-government, what more could he do? He could not disregard or threaten. Pressing steadily for reform, he must wait until Congress and its abettors saw the necessity of giving him military powers which an assemblage, and especially that one, could not discharge. Short of political or military dictatorship, which was abhorrent to everyone, nothing could cure the case except time and costly experience. The country was at the end of its first wind and had not got its second; this came with conclusion of the French alliance, appointment of Greene as quartermaster general and Steuben as inspector general, and the proof of new strength against the enemy at Monmouth.

The icy winds of Valley Forge, the tattered troops, the pestilential log hospitals which for so many were but way stations to the graveyard are in Washington's letters imploring redress of grievances lest the army "Starve, dissolve, or disperse."[8]   But still more these miseries are read in the feckless ruminations, ignorant gropings, and heedless stop-gap measures of Congress. One must sit down with the Journal of that body—its autobiography of incompetence—to appreciate its persevering errors. The record is like a long anxiety dream, repetitious, remorseless, and foggy.[9] If the members had been kept waiting half an hour for their dinner in the snug town of York, Pennsylvania, they would have roused to more effective action than was provoked by the sufferings of thousands on "a cold bleak hill . . . under frost and Snow" at Valley Forge.

The reason for recalling this imbecility is the object lesson it furnished to Alexander Hamilton as he shared the trials of that winter camp. He knew at only one remove the frustrations of Washington. That Gates, who had vexed him at Albany, had been called thence to head the new Board of War[10] laid the whole of the proceedings of Congress under special suspicion. Hamilton devoted a long letter to Governor Clinton to the "degeneracy of representation in the great council of America." Many members were able, but "Folly, caprice, a want of foresight, comprehension, and dignity" described the body as a whole. He had special opportunity of knowing that "Their conduct, with respect to the army . . . , is feeble, indecisive, and improvident—insomuch that we are reduced to a more terrible situation than you can conceive. . . . At this very day there are complaints from the whole line of having been three or four days without provisions." The chief cause of decay of Congress was the preference of able men for leadership in their own states; this sacrificed "the common interests of the Confederacy."[11] Hamilton had enough other proofs of the fumbling of boards and committees, but his in-

sistence, a little later, on administration of the great public departments by single, able and responsible men must have owed much
to the Congress at York.   Indeed, his whole emphasis upon the
executive, which was a recurrent theme with him throughout the
rest of his life, may trace back to that dreadful winter.   A legislature of one house, feeble and opinionated, was a demonstration of
the way to lose the name of action.

When Hamilton was in the highlands pressing forward the
troops he had extracted from the reluctant Gates, he did not know
that Washington himself was beginning to strike back at the Albany commander and the latter's accomplices.   This was in a
frosty note of two sentences to Conway:

"Sir: A Letter which I received last Night, containd the following paragraph.

"In a Letter from Genl. Conway to Genl. Gates he says: 'Heaven
has been determined to save your Country; or a weak General
and bad Councellors would have ruind it.' "[12]

The sequel to this involved a slander on Hamilton, though he
did not get wind of it until later.   At this point we must fill in
the story.   Colonel James Wilkinson, Gates's adjutant, on his
leisurely way to Congress to justify the terms of surrender given to
Burgoyne, stopped at Reading and spent an agreeable day with
Stirling and his Lordship's aides.   As Wilkinson described the
convivial occasion, the conversation "became general, unreserved
and copious," and the tenor of Stirling's discourse "and the nature
of our situation [read a little typsy all around] made it confidential."   He could not recall particulars, but would "acknowledge
it is possible in the warmth of social intercourse, when the mind
is relaxed and the tongue is unguarded, that observations may
have elapsed which have not since occurred to me."[13]

When Wilkinson arrived at Valley Forge he discovered that one
of his relaxed remarks had flown before him.   Conway, though
less troubled than he might have been, taxed Wilkinson with the
awkward disclosure.   Conway "had been charged by General
Washington, with writing a letter to Major-General Gates which
reflected on the General [Washington] and on the army."[14]   The
commander in chief's information had come to him in a letter
from Lord Stirling, who, thinking it his duty to detect "such
wicked duplicity of conduct," had passed on Wilkinson's remark

to Major William McWilliams, Stirling's aide.[15] Mifflin, at
Reading where Wilkinson bore the tale, had forewarned Gates
that a storm would break about his head. "An extract from General Conway's letter to you has been procured and sent to head
quarters," he reported. The sentiment was "such as should not
have been entrusted to any of your Family." Washington had
enclosed the quotation to Conway. "My dear General," Mifflin
begged, "take Care of your Generosity & Frank Disposition; they
. . . may injure some of your best friends."[16]

Gates added an anxious postscript to a cordial letter to Conway. He had just been tipped off by Mifflin. "I intreat you
. . . to let me know which of the letters was copied off. It is of
the greatest importance, that I should detect the person who has
been guilty of that act of infidelity: I cannot trace him out, unless
I have your assistance."[17] But he did not allow himself to remain
long in doubt. Ignoring his own indiscretion and Wilkinson's
loose tongue, Gates fixed his suspicion on Hamilton for having
revealed Conway's slur to Washington. No sooner did Wilkinson return to Albany than Gates, with sour relish, announced to
him, " 'I have had a spy in my camp since you left me!' I did
not comprehend the allusion," Wilkinson wrote, "and he explained by informing me, 'Colonel Hamilton had been sent up
to him by General Washington; and would you believe it, he pur-
loined the copy of a letter out of that closet,' pointing to one in
the room. I answered him that 'I conceived it impossible.' "
Gates insisted, explained that when the family was called out on
business, " '. . . Colonel Hamilton was left alone an hour in this
room, during which time, he took Conway's letter out of that
closet and copied it, and the copy has been furnished to Washington.' "

But it took more than piercing recollection of his own error to
discomfit Wilkinson. While affecting to defend Hamilton, he
tried to involve him in the suggested complicity of Troup, Gates's
aide. Gates knew the confidence of Troup in Hamilton. Wasn't
it probable that Troup had innocently communicated the import
of Conway's letter to his friend, by whose agency it reached Washington? Gates, however, would accept no palliation. Hamilton
had perpetrated the deed. Gates had adopted a plan " 'which
would compel General Washington to give him up, and . . . the

receiver and the thief would be alike disgraced.' " The prospect
of Gates coercing Washington to yield Hamilton as the culprit
must have shaken Wilkinson, for, in recounting the episode later,
he was voluble in excusing himself. Gates had not considered
Conway's letter as confidential "because he had read it *publicly* in
my presence," said Wilkinson, "as matter of information from
the grand army . . . and therefore I did not dream of the foul
imputations it was destined to draw down upon me. . . ."[18]

Gates at once insinuated to Washington his accusation against
Hamilton. ". . . I conjure your excellency, to give me all the
assistance you can, in tracing out the author of the infidelity
which put extracts from General Conway's letters to me into your
hands. Those letters have been *stealingly copied.* . . . It is
. . . *in your . . . power* to do me and the United States a very
important service, by detecting a wretch who may betray me,
and capitally injure the *very operations under your immediate
direction."* With more of the same admonition, he explained, in
a solicitude for clues that Washington did not appreciate, that he
was sending a copy of his letter to the President of Congress.[19]

Washington replied with a candor that made Gates squirm, as
we know from the latter's response and subsequent recriminations
on Wilkinson. Washington ignored the ill-concealed thrusts at
his aide, Hamilton, and recited that Stirling, "from motives of
friendship," had rehearsed what Gates's confidant, Wilkinson, had
repeated at Reading. Washington ended with a reprimand for
Gates, the more severe because sorrowful. Until he discovered
Gates on the prowl for a traitorous offender, the commander in
chief had supposed that Gates had meant to forearm him against
"a dangerous incendiary . . . Genl. Conway. But, in this, as
in other matters of late, I have found myself mistaken."[20]

Gates answered from York, where he had gone to take post as
President of the Board of War. His new pinnacle was a pivot on
which he gyrated. The paragraph quoted to Washington was
"spurious . . . a wicked forgery." Conway's letter mentioned
neither the weakness of any general nor bad counselors. Gates
now disowned suspecting Hamilton, and arraigned the faithless
Wilkinson, who ought to be punished.[21] We may reasonably suppose that Hamilton had a hand in Washington's dissection of this
shifty document. It was just, acute, observant of what Gates had

written, and left the poor man no refuge from his own attempts at evasion and deception. Gates at first accepted the authenticity of a charge, the existence of which he then denied. If Conway's letters were innocent, why had not Gates produced them? The fact was that Conway, by his silence under Washington's indictment, had practically admitted the authorship of the passage.[22] On Gates's disclaimers, Washington was willing to bury their correspondence in silence, "and as far as future events will permit, oblivion."[23]

The sequel, a half-hearted challenge by Wilkinson to Gates and an empty threat to have the blood of Stirling, was an accurate comment on the episode. Wilkinson, returning from Albany to Pennsylvania, learned that Gates had denounced him "in the grossest language." Expostulating his innocence and his sacrifices in the service of Gates, he demanded that the general meet him behind the English church prepared to shoot it out. Gates accepted, but at the last minute sent a request for an explanation. As they walked in a back street Gates burst into tears, and in a lachrymose exchange Wilkinson was satisfied.[24] He was even quicker to find appeasement in the dignified reply of Stirling.[25]

The suspicious scheming of Conway and his friends was in contrast to the good will and honest, arduous accomplishment for the army of Baron Frederick William von Steuben. He arrived at Valley Forge at the end of February 1778, and from the first an affectionate attachment grew between him and Hamilton. They had many bonds—painstaking devotion to the common cause, eagerness to introduce system into the military organization, a strong wish to combine field action with staff duty, and a knowledge of French (Hamilton's superior to the baron's). The distinctions between them mattered not at all: rank, age (Hamilton was twenty-three, Steuben forty-eight), or the faculty of the first for economy, and the open-handedness of the latter, especially with borrowed funds, his usual reliance; in fact, these differences proved further cement to their friendship. Nearly everyone liked the baron, in spite of the prickly duties of inspector general which he soon came to discharge; but in addition to official congeniality was the personal loyalty he inspired in his closest associates, such as Hamilton, and especially Major Benjamin Walker and Colonel William North, his aides.[26]

Hamilton saw Steuben not only as a cordial, true man, but as the instrument of instilling discipline and order into a weak, sick, discouraged army. Punctuality, knowledge, practice, and pride were to offer the anodyne to misery. Conway, appointed inspector general on December 13, 1777,[27] and resigned April 28, 1778,[28] had not occupied the assignment more than nominally,[29] indeed was worse than no one because of his vainglory, utter lack of tact, and his forfeiture of the confidence of the commander in chief.[30]

Steuben's "fondness for . . . importance," as Hamilton put it,[31] prompted the baron's complicity in the amiable deception that he had been "a lieutenant general in foreign service."[32] However, this was his single specious claim, and he offset it by offering as a volunteer under Washington without particular rank or command. Warned by the French war minister, St. Germain, that preferment of foreign officers had caused discontent among Americans, "I foresaw the necessity," Steuben told Hamilton, "of pursuing a different course from that . . . adopted by my predecessors, in order to gain admission into your army."[33] In this Steuben went too far, for the modesty of his proposals led, some years later, to serious question whether Congress had made any agreement with him. This produced embarrassment to Hamilton's persevering, skillful efforts to secure for Steuben the compensation he deserved.

Before there was prospect of acquiring so able an inspector general as Steuben, the commander in chief had planned a reorganization of the army. He required of the general officers at Valley Forge that they submit their ideas in writing. These papers, with Washington's own wishes, were worked up by Hamilton into a long report which Washington signed and offered January 29, 1778, to the congressional committee of conference which visited camp.[34] It was first necessary to reanimate the loyalty and zeal of the officers, else their languid example would descend to all ranks. A settled plan of half-pay or other pension on retirement seemed the essential means. An annual draft of troops, with a small bounty for reenlistment only, was proposed, but with limited power of engaging substitutes. A consolidation and reduction of the number of weak regiments was urged.[35] Expansion of the cavalry, of the inspector general's office, and establishment of a provost-marshalcy were recommended. Rank had been conferred lavishly, without uniformity, resulting in endless confusion, contention, and obstruction of the service; hence cures were enjoined.[36]

Sufficient clothing could be had only through national contracts with the French government. Home supplies and commercial purchase abroad would not serve.[37] The extraordinary importance of prompt appointment of a quartermaster general, to fill the vacancy since Mifflin's resignation nearly three months before, and the need for reducing supernumerary subordinates in the department were emphasized. Dr. Benjamin Rush and others had used the hospital department to make mischief for Washington. In this report the commander in chief was charitable and wise enough to lay the trouble fundamentally to lack of supplies and facilities. The bad effect of frequent failure of prompt pay for the troops was enlarged upon. The army was not sufficiently disciplined to withstand this strain on men's tempers.[38] The review ended with Washington's assurance that unless remedies for sufferings and discontents in the army were applied at once, "the most alarming . . . consequences" would follow.[39]

Steuben soon came to know the evils which Washington and Hamilton sketched, and he was the instrument of correcting many of them. When he first came to camp, however, a total stranger and knowing nothing of the language, he observed the utter lack of uniformity in military units, which must impede his instruction. The ravages of casualties, desertions, illness, and furloughs, with no recruits coming on, were startling. ". . . the words company, regiment, brigade, and division . . . did not convey any idea," the baron wrote, "upon which to form a calculation. . . . They were so unequal in their number that it would have been impossible to execute any maneuvers. Sometimes a regiment was stronger than a brigade. I have seen a regiment consisting of thirty men and a company of one corporal." The description of dress was easy, for some of the men were literally naked. "The officers who had coats, had them of every color and make. . . . With regard to . . . military discipline, I may safely say no such thing existed."[40]

An officer less eager to bring system to this army would have thrown up his distantly conceived project on the spot. One less willing to content himself with a few reasonable rules, and to begin with these on the smallest scale, would have failed from the first. Fortunately, this Prussian was as full of judgment as of knowledge. The virtue of adaptability combined with resolution never had a more shining example, or achieved a more substantial success. The first pertinent order was Washington's adding a hundred chosen men to the commander in chief's guard to form a model corps "to be instructed in the Manoeuvres necessary to be introduced in the Army. . . ."[41] With this detached corps, assisted by most carefully selected subordinates, Steuben began working at once. In ten days general orders announced that, pending approval of Congress, Steuben would serve as inspector general, with Lieutenant Colonels William Davis, of Virginia; John Brooks, of Massachusetts; and Francis Barber, of New Jersey; and Jean Baptiste Ternant as subinspectors. Hamilton may well have influenced the selection of his old teacher Barber.[42] Matters went on prosperously, Steuben training the experimental company himself, until, on April 30, 1778, Washington asked of Congress ratification of his arrangement and the commissioning of the baron, whom he praised, as major general. This action of Congress was announced in orders May 9, 1778.[43]

The ample powers which the commander in chief gave to Steuben at the outset, needed to install the new system, soon provoked protests that the baron was trenching on field officers' preserves. "Their jealousies and discontents were rising fast to a height that threatened to overturn the whole plan."[44] Washington felt obliged to issue general orders which, while they insured the uninterrupted influence of the inspector general and his deputies, protected unit commanders in what they regarded as their prerogatives.[45] These orders were sent to Congress, and the baron, going for an audience at York, was enjoined to modify his own further proposals with a view to avoid unnecessary conflict.[46]

Undoubtedly at Washington's suggestion, Hamilton wrote his own letter to William Duer, a member of Congress, dispatching it by the baron. It made two points that Washington could not put to Congress himself. The first was that Steuben, able and well intentioned, was apt to seek too large a sphere, and by no means should be given disciplinary powers, which belonged to commanders, ultimately to Washington. The second was that Washington's authority to alter regulations, as circumstances required, subject to later approval of Congress, should not be prevented. When Conway was made inspector general, he had been given practical independence of the commander in chief, which was resented by the army.[47]

We are unable to say what part Hamilton had in the preparation of Steuben's written instructions that later became *Regulations for the Order and Discipline of the Troops of the United States*.[48] Manuscript copies of the earliest directions for drill of the infantry were hurriedly made for the use of sub- and brigade inspectors,[49] and Hamilton's services as translator and editor may well have been requisitioned.

In any event, first fruits of Steuben's teaching were evident in the remarkably improved response of the troops to orders at the battle of Monmouth, where this kind of automatic obedience was never more needed.[50]

Hamilton, from beginning to end, tried to promote Steuben's services to the army, and later to present his claims to Congress. This involved double tact, in curbing the baron's pretensions and in conciliating line officers and legislators who considered his proposals improper. Fortunately for Hamilton's efforts, the pomposity of the Prussian volunteer was harmless in light of his undisputed merits. His occasional choler was on the surface of abundant good will and good humor. Washington appreciated his competence and zeal, and was profoundly grateful to him for his contributions. Hamilton could suggest, when the commander in chief could not, a little flexibility in interpretation of orders, to keep the baron happy and useful. Thus he wrote to Boudinot even more intimately than to Duer when Steuben posted to Congress with his demands, "almost resolved to quit the service" unless they were satisfied. At the battle of Monmouth Steuben had been a severe critic of Charles Lee's behavior, and Lee had retorted that the inspector-general hung back from danger.[51] This likely played a part in Steuben's reluctance to relinquish command of a division on the march from New Brunswick, which Washington had chosen to give him temporarily. Washington's separation of staff and line assignments must be followed as a rule, but was it possible, Hamilton asked of Boudinot, that Congress might content the baron by enlarging the inspectorship? Pending that, Congress might give him the right to be employed on detachments, which would please him and not offend others. "I need not caution you," the aide added, "that this is a matter of great delicacy and importance, and that every step taken in it ought to be well considered."[52]

As Lodge observed, Hamilton "wrote for everybody,"[53] though he was junior to most of them, and all, save Washington, were less busy than he. Some of his aptest letters and petitions fall in this category, evidence of the sympathy with which he entered into another's problems. Likely in more cases than not he had proposed the paper in the first place, so that the communication belonged to him as to the *soi-disant* author. On his list of clients were Henry Laurens, president of Congress, and Baron Steuben. His memorial to Congress for the latter[54] so absorbed him that he started to sign his own name before he substituted the baron's. This petition was the harder to compose because Steuben, in his frequent prior applications for back pay and losses in military service, had acquired the reputation of being unreasonable and importunate. Hamilton struck just the right tone, between request and reproach, between respectful submission and injured demand.

Twice, in afteryears, Hamilton asked Washington's powerful help toward favorable action on Baron Steuben's claims. Probably only his care for the opinion of our government in Europe moved him to the request for influence which Washington, on principle, was chary of using. "The poor *Baron* is still soliciting Congress," Hamilton wrote, "and has every prospect of indigence before him. He has his imprudences, but . . . he has rendered valuable services, and his merits and the reputation of the country alike demand that he should not be left to suffer want." Could Washington write to his friends in Congress?[55] Two years later it was at Steuben's request that Hamilton wrote again, and in more detail. "Our reputation abroad is not at present too high. To dismiss an old soldier empty and hungry, to . . . complain of unkind returns and violated engagements, will . . . not tend to raise it." Hamilton felt inclined "in this case to go further than might be strictly necessary, rather than drive a man, at the Baron's time of life, who has been a faithful servant, to extremities."[56]

Hamilton's association with Steuben in the Society of the Cincinnati (where the baron was in his element) is described elsewhere.

I·I

Brand from
the Burning

FOR the British, from Meschianza to Monmouth was pride before
a fall. For the Americans, after the misery of Valley Forge, camp-
ing on a battlefield they had won was bright achievement, moral
as much as military. The battle of Monmouth, June 28, 1778, in
all points of view was the most dramatic of the war. That of
Trenton, its nearest competitor, was the surprise capture by a small
force of a still smaller one; the plans of the patriots, laid in calm
courage, worked out well. At Monmouth the brand was snatched
from the burning, shame was turned to success. The disaffection
and disgrace of General Charles Lee, America's second in command, further distinguished Washington's rescue of the day. This,
for the sake of contrast, is a short description of events on that
blistering field. First failure, to be sure, led to victory only qualified, but such was fortune, more enthralling than pat perfection.[1]

The case of the two armies was reversed as compared with eighteen months before. Instead of the enemy pursuing Washington's
depleted force westward across New Jersey, the Americans, in equal
strength, were now in chase eastward. In fact, the mischance of
the campaign, from General Washington's standpoint, was that
he must come up with a fleeing foe. Washington must divide his
army to find, before he could fight, his enemy. The opposition of
most of his officers to risking a full-fledged encounter further perplexed the commander in chief's problem.

[158]

We have a full record of Hamilton's part in preparation for, during, and as a result of the Monmouth battle. His service as aide to Washington, in camp and field, and as his champion, is illustrated in this conflict. The engagement brought him into close personal contact with all of the leaders. So involved was he that the history of the battle may be written in terms of his doings. He had already helped provide for occupation of Philadelphia,[2] and had prepared for the commander in chief information and queries placed before the last Valley Forge council of war, mapping plans in consequence of the enemy quitting the city.[3]

We can follow Lieutenant Colonel Hamilton day by day, and in part hour to hour, from his leaving Valley Forge with Washington soon after sunrise June 19,[4] 1778, to his arrival on the field of Monmouth on the 28th. During this period of watchful pursuit of Clinton's force he was constantly assisting Washington, and soon Lafayette, to gather news of enemy movements and organize obstruction by militia and detached parties. The march commenced agreeably enough before it became vexed and then frantic. James McHenry, the fellow aide who in his diary frequently addressed sportive remarks to Hamilton, pictured the pleasant scene at the first camp, "8 miles from Moors & 25 from Philad.ᵃ [.] Head quarters at a Jonat.ⁿ Fells. [Doylestown] A raining evening." The "Company . . . within Doors" included "a pretty, Fullfaced, youthfull, playfull Lass, & a Family of Quakers meek & unsuspicious. Hamilton thou shalt not tread on this ground, I mark it for my own."[5]

The next day, Saturday the 20th, "A Rapid Mornings March" was made in spite of weather "excessive hot. Some of the soldiers die suddenly."[6] Thus began the torture of humid heat that fevered the advance to the day of Monmouth, when the mercury stood at 96 degrees. Hamilton was doubtless with Washington when the general reached the ferry at noon on Sunday the 21st, soon crossed and took quarters at Holcombe's house. "Here are some charming Girls," recorded McHenry, "but one of the Drums of the General's Guard more a favorite than Hamilton."[7] Neither aide could have dallied long, however, for both had writing to do for Washington. Reports of the enemy's movement, to Moore's Town and Mount Holly, coupled with departure of their shipping, indicated that

Clinton would "traverse the Jerseys." Hamilton explained this, for Washington, to Gates, who commanded at Peekskill.[8] The route Clinton would take—whether to some point on the Raritan River or Bay, or to Sandy Hook—was yet a mystery which Washington sought to solve by every means of information he could rally. Difficulties in knowing the enemy's whereabouts are today hard to understand. Clinton with some 10,000 men and a provision and baggage train twelve miles long (because the roads were few and narrow) was moving at snail's pace, five or six miles a day, with New Jersey militia and detached Continentals, some mounted, hanging on his flanks. Deserters in large numbers came in to the Americans, and the maximum area involved was a hundred miles one way and thirty or forty the other. Of course, where Clinton would ultimately point remained a further question.[9] Hamilton soon became a vital part of his general's intelligence system.

Brilliant results might impend if the enemy, vulnerable because encumbered and on the move, was attacked in force. Since Burgoyne's surrender, only Clinton's army remained to be destroyed and the war would be won. On the other hand, Washington's troops, only partially recovered from the distresses of Valley Forge, and scattered to provide against unknown contingencies, might prove the victims. Should this risk be run when the French alliance, with the arrival of D'Estaing's fleet, was already a military fact? Caution would reap a more certain though more patient reward. How far this would be deferred, by enemy resistance, problems of American-French land and naval cooperation, and by involvement in jealous European diplomacy, Washington could not foresee. This was the portentous speculation that obsessed headquarters in those anxious, toilsome, watchful days of June.[10] Hamilton, among the juniors, and Wayne and Cadwalader were for chancing it, and as the two armies crept forward the judgment of Washington, Lafayette, Greene, and Steuben hardened to this resolve.

A short march the morning of June 23 brought the army to a halt at Hopewell Township "near the Baptist Meeting," a dozen miles west and north of Princeton. Clinton's force had reached Black Horse[11] or perhaps even Allen Town,[12] the latter less than ten miles southeast of Trenton and some twenty-five from Washington's position. Hamilton promptly expressed the uncertainty in Washington's mind that was to keep him at a pause for two days.

"It was my intention to have taken post nearer Princeton," he wrote for the general, "but finding the enemy are dilatory in advancing, I am doubtful of the propriety of proceeding any farther, till their intentions can be ascertained." He wished to know of obstructions placed in their way so he might judge whether they delayed from choice or from necessity. If from choice, it meant the enemy wanted to draw him into a general action, or designed to coax him from the Delaware, flank his right, and gain his rear. He wished to be immediately advised of every movement and appearance of the king's army, dispatches to bear the precise hour.[13]

In spite of first orders to be ready "for a march or Action very early in the morning" of the 24th, the army was held over, disposed of heavy baggage, cooked rations, cleaned arms, and rested while Washington awaited developments and placed possibilities before his general officers[14] for their advice. Hamilton was an absorbed auditor as one after another gave his answer to the commander in chief's queries: Should he choose to hazard a general action? If so, how? If not, what safe means would annoy the enemy's march? Hamilton wrote out the decision, signed by all but Wayne, who wanted to bring on a decisive battle; others, outwardly at least, were content with advancing 1,500 more men to worry the enemy's left flank and rear, while the main body remained nearby to be governed by events. This result of the council, "unluckily called," said Hamilton, "would have done honor to the most honorable society of midwives, and to them only. The purport was, that we should keep at a comfortable distance from the enemy, and keep up a vain parade of annoying them by detachment."[15]

General Charles Lee's inhibitions, delivered with authority, ruled many: let Clinton cross New Jersey unhampered; the French alliance was America's promise of victory; equal numbers of Americans could not battle successfully with trained European soldiers. Others of bolder purpose so far yielded as to accept the compromise of sending forward a skirmishing party.[16] Those that were not dissuaded from their own views[17]—Lafayette, Wayne, and Greene —individually wrote to Washington urging that he disregard timid advice.[18] The story that after the council of war broke up Hamilton urged Greene to go with him to beg Washington to give battle is doubtful; the addition that the commander in chief agreed, and thus "an attack was decided"[19] is more so.   However, the young aide was surely the cordial supporter, if not the actual companion, of General Greene in efforts to produce a blow.   A score of years later, honoring Greene's memory, Hamilton stigmatized the faint-hearted cautions others gave Washington before Monmouth. He condemned "those impotent councils, which, by a formal vote, had decreed an undisturbed passage to an enemy . . . dispirited by desertion, broken by fatigue, retiring through woods, defiles, morasses, . . . in the face of an army superior in numbers, elated by pursuit, and ardent to signalize their courage."   But the courageous Greene "left nothing unessayed . . . to frustrate so degrading a resolution."[20]

Making the best of the decision of his council of officers, Washington from Hopewell the 24th sent Brigadier General Charles Scott forward with nearly 1,500 good troops to cooperate with smaller detachments[21] "to gall the enemys left flank and rear."[22] Morgan was to gain the right flank,[23] while small bands of foot under General Cadwalader and of horse under Colonel White were pressing up.   Thus far Washington had acted in accordance with the advice of his generals, but with the move of the army the morning of June 25 to Kingston,[24] four miles northeast of Princeton, he began to assert his command, moral and military, as necessity plainly required.   Lafayette, with a new force of 1,000 under Wayne, was advanced to attack, all of the American detachments, amounting to about 6,000 troops, to take the marquis' orders. He was empowered to commit them all in an engagement.[25] Washington, seeing that the British were taking the shortest route to the sea, by Monmouth Court House,[26] and would soon escape him, left off pestering and prepared to punish them.

Lafayette and Wayne were leaders eager for action.   Washington gave command to the marquis only after he secured the acquiescence of Charles Lee.   Hamilton described the vexing exchanges brought on by self-esteem.   "General Lee's conduct . . . was truly childish.   According to the incorrect notions of our army, his seniority . . . entitled him to the command of the advanced corps; but he in the first instance declined it in favor of the marquis. Some of his friends having blamed him for doing it, and Lord Stirling having shown a disposition to interpose his claim, General Lee . . . inconsistently reasserted his pretensions.   The matter was a second time accommodated, General Lee and Lord Stirling agreed to let the marquis command. General Lee, a little time after, recanted again and became very importunate. The general [Washington] who had all along observed the greatest candor in the matter, grew tired of such fickle behavior, and ordered the marquis to proceed." However, Washington did in the end feel compelled to put Lee, with additional brigades, in command of the whole forward body. To save the feelings of Lafayette, who was creditably amenable, Lee was not to interfere with any design Lafayette had in hand, but was to aid it.[27]

Now began for Hamilton four days of riding, gathering and giving intelligence as liaison officer between scattered portions of the army that must be concentrated for action against the enemy. At no other juncture in the war was his field service as aide so varied, intensive, and protracted. On June 25 he went ahead of Lafayette,[28] to whom he was assigned, to Cranbury. Here he was equidistant, a dozen miles, between Washington at Kingston to the north, the moving column of Clinton about Allen Town to the south, and English Town, the main army's future camp, to the east. Woodsy tracks connected the dispersed villages.[29]

Hamilton's first care was to inform Lafayette, as best he could, on the positions of enemy and American forces. The British rear was five miles east of Allen Town on the Monmouth road. Hamilton would appoint a place of rendezvous and notify Maxwell at Hyde's Town (Hightstown), Dickinson and Morgan, "said to be on the enemy's right flank; but where, cannot be told," and Scott who "from circumstances . . . is probably at Allen Town." Meanwhile, Lafayette should move toward Cranbury. The letter should be sent back to Washington. Hamilton was galloping to meet Maxwell and would report further. He added a postscript that Scott, at five o'clock in the afternoon, passed Hooper's Tavern five miles from Allen Town.[30]

Difficulties increased next day. Hamilton was with Lafayette's force at Robin's Tavern, eight miles east of Allen Town. As the enemy had passed the fork to South Amboy, he wrote to Washington, they were making toward Shrewsbury (Monmouth on the way). The troops were out of provisions; Wayne's men, particularly, were famished, and rebelled against moving from the present halt until commissary wagons came up. The intelligence system—

which Washington had striven to provide—had been neglected; the enemy had escaped Lafayette's pursuit, now brought to a stop by hunger. Worse, Hamilton continued, "We are entirely at a loss where the [main] army is. . . . If the army is wholly out of supporting distance, we risk the total loss of the detachment in making an attack," which they were anxious to undertake within the limits of prudence.[31] Lafayette added (7:15 P.M., June 26) that Hamilton had ridden the whole of the night before, without finding anybody that could give him reliable information. Lafayette learned otherwise that the enemy were in motion, their rear seven or eight miles away. He was going after them and might attack in the morning if they did not elude him in the night, "which I much fear, as our intelligence are not the best ones." He would be confident of striking a blow if Washington was near him.[32]

Prudence was stressed by Washington in his prompt replies that day. The eagerness of Lafayette, stimulated by that of Hamilton, might precipitate a premature stroke. The troops should not be pushed too hard in the heat. Food was on the way, but his own army was halted for the want of it.[33]

Hamilton replied, the night of the 26th,[34] giving important information and reassuring the commander in chief on the score of Lafayette's caution. The enemy was encamped with the van slightly beyond Monmouth Court House. To attack them without support of the whole army would be "folly in the extreme," especially because they had rearranged their march to put the baggage in front and close the rear with their best light troops, with a guard of a thousand men a quarter-mile back of the main body. However, a plan of assailing them, if Washington was prepared to come up, was outlined.

Hamilton had written this far when Lafayette received an order, from Washington at Cranbury,[35] to march to English Town where the main army could better support his attack or cover his retreat. Lafayette's detachment would be put in motion, accordingly, said Hamilton, at three o'clock next morning (the 27th).[36] Hamilton was still preparing for Lafayette's corps to assail the enemy rear. He dashed off a dispatch to Brig. Gen. Scott: "This part of the troops marches instantly—We are to join in the Monmouth road one mile this side of Taylor's tavern [.] You will govern yourself accordingly. If you can find Morgan let him be desired again to keep close to the enemy and attack when we attack [.]"

Lafayette, however, replied separately that in consequence of Washington's instructions he had given up the project of attacking, wished only to join Lee, and would march at two next morning. He could not resist adding, "I do not believe General Lee intends to make any attack tomorrow, for then I would have been directed to fall immediately upon them without making eleven miles entirely out of the way. I am here as near as I will be at Englishtown."[37] At English Town Lafayette and Hamilton were reunited with the main army under Washington.

What happened at Monmouth is readily understood if the physical features of the battlefield are clearly in mind. It was[38] an open plain some two and a half miles long and a mile wide, with the village of Monmouth Court House (since Freehold) at the eastern end, with hills enclosing the western end, the highest in the center, crowned by Tennent Church (still standing). However, of special importance, the field was cut, roughly north and south, by three ravines—one directly in front of the village, one in the middle, and the last below the eminence on the west. The boggy bottom of each was spanned by a single narrow causeway. English Town, where the main army, including most of the force under Lee, lay the night before the action, is four miles west and a little north of Tennent Church; that is, at the beginning nearly seven miles separated Americans and British.

We shall not be concerned with details of the engagement except as Hamilton figured in giving or helping to execute orders. Lee, commanding the large detachment, marched from English Town something after five o'clock[39] and came up with the enemy about eight o'clock in the morning of June 28.[40] It was probably a couple of hours after this that Hamilton was sent by Washington from English Town to reconnoiter. He fell in with Lee some distance west of the Court House, his troops in confusion. Hamilton urged Lee to order Lafayette to attack the left flank, which was done. Hamilton returned to Washington to report.[41] He met the general advancing at the head of the main army not far west of Tennent Church. Lee, Hamilton declared, would soon engage. He recommended, with reasons "which were thought good," that the right wing, under Greene, should be thrown to the south "and

. . . follow with the left wing [under Stirling] directly in General Lee's rear to support him."

This order was being given when a countryman brought news of a retreat. Washington could not believe it even when a soldier gave the same tidings. He was soon face to face with the ugly fact. Lee, when he found his tongue, offered explanations which Washington dismissed as fast as uttered.[42] Soon Lee was sent to the rear while Washington, on the hillside below the church, reversed the retreat, gave swift commands for artillery support from the flanks, put vigor in all, and drove the enemy from the field. "I never saw the General to so much advantage," said Hamilton shortly after. "America owes a great deal to General Washington for this day's work. A general rout, dismay and disgrace, would have attended the whole army in any other hands but his. . . . Other officers have great merit in performing their parts well, but he directed the whole with the skill of a master workman. He did not hug himself at a distance and leave an Arnold to win laurels for him, but by his own presence he brought order out of confusion, animated his troops, and led them to success."[43] The attempt of Gates's friends to remove Washington from command had already been much weakened, said Lafayette, "but from that day [Monmouth] it totally vanished away."[44]

Hamilton's part in battle was assumed in the emergency. To Lee and Washington he proposed dispositions of troops, but he helped Livingston and Olney, especially the latter, in posting their men for protection of artillery pieces which were in danger of capture in the enemy advance. After the forming of Olney's line Hamilton's horse was shot and in the fall the colonel was so hurt that he was compelled to retire from the action.[45] ". . . your friend Hammy," wrote McHenry to Boudinot, "was incessant in his endeavours during . . . the whole day—in reconnoitering the enemy and in rallying and charging." Hamilton and Laurens "seemed to court death . . . and triumphed over it as the face of war changed in our favor."[46] Hamilton was doubtless with the others of Washington's staff who, as "Night set in and we failing in our attempt to turn the Enemy's flank, composed ourselves to sleep behind the line of Battle under a large Tree." The following day, the British having decamped, was given to burying the dead and caring for the wounded.[47]

Hamilton's condemnation of General Charles Lee's retreat at Monmouth sprang from several causes. First, Hamilton penned, for Washington, the written order to attack, which Lee disregarded. Hamilton's accuracy in embodying Washington's intention and in reporting to the court-martial his recollection of the text were impugned when Lee disputed the wording. Second, Lee disparaged the military and personal conduct of the commander in chief on the field, both of which Hamilton admired. Third, Hamilton all along had been for giving the enemy a blow; he had deplored the obstructionist influence of many of his elders, and had worked manfully, before and in the battle, to organize the attack. Fourth, Hamilton's close association with Lafayette in these operations gave him a care for that spirited officer's reputation, which was injured by Lee's distracted or faithless command of the advance troops. Hamilton at no time drew out these reasons in so many words, but they are fairly inferred from circumstances.

Even had not Lee, in the sequel, written Washington contemptuous letters, he might have been ordered to trial; his actions after the battle made it inevitable.[48]

Hamilton testified twice at the court-martial, first the opening day, July 4, at New Brunswick, and on the 13th at Paramus.[49] Both times his testimony was important—as evidenced, for example, by Lee's cross-examination of him—and must have carried weight with the court. The essential information sought to be drawn from the witnesses Scott, Wayne, Fitzgerald, and Meade was whether Washington had ordered Lee to attack, if so with intent to bring on a general engagement, and what degree of discretion was allowed to Lee by the commander in chief. Hamilton was the first who could so much as refer to a written order.

He explained, in answer to the judge advocate's question, that he wrote Lee the night before the battle a letter "by General Washington's order, a copy of which I have not; but it was conceived in the spirit, as I understood, of former orders that had been given by him to General Lee, and was occasioned by an apprehension (as declared to me by General Washington) that the enemy might move off . . . and get out of our reach, so that the purpose of an attack might be frustrated. . . . the order directed that General Lee should detach a party of 600 or 800 men to lie very near the enemy . . . in case of their moving off to give the earliest intelligence of it, and to skirmish with them so as to produce some delay, and give time for the rest of the troops to come up." Lee was to direct Morgan, in case the enemy had marched, to attack with the same object, "and yet not so as to endanger a general rout of his party, and disqualifying them from acting in concert with the other troops when a serious attack should be made. This, I understood from General Washington, was in pursuance of his intention to have the enemy attacked." The letter was sent by a lighthorseman and Hamilton had given the purport of it to the best of his recollection.[50]

Lee took pains to bring out, in questions put to Hamilton and through testimony of his own aides, Captains Mercer and Edwards, that Washington's orders reached him at a late hour, one or two o'clock in the morning.[51] The implication was that Washington, or certainly Hamilton, had been tardy and that the commander in chief had not signed the order. In the hurry of those last hours the usual rule of keeping a copy of dispatches had been disregarded. Lee did not produce the orders at the trial, which means there was nothing in them to contradict Hamilton's recollection, and this most crucial document in the affair of Lee has never turned up from that day to this. The episode shows the trust reposed by the commander in chief in his aide, Hamilton, to embody the general's intentions in accurate language that would yet comprehend the several contingencies in the situation. Probably some letters that Hamilton wrote for Washington and for which the latter held himself responsible were never seen by the general. Battle preparations demanded not only intelligence in transmitting orders, but good faith in executing them. It was in this essential that Lee offended. Even had the written orders been offered in evidence, and proved precisely what Hamilton reported, Lee, judging by all his conduct on this and previous occasions, would have sought to justify his departure from directions.

Lee pressed Hamilton, in cross-examination, to say that Washington left Lee a measure of discretion, this being essential to Lee's whole defense. Lee cited a hypothetical case; Hamilton readily declared that Washington did not bind Lee under all, unforeseeable, circumstances, and that his own language given to the court was more explicit and full than he had ever used in written or spoken word to Lee. But, he ended, "from everything I knew

. . . General Washington's intention was fully to have the enemy attacked on their march, and that the circumstances must be very extraordinary . . . which, consistent with his wish, could justify the not doing it."[52]

Hamilton's next testimony bore harder upon Lee for his conduct on the field, and drew from that officer, later, sarcastic jibes against Washington's young aide. Lee, said Hamilton, had under his command more than half the army, 5,000 troops plus 1,400 that had been told off to cooperate with him. Sent by Washington to reconnoiter the country between him and Lee's corps, Hamilton found the latter in some confusion. He suggested to Lee to order Lafayette to attack the enemy's left flank, which was done. Hamilton "saw nothing like a general plan or combined disposition for a retreat. . . ." In the two orders he heard Lee give, Lee seemed "under a hurry of mind," and lacked the calm and steadiness necessary to support an officer under such critical circumstances.[53] As Lee was claiming that his retreat was deliberate strategy, he must confute, if he could, statements of Hamilton and others that he and his troops were in confusion. In his defense he ridiculed Hamilton's hot declaration to him, on the field, that they must do or die; Hamilton was in "a sort of frenzy of valor."[54]

Aside from the story of "Molly Pitcher," a heroine of several names, but authentic,[55] mention of Monmouth calls to most minds excoriating language of Washington when he met Lee and countermanded the retreat, though the fact is doubtful. Hamilton was present, described the encounter to the court, and said nothing of angry words. Years later he answered the question whether the commander in chief had cursed Lee: "Washington was modest. He was careful of his words. He had not time to curse. He had to retrieve the day." Washington urged Lee to remain there and check advance of the enemy. Hamilton himself, much engaged in assisting Livingston and Olney to reform their troops for counterattack, was near Lee, but "heard no measures directed, nor saw any taken by him to answer the purpose. . . ."[56]

The court-martial found Lee guilty as charged on two counts— disobedience of orders in not attacking the enemy, and disrespect to the commander in chief—and substantially so on the third charge of an unnecessary retreat, though Washington's word "shameful" was omitted in the judgment. He was sentenced to suspension from any command in the army for twelve months,[57] which by many was thought too light for guilt, too heavy for censure.[58]

Lee's retreat at Monmouth, his ill-deserved letters to Washington, and his trial had sequelae in which Alexander Hamilton figured. Hamilton's friend and fellow aide Lieutenant Colonel John Laurens was particularly resentful of Lee's expressions to and about Washington. With doubtful propriety he passed on his anathemas to his father, Henry Laurens, then President of Congress, while the sentence of the court-martial was pending before that body.[59] The younger Laurens applied to Hamilton from Philadelphia, probably Dec. 5, 1778, to answer Lee's publications, especially his "Vindication" that had appeared two days before. With the help of material that could be supplied by "the ancient secretary" (R. H. Harrison), said Laurens, Hamilton could conclusively show the inconsistency and falsity of Lee's defense.[60]

John Laurens with excessive zeal assumed the role of Washington's personal champion, and challenged Lee to a duel. Hamilton acted as Laurens's second, Major Evan Edwards as Lee's, when the principals met in a wood four miles south of Philadelphia on December 23. Lee received a slight wound in the side, and further shots were discountenanced by the seconds.[61]

Hamilton was constantly at Washington's side in planning reorganization of the army and the campaign of 1779. He was with the commander in chief in Philadelphia from December 22, 1778, to February 2 of the new year,[62] and prepared the queries which were discussed with a committee of Congress of which Duane was chairman and Gouverneur Morris was a member. While different courses were ostensibly left open for decision, the bent of the agenda was toward defensive operations. This choice would be economical, permitting preparation to utilize French aid, when available, in a more ambitious plan to drive the enemy from the continent. Repeated references to the necessity for supplying rather than spending resources point to Hamilton's preoccupation, which was one with Washington's. "Will not the situation of our affairs," it was suggested in summary, "on account of the depreciated condition of our Money, deficiency of Bread, scarcity of Forage, the exhausted state of our resources in the Middle department, and the General distress of the Inhabitants render it advisable for the main body of the Army to lye quiet in some favourable position for confining . . . the enemy to their present posts (adopting at the same time the best means in our power to scourge the Indians and prevent their depredations) in order to save expences, avoid New Emissions, recruit our finances, and give a proper tone to our Money for more vigorous measures hereafter?"[63]

America, in its then depleted state, was unequal in men and money to expelling the enemy from Rhode Island and New York, or to the scarcely less costly project of a full-scale assault on the frontier posts. But total lack of military activity would injure morale at home and credit abroad.[64] In this situation Congress concluded that an expedition against the Iroquois of western Pennsylvania and New York was most eligible. It would occupy attention without draining supplies, and could be accomplished by detachments from the main force. It would quiet the distressed frontiers by pressing back the hostile tribes and destroying their towns, though the British posts from which the Indians were munitioned and led, principally Niagara, would remain.[65]

Washington (Hamilton writing the letter) asked Gates to command the expedition,[66] but he declined with characteristic ill grace: "The Man who undertakes the Indian Service, should enjoy Youth and Strength, requisites I do not possess, it Therefore Grieves me that Your Excellency should Offer me The only Command, to which I am intirely unequal."[67]

Hamilton took satisfaction in the assignment of General John Sullivan to lead the expedition against the Six Nations.[68] The two were friends all along, exchanging good offices. Shortly before, Hamilton had exerted himself, in tactful persuasions for Washington, and in letters of his own, to close a breach which Sullivan had opened with our French allies. In August 1778 a combined attack on Rhode Island[69] was thwarted when Count D'Estaing took his fleet out of Newport to intercept that of Lord Howe. Instead he met a storm which crippled his ships. When he limped back to the coast, Sullivan and Greene, already in position, begged him to remain, but he insisted on departing for Boston for repairs. "Our troops," as Hamilton wrote Governor Clinton for Washington, "were still on the Island, and of course in a very precarious situation."[70] From this Sullivan extricated his army

by a well managed retreat just ahead of heavy enemy reinforcement by Sir Henry Clinton, of which Washington by Hamilton's
hand had warned.   But another prescient caution from headquarters Sullivan did not receive in time.   "Should the expedition
fail, thro' the abandonment of the French fleet," Washington reminded in Hamilton's words, "the Officers . . . will be apt to
complain loudly.   But prudence dictates that we should put the
best face upon the matter and, to the World, attribute the removal
to Boston, to necessity" in order to prevent disgust from producing a sad rupture.

However, Sullivan's Irish ire, ill-concealed before, burst out in
general orders in a hope that "the event will prove America able
to procure that by her own arms, which her allies refuse to assist
her in obtaining."[71]   Lafayette, commanding, with Greene, under
Sullivan, was acutely distressed, and regrets and alarms flowed to
Washington.   In letters for the commander in chief Hamilton
was the instrument of quieting offended and offending.   Sullivan
was kindly admonished, "The disagreement between the army
under your command and the fleet has given me . . . singular
uneasiness.   The Continent at large is concerned in our cordiality.
. . . In our conduct towards [the French] we should remember
that they are a people old in war, very strict in military etiquette
and apt to take fire where others scarcely seem warmed.   Permit
me to recommend in the most particular manner, the cultivation of
harmony and good agreement. . . ."[72]

Hamilton counseled with his perceptive friend Elias Boudinot,
in Congress, who, also part French, understood Gallic umbrage.
The letter was semipublic, one of those which Washington could
not write.   ". . . the imprudence of General Sullivan . . . was
the summit of folly, and has made a very deep impression upon
the . . . Frenchmen in general, who naturally consider it . . .
an unjust . . . reflection on their nation.   The stigmatizing an
ally in public orders . . . was . . . a piece of absurdity without
parallel."   The French would expect that Congress reprimand
Sullivan, but this would be a delicate business because most people
shared his indignation and all applauded the skill of his escape
when left in the lurch.   Hamilton was mindful not only of a state
of facts, but of how they would be viewed by a hasty and generally warmhearted public.   He was this sort of democrat, at

least. Improving a recommendation of Lafayette,[73] Hamilton enlarged on the bravery of Major Louis Toussard, who had been introduced to Boudinot by Hamilton, and who lost an arm in his one-man attempt to capture a field piece in the repulse of the enemy on the northern part of Rhode Island. Hamilton gave Boudinot liberty to publish his praise of Toussard's splendid courage, which deserved recognition of Congress and country.[74] This would be balm on more than Toussard's wound.

Probably D'Estaing did not miss Hamilton's part in headquarters zeal for *rapprochement,* and in response to one of Washington's reassuring letters made occasion to compliment the aide whose "talents and . . . personal qualities have secured for him for ever my esteem, my confidence, my friendship."[75]

As early as the opening of the year 1779 secret preparations were being made for the punitive march into the Indian country. Particularly General Schuyler had been queried on every phase of it,[76] and had answered fully from his special knowledge. Quartermaster General Greene had been alerted for information on boats and stores,[77] and Brigadier General Lachlan McIntosh at Fort Pitt had been brought into plans (afterward abandoned) for penetration from that point.[78] It was not until five months later that Hamilton wrote Washington's instructions to Sullivan for the push against the Indians. He was to assemble his main force at Wyoming on the Susquehanna and proceed to Tioga, thence to penetrate the farther interior. General James Clinton's brigade would rendezvous at Canajoharie, and, on Sullivan's orders, would either join him on the Susquehanna by way of Otsego, or would go on up the Mohawk. (The former plan was followed.) The villages of the savages should be laid waste ("not be merely *overrun* but *destroyed*") ; leaders of past incursions should be seized. Washington, from his own experience on the frontier, gave directions for copying the Indians' mode of fighting, "to make . . . attacks . . . with as much impetuosity . . . and noise as possible, [the troops] to . . . act in as loose and dispersed a way as is consistent with . . . mutual support." Hamilton, after his delicate military diplomacy with the French, obviously enjoyed instructions for rushing on with the war whoop.[79]

Always alert to economic and political debility that sapped military strength, Hamilton for Washington just at this time rejected an ambitious plan of Gouverneur Morris for the coming campaign. "The rapid decay of our currency," he reminded, "the extinction of public spirit, the increasing rapacity of the times, the want of harmony in our councils, the declining zeal of the people, the . . . distresses of the officers of the army . . . are symptoms . . . of a most alarming nature." A patriotic statesman at this juncture could best replenish the skeleton army by endeavoring "to pacify party differences, to give fresh vigor to the springs of government, to inspire the people with confidence, and above all, to restore the credit of our currency."[80]

Accumulated distresses were topped for the commander in chief by the practical refusal of the officers of the 1st New Jersey Regiment to march with Sullivan's expedition against the Indians as ordered. Maxwell gave Washington the memorial of the officers notifying the state legislature that unless they and their troops were paid within three days they must be considered as out of the service, though they would allow a reasonable time for appointment of other officers. Here was gross insubordination if not, under the conditions, mutiny. Washington's reply, May 7, 1779, composed by Hamilton, used earnest remonstrance and appeal to the officers' sense of duty rather than threat or peremptory reference to a collective court-martial. For as he wrote, by the same hand, four days later to the President of Congress, his rebuke of "highly blameable" conduct had to be "mild, when our situation is considered. The causes of discontent are too great and too general and the ties that bind the officers to the service too feeble to admit of rigor." Three hundred officers had recently resigned. Jay passed on to Hamilton the regret of the usually zealous John Lamb should he feel obliged to quit the service at that late day, "with a shattered constitution, and mutilated carcase, [and] leave others to enjoy the fruits of my exertions. . . ."[81]

Hamilton's politic wording to the recalcitrant officers lamented the "hasty and imprudent step, which, on . . . cool consideration they will themselves condemn. I [Washington] am very sensible of the inconveniences under which the officers . . . labor; and . . . my endeavors to procure relief are incessant." The means of government were straitened; "the situation of our money is no small embarrassment, for which . . . remedies . . . cannot be the work of a moment. . . . The patience and perseverance of the army have . . . inspired me with an unlimited confidence in their virtue, which has consoled me amidst every perplexity and reverse of fortune. . . ." A change of conduct now would argue a change of principles, "a forgetfulness as well of what we owe to ourselves as to our country. Did I suppose . . . this could be the case even in a single regiment . . . , I should be mortified . . . beyond expression." Would they wound his own honor, embarked with that of the army at large? Hamilton's personal attachment to New Jersey and close friendship with Governor Livingston, Boudinot, Barber and more, prompted combining appreciation with appeal: "The Jersey officers have not been outdone by any others in the qualities either of citizens or soldiers; and I am confident no part of them would . . . intend anything that would be a stain to their former reputation. The gentlemen . . . have only *reasoned wrong about the means of obtaining a good end;* and on Consideration . . . will renounce what must appear improper . . . when under marching orders, for an important service. . . ."[82]

To this persuasion the officers responded that they meant to obey commands, but only until substitutes were named.[83] Washington (Hamilton and his fellow aide Meade concluding the correspondence) called this a persistence in bad principles. However, he could offer no more arguments, and, so long as they did their duty, he would leave them to their own repentance.[84]

Aside from the ambush of a scouting party, the only engagement of Sullivan's campaign was the defeat of the British and Indians at Newtown (near present Elmira, New York) on August 28, 1779. The American commander's letter two days later furnished Hamilton facts to which he added "a few of the usual embellishments of a newspaper paragraph" in "Mr. Lowdon's paper."[85] A treacherous attack on Niagara by the Indians as a peace offering to the Americans had been suggested in Sullivan's instructions, but half-heartedly, and it was not attempted. Hamilton had a hand in a very different military project at this time.

He and John Laurens were constantly eager to promote each other's plans and prospects. These were not so much personal (though there was abundant inclination for that), as they were intended in the public interest, for, by the untimely death of Laurens, their friendship was embraced within the war years. A few months after Hamilton seconded Laurens in the duel with General Charles Lee, he supported his colleague in another sort of encounter, with the governor and legislature of South Carolina. Many were ready to say that this object, the arming of Negro slaves to recruit the scanty forces for liberation of the state, was as quixotic as the former. Necessity seemed to compel the expedient, but, more than that, the effort of the two complimented their lack of race prejudice. Remember that each grew up in a slave society, where the combination of scorn and fear of the blacks was all but universal. Generations later Colonel Robert Gould Shaw, of Massachusetts, had merit in leading Negro troops, but his justification, to himself and to his public, was easier than in the case of the gallant young South Carolinian.

John Laurens's education abroad (in Geneva and London) doubtless gave him a detachment which assisted his hatred of slavery. He despised the selfish arguments with which the institution was supported by planters with whom he had talked, in South Carolina and the West Indies. ". . . we have sunk the African[s] and their descendants below the standard of humanity," he wrote to his father, "and almost render'd them incapable of that blessing which equal Heaven bestow'd upon us all." However, his idealism was not so glowing but that he recognized slaves must be brought to freedom by "shades and degrees."[86] Enrollment in the Revolutionary Army, with the promise of liberty to those who survived the service, offered such a step toward emancipation.[87] This proposal, after he joined Washington's staff, he vehemently urged on his father, Henry Laurens, not only as President of Congress but as an individual slaveholder. The young man would take his patrimony in Negroes contributed to a black battalion in defense of South Carolina. The elder Laurens was anxious for manumission in principle,[88] but pointed out practical obstacles to his son's scheme. He feared that, if precipitately put to the test, the proposal might "soil [his] excellent character with a charge of . . . Caprice," and he "would not have heard the last jeer till the end of [his] life."[89]

In response to such pleas John Laurens renounced "this excentric Scheme,"[90] but only temporarily. The critical danger of South Carolina[91] drew him homeward on a renewal of his project, stopping at Philadelphia in his way. Hamilton gave him a letter to John Jay, the President of Congress, intended to secure the formal sanction of that body and the promise to take two, three, or four battalions of slaves, if enlisted, into Continental pay.[92] He did not know how invasion of South Carolina could be repelled (Savannah[93] and Augusta had both fallen) without such recruits. Negroes would make excellent soldiers with the intelligent management Laurens was prepared to give. ". . . I have frequently heard it objected to the scheme of embodying negroes," Hamilton observed, "that they are too stupid to make soldiers. This is so far from . . . a valid objection, that I think their want of cultivation (for their natural faculties are as good as ours), joined to [their] habit of subordination . . . , will enable them sooner to become soldiers than our white inhabitants. Let officers be men of sense and sentiment; and the nearer the soldiers approach to machines, perhaps the better."

Habitual contempt for Negroes made men "fancy many things that are founded neither in reason nor experience," and the incentive to clutch at valuable property "will furnish a thousand arguments to show the . . . pernicious tendency" of a project sacrificing self-interest. It was designed to require owners to contribute slaves in proportion to the numbers they possessed. The enemy would arm them if the Americans did not do so, of course giving them "their freedom with their swords. This will secure their fidelity, animate their courage, and . . . have a good influence upon those who remain, by opening a door to their emancipation. . . . the dictates of humanity, and true policy, equally interest me in favor of this unfortunate class of men."[94]

In spite of arduous and repeated efforts with the legislature, of which he was a member, John Laurens met with no success in South Carolina.[95]

Congress formed a plan, supposed to be kept secret, for procuring flour to supply the French fleet on arrival. Samuel Chase, a Maryland delegate, was identified as having violated the confidence in a disclosure to commercial confederates who intended to profit by forestalling the article, raising the price, and jeopardizing the public safety. This discreditable episode drew from Hamilton three letters of remonstrance, signed "Publius," in Holt's *New York Journal* in October-November 1778.[96] The weakness of government and currency depreciation were threats enough, without a

member of Congress abusing his privileged position for mean
advantage.   However, the wrathful indignation that led Hamilton
to hold the faithless legislator up to censure would have been better
expressed in less reiterated vituperation, and over his own name.
As rarely with him, his facility lapsed into an extravagance of language until the indictment—merited in itself—lost meaning.
Thus: "Were I inclined to make a satire upon the species I would
attempt a faithful description of your heart.   It is hard to conceive
. . . one of more finished depravity."   However, Washington,
too, excoriated "those murderers of our cause (the monopolizers
. . .)," the "most atrocious" of whom he wished "was hung . . .
upon a gallows five times as high" as Haman's.   A friend of Chase
tried in vain to persuade James McHenry to give up the identity
of "Publius."   Hamilton replied that his attack was dictated by
concern for the public good, and that he still believed Chase guilty,
in spite of formal exculpation.   However, if he revised this opinion,
he would "make . . . the most explicit . . . retribution."   Hamilton was uncandid in his anonymous abusive diatribe, even if Chase
was at fault.[97]

Other parts of these letters, amounting to his definition of the
good legislator, were sober and significant of sentiments he held
throughout his career.   They repel, so far as solemn avowal of his
principles can do it, loose charges that later he condoned conduct
of Duer, called reprehensible, and made his own control of the
Treasury benefit the speculations of his brother-in-law, Church.
A member of Congress "is to be regarded not only as a legislator,
but as a founder of an empire.   A man of virtue and ability,
dignified with so precious a trust, would rejoice that fortune . . .
placed him in circumstances, so favorable for promoting human
happiness. . . . To form useful alliances abroad—to establish a
wise government at home—to improve the internal resources and
finances of the nation—would be the generous objects of his care.
He would not allow his attention to be diverted from these to
intrigue for personal connections to confirm his own influence; nor
would he be able to . . . confound in the same person the representative of the commonwealth and the little member of a trading
company.   Anxious for the permanent power and prosperity of the
state, he would labor to perpetuate the union and harmony of the

several parts. He would not . . . court a temporary importance by patronizing the narrow views of local interest. . . ."[98]

Hamilton relied upon representative democracy, but was alive to the storms and lulls of popular sentiment which at times questioned the wisdom of the people in governing themselves. Overexcitement was apt to be followed by inattention. This invited the arts of the demagogue, who got into office through confusion, and through inertia was suffered to remain. "There are seasons in every country," he remarked, "when noise and impudence pass current for worth; and in popular commotions especially, the clamors of interested and factious men are often mistaken for patriotism." When "a temporary caprice of the people leads them to make choice of men whom they neither love nor respect . . . they afterward, from an indolent and mechanical habit natural to the human mind, continue their confidence and support merely because they had once conferred them."[99]

Always tender of his honor, immediately tracing and demanding retraction of any report of false utterance or conduct of his, Hamilton as a young man was bumptious. Such resentments, with courting of "the code," ran highest in military circles; as someone said, the epaulette readily became a chip. Hamilton in his zeal was self-important, "found quarrel in a straw." Acting as intermediary for others, such as John Laurens in the latter's duel with Charles Lee (above), he preserved better sense of proportion and in instances of which we know counseled explanation and peace.[100] As he grew older he was as firm but more considered in claiming satisfaction, and must have passed over many political imputations as unworthy of cavil.

In the career of a man who met death in a duel, any incident threatening violent personal encounter is to be noted. Hamilton's earliest exchange of this sort of which we have record was with a clergyman, Dr. William Gordon (1728–1807). He was a gossipy Britisher, companion of the critics of Washington, with ear cocked for whatever could enter the history of the Revolution he was to publish. Hamilton's passage with Dr. Gordon betrayed touchiness but also, most likely, the physical fag that helped produce it. This oversensitivity showed itself, a year later, in his sudden resentment of a monitory word from Washington. His critical and varied work for the commander in chief, plus assignments that were self-imposed, would have strained a stronger frame.[101]

Though Hamilton numbered the letters in the usual style of those portentous progressions, a good part of the Gordon correspondence is missing.[102]   The whole involved Massachusetts men, the offenders among them identified by Hamilton with the cabal against the commander in chief.   It appears that Colonel John Brooks mentioned to Hamilton a report that in a coffeehouse in Philadelphia (it would have been about midwinter 1778–1779, when visiting Congress with the commander in chief), Hamilton "declared . . . that it was high time for the people to rise, join General Washington, and turn Congress out of doors."   Brooks said F. W. Dana was his informant.[103]   Hamilton queried Dana on this in a letter delivered by Colonel David Henley, of Boston, who, as Hamilton's friend, was to "press for a speedy answer."[104]   Dana answered that he did not "recollect or imagine that he threw out the observation," and that Brooks must have mistaken him for another in the company.   Thereat Hamilton, "anxious to have this affair developed . . . in a clear and unequivocal manner," begged Brooks to review his memory.   Brooks still pinned it on Dana, and Dana "gave up" Dr. Gordon, of Jamaica Plain.[105]

Again using Henley's good offices, Hamilton forthwith taxed Gordon with passing "the calumny" to Dana and demanded his authority in "an immediate, direct, and explicit answer; sensible that the least hesitation or reserve may give room for conjectures which it can be neither your wish nor mine to excite."[106]   Dr. Gordon said he would disclose his author if Hamilton would pledge his honor "neither to give nor accept a challenge . . . nor to engage in any encounter that may produce a duel."   Hamilton "insisted on the author, on the principle of unconditional submission."[107]   Gordon returned that he must consult with his informer, evidently to discover whether he would give an apology or be game for a duel.   This took nearly two months, when Gordon's report proved to Hamilton, what he suspected from the first, that the "old Jesuit" had been acting a "rediculous farce," and was himself the inventor of the charge.   "Such I consider . . . and . . . shall represent you . . . and the notorious byass of your disposition to duplicity and slander will give it sanction with all who are acquainted with you. . . . I only lament that respect to myself

obliges me to confine the expression of my contempt to words."
Gordon's threat of an investigation by Congress of Hamilton's
conduct—welcome if Congress wished—was a further evasion.
Hamilton was ending the business.[108]

The following spring Dr. Gordon complained of Hamilton to
Washington, and Hamilton, with regret that the commander in
chief should be troubled with the affair, explained that so far
from complying with Gordon's conditions to escape inquiry, he
was afraid that Gordon would not go through with it. This was
the case, and Hamilton was left to "speak of him in those terms
which a sense of injury and a conviction of his unworthiness
dictate."[109]

Affairs of State
and Morristown Romance

THE capture of Stony Point on the Hudson the night of July 15–16, 1779, by an intrepid detachment under General Wayne was the kind of exploit after which Hamilton hankered. While he was as yet confined to headquarters assistance, at New Windsor a few miles up the river, in this capacity he helped the commander in chief form the stealthy plans for "Mad Anthony's" startling coup. In the preceding November Hamilton had written Washington's orders to McDougall to take command of all posts from Poughkeepsie downward, and directing that an enclosed redoubt, with guardhouse, be constructed at Stony Point on the west side of King's Ferry and a similar work at Verplanck's on the east.[1] When the enemy took and strengthened these, laborious fortification in the Highlands was negatived if not imperiled.

Hamilton wrote for Washington to Schuyler that the companion forts in British hands "will interrupt our easiest communication between the Eastern and Southern states, open a new . . . door to distress . . . the country." We had the mortification to be spectators of what we were powerless to counteract.[2] But few projects of daring and dispatch were beyond the capacity of Washington and Wayne working together. Washington's orders to Wayne for command of the light infantry, at Fort Montgomery (Hamilton the writer), included a proposal that bore fruit: "If . . . you see a favourable opportunity for . . . an advantageous

[182]

stroke, you have my permission for improving it. . . ."[3] In a confidential letter (also by Hamilton), Washington selected Wayne's objective. "The importance of . . . Verplanks and Stoney points to the enemy is too obvious to need explanation. We ought if possible to dispossess them. I recommend it to your particular attention, . . . to gain as exact a knowledge as you can of the number of the garrisons, . . . the nature of the ground . . . and the precautions . . . which the enemy employ for their security. It is a matter I have much at heart to make some attempt on these Posts. . . ."[4]

Promptly Tryon's Tories ravaged New Haven, Fairfield, and Norwalk. This further provoked the "advantageous stroke." Hamilton again took pen, for Washington, to Wayne: "While the enemy was making excursions to distress the country, it has a very disagreeable aspect to remain in a state of inactivity on our part. The reputation of the army . . . exact[s] some attempt from it. The importance of Stoney Point to the enemy makes it infinitely desirable that should be the object." He gave a deserter's report of an approach on the south flank of the works. The storming should be "by . . . surprize in the night."[5]

The aide acknowledged Wayne's swift report on means of penetrating the Stony Point defenses. Washington would join him for a reconnoiter "very early in the morning" of July 6.[6] In the following week every precaution was taken for secrecy of the assault.[7] This was evidently imminent when Hamilton as aide ordered Major Lee, and in his absence Captain McLane, "to have patrols kept from this till morning" seven or eight miles along the shore to guard against a party of the enemy above Tarrytown. "This may be a critical night and demands the greatest vigilance."[8] Beyond this, the story of the successful storm—bayonets against bullets and cannon fire—belongs to Wayne, Hamilton's friend Fleury who struck the British flag, and their companions. Hamilton was at the captured fort two days later, ordering McLane, in the general's name, to collect wagons to remove the wounded, cannon, and stores.[9] For Washington, he had the pleasure of commending Fleury to Congress and to the French envoy, M. Gérard.[10]

Hamilton had prepared the general's orders for an attack on Verplanck's Point, but this plan miscarried.[11]

Headquarters at Morristown knew no interval of exhilaration mingled with anxiety equal to that in the spring of 1780 following the return of Lafayette from France. Washington sent forward his welcome "with all the joy that the sincerest friendship could dictate," informed of precautions for the marquis' safe journey, and added the homely assurance that "a bed is prepared for you."[12] Lafayette was bringing news of fighting forces for America, an army of 6,000 under Rochambeau and a fleet commanded by Destouches. Moral support, then money and matériel had been grateful precursors; now were to come the longed-for companions in arms.

No sooner had he made acknowledgment to the French minister, Luzerne,[13] and bespoken the thankful greeting of Congress when Lafayette should present himself there,[14] than Washington set about rousing this country to practical response by doing its full military part. Deference to civil authority, perhaps too patient in the past, was not laid aside, but means were taken to animate and guide legislative action. Hamilton's help to the commander in chief was felt in this delicate and exigent task.

Efforts to ready America for cooperation with the French reinforcements began with priming trusted members of Congress. Almost identical promptings went to Joseph Jones, of Virginia, and to James Duane, of New York.[15] The prospect of men and ships from France contrasted with our distracted finances and empty magazines; "a plan must be concerted to bring out the resources of the Country with vigor and decision. . . ." This demanded that Congress vest full powers in a small committee posted near headquarters to "act with dispatch and energy" impossible in a deliberative body at a distance. "The conjuncture is one of the most critical . . . we have seen. . . . We shall probably fix the independence of America if we succeed," but failure, from hesitancy and fumbling, would doom our resistance. General Schuyler was Washington's first choice for this plenary committee.[16] These were plain hints for his correspondent's exertions in Congress.

Hamilton reinforced the general's proposal with a characteristic plea of his own to his friend Duane. "For God's sake, my dear sir, engage Congress to adopt it. . . . We have not a moment to lose." The urgency of headquarters preparations spoke in his phrases. Within a month men must be collected, magazines formed, "and . . . a thousand things of as much difficulty as importance" must be accomplished in order to profit by French assistance. He conveyed what Washington himself could not say —that the committee of Congress at camp must have authority to hand over power, for quick decisions, to the commander in chief. "The fate of America," he entreated, "is perhaps suspended on the issue; if we are found unprepared, it must disgrace us . . . , defeating the good intentions of our allies, and losing the happiest opportunity we ever have had to save ourselves."[17]

The commander in chief broadcast the news of expected French reinforcements to Generals Heath and Lincoln, and to Governors Bowdoin, Jefferson, Clinton, and Rutledge. The last should get the information to the besieging enemy, as if by accident, if this would prevent the fall of Charleston.[18]

Meanwhile Hamilton had evidently been set to collecting all knowledge of the vulnerable situation of the British at New York. He wrote Washington's instructions to Lafayette, to be passed to the French commanders on their arrival, hopefully in a few weeks. New York should be the object of concentrated attack if Sir Henry Clinton had not sailed back from the southward with three ships of the line and 7,000 land troops.[19] (Unknown at the time, this happened, for Charleston had fallen four days before, May 12.)

Not only Congress, but the states must be spurred to immediate efforts. The legislature of New York was in danger of adjourning before calls of Congress for men and supplies could be received. Hamilton wrote for Washington, begging Governor Clinton to hold the Assembly together, a matter "of infinite importance." The governor should not disclose that Washington was anticipating action by Congress.[20]

As days wore on, expectation of reinforcements from France was mocked by the torpid state of American preparations for the joint campaign. May at Morristown was clouded by wretched apprehensions, recruitment dragging, and little food and no pay for the troops already under arms. With "infinite pain" Washington told Governor Trumbull of Connecticut that "we are reduced to . . . extremity for want of meat. On several days of late the Troops have been entirely destitute of any," and before that had been "at a half, a quarter, and Eighth allowance. . . ." But

human nature could not endure further. The proof was that
only the night before two regiments of the Connecticut line "got
under Arms" and threatened to go home for the want of meat
and money. Expostulations of their officers barely sent them back
into their huts. A repetition of the rebellion, with worse results,
would happen unless relief came.[21] Approving the appeal to the
states by the committee of Congress, the commander in chief
ruefully confessed that French succor was like to become our ruin,
for attempts to equip promised to be too little for success, too
much to inspire further struggle. "The Country exhausted; The
people dispirited; the . . . reputation of these States in Europe
sunk; Our friends chagrined and discouraged; our Enemies
deriving new credit; new confidence, new resources." Only the
utmost effort could meet the emergency.[22]

This was the case when Hamilton unburdened Washington's
thoughts to President Joseph Reed of Pennsylvania. Here was no
complaint nor fevered exhortation, but solemn reflection on the
plight of America. The distress, as Bryant said of the ebbing tide,
was "too deep for sound or foam." False hope was dismissed for
noble candor. However dismaying, the simple truth was told.
The melancholy fact went beyond the perils of the moment.
Contrasted with the portentous future, these miseries seemed
minor, almost blessed anodynes to profounder sorrows. Putting
his name to Hamilton's words, Washington came his closest to
despair. Until now, rescue so near at hand, yet so beyond the
country's grasp, had made the irony. But this became an incident in the tragedy, unless, unless . . .

It was Washington's letter, a report of his foreboding. Still,
first and last it was Hamilton's, remarkable not only for perfect
sympathy with his commander, but surpassing this with understanding of counterpoised forces. This was the work of the first-
rate political economist. Young as he was, and brief though the
treatment, Hamilton never gave better proof of his insight into the
strength and weakness of nations.[23]

Estimate is useless without contents, yet mere abstract, with
selective quotation, is an abuse of what should be read in entirety.
Reed was thanked for Pennsylvania's aid in sending provisions.
However, he could not know, without being on the spot, the pass

to which the army had come. "All our . . . operations are at
a stand and unless a system very different . . . be immediately
adopted throughout the states our affairs must soon become desperate beyond the possibility of recovery. . . . Indeed I have
almost ceased to hope. The country . . . is in such a state of
insensibility . . . to its interests, that I dare not flatter myself
with any change for the better." He doubted whether the plea of
Congress to the states would take effect, "and if it does not I shall
consider our lethargy as incurable" and that "motives of honor [,]
public good and even self preservation have lost their influence
upon our minds." This was the most decisive moment America
had seen.

The poor prospect of naval superiority over the enemy took him
into a comparison of the resources of Great Britain, France, and
Spain. Those of the first were greatest and most at command.
"Though the government [of England] is deeply in debt . . . ,
the nation is rich and their riches afford a fund which will not be
easily exhausted." Nor could the destruction of public credit,
as the price of victory, discomfort the crown. On the contrary,
military success would confer political power to make bankruptcy
itself the welcome means "to climb to absolute authority" and "to
triumph . . . over the constitution."[24]

By contrast, the superior fiscal position of France was illusory.
War taxes would drain the shallow well of national wealth and
invite ruin. Spain he quickly dismissed. Revenue in precious
metals was less than supposed, but "Commerce and industry are
the best mines of a nation; both are wanting to her" and her
temper was "too sluggish to admit of great exertions." Her heart
was not in the war.

Thus the circumstances of America and her allies cried for
peace. Unless it was achieved in the coming campaign, the last
increment of help from France would be worse than wasted, for
America would sink under the very attempt to use it. Only the
exertions of Pennsylvania could save us. While other states were
depleted, she was "full of flour. . . ." Forgetting internal political dissension, she must yield it. "The matter is reduced to a
point. Either Pennsylvania must give us all the aid we ask of her,
or we can undertake nothing." Would the legislature vest the

executive with plenipotentiary powers? "This is not a time for
. . . ceremony. The crisis . . . is extraordinary and extraordinary expedients are necessary."[25]

Fortunately, Pennsylvania responded promptly and with a will.[26]

By the end of August 1780 the demand for immediate cooperation with our ally in an attack on New York had been removed
by British blockade of the second division of the French fleet at
Brest.[27] While America's military preparations must still be
pressed, the unforeseen breathing space turned thoughts to more
than men and munitions. A series of inconclusive conferences
between the states, stretching from 1776, had canvassed means to
bolster currency and credit and strengthen political union. The
latest of these, held that month, though enlisting only Massachusetts, Connecticut, and New Hampshire, reflected the mounting
alarm in ringing resolutions. The sum of them was that Congress
be vested "with powers competent for the government and direction of all those common and national affairs which do not, nor
can come within the jurisdiction of the particular states. . . ."[28]

Washington was quick to encourage this prospect of underlying
remedy. Hamilton, with feeling concurrence, wrote for him to
President [Governor] James Bowdoin that the recommendations
"if . . . carried into execution will be the most likely means . . .
to rescue our affairs from the . . . dreadful embarrassments
under which they labor. . . ."[29] But this solution, if limited by
adherence to the Articles of Confederation, must be insufficient.
Promptly, in letters of his own to influential figures, Hamilton
urged a general convention to frame an organic union, the central
government to have independent authority and a machinery of
efficient administration.

We have seen that in letters from headquarters to the committee
of correspondence of the New York Convention, Hamilton concerned himself with more than a report on military matters, and
volunteered his opinion of the new constitution then offered for
the state. Eagerness to make constructive criticism of what
others had done was multiplied in his own proposals for governmental and economic renovation which he brought to the notice
of Duane and Robert Morris in long letters in 1780 and 1781.
These similarly were written from camp, in addition to multiform
other duties, and in the information they marshaled and the

analysis they applied to primary issues of the national welfare, were *tours de force.* Taught by demonstration at headquarters of the needs of the country, his recommendations lost the tentative, speculative quality of his comments on the New York constitution, and took on decision and vehemence. He must have been influenced by the conventions that had been held, putting forward means of invigorating the economy and the general government. But Hamilton's comprehensive remedies went beyond the last and most positive resolves, of the meeting in Boston, August 1780.[30] These letters, private though they were, may be called, from their subject matter and method, his first state papers. They were rehearsals for the call from the Annapolis convention, his arguments in the Philadelphia constitutional gathering, the expositions in *The Federalist,* his pleas at Poughkeepsie for ratification by New York, and his first reports as Secretary of the Treasury. Considering the adverse circumstances under which these volunteered letters were prepared, and the early date of their production, they are little inferior to his later famous documents.

These little essays, the first of some 6,500 words and the second twice as long, illustrate several features of Hamilton's work. First, his conclusions were a growth, expressed, tested in the light of further developments, corrected, enlarged, and confirmed over a period of years. Here, leaving aside earlier intimations, was a clear decade, from 1780–1781 to 1790–1791, in which his probing and proposals were assuming finished form. What he came out with, at any stage, was surprising in one of his years, but it is to be remembered that he went to the Treasury with his diagnosis and remedy already shaped. Second, his prompting was practical, to cope with a confronting situation of which he had intimate, troublesome experience. Third, he surveyed his problem with the assistance of the best applicable writings he could come by, ranging over the history of many countries in ages from the ancient to the contemporary. Thus he escaped, on the one hand, rueful repetition, and on the other hand, unguarded espousal. His education in books had not been for nothing. Fourth, these letters show that his gifts, as distinguished from his acquirements, manifested themselves early. Some of the most memorable of his phrases, summing up a deal of observation and thought, occur in these pages, to be ramified, but not surpassed, to his latest day.

First we must notice what is evidently the earliest in this group of papers. It is found only in draft, unaddressed and undated, with two portions missing.[31] It was undoubtedly intended for Robert Morris as the fittest man to be named by Congress Minister of Finance. Hamilton afterward explicitly urged Morris's appointment and acceptance. The date of composition is more in question. Hamilton explained at the outset that he preferred not to explore disorders in the currency in the newspapers—"the discussion itself increases the evil"[32]—but chose to submit his proposals "to a member of that body, in whose power alone it is [surely Congress] . . . to extricate us from our embarrassments." Morris completed his allowed term in the old Congress in November 1778. But we are tempted to put the letter earlier, for Hamilton, not wishing to be identified (as aide of Washington?) directed that an answer "to James Montague, Esquire, lodged in the post-office at Morristown," would receive immediate attention. If Morris was in Congress and Hamilton was at Morristown, the letter must be prior to May 1777, when the army ended the first encampment at that place. This period is further favored because Hamilton referred to his "reading on . . . commerce and finance" as though recent. We know of this reading, presumably early in 1777, and the letter reflects Postlethwayt and European continental experience which we find in his notes near that time.

On the other hand, allusion is made to measures to procure a foreign loan, and to other developments as late as 1779,[33] when Hamilton was again at Morristown, though Robert Morris had then left Congress. It may be that parts of the letter were written at earlier and later periods, spring of 1777 and winter of 1779–1780.[34] It may never have been completed. Probably it was not sent, for no fair copy has turned up in Morris's papers or elsewhere,[35] no acknowledgment is found, and Hamilton would not have repeated numerous observations in his subsequent letter to Morris in April 1781. In any event, this production has an inconclusive, even confused, character which could not have satisfied the writer.

Hamilton offered Morris a plan for rescuing the currency and public revenue; it was "the product of some reading on the subjects of commerce and finance, and of occasional reflections on our particular situation. . . ."[36] In his (sent) letter to Morris, more than a year later, he explained he was obliged "to depend on memory for important facts, for want of the authorities from which they are drawn." As will appear from the detail of his presentation then, in facts and figures, he must have been able to refresh his recollection from notes. His reading, especially as shown in his second letter to Morris, is harder to explain than his reflections. With all his perception of what would serve America, he did have models, the experience of numerous countries to guide him.[37]

The principal concern was with inflation. The original rise in prices and wages (or loss of value in the circulating medium) was due to scarcity, the inadequacy of the country's resources to the sudden war demands. This would have happened even had the currency been gold. Later, but only later, "the badness of the money" contributed to the depreciation. We formerly had in circulation about $30,000,000, which was barely sufficient for normal requirements. Not enough of this sum could be drawn to government, in taxes and domestic loans, to meet war expenditures, without depriving commerce. The richest countries of Europe were always obliged to have recourse to foreign loans, and we could not avoid this expedient.[38]

A foreign loan at an earlier stage would have been salutary in preventing excessive paper emissions, but it was now imperative. The proceeds of the loan should not be used in an effort to extinguish the superfluous paper: speculators would push up the price of the paper in specie and sterling bills, but the prices of commodities would not fall correspondingly. Prejudice against the money in circulation was inflated more than the circulation itself. Statesmen must reckon on the slow correction of this want of popular confidence. It would be preferable to convert the loan into merchandise and import it on public account, but, for reasons which he gave, neither would this answer.[39]

"The only plan that can preserve the currency," he urged, "is one that will make it the *immediate* interest of the moneyed men to co-operate with government in its support." John Law had this capital notion in his Mississippi scheme, but his good plan was defeated by excesses.[40] To restore paper credit and furnish a permanent fund for the needs of government, Congress should establish the Bank of the United States. The popular subscription, reduced to specie value, was to be $10,000,000, and the government should throw in its foreign loan of £2,000,000. Bank notes were to be offered for the depreciated paper at the rate of one to sixty; the charter was to run for ten years. The Board of Trade (patterned on the Royal Council of Commerce, which he found in Postlethwayt) should be the government's representative in managing the Bank, but for executive departments proper he demanded single heads. He trusted that Congress would choose Morris as Minister of Finance.[41]

The second of this series was the letter to James Duane, a New York member of Congress, dated Liberty Pole (now Englewood), New Jersey, September 3, 1780.[42] Hamilton knew, or knew of, Duane as influential in the early struggle for independence in the state, later was his familiar, and frequently asked his help in presenting proposals to Congress.[43]

In the interval of nearly a year since drafting remedies, presumed to have been intended for Robert Morris, but not sent, Hamilton had made progress in his diagnosis of the country's crisis. His emphasis had shifted from monetary to political reform. The secret of rescue lay in bringing governmental authority to a focus. The old Continental currency had been practically repudiated in March of that year, but now mechanical instruments, even a national bank, became with him secondary.

"The fundamental defect," he began to Duane, "is a want of power in Congress." The central authority was diffident and impecunious; the states were grasping and made the army dependent on them individually.[44] Congress had descended from its original acts of the highest sovereignty, and should have continued to consider itself charged "to preserve the republic from harm." Here was Hamilton's doctrine of "discretionary powers, limited only by the object for which they were given; in the present case the independence and freedom of America."[45] This was to reappear regularly in his constitutional opinions—really in his conception of effective government—most notably in his validation of the Bank of the United States, and was to be adopted by Chief Justice John Marshall as the leitmotif of his formative decisions. It was Hamilton's application of the best sanctioned principle that "the letter killeth, but the spirit giveth life."[46]

The Confederation then pending was "neither fit for war nor

peace," and required to be altered. The army, "an essential cement of the union," ought to look up wholly to Congress, instead of being partitioned by mandates of the states. This would not be dangerous to liberty, for, said Hamilton, the risk was that the federal government would be weak, not that it would usurp the rights of the people. The likelihood was that the states would prevent "the pursuit of a common interest."[47] Worse, as the states increased in strength, "we shall have all the . . . opportunity we can wish, to cut each other's throats." Prompted by evidences before him, this was a forecast, eighty years in advance, of the Civil War. Only the framing of a union competent to compel "the obedience of the respective members" could prevent the peril he saw. This lights up his contention, in the Philadelphia convention seven years later, for a constitution conferring more coercive powers on the central government. If his plan involved some political violence, that we adopted obliged us to pay a high price in military violence for eventual unity.

Congress must have independent, permanent, and certain revenues. Designed for deliberation and debate, it must not attempt to play the executive; administrative boards were little better; the great departments must be placed in the hands of single able, responsible men. By this last means we might "blend the advantages of a monarchy and republic in our constitution."[48]

He spoke by the book, and in full concurrence with Washington,[49] in declaring that the army, fluctuating and ill provided by state purchases, was "a mob . . . ripening for a dissolution."

Characteristically, he went on from recrimination to remedy. Resumption of imputed powers which Congress had so long forfeited was probably not feasible. He swept aside the tentative Articles of Confederation and called for a constitutional convention at the earliest moment, the delegates to be explicitly empowered "to conclude finally upon . . . a solid coercive union." He ticked off the areas of national authority (since familiar to us), including the option of establishing banks. He proposed the appropriate administrative departments, with a capable individual at the head of each, for example, General Schuyler for War, McDougall for Marine, Robert Morris (who "could, by his own personal influence, give great weight to the measures he should adopt") for Finance.[50] The departments he took from the French model; an army recruited for the war, and paid directly by Congress, from successful Swedish experience. He believed a standing army, attached to Congress, "essential to the American Union."[51]

He turned from governmental structure to economic recruitment. Four conjoint means were necessary: "a foreign loan; heavy pecuniary taxes; a tax in kind; a bank founded on public and private credit." The endeavors of Congress for a loan would be clinched by telling France that without it we must make terms with Great Britain. France was too far committed not to respond, and the loan would further attach France to us.[52] Heavy taxes—especially a tax in kind, since the circulating medium was insufficient to represent the real wealth of the country—would be borne the more readily because of our democratic government. "It has been a constant remark that free countries have ever paid the heaviest taxes."

A bank with joint public-private resources ought by all means to be tried. This was the only way to support a national paper credit; the promise of profits to moneyed men who were stockholders would be an inducement where patriotism alone must fail. He cited the Bank of England and the banks of Venice and Amsterdam. Beginning on a modest scale, the bank would grow, serving government by contracting to furnish supplies, benefiting commerce by issue of a note circulation. The fund recently subscribed in Philadelphia for purchasing rations for the troops was no bank, for the directors spent their stock instead of floating their notes, but the participants in that scheme offered a nucleus of private interest in the institution he outlined. It should be remarked here, in view of hostile criticism of the Bank of the United States later, that Hamilton in his earliest proposals, as afterward, placed public objects first, the private participation being a means to this end.[53]

This review of sorrows and succors closed with remarks deserving recollection because Hamilton later reverted to them. He said, almost in so many words, that wealth and prosperity are the results of good government; men are controlled by opinion, and opinion should be marshaled "by sensible and popular writings" —*vide* the *Federalist* papers—to accept a new constitution.[54]

Duane at the time did not agree fully with Hamilton's remedies, and feared that those which were proper were impracticable of application. But Hamilton was firmly optimistic. "Convinced, as I am," he replied, "of the absolute insufficiency of our present system to our safety, if I do not despair of the republic, it is more the effect of constitution than of judgment."[55]

When he wrote his longer letter to Morris, April 30, 1781,[56] Hamilton had been for two months out of General Washington's military family, was with his wife at De Peyster's Point on the Hudson, and was asking the commander in chief for a field command.[57] He made no allusion to a former letter. Morris had been named Superintendent of Finance (February 20, 1781), and Hamilton hoped that Congress would agree to the reasonable conditions Morris attached to acceptance. Morris, he believed, could establish American independence, for "'T is by introducing order into our finances—by restoring public credit—not by gaining battles, that we are finally to gain our object. 'T is by putting ourselves in a condition to continue the war—not by temporary, violent, and unnatural efforts to bring it to a decisive issue, that we shall, in reality, bring it to a speedy and successful one."[58]

Assuming that the real wealth of a nation, its commodities and labor, was represented by its circulating cash, he found that governments generally were able to obtain about a fourth of this.[59] America should yield between six and seven millions of dollars in public revenue. Two and a half millions were necessary for the civil establishments, national and state, and eight millions for the war. This left a deficiency of between four and four and a half millions to be supplied by credit, foreign or domestic, or both. He canvassed the prospect and concluded that no source of loans, governmental or private, in the then disordered state of our finances, was promising.[60]

The only expedient was what he had urged before, a scheme that would invite credit by uniting private with public advantage —in other words, a national bank. This would support government, facilitate commerce, and thus be an engine of prosperity,[61] as had been demonstrated abroad, especially in the Bank of England. He scouted the notion, then advocated by some, that we should abolish all paper credit and depend on specie. Awkward and wasteful barter would be the result. The health of a commercial state "depends on a due quantity and regular circulation

of cash, as much as the health of an animal body depends upon the
. . . circulation of the blood." Good paper money must not be
condemned with bad.[62] Ours had depreciated "because it had no
funds for its support, and was not upheld by private credit."
Both of these essential features could be supplied in the plan of a
bank he described.[63]

The stock, he now thought, ought to be three millions of pounds
lawful money, the charter should run for thirty years. In stating
the twenty articles of the bank, he gave an explanation of each.
From defect of liquid funds for bank stock, he gave a much larger
place to the pledge of landed property than he later approved.
His belief in the dynamic growth of the country persuaded him
that all public war debt could readily be paid off in a generation.
It was in this connection that he remarked: "A national debt, if
it is not excessive, will be to us a national blessing. It will be a
powerful cement of our Union. It will . . . create a necessity
for keeping up taxation . . . which . . . will be a spur to industry. . . ."[64]

Alexander Hamilton was married to Elizabeth Schuyler, the second daughter of General Philip Schuyler and his wife Catherine,
at the bride's home at Albany, December 14, 1780.[65] The bride
was just over twenty-three,[66] the groom nearly twenty-six. His
courtship at Morristown before their engagement in March of
that year was brief. Elizabeth's consent had certainly been given
before Hamilton left headquarters, March 9, 1780, for a parley
with the British on exchange of prisoners, at Amboy, for he wrote
her from there on the 17th in tender possessiveness. He had
heard from Colonel Webb that she planned a visit to Philadelphia;
"I beg . . . you will not suffer any considerations respecting me
to prevent your going, for though it will be a tax upon my love to
part with you so long, I wish you to see that city before you
return."[67]

He probably had not met her before she came to Morristown on
a visit to her aunt, Mrs. John Cochran, wife of the surgeon-
general of the Middle Department.[68] Her parents, with their
youngest daughters, had gone to Philadelphia, where General
Schuyler took his seat in Congress. Elizabeth remained behind
to come on later with her sister, Mrs. Carter, to Morristown.[69]

Though Mrs. Cochran had all the means of introducing Elizabeth to headquarters society, her father had made her the bearer of a letter to Baron Steuben, "one of the most gallant men in camp." In the baron's absence on an inspection tour his aide, Captain Benjamin Walker, sent the letter along, regretting that his own shabby coat and hat prevented him—which was probably not the case—from filling the baron's office.[70]

Some have supposed that they met at Albany in 1777 when Hamilton was on his mission to Gates. Hamilton surely knew General Schuyler before his visit to Gates, but at that time seems not to have been introduced to his family. Writing to Mrs. Schuyler in April 1780, Hamilton is sorry that "I have not the happiness of a personal acquaintance with you. . . ." He could hardly have known Elizabeth without knowing her mother, as the Schuyler home at Saratoga (now Schuylerville) had been burned by Burgoyne and the family was occupying their house at Albany. Nor is there any allusion to Elizabeth in any of Alexander's letters previous to 1780 at Morristown, though he was writing to the Livingston girls who were her relations and close friends.

We do not know how early, but we may be certain from his letters shortly after, how ardently Hamilton pressed his suit. He had but just returned to headquarters from his fruitless efforts, with Duportail, to persuade D'Estaing to cooperate with the American forces, and must have been glad to direct his pleas in a more hopeful quarter. He was at this time taxing the shifty Dr. Gordon with that reverend historian's equivocations, and we may suppose that he was as pointed in his determination that fairer quarry should not elude him. Tench Tilghman, already a friend and admirer of Betsey, but with a detachment that preserved him a bachelor for some years yet, would have been the first to introduce these two.[71] "I was prepossessed in fav.^r of this young lady the moment I saw her," Tilghman wrote after a visit to the Schuylers at Albany in 1775. "A Brunette with the most good natured lively dark eyes . . . which threw a beam of good temper . . . over her whole Countenance." On a picnic jaunt to Cohoes Falls she disdained assistance in clambering over rough, steep ground, and laughed merrily at reliance of the other girls on male support.

However, numerous parties, private and public, including subscription dances at the commissary storehouse, and sleigh rides between headquarters and the country homes of the Stirlings, Mortons, and Boudinots in the neighborhood, would have brought Alexander and Elizabeth regularly together. Early in their acquaintance Hamilton reported that Betsey "found out the secret of interesting me in everything that concerns her. . . . She is most unmercifully handsome and so perverse that she has none of those pretty affectations which are the prerogatives of beauty." She had good nature and vivacity without frivolousness. She was fast unmaking philosophers in the camp, he among them. "It is essential to . . . the tranquility of the army . . . either that she be immediately removed from our neighborhood, or that some other nymph qualified to maintain an equal sway come into it."[72] "Hamilton is a gone man," wrote Tilghman, hinting that when he fell in love with Betsey he disappointed the hopes of "poor Polly," who had no title to be jealous, since Betsey admired her.[73]

When the Schuylers came up from Philadelphia, joining the Cochrans at Morristown, Hamilton had already won acceptance in the household. The two-story frame dwelling which was the scene of Alexander's romance yet stands a quarter-mile toward the village from the Ford Mansion. It has been restored as a memorial to the Schuylers; Betsey's portrait is a feature of the friendly living room. Hamilton should be included in the remembrance, for he must have spent every off-duty waking hour there.[74] A part of his commendation was surely his exchanges with General Schuyler, who was at headquarters as a member of the Committee of Congress, about lacks of the army for the coming campaign. Judge Jacob Ford, at that time a lad in his father's home which was Washington's headquarters, told an anecdote of Hamilton's absorption in his wooing. Washington would give the boy the countersign so that he could pass the guard after play in the village in the evening. One night Hamilton, returning from the Schuylers', could not remember the magic word when challenged by the sentry. Expostulation was no good against a bayonet, and the colonel for once was put to it, until he spied his young housemate, held a whispered conversation, and then, with full assurance, gave the open sesame.

A year earlier, before he so much as knew Betsey Schuyler, in a frisking mood, Hamilton had commissioned his friend John Laurens to get him a wife in South Carolina, and gave specifications of his requirements.[75] In the end he asked, "Do I want a wife? No. I have plagues enough without desiring to add to the number that greatest of all; and if I were silly enough to do it I should take care how I employed a proxy." But before that he gave his commands for a girl not different from the Betsey he was to find: "She must be young—handsome (I lay most stress upon a good shape) Sensible (a little learning will do)—well bred . . . chaste and tender (I am an enthusiast in my notions of fidelity and fondness) of some good nature—a great deal of generosity (she must neither love money nor scolding, for I dislike equally a termagant and an oeconomist)—In politics, I am indifferent what side she may be of—I think I have arguments that will safely convert her to mine—As to religion a moderate stock will satisfy me—She must believe in god and hate a saint. But as to fortune, the larger stock of that the better—You know my temper and circumstances and will therefore pay special attention to this article of the treaty—Though I run no risk of going to Purgatory for my avarice, yet as money is an essential ingredient to happiness in this world—as I have not much of my own—and as I am very little calculated to get more . . . , it must needs be that my wife . . . bring at least a sufficiency to administer to her own extravagancies."

These flourishes about finding him a wife were likely added to the letter for a reason which Hamilton did not mention, a wish to distract Laurens from what might seem a remonstrance. Laurens had been given a predated commission as lieutenant colonel in the line, and accepted it reluctantly while he knew that Hamilton was eager for similar transfer from staff assignment. Further to disavow any jealousy, Hamilton hastened to his little extravaganza. Incidentally, in this and other instances he had small turn for the purely playful. He had words for wit, but he never could abandon himself to the ridiculous for its own sake. He was perfectly at home with cogency, but not with comedy.

His prescription, combined with other circumstances, has encouraged some biographers—who did not require prompting from him—to remark that Hamilton in choosing a wife had an eye to

fortune and family.   Many a true word, they observe, is spoken in
jest.   Able and ambitious, but born out of wedlock, and a young
stranger in a strange land, his future would be furthered, in
resources and respectability, if he became the son-in-law of General
Philip Schuyler, whose social position and wealth were con-
spicuously established.   To enter that interlocking kinship would
remove a curse, and the political influence thus opened was a
prize.   Betsey's own qualities, while happily acceptable, were
secondary, runs this commentary.   Intellectually she was his
inferior, and her formal education, as shown in her faulty spelling,
had been small.   She has been compared, to her disadvantage,
with her unusually sprightly older sister Angelica, Mrs. Church,
whose letters to Hamilton have been thought to betray a more
than sisterly affection, which, by similar supposition, he returned.
Betsey was even dull, and found in fidelity, religion, and good
works a satisfaction that would not have contented one of acuter
mentality and feeling.

What we know gives the lie to these insinuations of motive.
Hamilton's letters to Betsey, from his courtship at Morristown to
the last hours of his life, show a tenderness, confidence, and deepen-
ing regard.   She shared his plans, perplexities, and his triumphs.
His conjugal lapse—perhaps more fully self-documented than that
of any famous figure—was to his discredit, not his wife's.   Her
faithfulness and whole deportment in the sequel had a glory to
equal any achievement of his life.   Hamilton, prescient and calcu-
lating on the public account, was not always deliberate in his
private affairs, where his strong emotions took command.   Prudence, let alone design, is not the notorious accompaniment of
falling in love, and Alexander Hamilton, by all the signs, fell in
love and remained in love with his Betsey.   Certainly his prospects
improved by marriage into her family and connection, but at no
point in his career, before he had this powerful help, was he at a
loss for opportunity, or ability to profit by it.   When he met
Betsey, he was already a favorite among those of his own age and
admired and trusted by his elders, who included many of the
country's principal men and women.   Well educated, of creditable military performance, acknowledged by all who knew him
to be full of promise, he stood in the closest confidential relationship to the supreme man in America.   In any sensible estimate,

he had as much to offer as to ask in a marriage—supposing, what is most unlikely, that his Cupid was so canny.

The notion that Hamilton meant to wed fortune rather than earn it is refuted in a warning he gave Elizabeth three months before their marriage, and an equal time after their engagement. The winter might produce a peace, and then housekeeping would replace the "fame" of headquarters society. "Tell me," he asked, "Do you soberly relish the pleasure of being a poor man's wife? Have you learned to think a home spun preferable to a brocade and the rumble of a wagon wheel to the musical rattling of a coach and six? Will you be able to see . . . your old acquaintances flaunting it in gay life—tripping it along in elegance and splendor —while you hold a humble station and have no other enjoyments than the sober comforts of a good wife? . . . If you cannot my Dear we are playing a comedy of all in the wrong, and you should correct the mistake before we begin to act the tragedy of the unhappy couple."

Though he asked these questions "with an air of levity, they merit a very serious consideration, for on their being resolved in the affirmative stripped of all . . . imagination our happiness may absolutely depend. I have not concealed my circumstances from my Betsey—they are far from splendid. . . . An indifference to property enters into my character too much and what affects me now as my Betsey is concerned in it, I should have laughed at or not thought of at all a year ago. But I have thoroughly examined my own heart. Beloved by you, I can struggle with every embarrassment of fortune with patience and firmness [.] I cannot however forbear intreating you to realize our union on the dark side and satisfy, without deceiving yourself, how far your affection for me can make you happy in a privation of those elegancies to which you have been accustomed. If fortune should smile upon us, it will do us no harm to have been prepared for adversity; if she frowns upon us [,] by being prepared, we shall encounter it without the chagrin of disappointment."

He reiterated his caution in sober language: "Your future rank in life is a perfect lottery—you may move in an exalted [,] you may move in a very humble sphere—the last is most probable; examine well your heart." She must not indulge the "pretty dreams . . . very apt to enter into the heads of lovers when they think of a con-

nection without the advantages of fortune." The vision of shepherdess and swain must not distort her calculation. "You must
apply your situation to real life, and think how you should feel in
scenes of which you may find examples every day. So far My
Dear Betsey as the tenderest affection can compensate . . . in
making your estimate, you cannot give too large a credit for the
article. My heart overflows with every thing for you that admiration [,] esteem and love can inspire. *I would this moment give
the world to be near you and only to kiss your sweet hand."*[76]

The Schuylers did not consider that in approving the match they
placed any strain on their self-esteem, generosity, or wisdom.
"You cannot my dear Sir," wrote Schuyler, in reporting his wife's
consent also, "be more happy at the connection you have made
with my family than I am. Until the child of a parent has made
a judicious choice his heart is in continual anxiety; but this anxiety
was removed the moment I discovered on whom she had placed her
affections. I am pleased with every instance of delicacy in those
who are dear to me, and I think I read your soul on that occasion
you mention. I shall therefore only entreat you to consider me as
one who wishes in every way to promote your happiness, and I
shall."[77]

So far from Hamilton courting Elizabeth Schuyler from ambition
rather than love, it was wryly suggested at the time that ulterior
design was on the other side. A spontaneous romance between
young people, if highly connected, could draw a sour comment then
as since. Arthur Lee, just returned from France, and elected to
Congress, in an intercepted letter printed in the *Royal Gazette,*
threw out: "If Schuyler is with us he may give his daughter to
Hamilton to gain a sway over Washington or be in the military
plot with him to surrender America back to great Britain and become Monks themselves."[78]

Acceptance of Hamilton by Elizabeth's family was not more
cordial in the promise than in the performance. No one will ever
know what was the "instance of delicacy" which pleased the prospective father-in-law, but one may guess that it was Hamilton's
disclosure, suitable under the circumstances, that he was an illegitimate son.

The fact was that the Schuylers embodied the gentility that
places value on individual worth. General Schuyler, earlier, had

preferred Hamilton among Washington's aides.[79] Their other
daughters married young men of notable position and wealth, but
these assets seem to have moved the parents no more than did
Alexander Hamilton's talents and integrity alone.   Indeed, of the
four girls, only Betsey married with her parents' knowledge, let
alone consent, which was a temporary wound to their affections,
though in no case did it prove an ill omen.   Alexander and Betsey
were anxious to be married at headquarters, which meant soon, but
Schuyler wrote, from Philadelphia, "You will see the Impropriety
of taking the dernier pas where you are.   Mrs. Schuyler did not see
her eldest daughter married.   that also gave me pain, and we wish
not to experience It a Second time.   I shall probably be at Camp
in a few days when we will adjust all matters."   Angelica, like
numerous other spirited young women of the first families, had
eloped.   "Carter and my eldest daughter ran off and were married," Schuyler had complained to Duer, who had introduced the
offending groom.   "Unacquainted with his family connections and
situation in life the matter was . . . disagreeable and I signified it
to them."   "Carter" was the alias of John Barker Church, who had
skipped England following a duel, and was a young man of excellent parts and prospects.   He and Angelica simply crossed the river
for nuptial rites at Rensselaerwyck.   Later Elizabeth's next younger
sister Margaret scampered off with Stephen Rensselaer, who had
abetted the Churches.   Later still Cornelia, the last of these graces,
staged an elopement (with the forbidden Washington Morton)
right out of fiction, with rope-ladder, waiting skiff, coach and pair
complete.[80]

Schuyler, looking forward to a decorous home wedding for
Elizabeth, went on to impart with a pride in Hamilton which was
to be stirred on so many future occasions, "You have been mentioned in private conversation [in Congress] to go as Secretary to
the Embassy at the Court of Versailles; there is but one obstacle
which prevents me from making up my mind on the subject; that
you will know when I have the pleasure of seeing you.   In the
mean time revolve the matter in yours."[81]

Unhappily, few of Hamilton's letters to Elizabeth before their
marriage have survived.[82]   Those that we have are ardent.   Besides, they pay her the compliment of including news and views of
public happenings.   Perhaps it was inevitable that a young man

who was just then laying before principal persons, such as Morris
and Duane, plans for reforming the economy and government of
the country, should slip into his love letters here and there a monitory passage looking to Elizabeth's education.   His proprietary interest was its own excuse, and doubtless a young woman at such
a time would accept in affection what another—or she herself later!
—might consider gratuitous.   Of course he would write her verses;
the muse that had stirred him in St. Croix to indite to a hypothetical maiden, or in Elizabethtown in a melancholy cause, now stood
much closer to his elbow.   Eight lines, "Answer to the Inquiry
Why I Sighed," are certainly of the period of their engagement:

> ". . . Completely wretched—you away—
> And but half blessed e'en while you stay.

> ". . . No joy unmixed my bosom warms
> But when my angel's in my arms."[83]

"I love you more and more every hour," he wrote her from Morristown when she was on a visit in the vicinity.[84]   "The sweet softness and delicacy of your mind and manners, the elevation of your
sentiments, the real goodness of your heart—its tenderness to me—
the beauties of your face and person—your unpretending good
sense and that innocent simplicity and frankness which pervade
your actions, all these appear to me with increasing amiableness,
and place you in my estimation above all the rest of your sex."
Then he went on to paint the lily.   She must not neglect the
charges he gave her, including that of "employing all your leisure
in reading.   Nature has been very kind to you, do not neglect to
cultivate her gifts and to enable yourself to make the distinguished
figure in all respects to which you are entitled to aspire.   You excel
most of your sex in all the amiable qualities, endeavor to excel them
equally in the splendid ones.   You can do it if you please, and I
shall take pride in it,—It will be a fund too to diversify our enjoyment . . . and fill all our moments to advantage."[85]

But ere long he was back to his excitement without exhortation obtruding.   "I . . . love you too much.   You engross my
thoughts too entirely to allow me to think anything else.   You
not only employ my mind all day, but you intrude on my sleep.
I meet you in every dream. . . 'Tis a pretty story . . . that I

am to be thus monopolized by a little *nut brown maid* like you and from a soldier metamorphosed into a puny lover." He is impatient at delay in joining her at Albany, but could not leave the general shorthanded, with Harrison gone to bury his father and Meade to marry a wife. He would not be detained past November. Because the groom's part in a wedding is of no consequence to anyone except the bride, the only question he had to pose about it was a "trifle, . . . whether you would prefer my receiving the nuptial benediction in my uniform or in a different habit. It will be just as you please, so consult your whim and what you think most consistent with propriety. . . ."[86]

In the interval of their engagement Hamilton was obliged to be absent several times from Morristown and subsequent headquarters, and Elizabeth seems to have chosen these periods for her own visits to Philadelphia and elsewhere. The most memorable of his errands was with the commander in chief to Hartford to meet Rochambeau on September 21. The sequel, in cruel contrast to the gratifying prospect of cooperation between the American and French armies, is more famous—their arrival, on the return journey, at Robinson's house opposite West Point at just the moment to discover Arnold's treason. Among the most particular accounts of these crowded, consternating hours, and of the imprisonment, trial, and execution of André, are those Hamilton wrote to Elizabeth, and a longer one in a letter to John Laurens, of which he sent her a copy.[87] Hamilton's witness to the occurrence, and his fruitless effort to capture Arnold in his flight, are dealt with in another place. His description of Mrs. Arnold's distraction bespoke his tender feelings for Elizabeth, though even so he was not so infatuated but that he mentioned the possibility of Peggy's complicity in the plot.

Other public developments entered into his letters to his sweetheart, such as the defeat of Gates at Camden. The serious portent of this was mingled in his mind with pointed satisfaction that Gates, in his expeditious flight from the scene of disaster, had proved the unworthiness which Hamilton had imputed to him. This had special meaning for Elizabeth because her father had been displaced for Gates, and the battles around Saratoga had been in her back yard, as it were. In addition, her lover and her father had surely given her the particulars of Gates's conduct toward Hamilton, obstructing the reinforcement to Washington, and accusing Hamilton of rifling his papers.

Other incidents of these months, even more personal to Hamilton, he must have shared with her. The chief was his renewed application to Washington to be given a field command, this time for the planned (but abandoned) attack on New York, with the dispositions for which Hamilton had had much to do. This happened just prior to[88] Elizabeth's marriage, and the disappointment was probably Hamilton's far more than hers. Not long before, John Laurens and Lafayette had urged Hamilton as envoy to France to arrange the loan which he had considered indispensable. This mission being given to Laurens, in spite of Laurens's protests in favor of his friend, Hamilton was recommended to Washington by Lafayette and Greene to become Adjutant General, but Hand had just been chosen. These proposals for Hamilton's promotion (treated elsewhere), though they miscarried, must have given Elizabeth Schuyler and her family keen pride. Hamilton's cooperation with General Schuyler to promote a firm, effective national union commenced before the wedding, and was an augury of the lifelong teamwork of the two men. In letters they wrote to others, on the same topics, is clear evidence of their exchange of views.[89] The evenings at the Schuyler home at Morristown were not devoted exclusively to Betsey. Doubtless she shared in his conversations with her father and mother about the state of the army and the country, and probably, like it or not, she had to take a deal of politics with Hamilton's gallantries to her. From her assistance, later, in copying reports he was preparing, and from her anxiety, after his death, to see the story of his public services published, it is clear that she entered into more than her husband's domestic and social life.

Alexander and Betsey were married in the drawing room of the Schuyler mansion in Albany. The occasion was not the least that lent distinction to that house and home.[90] James McHenry, Hamilton's colleague of Washington's staff, was present, and wrote an ode in celebration.[91] Their honeymoon, spent at Albany,[92] lasted until after the holidays, when they both repaired to headquarters.[93] Chastellux was a guest at the Schuyler mansion immediately after the marriage of Alexander and Betsey, and has left us a picture of the animated company there assembled. He and his companions crossed the river amidst snow and ice Christmas eve to be welcomed with warmth, food, wine, and the special satisfaction of finding as fellow guests his countrymen De Noailles, Damas, and Mauduit.   Chastellux brought letters of introduction from Washington and Mrs. Carter (Angelica Schuyler), but these he did not need, for he had a rendezvous there with Hamilton, whom he described with appreciation of his talents and his services to the French forces in America.   Mrs. Hamilton "has a mild agreeable countenance," and her younger brothers and sisters are "the handsomest . . . you can see."   The yuletide party included journeys by sleigh to neighboring points of interest.   In the evenings Schuyler opened to the French visitor his military and political correspondence, especially that bearing on Burgoyne's invasion.   One of the attendants assigned to Chastellux was Major William Popham, who remained an attached friend of the Hamilton's and who, fifty years after Betsey's marriage, was to assist her in obtaining her husband's military pension.[94]

Elizabeth Hamilton was a blessing to her husband.   She was summoned to be the companion, as well as the comfort, of a man of genius.   In that day of limited formal schooling for girls, she made the higher virtues of understanding and devotion the means of sympathy.   Of trouble she had more than her portion.   But her courage was equal to all.   She was the projection of the long tradition of responsibility in the Schuyler family, of which opportunity and her own qualities made her the flower.   The relation of husband and wife that began that December day was hardly closer than that of a new son in an affectionate household.   It is not possible to separate Hamilton's marriage to Elizabeth from his union with her family.   His own fragmentary domestic life as a child was now made whole.   To Philip and Catherine Schuyler he was an added fulfillment.   General Schuyler, in spite of his public services, was treated at times to prejudice and ingratitude.   These disappointments he met with the minimum of complaint and the maximum of forbearance.   His satisfaction in Hamilton's achievements, to which he notably contributed, was a sufficient compensation.   Here was a new graft on an old stock, which bore even better fruit.   If ever a patriarch enjoyed the generations after him, he was Philip Schuyler.   Schuyler was a large man of high forehead and prominent nose verging on the bulbous.   He was lord of the headwaters of the Hudson, skillful in treating with the Indians, and inevitably called on to fend off the foreign invader. New Englanders were his public foes, from suspicion bred by differences of culture. Gout was his inveterate private enemy, by inheritance and his own good living.[95]

Washington was Hamilton's chief public sponsor, as Hamilton, in much, was Washington's main support. Next to this tie, Hamilton's relationship to Schuyler was the most propitious and productive of his life. It was filial and companionable in ways not true of his association with Washington. He and Schuyler felt as well as thought alike. Schuyler's warmth was the match for Hamilton's fervor. Besides family affections, they had the same friends and identical political principles. Of practical importance in this partnership was the fact that they were of, and represented in public offices, the same state. It is easy to say that they were both aristocrats, the older man by descent, position, and possessions, the younger by preference. The meaning of this bond was their equal acceptance of obligation—toward persons, local community, and the American nation. Privilege, to them, implied discharging, indeed seeking, responsibilities. This was anything but haughty or disdainful. Mrs. Schuyler was as competent as mistress of a large household and extended domain. We know of her prowess as a chatelaine, feeding Indians come for treaty and trade, entertaining every distinguished visitor to Albany—American and French officers, and, after the surrender at Saratoga, General Burgoyne and his staff, Baroness Riedesel and her children. As Catherine Rensselaer, she was born to private expectations and public commitments similar to those of her husband.

We have ample evidence of the domestic love and trust that flowed between the Schuyler home and the Hamiltons. Testimony to the concert of political plans between Hamilton and his father-in-law would be fuller if the bulk of their correspondence with each other, found in a trunk at Albany, had not been burned by the son of a Schuyler executor in one of those monstrous acts of private prerogative.[96]

Witness

to Treason

HAMILTON'S first-hand reports of the discovery of Arnold's treason and of the fate of André have been oftener quoted than others. With the commander in chief, he chanced to be on the spot, took part in the fruitless chase after the miscreant, witnessed Mrs. Arnold's "mad scene" (mock or genuine), and tried to save André from the ignominy of the scaffold. His eager pen was sympathetic to the sufferers in the plot—to the traitor's lovely young wife because Hamilton was about to be married himself, and to the spirited British adjutant whose grace and talents matched his own. His most sustained account, in the form of a letter to his friend John Laurens, was widely published in the newspapers. It amounted to a semiofficial declaration to the world that Arnold's defection was individual and argued no crumbling of the morale of resistance.[1]

This stage of the war was another justifying the adage about raining and pouring. The army, like a grazing herd, must move as it ate, for Greene had quit as quartermaster general, transport had broken down, and local farmers, refusing the currency, compelled the alternative of impressment.[2] Washington had to turn back recruits he could not feed. Officers resigned or were so jealously troublesome that the general could almost wish they would act on their threats to leave. Hamilton wrote for him to Congress that "if something satisfactory be not done, the Army

. . . must either cease to exist at the end of the Campaign, or it will exhibit an example of more virtue, fortitude, self denial, and perseverance than has . . . ever yet been paralleled in the history of human enthusiasm."[3]   The French allies were stationary at Newport, awaiting arrival of a second division blockaded at Brest, and ignorant of what could be expected from Admiral de Guichen, still in the West Indies.   Meanwhile General David Forman, from his Jersey lookout, reported Rodney at Sandy Hook with a dozen ships of the line and four frigates to add to enemy naval superiority.   Would not the British now polish off their conquest in the Carolinas where Gates, the month before, had come to grief against Cornwallis at Camden?[4]

This was the discouraging outlook when Hamilton took horse on Sept. 17, 1780, at headquarters at New Bridge, New Jersey, to accompany Washington, Knox, Lafayette, McHenry, and other aides to a conference with General Rochambeau and Admiral De Ternay at Hartford.   Making for King's Ferry, they lodged that night at the home of Joshua Hett Smith, nearby.   Here a dinner guest was General Arnold, and through his audacity (or prudence, as he must have put it to himself) Washington and his party were introduced to treason without suspecting it.   Arnold affected to consult Washington about letters just received from Colonel Beverly Robinson,[5] written that day[6] from the British sloop of war *Vulture,* "off Tellers P[oint]."   That to Arnold enclosed one to General Putnam, asking for an interview on a private matter.   If Putnam was not in reach, would Arnold see him?   Washington disapproved the application, observing that Robinson should be referred to the civil authority.[7]

As Hamilton remarked, in retrospect, "This . . . fortunately deranged the plan, and was the first link in the chain of events that led to the detection.   The interview could no longer take place in the form of a flag, but was obliged to be managed in a secret manner."[8]   This was carried out the night of September 21.   Arnold directed Smith, whom he and General Robert Howe had used in obtaining military intelligence, to row out to the *Vulture* with a letter, which Smith said he believed was for Robinson.   He was to bring Robinson off for a meeting with Arnold.[9]

Meanwhile Washington and his party had gone on to meet the

French at Hartford. Civilities apart, little could be done but put proposals that hung on contingencies.[10] On the return, the general was delayed at Fishkill,[11] from which he set out, on September 25, before breakfast, for Arnold's headquarters and an inspection of West Point. Hamilton seems to have remained with Washington, Lafayette, and others when they turned off, near the river, to examine two redoubts on the east bank.[12] McHenry and Shaw, aides of Lafayette and Knox, were sent ahead to give advance notice to Arnold, his staff and household, of the general's expectation of breakfast.[13] When the commander in chief arrived with his party they were told by Arnold's aides, Lieutenant Colonel Richard Varick and Major David Franks, that Arnold had been called across the river to the fort and would return within the hour.[14]

After breakfast Washington and the other generals went to West Point. Hamilton, remaining at Robinson's, was alerted an hour later by "Mrs. Arnold's unhappy situation [which] called us all to her assistance."[15] She sent the housekeeper to inquire after Varick's health, but instantly caused alarm for her own by her "hysterics and utter frenzy." "Raving distracted," she talked deliriously of hot irons on her head, charged that Varick had ordered her infant killed, and knelt to him to spare the babe's life.[16] To assurances that all were her friends, and that Arnold would soon return, she cried, "No, no, he is gone forever!"[17] Whether Hamilton attempted consolation at this point we do not know; Franks and Varick were hovering, and Dr. Eustis was in attendance. It is unlikely that the two aides of Arnold shared with Hamilton shocking suspicions that were sprouting in their minds. As they coupled their general's sudden departure with his wife's alarms, including her exclamation that he would never come back, they feared he had gone to the enemy. The report "of a spy . . . being detected nigh our lines" added to the dismay because his name, John Anderson, had figured in Arnold's correspondence. Moreover, Arnold's barge had been seen going downriver.[18]

Not till later did Hamilton learn the particulars of Arnold's precipitate exit. An officer had brought him two letters. Soon he went upstairs to Mrs. Arnold. Two minutes afterward came Washington's servant announcing the commander in chief was close at hand. Franks went up to inform Arnold, who "came down in great confusion, and, ordering a horse to be saddled, mounted him and told me to inform his Excellency that he was gone over to West Point. . . ."[19]

The staggering letter that sent Arnold to his wife, then to his horse and barge, was from Lieutenant Colonel John Jameson, at the outpost of North Castle, saying one John Anderson had been captured, and that papers found on him had been dispatched to Washington.[20] This left Arnold but an instant for his escape.[21] That was his surging fright, but by mischance the messenger to Washington had been delayed by taking a circuitous route. He had made for the lower road, by Danbury, while the party from Hartford had come by the upper.[22]

Captain Jeronimus Hoogland, Jameson's courier, reached Robinson's house in Washington's absence at West Point. Hamilton took charge of his packet, but did not open it.[23] However, he was disturbed. He knew that Arnold had left the house unaccountably on notice of Washington's approach. He must have heard— if Franks and Varick did—rumors of a spy being taken. Mrs. Arnold's vocal distress was louder. Now came messages from the lines toward the enemy. And the messenger would not be mum about his errand.

When Washington returned to the Robinson house in midafternoon he must have been perturbed, though with suspicions less sharpened. Arnold was not to be found at the fort. Many of its defenses were neglected and vulnerable, and the garrison was scattered and employed on less essential tasks.[24] But the general was unprepared for the contents of the packet Hamilton handed him— a pass for John Anderson in Arnold's hand; a plan of the fortifications of West Point; an engineer's report on attack and defenses of the place; a return of garrison, ordnance, and stores; and a copy of the minutes of a council of war held by Washington three weeks before.[25] The covering letter of Jameson[26] must have said that these documents were found in the stocking feet of a southbound traveler arrested by militiamen near Tarrytown. If all of this did not proclaim Arnold's intended betrayal of West Point, an ingenuous letter from the prisoner himself to Washington all but clinched it. He identified himself as Major John André, Adjutant General of the British Army; ashore from the *Vulture,* seeking military intelligence, he had been forced, against his will, to come within American posts and to put on civilian clothing as a disguise. He wanted to rescue himself "from an imputation of having assumed a mean character for treacherous purposes. . . ." He did not name Arnold as the person with whom he had negotiated,[27] but the connection was not far to seek.

The shocking news was given to Hamilton,[28] and he and McHenry immediately took horse for Verplanck's Point, a dozen miles by the then road, to try to intercept Arnold, who in his barge had surely made for the *Vulture*.[29] They arrived "much too late,"[30] for the traitor had escaped to the sloop of war.[31]

From Verplanck's Hamilton dashed off a note to Washington. A line was enough to lament they had missed the quarry; the rest concerned rapid precautions lest the enemy, in spite of discovery of the plot, strike against West Point that night. He would advise General Greene (commanding in New Jersey) to be ready to march, and to detach a brigade to King's Ferry. He would try to find (Colonel R. J.) Meigs, start him to the garrison, and would prepare Verplanck's. He hoped the general would approve these emergency steps.[32]

It is probable that what Hamilton enclosed to Washington were letters that had come from the *Vulture* by flag, from Arnold to the commander in chief and to Peggy, and one from Beverly Robinson, Arnold's loyalist accomplice.[33] Hamilton would not need to read them to know their import. His later perusal of Arnold's profession of high motives in low acts, and Robinson's "frivolous" pretense that the British spy was covered by a flag of truce, entered into his description of the treason.[34]

Hamilton missed dinner at the Robinson house at four o'clock, for at that time he was pelting toward Verplanck's. Anyhow, it was one of the most melancholy meals to which a dozen men ever sat down. In spite of his high fever, Varick presided, and said no worse of it than "Dull appetites surrounded a plentiful table." Franks darted back and forth between guests downstairs and the distracted Peggy Arnold above. Only Washington, as yet keeping his own counsel, behaved as if nothing were amiss.[35] This was the more remarkable because Arnold's apprehensive aides, at Peggy's importunity, had taken the general to her bedside just before they sat down. To let him see her—"Poor . . . frantic, and miserable lady"—was the way, they thought, to convey their unspoken fears

that her husband had betrayed his trust.   Even Washington's assurances that she would not be harmed proved no therapy.[36]

Back from his disappointed dash after Arnold, Hamilton's sympathies were wrung by the sorrows of Peggy.   But he had little time
for delirium, for he must aid his chief in rapid issue of orders for
the safety of West Point.   First, Hamilton's message to Greene was
confirmed, at seven-thirty.   Greene must at once put his left division in motion for King's Ferry, coming on light for speed.   Hold
all other troops in readiness to march on shortest notice.[37]   Command at West Point devolved on Colonel Nathaniel Wade, who
must be vigilant in emergency preparations; directions to him were
not completed until 2:00 A.M. of September 26.[38]   Meanwhile,
André was to be brought to West Point for the closest watch upon
him,[39] and Gouvion scoured for Fishkill to gather in Joshua Hett
Smith,[40] whom Arnold, in his letter from the *Vulture,* had exculpated as his go-between.

Next day, Tuesday, September 26, offered no rest for Hamilton
and the other weary officers at Robinson's house.   Smith, expostulating, was brought under guard before eight o'clock that morning.[41]   He was a brother of William Smith, Chief Justice (and
chief propagandist) of the British in New York.   Washington gave
him a preliminary examination in the presence of Knox, Lafayette,
Hamilton, and Harrison.   "The General expressed himself with
some warmth," said Hamilton with evident restraint.[42]   Smith,
however, in spite of sudden arrest, night ride, and chills doubtless
mental as well as physical at finding himself questioned under such
circumstances, was wary in his answers and even offered himself as
a character witness in his own defense.   He explained volubly that
he had served General Howe and then Arnold as courier in their
contacts with spies.   The night of September 21, at Arnold's direction, he had rowed out to the *Vulture* with a letter, expecting to
bring off Beverly Robinson, who would give information in return
for favor in regaining his estate.   Instead, Smith was given as
passenger a cloaked man who, when landed, clambered up the
bank and talked long with Arnold in the fir trees.

The dark tryst concluded, the tired boatmen refused to row the
mysterious stranger back to the *Vulture.*   The principals, with
Smith as messenger, did not press them overmuch.   Arnold and
André rode to Smith's house to bide the day.   With morning

light, Fate took a hand. American guns at Teller's Point fired
on the British warship, compelling her to drop down the river to
Sing Sing—a few miles only, but enough to make the difference
between life and death for the spy, success and ruin for the traitor.
On the night of the 22nd, Smith escorted his charge, with Arnold's
pass, across King's Ferry, and set him on his way by land for New
York, in the guise of a merchant. Near Tarrytown, Anderson
(André) was challenged by three American militiamen, in panic
avowed himself a British officer, and was forced to yield up the
damning papers he carried in his stockings.

Washington, after interrogating Smith at Robinson's house,
found him "to have had a considerable share in this business,"[43]
even that he had "confessed facts sufficient to establish his guilt."[44]
Hamilton's part in this questioning was rehearsed, and more was
given, in his testimony at Smith's formal trial.[45]   Smith said later
that Hamilton's "evidence was perfectly correct," yet he "artfully
threw in a chain of reasoning, tending to prove my being in full
knowledge of General Arnold's intentions."[46]   This reference was
probably to Hamilton's depiction of Smith's political behavior in
the preliminaries of the Revolution in New York.   Hamilton
thought that his first sincerity in the Whig cause passed into "an
intemperate zeal" and "excessive warmth" that raised doubts
whether his professions were genuine.[47]   In the end the court-
martial acquitted Smith for lack of evidence "of his being privy
to . . . Arnold's . . . traitorous . . . designs," but in fact the
suspicions held by Washington, Hamilton, and many more were
not erased.[48]

Hamilton's tenderness for Betsey spoke in the phrases, in his
letter to her, in which he described his compassion for Mrs.
Arnold's "suffering innocence."   Though she had been "frantic
all day, . . . and exhibiting every . . . mark of the most genuine
and agonizing distress,"[49] it was not till evening, when he returned from the pursuit of Arnold, that Hamilton encountered
her frenzies.   Then his disappointment at escape of the traitor
was all but lost in sympathy for the distracted young wife.   ". . .
it was the most affecting scene I ever was witness to.   She . . .
entirely lost herself.   The General went up to see her, and she
upbraided him with being in a plot to murder her child.   One
moment she raved, another she melted into tears.   Sometimes she

pressed her infant to her bosom, and lamented its fate, occasioned by the imprudence of its father, in a manner that would have pierced insensibility itself. All the sweetness of beauty, all the loveliness of innocence, all the tenderness of a wife, and all the fondness of a mother showed themselves in her appearance and conduct. We have every reason to believe that she was entirely unacquainted with the plan, and that the first knowledge of it was when Arnold went to tell her he must banish himself from his country and from her forever."

Varick found Peggy "raving, mad to see him [Washington], with her hair disheveled and flowing about her neck; her morning gown with few other clothes remaining on her,—too few to be seen even by a gentleman of the family. . . ." Hamilton added to his letter to Elizabeth that next morning he found Peggy "more composed," but not convinced, by his best persuasions, that "the resentment of her country" would not "fall upon her (who is only unfortunate) for the guilt of her husband. . . . her sufferings were so eloquent, that I wished myself her brother, to have a right to become her defender." Arnold was the more despicable "for acting a part that . . . forfeited the esteem of so fine a woman."[50]

Hamilton recorded later that Mrs. Arnold had the solicitude of "all who were present. She experienced the most delicate attentions and every friendly office, till her departure for Philadelphia."[51] Washington did not suspect her of complicity in the treason,[52] though it was hardly on Arnold's assurance that he exculpated her.[53] Was Alexander Hamilton taken in by Peggy Arnold? He was only a few years older than she, and ready to ascribe Betsey's virtues to a lovely girl in distress. Did his chivalry get the better of his wits? Others present and later chroniclers were as prompt to call her guiltless.[54] Recent inquirers, with access to Sir Henry Clinton's files, have called her a deceiving little piece who aided her husband's treason all along, if indeed she did not draw him into it in the first place.[55] Explicit documentary evidence is lacking. The chief support of plausible inference is the fact that part of Arnold's correspondence with the British passed through her hands.

If Hamilton was deceived in the character of Mrs. Arnold, he was in no doubt about the guilty intentions and conduct of André. He branded as sophistry the pleas of the British that André ought to be released because he had come ashore under a flag of truce from the American general commanding the district, and had changed into civilian clothing and entered our posts on demand of that officer.[56] "Never . . . did a man suffer death with more justice, or deserve it less," was Hamilton's comment. The cynical practices of war authorized his deceptions, while he stood condemned on moral counts, including his willingness "to prostitute a flag."[57] Hamilton's appreciation of André's talents, and of his ingenuous behavior while a doomed captive in American hands, did more than any other description to fix him in the compassionate memory of his enemies. The phrases might have applied to the writer of them: "he united a peculiar elegance of mind and manners, and the advantages of a pleasing person. . . . His sentiments were elevated, and inspired esteem: they had a softness that conciliated affection. His elocution was handsome; his address easy, polite, and insinuating. By his merit he had acquired the unlimited confidence of his general. . . ."[58] Hamilton visited André several times during his confinement at Tappan, New York, near Washington's headquarters,[59] and was surely one of the American officers who drew the Englishman's special thanks for courtesies shown him.[60] Hamilton was the bearer of the prisoner's request to Washington to be allowed to write to Sir Henry Clinton; André explained to Hamilton, in affecting language, how he wanted to free his chief of blame for his predicament.[61]

However, there is reason to doubt a story that Hamilton lent himself to a proposal that Clinton give up the traitor Arnold in return for the spy André. The assertion rests on reminiscences of two actors in the scene, on the diary of a third, and on a letter said to be by Hamilton in a disguised hand. Captain Aaron Ogden,[62] at Tappan, was ordered to report to the commander in chief at eight o'clock on the morning of September 30, 1780. He was met by Washington alone at the door of the tent,[63] who gave him a packet addressed to Sir Henry Clinton. With an escort of twenty-five dragoons, under a flag of truce, he should deliver this at the nearest enemy post, calling first on Lafayette for special instructions. Lafayette directed that he should arrive at Paulus Hook (Jersey City) so late in the evening that he must spend the night; he should let fall to the commanding officer that if Clinton allowed Washington to get Arnold within his power, André would be at once released. At this assurance the commandant crossed the river, but returned in two hours with the message from British headquarters "that a deserter was never given up," and that Ogden's horse would be ready for him in the morning.[64]

Simcoe, commanding the Queen's Rangers, who had appealed to Henry Lee in André's behalf,[65] recorded that amongst the letters which passed from American to British headquarters, "a paper was slid in without signature, but in the hand writing of Hamilton, Washington's secretary, saying 'that the only way to save André was to give up Arnold.' "[66] It was possible, not probable, that the letter in question was delivered by Ogden at Paulus Hook in his packet. William Smith, Chief Justice of New York under the British, by implication put the furtive transfer of the letter at Dobbs Ferry the next day, October 1. When Lieutenant General Robertson, Smith, and Lieutenant Governor Andrew Elliott, in the *Greyhound,* anchored off Corbet's Point in the afternoon to make an oral plea to the Americans, they were told that General Greene was present to receive General Robertson and his aide, Murray, but that the others should not land. "A long Conference ensued," wrote Smith, "while Murray walked elsewhere with Hamilton[,] Washington['s] Aid de Camp & two other Rebel officers."[67]

Smith was too distant to see any sleight of hand by Hamilton, but here, if at all, is where it occurred. The letter itself is endorsed by Clinton, "Hamilton. W[ashington's] aid de camp, received after A['s] death." Signed *AB*, it is dated September 30 and proposes that André "might be released for General Arnold. . . . Major André's character and situation seem to demand this of your justice and friendship. Arnold appears to have been the guilty author of the mischief; and ought more properly to be the victim, as there is great reason to believe he meditated a double treachery, and had arranged the interview in such a manner that if discovered in the first instance, he might . . . sacrifice Major André to his own safety. No time is to be lost."[68]

The uncertainty of Hamilton's authorship is because of features of the letter itself, in a disguised backhand if his at all,[69] and because it is contrary to his known sentiments. He wrote to Laurens that the surmise of "double treachery" plotted by Arnold might, in the opinion of some, induce Clinton to give him up for

André. When a gentleman suggested that André might propose this to Clinton, André declined it. "The moment he had been guilty of so much frailty," declared Hamilton, "I should have ceased to esteem him."[70] To Betsey, Hamilton was more specific. He was picked to broach the expedient to André, but refused to offend the doomed man's honor or to convict himself of "the impropriety of the measure."[71]

Hamilton did heartily second André's plea that he be shot and not suffer the shame "to die on the Gibbet." This André begged after he listened to the report of the court-martial that he "ought to be considered as a Spy, . . . and . . . agreeable to the Law and usage of Nations . . . he ought to suffer Death."[72] His petition was renewed in a moving letter to Washington the day before his execution.[73] Both court and commander thought the indulgence could not be granted, as contrary to the customs of war, but forbore to give an answer, "to spare him the sensations which a certain knowledge of the intended mode would inflict."[74] As Hamilton had conveyed his quick sympathy for André personally—the condemned man in one of their conversations had broken into tears in spite of himself—[75] the entreaty to be spared hanging was doubtless a topic between them, and probably ended in Hamilton delivering the letter to Washington. Certainly Hamilton "urged a compliance" with a request which he did not think "would have had an ill effect"; he commented with bitterness that "some people are only sensible to motives of policy, and . . . from a narrow disposition, mistake it."[76]

To make his narrative complete, Hamilton described the execution of André, but he did not witness it, for Washington and his staff stayed away.[77]

Americans exulted that more than the Highlands stronghold was preserved to them. The conjecture was common that Arnold and Clinton had expected to include Washington, Lafayette, and Knox in the coup. Along with others of their closest attendants, Hamilton would have been thrust in the British bag.[78] It was soon known that Arnold had notified the enemy of Washington's movements in the vicinity.[79] Sir Henry Clinton's boast was, for the time, confined to the breast of his confidant, William Smith. Had not André been "catched with his Papers which forced Arnold to come off before the Design was accomplished," Clinton would have made "an instantaneous Termination of the War—said he should have had both Washington & Rochambeau Prisoners for they were both there now."[80]

However, aside from raising Washington higher in the gratitude and pride of his countrymen, his "escape" by the exploding of Arnold's treason was fanciful. Hamilton, though recording that "Arnold was very anxious to ascertain from [Washington] the precise day of his return," discounted the supposition that Washington's capture was a part of the plan. Coordination of British movements with Arnold's collusive disposition of troops in and about the fortress, which must be contrived clandestinely through the lines, was too complicated to include Washington in the clutch except by lucky coincidence. Unless in the improbable event of complete surprise, Washington would have taken command and, in spite of weaknesses, defended the fort.[81] Had not Arnold been forced, by flight, to confess his treachery, Washington would surely have circumvented it when he saw the suspiciously unready defenses of West Point. Further, the commander in chief spent the night of September 25 at the Robinson house, in its exposed situation, in spite of known dangers.

A sequel of Arnold's treason, in which Hamilton was made to figure, was the preposterous attempt of the British propaganda to throw blame on Washington for André's death as a steppingstone to his own desperate ambition. It was an instance of the familiar effort of an enemy to snatch at the most far-fetched claim if it could be given credit and currency among supporters. A long review of André's case, published by Rivington the next month, declared that Washington could not have been instigated by personal resentment against the young officer in his power. André's last letter was quoted, that he was "the victim of policy." The object of this "political stroke," this "dark scheme," was revealed in an intercepted letter of Hamilton to Isaac Sears.[82] Written "near the time when Major André was executed . . . by General Washington's confidential friend, . . . we cannot doubt of its containing that General's sentiments." Sears, often employed by abler heads for "bellowing at popular meetings," was a chosen instrument for devious design.

Replying to Sears' recent observation that "the same spirit of indifference to public affairs prevails" in Boston, Hamilton offered his habitual remedies in a contest that could not "be much longer supported on the present footing. We must have a government with more power. . . . We must have an administration distinct from Congress, and in the hands of single men under their orders." Ignoring all features of the exhortation that did not suit enemy purpose, the British threw up the question, Who could better expect to be thrust forward in the crisis, as protector or king, than Washington? "Now what can be conceived more . . . adapted to . . . these purposes, than the putting Major André, Adjutant General of the British Army, to death?"[83]

Hasty Words and
Quitting of Headquarters

WE can read Hamilton's restlessness in the autumn of 1780 in his efforts, and those of friends on his behalf, to find an assignment more exciting, honorific as he thought, or calling for more prowess than correspondence from headquarters.[1] As aide for three and a half years, he had discharged every kind of responsibility which that position presented. He had seen companions who remained in field command advanced in rank and seniority. He was soon to be married, which moved him to a fresh inspection of his future. The army would be going into winter quarters, which would reduce his duties toward routine and fasten him again to "the desk's dead wood." The domestic situation, economic and political, bore a dreary aspect, and plans for the next military campaign hung on perplexed guesses about Sir Henry Clinton's intentions. The young officer of the commander in chief's staff wanted to cope with more than lay at hand, which likely explains why he prepared his long letter to James Duane in Congress exploring means of rendering the country fitter to prosecute the war.

Lafayette, also, was itching for enterprise, as ever, and, being a major general with the right to expect attentive ears, and not an aide who was militarily immured, he used his scope. He revived the project—repeatedly proposed, planned, and rejected—of an attack on New York. French opinion would rally to this American success. Fort Washington would be the first object.[2] Washington replied (Hamilton his mouthpiece) that such a brilliant stroke was then beyond our means, that we had better bear the ills we had, and so on.[3] But the scheme would not down and, with a change of appearances, was actively resumed, Hamilton and Tilghman drawing orders for a sally against Manhattan and its dependencies.[4] Two nights hand running Lafayette and Hamilton concerted plans. Boats with muffled oars were to carry a thousand men to Staten Island. Washington's approval gave Lafayette license to discuss the whole with G[ouvion], the engineer, "who was charmed with the beauty and propriety of the thing." But what most absorbed Hamilton was that he, in the enthusiasm of the collaboration, was to command two hundred men in an attack. Wanting for this was Washington's permission. "To-morrow," Lafayette finished, "we must carry your private affair. Show me your letter before you give it."[5]

The two of them got their heads together over a reasoned request. Hamilton reminded the general that he had twice before asked for opportunity in combat. A year earlier he had applied to be assigned in the units going to the south; Washington had promised to gratify him when a convenient chance presented. The expedition to Staten Island in January 1780 had seemed to Hamilton favorable, and Lafayette inquired on his behalf, but Washington thought not, on two counts. Other officers would complain if Hamilton was given a whole battalion, and if his aide should come a casualty in the action Washington, in the then state of the headquarters staff, would lack necessary assistance.

The present project against New York offered neither of these objections. The command would not be beyond his rank; his 150 or 200 men would be made up from several corps, not be taken all from the light infantry. Further, the headquarters work could not suffer, for Hamilton was to be absent anyhow (evidently he' would shift his marriage for martial engagement). He hoped to lead his detachment against Bayard's Hill, the chief fortification of lower Manhattan, with which he was familiar. If the feint against Staten Island brought him too late for that prized attempt, he would like to form the van of another attack.

He chose to write to avoid the embarrassment of an interview. Ardent though he was, he did not want to take advantage of the general's disposition to favor him.[6] As it happened, this time

Washington was not called on to agree or refuse, for, as suddenly
as projected, the scheme was abandoned.[7]

Prospects of Hamilton's employment in official posts more important, to outward view at least, than that of aide, were promoted
by his friends Lafayette, Greene, and John Laurens. Hamilton
was hesitant to be urged for appointment as adjutant general, or,
immediately afterward, to be chosen by Congress for a special
mission to France to solicit monetary and military help for the next
campaign. Had either proposal matured, his break with Washington, which soon happened, would have been avoided. Had he
remained in the general's family he probably would not have had
his chance for capture of a British redoubt at Yorktown. Further,
his brief preparation for and admission to the bar would have been
deferred, nor would he have had valuable experience as a fiscal subordinate of Robert Morris.

In any event, Greene wrote to Washington that in the likelihood
of Colonel Alexander Scammell returning to his regiment, "a new
adjutant-general will be necessary; and I . . . suggest the propriety of giving this appointment to Colonel Hamilton. His services may not be less important . . . in your family business, if he
only employs a deputy extraordinary."[8] Washington replied that
"without knowing Colo. Hamilton ever had an eye to the office of
Adjt. General," he had recommended Brigadier General Edward
Hand. Besides, the adjutant-general took rank of the subinspectors, and full colonels among these would have objected if a lieutenant-colonel was put over them.[9]

Lafayette, similarly, found the prior preference for Hand, whom
Hamilton had favored, blocked efforts for his friend. The marquis,
from Paramus, November 28, 1780, wrote Washington cordially of
both General Hand and (Wm. Stephens) Smith, his own adjutant, but went on: "Unless [that is, if] however, you was to cast
your eye on a man, who . . . would suit better than any other
. . . , Hamilton is . . . the officer whom I should like to see in
that station. . . . his knowledge of your opinions and intentions
on military arrangements; his love of discipline the advantages he
would have on all the others principally when both armies will
operate together, and his uncommon abilities would render him
perfectly agreeable to you." Lafayette, like Greene, was aware
that, ironically, Hamilton's peculiar usefulness to the general as

aide stood in the way of his advancement.   So he added, "An adjudant general ought allwais to be with the commander in chief. Hamilton should, therefore, remain in your family," and his industry would allow him to fill both functions.[10]   At the same time Lafayette informed Hamilton of this and assured him: "I know the General's friendship and gratitude for you, . . . both . . . greater than you perhaps imagine.   I am sure that he needs only to be told that something will suit you, and when he thinks he can do it he certainly will.   Before this campaign, I was your . . . very intimate friend. . . . Since my second voyage, my sentiment has increased to such a point the world knows nothing about."[11]

However, mischances happened.   Lafayette wished Hamilton had permitted him to speak immediately with Washington; "this curs'd way of a letter you have insisted upon has been the Cause of my miscarrying. . . ."   Gouvion took Lafayette's letter to Washington straight to headquarters at New Windsor, but the general had altered his mind and gone to Morristown.   Here "another misfortune threw Hand in his way; and remembering your advice . . . , he hastened to make him the proposition, and in consequence . . . wrote his letter to Congress."   The marquis, after a circuit, caught up with Washington.   When he discovered that, much influenced by Hamilton, the general had settled the matter with Hand, Lafayette in his warmth offered to send an express to retrieve the letter to Congress, but Washington thought better not.

Failing to get the aide made adjutant, Lafayette posted to Philadelphia and immediately lobbied for Hamilton to be sent as envoy to France.   "I have already spoken to many members" with effect, he said, and, thus encouraged, would spend two more days "in paying visits."   If Hamilton was chosen, Lafayette would send for him by express, and speed him to France with "many private letters."[12]

John Laurens, too, had been urging the selection of Hamilton, who had proposed the mission for Lafayette, until the marquis preferred a command in the southern campaign.   "But, unfortunately for America," Laurens wrote to Washington, "Colonel Hamilton was not sufficiently known to Congress to unite their suffrages in his favor"; to prevent the business from being abandoned, Laurens, when asked, consented to go.[13]

Before he could have heard of this outcome, Alexander Hamilton was married to Betsey Schuyler. A visit to France, though in a winter voyage, would have given them a longer honeymoon than they enjoyed in the young aide's brief respite from headquarters duties.

Envy was not a part of Hamilton's nature, which, particularly in his youth and early manhood, was outgoing and enthusiastic. Besides, he felt resources within himself equal to his ambitions. At a later period, convinced that he better than another could marshal the country's defenses against a foreign threat, he coveted being placed first in command, as inspector general, under Washington, to the prejudice of Knox. He was overwrought to an ungenerous and unwise claim to preference. Had he been more relaxed, he would have saved himself excessive labors which would have been competently performed by the friend whom he shouldered aside.

Now, however, though disappointed in his hopes of leading troops in the field, he was in no wise jealous of those who were given other opportunities for which he was thought eligible. He agreed cordially with Washington's recommendation of Hand as adjutant general, and did all in his power to prosper the mission of John Laurens to France. Indeed, such was his brotherly affection and admiration for the South Carolinian that any notion of rivalship was out of the question, and the same was true of Laurens toward Hamilton.

This zealous support was expressed in the proposal, Lafayette agreeing, that the commander in chief furnish the special minister with a letter, to be presented to the French authorities, reinforcing and defining the objects of Congress. Hamilton prepared this, and Washington, having added a bon voyage, copied the whole to give it the benefit of his autograph, which leaves no question that it had his perfect sanction.[14] It is a cogent analysis of the state of the contest and declaration of the assistance from France necessary to accomplish allied victory. It is not so much a set of instructions to the American envoy as it is a plea to the French ministry. The major portion, setting forth the economic disabilities of the United States, while intimately and ruefully known to Washington, would not have originated with him.[15] Concerning ways and means, the whole is a remarkable forecast of the reasoning Hamilton used a decade later when Secretary of the Treasury.

In pressing the war, he began, the country had exceeded its

natural abilities. Mistakes had been made in the finances, but decay of public credit was due primarily to lack of wealth, or of funds for the redemption of paper. By now the popular contempt for the currency was itself an obstacle to its restoration. Efforts to support the army by collections of food and forage had proved unworkable. Domestic loans could yield little, for the few monied men could and would invest more profitably otherwise. The distresses of the army demanded speedy relief to prevent disastrous results, and he reminded of recent mutinies. War burdens were producing fears in the people that a struggle for liberty had become endurance of oppression from their own government.

The consequence was "The absolute necessity of an immediate, ample and efficacious succour of money; . . . enough to be a foundation for substantial arrangements of finance, to revive public credit and give vigor to future operations." Some months before, in a mood near disgust, Hamilton had written to John Laurens, who as a paroled prisoner of war (captured at Charleston) had been removed from the scene: "You have . . . heard how we have made a very good show with very little substance. . . . our countrymen have all the folly of the ass and all the passiveness of the sheep. . . . They are determined not to be free. . . . If we are saved France and Spain must save us. . . . the conduct of the states is enough to make a wise man mad."[16] The coming campaign, the instructions continued, must witness a fatal blow to the power of the enemy, or American resistance was finished. "Next to a loan of money a constant naval superiority on these coasts is the object most interesting." This would cut off enemy supplies from Europe and enable the allies to take the offensive. Besides, for reasons given, France would be wise to transfer the naval war to America.

Our ally must not conclude that our desire for independence or resources to secure success were extinguished, if only a spring could be supplied by outside help. We could repay our borrowings. "Our debts are hitherto small. The vast . . . tracts of unlocated lands,[17] the variety and fertility of soils; the advantages . . . we possess for commerce, insure to this country a rapid advancement in population and prosperity and a certainty, its independence being established, of redeeming in a short term of years, the comparatively inconsiderable debts it may . . . contract." What Washington and Hamilton agreed that Laurens should say had been put more bluntly by Rochambeau to Vergennes: "Send us troops, ships and money, but do not depend upon these people [the Americans] nor upon their means; they have neither money nor credit"; their resources for resistance are "only momentary."[18]

Laurens's efforts could not have been better rewarded. He promptly secured a loan of 10 million livres to be opened in Holland with French guarantee (4 million appropriated to cover bills drawn by Congress on Franklin, 6 million granted for military supplies), and the indispensable French naval reinforcements for what thus proved to be the closing campaign.[19]

Disappointed attempts at employment more independent than that of aide led on to quitting of the headquarters family.

Our knowledge of Hamilton's only emotional clash with Washington—it was in February 1781—is almost entirely from the self-justifying account given by the younger man to his father-in-law, Philip Schuyler.[20] Other close friends of Hamilton, who had the particulars from him orally, naturally made only veiled allusions to the incident in letters. Washington said nothing, referred to it in writing only twice, to Lafayette when the latter broached the subject, and, most considerately, to Hamilton himself, as we shall see.

Commander in chief and aide passed each other on the stairs at headquarters at New Windsor. "He told me he wanted to speak to me," Hamilton recounted. "I answered that I would wait upon him immediately. I went below, and delivered Mr. Tilghman a letter . . . of a pressing . . . nature. Returning to the General, I was stopped on the way by the Marquis de La Fayette, and we conversed together about a minute on a matter of business. He can testify how impatient I was to get back, and that I left him in a manner which, but for our intimacy, would have been more than abrupt. Instead of finding the General, as is usual, in his room, I met him at the head of the stairs, where, accosting me in an angry tone, 'Colonel Hamilton,' said he, 'you have kept me waiting . . . these ten minutes. I must tell you, sir, you treat me with disrespect.' I replied, without petulancy, but with decision: 'I am not conscious of it, sir; but since you have thought it necessary to tell me so, we part.' 'Very well, sir,' said he, 'if it be your choice,' or something to this effect, and we separated. I sincerely believe my absence, which gave so much umbrage, did not last two minutes."[21]

Within the hour Washington sent Tilghman to the offended aide, "assuring me of his great confidence in my abilities, integrity, usefulness, etc., and of his desire, in a candid conversation, to heal a difference which could not have happened but in a moment of passion." Hamilton gave Tilghman a return message that he must have been pondering, for it was in five parts. His resolution was not to be revoked. He begged to be excused from an interview that would be mutually disagreeable. Out of the family, he would conduct himself toward the general as while in it. He would not embarrass Washington's business by quitting him until absent aides returned. Meanwhile, he proposed that they behave toward each other as if nothing had happened. The general let it stand at that, with thanks for Hamilton's promised interim assistance.[22]

Hamilton explained to Schuyler that he rejected the overture to accommodation because he "always disliked the office of an aid-de-camp as having in it a kind of personal dependence." Early in the war he had refused invitations of two major generals,[23] but "an idea of the General's character which experience taught me to be unfounded overcame my scruples. . . . It was not long before I discovered he was neither remarkable for delicacy nor good temper, which revived my former aversion to the station . . . and it has been increasing ever since." Held by a sense of duty, he resolved that if a breach happened he would not seek to repair it. He believed Washington would bear a grudge against him.

Though holding Washington's confidence, "for three years past I have felt no friendship for him and have professed none. The truth is, our dispositions are the opposites of each other, and the pride of my temper would not suffer me to profess what I did not feel." He had let it be apparent that he "desired to stand rather upon a footing of military confidence than of private attachment." He thought this hurt Washington's self-esteem. Hamilton continued objectively: "The General is a very honest man. His competitors have slender abilities, and less integrity. His popularity has often been essential to the safety of America, and is still of great importance to it. . . . I think it is necessary he should be supported."[24]   Hamilton hoped and believed his own alienation would make no difference in Schuyler's friendship for Washington. Nothing should be said publicly of this rift between general and aide.

Written all over this is the effect of fatigue and anxiety on both of them.   The strains of war, long drawn out, had reached a new point of exasperation and alarm—treasury empty, mutiny of old troops, negligent recruiting of new, the enemy in Virginia threatening to cut off supplies from Greene's tenuous force to the south.[25]   Ironically, the worry was worse because of hopeful portents.   Maryland's adherence had made the Confederation a political reality, effective executive departments had been authorized, and the ceding of back lands loomed as a basis of government credit.   John Laurens might return with substantial instant financial help from France.   The French fleet at Newport, with the hope of splendid reinforcements under De Grasse, offered prospect of "speedy and glorious termination of the war. . . ."[26]   If only economic and military collapse could be staved off until reform within and help from without rescued the day!

Hamilton and undoubtedly Washington had worked until midnight February 15, the eve of their flare-up, preparing dispatches to be forwarded to Rochambeau and other French officers at Newport, "very early in the morning with the most positive directions concerning expedition."[27]   Under these circumstances a trifling mischance would easily produce a sudden reproof by the general and a sharp retort by the aide.   The wonder is that we have not more recorded instances of protracted strain leading to petty strife.   Mrs. Hamilton was at headquarters, which explains why Hamilton's particular written account of the break was addressed to her father, not to her.   She said that Washington "expressed himself as not having been treated, for some time, with proper respect."   Lafayette, distressed when he knew that he, however innocently, had caused the hot words, "explained the delay" and "privately expressed to each of them his own feelings. . . ."   However, "he found each disposed to believe that the other was not sorry for the Separation."[28]

If either was to blame, it was Hamilton.   Not that the delay, shorter or longer, in obeying Washington's summons was his fault. Detention by Lafayette was the merest accident.   But the younger man, with all of his remarkable qualities, did not show the forbearance required in his position. Surprised to find the general awaiting him at the head of the stairs in angry mood, the word of apology died on Hamilton's lips, and he answered in kind. And yet his response had been preparing. He wanted to be leader in a physical exploit, not auxiliary in headquarters administration, conference, and planning. That the pen was mightier than the sword he would have agreed, impersonally, but he had held the one too long and the other too little. Fellow aides had quit the "family" for the field—Baylor, Fitzgerald, Webb, Laurens, Scammell. He sensed, and said to Schuyler, that the war would soon be over; his coveted chance for a return to line command must be in the coming campaign or not at all.[29]

The motive belonged to youth. When Washington sent Tilghman to his aide with "his desire, in a candid conversation, to heal a difference which could not have happened but in a moment of passion," the general was acknowledging his own error, but more, he felt that Hamilton was making a mistake. Assurance of the young man's "abilities, integrity, usefulness, etc." (and we must supply Tilghman's elaboration), meant that he filled a special place in "the General's confidence and counsels," while others could act with equal distinction in march and in battle. Neither could foresee quite the crucial assignment that would fall to Hamilton's lot at Yorktown; but even so, in those few minutes of perilous assault, Gimat, Laurens, Barber, and others were no less spirited.

Schuyler, though finding no personal impropriety in Hamilton's conduct toward Washington, was "afflicted" by his wish to quit the general's staff, and hoped "that the unhappy breach should be closed, and a mutual confidence restored." The difference between commander and confidential aide, added to other divisions observed among the Americans, would have bad effect, "especially with the French officers, with the French minister, and even with the French court." Washington by his overture for reconciliation had acknowledged and repented of his haste. Hamilton should remember that "It falls to the lot of few men to pass through life without one of those unguarded moments which wound the feelings of a friend." He should blot out the incident. "Your services are wanted . . . in that particular station which you have

. . . filled so beneficially to the public, and with such extensive reputation."[30]

The larger question with which a biographer must deal is posed, not by the outburst of irritation, but by Hamilton's declaration to his father-in-law of his lack of personal attachment to Washington. It is true that at the time of writing, two days after the incident, his resentment had not cooled, or at least his obstinacy against a reconciliation, though invited by Washington and urged by Lafayette, Tilghman, and perhaps others, had not yielded. Thus his picture of Washington was colored by anger, and by his wish, himself, to stand in a fair light. But, in spite of this allowance for bias in saying that the general was "neither remarkable for delicacy nor good temper," and that he (Hamilton) had "felt no friendship for him," the report of imperfect sympathy was accurate. Paradoxically, the older man, of English reserve, was more outgoing in their relationship than the youngster from the tropics, who often was impulsive.

Washington was always not only fully appreciative of his brilliant junior associate, but many times expressed affection for him, in word and deed. Hamilton, on his part, was colder and less just. His self-esteem diminished his perception of Washington's greatness. This disability extended to some of Hamilton's particular partisans, notably Pickering. The fact of Washington's prime importance to the country's cause Hamilton fully declared, but the reason for it, in Washington's complete devotion, Hamilton, with all of his insight, did not quite grasp. Harrison, Tilghman, Meade, and more of his headquarters intimates who were in Hamilton's station, did honor to themselves in recognizing eagerly what Hamilton failed to catch. Hamilton was too capable, and not enough self-abnegating, to share their wisdom and their consequent personal attachment.

This is not the place to contrast Washington's mental aptitudes with those of Hamilton. The differences must appear in the recital of instances in which their complementary faculties were plied with success. Washington was less intellectual, was equal in reasoning power, superior in judgment. He was not so quick, but was surer. What he lacked in detail of information he more than made up in the sum. What glittered in Hamilton was gold, but had its modicum of alloy. Washington's metal was purer.

Hamilton was susceptible to infatuations to which Washington did not fall victim. This is not to make Washington the adulated symbol of all virtue, the measuring rod by which to gauge the shortcomings of another. The distinction was genuine and material.

Hamilton loved Laurens, Lafayette, Troup, Meade, and more. It was not only that they were of his age, for he was as devoted to elders like Schuyler and Boudinot. Numbers who were not his equals in talents enjoyed his loyal esteem; such were McHenry, Wolcott, and Nicholas Fish. Washington had the same place in Hamilton's allegiance, but, for whatever reasons we care to assign, not in his affection.[31]

Hamilton's exit from the family was an inconvenience to the general, not more, for the war was drawing to a close. The opportunity it gave Hamilton for return to command in the final scene of conflict, at Yorktown, had more importance for him in his aftercareer. Without the dangerous service he then performed, brief but brilliant, Washington could hardly have appointed him over Knox and other senior field officers seventeen years later. Superior still was the place he won in his own estimation, and the standing it gave him in the political councils of the country.

Noah Webster, seven years after the event, asked Washington to settle the controverted question whether in 1781 he ever meant to assault New York or whether a blow in the south was all along his object. Washington replied briefly, generally, and from memory "that it was determined by me (nearly twelve months before hand) at all hazards to give out and cause it to be believed by the highest military as well as civil officers that New York was the destined place of attack, in order to spur the Eastern & Middle states to greater exertions in furnishing specific supplies, and to render the enemy less prepared elsewhere. . . . New York was thought to be beyond our effort & . . . the only hesitation that remained was between an attack upon the British army in Virginia or that in Charleston. . . . That much trouble was taken . . . to misguide and bewilder Sir Henry Clinton in regard to the real object . . . is certain. Nor were less pains taken to deceive our own army. . . ."[32]

This seems to answer the speculations of the time, and to render unnecessary the elaborate recitals since of Washington's supposed quandary.[33] However, can we not trust what he wrote in his private diary at the time? As late as May 22, 1781, his memorandum of the "plan of Campaign" fixed upon with Rochambeau gave preference to the capture of New York.[34] Not until August 1 did he tell himself that failure of the states to furnish men had set awry his purpose. "Thus circumstanced . . . I could scarcely see a ground upon wch. to continue my preparations against New York . . . and therefore I turned my views more seriously (than I had before done) to an operation to the Southward. . . ."[35]

Read in the light of Washington's declared design to mislead "the highest military as well as civil officers," including "our own army," numerous happenings no longer appear experimental and indecisive, but testify to the subtlety of his operations. His words to Webster authorize us to believe that in this crisis of the war he shared his determination with no one; more, that all of his contrary propositions and conditional suggestions were put to his closest associates with the purpose of concealing as long as possible his true aim. Are we to conclude that when Washington reviewed this stressful period, the particulars of doubt and hesitancy, the possibilities that did not mature, tended to drop out in favor of the resolve that ended in glorious success?

Washington's secret, whenever he determined on it, was close kept if Hamilton did not know it, for the aide was privy to all that entered and left headquarters. The sole military aim of the commander in chief could not escape him. Indeed, he wrote for Washington letters disclosing it (see below).

Hamilton gave a double twist to Washington's deception of Sir Henry Clinton, according to an incident narrated by his son. An American spy, found to be in British pay, was allowed at headquarters to see a map marked for a pretended land and naval attack on New York. To confirm his belief, the spy inquired of Hamilton the destination of the army. Confident that the truth, under the circumstances, would be most misleading, Hamilton replied, "We are going to Virginia." Clinton made the expected deduction.[36]

Betsey Hamilton did her excellent best, as hostess at New Windsor headquarters, to carry off the situation as if there had been no rift between her husband and the general. At the first of March she "served . . . Tea with much grace" to Washington, Knox, and the aides, the special guest being Baron von Closen, who had arrived from Newport with letters from the French commanders.[37]

Almost Hamilton's last service as military aide was in Washington's journey from New Windsor to Newport to visit Rochambeau and Destouches to speed the departure of the latter's fleet for Virginia waters. The object was nothing less than the salvation of American hopes in the southern theater. De Tilly, dispatched from Newport three weeks earlier with a ship and two frigates in an ill-considered first attempt, had not been able to dislodge Arnold from Portsmouth. Now Admiral Destouches was sailing for the Chesapeake, as asked earlier by Washington, with the whole French fleet at Newport and 1,100 troops supplied by Rochambeau. The effort was to reach there before the British Admiral Arbuthnot could arrive from Gardiners Bay. Thus supported at sea, Lafayette could drop down from Head of Elk to cooperate with Steuben against Arnold and then move into North Carolina to "intercept if possible Cornwallis and relieve General Greene and the Southern States."[38]

At the end of the first day's eastward ride, March 2, from Colonel Andrew Morehouse's near the Connecticut line, Hamilton wrote for Washington to Rochambeau and Destouches giving notice of the visit and advance thanks for renewing the attempt in the Chesapeake.[39] Expresses hurried these dispatches along the route of the general, Hamilton, and Tilghman—Litchfield, Farmington, Hartford, Bolton, Norwich, and two ferries to Newport, the destination reached the 6th.[40] At the conference with the French officers, land and marine, Hamilton was surely an interpreter, along with Baron von Closen, who was in Washington's party in the journey to French headquarters. Washington reviewed the resplendent French troops, in such contrast to his own shabby Continentals and coatless militia, and the town of Newport, receiving him for the first time as commander in chief, offered him an address as glowing as the candled illumination of the evening. Hamilton was assigned to prepare Washington's acknowledgment of this welcome.[41] It embraced, in grateful, graceful sentences, just the appropriate compliments and thanks to French forces and nation, commiseration to Newport for injuries suffered when in enemy hands, and promise of full restoration.[42] Washington added to Hamilton's draft but a single appreciative word. This was the last of a long series of formal responses penned by the aide for his chief during the war, and unimportant except that it presaged others of more consequence, in civil capacity, ending in Washington's Farewell Address. Hamilton was pressed to be present at a conference of Washington with Rochambeau and his engineer, and on the 8th rode with the general and his hosts to the point to see the fleet pass out with a fair wind at sunset.[43]

When Washington had finished his business at Newport he set out, on March 11, by way of Bristol, Providence, and Hartford, through heavy roads and foul weather, for what he called "my dreary quarters at New Windsor."[44] Probably Hamilton was not with him on the return journey, as after March 8 none of his letters is in Hamilton's hand, all being written by himself or, oftener, Tilghman. Back at headquarters on March 20,[45] Humphreys began to share the work, and George Augustine Washington was occasionally pressed into service.[46] When Harrison, the "Old Secretary," went to headquarters on March 23 to say goodbye, Hamilton was not there, but was with Mrs. Hamilton and the Schuylers at Albany.[47] Washington's route by Providence was out of Hamilton's way homeward.[48]

Hamilton was back at headquarters at New Windsor, three weeks after the general's return from conferences with the French officers, for brief final service to Washington as aide. With the exception of one most particular letter (below), what he wrote for the general concerned principally exchange of prisoners, with the antecedents of which he was familiar.[49] Several letters conveyed Washington's perplexities to find commands for deserving officers; writing them informed Hamilton of the difficulties he was soon to encounter in his own application. The most illustrative was to Lafayette, explaining that if the marquis preferred to return to headquarters from Virginia, which he had full permission to do, Washington did not know how to find him a new field assignment.[50]

Meanwhile Hamilton was receiving the regrets of closest friends that he was leaving the general's family. Lafayette, from Head of Elk, hoped it had not happened; Hamilton would be more important at headquarters, but, failing that, Lafayette broadly hinted, Hamilton should head the artillery in a new light corps which the Frenchman proposed.[51]   Lafayette soon expressed to Washington his concern at the rift between general and aide.   He was the first to know of "a circumstance lately happened in your family" and from that moment used all means in his power "to prevent a separation which I knew was not agreeable to Your Excellency," but had waited for Washington to confide in him.[52] Washington answered in his own hand that he would at once have told Lafayette of the difference "had it not been for the request of H—— who desired that no mention should be made of it: Why this injunction on me, while he was communicating it himself, is a little extraordinary! but I complied, and religiously fulfilled it."[53]   In saying this, Washington probably did not know, unless Tilghman told him, that Lafayette, stopping Hamilton on his way to do the general's bidding, had been the unconscious cause of the tiff, and thus it was natural for the marquis to learn of it, from Hamilton, from Tilghman, or even by what he overheard.

Hamilton did not mention to Greene his impending separation from Washington until April 11, 1781; then he wrote briefly and vaguely, as letters from headquarters were often intercepted and "hung up in *Rivington's Gazette.*"   His departure from the family was "not an affair of calculation, but of feeling.   You may divine the rest. . . ."   Was there any post for him in the southern army? He would "hate to be nominally a soldier."[54]   Fleury knew from some source that Hamilton would soon quit as aide, for he inquired from Newport, April 10, ". . . are you already, out of the general's family? in what capacity do you serve?"[55]

At this time, the middle of April, 1781, expecting to leave his headquarters employment, he intended to take lodgings for Mrs. Hamilton, probably across the river at Fishkill (see below).   He asked Colonel Jeremiah Wadsworth, at Hartford, to send by the express a pound of good green tea and a dozen knives and forks "such as you purchased for Mrs. Jacob Cuyler at Albany."[56] Looking forward to new expenses, he was trying to draw some hard money from Philadelphia.[57]

Two of Hamilton's last letters for Washington, in his capacity of aide, appropriately enough forecast unmistakably the focus on

Cornwallis in Virginia which brought victory. Lafayette was disabused of his lingering belief that New York was to be the target. It was most probable, said the general, that "the weight of the war this campaign will be in the Southern states, and it will become my duty to go there in person. . . . Of this I would not have you to say anything."[58] The next day he reinforced this. Lafayette need not expect "a certain event"—an attack on New York. "The danger to the Southern states is immediate and pressing; it is our duty to give them support. . . ."[59]

Had Hamilton been available at headquarters immediately after the return from Newport, he might have saved the commander in chief an embarrassing incident. This was produced by a slur of the general on French cooperation. Washington was almost never imprudent; Hamilton frequently was; but in this instance the latter, less harried, might have interposed a caution which Tilghman did not use. In a private letter to his kinsman and Mount Vernon manager, Lund Washington, on March 28, he deplored the fact that the expedition of the French fleet and detachment which he had just seen sail from Newport was not undertaken "when I first proposed it to them; the destruction of Arnolds Corps would then have been inevitable before the British fleet could have been in a condition to put to Sea. instead of this the small squadron . . . was sent, and could not, as I foretold, do anything without a Land force at Portsmouth."[60] This letter, with others from headquarters,[61] was taken from the post rider next day at Smith's Clove, and was promptly published in Rivington's *Gazette.*[62] Lafayette, learning of this on his way to Virginia, sent Washington his feeling regret, verging on remonstrance: "A letter from you relating to the delays of the French makes a great noise at Philadelphia. Indeed it gives me pain on many political accounts."[63]

Rochambeau took longer in presenting his dignified protest. If Washington's expostulation was not a forgery, it was overturned by the facts in the case, which Rochambeau recited to show that the French had not been delinquent in obeying Washington's orders.[64] Washington called on Hamilton to draft his reply. Though the general made his own revisions, as an explanation it could not be a success. Beginning with the caution that the enemy, fond of damaging forgeries, may have changed some of his expressions, and the mitigations that his letter was private and no such complaint against the French allies had been offered to a public body, he was obliged to admit "the general import to be true." He hoped his indiscretion would not disturb the harmony between them.[65] No more could be said. Fortunately, Rochambeau's habitual generosity[66] canceled a slip of Washington that might have been injurious.

Hamilton drew for Washington recommendations for revising punishments in the army and prescribing modes of furlough and discharge that would discourage desertion.[67] The main point was that the death penalty was often ordered because 100 lashes—the highest number then authorized—were insufficient for certain crimes. But capital sentences, thus unreasonably imposed, were usually rescinded, which encouraged the more serious infractions of discipline. Could corporal punishment be extended to a maximum of 500 lashes? This savage recommendation is little mitigated by remembering that the floggings were distributed over a number of days. Perhaps recognizing this, it was proposed that some delinquents be put at public works, and deserters might be transferred to the navy, "where they have less opportunity to indulge their inconstancy." Other means of preventing, rather than penalizing desertion, were suggested. The matter was referred by Congress to a committee.

Previously, brutal punishments had entered into complaints that encouraged the Conway cabal. As one reads the reports of courts-martial as they came to the commander in chief for action, the suspicion is that soldiers' misdeeds were chargeable in great part to their misery. If erring individuals were to be corrected, a few stripes laid on the bare backs of some members of Congress might not have gone amiss. Washington and his officers, inflicting oversevere penalties, were victims of the same sunken morale; in desperation they went to extremes. We do not know how far Hamilton approved of the whippings. It is not fanciful to suppose that his opposition to slavery owed something to the harsh treatment of Negroes in the West Indies.

In this connection, his earlier compassionate plea for André to be shot rather than hanged may be recalled. A sequel was his later (June 1782) and more pointed intervention to save Captain Charles Asgill, an innocent young prisoner of war, from retaliatory execution. Captain Joshua Huddy, commanding an American blockhouse in New Jersey, captured by loyalists, had been hanged on a charge which Washington, his council of officers, and Congress were convinced was false. All concurred in a vain call on Sir Henry Clinton (and later Sir Guy Carleton) to give up Captain Lippincott, leader of the guilty party. Washington ordered that a British captain in American hands be selected and sent to headquarters as a hostage. The lot fell on Asgill, a mere boy and (which figured in the event) of titled birth and promising prospects. When Lippincott was acquitted by the British, young Asgill was slated for death.

While Washington feelingly begged that General Carleton would spare the innocent by making the guilty suffer, he was obdurate in his resolve for American revenge.[68] Had Hamilton been still at headquarters, in his old relationship to the commander in chief, he would have urged the impolicy of this at an earlier stage. As it was, he interceded through General Knox, whose advice had weight with Washington. Such a sacrifice of the innocent was and would be considered in Europe "wanton and unnecessary," and "unfavorable to the General's character." The war was all but won, and we should not at this late day commit an act of fury. Pretext could readily be found for Washington to relent of his oath. Carleton would offer apology and promise of prevention in future. Humanity would approve accepting these concessions.[69] This course was followed, though not until five painful months had elapsed, in which Lady Charles Asgill appealed to the King and Queen of France to save her son. Vergennes passed the royal plea to Washington, and Congress, with minimum face-saving, ordered the doomed youth liberated.[70]

The pageant at Newport and the short sequel at New Windsor headquarters closed the chapter of Alexander Hamilton's lively duty to the commander in chief as aide de camp. He had held the post for four years and one month. In that span, including all of the worst of the war except the desperate days of the winter of 1776 on the west side of the Delaware, he had seen many enter and leave the headquarters family. In the sifting, three always remained besides himself—Harrison, Tilghman, and Humphreys. While each of these had his special fitness, and each would have declined a distinction, Hamilton had come to be in fact what the

Spanish envoy Rendon called him, "first Aid . . . of General Washington."[71]   Little of his work had been routine, and none of it was performed in a routine manner.   He had not only anticipated Washington's wants, but, with his quick perception of the situation, military, political, and economic, was the general's counselor in becoming ways.   This is evident in contributions that he volunteered, in proposals that the commander sanctioned (such as the instructions to John Laurens in his mission to France), and appears in a hundred occasions when Hamilton's words were the prompting as much as the report of Washington's wishes.   With striking differences, their mental and moral qualities so blended during their war association that each was peculiarly welcome to the other.   In these years the partnership, as it may be truly called, was that of senior and junior, in all that the words imply. Then an interval in which the apprentice became a journeyman. When their active collaboration recommenced in the first cabinet, all of their mutual aid was redoubled.   Without the tutelage that Hamilton received at Washington's side during the war, and without the confidence of Washington which he then earned, their later hand-in-glove cooperation could hardly have been possible.

Hamilton seems to have moved from headquarters at New Windsor across to the east bank of the Hudson at De Peyster's Point[72] the middle of April 1781 or not long after, when he was joined by Elizabeth, who probably had left New Windsor for Albany when Hamilton went to Newport.   Copies of some of his letters at this time are partly or wholly in her hand.[73]   We have no evidence of his being at headquarters after April 22 except for his draft of Washington's reply to Rochambeau of the 30th; this undoubtedly required a conference for which the aide was haled back.[74]

Six weeks earlier he had written to Schuyler that though he was leaving his post as aide, "I cannot think of quitting the army during the war."   He was balancing between reentering the artillery, and taking "a handsome command in the campaign in the light infantry" should one offer.[75]   He now applied directly to General Washington.   He no longer had the hindrance of holding a staff commission, nor did Washington have the motive of preferring to keep a valuable headquarters aide.   But new difficulties loomed, which Hamilton sought to set aside.   He recited that in consequence of the resolution of Congress for granting commissions to previous aides-de-camp, he had obtained that of lieutenant colonel in the army of the United States bearing rank since March 1, 1777. He was ready for active duty whenever the forces should take the field. Could the general foresee an assignment for him in the coming campaign?

Unconnected with any regiment, his only command must be in a light corps, but for this he thought his pretensions good. He reminded that he had been in service since the beginning of 1776, and that had he remained in the line his rank would have been better than he now held. He anticipated objections that he well knew might be raised to naming to commands "officers not belonging to what is called the line." He hoped he stood well enough with the officers in general so that none would wish to debar him. As the light infantry already formed was detached to the south, a vanguard would be needed for the northern army.[76]

This request, for which Washington was prepared, crossed the river and had the general's regretful, and qualified, refusal the same day. Hamilton must recall the "ferment in the Pennsylvania line last Campaign" over the appointment of Major (Wm.) Macpherson,[77] and he knew "the uneasiness which at this moment exists" among New England officers because commands were given—of necessity—to Colonel Gimat and Major Galvan.[78] If any advanced corps was formed, it would be small, composed of Eastern troops, and the discontent of officers in those lines, should one of Hamilton's rank be given command of or in it, might have serious consequences. Possibly it crossed Washington's mind that the New Englanders' animus that displaced Schuyler from the northern command prior to Saratoga would be revived if his son-in-law was now given a preference in their ranks. Washington maintained his right to override objections, but, in a democratic army at a critical juncture, prudence forbade him to press too far. Hamilton's merit could not be disputed, but neither could that of others who had provoked protest. Commanders who had trained troops were jealous of opportunities for special enterprise, and repelled the intrusion of "Brevet Officers."[79] Finally, with fatherly solicitude, Washington tried to remove a suspicion which his young associate, still of touchy temper, might harbor: "My principal concern," he said, "arises from an apprehension that you will impute my refusal . . . to other motives than those I have expressed, but I beg you to be assured I am only influenced by the reasons which I have mentioned."[80]

Hamilton in his reply, which he delayed a few days in writing,[81] did not press the general for an early appointment to command, though he tried to argue away objections to it should another light corps be formed. He showed in some detail how his own claims were on a different footing from those of Major Macpherson, and how the appointments of Gimat and Galvan need not militate against him. He was anxious that Washington should not think him capable of asking what he knew was inconsistent with the good of the service.[82]

The shift from Washington's family and removal of the early prospect of other military employment did not leave Hamilton idle.

We do not know how long he had been at work on his second essay-letter to Robert Morris, outlining a policy and program Morris might choose to follow should he, as Hamilton devoutly hoped, accept the election as Superintendent of Finance. It was sent from De Peyster's Point, April 30, 1781, though it has been treated earlier in these pages in connection with his previous of-ferings on the same general topic to Morris and to Duane.[83] It is probable that it was commenced at Albany after Hamilton went there from Newport toward the end of March, when he had a fort-night's interval before returning to headquarters; here his work on it was doubtless continued, his duties for Washington being light, and he completed it when he moved to lodgings with Mrs. Hamilton across the river.[84] This is only one example of his ability to combine efforts of different sorts—the casual with the deliberate, the limited with the broadest. His present prescrip-tion for the financial rescue of the country was the result of all he had read, observed, and thought before, but especially was an enlargement upon the brief with which, for Washington, he had supplied John Laurens in his economic mission to France.[85]

We do not certainly know Hamilton's whereabouts in the next few weeks, after failure of his application for field command. In a letter of May 18, 1781, from Newport, his brother-in-law, John Carter (Church),[86] showed that he was not posted on Hamilton's latest plans, but supposed that he would accompany Washington

to the impending conference with the French officers at Wethersfield, and so sent the letter by the hand of General Chastellux.[87]
The talks resulted in the movement of Rochambeau and his army
to the lower Hudson and the projection of the more important
later cooperation with De Grasse's fleet, but whether Hamilton
was of Washington's party, May 18–25, is doubtful.   He was not
mentioned in Washington's diary or other accounts of the journey
and meeting.[88]

Schuyler showed no regret at the news of Hamilton's dim prospect of a new military assignment.   Instead, Hamilton could prepare to go to Congress, for the New York legislature, which
Schuyler would soon attend, would doubtless elect him a delegate.[89]   At the same time, Hamilton had an appreciative acknowledgment from Robert Morris of his recent "performance"
outlining plans for revenue and particularly for the foundation of
a national bank.   This time Morris was not writing to an unknown, for, as may have come to his ears, Hamilton had been in
contemplation of some for the very place Morris occupied (see below), and moreover the young man was familiar as the son-in-law
of Schuyler on whom Morris intimately relied.[90]

This exchange may be thought of as the proximate beginning of
the confidential association of the two men whose names are most
prominently identified with early American public finance.
Morris was reassured to find that many of Hamilton's suggestions
coincided with his own ideas.   However, the plan of a bank,
which Hamilton would soon see, fell short of the scale which the
latter had urged.   Morris was sure of the wisdom of beginning
with a small capital which could be collected rather than aiming
at more than could be raised, for this would be fatal.   Once
prosperously begun, the "future increase of capital" was certain.
For equally sound reasons he rejected the notion of "interweaving
a landed security with the capital. . . ."   Morris would give
Hamilton's proposals to the bank directors, and plainly offered to
accord him the recognition he deserved with the public, a pledge
which Morris later handsomely fulfilled.[91]

Probably about the middle of May, 1781, or later, Alexander
and Betsey went to the Schuyler home in Albany.[92]   If so, it was
here, in spite of the distractions of young nieces and nephews,[93]
that he wrote the first four numbers of *The Continentalist*.[94]   Ten

months earlier he had observed to Duane that "If a Convention is called [to form a closer union], the minds of all the States and the people ought to be prepared to receive its determinations by sensible and popular writings. . . ."[95] In the present papers his object was to persuade to the fullest use of the Articles of Confederation to give necessary power to the central government, though the last number did not appear until within a fortnight of the resolutions of the New York legislature, drafted by Hamilton, calling for a constitutional convention.[96] The method was the same he later used in the more elaborate *Federalist* series, with the difference in subject matter that he was now urging certain policies and practices in a going government rather than approval of a projected new one. As always in Hamilton's appeals in the public behalf, one led to another. *The Continentalist* is the sequel to the letters to Duane and Robert Morris and the memorandum for John Laurens's mission to France, and it anticipates the New York resolutions, the report of the Annapolis convention, and the *Federalist*. This short series is notable for simplicity of the treatment, except in certain passages discussing the incidence of taxes; for the moderation and practicality of his recommendations; and for the succinct statement of his Mercantilist inspiration. Many of the arguments were to be repeated in fuller form in later productions and debates.

He contrasted the nobility of "a great Federal Republic, closely linked in the pursuit of a common interest," with the contemptible prospect of "a number of petty States, with the appearances only of union, jarring, jealous, and perverse, . . . fluctuating and unhappy at home, . . . insignificant by their dissensions in the eyes of other nations."[97] Durable union required authority in Congress, but this we lacked because our popular revolution was jealous of bestowing power. But vigor in executing the laws was as needful as precautions against encroachment on rights. The danger with us, in a federal government, was that "the members [states] will be an overmatch for the common head. . . ." The citizen was more attached to his individual state than to the union; officers of a state promoted its consequence to flatter their own. Ere long the larger commonwealths would be strong enough, and, encouraged by foreign machinations, unwise enough, to promote rival confederacies. Already, in the midst of war

perils, some had flouted the just demands of Congress, which had
not been firm enough in maintaining "the powers implied in its
original trust." We ought to enlarge the competence of Congress. "Every plan of which this is not the foundation will be
illusory."[98]

The prime lack of independent revenue for the United States
should be cured by commissioning Congress to regulate trade
through its own customs officers, to collect moderate land and
head taxes, and to sell unlocated land for the national treasury.
"While Congress continue altogether dependent on the occasional
grants of the . . . States, . . . it can neither have dignity, vigor,
nor credit." Credit in our case required not only permanent
funds for punctual payment of interest, but for redemption of
principal in a given period. The wealthiest nations were obliged
to pledge funds to obtain credit. If this pledge, in America, was
to attract loans, the funds for interest and principal must be at
command of the national government. Foreigners capable of financial assistance did not "distrust . . . our becoming independent, but . . . our continuing united. . . ." A Congress with its
own resources would go far to reassure prospective creditors.

The war could not be carried on without borrowing. Domestic
revenue that could be drawn in annually would fall millions short
of annual needs, civil and military. Any debt we were likely to
incur could be paid off in twenty years of peace. He praised the
supplanting of the Board of Treasury with a single Financier in
the person of Robert Morris, whose proposed national bank united
"the influence and interest of the moneyed men with the resources
of government. . . ." But "Congress should have it in their
power to support him with unexceptionable funds." Had this
been begun four years earlier we would have escaped the pernicious
depreciation of the currency.[99]

Thus far had Hamilton written before the Yorktown campaign.
By the time he came to the fifth number of *The Continentalist*,
printed in April 1782, refusal of certain states to give Congress
its own revenue from import duties threatened to thwart the independence, economic as well as political, that was in prospect.
He threw his weight against this recalcitrancy. He rejected the
notion—"one of those wild speculative paradoxes, which have
grown into credit among us"—that trade would regulate itself,

and would not be benefited by encouragements and restraints of government. This was contradicted by experience and practice. "To preserve the balance of trade in favor of a nation ought to be a leading aim of its policy," and individuals must be prevented from running counter to this. Government intervention, promotional and punitive, was contemplated by David Hume, who sometimes, by misapprehension, was quoted to the contrary.

Hamilton justified a "general superintendence" of trade as against regulations by the several states. Moderate duties on commerce were "one of the most eligible species of taxation," best administered by the central government. However, he conceded to the shrill clamor of the states that the duties raised in each should be credited against its quota of contribution, which was based on land. But, said some, the import duty was passed along to consumers, and thus nonimporting states would bear part of the taxes of their neighbors through which foreign goods entered the country. To this Hamilton opposed the reciprocal relation of prices of foreign and home-produced commodities. Gain or loss of a particular state in trade with its neighbors would depend in the end on its own industry and frugality. The reasoning he used is of less importance, and perhaps of less validity, than his recognition of the multiple practical exceptions to "nice and abstract distinctions." In any event, national benefit must supersede local advantage.[100]

Without import duties, impositions on land would be burdensome. Such were to be avoided because they would make labor dear, both by raising the costs of necessaries of life and by inducing migration from old settlements to new. He repudiated, in its dogmatic form, the physiocratic contention that as all taxes ultimately rested on land they were most economically collected at the source. Measurably this was true, and he cited Petty for proof; at the same time, agriculture and commerce were mutually dependent, and if one was penalized the other suffered.[101]

The later part of *The Continentalist* foreshadowed Hamilton's efforts, under Robert Morris, to improve the system of taxation in New York. Without mentioning Adam Smith, Hamilton subscribed to his canons: contribution according to ability, and condemnation of all capricious and arbitrary assessment.[102]

These papers form a summary of Hamilton's views, political

and economic. Later offerings were longer, more analytical, and surer on doctrinal points, but for a succinct statement of his prescription for America, *The Continentalist,* from title to conclusion, serves admirably. The connotations are larger than appeared to his contemporaries who read the pieces in the *New York Packet.* In seeking to shape the solidity and prosperity of his new country he refused and refuted *laissez-faire* teachings, already beginning to echo, as inapplicable here, and found surer guidance in the maxims that had made strong nations in Europe.

15

Capture of
the Last Redoubt

HAMILTON's public life may be said to have commenced with his brilliant exploit in the siege of Yorktown. From the instant he mounted a redoubt in Cornwallis's lines America never lost sight of him. What went before, with all his precociousness and eager discharge of responsibility, was preparation. He had attracted powerful friends and sponsors, whom he had rewarded with loyalty beyond the call of duty. His own work, where known, though often original, had been under their aegis, mainly in the name of Washington. Now he was to be lifted from that matrix. The mold was always to stand him in stead. He could never have developed and applied his own force and accomplished his purposes without the contribution, early and late, of his closest associates, particularly the elders among them. But now he became a national figure on his own account. As his uniform was shed, his attributes became more numerous and more conspicuous.

Yorktown, after all, was the birth of the nation. Growing up lay ahead—formal completion of the war, acknowledgment of independence, a doubtful period with a trial government, the throes of a new Constitution, and after that the establishment of institutions permanent and proliferating. As our young officer sprang to the rampart he announced himself eligible to have a hand in the sequel to victory. First, it was fulfillment for him of his restless wish for field command. This was possible only because he had separated himself from Washington—and because Washington, with magnanimity and good sense, would not be separated from him. It was fulfillment, too, of his buoyant hope for success of the Revolution, from the time, six years before, when he refuted the "Farmer" and dared to address the meeting in the Fields in New York. Never lacking confidence in himself and in the causes he joined, here at Yorktown was proof of competence, his own and his country's.

While on this theme, we may notice that the officers who acted most closely with Alexander Hamilton in the storming attack at Yorktown were Frenchmen who, though they took with them the gratitude of America, soon melted from the scene. Two of his American companions in those dangerous minutes, Barber and Laurens, were to lose their lives before the war was over. Hamilton, with regret for his friends, remained the visible emblem of the dash that determined the result of the siege and thus the result of the war.

It was a debut only, but a most auspicious one.

The Allied demonstration before New York having proved abortive, Washington settled his force of some 6,000 at Dobbs Ferry, the French to the east of him. Here they were at a stand; the British, withdrawn to Manhattan Island, were too strong to assail; news from Virginia had Lafayette and Steuben dodging Cornwallis, while Tarleton, in a deep raid on Charlottesville, sent legislature and Governor Jefferson scampering through the mountains to Staunton and temporary safety. This was the posture of affairs when Hamilton came to the American camp, July 8, still hoping for an opening. When "nothing was said on the subject of a command," he wrote General Washington, enclosing his commission. The answer came promptly in a visit from Tilghman, who in Washington's name urged that he retract his resignation and an assignment as near as possible to his wishes would be found for him. This was another mark of Washington's cordiality, both in the promise and in the manner of making it. Hamilton wrote to his wife that, in spite of her preference, his honor obliged him to accept.[1]

Three weeks brought his appointment. General orders of July 31 announced that "The Light Companies of the first and second regiments of New York (upon their arrival at Camp) with the two companies of York levies under the command of Captains

[William] Sackett and [Daniel] Williams will form a Battalion under command of Lieutenant Colonel Hamilton and Major Fish." When formed, Hamilton's battalion would join the advanced corps under Colonel Scammell.[2] Here was just what he had wanted, command equal to his rank, of New York troops in the light infantry, in the advanced corps, with his old friend Nicholas Fish as his immediate subordinate, and the universally popular Alexander Scammell, late adjutant general, as his superior.[3] He immediately set about equipping his men. With his old jealousy for their welfare and efficiency, he applied to Tilghman for an order for shoes for the two companies of levies. Because Tilghman was doubtful, Hamilton cited to Washington that the advanced corps enjoyed such a preference in the last campaign, and that such troops could not perform their specially active duty unless shod.[4] Washington agreed, stipulating strict accountability.[5]

We cannot say how early Hamilton knew that his light corps, in advance of the main force of Americans and French, would move south to the penning of Cornwallis. Washington had written in his diary on August 1 that, not receiving the troops he needed for an attack on New York, "I turned my views . . . to an operation to the Southward. . . ."[6] By August 17 or before, he had the announcement from Lafayette that Cornwallis was fortifying himself at Yorktown.[7] Some days before the Americans crossed the Hudson, Hamilton informed his wife of a greater prospect of activity, and, having thus prepared her, in his next letter broke the news that he was going to Virginia. In the midst of preparations, he could not leave his command to visit her. He lessened her alarm, as far as he could, by venturing that "ten to one . . . our views will be disappointed, by Cornwallis retiring to South Carolina by land." At all events, operations would be over by the latter part of October, and he would fly to his home. He cautioned: "Don't mention I am going to Virginia."[8]

Just before marching, Hamilton got an accession to his corps of two companies, each of a captain, two subalterns, four sergeants, and fifty rank and file ("good men engaged either for the War or three years"), formed from the Connecticut line.[9]

Hamilton's battalion arrived with the remainder of the advanced corps at King's Ferry about one o'clock on August 20, immediately began to cross,[10] and must have been at Haverstraw that afternoon. We can follow Hamilton from camp to camp in the southward course, leaving the Hudson on August 25, in General Lincoln's van, and going to Paramus and Springfield. British spies eagerly darted to Clinton with information that Washington and Rochambeau intended to attack him by way of Staten Island, else why were bread ovens built at Chatham, and why else would thirty flatboats, mounted on carriages, be hauled along unless to support a bridge across the Kill van Kull?[11] This deceiving dalliance might hold for one more march, thought Washington on the 30th; the light infantry led the left of three columns by Brunswick and Trenton.[12] Here on the Delaware Hamilton may have had a reunion with his dear friend John Laurens, on his way from Boston to Philadelphia to report to Congress his successful plea for further French aid. Laurens had accomplished what Hamilton, in Washington's name, had enjoined. News of his arrival in camp would have flown quickly,[13] and to no ears sooner than to Hamilton's. The march was on to Philadelphia with a parade through the city the afternoon of September 2. The choking dust was kind in hiding the nondescript clothing of the Americans, but could not have helped the French, "in complete uniform of white broadcloth, faced with green."[14]

Hamilton was probably not so removed from headquarters news but that he shared Washington's worry over what was happening in the Chesapeake, where the French fleet of Barras, hopefully joined to the larger one of De Grasse, must block the escape of Cornwallis. General Forman, Washington's faithful marine observer on the dunes of Sandy Hook, had notified that twenty British sail of Admirals Graves and Hood had passed out. Would they reach Virginia waters before the French, and reinforce or rescue Cornwallis? Or would they find Barras alone and make him easy prey before De Grasse could arrive with overwhelming strength?[15] These troubling speculations were not at once relieved for Hamilton when Washington met an express, south of Chester on September 5, which quieted every fear. De Grasse was within the capes with twenty-eight ships of the line, four frigates, and 3,000 land troops to be immediately debarked at Jamestown for a junction with the Americans under Lafayette.[16] The next day, at Head of Elk, Hamilton did know, for he wrote to his wife, "Circumstances that have just come to my knowledge assure me that our operations will be expeditious, as well as our success certain." He was embarking next day for Yorktown, with a heavy heart for the wider separation from Elizabeth.[17]

Washington could procure shipping for fewer than half his troops. If Hamilton's light infantry, among the first that would be needed at the Virginia end, were embarked according to his expectation, their passage was probably slow and certainly uncomfortable. An interruption, at Annapolis, was ordered by Washington on September 12 when he learned that De Grasse had sailed from the Chesapeake to engage the British fleet, with unknown result. It was necessary to halt the southward movement of the flotilla until French protection of the bay was restored.[18] Ashore at Annapolis, where he could again put pen to paper, Alexander tried to reassure Elizabeth, now five months pregnant. In the process he had to reassure himself that he had not parted with happiness for a shadow. But he was going to do his duty. Her fortitude would be bolstered by knowing that "operations will be so conducted, as to economize the lives of men."[19] At Williamsburg, the point of concentration of all forces prior to beginning of the siege, he must have met his old teacher, Lieutenant Colonel Francis Barber, who had made the Virginia campaign with Lafayette.[20]

However, when the light infantry was brigaded on the 24th, Barber's battalion, with those of Vose and Gematt [Gimat], were placed under Muhlenberg, while Hamilton's battalion, with the regiments of Scammell and Hazen, were commanded by the latter.[21] Laurens was here, drafting for Washington the kind of letter that regularly had fallen to Hamilton's lot. De Grasse was begged not to withdraw his fleet from the Chesapeake, no matter how threatening he fancied the British squadron: "Our success . . . against York[town] under the protection of the . . . fleet is as certain as any military operation can be rendered by a . . . superiority of strength and means—it is in fact a matter of mere calculation—and our progress from the opening of the trenches to the capitulation . . . of the british General . . . must necessarily go a great way towards terminating the war. . . ."[22] Two agonizing days, thankfully the last that Washington was to suffer, ended on September 27 when De Grasse, without having received the American general's entreaties, replied that his own officers had dissuaded him from seeking sea-room. Instead, he was doing all that Washington could wish—anchoring the major fleet in the York River, patrolling the James, acting "in concert for the good of our operation. . . ."[23]

Hazen's brigade, with Hamilton's light infantry, marched in second place from Williamsburg for Yorktown on September 28.[24] Ten miles through woods with now and then clearings for corn and tobacco brought the column within a mile of the enemy's left outer line of defenses, where the battalion lay on their arms that night. Next morning Hamilton drew up his troops behind the morass bordering Great Run, crossed over to within a half-mile of the outworks, and was at once saluted with cannon fire in which one of the infantrymen lost a leg.[25]

Probably not until he reached Yorktown did he get news of mid-September from Albany, when General Schuyler wrote that Elizabeth "is in good health but was so sensibly affected by your removal to the southward that I apprehended consequences. She is now at ease." Mrs. Carter (Angelica) had given birth the day before to a fine boy, and the general hoped "her sister will give me another."[26]

The soldiers readily dug shallow trenches, and the bank of sandy soil thrown up was thought protection enough until the real siege operations commenced a week later. From his post Hamilton could see nothing of the village except a church steeple and the roofs of a couple of large houses. If he walked to the right to the river escarpment he could make out, dimly, some of De Grasse's vessels that blocked the seaward exit.[27] Yorktown lies on the high southwest bank, a bulge where the river enters Chesapeake Bay. Half a mile across is the sharper, low-lying Gloucester Point. For six weeks Cornwallis had been fortifying both places, principally Yorktown, where lay 5,000 of his 6,000 troops. The village is partially enclosed by creeks above and below which, like spread curved calipers, enter the river through deep ravines. Between them is a plain, half a mile wide, which provided the siege approach.

The American-French concentration, land and naval, that cornered Cornwallis and compelled him to surrender or be annihilated, excellent as it was in celerity and unity of execution, would not have been possible without bungling by the British. Cornwallis in Virginia, though under command of Sir Henry Clinton at New York, was perforce allowed discretion in critical choices. In the antecedents of the campaign the further sharing of decisions with Lord George Germain and the king, at hopeless distance, was a handicap. Cornwallis was directed to pitch upon a post that would afford protection to British ships, instead of, as the case demanded, one which ensured naval defense of his army. Yorktown, without sure naval superiority, was a poor selection anyhow. Having gone there, Cornwallis early withdrew from the commanding positions from which he was afterward besieged, and hemmed himself between ravines on two sides and water on a third. He began his defensive works late, and was pressing them to completion when better judgment would have told him that he should use the interval to escape, northward or southward, or to attack Lafayette's force before Washington could join the marquis at Williamsburg. The failure of Admiral Rodney to circumvent arrival of De Grasse's fleet in the mouth of the river put the finish to British chance of exit or of resistance until reinforcement could arrive from New York.

This is not to detract from the wisdom of Washington's plan of allied envelopment, or the steadiness with which it was accomplished. The American general, now supplied with important French army reinforcement, but especially with overwhelming naval help which he had hitherto woefully lacked, was able to take the offensive when the enemy was in worst plight. Yorktown, more than most complicated actions long in preparation, was a coincidence of error on one side and correctness on the other.[28]

The second morning, September 30, Colonel Alexander Scammell, Hamilton's fellow commander, reconnoitering as officer of the day, was taken prisoner and mortally wounded.[29] This made Huntington's battalion larger than Hamilton's and brought a proposal from Lafayette to Washington that the two be equalized, "and put the eldest of the two lieutenant colonels [Hamilton] upon the right of the brigade."[30] Scammell's death made Hamilton eligible for the signal part he soon played in the assault.

The scheme of siege, for which Washington relied, among his own officers, on the engineering skill of Duportail and Gouvion, and the practical experience of Steuben, was by two parallels. These were trenches 3½ feet deep and 7 feet wide, the embankment of loose soil in front strengthened by materials they could get from the woods.[31]   Hamilton's corps was assigned to provide 70 fascines (bundles of sticks), 21 gabions (wicker cylinders to be filled with earth), 21 saucissions (baskets) and 210 pickets for staking the last.   All troops not otherwise engaged were constantly employed in making these reinforcements.

At intervals were redoubts and other batteries.   The first parallel, 600 yards from the enemy's works, was opened October 6, finished the 9th, when artillery of all sorts played on the invested foe.   The second parallel, at half the distance, was opened the night of the 12th.   But work on this closer line, as it was pushed toward the right, was dangerously hampered by enfilading fire from the two enemy advanced redoubts.[32]   The nearer was 200 yards in from the river and 300 yards from the main line of British defenses.   The other was on the brow of the cliff.   Each was protected by an abatis of felled trees, the sharpened limbs toward attackers.   The redoubt in from the river, which came to be known as No. 9, was the stronger, pentagonal with a deep fosse and a fraise of pointed stakes planted at right angle in the rampart.   That at the river, No. 10, was smaller, square, and lacked the fosse, but was otherwise the same.[33]

Unless these menacing redoubts were taken, the second parallel could not be completed without progressive losses in the entrenching parties.   They were too far from the first parallel for feasible storming across open ground.   The decision was to construct a special epaulement or "shoulder" as close as possible from which attackers could, in later phrase, go "over the top."[34]

On October 11 the enemy did not return a single shot; it was concluded that constantly increasing Allied fire was driving them from their embrasures.[35]   However, the night of the 13th and during the 14th the British artillery was busy, cannon and royals; a new five-inch shell was especially dangerous.[36]

During the 14th the old batteries pounded the abatis and salient angles of the two redoubts that stood in the way of capture of Cornwallis until in the afternoon the engineers thought they were sufficiently reduced in preparation for storming.[37]   Then came the question of assignments for this task.   A fortnight earlier Lafayette had solicited Washington to give him command of the right, American, wing of the combined armies for the siege, displacing General Lincoln who, the ambitious young Frenchman suggested, could console himself with directing operations across the river or higher up, at West Point.[38]

Washington conceded nothing so impolitic, not to say improper, but, as often happened, he found a suitable way to gratify the applicant. Rochambeau should make his own choice for the assault on No. 9 redoubt,[39] and Lafayette should take charge of the attack on No. 10 by the American light infantry of his division. The marquis, for command of his five battalions in the storm, designated Lieutenant Colonel Gimat, his former aide. This was because Gimat, and three of the battalions, "had made the whole Virginia campaign," while Hamilton, leading the two others, had "just come from the Northward." Hamilton saw his long-sought chance for distinction in battle slipping from him. He instantly took his counterclaim to Lafayette. That day was his tour of duty, he was senior to Gimat. Lafayette laid the issue before the commander in chief, to whom Hamilton posted to plead his right. We may imagine the ardor of his argument. Washington did not need to be reminded of his former aide's repeatedly disappointed ambition. Soon Hamilton burst from the tent and embraced Fish, exclaiming "We have it, we have it!" Lafayette objected little "to the gratification of a friend, the less so as his own former aid de camp was not excluded."[40] Lieutenant Colonel Gimat should lead his own battalion in the right column, followed by Hamilton's battalion under Major Fish. Lieutenant Colonel Laurens was to command the left column, a detachment of eighty men to circle to the rear of the redoubt, "take the enemy in reverse, and intercept their retreat."[41] Washington ordered distracting feints for the French left and at Gloucester Point, approved the orders of Vioménil and Lafayette, and made a personal appeal to the latter's troops for courage in the crucial assault.

Allied trenches and camp were expectant of "something grand to be done by our infantry."[42] When night fell,[43] at the signal of six cannon fired in rapid succession from the French batteries,[44] the two storming parties, of four hundred each, sprang from their separate defenses.[45] For silence, Hamilton's men advanced with arms unloaded, relying on the bayonet.[46] Captain James Gilliland with a few sappers and miners was in Gimat's van to remove obstructions, but delay for this was avoided when the troops impetuously passed over abatis and palisades.   Under heavy fire from above, Hamilton leaped to the parapet, called to his men to follow, and was the first in the work.   Lieutenant Mansfield and Captain Olney of Gimat's battalion were on his heels. Laurens came in from the rear on the instant, and Fish, who had unlocked to the left, entered from that quarter.   "The redoubt was in the same moment enveloped and carried in every part."

The enemy were "entitled," Hamilton reported, "to the acknowledgment of an honorable defence."   Major Campbell, commanding the fort, was made prisoner by Laurens; a captain, ensign, and 17 others were captured; 8 were killed or wounded (none after he ceased to fight), and the remainder of the garrison of 45 British and Germans escaped.   Hamilton's casualties were five times as high—a sergeant and 8 rank and file killed (all but one in Gimat's battalion), and 5 officers, a sergeant, and 25 rank and file wounded, a total of 40.   "The rapidity and immediate success of the assault," Hamilton reported to Lafayette, were "the best comment on the behavior of the troops."   He paid tribute to all in his command, particularizing the leaders, several of them for their wounds—Lieutenant Colonel Gimat, Captains (Stephen) Olney, (Stephen) Betts, (Thomas) Hunt, and (David) Kirkpatrick, and Lieutenant (John) Mansfield.   In haste of drafting he failed to include the supporting units under Generals Muhlenberg and Hazen; he might have been expected to speak of Lieutenant Colonel Francis Barber, who, first in this column, was detached to the aid of the advance, arrived, as Lafayette declared, "at the moment they were getting over the works," and was slightly wounded.[47]

Contemporary historians were apt to put in their volumes hearsay chaff that the years winnowed out.   William Gordon, who was called to account by Hamilton for other misdeeds, related that Lafayette, with Washington's acquiescence, ordered the storming party "to remember New London, and to retaliate by putting the men in the redoubt to the sword after having carried it."   He added that the humanity of Laurens, Hamilton, and their followers compelled them to disobey the command and spare the prisoners.[48]   More than twenty years later, when the tale was revived in newspapers here and in Europe, Hamilton was at pains to contradict it publicly in the most explicit fashion.[49] This drew a grateful acknowledgment from Lafayette.[50]

The capture by the French of the other redoubt was similarly brave, though not as swift for several reasons: the fort was stronger, had a garrison of four times as many, its abatis, palisade, and fraise were more intact and had to be cut away by carpenters before the troops could reach the ramparts. The French attack was earlier discovered, which, with the enemy cannonade of the redoubt when taken, helped account for the higher losses, 46 killed and 68 wounded. Of the enemy 18 were killed, more than 40 were made prisoners, including three officers, but the lieutenant colonel commanding and 120 men escaped. The French troops were principally chasseurs and grenadiers of the Gatinais and Deux-Ponts regiments.[51]

Washington's praise of the attacks must have given Hamilton peculiar satisfaction: "The bravery . . . was emulous. . . . Few cases have exhibited stronger proofs of Intrepidity, coolness and firmness than were shown upon this occasion."[52] That very night the captured redoubts were incorporated in the second parallel, the forts were hastily rebuilt on the exposed sides, and their guns were turned on the inner defenses of Cornwallis's garrison. The success in capturing the redoubts on the enemy's left flank, Washington wrote to Greene, "will prove of almost infinite importance in our Approaches. . . ."

The advanced redoubts lost, "My situation now becomes . . . critical," Cornwallis reported to Sir Henry Clinton, October 15, in cipher; "we dare not show a gun to their old batteries, and I expect that their new ones will open to-morrow morning; . . . we shall soon be exposed to an assault in ruined works, in a bad position, and with weakened numbers . . . I cannot recommend that the fleet and army should run great risque . . . to save us." Escape across the river held briefly the last hope. "A retreat by Gloucester," said Tarleton, "was the only expedient . . . to avert the mortification of a surrender, or the destruction of a storm." However, when Hamilton wrote to his wife, two days after the attack, that she need fear no repetition of such dangerous action, he did not know how promptly Cornwallis would crumple. Indeed, this was a surprise to Washington and others.[53] The storming attacks were the beginning of the end of the siege, which was all but the end of the fighting war.   The French drove back a British sally into the trenches in the early hours of the 16th, and wind and rain drove back the boats of the forlorn attempt at extrication across the river that night.   Next morning, the 17th, a red-coated drummer, amidst roar and smoke, mounted the horn work, and then an officer waving a white handkerchief.   The guns fell silent. Cornwallis, in a single sentence, asked for terms for his surrender.[54]   This line or two of script, penned in the cave in the protecting cliff in which his Lordship had taken refuge, is the most dramatic document of the war.   In turning the manuscript memorials of the siege, though one is prepared for Cornwallis's capitulation, he comes upon it with a start.   Triumph and tragedy are in the terseness of it.   So much of resistance to British power had gone before, so much of national fulfillment was to follow.

Old Elias Boudinot, proud of his protégé and writing long after the events, gave Hamilton a rôle in the surrender not elsewhere revealed, but not to be discredited out of hand.   He said Washington wanted to avoid storming the remaining works, with heavy loss of life, to which he must resort because De Grasse threatened to withdraw troops he had brought to the siege.   The commander in chief sent Hamilton and other officers under a flag to meet the British, and in the course of business to hint that an offer of surrender would be generously met.[55]

Hamilton's friends Laurens and De Noailles settled terms with their British counterparts in two days.[56]   Cornwallis perforce signed.   In the redoubt that Hamilton's troops had stormed,[57] Washington, Rochambeau, and Barras put their names to the document.   No evidence is found for the story that Hamilton, as officer of the day October 19th, supervised the ceremonies in which the enemy laid down their arms.   Lossing related that British officers demurred at handing over their cased standards to sergeants, and that Hamilton resolved the embarrassment by directing that the youngest ensign in the American army receive the flags and pass them to the enlisted men.[58]   In any event, General O'Hara, who deputized for Cornwallis at the ceremony, had no need of Hamilton's good offices (engaged years before if he should become a prisoner), for Washington at once invited him to dinner.

Hamilton did not linger at the scene of triumph. True to his promise to his wife on setting out for Virginia, he had left York-town, within a week of the surrender, for Albany.[59] ". . . he thought of nothing but reaching [his wife] the soonest possible," Schuyler later reported from Albany, "and Indeed he tyred his horses to accomplish it, and was obliged to hire others to come on from Red Hook."[60] Discontinuance of active military duty at an officer's wish was then a casual affair.[61] This, as it turned out, was Hamilton's last field service, but he wanted to retain his rank in case events recalled him. He asked Washington, the following spring, to explain his desire to Congress. He renounced "all claim to the compensations attached to my military station during the war or afterwards."[62]

Tench Tilghman had reached Congress, with Washington's of-ficial announcement of the reduction of Cornwallis, on October 24. Boudinot mentioned in this connection a circumstance that forecast Hamilton's next sphere. "When the Messenger brought the News of this Capitulation . . . it was necessary to furnish him with hard money for his expenses. There was not a suf-ficiency in the Treasury to do it, and the Members of Congress, of which I was one, each paid a Dollar to accomplish it."[63]

16

Apprenticeship
with Robert Morris

ROBERT MORRIS having stipulated for a free hand in selecting his subordinates in the new Office of Finance, chose his receivers in the states with particular care.[1] As his intermediaries with the legislatures, which were in fact sovereign in furnishing or refusing tax revenues, they occupied critical posts. They must be both persuasive and firm. At the outset Morris may have been indebted to Hamilton for the provision in the act of November 2, 1781, which allowed him to have his own receivers in the states rather than depending on the loan office commissioners. Hamilton had suggested to Duane, more than a year earlier, that a "Continental Superintendent" in each state oversee the collection of taxes, and Duane had taken a leading part in defining the new fiscal system.[2]

Hamilton was Morris's inevitable appointee for New York, for reasons which the Financier himself gave. Now free of military duties, Hamilton knew the needs of the army, and had the connections in the state and the address to induce the legislature to meet its responsibility in the crisis.[3]

However, when Morris invited him, May 2, 1782, to accept the place,[4] Hamilton at first demurred. Time was precious to him in preparing himself for the law. With the best disposition to serve the public in a promising civil capacity, he declined to be interrupted for the small commission, which he thought would not exceed a hundred pounds annually while the war lasted, or twice that when peace was established.[5]   Morris understood his objections, but removed them.   Hamilton's commission for the current year would be paid on the whole state quota, even though the taxes were not collected,[6] and Morris believed the duties would not interfere with study.

Hamilton thereat promptly accepted, but now with the scruple that in the present state of things his service would not equal the compensation.[7]   He had been informing himself, and concluded that "the whole system (if it may be so called) of taxation in this State is radically vicious, burthensome to the people, and unproductive to Government. . . . there seems to be little for a Continental Receiver to do," for, even were the county treasurers more amenable, no appropriation had been made for continental purposes.   His only prospect was in seconding the Financier's applications by personal efforts with the legislature, which would meet within a few weeks.   Meanwhile he begged instructions and promised immediate exploration of his task.[8]   Morris, forwarding the credentials July 2, found Hamilton's idea of the rôle of Receiver precisely to his liking, and gave encouragement equal to his appreciation.   Amidst all the reluctance and refusal that wrapped the problems of finance, here was a young man who ran to meet him.   Hamilton brought knowledge, and purpose imbued with contrivance.   This was the beginning of official association of the two public servants best fitted to liquidate the war.[9]

Even this partnership of talent and patriotism was unequal to punctual accomplishment in face of the jealousies and studied neglect that reigned.   Morris, by main force, had supplied the material means for military success at Yorktown.   The bank he established and the reforms in state contributions that resulted from his exhortations were hopeful but partial aids in the stubborn aftermath.   He was to quit in exasperation close to disgust.   But out of his failure came Hamilton's eventual triumph in what had been their common resolve.   Time was the controlling factor. Wars are not so quickly ended as begun.   The military campaign of the Virginia peninsula was a masterful effort, but was shorter and simpler than the fiscal and political campaign that became its necessary sequel.   This stretched into a decade of devoted diligence.   Robert Morris, taught by events, knew this as poignantly as Hamilton did.   But, nearly sixty, he had been ready to retire when he accepted the assignment of Financier, and at the end of his arduous service lacked the energy demanded by the tasks that remained.

Fortunately Hamilton, his helper in these first trials, was half his age and could complete the mission. As has often happened, the apprentice outdid the master. Yet we must pause over their fruitful friendship and joint exertions, which continued after they changed places and Morris filled the supporting rôle. In the brief months of Hamilton's receivership the quick cooperation of the two grew into free and full mutual confidence. Their only difference on immediate policy was, as we shall see, on a technical point, in which Hamilton readily yielded to Morris's superior wisdom, experience, and responsibility. Another variation of view remained latent in the period of their official connection. Morris, with the training and interest of the great merchant, spontaneously relied upon individual initiative for the general benefit. Hamilton, primarily an executive in the public service, approved economic controls to which Morris would not assent.

However, these divisions between them were minor as compared with their overwhelming identity of commitment and method. The true correspondence of these chief figures in American fiscal statesmanship lay in their moral code, inseparable from their intellectual penetration and administrative skill. What set them apart and bound them to each other was their courage in situations confusing to minds less honest.

Hamilton no sooner received his commission from Morris, July 13, 1782, than he put out for Poughkeepsie, where the legislature had just met in special session.[10] Governor Clinton had called it for conference with a committee of Congress "on the Necessity of providing competent Means for a vigorous Prosecution of the War."[11] Ostensibly this was a promising beginning, though the previous session, also specially convened on urgent pleas of Congress, the commander in chief, and the Superintendent of Finance, had furnished no aid to the Continental cause.[12] Hamilton would take every step in his power with the inhibited legislators, but "without very sanguine expectations." To extract even a little from them, "mountains of prejudice . . . are to be levelled"; for anything sufficient, their entire system must be renovated.[13]

Immediately he reached Poughkeepsie, Hamilton sent a copy of his warrant to Governor Clinton, with a request to meet a committee of the two Houses.[14] Clinton and legislature at once complied.[15] In his interview Hamilton pointed out "the defects of the present system" that prevented "a solid arrangement of finance." All were convinced, as was Clinton,[16] that something was wrong, but few were willing to remedy the mischief when defined. We do not know how far Hamilton's arguments and importunities were responsible for the tax act to raise £18,000 in specie, bank notes, and Morris's notes, appropriated to the Financier's order.[17] Hamilton feared this fund would be diverted to supply forage begged by Washington.[18] He had been able thus far to prevent this, but was obliged to leave to prepare for his bar examination. At best, the tax would not bring more than half the sum into the treasury, from vices in the scheme of collection. He did not mention his undoubted agency in a bill of the Assembly, then before the Senate for concurrence, "to compel the Payment of the Arrearages of Taxes."[19] But it was at his instance that the legislature had appointed a recess committee to devise, in conference with Hamilton, a more effectual system of taxation, in which payment would be truly compulsory and collection economical.[20]

In addition to other difficulties, Hamilton had to encounter the personal and political resentment of Abraham Yates, Jr., of Schenectady, the New York loan officer. Yates was persistent in protesting to all that he should have been given the post of Continental Receiver which went instead to Hamilton. He believed the law of Congress contemplated making the loan commissioner in each state the first choice. He had served diligently for deferred pay, was "Dayly obliged to shift for the necessarys of life," while Hamilton was preferred, with a "generous and Immediate salary (it is said between three and five hundred Pounds). . . ." Would Duane, the New York delegate who was chairman of the committee of Congress to inquire into proceedings of the Superintendent of Finance, find out the cause of this shabby treatment and say how he could "obtain redress"?[21] Duane comforted Yates's pride but repeated Morris's reasons for naming receivers who were not loan officers.[22] Still disgruntled, Yates complained to Hamilton himself and to more. Finally Robert Morris

squelched Yates politely but firmly,[23] though noting in his diary
that a committee of Congress was questioning his appointments
to the receiverships.[24]

The hostility of Abraham Yates at this early period was an ill
augury for Hamilton's influence with upstate politicians of the
Clinton faction. It could not be helped. Hamilton's opinion of
Yates just at this time was given to Morris: his "ignorance and
perverseness are only surpassed by his pertinacity and conceit.
He hates all high-flyers," which was his name for men of another
temper. "The people have been a long time in the *habit* of choosing him in different offices," and he was "preacher to their taste.
He assures them, they are too poor to pay taxes"; he "deserves to
be pensioned by the English Ministry."[25] Leonard Gansevoort
gave a harsher estimate of Yates, who was "opposed to grant in
Congress an Impost to enable them to discharge their . . . Engagements. . . ."[26]

Hamilton's efforts to convert the New York lawmakers to the
necessity of supplying funds to Congress bespoke the vigorous discharge of his immediate assignment as Continental Receiver. He
reported to Morris, impersonally, a more significant achievement
which was his work, in conjunction with Schuyler. His mind ran
steadily on thorough remedies, no matter how remote the prospect
of realization. The vexations at hand led him to press for the genuine cure. He and Schuyler, in the sympathy that marked their
thoughts and actions, produced a call by the New York legislature
for a constitutional convention to revise the Confederation to give
effective powers to Congress. The resolutions, unmistakably written by Hamilton, were the sequel to his plea to Duane two years
earlier and to the *Continentalist* adjurations which ceased to appear almost within the fortnight. As the first demand by a public
body, this was a step that conducted to the conventions at Annapolis and Philadelphia and the establishment of the new federal
government.

Schuyler, as leader of the Senate, on July 19, moved that the
house go into committee of the whole on the state of the nation,
and the next day Ten Broeck reported the declaration. After
solemn consideration of the posture of affairs domestic and foreign,
nine resolves proclaimed:

"That the Situation of these States is in a peculiar Manner

critical and affords the strongest Reason to apprehend from the Continuance of the present Constitution of the Continental Government . . . a Subversion of public Credit . . . and Consequences highly dangerous to the Safety and Independence of these States." Further pecuniary aid from our Ally is in doubt and the states are not capable of carrying on the war "while there is an Adherence to the Principles which now direct the . . . public Measures." The present plan of Congress for the finances "is founded in Wisdom and sound Policy, and . . . a Failure in this System, for Want of the Support which the States are able to give, would be productive of Evils too pernicious to be hazarded." Final victory is in prospect if the states "unite in some System . . . for producing Energy, Harmony and Consistency of Measures. . . ." Therefore, it is "Resolved, That . . . the radical Source of most of our Embarrassments, is the Want of sufficient Power in Congress" to secure "ready . . . Cooperation of the different States, on which their immediate Safety and future Happiness depend." Demonstrated defects ought to be promptly "repaired, the Powers of Congress extended, a solid Security established for the Payment of Debts already inured [incurred], and competent Means provided for future Credit, and for supplying the current Demands of the War."

These ends "can never be attained by partial deliberations of the States separately [as had been tried]; but . . . there should be as soon as possible a Conference of the Whole on the Subject; and . . . it would be adviseable . . . to propose to Congress to recommend, and to each State to adopt the Measure of assembling a general Convention . . . especially authorized to revise and amend the Confederation, reserving a Right to the respective Legislatures to ratify their Determinations."[27] The Assembly concurred, and the resolves were ordered sent to Congress and the executives of the states.[28]

It was the boldness, not the pertinence, of these recommendations that made Hamilton dubious of their practical result. Considering the warmth of his advocacy, he viewed with detachment the unpromising outlook. The expedient was necessary, but he did not expect concurrence of the other states. "Urge reforms, or exertions," he lamented to Morris, "and the answer constantly is, What avails it for one State to make them without the concert of the others? It is vain to expose the futility of this reasoning: it is founded in all those passions which have the strongest influence on the human mind."[29]

In his modest rehearsal of transactions at Poughkeepsie, Hamilton did not mention his own election to Congress on July 22, two days after the resolves for a constitutional convention were adopted. This was a compliment to the impression he had made on the legislature by his solicitations for the Financier in the days just preceding. He owed his choice, as the only new delegate (the others were reelected) to the Assembly; Schuyler was nominated by the Senate, but at once withdrew in Hamilton's favor.[30] This removed him, when his term should begin, from the office of Continental Receiver, but gave him a superior opportunity to urge the political reforms which were the conditions of satisfactory revenue.[31]

In his brief preparation for the bar Hamilton had the assistance of his old friend Robert Troup, who was practicing at Albany and was invited to live with the Hamiltons during this period. Hamilton read—mainly Blackstone, surely—"while walking to and fro" almost long enough to have marched from end to end of the Confederacy.[32] As though striding through the texts was not enough, he reduced his reading on practice to a manual which was used by other students and became "the ground work of subsequent practical treatises by others on a larger scale."[33] The only known copy, 177 pages in an unidentified hand, is headed "Practical Proceedings in the Supreme Court of the State of New York," with Hamilton's name written below.[34] It is a handbook covering rules of the court, steps in a variety of pleadings, and deals only incidentally with substantive law. Twoscore shorter or longer sections treat of Process, Venue, Release, Covenant, Judgment and Execution, Scire Facias, Habeas Corpus, Joint Partners, Trespass in Ejectment, and so on. The authorities he used—reports, manuals of procedure, collections of statutes—were English,[35] with occasional corrections to conform to diverging American (specifically New York) practice. Where he found his sources in conflict he offered his own solutions; though these are indications of his independence of mind, they are too brief and tentative to have positive value.

When Hamilton declined Morris's first offer to become Receiver it was because he had a limited time in which to qualify for the bar. Only a week before, he had presented himself before the Supreme Court of Judicature, sitting at Albany, and asked indulgence in his case. By an earlier rule, a clerkship of three years was a prerequisite to admission as attorney. In January, however, this demand was suspended "in favor of such young Gentlemen who had directed their Studies to the profession of the Law, but upon the breaking out of the present War had entered into the . . . defence of their Country," but the extension was only to the end of April term. Hamilton declared that he belonged to the exempt candidates but that "being unprepared for an examination, he prayed . . . that the . . . rule . . . may be further suspended until October Term next." This was granted as to him.[36]

His petition gives the only indication that Hamilton, before entering the army, had determined to be a lawyer, if we give his words their strict construction. This was natural enough. He early abandoned the notion of medicine; his devotion to religion was superseded by absorption in politics; later his resolve was strengthened because the prospect of a further military career was nil, and he did not seek public office. He had no resources of his own for going into business, which was disordered. Several older friends were successful lawyers, especially Boudinot and Duane, and younger ones, particularly Troup and Brockholst Livingston,[37] were preparing for that profession. Education, inclination, and aptitude pointed him to this course.

The extension Hamilton obtained from the court was sufficient, in spite of his diversion to the duties of Receiver of Taxes, for him to complete his law reading, for he was "admitted [as attorney] July 1782."[38] Further, in spite of misgivings,[39] he was able to pass the examination for the "degree of Counsellor" by October, and was admitted to this more privileged status on the 26th.[40]

His admission to the bar accomplished, Hamilton laid himself out, as he had promised,[41] in Morris's service. His efforts became more comprehensive than before. He at once called on Gov. Clinton for the specific information on New York's past and pending contributions to the Continent and the condition of the state's treasury and circulation, as requested a year earlier by the Financier.[42] Urgent as he was, he anticipated delay in Clinton's compliance, and the same day stirred Colonel Udny Hay, the Deputy Quartermaster General for New York, to answer as far as he was able.[43]   He dug deeper and more widely by applying to the county treasurers for their receipts and expenses of collection.[44]   He prodded Robert Benson and McKesson, clerks of the Senate and Assembly, for essential returns.[45]   He had already asked of W. E. Bancker, the state treasurer, the overdue first payment on New York's quota, with brisker collection for the future.[46]

Before he heard from these sources he fulfilled his promise[47] to give Morris a report of the situation and potentialities of New York.   His lengthy review opened with a plea in extenuation. The equivalent of only four of the fourteen counties remained out of the hands of the enemy, loyal, and intact.   The population that could be commanded was not correspondingly reduced, but labor was dearer than before the war.   The state had made great efforts in the common cause, though sometimes more distressing in the mode than need have been.   Expenditures for the army were some $180,000, but the people paid out more than this in trade with other sections, leaving *"an extreme* and *universal* scarcity of money."[48]

The government of New York exhibited "the general disease which infects all our constitutions—an excess of popularity. . . . The inquiry constantly is what will *please,* not what will *benefit* the people."   This foredoomed to folly.   Taxes were fixed not by property ownership, but by "the discretion of persons chosen by the people themselves to determine the ability of each citizen." The desire to overburden Tories had recoiled and rendered assessment of Whigs most unequal.   He pictured the practices of levy and collection—distracted and unproductive; and all attempts to amend the iniquity "without totally changing it are fruitless."[49]

The authorities, well disposed toward the Continent, were in danger of contenting themselves with caring for local government and providing the state's quota of troops.   Confidence in Morris personally was high, but Hamilton had been obliged to busy himself counteracting resentment because Morris was held to have reflected on the exertions of New York.[50]   However, a third of the people still wished, secretly, for enemy success, while "the remainder sigh for peace, murmur at taxes, clamor at their rulers, change one incapable man for another more incapable," and if left to themselves would purchase peace at any price. Popular resolve might stiffen if the legislature could be brought to a wise plan in its finances. This done, the state could furnish £40,000 to Morris, but only a third as much if commerce continued clogged "for want of . . . a sufficient medium." He would strive to convince the legislative committee "that a change of measures is essential."[51]

Hamilton then gave the Financier his confidential estimate of leading public men in New York state, by way of informing him more particularly of what exertions could be expected toward furnishing revenue to the Continent. Hamilton here offered certain strictures on temper and conduct,[52] with one aspersion of moral integrity such as, years later, drew, literally, the fatal fire of Aaron Burr. His openness now shows how rapidly his friendship with Morris had grown since he wrote the latter, anonymously, from camp at Morristown two years before.

Hamilton found no man who had "a decided influence in" the state government. Governor Clinton had declined in popularity, partly from vigorous law enforcement that did him honor. "He is . . . a man of integrity and passes with his particular friends for a Statesman; . . . without being destitute of understanding, his passions are much warmer, than his judgement is enlightened. The preservation of his place is an object to his private fortune as well as to his ambition; and we are not to be surprised, if instead of taking a lead in measures that contradict a prevailing prejudice, however he may be convinced of their utility, he either flatters it, or temporises, especially when a new election approaches." Schuyler had more weight in the legislature than the governor, but was frequently mortified to see his measures miscarry. "Mr. [John Morin] Scot[t] . . . has his little objects and his little party. Nature gave him genius; but *habit* has impaired it. He never had judgment; he now has scarcely plausibility. . . ."

Scott, on occasion, was governed by (William) Malcolm, who was resourceful and expert in business, but yielded to his vanity. "He has it in his power to support or perplex measures as he may incline, and it will be politic to make it his interest to incline to what is right." For that reason Hamilton had proposed him "for a certain office," probably that of Receiver to succeed himself.[53]

Lansing, who later was to be Hamilton's opponent in Philadelphia and Poughkeepsie conventions, "is a good young fellow and a good practitioner of the Law; but his friends mistook his talents when they made him a statesman. . . . The county of Albany is not of my opinion concerning him."[54]

Hamilton did not require to have his exertions to find money for Morris stimulated by a demand upon him of Pickering, Quartermaster General, to take up some of the Financier's bills of exchange.[55] A few days later he was embarrassed to confess to Morris that so far from funds, he was still seeking information when they might be had,[56] and at the same time begged this from Governor Clinton.[57] Morris understood Hamilton's discouragements, but "knowing that your abilities and Zeal to promote the public Good are equal to the most arduous Undertakings I have no doubt that your Endeavours will be successful."[58]

Soon Hamilton was giving proof of this by applying directly to the county treasurers to exhort the collectors so that the state tax for Continental use might be paid punctually.[59] He gave Morris all the particulars he had been able to gather of New York laws, contributions to the Continent under them, and the quality of the currency—materials Morris had been begging since a year before Hamilton's appointment began to produce them. Opposite the laws for loans and levies, Hamilton set down the sums collected under each. Though this was a story of state revenue, principally, the exasperating showing bore out Hamilton's contention that little could be expected for the federal treasury unless the tax system of New York were remodeled. A law of November 1, 1781, "for raising £25,000 in specie . . . has yet produced but [£]64.10." Brought in for taxes were state agent's certificates, forage and quartermaster notes, and depreciation notes. Nor could full information be had until Morris appointed a commissioner to settle accounts with New York.[60]

Always anxious for abundant circulating media, Hamilton proposed to Morris means of keeping the latter's notes in active, widespread use; this object would be aided if the notes were of smaller denominations than twenty dollars.[61] He hoped in vain for Morris's instructions before meeting the legislative committee on taxes, but was prepared to anticipate them.[62] Within some weeks he had Morris's full views. The Financier still had not seen the

New York resolves for extending the powers of Congress, but "A firm, wise, manly system of federal government" was "what I dare not expect, but what I will not despair of."[63]   He pointed out that New York was not so exhausted as Hamilton had pictured, and used Hamilton's own observations to prove that the state, by curtailing private luxuries and public extravagance, could turn in more to the Continental revenue.   A month later Morris found Hamilton's "Prospect [for] the Receipt of Money for Taxes . . . very unpleasing," and again foretold "dangerous . . . Consequences" unless the states laid, collected, and transmitted taxes.[64]

Only Morris, in the realm of public finance, was able to give Hamilton fatherly correction.   Others, later, objected violently enough to Hamilton's reasoning, and promptly had his counterarguments.   From Morris he accepted instruction, not only because this was becoming but because the teaching was as good as it was kindly.   Thus Morris explained that the large denominations of his notes were deliberate, to channel them quickly to the hands of receivers and collectors, and to confine them to the use of merchants.   With all precautions, they had depreciated, at first, in the Eastern states.   If thrown at once in the way of people who suspected all paper money, their value would have been rapidly destroyed.   Farmers would not accept paper merely because it would pay taxes which they were determined to avoid anyhow.   Confidence grew slowly; Morris wanted to bring it, with patience, to the maturity where tavern and storekeepers would take his notes, for only then would his paper enjoy full credit in common use.   Hamilton was persuaded by Morris's reasons that the denominations of the notes generally should not be lessened, but thought a part should be of smaller amount.[65]

Hamilton had recommended Malcolm to succeed himself as Receiver for New York, but Morris, for reasons he considered sufficient, had fixed on Dr. Thomas Tillotson for the place.[66]

We often have occasion to notice how Hamilton, responding to temporary demands, lost no opportunity to provide permanent solutions.   A meeting of public creditors at Philadelphia pleaded with Congress to resume interest payments on their loan office certificates.   Hamilton determined to enlarge this into a concerted demand from all the states for a restoration of Continental credit which he hoped might lead to a new constitution strengthening the central government. A meeting at Albany was presided over by Schuyler. Hamilton told Morris about it briefly.[67] A state convention at Poughkeepsie and a general one at Philadelphia were proposed. Petitions went to the legislature and to Congress, and Hamilton prepared an address to the public creditors of New York. The whole was a bold, risky move.[68] If consolidated, creditors already disgruntled might become disaffected, shutting off further financial aid from that quarter and clamoring for concessions to secure a swift peace. A few months later Hamilton was to indulge the notion, momentarily, that the unpaid army might usefully coerce Congress. This would have invited mutiny and internal revolution, hazarding vastly more than could flow from the most vehement protest of security holders.

Perhaps from his own apprehension of ill results, the address Hamilton composed was persuasive, not peremptory. Public creditors, whatever their degree of patriotism, had an equal claim upon the plighted faith of government.[69] Long violation of the public engagements was due not to bad intent, but to bad management. Needs of the treasury could not be supplied from taxes, nor from further loans from the French government. Individuals at home and abroad must be induced to lend, and this could only be by "the punctual payment of the interest, by substantial funds, permanently pledged for that purpose."[70] The country could command the moderate sum to fund the debt, old and new. Such a measure could lighten the burdens of all. Public securities, rendered valuable and negotiable, would be a medium quickening commerce.[71] Those unwilling to lend to the public must be solicitous for fair treatment of men who had loaned, else government, without other recourse, must lay swingeing taxes. Finally, purity of faith must belong to the young republic, "especially on . . . first emerging into political existence." Resort to loans was a favorite theme which reappeared often in his later, better known advocacies. At this time Morris was more insistent than Hamilton was on supplying the treasury by energetic taxation, even at the expense of commerce, rather than by loans.[72]

After his meetings with the committee of the legislature,[73] Hamilton set down a plan of specific taxation for New York. With changes dictated by expediency, it shows in detail what he must have urged on the committee.[74] In this as in other instances he was guided by the recommendations of Robert Morris, though he departed from them as his own judgment suggested. The Financier's "principles and arguments [,] as luminous as they are conclusive," as Hamilton called them, require to be studied if one is to understand the younger man's debt to the older, not only in the present case but projected into the future.[75] The purpose was to substitute taxes, at declared rates on classified objects, for the loose quotas and arbitrary assessments that prevailed in the state, and to make the collection certain and economical. Much that Hamilton now embodied was to reappear, with necessary changes, in his Treasury reports (and accompanying bills) offered to the national Congress a decade later. Not only did he particularize the taxes of every sort; for all except duties on imports he estimated the yield.[76]

He proposed taxes on general property—lands, houses, and luxury possessions, excises on salt and tobacco; tavern licenses; polls of servants; stamps for legal documents; and import duties in addition to those granted to Congress. All taxes, where possible, were graduated with respect to presumed ability to pay. Property owners were to declare their lands, on oath, and to give information concerning their carriages and servants. Houses were minutely classified as to size and quality, and collectors were to visit them annually for the levy. All taxes being specific, there was not properly any assessment, but times of laying and paying were definitely provided. He pressed the committee for an excise on distilled liquors, but was forced to be content, in his written scheme, with charges for tavern licenses, graduated according to sorts of liquors sold. Taxes on land were 3d. per acre on meadow, 2d. on arable, and 2s. per hundred acres on wood and waste. Proceeds of the different taxes were appropriated to specified purposes—those arising from lands to support of the state government, the house tax to Congress.[77] The scheme was devised in the emergency to raise revenue, sufficient and certain.[78] However, with the exception of the salt tax, it also accords with modern canons of justice in taxation.[79]

Hamilton had told Morris his doubts whether, though prepared with materials, he could induce the committee of the legislature to "enter cordially into right views."[80] Six weeks later, when he met with the committee, he reported that some members had their favorite plans to protect, while others had nothing to propose except objections.[81]   However, it was agreed there should be "an actual valuation of land, and a tax of so much in the pound. . . ." The committee would not listen to Morris's proposal, to Congress, of a flat tax of one cent an acre,[82] but came nearer to Hamilton's classification into meadow, arable, and waste.   Others of Hamilton's levies were accepted in principle, but funding by New York alone was not approved.[83]

The Superintendent of Finance anticipated collections of taxes, specie, by issuing his own notes drawn to the order of John Swanwick, his partner.   Hamilton tried in vain to maintain these at par with notes of the Bank of North America.[84]

As Hamilton was about to relinquish office under Morris in order to enter Congress, he rendered the Financier his cash account, showing that he had received $2,500, most of which had been or would be exchanged with Colonel Pickering, the Quartermaster, and Duer, the army contractor, for Morris's notes.   He wanted to turn his records over to Dr. Tillotson, his successor. For the last quarter of 1782, according to the accounts of Morris, Hamilton did twice as well as New York Receiver, though Tillotson's collections and payments, beginning with the first quarter of 1783, were somewhat better.   However, a year after Hamilton gave over, Morris, little pleased with Tillotson's recent report, offered a reflection that described Hamilton's trials as well. "Clamors against poor Tories," observed the Financier, "form an easier Testimony of Whiggism than the vigorous pursuit of continental measures.   The apprehension of New York being over from the efforts of the enemy, they will I suppose continue . . . as indifferent about the public service as they have been for a long period of Danger."[85]   And Hamilton, as a result of his efforts to extract taxes, was sure the states were "in no humor for continuing exertions."   If the war lasted, he wrote to Lafayette in Paris, it must be carried on by external aid.   "I make no apology for the inertness of this country: I detest it: but since it exists, I am sorry to see other resources diminish" (meaning removal of the French army).[86]

17

"We Must Pledge
an Ascertained Fund. . . ."

AMERICA won the war when Cornwallis surrendered at York-town. The king's ablest general was taken captive with the largest body of enemy troops. This military finish of the Revolution was plainer later than then. The South was cleared but exhausted, and still demanded safeguarding by Greene. New England, in fact freed three years earlier at Bennington and Saratoga, suffered the sting of Arnold's raids along the Sound. The British held New York City and its productive environs. They were naval masters of the West Indies, which might be the launching stage for fresh attempts. The stubborn foe had recruited from disaster before, might do so again. News from the prideful Parliament, subject to a sullen king, was slow and uncertain. America was flushed but almost spent; British fury might yet command resources. The attempt of desirable colonies to wrench free from the world's dominant empire remained of doubtful issue. Washington, with-drawn to the Hudson Highlands, stood sentry.

Troubled patriot hope, ready to rise to expectancy, was not supported by renewed preparation, should fighting be resumed. Washington, alert to the danger, psychological as well as military, exhorted in vain. The concentration of force, American and French, that ringed Cornwallis and battered him into submission, was followed by lassitude. This was the historical hazard of the Revolution. When the American Mars loosened armor, he was found to be wearing political diapers. Victory for independence,

though it seemed long deferred, came quicker than national maturity. Excitement cooled; resolve did not warm. An established country copes with the aftermath of war, but the infant
republic was threatened by the trauma of battle birth.

Though Hamilton climaxed campaigns when he sprang to the
last enemy parapet, others, by age and talents, outranked him in
military achievement. His heroism, that singled him out in a
superb company, was far different: the nurture of the new nation.
None surpassed him in swift anticipation of crises, or in skills for
meeting demands. In the next chapters we shall see him strug-
gling against the obfuscation of those of slower mind, and not a few
of perverse disposition. Not his least remarkable feature, amidst the
disabilities of Congress and Confederation, was his patience, for he
was so clear-eyed, determined, and so young. He is sometimes regarded as precipitate, with the faculty of force rather than fortitude.
But he was not egotistically captious at the ineptitude of many, nor
disillusioned from his task by rebellion in influential quarters. He
dealt, undismayed, with each immediate difficulty as it arose, seeking the while to make every solution contribute to a foreseen end.
Jefferson, when needed in Congress, retired to his Virginia countryside, to codify local statutes and classify native fauna and flora.
Perhaps this was the higher wisdom, which relies on time to cure
all ills. Other philosophers deserted the crucible for the closet.
Congress was the loser by their retreat. Time, abandoned to its
devices, would have produced a pattern, but it might have been
disastrous, or might have vastly delayed the rise to national competence. Someone must be on hand, to resist, to prompt, to
realize a plan. Luckily there were several of high capacity, nor
were they poorer patriots, nor worse philosophers, for buffeting in
the political melee. Without them the promise of America might
have vaporized. The lack of their sort was the tragedy of the
French Revolution, which lapsed from democracy into despotism,
and in the end bore its fruits in pragmatic England rather than
in levitation of egalitarians.

Hamilton's ability to bear with opponents while he combated
their views did not limit him to opportunism. He improved the
moment for the sake of the future. But when the hour was not
shining, as was mostly true, he hastened his designs. When the
interval was propitious, when temporizing devices had demon-

strably failed, he came forward with a more comprehensive, candid scheme ready formed. On such occasions his moral fervor was brought into play, abundantly supported by argument, and aided by ingenuous persuasion. Technical management and operational means, in which he was expert, did not obscure his reliance on first principles, few and simple. His prescription for national prosperity was good faith, work, and union. Each of these had connotations which must appear as we proceed.

So much for introduction to the postwar period and Hamilton's leading part in constructing the American commonwealth. The depth and devotion of his purpose are not conveyed in abstract statement. We need to track his day-to-day doings to know the discouragements that produced his triumphs. This means inspecting public proceedings (few in his life were purely private) in detail. Grand summary would be nothing without particular recital of what went before. His obstacle race, rightly seen, holds more excitement than witnessing the finish on the straightaway.

Hamilton was elected to Congress by the New York legislature on July 22, 1782, along with James Duane, William Floyd, Ezra L'Hommedieu, and John Morin Scott for the term of a year beginning the first Monday in November.[1] Three weeks passed before he took his seat on November 25.[2] Floyd followed on the 27th, and on the same day Duane and L'Hommedieu received leaves of absence.[3] They bequeathed to the replacing delegates, besides a history of personal pecuniary distress, and concern for the condition of Congress and the country, a special anxiety lest the supposed interests of New York should be injured by possible recognition of the independence of Vermont.[4]

From his scene of domesticity in Albany, on the eve of setting out for Philadelphia, Hamilton wrote, in a familiar letter to Lafayette: "I have been employed for the last ten months in rocking the cradle and studying the art of *fleecing* my neighbors. I am now a grave counsellor-at-law, and shall soon be a grave member of Congress. . . . I am going to throw away a few months more in public life, and then retire a simple citizen and good *pater familias*. . . . You are condemned to run the race of ambition all your life. I am already tired of the career, and dare to leave it."[5] He was not so disdainful of his approaching new assignment when writing to his even closer friend John Laurens: "This State has pretty

unanimously elected me to Congress. . . . Peace made, . . . a
new scene opens. The object then will be to make our independence a blessing. To do this we must secure our Union on solid
foundations—a herculean task,—and to effect which, mountains of
prejudice must be levelled! It requires all the virtues and all the
abilities of the country. Quit your sword . . . ; put on the
toga. Come to Congress. We know each other's sentiments;
our views are the same. We have fought side by side to
make America free; let us hand in hand struggle to make her
happy."[6]

Laurens probably never got his comradely summons, more was
the pity, as he was killed in a chance engagement in South Carolina less than a fortnight later. He fell, with a score of companions, when ambushed by a British foraging party on the Com-
bahee River. He had been dancing at a home in the neighborhood to within two hours of mounting his horse to answer the
alarm. "Poor Laurens has fallen in a paltry little skirmish,"
wrote Greene to Williams. "You knew his temper, and I pre-
dicted his fate. The love of military glory made him seek it upon
occasions unworthy of his rank. This state will feel his loss."
Hamilton received the news with "the deepest affliction," for
Laurens was "a friend I truly and most tenderly loved, and one
of a very small number."[7]

The untimely death of Laurens, besides a personal distress, was
a blow to Hamilton's political projects. The two friends, working together in Congress, conventions, and later posts, would have
been a partnership of matching talents and patriotism. That
Laurens was from South Carolina would have proved a capital
asset to the combination. We may not speculate too far, but
Laurens's hatred of slavery might have served, when the Constitution was made, to dilute the mischievous demands of his state
which preserved that institution. As it was, Hamilton had sympathetic, even devoted, helpers in South Carolina in the Federalist
program, such as William Smith and the Pinckneys. But they
were of later attachment and had not the same intimate, wartime
personal ties with him. Besides, Laurens possessed a superior
idealism and versatility. His heritage, intelligence, and courage
might have made him such a leader to the southward as Hamilton was in the Middle States. The deprivation was greater be-

cause, as it happened, few of Hamilton's college and army companions, of his own age and sharing his views, participated actively with him in the political scene.   Troup tended his law practice; Meade became the country gentleman; the sphere of Fish remained local.   Madison and Marshall, the former only four years
Hamilton's senior, the latter exactly his age, were signal allies,
though with the difference between them that Madison soon fell
away from Federalism, while Marshall's principal efforts in that
behalf registered after Hamilton's death.   Hamilton was ever able
to cooperate cordially with men older than himself, for his gifts
canceled divergence in age.   However, a certain spring and joy-
ousness would have been added had young Laurens and more like
him been at Alexander's side in the pitch for union.   One does
not forget the loyal Wolcott and the alert Fisher Ames.

Another on whom Hamilton relied for counsel as he entered
Congress was Nathanael Greene.   There, he invited, "I shall be
happy to correspond with you with our ancient confidence; and
I . . . entreat you not to confine your observations to military
subjects, but to take in the whole scope of national concerns.   I
am sure your ideas will be useful to me and to the public."[8]   But
here too Hamilton was disappointed in his hopes of an able col-
laborator long his familiar, for Greene died just as the new
national government was formed.

After nine months as delegate, "I have been making a short apprenticeship in Congress," he told John Jay, but was preparing to
take leave of public life.[9]   Hamilton did not "throw away" his
term in the national legislature.   On the contrary his "apprenticeship" there was fruitful of later masterworks in the call for a
new basis of union, in leading the fight for ratification of the Constitution, and in equipping the national authority with resources.
In the Continental Congress he experienced the obfuscation and
near futility into which the councils of the country had fallen.   In
Philadelphia, Hamilton was no longer viewing the defects of Congress from distressed military camps, nor lamenting in the press,
nor sharing the pains of the Superintendent of Finance as he
sought to collect Continental revenues in New York.   Now he
was an immediate participant, at grips with grave problems for
the meeting of which he and his companions had more responsibility than resources.   His tour of duty in Congress freshened and

confirmed his knowledge of the insufficiency of the Confederation, and determined him to cure the evil.

Efforts have been made to rescue the reputation of the Confederation and Old Congress from the discredit into which John Fiske's memorable *Critical Period of American History* cast it.[10] This has included accusing Fiske of poor scholarship if not disingenuousness. But the degree of real revision is not in proportion to the industry expended in the fuller review of evidence. Issues confronting the government between Yorktown and the Philadelphia convention, and the consequences that hung on them, were not imaginary. A succession of men, honest and able (though certainly not divested of private prompting), from all the states over this postwar period, struggled to resolve the country's problems. The result was abandonment of the Articles of Confederation and construction of a very different constitution. By admission of Congress and the country the Confederation failed and deserved to be superseded. The new national government was not a "plot" but a plan that emerged from travail. It is inevitable that the clay feet of those who marched in a new direction —toward national competence—should seem to track the stage with more mud than was left by their opponents who were content to stand still. But the fact is that patriotic purpose, however defiled, was superior to selfish interest on both sides. It is impossible to read the record of the Continental Congress without being persuaded that it was expected to make bricks without straw. What is here said in countercry applies substantially to Charles A. Beard's *Economic Interpretation of the Constitution* as it views the Confederation in retrospect, but that celebrated and influential work is best judged in discussing the Philadelphia convention of 1787.

The months November 1782 through July 1783, when Hamilton had his seat, found Congress on its pivot. Until then the urgency of war had obscured the political problem. Others of nationalist persuasion withdrew about the same time he did, leaving Congress to its own uneasy contentment which became the country's contempt. But in this brief interval issues were joined. The effort to secure stable revenue for the interest and ultimate extinguishment of the public debt was hopelessly disappointed when Virginia added her caprice to Rhode Island's recalcitrance in refusing the 5 per cent import duty. The dispute between New York and the Vermonters over the New Hampshire Grants threatened internal war which would have flouted the national jurisdiction Congress had invited. This was the period of anxiety over the peace, with tragicomic inability to hale enough delegates to ratify a treaty so long sought.

Conditional clauses in land cessions, at first deferred, were now to be faced. The army, unpaid but undisbanded, became a threat to civil law and even to the prestige of its commander in chief. Congress, its hall surrounded by mutinous troops, found the local authority a broken reed, and decamped to the rural protection of Princeton, where a diminished number of delegates sighed for a permanent place of safety. Requisitions on the states for money, always a poor reliance, now failed altogether for a solid year. As he left this focus of confusion Hamilton reported:

"We have now happily concluded the great work of independence, but much remains to be done to reap the fruits of it. Every day proves the inefficiency of the present Confederation; yet the common danger being removed, we are receding instead of advancing in a disposition to amend its defects. The road to popularity in each State is to inspire jealousies of the power of Congress, though nothing can be more apparent than that they have no power; and that for the want of it, . . . we at this moment experience all the mischiefs of a . . . ruined credit. It is to be hoped that when prejudice and folly have run themselves out of breath, we may return to reason and correct our errors."[11]

During Hamilton's tenure Congress was habitually "thin" for ordinary business, and the nine or thirteen states whose consent was required for crucial action could scarcely be dragooned into attendance. A few of conspicuous talents were among his fellow delegates, for longer or shorter stays—Oliver Ellsworth of Connecticut, James Madison of Virginia, James Wilson of Pennsylvania, John Rutledge of South Carolina. Elias Boudinot was President of Congress during the whole time Hamilton was a member. Others who may be thought of as "high in the second order of ability," who would have carried weight in any assembly, were Oliver Wolcott of Connecticut, Daniel Carroll and James McHenry of Maryland, Nathaniel Gorham of Massachusetts, Thomas FitzSimmons, Thomas Mifflin, and Richard Peters of

Pennsylvania; Ralph Izard of South Carolina, and Hugh Williamson of North Carolina.   It may be that the legislatures of certain
individual states commanded as much capacity as did Congress.
The attendance at any one time rarely numbered more than
twenty delegates, and of these the same few took the leading part
in debate and committee work.[12]

Hamilton from the start figured with determination and industry in every move to bolster the respectability of the Confederation.   Most of the members, judging from their reports to their
governors, considered themselves ambassadors from the several
state governments, engaging in diplomatic exchanges and seeking
local advantage from such collective authority as existed.   Hamilton and Madison were almost alone in their willingness to re-
monstrate with their home legislatures and executives when the actions of these ran counter to the harmony and needs of the whole.
Hamilton used a combination of force and forbearance in pressing
his principle of strengthening Congress, because the constitutional
fabric on which he must depend was frail.   The levers he devised
were powerful, but when one was plied it threatened to crush
the poor fulcrum.   In the day-to-day debates, parliamentary
maneuvers, and proposals of his committees he was convincing
himself, after honest trial, that no amount of patience and ingenuity would render the Confederation equal to its obligations.
These months were the school of his afterrôle in accomplishing
national sovereignty.   One can see his resolution mounting with
every disappointed design.   When later he employed with swift
vigor the tools that lay to his hand, it was because he had forged
them with pain.

A constantly recurring effort of his opponents was to use the ob-
structive power of the states.   The most tormenting drive was that of
the delegates from Rhode Island to block the 5 per cent general import duty, which was to say the ability of the central government
to meet its financial requirements.   This included the imminent
business of satisfying a clamorous army which demanded to be discharged but would not be demobilized without some pay at once,
and the prospect of arrearages and pensions.   In this fight Hamilton
was in unison with a great part of Congress.   Madison's reproach
was characteristic: "The prospect . . . from the impost . . .
seems to be . . . blasted by a . . . final veto of the Assembly of

Rhode Island.   This State . . . voted in Congress that 6 million of Dollars were necessary for the year '83, that 2 million were as much as the States could raise . . . and that applications for loans in Europe ought to be relied on for the residue.   And yet they absolutely refuse the only fund which could be satisfactory to lenders.   The indignation against this perverse sister is increased by her shameful delinquency in the . . . requisitions."[13]

However, Hamilton was more alert than most to the danger that lurked in another and delusive quarter.   This was the willingness of some states—well enough disposed but despairing of the resources of Congress—to subtract from the national commitment by satisfying their own troops or otherwise accepting financial responsibility, at least temporarily.   This hindrance in the guise of help was difficult to reject.   The offer now seemed economical, but was to take on political import in the struggle a decade later over national assumption of state debts.

Little more than a week after Hamilton took his seat (December 2) the Rhode Island delegates moved that Congress recommend to the states that they individually settle with their temporary troops and charge the accounts to Congress.   This dodge of Rhode Island to avoid the impost was promptly countered by a motion, seconded by Hamilton, to postpone, which was carried 7–1.[14]

Because of particular knowledge, Hamilton served on numerous special committees to deal with applications from the army.   First assignments were minor, but might be embarrassing, such as refusal of prior payment to foreign officers stranded here.[15]   Soon he was in the midst of the crisis of defection at Newburgh and mutineers' menace to Congress.

Before Hamilton's arrival the New York delegates (Duane, L'Hommedieu, and others) had stoutly upheld the claims of New York in the country west of the Connecticut River called the New Hampshire Grants against the pretensions of Ethan Allen's Green Mountain Boys and the independent state of Vermont.   In the long dispute, rival land titles of New England Yankees and of Yorkers were held by genuine settlers and by even more contentious speculators.   McKean of Delaware, at this middle stage of the wrangle, offered a motion, written by Hamilton, condemning recent depredations on alleged New York citizens, calling for "immediate and decided interposition of Congress, . . . for preserving peace . . . until a decision shall be had of the controversy," and promising effectual enforcement by the United States if restitution was neglected. Howell of Rhode Island moved to strike out the enforcement threat, but lost. In fact, Hamilton's strong wording was too popular, for when Madison and McKean wanted to soften the phrases expressing the alarm and demanding the intervention of Congress, Hamilton and Floyd were for acquiescing, but the original motion was agreed to unimpaired.[16] Hamilton, earlier than other New Yorkers, as will appear, favored concessions looking to peaceful settlement, and a decade later he was quick to welcome Vermont to statehood.

On December 6 the perverse refusal of Rhode Island for almost two years to grant the impost resulted in a new demand upon her, followed by detection of Howell, her dominant delegate, in a disingenuous attempt to prevent her compliance. Hamilton moved a resolve renewing the call on the states for requisitions and dispatching emissaries to Rhode Island to plead for consent to the impost which the lower house of the legislature had rejected. The more determined parts of the motion were penned by Hamilton, with a few sentences in Madison's hand. The demand for payment of requisitions was unanimously passed, and only the Rhode Island pair of delegates objected to the deputation. Osgood of Massachusetts, Mifflin of Pennsylvania, and Nash of North Carolina were named for the mission; they came from the three parts of the country and all were of states that had agreed to the impost; they were to go with full information from the Superintendent of Finance and the Secretaries of War and Foreign Affairs.[17]

Now was the biter bit. For this same day, a newspaper publication, ostensibly by a gentleman in Philadelphia, that "had been handed about for several days," was pinned on David Howell of Rhode Island. It misrepresented congressional loans as prospering and betrayed the secret proposal of Sweden to enter into a treaty "with the view," said Madison, "of disproving to the people of R. Island the necessity of the Impost of 5 P C^{t}. . . ." The author declared, in Providence and Boston gazettes, that the loan Adams was negotiating "fills as fast as could be expected. The

Dutch are very friendly. . . . Another Northern Power has solicited the Friendship and Trade of the United States; and a . . . Treaty may be expected soon to take Place there. . . . The national Importance of the United States is constantly rising in the Estimation of European Powers. . . . Such is their Credit, that they have of late failed in no Application for foreign Loans." Not very oblique methods were used to compel Howell to confess these illicit disclosures which, as to the loans, were perfectly false. "Mr. Howell was visibly perturbated but remained silent."[18]

Hamilton was now drawn further into defense of the impost. On December 11 was read a letter from the speaker of the lower house of Rhode Island to the President of Congress announcing that the state would not accede to the impost and reciting reasons that had been furnished by Howell and Arnold in more hortative form.[19] 1. The impost would bear hardest on commercial states like Rhode Island. 2. "It proposes to introduce into this and the other states, officers unknown and unaccountable to them, and so is against the constitution of this State. . . ." 3. The standing grant to Congress would prevent Rhode Island from raising its quota of public taxes in whatever way it thought most proper. The Rhode Island delegates followed by moving that the deputation to their state be countermanded. The New Yorkers got this defeated; delay of departure, pending further orders of Congress, was referred to a committee of Hamilton, Madison, and FitzSimmons.[20]

This committee reported five days later on the refusal of Rhode Island to approve the impost. The manuscript, almost entirely in Hamilton's hand, is a model of exposition, a tabloid treatise on public finance, wise politically and economically. It contains in compact statement many of his leading ideas, which were to reappear often in elaborated form. It is impossible to believe that this earnest, lucid paper is the work of an unworthy schemer. There is not room in one man's mind for such competence and complicity too. His overwhelmingly sympathetic audience was sure to give moral support. Like all of his best writing, without a wasted word, this rebuttal to the Rhode Island objectors is difficult to condense. He replied to the three arguments in turn:

1. (That the impost was unfair to the commercial states.)
Not so, since "every duty on imports is incorporated with the price
of the commodity, and ultimately paid by the consumer with a
profit on the duty itself as a compensation to the merchant for
the advance of his money." The duty is no more a charge on the
importing state than on the merchant, for using states pay in proportion to their consumption, or to their population and wealth.
Characteristically, he contented himself with stating the tendency
in shifting and incidence of the intended import tax. As many
times later, he refused to enter on detail that was disputable and
irrelevant. "Over-nice and minute calculations in matters of this
nature are inconsistent with national measures. . . . Absolute
equality is not to be attained: To aim at it is pursuing a shadow
at the expence of the substance. . . ."[21] Madison, on Hamilton's
committee, might have taken a lesson for afteruse when he insisted
on fiscal purity to the sacrifice of practicality.

2. (That the impost would introduce alien officers into Rhode
Island.) "The legislature must always have a discretionary
power of appointing Officers, not expressly known to the constitution, and this power will include . . . authorising the Federal
Government to make the appointments . . . where the general
welfare may require it." Must the federal government have no
internal officers? This was absurd. "The truth is, . . . no Federal constitution can exist without powers, that in their exercise
affect the internal police of the component members." The impost was a necessity. Revenue to be raised within the states was
inadequate. The lack could not be supplied by loans. Applications to foreign countries had fallen short of success. Individuals "will neither be actuated by generosity nor reasons of state.
'Tis to their interest alone we must appeal. To conciliate this, we
must not only stipulate . . . compensation for what they lend,
but we must give security for the performance. We must pledge
an ascertained fund, simple and productive in its nature, general
in its principle, and at the disposal of a single will." This required that collection as well as appropriation be under control of
the United States.

3. (That Congress would become independent of its constituents.) In answer to this last objection to the federal impost,
Hamilton explicitly foretold his policy of redeeming the debt.

Had his authorship of this report been remembered in interested quarters, there need have been no doubt, a decade later when he was Secretary of the Treasury, that he would do his utmost to honor the public obligations. However, his commitment was lost in the anonymity of congressional minutes, and was given in a cause that failed.

That its own revenues would ensure for Congress autonomy, subject to the suffrages of the states in electing members, was true. It had no weight in this case because the fund was limited to redemption of the war debt and the duty had a fixed rate. No one meant to perpetuate the debt any more than to repudiate it. The ability to discharge the war debt in a moderate time could not be doubted. The government, limited by frequent elections and rotation in office, "ought to have the means necessary to answer the end of its institution. By weakening its hands . . . it may be rendered incapable of providing for the interior harmony or the exterior defence of the State." The capital of the debt could be met only by degrees, "but a fund for this purpose, and for paying the interest annually . . . ought to be provided. The omission will be the deepest ingratitude and cruelty to a large number of meritorious individuals, who . . . have adventured their fortunes in support of our Independence. It would stamp the national character with indelible disgrace." Since it was not possible to pay off the principal forthwith, "the next expedient is to fund the debt and render the evidences of it negotiable." By this means "the active stock of the nation [basis for private borrowing] would be increased by the whole amount of the domestic debt. . . . The national credit would revive and stand thereafter on a secure basis." Any surplus of designated revenues should go to "form a sinking fund, . . . inviolably appropriated to the payment of the principal of the . . . debt, and shall on no account be diverted to any other purpose." Cling to the old frustrated finance, and the result would be war protracted, Congress harassed, and "the national . . . safety at the mercy of events."[22]

Here was most of Hamilton's fiscal philosophy in a nutshell. National honor would be rewarded by prosperity and security, without sacrifice of liberty. The debt, once funded, would be not a burden but a benefit. This splendid paradox expressed Hamilton's insight and optimism, in contrast to the political distrust and

financial reluctance of the smallest state. Even the delegates from
Rhode Island were won to the logic of it, for they voted with the
others, eight states present, in unanimous approval, "a few trivial
alterations only being made in the course of discussion." However, Arnold voiced his private spleen to his governor. The answer of Hamilton's committee to Rhode Island was "a very lengthy
performance, wherein a State of Public Affairs . . . was labo-
riously wrought up to the liking of a majority of Congress, who
. . . approved it. . . ." The impost was "extolled as the in-
fallible grand Political Catholicon, by which every evil was to be
avoided, and every advantage derived."[23]

Hamilton pressed the indictment of Rhode Island and of
Howell, her chief spokesman in Congress.[24] He drafted a motion
condemning the letter in the *Boston Gazette* of November 10 as
injurious to the financing of the war; it was the sense of the house
that the author misrepresented facts and violated the secrecy enjoined on members. The governor of Rhode Island was to be
called on by the Secretary of Foreign Affairs to disclose the author.[25] He secured approval of his committee report, that the
deputation to Rhode Island should proceed as soon as possible.[26]
Howell now acknowledged that he wrote the letter, and Daniel
Carroll moved that the governor of Rhode Island be not addressed
on the subject. "The state in w,^ch such a vote would leave the
business unless the reason of it was expressed, being not adverted
to by some, . . . this motion was incautiously suffered to pass.
The effect of it however was soon observed, and a motion . . .
[was] made by Mr. Hamilton, to subjoin the words, 'Mr. Howel[l]
having in his place confessed himself to be the Author of the publication.' " Ramsay of South Carolina, to avoid a stigma on
Howell that might martyr him and confirm Rhode Island's opposition to the impost, moved another wording. Hamilton
opposed this and called for the yeas and nays on Ramsay's substitution. Thereupon "Mr. Howell grew very uneasy at the
prospect of his name being . . . brought on the Journals," and
asked that the matter be suspended till next day.[27]

Then (December 18) Howell read a defense of his conduct.
His accusers were overbearing; their censure was destructive of
his liberty to communicate with his constituents. He moved to

revoke the call on his governor to disclose the author of the letter, but only his immediate colleagues voted with him. His "behaviour was extremely offensive, and led to a determined opposition to him. . . ." He was willing to withdraw his protest if he was not named on the Journal, "but the impropriety which appeared . . . particularly to Mr. Hamilton, in suppressing the name of the Author of a piece wch Congress had so emphatically reprobated, when the author was found to be a member of Congress, prevented a relaxation as to the yeas & nays."[28]

So far as Howell was concerned, the episode ended when he was followed in his defiant retreat to Rhode Island by a recital of the proceedings plus reports by our ministers abroad of the untoward state of our loans.[29]

The deputation to Rhode Island was aborted by news that Virginia had repealed her consent to the impost. The three delegates set out on December 22 armed with Hamilton's answer to objections.[30] They had gone half a day's journey when Abner Nash, one of the deputation, remarked, casually and belatedly, that unofficial word had reached Congress of Virginia's change of front. This was in a private letter of Edmund Pendleton which Madison[31] read to Congress.[32] The bad news was confirmed by letters of Randolph and Governor Benjamin Harrison.[33] "The most intelligent members," said Madison, "were deeply affected & prognosticated a failure of the Import scheme, & the most pernicious effects to the . . . duration . . . of the Confederacy." He himself refused to be dashed, hoped that Virginia would yet come into line; "Congress cannot abandon the plan as long as there is a spark of hope. Nay, other plans of a like principle must be added."[34]

An interlude, reverting to old business,[35] was debate on what should be done about redemption of Continental bills remaining in the hands of individuals. At what rate should specie certificates, bearing interest, be given for old tenor currency yet outstanding? States that had not sunk their proportions were to be charged with the deficiency. Mixed motives figured. States with more than their quotas outstanding wanted to protect their citizens with a tolerable rate, so long as Congress consented to be liable; otherwise they would resort to stoppages.[36] Southern states were for sinking the old currency, whatever the sacrifice to individuals. When the usual motion to postpone was rejected, Wolcott vainly sought to give the states discretion.

Hamilton, "on the principle of Policy," we are told by another member,[37] moved for the rate originally established, 40 for one, and got the full backing of the states with more than their proportion of the money still out (New Hampshire, Massachusetts, and Rhode Island), but was negatived elsewhere. The concession of 75 to one, from despairing New Englanders, fared worse, and the whole matter went over.[38]

The Congress of the Confederation was culpable in much, but often its members must have felt that body was punished beyond its deserts. Such a sorrowful concatenation of events fell in the beginning of the year 1783. Unalloyed failure would have been bad, but harbingers of splendid achievement mixed with fears of impending ruin to make distress excruciating. Two days before Christmas came official news that Great Britain, abandoning earlier slighting allusions to her erstwhile colonies, had commissioned Richard Oswald to conclude peace with the "Thirteen United States of America." Boudinot, the President of Congress, wrote with his usual optimism, "The Rubicon is therefore Past and . . . my Expectations are likely to be fulfilled. . . ."

A fortnight later Hamilton, and his friends Madison and Wolcott, still had misgivings. "Whether [peace] will take place . . . is a problem of difficult solution," Hamilton wrote. "The . . . unsteadiness for which Lord Shelburne is remarkable will not justify any confidence in his intentions; and the variety of interests to be conciliated in a treaty . . . must render it a work of difficulty."[39]

This was precisely at the time that the deputation to Rhode Island to appeal for reliable funds for Congress was recalled on warning that Virginia had retracted her consent to the impost. Five days later (December 29) a delegation from the army enlivened the holiday spirit with fresh importunities for pay ere they be discharged.[40] The committee from the camp at Newburgh—General Alexander McDougall and Colonels Mathias Ogden and John Brooks—circulated among members of Congress informally for a week, preparing them for the army memorial, signed by General Henry Knox and a dozen other officers of lesser rank.[41] This

was laid before Congress January 6, 1783. The very restraint of
its language betrayed disappointment threatening to become dis-
illusionment, disgust, and retaliation. The appeal was dutiful to
Congress "as our head and sovereign," but was dutiful to the
army also: "We complain that shadows have been offered to us
while the substance has been gleaned by others. . . . Our distresses are now brought to a point. We have borne all that men
can bear—our property is expended—our private resources are at
an end. . . . The uneasiness of the soldiers, for want of pay, is
. . . dangerous; any further experiments on their patience may
have fatal effects."[42]

In spite of Virginia's defection from the impost, practically removing that means, Congress was determined to persist in the
attempt for a permanent revenue. Hamilton was appointed
chairman of a committee, with FitzSimmons and Madison, to contrive steps to that end.[43] The result was a conglomerate proposal
embracing valuation of surveyed lands and improvements as a basis
of reapportionment of quotas, completed cessions of Western lands,
a variety of specific import duties, and revival of the impost besides. During the slow, baffled progress of these discussions, the
deputation from the disgruntled army, more restive by the day,
was a torturing symbol before Congress of its incompetence.

Congress was rarely without a convergence of problems, solutions to which were mutually dependent. At the present juncture,
how improve the pleasing prospect of peace while the army was
fearful of being disbanded before it was paid, and the Treasury
never emptier? Beneath this conflict, soon to flare in angry anonymous threats at Newburgh, was the fundamental political defect
of the Confederation, which prevented command of resources. In
seven years of struggle to wage war, income had been desperately
improvised. Ironically, now that the military immediacy was removed, financial ingenuity had become reluctance. Negotiation
of further foreign loans did not thrive beside negotiation of peace.
French francs were as hard to come by as Dutch gulden. Not
only did heavy debts discourage response to fresh applications, but
the peace designs of all parties were in doubt. Had Britain accepted defeat, or would she perhaps renew the war? Would
France discover an interest hostile to that of America, and if so
would we keep a faith which she gave signs of breaking? Spain

and Holland were supposed to have demands which might complicate a general settlement.

Moreover, while we continued to draw on our agents abroad for funds which they had not been able to recruit, our capacity to summon means at home hung in the balance. The Superintendent of Finance, despairing of requisitions, gave notice of quitting ere his own credit should crumble with that of the country. After collapse of the impost, intended to supply the national treasury with independent funds and to distribute the burden fairly among the states, how reform the old method of requisitions? This or that dodge for improved apportionment might be tried, and additional ingredients of revenue might be insinuated, but when all was said and done Congress lacked authority to exact. The Articles of Confederation left in the separate sovereignties too much freedom of choice, which they used for obstruction.

While Hamilton in Congress worked manfully to meet these vexations, his correspondence showed his conviction that temporary expedients would not serve. He knew that he was plying broken tools that could not be repaired, but must be replaced by a new machine. Thus he declared to the not very sympathetic Governor Clinton: "Every day proves more and more the insufficiency of the Confederation . . . and many of the most sensible men acknowledge the wisdom of the measure recommended by your Legislature" for the formation of a firmer union.[44]

18

". . . A Fatal Opposition
to Continental Views"

THE solemn remonstrance of the officers against turning the army off empty-handed compelled Congress to face its fiscal plight. Head-in-the-sand tactics could no longer be indulged. The state of the Treasury was not in doubt; but the prospect must be discovered, disclosed, and, by whatever means, improved. Woeful as it was, the case was to be worse before it became better, but efforts at redress fairly date from the army demand. The Grand Committee to which the memorial was referred met on the same day, and recognized that nothing could be done before conferring with the Superintendent of Finance on the following evening.

Robert Morris "informed them explicitly that it was impossible to make any advance of pay in the present state of the finances . . . and imprudent to give any assurances with respect to future pay until certain funds should be previously established." Openly acting under pressure from the army would inspire distrust of Congress and produce fresh importunities. Expedients the Financier had in view required secrecy; "the situation . . . within his department was so alarming that he had thoughts of asking Congress to appoint a Confidential Committee to receive communications . . . and to sanctify . . . such steps as ought to be taken." The conferees went into forebodings not relieved by agreement to meet three evenings later with the representatives from the camp, Morris to be present to document the distress.

Fateful parleys followed fast. Scarcely had the congressmen

braced themselves to confront the officers when debate on the floor, of the old maundering sort, was interrupted by Morris's fore-shadowed letter urging that a very special committee, of a delegate from each state, be empowered to advise him.   Possessed of pride, though out of pocket, Congress objected that this would commit it too far.   Instead, three members—Rutledge, Osgood, and Madison—were told off to listen to the bad news of the Financier and inform the whole body.

Immediately on adjournment the trio met Morris.   He quickly stated the problem.   He had already overdrawn expected Euro-pean funds to the extent of 3,500,000 livres; the only hope for further drafts was the friendship of France.[1]

Next morning Rutledge and his colleagues asked whether Con-gress was prepared to know the message of the Financier, which the committee must keep confidential unless disclosure was offi-cially required.   Authorization given, two sentences told the story. The Financier had overdrawn known funds.   Might he now draw on problematical loans?   The answer, with the stateliness of in-solvency, was Yes.   A telling touch was the caution that bills of exchange must not exceed "the amount of the money directed to be borrowed. . . ."[2]

In this posture of national credit, the audience with army sup-plicants was bound to be noncommittal, though the occasion sent apprehensions vibrating through Congress.[3]   However, if Con-gress could make no promises, the officers had a proposal.   De-livered with "peculiar emphasis" by McDougall, their spokesman, it was that Congress ponder "the debility and defects in the federal Gov., and the unwillingness of the States to cement & invigorate it. . . ."[4]

The hearing closed with naming a sub-committee of Hamilton, Madison, and Rutledge to report arrangements, in concert with the Superintendent of Finance, for satisfying the army.[5]   A stop-gap answer to the army memorial was the report of a grand com-mittee, drafted by Hamilton with some lines by Boudinot.   It provided for present pay as far as the Superintendent of Finance was able (an idle assurance), and the states and the Superin-tendent would settle arrearages.   However, the moral commit-ment was given that "the troops . . . in common with all the creditors . . . have an undoubted right to expect . . . security; and . . . Congress will . . . enter upon an immediate . . . consideration of" means of funding the whole debt of the United States.[6]

Resolution was easier than remedy. February 6, 1783, Congress came to cases. The Articles of Confederation recited that the common treasury should be supplied by the several states in proportion to all granted or surveyed land within each state, valued in such mode as Congress should point out. States laid what taxes they chose to make up requisitions which they treated with varying degrees of neglect, but Congress could at least direct the assessment of quotas. Now it was moved that the legislatures should divide their states into districts and appoint commissioners to estimate the value of lands and improvements. These valuations, transmitted to Congress, would dictate requisitions.[7]

This left the crucial determinations to the states, whose efficiency and good faith in assessments were alike suspect. Hamilton therefore moved, FitzSimmons seconding, a substitute plan, slower but surer, vesting control in Congress. Assessment should be deferred until Congress could afford the expense to "proceed to . . . valuation, by commissioners appointed by them and acting under their authority, upon principles uniform throughout the United States. . . ." Delay would be less hurtful than defective execution. Nor would the national assessment, and final adjustment of accounts, neglect "equitable abatements to such States as have been more immediate sufferers by the war." Meantime, the old quotas would stand. This substitute resolution was lost, but so too was the original proposal assigning assessment to the states.[8] Hamilton considered various expedients to keep as much power as possible in Congress, and to make the quotas reflect the true competence of each state.[9]

Congress resolved, on February 17, 1783, that states obtain an accurate account of lands and buildings and of white and black inhabitants. These were to be rendered by March 1, 1784, when Congress would appoint a grand committee, any nine of whom could agree on "a just and true estimate of the value of all lands in each of the United States." If approved, this would furnish the rule for adjusting all accounts with the individual states, and would operate for a term not exceeding five years in apportioning requisitions. This passed 9 to 2, Hamilton and Floyd of New York voting against it, as also Carroll, the only representative of Maryland.[10]

The discussion prompted Hamilton to explain to Governor Clinton and the New York legislature why in his view there could be no "general representative of the wealth of a nation, the criterion of its ability to pay taxes." Neither land nor numbers could serve. For illustration, the United Provinces, with more than half as much revenue as Great Britain, had not one fourth the land and less than a third the population. The Netherlands and the Swiss cantons were equal in territory and people, but the former were five times the latter in revenues. "The truth is, the ability of a country to pay taxes depends on infinite combinations of physical and moral causes which can never be accommodated to any general rule—climate, soil, productions, advantages for navigation, government, genius of the people, progress of arts and industry, and an endless variety of circumstances. The diversities are sufficiently great in these States to make an infinite difference in their relative wealth, the proportion of which can never be found by any common measure whatever."

Here was the advanced idea that what the older economists called the "opulence" of a country depends not on its physical features, property, and population, but on its total faculties, its organic functioning. The whole might be greater than the sum of its parts. Economic capacity had many ingredients, among others the gift for associated effort. This was a favorite conviction with Hamilton, several times through the years explicitly stated, and underlying all of his policy as a minister of state. Political economy, properly so called, depends on immaterial as well as on material elements, blended and directed with conscious art. The wisest of the Mercantilists knew this; the *laissez faire* school, just rising at this period, attended to it too little or not at all; the economic nationalists who followed Hamilton in time and influence built their recommendations upon it.[11]

The only possible way to make the states contribute to national expense "in an equal proportion to their means," Hamilton concluded, "is by general taxes imposed under Continental authority." Local burdens would be compensated and become diffused in the course of time and experience. Since Congress had the discretionary power of determining necessary revenue, it must have the power of taxation. As matters stood, the vice of inequality "will either, in its consequences, reform the Federal Constitution or dissolve it."

He described the defects of both plans—self-serving state assessment and vague, speculative valuation by Congress—to explain why he opposed the last as well as the first. He would never consent to amuse the states "by attempts which must either fail in the execution or be productive of evil. I would rather incur the negative inconveniences of delay than the positive mischiefs of injudicious expedients. A contrary conduct serves to destroy confidence in the government, the greatest misfortune that can befall a nation." At the very least, Congress should have its own commissioners in the states, acting "under the direction of that *body* which has a common interest." In the dawn of peace, plans should be uniform as they might be enduring. Finally, though he had given opposition, now that Congress had adopted a scheme, he hoped New York, for the sake of the Union, would comply cheerfully.[12]

Notwithstanding the decision to rest state quotas on land values, those in favor of a broader basis of requisitions and surer sources of revenue returned to the attack. Hamilton was a member of a committee (Gorham, chairman) which on March 6, 1783, renewed the proposal for an impost of 5 per cent on all imports, with a few exceptions, plus specific duties on imported wines, liquors, sugars, and teas for discharge of the war debts. The states were to appoint the collectors acting in their limits. Congress was to furnish an annual account of the whole, and credit each state, against its quota, with the amounts collected within it. The plan was to run for twenty-five years. A constitutional amendment substituted population for land as the criterion of requisitions, excluding slaves and Indians not taxed. However, this produced nothing more than confused debate.[13] The committee reported in further detail on March 18, adding some specific import taxes, and proposing requisitions to raise $1,500,000 a year, but the whole was negatived, 6 to 4, and two states divided.[14]

While arrival of the preliminary treaty of peace with Great Britain, on March 12, 1783, was an immense relief, and practically removed fears that the war would be renewed, most in Congress

were chagrined at information that our commissioners had negotiated without the knowledge of France.   A secret article setting
a more generous boundary to West Florida if it fell to Britain
than to Spain disregarded our repeated promises "to make the
most candid . . . communications on all subjects" to the ministers of France.

This ounce of bitter in the pound of sweet was officially notified
to Congress by Livingston, Secretary for Foreign Affairs, on March
18, and was the subject of a week's earnest and at times violent
debate (unrecorded except for Madison's notes).[15]   Leading
members from all sections of the country gave their views.   Should
Congress reprobate, to France, the course of our ministers in treating clandestinely with the common enemy?   Should the terms relating to West Florida be disclosed or altered, and how?   Most
Southern members[16] found excuses for our envoys, and were
joined by those from New England.   These last were tender of the
feelings and reputation of John Adams, who had been won over
by Jay and the two had drawn in Franklin.

It remained for Hamilton, Wilson, Peters, and Clark, from the
Middle States, to take a middle position.   They had to balance
cross-currents in Congress, gratitude to our envoys for surprisingly
favorable terms, our national honor, commitments of France to
Spain, and future dependence on our chief ally.

Hamilton "urged the propriety of proceeding with . . . circumspection."   It was possible to put a reasonable interpretation
on "the policy of France to procrastinate the . . . acknowledgm.^t
of our Independence on the part of G.B.," which contrasted with
"the past cruelty & present duplicity" of our enemy.   "He disapproved . . . highly of the conduct of our Ministers in not
shewing the preliminary articles to our Ally before they signed
them, and still more so of their agreeing to the separate article."
Britain would use this to produce distrust of us in France.   His
unflattering thumbnail sketch of Spain ended with the notion
that when the secret article was known she might resort to a
separate treaty.

"He thought a middle course best with respect to our Ministers; . . . they ought to be commended in general; but . . . the
separate article ought" to be revealed in France.   He saw both in-

justice and danger in recalling or reprehending trustworthy men.[17] Hamilton's motion[18] was much to the purpose of others offered by Peters and Williamson that day.   All papers and propositions were referred to a committee of five of moderate views, Hamilton a member.[19]   The situation was further embarrassed by disclosure of the secret article in American newspapers, and it was inferred that this discreditable item was known in Europe.[20]   The committee reported honest resolutions acknowledging our misconduct toward France.   But no action was taken[21] because next day, March 23, arrived news of the signing of a general peace,[22] and almost at once letters were received from Vergennes reproving the behavior of our negotiators, for which Franklin had apologized. Forgiveness was coupled with exhortations to us to establish "permanent revenues for paying our debts & supporting a national character."[23]

The clutching for revenue was rendered frantic, in the delayed, dazed way of Congress, by the groans and then the growls of an idle army fearful that peace would discharge them to their homes penniless and with no security for arrears of pay.   Arthur Lee, just arrived at Philadelphia from Virginia, gave his slant to Sam Adams: "Every Engine is at work here to obtain permanent taxes and the appointment of Collectors by Congress, in the States. The terror of a mutinying Army is playd off with considerable efficacy. . . . But to remedy temporary evils by permanent Ones is neither wise nor safe. . . . A majority of the Army . . . will . . . not lend themselves to the tory designs, as I verily beleive this is, of subverting the Revolution. . . ."[24]

At this juncture, with peace impending and the wearied but unpaid army viewing its advent with misgivings, the distracted Congress was between the devil and the deep.   The embarrassments in the situation are nowhere better revealed than in the correspondence between Hamilton and Washington.   Their exchanges were always frank, but now took on a perfect intimacy. These letters offer a microcosm of the relations of the two men, so similar and yet so different.   Hamilton, as always, felt free to point out a main line of conduct.   His manner was even didactic, unless one recalls that now, in Congress, Hamilton had information which he could reason from without disclosing in so many words.   The long relationship of chief and aide was for the nonce reversed. Hamilton was at political headquarters, while Washington was in effect on detail in the field. As ever, Hamilton was the one to cite possibilities, to raise doubts, to adventure what might prove effective, though dangerous just this side of possible disaster. Washington, on his part, with such assistance, knew how to choose the true course between diverging plausible paths. It will many times appear in this narrative that the younger man was quicker in perception, more fertile in resource, had the more multiplex mind. But the senior member of the extraordinary partnership was superior in steady, constant judgment. Hamilton's prism dispersed the spectrum into more shades of color, but Washington did not miss the bend of the arc.

The critical question was what part the army should play in persuading country and Congress to fund the debt and thus provide means of satisfying all of the public creditors. Should its entreaties rise to remonstrance and be allowed, even encouraged, to go on to threatened revolt as the instrument of coercion? Hamilton certainly toyed with this notion, to the knowledge of those about him, though he concluded that it was too perilous a game to be risked.

"The state of our finances was perhaps never more critical," Hamilton wrote to Washington in February.[25] Whether there was peace or war, "a few months may open an embarrassing scene. . . . It appears to be a prevailing opinion in the army that the disposition to recompense their services will cease with the necessity for them, and that, if they once lay down their arms, they part with the means of obtaining justice. . . . What is the true line of policy? The claims of the army, urged with moderation, but with firmness, may operate . . . to produce . . . the measures which the exigencies of affairs demand. . . . But the difficulty will be to keep a . . . *suffering army* within . . . bounds. . . . " Washington should intervene "to bring order, perhaps even good, out of confusion." General Knox would prove a prudent intermediary, assisting the commander in chief to keep the confidence of both army and people. The object must be "the establishment of general funds, which alone can do justice to the creditors of the United States (of whom the army forms the most meritorious class), . . . and supply the future wants of government."[26]

Washington in reply[27] rejected any use of the army as a lash to a reluctant Congress. If the army became their own providers it would "be productive of Civil commotions and end in blood. . . . God forbid we should be involved in it." He hoped that Hamilton's apprehensions, in case of peace, were misplaced. In any event he would pursue his "steady line of conduct" and trust that the army would not exceed the bounds of reason. Perhaps Congress should adjourn to allow members to explain to their constituents the defects of the constitution.[28]

By the time Washington wrote again, March 12, and before he had heard further from Hamilton on the subject, he reported that "a Storm very suddenly arose with unfavourable prognostics, which tho' diverted for a moment, is not yet blown over," nor was it in his power to know the issue. He was obliged "to arrest . . . the foot that stood wavering on a tremendous precipice, . . . and to rescue [the officers] from plunging themselves into a gulph of Civil horror. . . ."

The storm was the result of two anonymous letters that appeared in camp, inciting the officers to abandon the country if war continued or to use military force to compel Congress to stand and deliver if peace ensued. This advice was to be discussed at a meeting called for March 11. The second letter was the longer and more provocative. America had disdained the officers' cries, said the writer. "If this, then, be your treatment, while the swords you wear are necessary for the defence of America, what have you to expect from peace, when your voice shall sink, and your strength dissipate by division?" If officers, thus spurned, could "consent to wade through the vile mire of dependency," then "Go, starve, and be forgotten." The present moment must be seized. "If your determination be in any proportion to your wrongs, carry your appeal from the justice to the fears of government." If war was the portion, they should "retire to some unsettled country" and " 'mock when [the people's] fear cometh on.' "[29]

This second address, Washington informed Hamilton in a postscript, had just been "thrown into circulation. The Contents evidently prove that the Author is in, or near Camp," and not, as some had supposed, a member of a cabal in Philadelphia. He besought Hamilton to urge Congress to discharge its duty to the

army promptly; a large part of the officers "have no other prospect before them than a Gaol, if they are turned loose without a
liquidation of Accts." Delegates of delinquent states "must be
answerable to God and their Country for the . . . horrors which
may be occasioned. . . ." This same day, March 12, President
Boudinot informed Washington of the arrival of Captain Joshua
Barney bringing the preliminary treaty of peace signed by British
and American commissioners at Paris on Nov. 30, 1782.[30]

When Hamilton next wrote to Washington, in swift reply to
the above, on March 17, he knew only that Washington had fore-
stalled the irregular proceedings in camp with general orders for
a meeting of the officers on March 15. Hamilton was in suspense
for the result. However, he was glad that Washington was di-
verting, not attempting to stem, the torrent. It was true that
members of Congress had encouraged the idea of combinations
between public creditors and the army. And he confessed, "I
have myself urged in Congress the propriety of uniting the influence of the public creditors, and the army as part of them, to
prevail upon the States to enter into their views. I have expressed the same sentiments out-of-doors. Several other members of Congress have done the same." He had thought the discontents of the army could be turned to a good account, but "any
combination of *force* . . . would only be productive of the horrors of a civil war, might end in the ruin of the country, and
would certainly end in the ruin of the army."

His complaint was as ever of "prejudices in the particular
States opposed to those measures which alone can give stability
and prosperity to the Union. There is a fatal opposition to Continental views." Necessity alone could work a reform, but how
apply and control it?[31] He reported as pertinent to the officers'
demands two actions of Congress, without noting his part in
them. The particular states were required to settle army accounts to August 1, 1780, the Superintendent of Finance, hopefully, to "take measures" for settling since that period.[32] Eight
and a half states had favored commutation of half-pay for life into
full pay for five years, which was actuarially about right.[33]

By the time Hamilton wrote again to the commander in chief
the affairs of the Confederacy wore a pleasanter aspect. Washington on March 15 had met the officers at Newburgh, had begged

their patience and confidence in Congress, and, in a resolution promptly drawn by a committee headed by General Knox, had been assured of the "good Sense and steady Patriotism of the Gentlemen of the Army."[34]

However, the officers, in responding to Washington's plea for restraint, declared themselves "convinced that the representatives of America will not disband or disperse the army until their accounts are liquidated. . . ." Meanwhile Robert Morris, exasperated by demands upon an empty Treasury, had announced that he would retire as Superintendent of Finance unless the states paid up. Hamilton was one of a committee that persuaded him to remain until arrangements were completed for discharging the army (see below).[35]

This tormenting unfinished business was ironically complicated by the grateful news, in letters from Lafayette, that peace had been signed between all of the belligerent powers on January 25 and that hostilities had ceased. Lafayette wrote on the same day ("Most Private") asking Hamilton to secure a resolution of Congress approving the marquis's assistance in Europe in concluding peace. Besides, having been considered at the British court "an enthusiastic rebel, . . . a young madman," he would prize being sent there "an Extraordinary Envoy from the United States" bearing the American ratification of the treaty. He was similarly solicitous for Hamilton, who should be chosen Minister to Britain. In addition to these private items, he implored revision of the Confederation "to invigorate the Continental Union; . . . this last stroke is wanting, and unless the States be strongly bound to each other, we have much to fear from British, and, indeed, from European politics."[36]

Congratulating Washington upon the conclusion of his military labors, Hamilton pointed to the equal need for his further exertions "to make our independence truly a blessing." Solid establishments within must perpetuate the Union and "prevent our being a ball in the hands of European powers, band[i]ed against each other at their pleasure. . . ." But this would be an arduous work, "for to borrow a figure from mechanics, the centrifugal is much stronger than the centripetal force in these States; the seeds of disunion much more numerous than those of union."[37] Washington answered in echo of Hamilton's hopes and fears. He was "deeply impressed with the necessity of a reform in our present Confederation. . . . No Man . . . has felt the bad effects of it more sensibly; for [to] the defects thereof, and want of Powers in Congress, may justly be ascribed the prolongation of the war. . . ." He wished for Hamilton's further thoughts[38] which were promised. This was the beginning of the peacetime collaboration between them which ended only with Washington's death sixteen years later. In the course of it Hamilton long remained the co-adjutor, until his contribution to the partnership marked him as all but Washington's *alter idem*. This, be it said, with a difference. Hamilton's contrivance of ways and means was essential to Washington's influence, just as Washington's prestige and approval were necessary to the success of Hamilton's proposals, economic and political. Divergence, toward the end, was due to the inability of Hamilton, in altered times, to wear the mantle of Washington. No more could anyone else do that.

Developments in Congress, the lull in the army's importunities, and impending peace furnished the background of Hamilton's next application to the commander in chief. The means of supporting public credit came forward again, on March 22, 1783, in a further report of Gorham's committee, on which Hamilton served. The proposal was that the proceeds of specific duties be credited to the states within which they were collected. Though of the committee, Hamilton moved, and James Wilson seconded, a substitute plan. After a preamble declaring the purpose of Congress to secure permanent, adequate funds, he included the general impost and the "specifics" of the majority bill, but added taxes on land and dwellings, the latter at graduated rates. The product of these property taxes should be credited to the states in which they arose. Not so, however, the proceeds of the import duties, which were "to pass to the general benefit of the United States," until the debt due by the United States at the termination of the war was discharged.[39] This scheme, ampler and more national than that of the committee, was rejected, 7–4, only New York, New Jersey, Connecticut, and Pennsylvania for it. After postponements until news of peace had been received, Hamilton revived a proposal of Madison substituting population for land as the basis of apportioning the public debt; the count was to be of all white and other free citizens (including indentured servants), and three-fifths of the slaves.   This was passed almost unanimously,[40] but it did nothing for present revenue.

Hamilton, for a committee of Congress, queried the commander in chief for advice on handling of the army claims.   "On one side the army expect they will not be disbanded till accounts are settled and funds established.   On the other hand, [Congress] have no constitutional power of doing any thing more than to recommend funds, and . . . these will meet with mountains of prejudice in some of the States."   Yet many mischiefs would follow from leaving the army intact but unpaid.[41]   This official application was enclosed in a personal and confidential letter of Hamilton of the same date.   Republican jealousy and ingratitude were likely to turn the army away empty.   But the army must submit to its fate, for force could not succeed without reversing the Revolution to dictatorship.   He was suffering a reaction from his exertions in Congress, and confessed to "an indifferent opinion of the honesty of this country, and ill forebodings as to its future system."[42]

Washington answered in his public capacity in a letter to Bland,[43] and separately replied to Hamilton that he had read his private misgivings about the good faith of Congress "with pain, and contemplated the picture it had drawn with astonishment and horror. . . ."   The idea of redress by force was too chimerical to have had a place in any serious mind in the army, but there was no telling what disturbances might result from distrust of justice. The fears of the army were "all alive," and Washington hoped the lines would not be disbanded until accounts were liquidated, or bad consequences would follow.

In confidence Washington informed Hamilton that leading men in the army suspected that Congress, or some members of it, wanted to use the army only to establish Continental funds; if plaints from Newburgh served this end, then the army might be sacrificed.   The Superintendent of Finance was supposed to be at the bottom of this scheme.   But the army in its irritable state was "a dangerous instrument to play with. . . ."   His summary advice was to "disband the Army as soon as possible, but consult the wishes of it. . . ."[44]

Hamilton, in reply, posed the cleavage in Congress on the public debts.   "There are two classes of men . . . of very different views—one attached to state the other to Continental politics.

The last have been strenuous advocates for funding the public debt upon solid securities, the former have given every opposition in their power and have only been dragged into the measures . . . now near being adopted by the clamors of the army and other public creditors." He was not surprised that he had been suspected of exploiting the demands of the army for the benefit of a comprehensive plan of finance. The truth was that the "advocates for Continental funds" had blended the claims of the army with those of other creditors with no design to abandon the army when its cries had served their turn. Provision for the army alone would not weigh with security holders whose influence in the creditor states was necessary to an inclusive scheme.

Beyond the problem of satisfying claimants of the moment, from whatever quarter, was that of "how to restore public credit." Taxes could not supply more than a fraction of needed income directly, but if explicitly pledged to meet principal and interest could induce further loans, then languishing, which were the only recourse. It was "necessary to combine all the motives to this end, that could operate upon different descriptions of persons in the different states. The necessity and discontents of the army presented themselves as a powerful engine." Those who rejected "continuance of the old wretched state system, . . . the men who think continentally," counted on the impost, if approved, to pay the interest on old and new loans in Europe.

He exculpated Robert Morris from the insinuation that he would play the army as a pawn. He was wise to resign unless funds were established within his generous time limit, else he would have brought down his private credit and the last prop of the public credit in one stroke. Only the publication of his letter of resignation was ill advised, for that had reanimated old passions against him.[45] "I believe no man in this country but himself," declared Hamilton, "could have kept the money machine a going during the period he has been in office. From every thing that appears his administration has been upright as well as able."[46]

Congress having been notified, March 24, of the cessation of hostilities, Hamilton bore an active part in conclusion of the preliminary articles of peace and worked zealously for their faithful observance by the United States in order to prevent any hitch in reaching the definitive treaty.[47] This was a difficult interval, for adjustment of our internal problems, political and economic, depended on ending the war, while that would be endangered by faulty compliance on our part with terms remarkably favorable. Prudence in this parlous period was essential.   But signatures and seals on parchment merely punctuated developments.   Even after the final treaty was ratified, our national life was to remain in suspension for six years until experience and effort gave us a new Constitution and truly promising prospects of independence.

Hamilton worked through these preparatory stages with his eyes fixed on the future of American greatness.   Present irritations, jealousies, and fears, should be composed so as not to hazard the enduring result.   The peace opened Hamilton's contribution to America.   Hitherto he had been patriot pamphleteer, soldier in the field, confidential aide of the commander in chief, and had wrestled with collection of revenue and vexations of wartime legislation.   This excellent service had been as junior partner to others of more maturity and authority.   Now he began to draw ahead and exercise his creative powers, rallying the assistance of colleagues who shared his views and supported his plans.   Hamilton's entry into this career was temporarily interrupted by his withdrawal from Congress to commence the practice of law, but this was a pause, not a diversion, and it led into his most active participation, beginning with the Annapolis Convention of 1786.   We may date his new direction from the spring of 1783, when Congress was closing the war chapter.

Early in April he was deputed by a committee for peace arrangements in the different departments of the government to inquire of the commander in chief what he would recommend for present defense and future military security.[48]   Congress ratified the preliminary treaty of peace with Great Britain on April 15, 1783, Hamilton having written the resolution calling for the draft form.   He also secured passage of a simple provision for the commander in chief to enter into preparatory arrangements with the British land and naval commanders for surrender of prisoners and evacuation of posts.[49]   This was later somewhat complicated.[50] Hamilton tried unsuccessfully to restore the mandate giving sole responsibility to Washington to meet military terms of the treaty,[51] but forthwith wrote to Washington as directed.   He conveyed the doubt of Congress whether *"the ratification of the treaty in*

America"—after which there should be no more confiscations, and hostilities should cease—referred to the provisional articles now endorsed or to the definitive instrument yet to be concluded. On this question depended the earlier or later liberation of prisoners. One would suppose that peace commissioners would use unmistakable language. Hamilton counseled the precaution of restoring prisoners only as the British forces were withdrawn.[52]

Meanwhile the search for income was compelling. The revenue scheme finally enacted by Congress on April 18, 1783, was a congeries of expedients arrived at by several compromises.[53] The ingredients of it had been made familiar in accumulating proposal and mounting debate—the general impost, numerous specific duties, requisitions of a total of $1,500,000 annually, and a recommended change in the eighth of the Articles of Confederation to make population instead of land and improvements the basis of apportionment. Duties and requisitions were limited to twenty-five years and to the purpose of discharging war debts. All of these revenues were conditional on unanimous consent of the states, which, once given, formed "a mutual compact" not to be broken by a minority. Land cessions were again enjoined. Though fearfully and wonderfully made, the measure represented a gain for central authority.

The act itself (really a set of recommendations to the states) gave evidence of Hamilton's efforts as one of the committee[54] that drew and guided it to passage. We may be sure that he urged that the collectors, though regrettably appointed by the states, should "be amenable to, and removable by the United States in Congress assembled, alone. . . ." The shift from land to population as a basis of apportionment of requisitions had been his frequent insistence,[55] nor could he have been brought to abandon the impost. Concessions he and other friends of the measure were obliged to allow, but how he breasted the opposition for main purposes is apparent.[56]

Hamilton's influence is plain in the frank and persuasive address to the states, prepared by a committee of Madison, Ellsworth, and himself, which was sent to the governors by President Boudinot, explaining the revenue recommendations. Legislatures not sitting should be speedily called for action on the proposals, and delegations in Congress be recruited to strength.[57] The whole amount of the debts was placed at $42,000,375; for the time being only the annual interest of $2,415,956 could be provided, but this must be done beyond peradventure. Requisitions "from time to time" on "thirteen independent authorities" could not serve. A general impost (again urged), with the specific duties, ought to raise nearly $916,000. This left $1,500,000 of interest to be made up by the states as they chose. Impost and requisitions, to establish public credit, must be joined in "one indivisable and irrevocable act." Domestic creditors were already entitled to the principal of their loans. Congress could not satisfy them except by assuring the payment of their interest, "to enable them, if they incline, to transfer their stock at its full value." If confidence in the funds was thus inspired, the capital of the domestic debt could be canceled by new loans bearing less than the prevailing 6 per cent—a clear gain. Principal must be discharged from expected increase in revenue, including sale of vacant territory.

The burden of the debt could and should be borne with pride. The holders, foreign and domestic, were all worthy. "To discriminate the merits of these several descriptions of creditors, would be a task equally unnecessary and indivious. If the voice of humanity plead more loudly in favour of some than of others, the voice of policy, no less than of justice, pleads in favour of all."[58]

These arguments had Hamilton's hearty concurrence, if he did not originate them. No discrimination between creditors, especially between first holders and transferees, emphatically was not Madison's idea when Hamilton urged it on the national Congress seven years later.

In spite of his important part in framing the measure, Hamilton was one of only four members of Congress voting against it.[59] He gave his reasons to Governor Clinton.[60] The compromises made the plan less potent and not more palatable; the states would consent as readily to a better proposal, and if the present one were agreed to it could not succeed in its purpose. All of the "capital articles of visible property" should have been designated, as this would make revenue increase with the increase of the country. The principal of the debt could not be paid in twenty-five years, when the funds would be cut off. He could not credit the good faith of collectors appointed by reluctant states. The whole of his later policy he now put crisply: ". . . for want of an adequate security the evidences of the public debt will not be transferable for any thing like their value; . . . not admitting an incorporation of the creditors in the nature of banks, will deprive the public of the benefit of an increased circulation, and . . . will disable the people from paying the taxes for want of a sufficient medium."

Still, he hoped New York, as a creditor state, would support the plan. Beyond this were superior motives—"the obligations of national faith, honor, and reputation."

With fiscal ruin or rescue hanging in the balance, Hamilton was one of a committee to confer with the Superintendent of Finance to persuade him to continue in office until at least an instalment of pay could be raised for the soldiers then on the point of dismissal.[61] Hamilton penned that part of the report, soon submitted, which stated Morris's difficulties but also his consent to serve, with the support of Congress. Hamilton included a plea that Congress "stimulate the most vigorous exertions of the states towards raising the necessary supplies of money," and that France should be appealed to for at least four millions in addition to the six millions lately granted. However, this was stricken in favor of a more noncommittal conclusion written by Boudinot and Osgood.[62]

At this juncture Hamilton tried to expedite the work of Congress by requiring that committees delinquent with their reports be obliged to offer reasons.[63] He sought in vain to have the doors of Congress thrown open, as "it is of importance in every free country, that the conduct and sentiments of those to whom the direction of public affairs is committed, should be publicly known. . . ."[64] He was successful, over South Carolina's objection, in removing the Virginia, Maryland, and Pennsylvania lines, the artillery and cavalry, under Greene's command, to their home states.[65]

Hamilton as chairman wrote the report of the committee that urged the soonest possible conclusion of a commercial treaty with Britain. As the object could not be accomplished by weaving commercial provisions into the peace treaty, it was recommended that a temporary commercial convention be entered into until a permanent one could be negotiated.[66] His concern to see our foreign trade resumed and extended at the earliest moment is evident.

As Hamilton was one of a small number of army officers in Congress, and understood administrative problems from his experience as aide to the commander in chief, he was oftenest turned to in planning demobilization of the troops. Liberal proposals for care and relief of disabled veterans[67] and for adjusting final rank of officers in meritorious cases[68] were subordinate to a fresh exhortation to the states for money to facilitate discharges.

Reporting for his committee on peace arrangements, Hamilton recommended an organization for the Department of Foreign Affairs. At the moment of entering the family of nations, with acknowledged independence, this essential agency of the government was in tenuous state. Robert R. Livingston could not be persuaded to withdraw his resignation as secretary unless his salary was increased to cover his expenses, and even so might prefer the place of Chancellor of New York.[69] Hamilton and his colleagues of the committee secured assent to continuance of the office, the holder to present to Congress from time to time plans "for conducting the political and commercial intercourse of the United States with foreign nations. . . ." Declaration that the Secretary should be head of the diplomatic corps, and provisions for consular agents abroad seem to have been postponed.[70]

On the eve of receiving the definitive Treaty of Peace Congress was distracted by questions of the relative powers to be assumed by the central government and those claimed by the states.[71] Hamilton's efforts were toward enlarging and confirming the former. In reply to his inquiry for a broad plan for a permanent military establishment, Washington proposed a small national army of some 2,600 to guard the frontier posts and West Point, and a militia.[72] All that Hamilton's committee got through Congress at this time was garrisons of three-years men, for a maximum of nine months, after the British evacuated the posts.[73]

Two days, May 21 and 22, 1783, were given to debating new instructions to be sent to Francis Dana, American representative at St. Petersburg. As acknowledgment of our independence was imminent, Hamilton wanted Dana's mission terminated, with no entry of this country into the Armed Neutrality or into a commercial treaty with Russia. We no longer required support in our contest with Britain, declined "to become a party to a Confederacy which may hereafter too far complicate the interests of the United States with the politicks of Europe," and could well postpone trade engagements with Catherine's government. Hamilton, though apparently present, did not vote on the final motion which authorized a temporary commercial treaty with Russia, omitting most of his precautions born of national pride.[74]

It was necessary to reduce the army, for its own sake and in order to save expense. Hamilton was chairman of the committee, with Peters and Gorham, that proposed that noncommissioned officers and privates enlisted for the war be conducted to their home states and there be discharged; it was also proposed that a proportionate number of officers should be allowed to retire. This provoked sharp reply from those who feared the war was not finished. In the end the whole problem was put over.[75]

Of more importance for the future than anyone recognized was Hamilton's motion that our peace negotiators endeavor to stipulate "that neither party shall keep any naval force on the lakes on the Northern and Western frontier." This took only two lines in the Journal;[76] it was not noticed, apparently, in the report of the committee to which it was referred, being forgotten in the welter over debts due British subjects and future treatment of Tories.[77] Few of Hamilton's proposals were more pregnant than this one for peace and easy commerce with Canada.

Much was in abeyance just at the juncture when the war was being wound up. Congress lacked a foreign secretary, could not summon attendance on its own sessions,[78] and was without means of paying off troops furloughed or discharged. Hamilton sought to mend the last, as far as possible, by providing that until lands promised to soldiers could be located and surveyed, they be given certificates of their claims.[79] He pushed this forward by seconding a motion of Bland accepting Virginia's cession of Western lands, dividing the whole into districts, and giving every soldier thirty acres for every dollar due him. The object of the movers went beyond this, to composing differences between the states over land cessions complicated by private company claims. All had to remain contingent on approval of Virginia and of the army, but pending this the admission of new states within the territory was projected.[80] In the debate, Hamilton joined with others for extending the control of the United States, and allowing the claims of the land companies. Progress was suspended till the Maryland delegates, who also took this position, were present.[81]

19

Champion of Congress
Against Mutineers

CONGRESS felt itself impotent enough without being compelled to decamp from Philadelphia because of the menace of mutinous troops. This enforced exit in the last days of June 1783 was the result of inability to pay the soldiers awaiting discharge; even the token month's wages, at length made available, were paid tardily. Refusal of Pennsylvania authorities and of the local militia officers to furnish protection was another evidence of the low estate to which Congress had fallen even in its own capital. Hamilton, as chairman of the committee of Congress to negotiate with the Executive Council of Pennsylvania, penning the appeals and remonstrances, had all the features of the disconcerting demonstration impressed on his mind. The episode underscored the need of Congress, particularly as it was discussed after the Constitution was adopted, for a preserve over which it would have complete governmental control. In addition, this vivid experience of local obstruction to federal demand could not have failed to influence Hamilton's constitutional convictions. It reappeared in his plans for a sufficient standing army, and for a degree of federal power over the militia of the states. The humiliating incident doubtless bore its part in determining him, a decade later, to assert central authority in collecting the excise in western Pennsylvania.

The qualms of Congress began almost a fortnight in advance of its being actually surrounded by mutineers. Apprehension was provoked by a letter of Washington of June 7 enclosing an address of officers complaining that they were to be turned off unpaid.[1] This was because soldiers and a proportionable number of officers, in consequence of a motion of Hamilton,[2] were being furloughed home in anticipation of final peace, though the states had not forwarded the taxes as begged in an earlier resolve Hamilton had introduced.[3]

The next warning of approaching danger was a remonstrance, about the middle of June, of sergeants of recent recruits in the barracks at Philadelphia against accepting their discharges until they were paid. Congress determined to take no notice of this irregular representation.[4]

Mutterings turned to mutiny on the morning of June 17. Congress knew it two days later when President John Dickinson, of the Executive Council of Pennsylvania, "immediately transmitted" letters received by him from Colonel Richard Butler, commanding the Third Pennsylvania Regiment, and from William Henry, of Lancaster.[5] These informed that eighty armed soldiers had broken away from their officers and set off for Philadelphia "to co-operate with those now in the city . . . to procure their pay (or perhaps to possess themselves of money at any rate)." They had thrown out hints that they might "rob the bank, the treasury, & c. & c."—though the latter must have been a sleeveless errand![6] Colonel Butler had explained to them in vain that they must remain at Lancaster to be paid, and that furloughs were at their option. Butler thought the defection had originated in Philadelphia, "and that the flame is supported by inimical . . . people." Putting prudence above pride, he had sent officers after the mutinous men to try to persuade them to return to Lancaster and their duty; he advised that if they persisted in applying at Philadelphia they be sent back empty-handed, or their success would encourage others in disobedience.[7] In orders dispatched to the marchers Colonel Butler warned, with prescience, that "your appearance at Philadelphia . . . will be justly construed into *menace,* rather than a proper mode of seeking justice. . . ."[8]

As soon as news of the mutinous march was given, Congress named a committee of Hamilton, Ellsworth, and Richard Peters to ward off the danger.[9] In the trying days that followed, Hamilton, as chairman, not only spoke for the committee and for Con-

gress, and wrote and delivered the reports, but it is plain from
internal evidence, especially from a long, retrospective remonstrance to President Dickinson, that he engaged himself whole-
heartedly, and did more than any other, to contrive the safety and
support the dignity of the national government.[10]

The committee immediately, on Thursday, June 19, while the
mutineers were still on their march, urged the Executive Council
to dispatch militia to intercept them before they could join the
already insolent troops in the Philadelphia barracks.   Hamilton
and his colleagues returned to the congressional chamber with the
disappointing verbal report[11] that the Council was reluctant to
call out any part of the militia, believing the latter unwilling to
act unless the troops committed some outrage.[12]   Unable to use
coercion, the committee had tried persuasion to turn back the
marchers.   Major William Jackson, the Assistant Secretary at
War, had been sent to meet them; his instructions, drawn by
Hamilton, were to assure them of every fair treatment when they
had returned to their officers at Lancaster; they could have provisions if they chose to stop where they were.[13]

The rebellious eighty rejected reason, pressed forward, and
reached the city on Friday morning, June 20.[14]   They joined the
troops at the barracks, who had been increased by a few companies of veterans that arrived the day before from Charleston.
The total in the barracks was about five hundred.   But all was
orderly, and Congress adjourned as usual on Friday afternoon till
Monday morning.[15]   Hamilton and his committee, meanwhile,
had arranged with the Superintendent of Finance for the prompt-
est possible payment of the unwelcome contingent, but only after
they returned to Lancaster.   General Arthur St. Clair, commanding the Pennsylvania line, was sent for.

Saturday morning, June 21, produced a different scene.   Sometime after noon a member of the committee notified President
Boudinot that the soldiers at the barracks had thrown off all authority of their officers, promised to be troublesome by evening,
and were suspected of a design to rob the Bank.   Thus advised,
Boudinot called the members of Congress to assemble at one
o'clock.   They passed sentinels posted at the doors of the State
House, where both Congress and the Pennsylvania Council met,
and must have seen that the building was surrounded by three

hundred or more soldiers, fifteen or twenty of them close to the south windows of the Council chamber.[16]   Congress lacked one member of having a quorum when President Dickinson, of the Council, came into the chamber and announced that the troops had made a demand on the Council which the Council had unanimously rejected.   The "non-commissioned officers and soldiers now in this city" peremptorily required of the Council "authority to appoint commissioned officers to command us and redress our grievances. . . . You will immediately," they demanded, "issue such authority and deliver it to us, or otherwise we shall instantly let in those injured soldiers upon you, and abide by the consequence.   You have only twenty minutes to deliberate on this important matter."[17]   Only seven sergeants commanded the rebellious troops, who surrounded the State House with bayonets fixed.

Previous to Dickinson's appearance, General St. Clair reached Congress and reported that the veteran troops from Charleston had been forced by the mutineers to join them and that all had disobeyed their officers in leaving the barracks.   St. Clair was ordered to attempt to march the soldiers to their quarters, but Congress would take no other action while menaced.   The members authorized the Secretary at War to secure from General Washington a detachment of troops to suppress the disturbances.[18]

Many of the mutineers were drunk, and threatened Congress by name.   After sitting surrounded for nearly three hours, the members rose and walked through the cordon without incident. St. Clair succeeded in persuading the rebels into the barracks, promising that they might designate officers to represent them in dealing with the Executive Council.   However, the mutineers held the powder house, some other arsenals, and possessed themselves of several field pieces.   Alarmed, and suspecting that the militia would not be called out or would not respond, Congress met again in the evening.   It was resolved that the President and Executive Council of Pennsylvania be informed that the authority of the United States had been insulted, that the peace of the city was endangered, and that effectual counteracting measures must be taken at once.   The committee of which Hamilton was chairman was to consult with the Pennsylvania Council to this end; if satisfactory assurances were not given, they might advise the summoning of Congress the following Thursday, June 26, at Trenton or Princeton.[19]

The appeal to General Washington to march in a detachment of reliable troops was confirmed, but Boudinot wrote the commander in chief late that night that the steps of Congress were to be kept secret until the disposition of the Pennsylvania Council was known. Hamilton and Ellsworth visited President Dickinson, read him the resolutions, and received his promise to call the Council to meet them next (Sunday) morning, at the President's house.

At this interview Hamilton again read the resolutions of Congress, proposed that sufficient militia be embodied to end the danger, and informed that Congress had suspended its meetings in Philadelphia until they could be held with safety. "The council, after some conversation, informed the committee, that they would wish, previous to a determination, to ascertain the state and disposition of the militia, and to consult the officers for that purpose."[20]

Dickinson, in his report to the Pennsylvania Assembly, six weeks later, expanded on the misgivings of the Council about calling the militia. He listed inhibitions which could not be thought creditable in the Pennsylvania authorities, but went on to say that Hamilton and Ellsworth found "great weight in these observations" and were willing, unless the militia would act quickly and reliably, to wait for the detachment General Washington was sending.[21] Hamilton rejoined that the committee of Congress never made "concessions in favor of the conduct of the Council," and were so far from concurring that they "strongly urged the expedience and necessity of calling out the militia . . . against an unofficered and disorderly body of mutinous soldiers." He appealed to his notes, made at the time.

Probably it never occurred to Dickinson that Hamilton would be moved to his searching reply, which is characteristic of his answers on occasions when he considered he and those for whom he spoke—Congress in this case—had been misrepresented. The recital of particulars could not obscure his abiding concern for the repute of the central government. This took full account of the need of maintaining good federal-state relationships. ". . . I

viewed the departure of Congress as a delicate measure," he reminded, "including consequences important to the national character abroad, and critical with respect to the State of Pennsylvania, and . . . the city of Philadelphia; . . . the triumph of a
handful of mutinous soldiers, permitted in a place which is . . .
the capital of America, to . . . imprison Congress, without the
least effort on the part of the citizens to uphold their . . . authority, so as to oblige them to remove . . . would . . . be viewed at
a distance as a general disaffection of the citizens to the Federal
Government, might discredit its negotiations [for peace], and affect the national interests. . . ."[22]

Disappointment was in store for Hamilton and his committee
when they waited on the Council the next morning, Monday.
Hamilton presented the resolves of Congress in writing, and,
taught by behavior of the Council the day before, asked for a
written answer.[23] This the Council refused, "alleging that it had
been unusual on similar occasions. . . ." Their verbal reply, as
Hamilton reported it, voiced high respect for the "representative
sovereignty" of the United States, wished to support it, regretted
the insult that had happened, but were convinced that nothing was
to be expected from the militia unless Congress suffered a greater
outrage. The Council thought the mutineers showed signs of
submission. Hamilton rejected this easy optimism, pictured the
mounting danger, and said that Congress must use its own coercion to place the rebels in the power of government. The Executive of the state had failed to support public authority, and unless
matters took a better turn by the following afternoon, the committee was bound to advise removal of Congress to Trenton or
Princeton.[24]

Dickinson's account of this meeting, as given to his own Assembly afterward,[25] bears out Hamilton's conclusion that the state
government would not protect Congress. Dickinson hugged the
sovereignty of Pennsylvania with what Hamilton called "an unbe-
coming stateliness" and "overwhelming nicety."[26] The incident
has meaning for its portrayal of Hamilton's theory of dealings between the nation and one of the states. The national authority,
in national matters (in this instance the safety and dignity of Congress), was paramount. "Reserve" on the part of a state was
"uncandid," and obstructed the functioning of the federal system.

The tilt between Congress and Pennsylvania Council was exacerbated because at close quarters. In such exchanges Hamilton often caused outcry by the force of his thrusts, but he was almost never plagued by ambiguity of his phrasing. He now gave unintentional offense by reporting that the state Council regretted the insult "with this additional motive of sensibility, that they had themselves had a principal share in it." Pennsylvania delegates were quick to note that the expression "principal share in it" was misleading. Ellsworth, for the committee (Hamilton being absent), promptly soothed with a resolution assuring that "Congress do not conceive the committee had the most distant intention to insinuate that the Executive Council had any share in promoting . . . but that the . . . Council had shared . . . in receiving the insult."[27]

Hamilton's willingness to delay recommendation that Congress remove from Philadelphia was not met by submissiveness of the mutineers. Instead, the secretary of the board of sergeants instructed the six commissioned officers chosen to negotiate for them with St. Clair and the Council: ". . . every effort in your power must be exerted to bring about the . . . most ample justice; . . . use compulsive measures should they be found necessary—which . . . we will support you in to the . . . utmost of our power. Should you . . . not . . . do all in yours, Death is inevitably your fate."[28]

Consequently Hamilton's committee on Tuesday, June 24, urged that Congress meet two days later at Princeton.[29] President Boudinot immediately issued a proclamation citing the peril in which Congress yet stood and providing for the removal.[30]

The sequel is quickly told. Finally aroused by the departure of Congress, and finding the soldiers still "in a very tumultuous disposition," the Pennsylvania Council busied itself mightily to muster five hundred militiamen "as a measure indispensable and immediately necessary to secure government from insult, the State from disturbance, and the city from injury." The mutineers, learning that a detachment from the northern army was nearing, and deserted by two officers who had been their instigators, downed their arms and capitulated. The Lancaster contingent marched back to their post. The remaining four officers of the rebels' committee were arrested. In time to avoid bloodshed but too late to prevent discredit, the Pennsylvania authorities exacted "dutyfull submission to the offended Majesty of the United States."[31]

The Philadelphia newspapers, during the disturbance and afterward, reflected the local desire to minimize the danger, exculpate city and state authorities, and blame Congress as alarmist. The information they gave was late, little, and misleading. Particularly the effort was to show that the demonstration of the soldiers was directed to the Pennsylvania Council and in no way threatened Congress, toward which, if anything, the discontented troops were friendly. Benjamin Rush mocked a member of Congress: "If you remain one week longer at Princeton feeding one another with ideas of . . . wounded dignity . . . you may loose Pennsylvania forever from your plans of continental revenue." And John Armstrong, Jr., ever ready with rhetorical sarcasm: "The grand Sanhedrin of the Nation, with all their solemnity & emptiness . . . have removed to Princeton, & left a State, where their wisdom has been long questioned, their virtue suspected, & their dignity a jest."[32]

In the aftermath, Hamilton took means to correct the charge that he had been quick to recommend the removal of Congress from Philadelphia in order to further the claims of New York as the place of later residence, temporary or permanent. He asked Madison's full testimony on the point: "Did I, as a member of the committee, appear to press the departure, or did I not rather . . . postpone that event as long as possible, even against the general current of opinion?"[33] None who had his report to Congress on July 1 could have doubted his reluctance to promote removal, as that would strain relations with Pennsylvania and invite damaging suspicions abroad.[34] In contrast to Hamilton's scruple, even President Boudinot had been ready to improve the event for the advantage of his own state. Would his brother Elisha prepare his "Troop of Horse . . . to meet us at Princeton [?]" Jersey's show of succor "may fix Congress as to their permanent residence."[35] The New Jersey authorities, state and local, chorused their welcome, and were thanked by Congress with overtones of reproval of their hesitant neighbors across the river.[36] The Pennsylvanians were soon repentant, and begged the return of Congress to Philadelphia.[37] However, long before this, indeed almost as soon as Congress convened at Princeton, Hamilton wrote and seconded a motion of Mercer of Virginia that Congress should return to Philadelphia until a permanent residence was selected, since Howe's troops would make the city again safe. This conciliatory intention was set aside by a substitute motion of South Carolina and Massachusetts delegates condemning Pennsylvania recalcitrance and demanding assurances.[38] Of course, as events developed, Congress moved to Annapolis in November 1783, to Trenton a year later, thence to New York City, and did not go back to Philadelphia until seven years after the mutiny that drove it out.

The lessons impressed on Hamilton by his service in Congress resulted in a reasoned proposal for the calling of a constitutional convention that would eliminate the grave defects of the Articles of Confederation as they had become evident by bitter experience. The manuscript is endorsed, in his hand, "Resolutions intended to be submitted to Congress at Princeton in 1783 but abandoned for want of support," and is dated June 30, 1783.[39] This was the first day Congress, after adjournment to Princeton, had a quorum, and hence an accumulation of matters growing out of the mutiny then came before the body for report and action.[40] This press of business, amidst confusion in Philadelphia and at Princeton, plus thin attendance on Congress,[41] disinclined members to consider such a thoroughgoing proposition for reorganization of the government, and Hamilton left Congress not long after his resolves were penned. The spirit of party, *"interest making and caballing,"*[42] roused by treatment of the mutiny perhaps had more to do with persuading Hamilton he must shelve his scheme at that time. The clash between the reluctant, or obstructionist, Pennsylvania executive and the claims of Congress as the national body had brought into sharp focus the autonomy of one state vis-à-vis the Union.[43] The example agitated the ever present question of relative rights and duties within the Confederation. The resentment of Congress at being driven out more readily expressed itself in sending federal troops to Philadelphia than in reconstructing the Constitution to give wider permanent central powers.

This was not the first time Hamilton bruited the need for reform of the governmental structure, and this analysis, fuller than those that went before, led on to others more elaborate and persevering.

The plea, abortive at the moment, was resurrected in the report of the Annapolis Convention three years later, in Hamilton's arguments in the Philadelphia Convention of 1787, and in the Federalist papers. His advocacies did not spring bright and complete from the brow of Jove. They developed in his thoughts as frustrating events taught him. The idea was in gestation for a long period, fed by a succession of experiences which were turned to account. Other instances were the proposals for a Bank of the United States and for funding the debt. Not only was all grist that came to his mill, in maturing particular recommendations, but his several projects supplemented each other.

Hamilton designated a round dozen of defects in the Confederation. The others hung on the first, which was "confining the power of the Federal Government within too narrow limits; withholding from it that efficacious authority . . . in all matters of general concern, which are indispensable to the harmony and welfare of the whole. . . ." Legislative and executive powers were confounded and judicial power was wanting; recruiting funds was defeated by the requisition system, and borrowing must be bottomed on taxation. Effectual means for defense and trade regulation were lacking, and treaties when made could not be supported. The government forfeited "system and energy" as long as nine states must assent to principal acts. He centered his peroration on the shameful inability to pay the army and other creditors, and concluded with a plea for a convention "with full powers to revise the Confederation," the states then to adopt or reject the amended instrument. The recommendation here, as in the call of the Annapolis Convention, was for alterations in the Articles of Confederation rather than for fashioning a new Constitution. However, the changes deemed imperative, spelled out in 1783, were so many and so fundamental as to imply a fresh start.[44]

This analysis of weaknesses of the Confederation is to be read in conjunction with two letters of Hamilton to Washington. The first, in March 1783, congratulating the commander in chief on the preliminaries of peace, urged that his labors were next needed in constitutional reform, "to make solid establishments within, to perpetuate our Union. . . ." Hamilton promised that he would later open himself on this subject.[45] Six months afterward he re-

verted to it. Before leaving Congress he had hoped that body
"might have been induced to take a decisive ground; to inform
their constituents . . . of the impossibility of conducting the public affairs . . . with powers so disproportioned to their responsibility. . . ." Having done this, he wanted Congress to adjourn
the moment the definitive treaty was ratified. Washington's retirement at the same juncture, with his admonitions on the necessity of a change in the government, would have given double incentive for curing old ills. Before he left, Hamilton had despaired
of Congress adjourning with a flourish, but he trusted that Washington's circular letter to the states—his political valedictory as
was supposed—would help mend matters. Washington had declared this was the moment for the people of the United States "to
establish or ruin their national Character forever, this is the favorable moment to give such a tone to our Federal Government, as
will enable it to answer the ends of its institution, or this may
be the ill-fated moment for relaxing the powers of the Union,
annihilating the cement of the Confederation, and exposing us to
become the sport of European politics. . . ." The circular has
echoes that may have come from Hamilton, though Washington
accurately referred to the proposal of larger power for Congress as
one that had been "frequently agitated."[46]

Hamilton pleaded in similar vein, at just this time, in his *Vindication of Congress,* against heaping censure upon a body that had
"the phantom, without the substance of power," for "the constitutional imbecility" of the Union must be apparent. Attention of the
people must be directed "to the true source of the public disorders
—the want of an EFFICIENT GENERAL GOVERNMENT . . . and a
CONFEDERATION capable of drawing forth the resources of the
country."[47]

Hamilton remained in attendance on Congress two and a half
months longer than suited his own convenience. In mid-May he
hoped that Governor Clinton would send on another delegate;
"Having no future views in public life, I owe it to myself without
delay to enter upon the care of my private concerns in earnest."
But he continued because he felt it obligatory to have New York
represented while the national credit, and the state's peculiar interest, hung in the balance.[48] Then he was detained by his leading part in dealing with the threat to Congress by the mutinous

troops.   Thereafter he tarried, sometimes at Princeton, sometimes at Philadelphia, waiting for Duane to join him, and for the definitive treaty of peace to arrive, until he finally left Congress at the end of July, 1783.[49]

Temple Hill at New Windsor, now lonely and vacant except for a marker and the replica of a log house used in the encampment, is a place of memories of the last months of the Continental army. Here Washington, by his feeling remonstrance, quashed the proposal that officers and troops use their swords and bayonets to pry pay from Congress.   Here too was formed, shortly afterward, the Society of the Cincinnati, regarded in certain quarters as a no less sinister, though more subtle, attempt to bring government under military domination.   The proposal of General Henry Knox for "a society to be formed by the American officers" before they separated led to acceptance of the "Institution" (constitution) in principle May 10, 1783, Baron Steuben presiding.[50]

For the sake of rough chronology, Hamilton's early connection with the society may be mentioned here.   The hereditary order, of officers American and foreign, who had served three years or to the end of the war, had as objects liberty and union of the states, fraternity, and charity toward members and their families falling on misfortune.   A limited proportion of honorary members might be elected.

Washington became President-General and so continued to his death, when Hamilton succeeded him.[51]   Hamilton was not among the original signers at New Windsor, having ended his military service eighteen months before, but he immediately became active in the New York Society, of which Steuben was the head.   Of course, many there were his special friends—Sebastian Bauman, Nicholas Fish, William North, Nathaniel Pendleton, William Popham.   However, he like many others was for a time in arrears for dues ($60, one month's pay at his rank).[52]   Hamilton was an enthusiastic member, and resisted certain concessions to popular antagonism.   Though to a less extent than the amiably pompous Steuben and Knox, he stood in the public eye as an emblem of the dangerous design of the Cincinnati to set up in the young democracy "an artificial and . . . decorated nobility," if not a criminal conspiracy.[53]   His aristocratic tastes and vigorous propagation of his political principles encouraged this notion that the Society fitted his hand like a glove.

Naturally, attacks on the Cincinnati commenced with its birth. Those of Aedanus Burke, the plethoric South Carolina judge,[54] the popular satirist Hugh H. Brackenridge,[55] and the egalitarian Mirabeau[56] came not so close home to Washington, the responsible President-General, as did the more private condemnations of John Adams,[57] the misgivings of Jay,[58] and the eager imputations of Jefferson. Preparing for the first general meeting of the Society at Philadelphia in the spring of 1784, Washington asked Jefferson for his own slant, and that of others in Congress, on the Cincinnati.[59] Jefferson, in reply, acknowledged the fraternal impulse that formed the society, and had "no suspicion" that the organizers "intended, those mischiefs, which exist perhaps in the foreboding of politicians only." This much said, he gave substance to every ingenious derogation. This order, attracting "all the men of talents, of office & wealth," seizing opportunities with military promptitude, and supported by foreign members and courts, was opposed to American constitutions built on "the natural equality of man." Civilian delegates in Congress viewed the baleful Cincinnati "with an anguish of mind . . . not . . . produced by any circumstance before." It could not be rendered unobjectionable without changes that "would amount almost to annihilation." He trusted that Washington would avoid the compromitting connection.[60]

Disturbed by dissent from many quarters, but particularly by Jefferson's criticisms, Washington successfully urged on the first general meeting, May 5, 1784, that the hereditary feature, accumulation of funds in the hands of the society, and the addition of honorary members, required "alteration in their very essence." The funds were to be loaned to the respective states, the interest to go to the charitable purposes of the Order. The "Altered and Amended Institution," thus voted, went to the state branches for action.[61]

The New York society this year deferred decision pending the report of a committee of which Hamilton was chairman. Washington wrote him in hopes the state branches would ratify the recommmendations to enable "the Cincinnati . . . to live in peace with the rest of their fellow citizens. . . ." Except for the obligation to foreign officers, and the charitable uses of the foundation,

Washington would have wished to rebuke unwarrantable prejudices "by abolishing the Society at once, with a declaration of the
causes, and the purity of its intention."[62]

This plea had only partial effect with the New York committee.
Hamilton reported on July 6, 1786, approving the motives of
amendment but rejecting the chief proposed changes. Without
hereditary membership there would be no certain continuance of
the society. However, this right should not be embodied in a legal
charter, for that might make the supposed danger from the institution more than imaginary. Succession should hinge not on primo-
geniture but on merit only. Further, the distinction between
regular and honorary members held up an ill founded distinction
in claim to patriot service. Funds should not be loaned to the
state, which might not wish to borrow, and the society could better
control its own treasury.

This resolution was adopted, but a year later Hamilton reported
that at the general meeting discussion had been postponed because
states disagreed on the need for any changes, and caution must be
preserved to keep Washington at the head of the society.[63]

After adoption of the Constitution of the United States, nothing
more was heard of reforming the order.

20

Devil's Advocate

It was natural in one of Hamilton's eager, sensitive make that vehement exertions to rescue the credit of Congress should be followed by intervals of disgust and near despair. Actually from his seat in the legislature he wrote to General Greene, on June 10, 1783, that he expected to leave Philadelphia shortly for Albany "and to remain there till New York is evacuated; on which event I shall sit down there seriously on the business of making my fortune. . . . There is so little disposition either in or out of Congress to give solidity to our national system that there is no motive to a man to lose his time in the public service, who has no other view than to promote its welfare. Experience must convince us that our present establishments are Utopian before we shall be ready to part with them for better."[1]

Hamilton was held in Congress beyond his expectation by the menacing mutiny of troops at Philadelphia, and the tenuous removal of the legislators to Princeton.[2] Betsey and the baby had left Philadelphia for Albany in the spring,[3] which increased Hamilton's impatience to follow. But, pressed to remain to ratify the definitive treaty of peace, daily expected, he had no prospect of setting out before July 26.[4] Further detained in Congress, he discharged a last responsibility by counseling Governor Clinton, in the interest of continental harmony, to modify New York pretensions to the New Hampshire Grants, and to permit the Western posts, when evacuated, to be garrisoned by national, not state, troops.[5]

However, August 5 found him in New York City. Business of

Mrs. Schuyler was the cause of his visit.   He had evidently started
out in haste, for he sent word back to a colleague to pay a small
tavern bill he had forgotten in Princeton.[6]   The definitive treaty
had not arrived, but numbers of city merchants were preparing
to depart.   They were alarmed by threats sent in by Americans in
anticipation of enemy withdrawal.   British allegiance would have
been no detriment had these merchants remained, but the British
guineas—maybe eight or ten thousand taken away by each—
would be a loss.   Said Hamilton, "Our state will feel for twenty
years at least, the effects of the popular phrenzy."[7]   Measures
were taking in earnest toward an evacuation.   This was Hamilton's first view of the city from which he had been driven, in
Washington's army, seven years before.   The shoe was now on
the other foot.   Political and social dismay of Tories of varying
degrees took the place of military consternation of patriots.
Henry Livingston, after a visit to the city, told Duane, "all is confusion, Horror and fear.   in short, they are a poor abject, cring-
ing sett . . . as ever lived. . . ."   And John Lansing, Jr., reported "violent commotions . . . to be apprehended."   Many
New Yorkers were resolved "that no Tories notoriously so shall be
permitted to reside amongst us."   If the legislature "do not comply
with their wishes they must try *their* Hands."[8]   Our young
lawyer, former soldier, and former legislator, in the next months
and years was to do more than others to defend the rights of individuals and a class suspected or hated.   His motives went beyond
the reward from fees, for he believed that reprisal was dishonorable and unwise.   Popular heat and legislative and executive vin-
dictiveness for a time were inevitable.   But Hamilton, in dis-
suading from violation of Constitution and treaty, was active in
shortening this phase of recovery from the tensions of war.

He reached Albany, and reunion with his family, on August
11, 1783.[9]   The Schuyler home, joyfully offered in such intervals,
was only incidentally a physical haven.   Here Hamilton always
found mental and emotional comfort.   If he and the Schuyler
household ever differed in domestic relations or in public desires,
the evidence does not exist in the long record that we have of their
affectionate mutual reliance.   With Washington, Hamilton had,
under varying circumstances, an identity of purposes, and similarity of solutions for particular problems; with Schuyler the coinci-

dence was even more cordial. Hamilton and his father-in-law were more alike in temperament, and their teamwork was promoted, of course, by the family bond. The balance of practical obligation was of the younger man to the older, partly because Schuyler had fewer public responsibilities, and found enough reward in Hamilton's accomplishments. No account of the latter can be just which does not point to the prompting and resourceful support which Schuyler constantly afforded to his brilliant friend. A stay in the Schuyler home at Albany was always a recruitment of Hamilton's powers and plans.

The interval this time before the Hamiltons set up their own establishment in New York was brief. Even so, Hamilton was occupied. As his mind continued to run on public issues, so did his pen. His "Vindication of Congress" probably belongs to October 1783.[10]

Making plans for entering on his profession of the law, he forswore future active military participation. To Washington he expressed the wish to preserve his rank in the peacetime army, but "without emoluments and unattached to any corps, as an honorary reward for the time I have devoted to the public service. As I may hereafter travel [evidently abroad, an expectation never realized] I may find it an agreeable circumstance to appear in the character I have supported in the revolution." The favor he now asked might be granted because Congress had declined to give his war contribution any notice "on an occasion, which appeared to my friends to entitle me to it. . . ."[11] Perhaps the allusion was to disappointed hope of promotion for his exploit at Yorktown.

Some have concluded, from scrutiny of Hamilton's personality, that military glory was his dominant ambition, the natural expression of his drive for power. It is true that he was zealous in the war, and always cherished his army friendships, as witness his eulogy on General Greene, and his prominence in the Society of the Cincinnati. But even when he became Inspector-General and was in command next under Washington in the mobilization against France, military means were subordinate to civic object. He was primarily a political, not a military man. In the midst of the Revolution, May 1777, he wrote from headquarters at Morristown to an unidentified woman correspondent: "I do not wonder at your antipathy to [war]. Every finer feeling of a delicate mind revolts from the idea of shedding human blood and multiplying the common evils of life by the artificial methods incident to that state. Were it not for the evident necessity; and in defence of all that is valuable in society, I could never be reconciled to a military character; and shall rejoice when the restoration of peace on the basis of freedom and independence shall put it [in] my power to renounce it."[12]

Hamilton's services as a lawyer were solicited even before the British evacuation of New York City, where he intended to practice. As early as May 30, 1783, he entered in his accounts that he had received £6 from Isaac Sears as a retainer and for advice in a cause expected to be commenced by one Soderstrom.[13]   Three months later Richard Soderstrom, of Boston, wrote Hamilton direct, seeking to engage him, along with Duane and Egbert Benson, as attorney in a suit as soon as civil government should be established in New York City and Long Island.[14]   Soon he was receiving work in the Albany area, drawing a memorial of the manor of "Renselaerwick" to the legislature.[15]   This was followed by a case as vexing from the personalities of the litigants, and Hamilton's cordial friendship toward both of them, as because of any legal complexities.   Robust old Robert Livingston, lord of the manor, objected to the erection of grist mills on the property by his kinsman, Chancellor Robert R. Livingston.   Brockholst Livingston urged that Hamilton be retained: "His opinion will be well worth having, & in case it be determined to pursue your claims by action, his assistance will be very material."[16]

At the beginning of his law practice in New York, before entering Washington's Cabinet, Hamilton had his home and office at 57 Wall Street, to which the family moved probably in November, 1783.[17]   He was one of thirty-five lawyers listed in David Franks' *New York Directory* for 1786.   Others who were his associates—now of counsel with him, now against—were located nearby.   Robert Troup was at 67 Wall Street, Brockholst Livingston at No. 12, John Lawrence at No. 15.   Aaron Burr was to be found at 10 Little Queen (Cedar) Street, Edward Livingston at No. 51, Richard Varick at 46 Dock Street, Morgan Lewis at 59 Maiden Lane.[18]

Fuller treatment of Hamilton the lawyer belongs to his return to practice after tenure of the Treasury, 1795.   The earlier span was little over half as long and was more broken by public assignments, sitting in conventions and in Congress. The records that we have, mostly fragmentary, of early cases, show that his practice was general. It varied from giving opinions to trying suits, mainly in civil but also in criminal matters. The latter included the defense of one Murphy, charged with horrendous assault on Margaret Russell, "with force and Arms to wit with Sword and Stones and Knives . . . with intent her the said Margaret . . . to Ravish and Deflour. . . ."[19] In the opening years he appeared in the mayor's court (where first sat his friend James Duane) oftener than on circuit,[20] drew memorials to the New York legislature and to Congress,[21] and handled affairs for clients in Europe.[22] From the beginning, Hamilton had a busy practice in the New York Supreme Court of Judicature, which met alternately in Albany and in New York City. After two years, at an Albany sitting, he had fifty cases of clients, often important names, in New York, Richmond, Queens, Suffolk, Westchester, and Washington counties. However, Lansing, Burr, and one or two others, longer at the bar, had more cases, sometimes two or three times as many.[23] In Hamilton's frequent enforced absences, as at the Annapolis, Philadelphia, and Poughkeepsie conventions, and in Congress, friends (Troup, Lawrence, Sill, De Haert) made motions for him.[24] His suits were mostly for debt, he appearing oftenest for the plaintiff.

His fees at the beginning were small, usually £1 as a retainer, and £5 a day and expenses for trying a case on circuit. Additional payments were sometimes contingent on his success for his client.[25] Later in his practice he was better rewarded, but refused cases which went against his professional principles, and fees which he thought excessive.[26] At the start a proportion of his legal work came to him from members of his family connection, as John J. Van Rensselaer, the manor of Rensselaerwick,[27] and especially from his wealthy brother-in-law, John Barker Church.[28] Friends often figured in his practice—Robert Morris, John Jay, Laurence Kortright,[29] Timothy Pickering,[30] Isaac Sears,[31] John Holt,[32] Benjamin Walker, [Lewis?] Pintard,[33] and more. The Bank of New York, of which he was a founder, continuously gave him business.[34]

In his surviving legal briefs and notes for argument are citations of the common authorities,[35] and numerous others, especially in the fields of public and international law, which were less familiar but were boldly brought forward as supports to his scrupulous interpretation of the treaty of peace.[36]   In 1785 he purchased and partly annotated Compton's *Practice Commonplaced; or Rules and Cases of Practice in the Court Arranged, Etc.*, published in London two years earlier.[37]

From the very first he was besought to receive into his office young men as pupil-clerks.   We know of a half-dozen whom he thus instructed before he suspended practice to take over the Treasury.   Pierre V. Van Cortlandt and Dirk Ten Broeck commenced in February, 1784, paying the usual fee of $150, and in May came Jacob A. Le Roy, but the payment was refunded to his father because he did not continue.[38]   John Adams, who at the time did not know Hamilton personally, entered his son July 20, 1789, but the $20 installment of tuition was remitted when Hamilton was called into Washington's Cabinet.[39]   Between these dates Samuel Broome, Jr., put in seven months.[40]   Joseph Strong served the full three years' clerkship "in the business of an attorney."[41]

We have an estimate of Hamilton as a practitioner from Chancellor James Kent, who spoke with peculiar knowledge not only of the New York bar but of American law.   Fortunately Kent's observation commenced almost with Hamilton's first appearance in the courts, and he left accounts of his impressions then, 1785–1788, as well as for the later period, 1795–1804, when Hamilton had returned from the Treasury to his profession. Kent was enough younger than Hamilton (eight years) to look up to him, but near enough of an age to cherish an intimate friendship.   Of the talented men who knew Hamilton best, none has left a more discerning picture of his qualities and achievements.   A declared admirer, Kent was always prepared to give reasons for his praise.

He described for young lawyers of another generation the legal personalities and character of litigation in the opening years after the Revolution.[42]   The leaders who had come to the bar in New York shortly before the war in many cases were preferred for public offices and did not return to active practice.[43]   The field was left to "a number of ambitious and high spirited young men" who went from musket and saber to quill. Kent hit off the qualities of the different ones—Burr was acute, terse; Brockholst Livingston, copious, fluent; Troup, sensible and thorough; Harison, scholarly and lucid; Jones and Benson, masters of older precept and practice. "But among all his brethren, Colonel Hamilton was indisputably pre-eminent," promptly earning recognition for his grasp and frankness. He benefited by the "most active business" in "the claims of real property" which opened with the peace, and at the same time helped inform American jurisprudence with reliable English precedents.[44] Robert Troup, Hamilton's closest lawyer friend, who had instructed him in the practice in the summer of 1782, observed that he was not stocked with case law. "Never failing to be busied . . . in politics, he had only time to read elementary books. Hence he was well grounded in first principles," which he applied "with wonderful facility, to every question he argued. But if you stated a Case to him, and allowed him time to examine the Reporters, he would . . . give an opinion that would bear the test of the severest discussion."[45]

The case in Hamilton's early law practice most significant for its influence on public policy was that of Rutgers versus Waddington. In this, as in others less known, he defended an erstwhile enemy against the claim of a patriot plaintiff. The principle transcended the practical matter in hand. What he really chose to uphold was the good faith of the United States in honoring the sanctity of the treaty of peace.

Before we can appreciate the elements involved in the suit we must glance at the rancor of New Yorkers against all who had stood with the British during the war.

On a Sunday in the spring of 1784 Hamilton wrote from New York to his bantering friend, Gouverneur Morris: ". . . I will, in the lump, tell you that we are doing those things which we ought not to do, and leaving undone those things which we ought to do. Instead of wholesome regulations for the improvement of our polity and commerce, we are laboring to contrive methods to mortify and punish Tories and to explain away treaties."[46] And a fortnight later, again to Morris, he reverted to the scene of "Discrimination bills, partial taxes, schemes to engross public property in the hands of those who have present power, to banish the real wealth of the State, and to substitute paper bubbles. . . ."[47]

This was an accurate sketch of the antics of New York lawmakers as the war drew to a close and in the years immediately
following the peace. He pretended to view the perversity with
patience, if not with composure. "Let us . . . erect a temple
to time," he remarked, "only regretting that we shall not command a longer portion of it to see what will be the event of the
American drama."[48] Actually, Hamilton was by no means relaxed in the face of untoward developments. He not only deplored the obstacles that his state put in the way of internal harmony, American union, and strict observance of the treaty, but
he exerted himself, in his private professional capacity and as public servant, to remove them. In the next years his successful efforts to build the new nation sprang from his position as a citizen
of New York. This could not be his arena earlier while he was
in the army, and later, when he entered Washington's Cabinet,
his connection with his own state became collateral. The short,
crowded span from 1782, when he was named Continental Receiver of Taxes for New York, until 1788 when he secured ratification of the Constitution at Poughkeepsie, witnessed his formative actions. His policies as first Secretary of the Treasury,
reaching into much besides his specific fiscal assignment, clinched
his earlier achievement. What we may properly call his first
New York period was, in the wide political sense, the most creative
of his career.

We may not appreciate his accomplishment unless we recall
the turmoil of the time and place. It was characteristic of Hamilton to begin where he was, and then to turn every local solution
to realization of his fondest national hopes. His faculty for making the immediate conduct to the ultimate was never better illustrated.

What was the complexion of New York in this troubled interval
of the mid-eighties? In respects it was peculiar,[49] though at the
same time similar to what was happening in Virginia, Pennsylvania, Massachusetts, and elsewhere. The chief elements may
be put down, too briefly, as Clinton, classes, and collapse. Governor George Clinton, completely elected (both governor and
lieutenant-governor!) in 1777 over Philip Schuyler and John
Morin Scott, and regularly reelected five times thereafter, was to
be Hamilton's foil. Sixteen years Hamilton's senior, and six

years Schuyler's junior, he earned his dominance in the state.   He
was the populist, only verging upon the demagogue.   His connections were fortunate.   Scotch-Irish with a wife of Dutch extraction (Cornelia Tappen, of Poughkeepsie), and himself a hus-
bandman, he appealed to two groups of upriver farmers.   Brigadier General of the New York militia, serving simultaneously in
fort, field, and executive chair, he was defender of the state he
ruled.   Not brilliant in either office, he was steadfast in both.
His manifest pride in the state was not unmixed with personal
preening, but this was taken by his followers as a compliment to
them, not as a demerit in himself.   He was scrupulous, even ingenuous, in putting down mob excesses, for he repressed the "doc-
tors' riots" in New York City and led state troops against the
border Shaysites.   He did not so much court common approval
that he refused to be a charter member of the Cincinnati.   He
had a broader base and firmer principles than most leaders of a
faction, to which his long reign in New York, and his later election to two terms as Vice President of the nation, bore witness.
His defects belonged to his virtues.   Often narrow, always stubborn, he was a patriot within his lights.   You always knew where
to have him.

His class was more accurately an interest, that of small farmers north of Westchester.   Generally the landed proprietors made
common cause with the merchants and mechanics of the metropolis and the larger towns, notably Albany.   Not always, however,
for the Livingston tribe later shifted allegiance.

The trade depression that followed the war was a pervasive
cause of political discontent as well as of economic grief.   It was
generated in destruction of public credit, disordered currency,
withdrawal of British and French forces, demobilization of the
American army, unwarranted land speculation, and severe losses
in foreign commerce, especially with the British West Indies in
consequence of the order in council of July 2, 1783.[50]   At that
beginning stage of our national development, individual states attempted their own means of counteracting business distress instead
of confiding needed powers to the central government.   This substituted harmful internal rivalries for salutary national measures
designed for fiscal solvency and benefit of trade, both interstate
and foreign.   Congress was impotent enough by constitutional

limitations, and was further frustrated by mischievous divisive actions of the jealous states. These dissentions had to run their
course before the members of the Union were persuaded of their
errors. By then the Confederation was wrecked beyond repair.
This was a blessing in disguise. It is true that the spell of bad
business had been weathered by the time the new Constitution
was submitted for ratification, though this was not so plain to
actors in the scene as it has become to the historian. In spite of
exit from the slump, however, the old scheme of government could
not have served. Its structural weaknesses would have remained
to plague the future. Judged by its results, a national shake-up
was demanded.

Business was peculiarly slack in New York City and in Albany;
the former was deprived of most of its West Indian commerce,
the latter forfeited the fur trade to Montreal while enemy garrisons continued to hold the frontier forts.

Of course loyalists, many of whom had formed military units
that laid waste the country, were hated and feared. They were
also expropriated. The process began with the Confiscation Act
of 1779 which attainted those on a long list and made their estates
forfeit.[51] This was followed by successive acts for the sale of condemned property, the only moderations being those to protect
lessees, mortgagees, and the like.[52] Debts due to persons within
the enemy's lines were stayed, or could be paid in loan certificates
of the state, practically worthless to the receivers.[53] Those who
in any way countenanced the enemy after the Declaration of Independence might not vote or hold office, and any convicted of
cleaving to the enemy, if found within the state, were guilty of
treason—that is, were banished.[54]

The war fury against loyalists did not pass with the peace. Instead, sales of confiscated estates continued,[55] debts due to the proscribed were authorized to be withheld,[56] and those that escaped
worse treatment were visited with double taxes.[57] Loyalists were
not permitted to practice the professions.[58] Petitions to be allowed to return from banishment, or for restoration of property,
were referred to committee and shelved.[59] Sometimes reasoned
remonstrance of the Council of Revision was accepted,[60] at other
times overridden.[61]

Hamilton, as legislator and lawyer, protested persuasively but

in vain against infractions of the treaty of peace, at that time provisional but, he held, no less binding. The state became responsible for violations by mobs and volunteer associations if it did not
restrain them. But worse, transgressions were "going on in form
of law," such as indictments under the Confiscation Act. This
broke the sixth article of the treaty, mandatory, under which we
engaged to do no future injury to those who had adhered to the
enemy. It was optional with the states to comply with the recommendation of Congress under the fifth article that they restore
loyalist property; Hamilton did not say what their behavior on this
head should be, but we may be sure he hoped they would conform. Without repudiating the treaty, the British, he reminded,
could evade parts of it. He foretold that they might retain the
frontier posts, hamper our fisheries, and invoke navigation laws
against our foreign commerce. Mere resentment on our part
ought not "to put those great national objects to the hazard. . . ."
He regretted the expulsion of "a great number of useful citizens"
(loyalists) to Canada.[62]

Soon the New York legislature refused to discharge its moral
responsibility. Governor Clinton submitted the proclamation of
Congress of ratification of the definitive treaty, but he offered no
comment on the national recommendation that the state restore
property and rights of loyalists.[63] In a vigorously worded answer
the legislature cited the war depredations of the loyalists, and declared that justice did not require, and the public tranquillity did
not permit, giving them back their citizenship. As for their property, New York was only following the example of the king, who
offered no compensation for damages.[64]

Hamilton's "Letters from Phocion," 1784, gave his public remonstrance against acts of the legislature that year confirming and
extending legal disabilities of Tories and those suspected of disloyal sentiments. The two essays were broad appeals "To the
Considerate Citizens of New York, on the Politics of the Times,
in Consequence of the Peace." Acceptance of his liberal arguments would bolster the chances of his clients of these classes in
his current court cases, and would enlarge the number of his
political supporters, but there is no evidence that either personal
result supplied his motive.[65] On the contrary, in few occasional
pieces did he put more ardently several policies and principles

fundamental to his conduct and creed. These included the pre-eminence of the treaty of peace and its faithful observance as proof of national honor, liberty by force of due process of law, and a propitious future flowing from liberal political and economic tenets. At this juncture, especially in New York, so long the seat of the enemy, temporary vindictive resentment threatened to trample individual rights which must be preserved for the permanent protection of all the people. He was jealous for social justice at the outset. " 'Tis with governments as with individuals; first impressions . . . give a lasting bias to the temper and character. Our governments, hitherto, have no habits. How important to the happiness, not of America alone, but of mankind, that they should acquire good ones!" If beginning with "a scrupulous regard to the Constitution, the government will acquire a spirit and tone productive of permanent blessings to the community. If, on the contrary, the public councils are guided by . . . passion, and prejudice; if from resentment to individuals, or a dread of partial inconveniences, the Constitution is slighted, or explained away, upon every frivolous pretext, the future spirit of government will be feeble, distracted, and arbitrary."[66]

The world's eye was upon America. Despotisms everywhere were shaken by our bid for freedom. We must justify our Revolution by its fruits. Merchants and artisans, instead of seeking to expel former enemies, in order to reduce competition, should want to keep and encourage them. More traders and mechanics, in the growing economy, would add to prosperity for all.[67]

In the prejudicial spirit of other measures, and in an effort to forestall the peace treaty,[68] the New York legislature passed the Trespass Act, March 17, 1783. This short law declared that any refugee from the enemy might "bring an Action of Trespass against any Person or Persons who may have occupied, injured, or destroyed his . . . Estate . . . within the Power of the Enemy. . . ." This promise was sweetened by the provision that "no Defendant nor Defendants shall be admitted to plead, in Justification, any military Order or Command whatever, of the Enemy, for such Occupancy, Injury, Destruction, Purchase or Receipt, nor to give the same in Evidence on the general Issue." The whole was buttressed by confining the decision to local magistrates sure to be sympathetic to aggrieved patriots, for "any such Action

. . . brought in any Inferior Court within this State . . . shall
be finally determined in this Court. . . ."[69]

After the evacuation, Mrs. Elizabeth Rutgers, a citizen of New
York, brought suit in the mayor's court against Joshua Waddington and Evelyn Pierrepont, British merchants, for £8000 damages in their occupancy, for five years, of a brew- and malt-house
in Maiden Lane in the East Ward.[70] The case was argued on
June 29, 1784, before James Duane, mayor; Richard Varick,
recorder; and five aldermen. Counsel for Mrs. Rutgers was
Jonathan Lawrence, assisted by Attorney General Egbert Benson,
(William) Wilcox, and Robert Troup. Alexander Hamilton was
chief counsel for the defendant, aided by Brockholst Livingston
and (Morgan) Lewis.[71]

The cards seemed stacked against Hamilton's client, the enemy
intruder who had enjoyed the property of a native daughter, and
widow at that. The prospects of recovery by hundreds of other
resentful New Yorkers hung on Mrs. Rutgers's success. On her
side was the able attorney general defending a perfectly explicit
state law which had the enthusiastic approval of almost every
citizen. This was to be the test case, in which a legal verdict for
the defendant would expose his champion to social and political
odium. Hamilton was appearing in this unpopular rôle in many
such suits. In appraising his course in accepting, at the outset
of his practice, loyalist and British clients, we must recall the
rancor of the times. Patriots, long expelled from their homes and
other property in the city, who had used up, in many instances,
their last resources, were poised to pounce on their hated despoil-
ers where these remained or had the hardihood to return to the
scene.

Mayor Duane, who was to preside in the Rutgers-Waddington
suit, received condolence because "the hands of violence and
rapacity, have these long years been raging through our State &
particularly your City . . . , where thousands have been ruined
. . . by these Barbariance. . . ." When he reflected "on the
. . . distress . . . so prevalent," Duane, instead of giving the
usual "publick Entertainment on the Investiture of the Mayor-
ality," asked aldermen and common council to distribute "for me
twenty Guineas towards the Relief of my suffering Fellow citizens
in your respective wards." The merchant William Constable just

at this time found "NYk . . . far different from what I could
have wished—no business . . . , the necessaries of life dear . . .
and political animosities disturbing every Society. . . ."[72]

Governor, legislature, and most state officers vociferously supported the intention to take revenge on those who had enjoyed
the British occupation. The "folly" of punitive statutes against
loyalists, Hamilton confided, "has afforded so plentiful a harvest
to us lawyers that we have scarcely a moment to spare from the
substantial business of reaping."[73]   In becoming devil's advocate,
Hamilton was moved by professional obligation, for he believed—
and proved—that the obnoxious Britishers had law on their side.
Moreover, he was prompted, with the proclamation of peace, to
let bygones be bygones, and wished to see the national government
preside over the new era of political integrity and economic progress.

Probably the magistrates—certainly Duane and Varick—however engrossed in the practical business of policing a disordered
city, were better prepared than others for the bold turn Hamilton
took in the defense of Waddington against Widow Rutgers.
Though New York was then the embodiment of state authority,
he lifted this local case to the plane of national and indeed international responsibility of America.   The concept of the nation as
a political unit was barely dawning,[74] and of course its law was
ill defined.   Beyond that, international commitment was in the
realm of rumor, a figment hopelessly remote from the demand for
damages on a brewhouse in Maiden Lane.

Lawrence, followed by Wilcox, opened for the plaintiff. They
stood on the statute, which was explicit.   Both of the parties
came within it.   Elizabeth was an inhabitant of New York City,
left it at the British capture, and never came again into the power
of the enemy, where her property lay.   Therefore she was made
worse and sustained damage, and so on.   Livingston, Lewis, and
Hamilton, successively, were heard for the defendant.   Hamilton's
argument embraced the others and made the overwhelming impression.

As was habitual with him, he began with the fundamental principle, though this was novel and unwelcome to his hearers.   The
case concerned the national faith and character.   Where were the
rules of international law found?   In the opinions of writers and

the practice of governments. The war was a "solemn" one, authorized by act of Parliament and admitted by our Declaration of Independence. It was not internal to the British empire, but was between nations, as we must be the first to maintain. The legal fact of war precluded objection founded on its injustice; war carried rights to the invader, including enjoyment of fruits of the area actually held by force of arms. New York City was captured, and British subjects, occupying property by authority of military commanders, were not liable to American owners for the period of enemy seizure. Among his materials for use in this and similar defenses against the Trespass Act is a manuscript copy of the order, December 1, 1780, of "James Robertson, Esqre Captain General and Governor in chief in and over the Province of Newyork," appropriating to the king's service the use of rents of "deserted Houses belonging to the People in Rebellion, or who reside among the Rebels. . . ." On the reverse is Robertson's authorization, January 1, 1781, to John Smyth as "Treasurer of the City of Newyork," who would collect the rents.[75] By the treaty of peace, Hamilton declared, all claims of either of the contracting parties, and of their subjects and citizens, by reason of damage relating to the war, were reciprocally and effectually relinquished, renounced, and released to each other. The treaty was the law of the land, binding on New York by the action of Congress in the name of the Confederation.

His brief notes for argument are revealing. At the outset he would pose the "IMPORTANCE of the case . . . from its influence on the national character—May be discussed in Europe; and may make good or ill impressions according to the event." Next was the *"Necessity* of preserving inviolate the rules which regulate the Great Society of Nations." He recognized that this, abruptly announced, would be startling in a mayor's court, therefore crossed it out and substituted a gradual approach in several steps.[76] Hamilton devoted a whole section of his speech to illustrating and enforcing the national sovereignty. "As well a County may alter the laws of the State as the State those of the Confederation." The subordination to national authority in all matters touching obligations to foreign governments was manifest. "Legislation of one State cannot repeal [the] law of [the] United States. All must be construed to stand together." To make the defendant liable "would be to violate the laws of nations[,] . . . a solemn treaty of peace & revive [a] state of hostility." It would be to infringe the Confederation "& endanger [the] peace of the union[.] Can we suppose all of this to have been intended by the Legislature[?] . . . And if it was intended the act is void!"[77]

Lawrence and Hamilton's special friends Troup and Attorney General Benson answered. They did not so much urge the merits of the case as they questioned the sanction of writers on international law and denied the power of the court to void a statute. Hamilton had cited the chief formulators and commentators with particularity. His opponents called these "philosophers" vague and at odds with each other; ". . . authorities from Grotius, Puffendorf, Wolfius, Burlamaqui, Vattel, or any other Civilians, are no more to the purpose than so many opinions drawn from sages of the Six Nations." And it was the function of courts "to declare laws, not to alter them. . . ."[78]

The magistrates reserved their decision for two months, until August 27, 1784, and then, in deference to "much public expectation," published it "to prevent misapprehension."[79] The mayor and his associates were self-conscious, as well they might be. "It were to be wished," they began, "that a cause of this magnitude" —which must "record the spirit of our Courts to Prosperity [posterity]" and embraced "the whole law of nations!"—"was not to receive its first impression from a Court of such a limited jurisdiction, as that in which we preside. . . ."[80] But equally they were courageous. While they faithfully recapitulated the pleas of both sides, they followed the reasoning of Hamilton. They caught his enthusiasm in apostrophes to international law and to the paramountcy of the Confederation in foreign relations. The high moral tone of it, braving local popular protest, was a credit to the court as well as to successful counsel. The judgment was for the defendant except in part, on a technical point[81] that gave no comfort to clamorous American citizens.

These last were not long in organizing to denounce the decision. A fortnight after, a number of New Yorkers meeting at the house of Mrs. Vandewater named a committee to issue an address on the baleful award.[82] The group was headed by Melancton Smith, who was nearly always opposed to Hamilton's views, and included

Jonathan Lawrence (with doubtful propriety, as he was of counsel for Mrs. Rutgers), Peter T. Curtenius (State Auditor), and Anthony Rutgers. After reviewing the case the committee declared "that the Mayor's Court have assumed and exercised a power to set aside an act of the state. That it has permitted the *vague and doubtful* custom of nations to be plead against and to render abortive, a *clear and positive* statute, and military authority of the enemy to be plead against the express prohibition of our legislature" in a fashion that threatened the liberties of the people. An appeal must be carried to the Supreme Court. Hamilton, it was more than hinted, was counterrevolutionary, building his greatness on the ruins of dear-bought freedom.[83]

This probably inspired a protest in the legislature at its next meeting. William Harper, Montgomery County, offered a resolution "That the adjudication . . . is in its tendency, subversive of all law and good order, and leads directly to anarchy and confusion. . . ." If courts could repeal laws, legislatures would become useless. Therefore it was recommended to the Council of Appointment at their next opportunity to name such a mayor and recorder "as will govern themselves by the known laws of the land."[84] Persevering opposition[85] was unable to prevent an order to Robert Benson, clerk of the mayor's court, to appear with the records. The House then condemned the judgment, 25–19.[86]

The successful defense of Waddington against the Trespass Act, inevitably gaining notoriety, branded Hamilton, in hostile quarters, as an Anglophile. The charge, immediately after the war, when patriot feeling was bitter, was personally damaging, but it faded, with the years, into a political reproach. This celebrated case was only first blood in Hamilton's long fight for respect for the terms of peace, which came to success eleven years later with approval of the Jay Treaty.

2 1

A "Money Bank"
for New York

ALEXANDER HAMILTON was one of the organizers of the Bank of
New York in 1784 and was thereafter its chief public champion.[1]
While thus a founder in the proper sense, he was not among the
earliest promoters.[2] Acting as agent for his brother-in-law, John
Barker Church, Hamilton advised on means whereby Church and
Jeremiah Wadsworth, both then in Europe, could establish their
private bank in New York. An interim plan was for Church
to buy, through Hamilton, 250 shares in new stock issuing by the
Bank of North America, in Philadelphia. This intention should
be kept secret or others might "prevent us [Wadsworth and
Church] from a preponderance in the Bank which is to us a very
capital Object. . . ." Afterward they might sell these shares
"if we want Funds for a Bank that we may establish in New
York. . . ."[3]

This latter project was threatened by announcement of the
Bank of the State of New York, inspired by Chancellor Livingston,[4] two-thirds of the capital of which was to be in pledges of
lands.[5] Livingston and his friends petitioned the legislature for
an exclusive charter.[6] Hamilton began an opposition to this
scheme on all fronts, for the benefit of the commercial interest
which would be served by the sort of bank Church and Wadsworth
intended. Perhaps it was Hamilton's objections that the chancellor denounced as "The endeavour . . . to sow distrusts between
the Landed & the commercial interests of this country," which

[346]

could "only originate in the extremes of ignorance or malice." Describing himself as "a mere speculative man," he recommended as bank directors those who had retired from active affairs, lest "the adventitious spirit that supports commerce" should command the institution's resources.[7] Hamilton had some difficulty in persuading the merchants themselves, and met so much resistance from country members in the legislature that he entered a formal petition there against the Chancellor's proposal.[8] He argued with the projectors, and doubtless prompted letters in the newspapers showing that a due proportion of specie was the only reliable bank reserve.[9]

The most concrete countermove was a subscription set on foot by some of the merchants "for a money bank." Hamilton hesitated before accepting their invitation to become a stockholder. He approved the object, but took a little time to conclude that Church and Wadsworth would do better to join in this enterprise, which had sound support, rather than embark on a rival one. During his delay a meeting had been held February 24, in response to a newspaper notice reading: "BANK. It appearing to be the disposition of the Gentlemen in this City, to establish a Bank on liberal principles, the stock to consist of specie only: they are . . . hereby invited to meet . . . at the Merchant's Coffee-House; where a plan will be submitted to their consideration."[10] A committee was appointed to receive subscriptions to a stock of $500,000 in gold or silver,[11] a thousand shares of $500 each. When half the shares were taken, the bank would be organized with president, twelve directors, and cashier. The holder of shares up to four should have one vote for each, for six shares five votes, for eight shares six, and for ten shares seven votes, which was the maximum no matter how many shares a stockholder owned. This was the situation when Hamilton entered the company. The limitation on a stockholder's votes would prevent Church and Wadsworth from enjoying "a proper weight in the direction."[12] Consequently, at "an after meeting of some of the most influential characters,"[13] Hamilton reported to Church, "I engaged them so far to depart from this ground as to allow a vote for every five shares above ten."

The required half of the capital was promptly subscribed, and at the organization meeting Alexander McDougall was elected

president and Alexander Hamilton one of the directors.[14] He
would hold the place until Church and Wadsworth arrived, and
if they chose to become partners in the bank he would make a
vacancy for one of them.[15] They did become considerable stockholders in the summer of 1784,[16] and Wadsworth became the second president of the bank, 1785–1786, following McDougall's
resignation, but Hamilton did not resign as a director until
1788.[17] He held only one share of stock.

Hamilton drew the constitution of the Bank of New York,
adopted at the organization meeting March 15, 1784. He accepted the general plan as he found it before he took an active
hand, but he extended the voting rights of larger stockholders,
prescribed particulars for protection of stockholders, and was probably responsible for immediate application for a charter.[18] The
directors were not to employ the resources of the bank to negotiate
foreign bills of exchange, or to make a loan to any foreign power.
Shares should be readily transferable. No stockholder could vote
for directors unless he had held his shares three months; proxies
were limited; directors must be stockholders, and could be proceeded against for malfeasance.

From the first Hamilton intended that the Bank of New York
should be incorporated. In fact, application for a charter, such
as was enjoined upon the president and directors, had already
been made before the constitution was adopted,[19] and, anticipating success, in the constitution he provided for limited liability of
stockholders.[20] The outline of charter provisions, doubtless prepared by Hamilton,[21] was to undergo changes before the legislature acted favorably seven years later. This first trial, on his own
responsibility, contemplated state and national governmental de-
posits, and consequently a procedure of official inspection. To
combat incorporation of a land bank, then before the legislature,
Hamilton in his application was propitiatory toward the agricultural interest,[22] but the "money bank" was to make and receive
all payments in gold or silver coin or bank notes only, and must
never engage in trade.

Meanwhile, while awaiting a charter, banking rules must be
adopted. William Seton, the cashier,[23] was dispatched to Philadelphia, then the only banking center, "to procure materials and
information in the forms of business." Hamilton furnished him

letters of introduction to Thomas FitzSimmons and Gouverneur
Morris, old friends and directors of the Bank of North America.[24]
Here was testimony to the utter inexperience of New Yorkers in
the actual operation of a bank. Since this was the first attempt,
it could not have been otherwise. Hamilton's reading and
thought had made him clear on the function of banks, but with
the day-to-day performance he and his associates could not be acquainted. Thus Hamilton, his mind running on the practicalities
of managing the Bank of New York, inquired of Morris for "the
best mode of receiving and paying out gold." He knew the evils
of the Philadelphia method, weighing in quantities, but had no
substitute, "unless there could be a coinage." This incident reminds how rapidly the independent life of America developed
after the war, and responsible public officials and businessmen with it. Within a few days Hamilton received a request
from Jefferson for aid in preparing a report on the subject
of coinage for Congress, a matter with which, as Secretary of
the Treasury and afterward, Hamilton was so prominently
identified.[25]

The remarkable fact is that, venturing as bankers in a partially
ruined city in the wake of war, with foreign and domestic trade restricted, they so quickly fell into sensible system and were successful. However, Seton was not at once to be satisfied in his
mission of inquiry in Philadelphia, for, temporarily, he was not
received at the Bank of North America. It was in straits because
its previous prosperity had raised up a dangerous rival. Two
months earlier John Chaloner had posted Hamilton on what was
brewing. "The Bank [of North America] have agreed to enlarge
their shares[,] the new subscriber to pay 500 Dollars[,] 50 of which
he gives to the Old Stock as a premium for coming into the partnership. This . . . has occasioned some of the wealthiest Merchants to combine & establish a new Bank[.] Subscriptions . . .
will be soon open at four hundred dollars a share. I have not a
doubt . . . that it will be as permanent[,] secure and profitable as the present one & will . . . have the preference whilst
the Old Stock is incumbered with the Clog of fifty Dollars
advance."[26]

Hamilton was of two minds about this competition of banks in
Philadelphia. He wrote FitzSimmons that for them to join forces

was "evidently the interest of both."[27]   But the same day he advised Gouverneur Morris to accept a duplication that was inevitable.   The erection of a new bank in Philadelphia did not appear to him an evil to the community.   The large profits of the old bank—they had averaged 14 per cent—would be reduced, but would remain enough, "and the competition will cause business to be done on easier and better terms in each, to the advancement of trade in general."   Businessmen would seize opportunity where they found it.   Let the two banks "live well together and manage their affairs with good humor and concert."[28]

The report from Seton, revealing the damage of disharmony, perhaps swung Hamilton back to his first notion that the two banks should consolidate.   Denied information from the Bank of North America on an excuse, Seton was sure the real reason was the withdrawals of gold and silver that had led to stoppage of discounting and abandonment of the new bank to save the old. Moreover, £60,000 sterling of Robert Morris's bills, drawn for the Dutch loan, were under protest; and the bank he had founded must support him, or it and the public credit would go down together.   Carrying further the spirit of cooperation, Gouverneur Morris was for making the Bank of New York a branch of the Bank of North America.[29]   Hamilton now confessed to Morris that he had been mistaken in the benefits to the community he had supposed would result from competition.   "I am very happy to hear of the union of your two banks. . . ."[30]

This episode of competition versus combination in Philadelphia banking has been rehearsed to show how Hamilton's uncertainty was followed by the conclusion that absorption of the new enterprise into the old was the fortunate result for all concerned.   In the beginning he felt that private investors' loss from competition would be the business community's gain.   Then he saw that individual injury might be so severe as to endanger the public, and he condemned the rivalry he had welcomed.   It would be mistaken to argue from this instance that Hamilton was offering a firm judgment applicable to American economic policy.   The case was peculiar to the inexperience and limited resources of the time and place.   One may not say from this that Hamilton discounted the benefits of competition and favored combination.   In fact, branch banking as provided in the first Bank of the United States, as we shall see, was not his idea. Still, the illustration, so far as it goes, has its bearing on much later developments—the excesses of "wildcatting" contributing to panic and depression in 1837, and the increasing extension of governmental authority over banking.

President McDougall advertised on May 1, 1784, that subscribers should pay in the first half of their shares on June 1 to William Seton, cashier, at 67 St. George's Square,[31] and here, in the "Walton house," the bank opened.[32]

The Bank of New York labored seven years for its charter. The legislature, dominated by the popular prejudice of Governor Clinton, was fearful that corporations, particularly those of financial and trade character, would abuse their privileged power by oppressing the community. Liberty, so soon after the war, was a shibboleth that stood in the way of economic organization. The business depression that immediately ensued intensified every suspicion of collective action by men of property, by mechanics, or by recent immigrants. The growth of the Bank of North America, rid of the threat of the abortive Pennsylvania Bank, was related in the average mind to hard times that followed, and led to an effort in the Pennsylvania legislature to withdraw its state charter. In March, 1785, in response to petitions which accused the bank of responsibility for business misfortune, the legislature appointed a committee to inquire "whether the bank established at Philadelphia was compatible with the public safety and that equality which ought ever to prevail between the individuals of a republic." The economic expositions of Pelatiah Webster and Thomas Paine and the constitutional examination by James Wilson show of how much instruction the suspicious public stood in need. Objections to this bank and to banks in general were answered with patient persuasion. Wilson's exculpation of the bank included the reminder that "The disagreeable state of our commerce has been the effect of extravagant . . . importation." The pamphlet war thus provoked had repercussions in New York.[33]

This was the atmosphere of hostility in which the Bank of New York applied for incorporation in the autumn of 1784. The petition is obviously, from logic and style, the work of Hamilton.[34]

It was suitable now to offer supporting reasons. The usefulness of banks in commercial countries had long been demonstrated; in Europe they were "regarded as one of the surest foundations of public and private Credit." This "forms a presumption in their favour, not easily to be outweighed by arguments that rest on speculation and Theory." The Bank of North America was serviceable in the Revolution, Massachusetts had lately chartered a bank in Boston, and the progress of New York in recruiting its industry and trade, after the checks of war, must not be hampered by failure to charter a similar institution.

This explanation of the service of banks is an early illustration of Hamilton's habitual method. He first equipped himself by study and reflection and then proceeded without pause to inform and influence public opinion. Little of his work remained *in camera.* Indeed, so eager was he to present his views for the knowledge of the community, that the problem is never to discover what they were but rather whence he derived them. Reading, inquiry, and correspondence of friends, and observation, plus creative capacity were his sources. When they are traced, as is often possible, the speed and dexterity with which he made and applied deductions provoke admiration. The reasons for his self-sufficiency as a public advocate are not far to seek. American policies and institutions were just forming, and to embody views in action they must be grounded in one's own conviction. Later, in the Treasury, Hamilton had assigned helpers, Tench Coxe and Oliver Wolcott, Jr., the chief, who were fully competent to conduct certain researches and prepare particular solutions. But even then the extent of Hamilton's own immersion in the raw data, let alone his facility in combining what others had produced in parts, is surprising.[35]

Hamilton on this occasion, when he saw that the outcome was doubtful, enumerated as benefits of a bank that it assists government with emergency loans, favors industry and commerce by increasing the circulating capital in the safest fashion, offers short credit demanding punctuality, and eventually lowers the rate of interest. For reasons which he called over, a bank "by promoting Industry and Commerce . . . necessarily promotes Agriculture and renders landed Property more valuable." In New York the scarcity of specie caused a peculiar need for a bank. "Paper struck by the mere Authority of Government . . . is hardly likely to regain . . . Confidence. . . . The cooperation of a Bank seems the only expedient left to . . . supply the deficiency of Specie by a Paper Circulation," and the Bank of New York had already justified itself.

This application for a charter was still pending in the legislature when, in February, 1785, almost three hundred citizens signed a memorial offering to appear before a committee in its behalf. The list, composed of five sections, evidently as different canvassing friends of the bank obtained signatures, includes the leading names of the city then, men of all callings and shades of opinion. Specimens in sequence are Philip Livingston, Isaac Sears, John Lamb, Wm. Duer, . . . S. B. Webb, Benjamin Walker, Robt. C. Livingston, . . . Wm. Constable, Robert Harpur, Melancton Smith. Names that figured from Hamilton's youth were John Cruger, Lawrence Kortright, Wm. Newton, and George Codwise.[36]

Just at this time, following the proceedings of the legislature with special concern for the Bank bill, Hamilton, for humanitarian and civil reasons, was surely alert to the progress of measures for emancipation of slaves in the state. Aaron Burr bore a forthright part in the movement, while another, Comfort Sands, more prominent in the affairs of the Bank, proved obstructionist. In the Assembly a bill for gradual grant of freedom was framed on application "of the people called Quakers," and was limited to those of Negro, mulatto, Indian, and mustee blood born in New York.[37] Burr, in committee of the whole, was for broadening this to declare that any "person of whatever description, age, or colour, now holden, or claimed as a slave . . . by any . . . inhabitant of this State, . . . hereby are . . . absolutely free." This was rejected by more than two to one.[38] Sands was for continuing the emancipated for long periods in the hands of former owners, with the rights of indentured servants.[39] Others successfully championed prohibitions on any Negro voting or holding office, and placed a fine of £100 on each party to a Negro-white marriage.[40] On objection of the Senate the Assembly partially receded from these restrictions. The Council of Revision disapproved the bill on grounds of civil rights, but with no other effect than that the measure was killed.[41]

The legislature had refused to incorporate an association of tradesmen and mechanics. The Council of Revision was upheld in its objections, which stand in contrast to the frequent demand, in industrialized America, that trade unions should be compelled to incorporate. Fears not altogether fanciful are evident in the charge that on the principle of this bill New York "may become a community of corporations, influenced by partial views, (under the direction of artful men) composing an aristocracy destructive to the constitution and independency of the State."[42] A society for encouraging emigration from Germany was similarly discountenanced.[43] The plea of Hamilton and his friends for a charter for a money bank would not draw a more cordial response. At least the even-handed lawmakers are to be praised for declining to favor wealthy applicants, numbers of them sitting in the legislative chambers, over poor workers and immigrants who were more distantly represented. John Williams reported (April 9) as the opinion of the committee of the whole that the bill "for incorporating the President, Directors and Company of the Bank of the State of New-York" should be rejected, and this was voted by the Senate.[44]

For nearly five years the Bank of New York did not renew its effort to obtain a charter. The neighboring Bank of North America was in the toils. In a period of financial stringency a private bank, like that of New York, was blamed for abetting if not actually causing widespread misfortune. Ignorance combined with suspicion to attribute to directors motives of selfish gain at the expense of worthy applicants for loans. Perhaps in such times all concerned in the Bank of New York were content to forgo a charter and thus not provoke a legislature which might start a hostile inquisition. Hamilton remained a director until 1788, but the increasing demands on him of his law practice[45] and his part in the Constitutional Convention, its antecedents and aftermath, probably left him little extra time for service to the bank.

Another application was rejected, by the Senate, in February 1790, but by only the casting vote of the chairman in the committee of the whole.[46] Returning prosperity, the excellent performance of the bank, and elevation of Hamilton to the Treasury must all have figured to lessen opposition.[47] The following winter

Seton, inquiring when a new petition and bill for incorporation should be filed, wrote with confidence that "The Directors . . . repose a firm reliance on the fullest . . . support of the City Members to an Institution whose . . . operations they must be sensible tend to the public good."[48] The bill was debated from time to time for five weeks, was amended in both houses, and passed March 21, 1791.[49]

Curtain Raiser for
Constitutional Convention

HAMILTON'S telling part in the Annapolis Commercial Convention, September 1786, is memorable because this meeting, otherwise abortive, proved the prelude to that of the following year which framed the Constitution. The gathering at Annapolis, and one preceding it, March 1785, at Alexandria and Mount Vernon, were due to the initiative and deep solicitude of James Madison. His wish was to reduce the means of trade rivalries between the states. These were conspicuous evidences of the jealousies and distrusts that flourished under the Confederation.

It is proper to trace Madison's promotion of the Annapolis meeting, because this led to Hamilton's potent collaboration with the Virginian. In the summer of 1784 in the Virginia legislature "A trial was made for a [federal] Convention," but met mischances and after two days of debate the resolution was negatived; ". . . Mr. [Patrick] Henry shewed a more violent opposition than we expected."[1] On Christmas day of that year Madison had not made close observations of "the project of a Continental Convention," but assured Richard Henry Lee that union was necessary to escape foreign danger and internal dissension. Three days later he was penning resolutions touching navigation and jurisdiction of the Potomac for Virginia commissioners named six months before.[2] Soon he took satisfaction in agreement of Chase and Jenifer, of Maryland, and Mason and Henderson, of Virginia, to report to the two legislatures in favor of a concurrent

[356]

control over Potomac and Chesapeake.[3]   The meeting of Maryland and Virginia commissioners at Alexandria was continued, at Washington's hospitable bidding, at his home nearby.   The plan "concerted at Mount Vernon, for keeping up harmony in the commercial regulations of the two States" was enlarged when Maryland invited in Delaware and Pennsylvania, "who will naturally pay the same compliment to their neighbours."[4]

The burdens and distortions of commerce, foreign and interstate, were both cause and consequence of the postwar economic depression beginning about 1785 and continuing for half a decade until the national government was introduced.   The mutual spite of New York and New Jersey was symbolic.   New York required that "every wood-boat and shallop from N. Jersey, of more than 12 tons, shall be regularly entered and cleared out at the custom house, in the same manner as if they had arrived from any other foreign port."   As this reduced the small profits of Jersey boatmen, they prevailed on their legislature to lay a swingeing tax (£30 per month) on the lighthouse and plot around it, on Sandy Hook, belonging to the corporation of New York City.[5]

Six months before delegates at Annapolis were to face the problem of producing order, Madison pointed Jefferson to "the present anarchy of our commerces"; he thought "most of our political evils may be traced up to our commercial ones. . . ."[6]   And in the retrospect of half a century he described how states without good harbors "were subject to be taxed by their neighbors, thro' whose ports, their commerce was carried on.   New Jersey placed between Phil^a & N. York, was likened to a cask tapped at both ends; and N. Carolina, between Virg^a & S. Carolina to a patient bleeding at both Arms.   The Articles of Confederation provided no remedy for the complaint. . . ."[7]   Connecticut laid heavier duties on imports from Massachusetts than from Great Britain.[8]

The unexpected speed with which men, once brought together, resolved on a radical remedy for the malfunctioning of American society testifies to the alarm spread by business letdown and political confusion.   Hamilton, Madison, and Washington saw the need and the means of rescue earlier than most others did, but the suddenness with which their colleagues were converted argues the evident weakness of the country under the Confederation.

This produced quick consent, at Annapolis and Philadelphia, to proposals for reform.

Some would explain this presto action by the intention of leaders to protect their own property claims, so dangerously threatened. The Constitution, runs the argument, was a political ruse. It was not magisterial, but mercantile; partook less of the council chamber than of the countinghouse. This too pat explanation is denied by the character of the discussion at Annapolis, the debates at Philadelphia, and the searching analysis to which the proposition for competent union was subjected in the process of winning approval by the states, as we shall see in course.[9]

New York, more than other states, required exit from the depression, and at the same time correction of her restrictive commercial policy. Hard times bore on New York the harder because the British, still holding the frontier posts, blocked and diverted the fur trade; the metropolis, so recently evacuated by the enemy, suffered in the slump in proportion to the city's trade importance. New York offended against its nearest neighbors, Connecticut and New Jersey, by limiting imports from them, even indispensable food and fuel. The poor state of business in New York City was cited by 543 petitioners (Hamilton not among them) as added reason why the legislature should suppress the newly opened theater in John Street. War destruction prefaced present burdens; "the private debts in which numbers are involved—the National Debt—The heavy arrears of Taxes—the growing Scarcity of Cash—and the deranged State of Trade, with many other evils under which we groan, evince the high impolicy of suffering the Theatre, which is a School of Dissipation, if not of Vice, to be erected among us at this Time."[10]   Nathaniel Hazard begged Hamilton's influence to protect the "unfortunate Corps" of American merchants against the rapacious demands of their British creditors. "Our humble Request is but to *be heard before* ruined; . . . we are dragged to Prison, by hungry british Agents who . . . hover like Cormorants over the devoted Carcasses of their captive debtors. Some of them are little illiberal insolent Upstarts . . . who [would] freely Coin their [debtors'] Life Blood into Guineas. . . ."[11]

When the Annapolis commissioners assembled, New York was the only state still rejecting the impost—or acceding to this long-sought provision for independent federal revenue with conditions attached which Congress could not accept. Efforts to sanction national, not state, collectors, and payment of duties in national, not state, currency, had been decisively beaten in both Assembly and Senate.[12]   This was followed by refusal of Governor Clinton, the month before the Annapolis meeting, to call the New York legislature in special session to undo the mischief.[13]   This was to precipitate Hamilton into another losing fight to rebuke such contumacy.[14]

So Hamilton went to Annapolis ready to overleap state recalcitrance, as manifested under the Confederation, and to improve the opportunity for a reconstruction of government, which had all along been his remedy.   He was not alone in this wish; his distinction was in moving for it decisively when others hesitated.[15] Madison gave Jefferson reasons why five states had not named delegates, and continued: "Many . . . both within & without Cong[s], wish to make this Meeting subservient to a plenipotentiary Convention for amending the Confederation.   Tho' my wishes are in favor of such an event, yet I despair so much of its accomplishment at the present crisis that I do not extend my views beyond a commercial Reform."[16]   Madison's caution before the meeting had not gathered much courage when poor attendance promised futility for even its limited assignment.   Full delegations were on the ground from only three states—Virginia, Delaware, and New Jersey—though "two Commiss[rs] attend from N. Y. & one from P[a]." (September 11).   Unless numbers suddenly increased, "it is proposed to break up the Meeting, with a recommendation of another time & place, & an *intimation* of the expediency of extending the plan to other defects of the Confederation."[17]

Hamilton's appointment to represent New York in the Annapolis Convention barely escaped legislative mischances, being almost the last act of the session, May 5, 1786.   Delays had been caused by trivia, and by the machinery of designating delegates who never attended.   Pervasive reforms are not to be ascribed to an individual, but had Hamilton not been deputed to Annapolis the thin assemblage there might not have called for the Constitutional Convention, without which we would have lacked the prompt creation of the national government.

In his message of March 14, 1786, Governor Clinton transmitted resolutions of Congress and the act of Virginia appointing commissioners to meet with those of other states "for . . . framing such regulations of trade as may be judged necessary to promote the general interest. . . ."[18]   The next day the Assembly, in committee of the whole, worded liberal instructions to five New York commissioners, any three of whom were to join in reporting to the states "how far an uniform system in their commercial intercourse and regulations, may be necessary to their common interest and permanent harmony. . . ."[19]

Not till April 20, 1786, were Hamilton, Robert C. Livingston, and Leonard Gansevoort chosen, with blanks left for two more delegates.[20]   The Senate added the names of James Duane and Egbert Benson, and Robert R. Livingston, in which the Assembly agreed.[21]

The Virginia delegates chose Annapolis as the place of meeting, avoiding the neighborhood of Congress and large commercial towns, "in order to disarm . . . adversaries . . . of insinuations of influence from either of these quarters."   Ironically Maryland, the host state, which had benefited from previous negotiation with Virginia, refused to name representatives to the Annapolis meeting.   Daniel Carroll told Madison this was "from a mistaken notion, that the measure would derogate from the authority of Congress" over commerce and revenue, which, as Madison remarked, was the reverse of the fact.   Probably Maryland, like other states not participating, believed "that the time had not arrived for such a political reform, as might be expected from a further experience of its necessity."[22]

It is probable that Hamilton, with the other dozen delegates, stayed at George Mann's "City Tavern," of one hundred beds and stabling for fifty horses.   When Washington had resigned his commission at Annapolis, Mann served the "elegant and profuse" congratulatory dinner to two hundred guests, provided the liquor and music for the grand ball tendered by the Maryland General Assembly and rendered a bill that incuded items of 84 knives and forks lost and 133 dishes and plates broken.[23]   Meetings of the commissioners were in the old senate chamber of the State House, since restored after a criminal remodeling in 1878.[24]   Probably no citizens cared to be admitted to the balcony to witness the proceedings.   The *Maryland Gazette* took no notice of the meetings except to say, on the day of adjournment (September 14), "Several gentlemen, members of the proposed Commercial Convention, are arrived in this city."[25]

Had attendance at Annapolis been fuller, the commissioners would have been disposed to confine themselves to the commercial object.   Probably, however, they would have listened to Hamilton and Madison had these urged that uniform trade regulations necessitated constitutional changes, which, in the report, should be broached to Congress and the states.   Several who were appointed but did not attend would have been helpmeets in strengthening the Confederation, to whatever extent.   One was George Clymer, merchant, firm Federalist, and colleague with Thomas FitzSimmons and Tench Coxe on the Philadelphia committee which more than a year before had favored regulation by Congress of "the general commerce of the United States, and an harmony of measures."[26]   Duane, of New York, would have thrown his weight in the same scale.   The absence of Melancton Smith, who within two years was to be Hamilton's chief antagonist on the floor of the Poughkeepsie convention, was not to be lamented by the friends of vigorous renovation.

The idea of snatching the brand from the burning by urging inclusive constitutional reform must have arisen spontaneously among the delegates when they found they had not enough states represented to deal with commercial frictions.   "I do not . . . recollect the member who first proposed it to the body," Madison wrote in distant retrospect.   "I have an indistinct impression that it received its first formal suggestion from Mr. Abraham Clark of New Jersey.   Mr. Hamilton was certainly the member who drafted the address."[27]   ". . . that the commission of the N. Jersey Deputation had extended its object to a general provision for the exigencies of the Union," said Madison, encouraged the few gathered at Annapolis to appeal for a constitutional convention.[28]   Clark, thus empowered, and eager to secure correction of New Jersey's complaints, must have arrived at Annapolis early, for he left home the first day of September.   Owing to the wait for other delegates, which must have sharpened his impatience, he did not get home until three weeks later. He had a right to feel that his charge to the state (at $4 per day, $80) was well earned.[29]

In his latest allusion (about 1835) Madison implied that Hamilton's wording of the address of the convention underwent considerable discussion; the report "was drafted by Col: H, and finally agreed to unanimously. . . ."[30] Particulars of preparation of the report are credited to Hamilton's colleague Egbert Benson. The draft was by Hamilton, though he was not a member of the committee named to compose it. Governor Edmund Randolph objected to the original statement "as too strong; whereupon Madison said to Hamilton: 'You had better yield to this man, for otherwise all Virginia will be against you.' " The indifference of a number of states and delegates prompted compliance, and thus the plea "was toned down . . . to suit tender stomachs, and in this . . . milder shape was adopted. . . ."[31] Hamilton himself (spring of 1789) described how the Annapolis gathering determined on its call for wider constitutional reconstruction. Too few states were represented to proceed with the commercial mission. In addition, those present "were unanimously of the opinion that some more radical reform was necessary," so "they, with one voice, earnestly recommended" the Philadelphia meeting "with power to revise the confederation at large. . . ."[32]

We may reconstruct the little company at Annapolis with the help of contemporary portraits of principal delegates.[33] John Dickinson was narrow-shouldered, with large nose, full lips, and a frown. George Read, whose house at New Castle, Delaware, accurately reminds of him, looked aristocratic, had ruffles at his wrists, and a copper-plate handwriting. Madison seemed a refined boy, with high forehead and regular features. Randolph had a handsome, oval countenance, with dark hair and eyes. Tench Coxe, just Hamilton's age, was one of the younger members; he looked a businessman version of Lord Byron, his dress, until evil days overtook him, appropriate to his striking profile. Benson's mobile, amiable face, eyes wide apart, and white hair, conveyed frankness and friendliness.

The minutes of the meeting reveal more plainly than the address the tussle that resulted in recommending that the ensuing convention of all the states be empowered to offer political as well as commercial remedies. The minutes that we have[34] (apparently one or two days of sessions are missing) are in the hand of Benson, in the rough form in which they were taken as talk proceeded. Deletions and substitutions register the tides of argument. It appears that the purport of the address, which was the sole and sufficient accomplishment of the gathering, was dictated by the full dozen commissioners to the drafting committee, though it is probable also that drafts, as submitted, were discussed on the floor. Benson dated the minutes September 11th, 1786 (substituted for 12th), and recited the object of the convention, from the resolution of the Virginia legislature, which was to consider recommending to congress "an uniform System in . . . commercial Regulations." After the commissioners present were listed and it was noted that Dickinson was unanimously elected chairman, the report on credentials recorded that only three states, not five, were legally represented, even after the delay of more than a week. New York had two commissioners present and Pennsylvania one, but "three Commissioners are required as a Quorum to represent these States respectively at this Convention."

This became an additional reason for undertaking no stated business, but we are sure that it made the participation of Hamilton, Benson, and Coxe, if anything, more effective because it was informal. Benson and Coxe were named, with Clark, Read, and Randolph, to "be a Committee to consider of and report the measures proper to be adopted by this Convention." Since Benson put his own name first, he was presumably chairman of this steering committee, and Hamilton, as his colleague, would have special opportunity to influence their report. We do not know how long this committee deliberated, but Benson gave the result on a fresh sheet, with a new pen, and in a more legible hand: "That in their Opinion it will be inexpedient for this Convention, in which so few States are represented, to proceed in the business committed to them— That nevertheless the Object of the present meeting appears . . . of too much Importance to the Interest and Prosperity of the United States not to be pursued, and under this Impression the Committee think it will be proper to recommend in strong Terms a future meeting of Commissioners from all the States—

"That . . . the Matters, intended for the consideration of this Convention, would essentially affect the whole System of Federal Government, and the exigencies of the United States, in other respects, are of such a Nature, as to render it advisable that the Commissioners, who may be appointed for the proposed meeting should be authorized to deliberate on all such measures as may appear to them necessary to cement the Union of the States, and promote the permanent tranquillity, Security, and Happiness— The Committee with this view submit the following Resolution viz."

To this point the draft, if we may judge from the manuscript, was received without demur. But now the apprehension aroused in some of the committee by the allusion to cementing the union for permanent tranquillity and security subjected the next words to close scrutiny. A committee should be appointed to prepare an address to the several states explaining why the commissioners now assembled were prevented from proceeding on the business entrusted to them, and proposing a future meeting of commissioners "to report to the respective States, all such measures as shall appear to them proper to render the Federal Government more adequate to the Peace Safety and Prosperity of the Union, and further recommending to the States that their Delegates in Congress be instructed to procure the Approbation of that Honorable Body to the proposed meeting."

This last about rendering the federal government more adequate was short and sweet, but it was stricken out, from what we know otherwise, probably at the urging of Edmund Randolph. In the margin is written the less explicit injunction that stood: the address should submit to the states "the Propriety of extending the Powers to be given to the future Commissioners to every other matter respecting the Confederation and . . . the Commissioners at such future meeting [should] be instructed to report to the United States in Congress assembled agreeably to the 13.th Article of the Confederation."

This ends the minutes, or notes, of Benson, as we have them. There may have been two, or possibly three days—the 12th, 13th, and 14th—of further discussion, in which the topic surely was the content of the proposed address. No record of the convention shows who was on the committee to draw the address, or whether the suggestion of a committee was abandoned and, from a volunteered original draft by Hamilton, the wording was hammered out in the meeting of all the commissioners.

The address of the convention was not different in substance from the report of the steering committee.[35]   Dated September 14, 1786, it was sent officially to the legislatures of the five states with commissioners present, but "from motives of respect" copies went also to Congress and to the governors of the other states. The differing powers given by states to their commissioners, described in the address, anticipated the authorizations of delegates to the Constitutional Convention.   In the smaller as in the larger meeting, the more liberal instructions encouraged the majority to venture on a bold program.   In this case the stipulations of New York, Pennsylvania, and Virginia were nearly the same.   Their representatives were to consider the desirability of a uniform system in their commercial intercourse and report to all the states an act which, when unanimously ratified by them, would enable Congress to provide for the object.   Delaware's turn on it was similar, except that the act was to go first to Congress and, if there agreed to, should be confirmed by the states.

New Jersey opened the prospect of general constitutional reform, directing its commissioners "to consider how an uniform System of their Commercial Regulations and *other important matters* might be necessary to the common Interest and permanent harmony of the several States."   An act, ratified by the states, "would enable . . . Congress . . . effectually to provide *for the exigencies of the union.*"

Since the commissioners of four states did not attend, and four more states made no appointments, those present preferred not to frame a commercial system that had presupposed a full representation.   Then commenced the language that swaddled but did not smother the infant proposal of a new federal constitution. "Deeply impressed however with the Magnitude . . . of the object confided to them . . . Your Commissioners cannot forbear to indulge . . . their earnest and unanimous wish that speedy measures may be taken to effect a general meeting of the States in a future Convention for the same and such other purposes as the situation of public affairs may be found to require."   Deferentially, this sentiment was "dictated by an anxiety for the welfare of the united States [and] will not fail to receive an indulgent Construction."   The idea of New Jersey of including "other Objects, than those of Commerce," deserved to be incorporated in the

purpose of a future convention.   Trade regulation was so comprehensive as to "require a Correspondent adjustment of other parts
of the Federal System."   The "embarrassments which Character-
ize . . . our National Affairs, foreign and domestic," warranted
the conviction that unsuspected shortcomings in the federal government needed "a deliberate and candid" canvass in united
councils.

The commissioners would not enumerate familiar national circumstances that rendered "the situation of the united States delicate
and critical, calling for an exertion of the united virtue and wisdom of all the members of the Confederacy."   A convention of the
states "for the special and sole purpose" of supplying defects was
recommended.   The delegates unanimously hoped that their own
states would persuade all to send deputies to Philadelphia the
second Monday in May following "to take into Consideration the
situation of the united States, to devise such further provisions as
shall appear to them necessary to render the Constitution . . .
adequate to the exigencies of the Union. . . ."   Congressional
approval and ratification by every state legislature was the suggested procedure.

Though the acid bite on his etching had been blurred by the
retroussage of Randolph, enough remained to make Hamilton's
delineation unmistakable.   There was no better illustration of
the determination and ingenuity with which he habitually used
one event to produce another that would advance his plan.   Here
at the slimly attended Annapolis Convention a balk to progress on
a limited program was made to open a wider prospect.   This was
not all Hamilton's doing.   Madison urged, Dickinson approved,
the New Jersey commissioners came empowered.   The vexing
results of competitive state trade regulations, the refusal of states
to allow Congress to raise a revenue on imports, the prevailing
hard times signalized in Shays' revolt in Massachusetts, and much
besides that was amiss in the Union had stirred apprehension and
called for remedy.   Suspicion of the real purpose of the Annapolis
meeting had been so strong as to amount to an invitation to the
commissioners to act upon it.   However, the failure of the commercial gathering needed someone with courage superior to lingering caution.   We read between the lines of the scanty records of
the meeting annoyance that commissioners who had been desig-

nated did not arrive, though their colleagues waited patiently. We easily suppose the conversations during more than a week of idleness. These were able and responsible men, all of them before and afterward actors in forming national policy, and they would not waste words when talking together on neutral ground. As they gathered in the State House, a mere dozen, and three of them technically without votes, the common query must have been, "What can we do?" At this juncture, Hamilton's rashness—as others were apt to term his resourcefulness—was a determining component. Now as at other times he precipitated in the report what was in solution in others' minds.

It seems likely that Hamilton and Madison rode together, after the meeting, from Annapolis to Philadelphia.[36] If so, their collaboration for the calling of a Constitutional Convention would be extended through several days of leisurely conversation. This may help to explain their teamwork in the Philadelphia gathering and in publication of *The Federalist*.

Madison's efforts were rewarded when the Virginia legislature was the first to approve, and almost unanimously, the call that issued from the Annapolis meeting, and placed Washington at the head of her delegates to the Constitutional Convention.[37] This last was a master stroke of policy, in which Hamilton joined by urging Washington to lay aside his inhibitions. Washington was reluctant to act in the Philadelphia convention because he had declined to attend the meeting of the Cincinnati to be held in the same city.[38]

Hamilton, as envoy from the Annapolis commissioners, did not meet with a similarly warm response from the governor of New York. On the contrary, Clinton "expressed a strong dislike" to the object of the report, "declaring that . . . no such reform . . . was necessary; that the confederation as it stood was equal to the purposes of the Union. . . ."[39]

However, the favorable reception by the New York legislature of the address of the Annapolis convention figured in the approval of the proposal by Congress. The latter body was at low ebb, dawdling along, when it could get a quorum, on post office and Indian affairs. The letter of Dickinson, transmitting the call Hamilton had prepared at Annapolis, was read promptly on September 20, 1786.[40] A committee of ten to report on these papers was not appointed until October 11,[41] was renewed and enlarged on February 12 and 13, 1787,[42] and reported February 21, by which time Madison had taken his seat.[43] The report, made the order of the day, was that Congress entirely coincided with the Annapolis commissioners "as to the inefficiency of the federal government and the necessity of devising such further provisions as shall render the same adequate to the exigencies of the Union. . . ." It was strongly recommended to the legislatures to send forward delegates to meet the proposed convention. At this point the New York delegates wished to postpone the report in order to move, in accordance with their instructions, a more specific recommendation to the states "for . . . revising the Articles of Confederation" and reporting to Congress and the states "alterations and amendments . . . to render them adequate to the preservation and support of the Union." When this motion was lost,[44] the Massachusetts delegates (Dane and King) who had favored it successfully proposed a more guarded wording—"for the sole and express purpose of revising the Articles of Confederation. . . ." Changes should become binding when agreed to by Congress and confirmed by the states.[45]

The Annapolis Convention was, politically, such a spring-back from discouragement as the battle of Trenton had been ten years earlier. In each case the sorry pass to which the country had come incited to a bold stroke. But with this difference, that Trenton was an early challenge to enemy power destined to remain strong for many years, while the forces opposed to a new Constitution were crumbling when the Annapolis plea was issued. The pertinence of the Annapolis demand was ready to be acknowledged, in spite of some lingering bluster. Earlier efforts for a remodeling assembly, in their iteration, had carried more conviction than appeared at the time. The impotence of Congress amidst the distractions of the states had been written larger with each passing year. The postwar economic letdown made the sickness of the Confederation conspicuous. Business depressions have frequently given America new directions, and none more so than this earliest in our national history.

Until this distress struck, many had complacently supposed that independence was enough, and did not address themselves to the problem of internal government. Freedom would somehow produce its own triumph.   The emotional attachment of these was to their separate states.   Their confidence was in the sufficiency, indeed supremacy, of state authority.   But the states were involved not only in internecine quarrels, covert and overt; they were also immersed in common trouble.   Civil war in Massachusetts, in Shays' Rebellion, was the fairest proof of incapacity of the individual commonwealth to preserve order, let alone promote prosperity.   Men assented to the logic of more central power because their preoccupation the other way had been discredited; their arguments were about exhausted.   A tottering Congress, strangulated trade, border warfare, domestic insurrection—time and events had worked with those declaring for reform before the fruits of the Revolution should be sacrificed.   It was the lesson of Samson—from corruption, sweetness.

From State Vexation
to National Solution

As a member of the New York Assembly, in the session of January–April, 1787, Hamilton was able to further several objects to which he had long devoted himself. The chief was the sending of delegates to the Constitutional Convention to meet in Philadelphia, of whom Hamilton was one. His effort to secure retraction of conditions on the impost was unsuccessful, but this made little difference, as measures were in train for a new federal government with adequate revenue powers. As the legislature sat in New York City, Hamilton was constantly present.[1] The first contest was characteristic, over the refusal of Governor George Clinton to call a special session of the legislature to expedite the national impost. The tilt came on the reply to the governor's speech. Clinton had submitted the resolutions of Congress of the previous August, "expressing their sense of our Act of last Session, for granting to them an Impost, and requesting an immediate call of the Legislature. . . ." He forbore remarks on a familiar subject except to declare that a "regard to our excellent Constitution, and an anxiety to preserve unimpaired the right of free deliberation on matters not stipulated by the Confederation, restrained me from convening you at an earlier period."[2]

Hamilton was on the committee, with Jones of Queens and Gordon of Albany, to draft a reply to the governor's message. The response, read to the Assembly by Hamilton, omitted mention of the governor's excuses, and thus condemned his obstruction of

[370]

the otherwise unanimous plan for federal revenue. The committee of the whole agreed, but Malcolm and others moved to ap-
plaud the governor's conduct. In spite of Hamilton's efforts, a
brief statement to this effect was incorporated.[3] He was not on a
large committee on the substantive matter of New York's adherence to the impost, but of course cast his vote for the enacting
clause of a bill to grant the duties, and it was agreed to, 29–28.
In accordance with provisions he himself had introduced in Congress, he approved having New York name its collectors, and,
when that was rejected, giving the power to Congress, which also
was rejected.[4]

Hamilton was chairman of a committee to consider laws governing debts due to and trespasses by persons who at the time had
been within the enemy lines. These were questions of honor and
right to which he had devoted attention in Congress and in his law
practice. He reported a bill making it lawful for a defendant
(actually one who had paid rent to the British for a patriot's
premises) to plead the military order.[5] He favored facilitating
payment of debts owing British merchants, but lost by two votes.[6]

Each member nominated five delegates to Congress; Hamilton
named Duane, Egbert Benson, P. V. B. Livingston, William Floyd,
and John Taylor. But the Clintonians had the votes, and only
Benson, of Hamilton's choices, was named by the Assembly.
Schuyler had been nominated by the Senate, but in the final joint
action John Lansing, Jr., on the Assembly list, was elected.[7]

Alexander Hamilton must have been sure that New York would
participate in the Constitutional Convention. Robert C. Livingston was chairman of a small committee to consider the report
of the Annapolis commissioners, and the act of Virginia, calling
for the assembling of delegates at Philadelphia May 2.[8] Later it
was resolved that New York members move in Congress for a convention to revise the Articles of Confederation.[9] The Assembly
had proposed that five delegates be appointed,[10] but two days later
concurred in the Senate's preference for only three.[11] The design of the upper house, by this means, to compose a deputation
committed against the Constitution is apparent in the brief record
of debate. Schuyler, in the Senate, made the motion for five
delegates from New York, giving a liberal description of their assignment. The motion of John Haring, faithful adherent of

Governor Clinton, for only three, passed 11–7. Further, an attempt of Abraham Yates, Jr., to preclude any changes in the Articles of Confederation if such changes were inconsistent with the constitution of the state of New York was defeated only by the deciding vote of the presiding officer, Pierre Van Cortlandt.[12]

When it came to choosing delegates, March 6, 1787, Robert Yates received a nomination from every member (52), Hamilton from all but himself, Samuel Jones, and Matthew Patterson (49); John Lansing, Jr., was third, with the preference of 26 members. Hamilton's other nominees were Duane and R. R. Livingston, who stood fourth and fifth in the combined Assembly list.[13] Had either of these been sent to Philadelphia, the majority of New York delegates espousing a strong central government, the Constitution might have come closer to Hamilton's views, and ratification at Poughkeepsie would not have hung so long in the balance. But that would be to suppose the weight of opinion in New York (or the influence of Governor Clinton) to be different from what it was.

The Senate also nominated Yates, Hamilton, and Lansing, so they were elected "for the sole and express purpose of revising the Articles of Confederation, and reporting to Congress . . . such alterations . . . as shall . . . render the foederal Constitution adequate to the exigencies of government. . . ."[14] Undoubtedly Hamilton was readily elected to represent New York in the Philadelphia convention because he was the one of two state delegates who had troubled to attend the Annapolis convention, and was known to have had a vigorous part in turning that otherwise abortive meeting to unexpected account. Further, his zeal for an effective national government was overbalanced, as the Clinton majority supposed, by sending with him two of their stalwarts, Yates and Lansing.

Other matters which Hamilton favored were of their own but less importance. He took the lead in enlarging the privileges of his alma mater, Columbia (formerly King's) College, and was successful in seeing the Regents given power to approve establishment of other institutions with the same rights.[15] He was active in having certain classes of buildings included in the yearly tax levies.[16] He favored a proclamation of the governor for the apprehension of Daniel Shays and other leaders in the revolt in Massachusetts,[17] but also supported the independence of Vermont, which had been brought on the national carpet by other rebels.[18] Hamilton was of the committee which granted the petition of John Fitch for exclusive privileges for a limited time of constructing steam vessels.[19]

Another item has its curious personal interest. The Council of Revision objected to a bill which forbade the guilty party in a divorce for adultery to marry again. The Council argued that the discipline of celibacy was understandable in a "cloyster," but that to condemn one who had already shown "an instance of frailty" to live celibate in society was to invite open violation of rules of decency. Hamilton voted with the majority to disregard the Council's caution.[20] This was in spite of the fact that his mother, under just such a law in the Danish West Indies, had been forbidden to remarry. Had it not been for this prohibition, Alexander might have been legitimatized by her marriage, which probably she would have chosen, to James Hamilton. Further, Hamilton himself, had his wife been a different woman, would one day stand in peril of this law for which he voted.

Hamilton's practical knowledge of the "feeble and distracted" condition of the Confederation informed his persistent efforts at remedy. The war years, spent at headquarters, taught him the incapacity of the Old Congress, acting through committees, and speaking to semisovereign states in the voice of appeal, not of authority. As Receiver for New York he found that reforms were obligatory before revenue could flow to the central treasury. In Congress in 1782–1783 he had intimate proof of the defect of power in that body. Now in the New York Assembly in 1787 the recalcitrancy of Governor Clinton and his majority illustrated anew the jealousy in the parts that defeated energy in the whole. This last experience, on the eve of his entry into the Constitutional Convention, bore in on him the dangers of boundary quarrels between the states. Unwillingness of the separate jurisdictions to compose commercial conflicts, at Annapolis, had been frustrating. But now he saw New York, Massachusetts, New Hampshire, and Connecticut ready to enforce their claims to disputed territory, even at the cost of bloodshed.

Hamilton helped to settle two of the wrangles of his own state with neighbors. His exertion in these contests, though ultimately

successful, was all he needed to send him to Philadelphia determined to find permanent means for "national concert."

The issue of the status of Vermont was joined between that demanding region and the counterclaims of New York, New Hampshire, and Massachusetts. Like other such differences, it had
rumbled during the Revolution and rose to major dissension after
the peace. The Green Mountain Boys were fit fellows to take
their own part. Refusing to be absorbed by New Hampshire or
to remain under New York, and irked by the temporizing injunctions of Congress, they declared the independence of Vermont in
January 1777. Their military exploits, while local, were early
and successful. Their hero in field and forum was the vehement
Ethan Allen, whose brothers served as bristling diplomatists. Since
Vermont was not accepted as a member state in the Union, their
negotiations with the British in Canada were canny self-protection
or treason to the country, depending upon the sympathies of the
beholder.

Hamilton brought the controversy to a head by introducing his
bill for acknowledging the independence of Vermont on condition
that it be incorporated in the Union.[21] He gave his reasons in
rapid succession.[22] These were answered a fortnight later when
Richard Harison, counsel for proprietors of land in the disputed
district, on motion of Hamilton was admitted within the bar of
the house.[23] This able lawyer, serving his clients, did not choose
to broach questions of policy which Hamilton promptly explored.

In his main speech, April 28, 1787, Hamilton had the advantage
that most of the arguments pro and con had been canvassed. He
had ticked off the favorable points in presenting the measure, had
handsomely introduced Harison, as counsel for the petitioners
against, and now was ready to close the debate with elaborate rebuttal and new reasoning peculiarly his own. While a minor performance as compared with some of his advocacies, it stands as
one of the most forceful. The very exacerbation of the controversy was turned to his hand. Governor Clinton had dealt in
protracted provocation against the Vermonters, yet had proposed
no practicable course of action. Meanwhile the interest of the
Union, and of his own state, *vis à vis* Vermont, had become more
pressing. The endurance of the treaty of peace was tenuous; the
British, still in possession of the frontier posts, by defection of the

Green Mountain region might lap a tongue deep into the country they had lost. The erstwhile enemy then would border the Connecticut, threaten the Hudson almost down to Albany, and divorce New England from the Middle States. The imperfect friendship between New York and New England could ill afford this peril. Further, Kentucky, with the blessing of Virginia, was about applying for statehood, and would add to the weight of the South in Congress.

With matters at this pass, candor was demanded. Hamilton insisted that the independence of Vermont was an accomplished fact. Contentions about constitutionality, land claims, and military coercion must be subordinated to this premise. His forte was in recognizing when a train of developments had reached the point that required decisive action, and in supplying a program that rescued from danger. For this the procrastinating called him precipitate. The truth is that he did not so much anticipate events as he defined, for minds slower and confused, what had already happened. His prescription in the Vermont puzzle was pragmatic. His opponent, for the private petitioners, had urged the dogma "that the chief object of government is to protect the rights of individuals by the united strength of the community." But this principle, Hamilton insisted, found limits in application. It must not be pursued beyond "a rational prospect of success." Was New York, whether or no, to vindicate the rights of its citizens in the disputed territory by reducing revolted inhabitants of that district? He brought the question to earth: "Can this be done? Is the State in a situation to undertake it? Is there a probability that the object will be more attainable at a future day? Is there not rather a probability that it will be every day more out of our reach. . . .? Is it even desirable, if practicable. . . .?"[24]

During the war New York was unwilling to repress the rebellion, from damage to national unity; now it was unable to do so, from its own prostrate condition. In the use of force New York would find no allies in New England, and her own citizens, on the principles of the Revolution, would be against "a contest for dominion over a people disinclined to live under our government." If nominally retrieved, these mountaineers could hardly be controlled, and had better be let go.

The silence of the New York constitution on the right of the

legislature to lop off a part of the state gave assent, certainly in
this case in which the territory was already lost.   Thus Hamilton
invoked, as often later, the implied powers of sovereignty.   Policy
dictated what the constitution permitted.   By the bill, independence would be acknowledged only if Vermont was incorporated
into the Confederacy, when the new state would help to bear the
public burdens.   Further, this would end overtures of the Vermonters to the British in Canada, who, in spite of the peace treaty,
were too likely to be responsive.   He cited his own wartime knowledge of this dangerous intercourse, and was sure it continued.[25]
Britain meant to keep the Western posts because they commanded
the fur trade; "degraded as we are by our mismanagement" and
obliged to "a change of government" before we could resist physically, we might expect indefinite retention of such vantage points
by the late enemy.   If it came to war again, Vermont would be
an acquisition to Britain.   Vermont might reject membership in
the Union, prefer annexation to Canada.   If this was her answer,
we would at least know where we stood.   If the nation was not
militarily able to recover Vermont, this admission "must operate
as a new inducement to the several States to strengthen the
UNION."[26]

If Vermont was in fact already severed from New York, citizens
of the latter could expect no compensation for lands forfeited, except in a federal court, which the bill contemplated.   Pleading
in the New York Assembly on an issue that Clinton had treated
as local, Hamilton's solicitude flew to the national welfare.   Our
affairs were critical; danger from abroad could not be risked.   He
closed with solemn sarcasm for colleagues ready "to attempt a
display of unprofitable heroism. . . . Those . . . who suppose
our government is full of energy, our credit high, and trade
and finances flourishing—will . . . see no room for . . . anxiety
. . . , and may be disposed to leave Vermont in its present state.
If the bill should fail, I hope they will never have occasion to regret the opportunity they have lost."[27]

Hamilton's bill, thus urged, passed the Assembly, 27 to 19,[28]
but died in committee in the Senate.[29]   It was too early for a final
determination, for the states composing the Confederation had not
so much as met in constitutional convention, public and private
claims to compensation were in the foreground, Clinton continued

his opposition, and Vermont itself remained to be convinced. Still, Hamilton, by his advocacy, had supplied the impetus toward a favorable conclusion, which he assisted the next year in exchanges with Nathaniel Chipman, who represented influential Vermonters.

Summary treatment is sufficient for the other boundary controversy in which Hamilton was involved, this time as lawyer rather than as legislator. Massachusetts claimed that, under her colonial charter, her breadth extended "throughout all the main land, . . . westwardly to the southern [Pacific] ocean."[30] This would have cut New York in two, and therefore she countered by putting forward her protectorate over the Six Nations occupying this area. By the autumn of 1786 agents of the two states had agreed upon judges to form a federal court to determine the controversy.[31] However, commissioners named by the disputants, with discretionary authority, met at Hartford and settled the matter December 16, 1786.[32] The bargain was that New York retained "Government, sovereignty and jurisdiction of the lands," but Massachusetts was accorded property ownership, or "the right of preemption of the soil from the native Indians," her grants to be exempt from most New York state taxes for fifteen years.[33]

Governor Clinton in his opening message to the New York legislature in 1787 announced with satisfaction that the differences with Massachusetts had been adjusted in all respects "otherwise than by a Foederal Court. . . ." He was sure that the terms of agreement, and accompanying map, could be approved, "and that adequate provision will be made for the services and expences . . . in laborious preparations for the trial, as well as in the final extinguishment of the contest."[34]

Hamilton was one of the lawyers (his friend Samuel Jones another) who prepared the case for New York against the pretensions of Massachusetts. His work anticipated trial before a federal court until it developed that he could serve as adviser to the commissioners at Hartford. As the record of lengthy proceedings there[35] has not been found, we do not know Hamilton's contribution to the settlement. We do have his autograph brief sustaining New York's side of the controversy. An elaborate recital of authorities, legal and historical, led to two conclusions: "One [,] That in the general sense of Mankind the colonies of the different

nations in America were measured not by their parchment boundaries but by the extent of their actual or reputed possessions and
settlements[.]   2. that The Country *commonly called New England*
lay between the Atlantic ocean and the Rivers St Lawrence & Hudson.   This last is of great importance to the right interpretation of
the last Charter of Massachusetts. . . ."[36]

Hamilton's service to the New York agents in managing the
controversy with Massachusetts, for which he was paid, perhaps
the final balance, as late as April 1789,[37] was doubtless similar to
that of his colleague, of which we have some particulars.   Jones's
charges covered "going to Boston and examining Records and
collecting Evidence there 25 Days at 64/ per Day," besides 24
days in New York.[38]

As a matter of fact, the speed and greed of land speculators in
both states entailed disputes in the sequel.   Hamilton's familiarity
with the dangers in this conflict between state sovereignties further
munitioned him for his campaign for national unity, so soon to
commence in the Constitutional Convention.

When the new Union became a fact, the early acceptance of
Vermont as a member state, which Hamilton had persistently
furthered, was a foregone event.   However, uncertainties, alive
enough at the time, remained.   Nathaniel Chipman and other
Vermont leaders, gathered at Chipman's house at Tinmouth,
feared that if the case ever went to a federal court the land claims
of New York would be upheld.   They resolved to appeal to influential New Yorkers, friends of a strong union, for speedy adjustment of the controversy, and admission of Vermont as a state.
Chipman's letter, July 14, 1788, was brought express to Hamilton at Poughkeepsie, where he was attending the New York convention that ratified the Constitution.   Vermont would come in if
Congress would compensate New York land claimants, and on
condition that certain of the proposed amendments to the Constitution were adopted.[39]   Schuyler, Benson, and Harison, who were
at Hamilton's quarters, helped formulate his reply.[40]

Hamilton followed these persuasions in a meeting with Chipman at Albany in the winter of 1788–1789, when agreement on
final procedure was reached.[41]   New York appointed commissioners, July 14, 1789, with full power to approve admission of

Vermont as a state;[42] Chipman was one of the corresponding deputies of Vermont.[43] After some backing and filling, the two sets of commissioners, in New York, October 7, 1790, agreed, and Hamilton had the satisfaction of witnessing the signatures of the New Yorkers.[44] In the Vermont convention at Bennington, January 1791, Chipman's excellent plea for joining the United States reflected Hamilton's influence.[45] Vermont was admitted to the Union on February 18, 1791.

Most of Alexander Hamilton's public life revolved about the national government, as at times the national government seemed to revolve about him. Though he had a keen concern in New York politics, this was chiefly as elections and other actions in his own strategically situated state and city bore on the national fortunes. He had little of the sectional and local attachment such as formed a prominent ingredient in most of his party colleagues of New England and with men of opposite persuasion in the South. To a singular degree he was a national figure.

Of course, the central feature of all that period was the Constitution of the United States. It has been said that Hamilton had the chief part in giving the Constitution its character.[46] This is too much praise, and inaccurate if we regard the actual construction of that document. His service to the Constitution was rather before and after the Philadelphia convention of 1787 than during it. He early recognized and with many others proclaimed the lacks in the Confederation. He seized the desperate opportunity of the Annapolis convention to bring dissatisfactions to a head and produce the deliberations at Philadelphia. Afterward, by means of the *Federalist* papers explaining the Constitution and rendering it congenial, and by securing the adherence of New York, he had a leading rôle in installing the national government. Then as first Secretary of the Treasury, an assignment to which he gave wide latitude, he took peculiar responsibility for adding to the general government "not only . . . a strong soul, but *strong organs* by which that soul is to operate."[47] Further, in justifying these instruments, particularly in defending the Bank of the United States, he broached the doctrine of implied powers of the Constitution which in John Marshall's hands enormously facilitated the functioning of the central government under its fun-

damental law. This last, an interpretation, invoking the spirit
rather than the letter, was equal in results to any provision written into the document.

Hamilton helped prepare for the making of the Constitution,
did his utmost to persuade the people to sanction it, and aided in
converting it from parchment into practice. What of his influence in hammering out the Constitution in the Philadelphia convention? Here he was helpless, so far as voting was concerned,
because his two colleagues in the small New York delegation,
Robert Yates and John Lansing, Jr., were virtual emissaries of
Governor Clinton, sent to protect state claims and to concede as
little as possible to national demands. During the six weeks that
they remained in the convention the vote of New York must be
divided on most critical questions. After they departed the state
had no vote, the secretary's column of ayes and noes being as con-
sistently blank for New York as for recalcitrant Rhode Island.
Besides, this habitual difference with his fellow New Yorkers put
him at a moral disadvantage in the convention, and injured his
prestige. The fear of delegates who wanted a strong central government that in the end New York would not approve such a constitution tended to undercut what Hamilton could say in support.
In this "disagreeable situation" he absented himself during the
middle third of the convention's duration. Five years later, describing his position in the convention, Hamilton wrote that he
"was the only member from the state to which he belonged who
signed the constitution, and, it is notorious, against the prevailing
weight of . . . official influence . . . and against what would
probably be the opinion of a large majority of his fellow-citizens,
till better information should correct their first impressions."
The final transaction of the convention listed 11 states as present
and assenting, and "Mr. Hamilton from New York."[48]

Though in steady attendance, he took only incidental part in
the proceedings for the first four weeks. In spite of the major
rôle he had played in promoting the convention, we can account
for his reticence, as he did, by the circumstances of his dissent and
by his comparative youth and inexperience.[49] Others in the convention, older and better known than he, were more silent
throughout. Among these were Robert Morris, Mifflin, William
Livingston, Rufus King, Charles Cotesworth Pinckney; Langdon,

of New Hampshire, arrived late, and George Wythe, of Virginia, was obliged to leave early; George Clymer and Thomas FitzSimmons, of Pennsylvania, were less prominent but had pronounced views and the right to speak them.[50] Hamilton's one major appearance, when his speech occupied the whole session of June 18, erred on the side of candor. It came near being a blast against friends as well as foes among the delegates. Though he caught himself toward the end, and brought his recommendations for an unshackled central government to what was feasible in America, he had unnecessarily invoked the superiority of a kingly system. The reports of his praise of the British constitution show that he knew he was out of bounds. He deliberately held up monarchical merits, not expecting to get them approved, but hoping to edge the convention closer to his ideal. He was confident that the people were learning to demand more authority in the general government than the most forward in the convention meant to offer them.

But, obstructed from a continuous, firm participation in the debates, he overdid his grand deliverance. One of his fellow delegates, William Pierce, of Georgia, in his character sketches of those in the convention, ended praise of Hamilton with the reservation that "His manners are tinctured with stiffness, and sometimes with a degree of vanity that is highly disagreeable."[51] Gouverneur Morris, years later, deplored Hamilton's indiscretion in bringing forward monarchical principles which could not find lodgment here.[52] Two French commentators, Luzerne and Otto, found Hamilton impetuous.[53] "When he comes forward," Pierce observed, "he comes highly charged with interesting matter, there is no skimming over the surface of a subject with him, he must sink to the bottom to see what foundation it rests on."[54] This was one of the times when the load in his musket exceeded the accuracy of his aim. A steadier fire, day after day, with the bead carefully drawn on the target that was up at the moment, would have been more effective. This is the wisdom of hindsight, and calculates without the temperament of the speaker and without the provocations under which he stood.

By contrast, other friends of a government "adequate to the exigencies . . . of the union" did better—Madison with his unremitting calm exposition, and Wilson with vehemence under good control.[55]   However, Hamilton, though a little perverse in his main presentation, was not dogmatic or stubborn, nor did he express the extremest antagonism to autonomy of the states.   Thus Read, of Delaware, two weeks before Hamilton's speech went further: "Too much attachment is betrayed to the State Govermts. We must look beyond their continuance.   A national Govt. must soon of necessity swallow all of them up.   They will soon be reduced to the mere office of electing the national Senate."[56] Gouverneur Morris showed how in other confederacies local jurisdictions destroyed common ties, and asked: "Do Gentlemen wish this to be ye case here.   Good God, Sir, is it possible they can so delude themselves.   What if all the Charters & Constitutions of the States were thrown into the fire, and all their demegogues into the ocean.   What would it be to the happiness of America."[57] And Madison, in more measured language: "Some contend that states are sovereign, when in fact they are only political societies. . . . The states never possessed the essential rights of sovereignty. These were always vested in congress.   The states ought to be placed under the control of the general government—at least as much so as they formerly were under the king and British parliament."[58]

Various members of the convention, known for prudence and poise, toward the end showed an obstinacy which was blended of weariness, sincerity, and egotism, but in any event betrayed a loss of judgment.   The almost uninterrupted sittings, six days a week through the whole hot summer, with caucuses and committee meetings when the convention itself was not putting their minds to the stretch, had frayed the nerves of some of the best.   George Mason, provoked by a minor point, declared "that he would sooner chop off his right hand than put it to the Constitution as it now stands."[59]   Gunning Bedford, of Delaware, at the nadir of the discussions, did worse in his unworthy threat against the large states for insisting on proportional representation in both houses: *"I do not, gentlemen, trust you.*   If you possess the power . . . what . . . would prevent you from exercising it to our destruction? . . . Is it come to this, then, that *the sword* must decide this controversy. . . .?   Will you crush the smaller states. . . .? Sooner than be ruined, there are *foreign powers who will take us by the hand."*[60]

Long time has obliterated short tempers in the convention, and has forgotten transient utterances of members who ran counter to the ultimate decisions of the constitutional fathers. Their lapses are recalled here because similar kindness has not been shown in the case of Alexander Hamilton. His proposals, whether meant to spur the delegates to thorough reformation of the government, or merely indiscreet, were elaborately argued, not seized upon by whim or spoken in passion. He had the good sense to retreat from them afterward. In popular history he has been the victim of his vivid purpose and forceful mind. Having ascribed to him the character of conservative, many who tell his story neglect the shadings. He is made to stand out in silhouette.

In depicting Hamilton's part in the Constitutional Convention in 1787—before, during, and after this supreme assemblage in American history—we meet at the threshold the celebrated contention, or discovery, of Professor Charles A. Beard that the motives of the overwhelming majority of the members were selfish, to rescue their own property claims. At least five-sixths of the delegates "were immediately, directly, and personally interested in the outcome of their labors at Philadelphia, and were . . . economic beneficiaries from the adoption of the Constitution."[61] Beard compared the project of the Constitution to the Norman conquest of England: "The point is, that the direct, impelling motive in both cases was the economic advantage which the beneficiaries expected would accrue to themselves first, from their action."[62]

It has become heretical to doubt that the Constitution was disingenuous, that its makers were self-servers rather than patriot publicists.[63] One writes himself down a worshipful innocent if he supposes that the fathers were engaged in another task than feathering their own nests. In accepting this rôle, it is pertinent to point out that Hamilton, who did more than others to produce the convention and to persuade the states to accept the Constitution, is the most embarrassing exception to Beard's thesis. He had no worldly goods, or property prospects beyond what his professional talents could earn.[64] Those less acquainted and scrupulous than Beard should be reminded that Hamilton's advocacy of an effective central government long antedated the Philadelphia convention, from the time (1780) when he was a young officer attached to Washington's headquarters; that his proposals took

varying forms and never coincided with the instrument as promul-
gated; and that his arguments for ratification, so far from forming
the strategy of a privileged clique, were directed to all of the people
of the country.

Others in the convention, who had more to do than Hamilton
with shaping the provisions of the Constitution, had no personal
property concern in their work. Such were Madison and Gouverneur Morris.[65] Contrariwise, principal opponents stood to gain
from the Constitution in their own estates; such were Yates,
Lansing, Luther Martin, Mason, and Gerry.[66]

Discredit of high political purposes of architects of the Constitution has led to attempts to rehabilitate the character of the Articles of Confederation and the record of the Continental Congress.[67] This is an unpromising enterprise, as is best proved by a
faithful reading of the journals of the Old Congress, its diplomatic
correspondence, and the letters of its members. Leaders in
achieving the new Constitution, such as Hamilton, Madison,
James Wilson, and many more, had first been disappointed in
valiant and patient struggles to make the old system serve the demands of solvency and union. The pernicious anemia that beset
the Congress promised to be fatal; the future further darkened
when separate states could no longer support the sovereignties
which they boasted (as in Shays' Rebellion), or settle interstate
land claims without violence. At this point foreign intervention
to partition the country loomed as more than an imaginary threat.
So far from Congress being flouted by the Constitutional Convention, the Confederation was carried out decently—on its shutter.

It was inevitable that the convention was composed of men influential in the public life of their states, which meant that a majority were lawyers, and from the seaboard, rather than mechanics
or inland farmers. Leisure to attend, by itself, required that they
be men of substance. This had been true in every delegate body
beyond the most local. Naturally such persons would possess
property—in loan-office certificates as a matter of patriotism, or
in lands as the habitual outlet for investment. To identify these
holdings and to proclaim a pocketbook theory of individual design in public councils is as extreme as to assert the opposite, that
men could plan in common with no relation to their private property pretensions.

Descrying an economic class interest as dominant in the construction of the Constitution is more valid and illuminating. But this "realistic" interpretation is modified by recalling prevailing political opinion of the time. Equalitarian thought, democracy in government, had made only anticipatory appearance in America, did not become conspicuous until shortly after in the French Revolution, and could not form the basis of a political party for two decades more. In Locke's philosophy, most influential in the convention, protection of property emerged as the purpose of government. This mandate of municipal law was a consequence of natural law, and had an ethical foundation. For Locke derived property from labor, which assumed different degrees of ability and industry. In Madison's words in recommending the Constitution, it is "The diversity in the faculties of men, from which the rights of property originate. . . . The protection of these faculties is the first object of government. From the protection of different and unequal faculties of acquiring property, the possession of different degrees and kinds of property immediately results. . . ."[68]

Just as Beard absolved Hamilton of personal pecuniary purpose in the design of the Constitution, so he agreed that Hamilton catered to the moneyed classes not for their sake but in order to strengthen the new government by attaching them to it.[69] His work in this regard was not so much in the convention, though there too, as later in his Treasury proposals.

Naturally Hamilton's reading as well as his experience and observation shaped his advocacies in the Constitutional Convention. He rarely quoted an author or (except in legal briefs) cited the authority of a writer in connection with a particular statement. Rather, the opinions which he owed to books, in whatever degree, were embedded and diffused in his mind. They must be identified by fair inference, assisted by his occasional mentions. Among the influential writers on political philosophy, Hamilton's closest affinity, perhaps, was with Thomas Hobbes, to whom he alluded in his early controversy with the Westchester Farmer. In reviewing Hamilton's expressions in the convention, one feels the contribution of Hobbes concerning the character and aims of government.

The correspondence between Hobbes and Hamilton in secularity, realism, and practicality, in aims, policy, and method is striking.   Both, living in times of civil war, placed prime emphasis on sovereign authority, domestic peace, and defense against foreign threat.   For each, morals derived from law, and conscience from obedience to constitutional rule, rather than the other way around. Both were concerned with institutions more than with ideologies. The subject made the sovereign, but this much said, a near absolutism invested the latter, whether king or parliament.   The divine right of the state was not ghostly, but was a modus operandi for security and contentment.   Sovereignty rested on consent, but once authorized, the presumption was in favor of the utility of the actions of government.   Government must be instrumental: "For seeing the Soveraign is charged with the End," said Hobbes, "which is the common Peace and Defence; he is understood to have Power to use such Means, as he shall think most fit for his discharge."[70]   Judicial determinations between disputants were worthless except as supported through police and militia.

The similarity of the presuppositions and policies of Hobbes and Hamilton was so close as to leave no doubt of the relation of teacher and taught.   Deductions, recommendations, and even phrases are often identical, or nearly so.   ". . . the Passions of men, are commonly more potent than their Reason," Hobbes observed.   "From whence it follows, that where the publique and private interest are most closely united, there is the publique most advanced."[71]   The dangers of demagoguery, or popular flattery to serve the purposes of private ambition, were stigmatized by both Hobbes and Hamilton.[72]   Perhaps most important in our comparison, the state, for both of these thinkers, was not simply protective, but was positive; was not only to keep the peace, but to promote collective prosperity.   Thus Hobbes said "a generall Providence" must overcome poverty.   The impotent, unable to work, "ought not to be left to the Charity of private persons; but to be provided for . . . by the Lawes of the Common-wealth." Those with strong bodies must be forced to work, "and to avoyd the excuse of not finding employment, there ought to be such Lawes, as may encourage all manner of Arts; as Navigation, Agriculture, Fishing, and all manner of Manifacture that requires labour."[73]

In sum, with both Hobbes and Hamilton, liberty was in law; due process was the means to private—because to public—happiness. That Hamilton enlisted the rich to benefit the public, and did not suborn public authority to serve privilege, is a major principle of his conduct that will be further established when we come to discuss the economic institutions he erected. The vulgar assertion to the contrary, that he was no better than the brilliant and plausible strategist of the moneybags, has been made many times. It has been said that he illustrated his unworthy intent by giving official information that furthered the speculations of relatives and particular friends. The finance minister of purest integrity, at that period of American history, could not have escaped such charges.

Of course, there were economic classes in this country; even though wealth and income were more equally distributed than in the Old World—chattel slaves at the bottom, laborers and small farmers next, mechanics and petty traders better off, and large planters, landholders, merchants, and a few financiers, with allies in professional callings, at the top. The more successful, whose fortunes were as insidiously threatened by national governmental weakness as they were openly imperiled by agrarian rebellion, took the lead in framing the new Constitution. Broadly they were the Federalists who operated under it for a dozen years, spelled it out in statute, treaty, and day-to-day policy. In this process their personal and public integrity was not impugned. Perhaps it is accurate to say that they were partisans in the public cause.

The wisdom of what the delegates of America did at Philadelphia needs no plea. The expanding economy and polity of a century and a half continued to prove the Constitution a serviceable instrument. That its makers saw no cause for being surreptitious in or apologetic for their handiwork was evident at once in the vigor of debate in the convention and the mode of the document's submission to the country. It invoked the name of the people and was placed before them—or the portion of them enjoying the suffrage at that time—for adoption or rejection in specially elected state conventions. The legislatures were not allowed to pass upon it for obvious reasons. It erected a new central power, acting, in national concerns, immediately upon the citizens. The states in their separate corporate capacities, as represented by their legislatures, could be expected to be hostile to a plan that seemed to diminish their consequence. The people, speaking as directly as was then permitted in any vote, after full scrutiny, adopted it. In New York, where the contest was closest, delegates to the Poughkeepsie convention were chosen by manhood suffrage. The airing and endorsement that the Constitution received must settle the fact that it was not a plot or imposture.

"No Man's Ideas . . .
More Remote from the Plan. . . ."

THOUGH Alexander Hamilton had had so prominent a part in the calling of the Constitutional Convention, he did not attend promptly on the day set for the opening, May 14, when quorums of representatives of only Pennsylvania and Virginia were present,[1] but arrived with Yates to take his seat on May 18.[2] In Philadelphia, Hamilton lodged, with numerous "gentlemen of the convention" at the Indian Queen tavern, in Third Street between Market and Chestnut.[3] This gave him an opportunity to learn and influence sentiments outside the convention hall; such topics had to be avoided when delegates dined out in mixed company, which must have been a welcome change from constant association with one another. Hamilton's early service in the convention was confined nearly entirely to formal matters. After Washington was conducted to the President's chair, Hamilton nominated Major William Jackson for secretary, and he was elected over Temple Franklin, five to two. Jackson had sought the place and proved a poor selection, as he kept the minutes without the expected care. John Beckley, of Virginia, was among the "several candidates" for the appointment, alluded to by Mason, and went to Philadelphia with Randolph in confidence of success.[4] Beckley, a violent partisan and busybody, afterward brought on much trouble for Hamilton. Hamilton was elected, with Wythe and Charles Pinckney, a member of the committee chosen the first day to report standing rules for the convention, and these were accepted with little change.[5]

[389]

John Lansing did not take his seat until June 2. Before this, Hamilton and Yates divided the vote of New York on the crucial question whether the convention was to frame a new and national government or was to amend the Confederation, Hamilton, of course, being for the former.[6] On matters less portentous they concurred. After Lansing with Yates made a New York majority against Hamilton, we find no more divisions recorded for the state, but a ballot contrary to Hamilton's view where we know it.[7]

Hamilton, like several others in the Constitutional Convention, took notes during the proceedings. But his are of a different sort from the others. Madison, what with laborious transcribing and supplementing after the sessions, intended his methodical full report for posthumous publication, while Yates, Lansing, King, and McHenry were in varying degrees systematic, conveying what was said and done. Hamilton's disconnected, laconic jottings reflected as much his own thoughts as those of the speakers. They obviously were made solely for his own use, primarily in defense of positions he meant to take. The sixteen sheets, often written on both sides, that have survived among his papers,[8] though without dates, have been painstakingly related to what seem to be the appropriate days of debate.[9] However, they throw little light on what transpired, except in his own eager mind. Sentences are left unfinished, for a second prompting crowded in on the first, and a third on both of them. These memoranda give only the record of a man talking to himself. Occasionally an idea stands out complete, as when he noted his objection to an argument offered.[10]

For example, when Wilson and Madison wanted larger election districts, of "such extent as to render combinations . . . of interest difficult" (blocking the issue of paper money), Hamilton noted his exceptions: "Paper money is capable of giving a general impulse. It is easy to conceive a popular interest pervading the E [astern] states. . . . Frequently small portions of . . . large districts carry elections—An influential demagogue will give an impulse to the whole—Demagogues are not always *inconsiderable* persons—Patricians were frequently demagogues." And further he reflected that though you attempted "to refine the representation of the People" by balloting over a greater area, "The Assembly when chosen will meet in one room if they are drawn from half the globe—& will be liable to all the passions of popular assemblies."

What Hamilton said in his principal and only comprehensive speech in the convention, June 18, is of importance for several reasons. Not offered until deliberations had been in progress for four weeks, his first participation in the debates had undoubtedly been awaited with expectation, for his profound dissatisfaction with the Confederation and his part in the calling of the convention were known. This deliverance was chiefly responsible for his influence on the character of the Constitution as it issued. He was opposing the expressed views of his own colleagues from New York, and for this reason he spoke seldom afterward. His proposals were offered when the delegates had already digested two plans, those of Randolph and of Paterson, which were distinct from each other. At the last previous session, on Saturday, June 16, Lansing, Paterson, and Wilson had contrasted these,[11] so that the convention was ready to receive a third scheme.

Hamilton's later brief appearances on the floor, his conversations and correspondence with fellow delegates, and his work in the committee on style bore their part in shaping the document. But his full-fledged argument, connected and spirited, occupying an entire day, was a point of reference for subsequent discussions. As his formal pronouncement on what the crisis of the country required, it remained then and for long in the minds of his hearers. Reports, biased by friends and foes, carried his sentiments of that day into the hot contests of the years that followed.[12]

Hamilton's speech lasted between five and six hours, in spite of the heat that June Monday. The convention met at eleven, ran through to about four without a break. Delegates fortified themselves with big breakfasts, made dinner the deliberate business of the late afternoon, and were ready at ten to drink and sup till midnight. Thus they were prepared for formidable oratory as the only air-conditioning. If Hamilton's hearers from eleven states were fatigued, which was not said, at least he did not, like Luther Martin after a three-hour discourse "diffuse, and . . . desultory," profess himself exhausted but generously promise the House more next day.[13] Gouverneur Morris called Hamilton's speech "the most able and impressive he had ever heard,"[14] and let it go at that, while William Samuel Johnson remarked to the convention that Hamilton, making his proposals "with boldness and decision, . . . has been praised by every body, [but] he has been supported by none."[15] This last was not quite true, for Read of Delaware "repeated his approbation of the plan of Mr. Hamilton, & wished it to be substituted for that on the table [Randolph's]."[16] Johnson offered his comment on Hamilton's failure to make converts only three days after the speech. The fact was that Hamilton's principles, and a number of his specific proposals, percolated through the discussions in the succeeding three months and won their way into the Constitution, even though he did not have acknowledged champions.

Without his projection of a dominant national authority, extreme as it was in the plan he urged, the final instrument would have been more equivocal as it came from the hand of the convention. His demand for centralized power had substantive virtue, but the psychological value of it was superior. Posting himself decidedly in advance of what others would accept, he beckoned forward and reduced inhibitions of delegates. His earnestness, and the thorough construction of his scheme, forbade any to call him quixotic or exhibitionist. As one reads the record of debates, it is his animating purpose, unhindered by ineligible particulars, which infused deliberations and helped bring them to a strong conclusion.

Hamilton's influence was greater because his colleagues Yates and Lansing flung off in a pet. Had they remained in convention, the force of New York would have been registered for looser federal ties. Had Hamilton continued with them, his steady dissent from the New York majority position would have furnished a spectacle of division within an important delegation, little calculated to encourage progress in the assemblage as a whole. As it was, his withdrawal over a period was not a handicap, for he had deposited his views, and the reason of his temporary absence was patent. Then his return for final discussions disposed the convention to him, for his effort was to conciliate the obstinate and to ready the draft of the Constitution, defective as he considered it, for favorable action by the states. The merit of concession, for the sake of cooperation in carrying a main idea, was rarely better illustrated. The favorable impression Hamilton made in the convention doubtless carried over into the reception accorded *The Federalist* papers by readers who knew the conduct of the principal author.

Though Hamilton did not write out his set speech in the convention, before or after delivery, we have tolerable knowledge of it from several sources. The most authentic is Hamilton's extended outline which, from the length of his address, he must have had in his hand at the time. The earlier and larger part of the outline consists of heads of topics and by itself tells little, but the later sheets contain more connected sentences.[17]

Next, we have reports made at the time by three of his hearers —Madison, Yates, and King. Madison later said that his account of Hamilton's address was almost unique among his records of the proceedings in having the speaker's approval of the form in which Madison cast it. ". . . Mr. Hamilton . . . happened to call on me," Madison wrote, "when putting the last hand to it, and . . . acknowledged its fidelity, without suggesting more than a very few verbal alterations which were made. . . ."[18] Yates, especially considering his own state-sovereignty commitment, in penning his report entered into the spirit of Hamilton's plea for strength in the central government. King's version of the speech was shorter, but confirms the others. Later recollections of members of the convention, though they probably harked back mostly to this main exposition, are founded on a good deal besides and are of no use for detail. They either accused Hamilton of advocating monarchy, an American pattern of the British constitution, or they defended him against this charge. Thus they emphasized what became, for party purposes, the significance of his deliverance before the convention.

It may well be that Hamilton, so long silent in the deliberations, but now prepared to unburden himself, asked John Dickinson, from the small state of Delaware but with strong national sympathies, to give him a launching platform for his speech. At the opening of the session Dickinson brought the committee of the whole back to first principles by moving to postpone consideration of Paterson's first proposition and to enter on the resolve "that the articles of confederation ought to be revised and amended, so as to render the government of the United States adequate to the Exigencies, the preservation, and the prosperity of the Union."[19]

Thus invited, Hamilton explained that he had not come for-

ward before on the business of the convention because he was reluctant to oppose the views of others of more experience, "and
partly from his delicate situation with respect to his own State,
to whose sentiments as expressed by his Colleagues, he could by
no means accede."   But the crisis of the country compelled him
to declare himself unfriendly both to the Virginia and to the New
Jersey plans.   "He was particularly opposed to that from N. Jersey, being fully convinced, that no amendment of the confederation, leaving the States in possession of their sovereignty could possibly answer the purpose."   At the beginning, however, he confessed his doubt whether from "the amazing extent" of America,
the desired blessings would flow from "any general sovereignty
that could be substituted."[20]   He was leading into his contention
that any federal plan, bottomed on democratic representation,
would prove insufficient; that class interests, rather than individuals in the mass, had to be represented.   When these had been
set off against each other, their balance could be maintained and
"a permanent *will*" could be furnished only by a hereditary monarch.

He recognized—here we are getting ahead of the unfolding of
his argument—that he was projecting "the best form of government—not as a thing attainable by us, but as a model which we
ought to approach as near as possible."[21]   This meant, in his
sketch of a constitution delivered with the speech, senators and
chief executive chosen indirectly by the people and holding office
during good behavior, plus confinement of state legislatures to local concerns and vigorous operation of the central authority on
individuals throughout the union.   However, his proposal of
what amounted to a permanent president (though subject to trial
on impeachment) was not his "final opinion," which "was against
an Executive during good behaviour" and favored one with "no
greater duration than for three years."[22]   .

His preference, when he made the speech, for a permanent president, with concomitant features of a constitution, he knew "went
beyond the ideas of most members,"[23] and later he said that it
"was brought forward to make it the subject of discussion, and
see what would be the opinions of different gentlemen on so
momentous a subject."[24]   As he spoke on the floor he acknowledged "despair that a republican form of government can remove

the difficulties," but "Whatever may be my opinion, I would hold it . . . unwise to change that form of government."[25]   Madison reported that Hamilton "did not mean to offer the paper . . . as a proposition to the Committee [of the Whole].   It was meant only to give a more correct view of his ideas, and to suggest the amendments which he should probably propose to the plan of Mr. R[andolph] in the . . . stages of its future discussion."[26]

Scouting the subtleties of argument on previous days, Hamilton believed the delegates had powers, or if not powers, the moral obligation to the country, "to do on this emergency whatever we should deem essential to its happiness.   The States sent us here to provide for the exigencies of the Union."[27]   He dwelt, as others before him, on the weaknesses of the Confederation.   These fatal defects could not be remedied by mere amendment, as in the Jersey plan, or in the federal system proposed by Virginia.   The essential basis of a *national* government was "an active & constant interest in supporting it,[28] but the states fastened the people to local loyalties.   Laws for coercion of states by the general government were lacking; this was wise, since attempts to use military force would produce war between the parties and an invitation to foreign intervention.   "To effect any thing" it was necessary that the central power reach individuals as well as the states, for "Passions must be turned towards the general government."[29]   The few and the many, creditors and debtors, had distinct interests.   This was in fact the texture of society.   He put much of his political doctrine in the assertion that the central authority must claim "the regular weight . . . it will receive from those who will find it their interest to support a government intended to preserve the peace and happiness of the community of the whole."[30]

He went on from analysis to advocacy.   "If [the states] were extinguished, he was persuaded that great oeconomy might be obtained by substituting a general Govt.   He did not mean however to shock the public opinion by proposing such a measure. On the other hand he saw no *other* necessity for declining it." The states as distinct entities were not necessary for commerce, revenue, or agriculture.   Though subordinate authorities would be required for local purposes, "cui bono, the vast & expensive apparatus now appertaining to the States."[31]   As matters stood, in a national government how prevent the turbulent, unreasonable many from tyrannizing over the few whose concern was security and constancy, and how stop the few, if they held sway, from oppressing the people? The solution was to place power in the hands of both, but they must be permanently separated. However, the motive of each group must "exist in full force, or it will not answer its end." Therefore they needed "a mutual check. This check is a monarch."[32]

His recommendation for America was a senate, during good behavior, for stability and prudence; an assembly "derived immediately from the people,"[33] and what amounted to a permanent president. "But is this a Republican Govt. it will be asked? Yes, if all the Magistrates are appointed, and vacancies are filled, by the people, or a process of election originating with the people."[34] However, he had no scruple in declaring "that the British Govt. was the best in the world: and that he doubted much whether any thing short of it would do in America." As Necker had said, the British constitution united "public strength with individual security." The hereditary king contributed to this result; he was placed above corruption.[35] Though in his own mind the British government "is the only proper one for such an extensive Country . . . we are not in a situation to receive it—perhaps if it was established it wd. maintain itself—I am however sensible that it can't be established by consent, and we ought not to think of other means—We may attempt a general & not a federal Govt:"[36] We should "go as far in order to attain stability and permanency, as republican principles will admit." The evils operating in the states must soon cure the people of their fondness for democracies, and whenever that happened they would not stop where Randolph's plan placed them, but would "go as far at least" as Hamilton was proposing.[37]

The supposition of Hamilton's poor opinion of the people has rested on such remarks as he now made. As reported by Yates, "All communities divide themselves into . . . the rich and well born" and "the mass of the people. The voice of the people has been said to be the voice of God," but "this maxim . . . is not true in fact. The people are turbulent and changing; they seldom judge or determine right. Give therefore to the first class a distinct, permanent share in the government. They will check the unsteadiness of the second, and as they cannot receive any advantage by a change, they therefore will ever maintain good government. Can a democratic assembly, who annually revolve in the mass of the people, be supposed steadily to pursue the public good? Nothing but a permanent body" can counter "the imprudence of democracy."[38]

Sixteen years later he still considered this plan "conformable with the strict theory of a Government purely republican," for executive and legislature would be elected by the people but hold their offices by a *"responsible"* but "temporary or *defeasible* tenure." He went on to remark that five states had favored, in the convention, an executive during good behavior, and believed that Madison (at the later period so much the democrat) had voted for it.[39]

We know beyond peradventure—or nearly so—the outline plan of a new government with which he ended his address. It was a brief scheme, of eleven articles, occupying only two pages of print, that he then read to the delegates. Two of his editors and biographers seem to have been mistaken in concluding, his son explicitly and Lodge less so, that he recited a much more detailed constitution, closer to the republican model.[40]

Parenthetically, we should note that his second plan, given to Madison three months after the first sketch was read to the convention, furnishes Hamilton's maturer design for the constitution. In drawing it up he had the benefit of further discussions on the floor and of his reflections on views that differed from those he initially held. If two minds are better than one, the fifty-five minds of delegates who first and last sat in the convention (or the average of forty in attendance at one time) were much superior. The whole convention showed development of thought, individual and collective. Provisions supposedly settled were reopened, in some cases several times; reference of vexed questions to a committee did not keep the delegates from critical review of the committee's report and from consequent remodeling of what had been submitted. In the course of the debates men made threats which they afterward withdrew, and issued hot ultimata which they retracted on cooler consideration.[41] The two conspicuous compromises of the convention, the first composing the clash between large and small states, the second reconciling differences between free labor and slave commonwealths, came subsequent to Hamil-

ton's chief speech, when his shorter plan was projected.   Also, at
the end of the meetings numerous prominent delegates, Hamilton
among them, declared that they would sign the instrument though
it did not meet their views, and undoubtedly more subordinated
their own preferences to the harmony which they believed essential
in proposing the document to the country.   Hamilton did not quit
the convention like his dissenting colleagues, Yates and Lansing,
or like the disgusted Luther Martin, of Maryland.   His opposition to the Constitution, as finally formed, was deeper and broader
than that of Gerry, Mason, and Randolph, the three who in the
end declined to sign.

Hamilton's purposes for America, whether in helping to formulate the Constitution, or in later administrative and policy decisions, were remarkably constant.   It was as though he knew his
career was to be foreshortened, and so he must follow his lode-
star.   But early determined principles did not prevent him from
altering his program as taught by experience.   This was notably
his case in the Constitutional Convention, where the ablest advocates, focusing on momentous questions, offered such a school for
information and wisdom as has rarely been held in so short a
period.   Hamilton consciously, as the convention proceeded,
changed his recommendations to meet the evident demand for institutions more popular than those of his predilection.

Thus, years afterward, nearly at the end of his life, he contrasted
the "highest toned propositions" which he offered in the convention with his "final opinion" in that body that the president, instead of continuing during good behavior, should be elected for
only three years, actually a shorter term than the Constitution
provided.   He had supposed that discussions were fluid, that proposals and votes of delegates were not "evidences of a definitive
opinion."[42]

His first sketch of a constitution, if we take Madison's copy of
it,[43] and mention only the pivotal points, provided a two-house
legislature "with power to pass all laws whatsoever. . . ."   The
Assembly was to be "elected by the people to serve for three years."
The members of the Senate were to be elected by electors chosen
by the people, and were to serve during good behavior.   The chief
executive, called governor, was similarly to be chosen by electors
selected by the people;[44] he was to have a negative on all proposed

laws, should solely appoint chief officers, and "have the direction
of war." Only the Senate could declare war. No vice president
was provided, but the president of the Senate would serve temporarily in the death or removal of the governor.

Federal judges, presumably to be named by the governor with
consent of the Senate, were to have adequate, permanent salaries
and indefinite tenure; the chief court was to have limited original
and a wider appellate jurisdiction, while federal courts in each
state should have "the determination of all matters of general concern." All officers, on impeachment for corrupt conduct, should
be tried by a court consisting of the chief judge of every state.[45]

Laws of the states contrary to the constitution or laws of the
United States were void. To prevent such laws being passed, the
president of each state should be appointed by the general government and have a negative on state laws. No state was to have
standing armed forces, and state militia were to be under exclusive
direction of the United States.

Hamilton explained these articles in a sort of afterspeech,[46] but
his oral observations on them must have been brief and left the
scheme of government as then presented terse on cardinal points
of federal power and vague or lacking on all others. Topics and
terminology alike indicate that this paper was struck off early in
the history of the convention, and, as Hamilton said, would be
elaborated in amendments he intended offering to Randolph's
plan.

Not so the complete constitution which he "drew up while the
convention was sitting," never offered to the delegates in meeting,
but left with Madison for his history. We are at no loss to know
why, in spite of its painstaking articulation, it was not presented
for discussion. His earlier speech and outline of a project had
made no converts; he could expect no support from his New York
colleagues while they remained in the convention, and after they
left, in the periods of his presence he had no vote. Charles
Pinckney's plan, though before the Committee of the Whole for
more than two months,[47] was never considered in any connected
fashion, and it was closer to Hamilton's views than the Randolph
or Paterson plans which were staples of debate. Hamilton's
pains in drawing up his scheme may be laid to his habit of casting
his projects into definite form, fit for adoption or operation, and

to his wish, since he took little part in the debates, to have his connected plan on record.

We cannot say, viewing the contents of his final plan, how far the provisions of it, entering into his statements on and off the floor, influenced the formation of the Constitution, and how far they were themselves reflections of the course of the debates. As explained above, parts of it were obviously set down late in the discussions, and that is all we can aver about the blend of first conviction and subsequent conversion.

Hamilton, in long retrospect, said that this draft constitution was predicated on three bases: (1) "That the political principles of the people of this country would endure nothing but republican government"; (2) That the republican theory should have here a fair and full trial; (3) For such a trial it was essential the government should have all the energy and stability that could be reconciled with the theory. "These were the genuine sentiments of my heart, and upon them I acted." He still hoped that the experiment might not prove disappointing through inattention to resource and firmness in the central authority.[48] This is a true short statement of his aims and conduct, in the Constitutional Convention and afterward—to enable representative government to succeed by endowing it with sufficient strength. A summary of Hamilton's detailed, revised plan of a constitution (that never formally offered) will show how he had accommodated himself to the results of debates. Even so, his ideal government was more centralized, more removed from immediate expression of the will of the people, than that framed in the convention. It throws light on his later purposeful support of a document which fell short of his wishes.

His constitution should be ordained and established by "The People of the United States of America."[49] The Assembly (House of Representatives) remained as in his original short sketch, elected by the people for three years, now with the added provision that this be the maximum term. The electors were to be all free male citizens and inhabitants, of the age of twenty-one, and all entitled to an equal vote. The first Assembly should consist of a hundred members variously apportioned to the states, running from two each for Rhode Island and Delaware to sixteen for Virginia. Thereafter apportionment, and direct taxes, should be according to a decennial census of free persons, except Indians not taxed, and three-fifths of all "other persons." Revenue and appropriation bills should originate in the Assembly but might be amended by the Senate.

Senators should be designated by electors chosen for that purpose by (male) citizens and inhabitants with a landed property qualification. Senators should be two-fifths of the number of representatives, and be apportioned to states, no state having less than one. (He opposed equal representation of states in the Senate.) Senators should hold their places during good behavior. The Senate had exclusive power of declaring war, and must consent to treaties (as in his shorter, earlier plan).

The chief executive he now called President, who, after the first (to be elected by plurality of the national legislature) was to be chosen by an elaborate cautionary scheme. After proper notice and delay, citizen electors with property qualification roughly three times as high as for the choice of senators, should choose, by states, first electors. These should in turn vote for a smaller number of second electors. These, from a list of nominees of the first electors, should declare the majority nominee President, or in case none had a majority, select from the three who stood highest.

The President would hold his place during good behavior, be removable only by conviction on impeachment for crime or misdemeanor. He could prorogue or adjourn the legislature and had an absolute negative on all bills. Though commander in chief of all armed forces, he should not actually take the field without the consent of the legislature. The President of the Senate should be Vice President of the United States.

The Supreme Court was to consist of from six to twelve judges, sitting during good behavior. Its original jurisdiction was widened to cover all causes in which the United States was a party (except for a controversy between the United States and a state over territory). Appellate jurisdiction, both as to law and fact, extended to all questions between citizens of different states and to "all others in which the fundamental rights of this constitution are involved." Thus he envisioned the power which the highest court came to exercise in interpreting the fundamental law. Justices of the Supreme Court were to be joined by chief justices of state courts in trying impeachments of the highest federal and state officers.   The President could be impeached by two-thirds of each house of the legislature.   Except in cases of impeachment, trial by jury was preserved.

The legislature had power "to pass all laws which they shall judge necessary to the common defence and safety and to the general welfare of the Union," but there should be no bill of attainder, ex post facto law, nor religious test for office.   While the President had the appointment of heads of federal departments, the Treasurer of the United States was to be elected by the legislature.   National laws and treaties were the supreme law of the land and should be so construed by the state courts.

As in Hamilton's shorter sketch of a constitution, the chief executive of each state was to be appointed "under the authority of the United States" and have a veto on all legislation in his state.

Citizens of each state should enjoy the rights of citizens of other states, and each state must give full faith and credit to the public acts of another.   Fugitives from justice across state lines must be delivered up.

No new state should be erected from existing ones without consent of the federal legislature and the legislatures of the states concerned.   The United States guaranteed to each state a republican form of government and protection against domestic violence and foreign invasion.   No state could enter into a contract with another or make a treaty with a foreign power without consent of the United States.

The constitution might be amended on proposal of two-thirds of the legislature (Congress) and ratification by legislatures or conventions in the same proportion of the states.

Finally, the constitution should be submitted to conventions in the states (no intermediation of Congress at this point being mentioned) and when "duly ratified" (no number of states specified) should go into effect.   This, then, was Hamilton's formal draft of a constitution after all of the evidence developed by the Philadelphia convention was in.[50]   He continued in the convention through June 29.[51]   This day he took part in the debate brought to a head by the proposal of Johnson and Ellsworth, of Connecticut, for the compromise of equal representation of the states in the upper house, and proportional representation in the lower.   While his opposition was in vain—for his New York colleagues, in the voting, placed that state in the majority against him—he had the satisfaction of hearing his general plan of government praised by Read of Delaware.[52]

Hamilton was not idle in behalf of the Constitution while absent from the convention. Promptly on July 3 he wrote to Washington from New York that his tests of the people's temper there and in New Jersey, as he traveled through those states, favored "a strong well mounted government . . . something not very remote from that which they have lately quitted" [i.e., the British administration]. Though the persons whose views he sampled were not yet ripe for such a plan as he advocated, there was no reason to despair of the public adopting one "equally energetic" if proposed by the convention. He was concerned (as in his last observations on the floor) at the parlous aspect of the convention when he left it, and feared lest "we shall let slip the golden opportunity of rescuing the American empire from disunion anarchy and misery—No motley or feeble measure can answer the end or will finally receive the public support. Decision is true wisdom and will be not less reputable to the Convention than salutary to the community." He had not compared sentiments with Washington during the sittings, but knew the President of the convention would welcome this sincere report of opinion out of doors.[53]

Washington answered, on July 10, that the "state of the Councils" was in "a worse train than ever," so that "I *almost* despair of seeing a favourable issue to . . . the Convention. . . . The Men who oppose a strong & energetic government are . . . narrow minded politicians, or are under the influence of local views." Their predictions of popular rejection of an adequate constitution were specious, but though present sentiment be what they warned, "the question ought nevertheless to be, is it, or is it not, the best form? —If the former, recommend it, and it will assuredly obtain mauger opposition." Washington's despondency was on the day Yates and Lansing retired permanently from the convention. They doubted their powers as delegates, they doubted the feasibility of a general government, they doubted whether the convention would alter the bad principles on which it was far embarked, and they doubted whether they could return.[54] The fact was that, under the command of Governor Clinton, they were both "narrow minded politicians" and obsessed by "local views." Their whole mental temper, while in the convention and in withdrawing from it, reminded of the slothful servant who, instead of putting his talent out to interest, wrapped it in a napkin.

Hamilton had written Washington July 3, that he would return to the convention in ten or twelve days if he would not be wasting his time, and Washington answered: "I am sorry you went away— I wish you were back —The crisis is equally . . . alarming, and no opposition . . . should discourage exertions till the signature is fixed."[55] The convention wrangled July 10, the day Washington wrote to Hamilton, over the apportionment of representatives to the states in the first congress, with much pulling and hauling for special advantage. Gouverneur Morris "regretted the turn of the debate. The States he found had many Representatives on the floor. Few he fears were to be deemed the Representatives of America."[56] Luther Martin described the impasse over representation in the Senate: "Every thing was now at a stand and little hopes of agreement, the Delegates of New York had left us determined not to return, and to hazard every possible evil, rather than to Yield in that particular. . . ."[57]

If, as Manasseh Cutler noted in his journal, Hamilton was back in Philadelphia on July 13, this could not have been in response to Washington's plea, for there would not have been time.[58] He probably returned according to his intention. But there is no evidence in the convention proceedings that he was present there.[59] The discussion was strained, on how far Negro slaves were to be counted as persons or as property, of course with both representation and direct taxation of the Southern states the issue. Gouverneur Morris helped bring "this struggle between the two ends of the Union" to a compromise, reached a few days later, by saying boldly that if each section cherished only its selfish views, "let us at once take a friendly leave of each other."[60] Hamilton, if present, would have approved Randolph's motion to make numbers of inhabitants cover wealth of the different states, rather than trying to estimate the two separately.

While in New York, Hamilton heard of insinuations of Governor Clinton against what was going forward in Philadelphia. Irked in the convention by the cross-grained Yates and Lansing, Hamilton had remained polite. But here was their inspirer, to whom he would give no quarter. In a long unsigned article in the *New*

York Daily Advertiser, July 21, 1787,[61] he condemned the governor because, by report, "in public company, without reserve [he] reprobated the appointment of the Convention," which according to Clinton, was "calculated to impress the people with an idea of evils which do not exist. . . ." Hamilton defended the convention under nine heads. From the action of the states in sending delegates it was plain that the present government was not equal to the purposes of the union; otherwise twelve legislatures would not have invited diminishing their own powers. Existing evils did not admit of dispute—a starved treasury, commerce stagnant because we could not retaliate against foreign discriminations, our national character degraded since we could not guarantee our own performance of treaties. The Union was nominal, "destitute of the necessary powers to administer the common concerns of the nation. . . ." This called for collective wisdom to provide remedy. The specially appointed body was less distracted, abler, and more disinterested than Congress. However justifiable beforehand, once the convention was called, it was *"unwarrantable and culpable in any man"* to try to prepossess the public against its measures.

This attempt to block Clinton's offensive at the outset was countered by "A Republican" in the *New York Journal,* Sept. 6, 1787.

In his rejoinder to Clinton's champion[62] Hamilton declared he had written the piece complained of, and had left his name with the printer to be furnished to anyone applying on behalf of the governor. Thus he had made an honorable attempt "to unmask . . . the pernicious intrigue of a man high in office, to preserve power and emolument to himself, at the expense of the . . . happiness of America." The governor had not denied the charge, in print or to Hamilton personally. He repeated that Clinton should not have prejudged the constitution. Nor should a citizen be blamed for criticizing official action. This right was "the bulwark of public liberty."

Hamilton sent his answer to Washington with a covering letter saying that the governor in effect admitted trying to discredit the convention. However, Clinton's party, to diminish Hamilton's influence, had undertaken to rob him of the reputation of enjoying Washington's confidence. The insinuation was that during the war Hamilton had "palmed" himself upon the commander-in-chief and left the military family because he was turned out of it. Hamilton asked for Washington's denial of these whispered accusations.[63] Clinton defended himself and disparaged the Constitution in seven letters of "Cato," which were answered by Hamilton ("Caesar").[64] This clash with Clinton boded ill for Hamilton's credit with him and his followers in future. Not much was to be expected in that way anyhow, but a public denunciation of the political leader of his own state before the Constitution was offered to the country made its acceptance by New York additionally difficult. Cooperation of Lansing and Yates with Hamilton in the convention, never promising, became impossible after Hamilton's attack on their leader. The dangerous results of the quarrel help to explain why Hamilton, after more experience, pitched *The Federalist* papers on a high plane of impersonal argument and exposition, and why he prepared so carefully to give the Poughkeepsie convention a propitious turn.

The convention was in recess for two weeks, July 26–August 6, to allow time for the Committee of Detail to do its work, which permitted Hamilton to remain in New York with good conscience. In this interval of public concerns he discharged a private office by acting as mediator in the threatened duel between his friend Auldjo and Major William Peirce. Taken in connection with his passage with Clinton, in the same days, it indicates the clear distinction Hamilton made between political and personal criticism.[65]

Hamilton was again in the convention on August 13. By then the compromise between large and small states over representation had been concluded, and attention turned to membership in the two branches of Congress, and the powers of each. The subjects debated that day were both close to him—the eligibility of foreigners for the House, and the exclusive right of the House to originate money bills. Hamilton seems to have expressed himself only on the first. He spoke to his motion to eliminate any term of citizenship for those elected to the House. The danger of persons with foreign attachments insinuating themselves into our councils was slight as compared with the advantages of encouraging immigration from Europe. Wilson supported Hamilton, withdrawing his own motion which required four years' previous citizenship. But Gerry, Williamson, and Butler were suspicious and chauvinistic, and the motion was lost, 7 to 4.[66]

Hamilton could not have remained long in the convention after his appearance there August 13, for we find him in New York on the 20th writing letters that indicate he had been home some days. "For the sake of propriety and public opinion" he offered to return to Philadelphia with Yates or Lansing if either of them would come down. He knew neither would do it; a quorum thus obtained for New York would have been footless anyhow because the vote of the state would have been divided on all important issues. However, Hamilton was eager to resume his place if a material change was made in the plan reported by the Committee of Detail, or if the convention was about to close its business, and asked Rufus King to inform him.[67] When King did not reply Hamilton renewed his request; he was anxious because he must be away on a circuit in a neighboring county for most of a week. He heard "that some late changes in your scheme . . . give it a higher tone."[68]

The "higher tone" referred to proposals tending to strengthen the central government in all departments, and not at all to a rumor that the convention was plotting to call the Bishop of Osnaburgh to head an American monarchy. This piece of gossip, started with mischievous intent, appeared in the *New York Daily Advertiser* on August 18.[69] Hamilton at once took pains to track the insinuation to its source, as he suspected "that it has been fabricated to excite jealousy against the Convention, with a view at [to] an opposition to their recommendations." As the letter was thought to have originated in Connecticut, he asked Jeremiah Wadsworth to make particular inquiry there, as he had "different reasons of some moment for setting it on foot." Crazy as the report was, it holds significance because Hamilton said it was "sent by one *Whitmore,* of Stratford, formerly in the Paymaster-General's office, to one James Reynolds of this city,"[70] who played a sorry part in Hamilton's story later.

The next mention of Hamilton in the convention proceedings is on September 6, which is probably as early as he attended.[71] In any event, since September 4 the convention had been pondering offerings from the committee of eleven (elected August 31)

which was to bring forward again in acceptable form all unfinished business. Chief debate was on the method of choosing
the President, than which no issue had been more disputed. As
the committee received the proposal, the President was to be
elected by a majority of the members of the two houses of Congress in joint balloting. The possible extremes were designation
by popularly chosen electors on the one hand, and by the states
in some fashion on the other. The committee presented a compromise: electors chosen as state legislatures should direct, and
apportioned to representation of each state in congress, to elect
the President; but in case of equal majorities or of no majorities,
the choice to fall to the Senate, the President to have a four-year
term and be reeligible.

This plan, though defended in different degrees by Gouverneur
Morris and others of the committee which had devised it, was generally condemned by delegates of various views otherwise, such as Mason, Wilson, Madison, Randolph, Pinckney, Williamson, Rutledge,
and Dickinson.[72] The main objection was that the proposed
mode made the President dependent on the Senate, which represented the states more directly than the people, gave to the
process an aristocratic cast, and invited to corruption.[73] Thus
matters stood on September 6. Hamilton's position, in his original scheme presented in June, and elaborated in his later plan,
gave the choice of President to popular electors, without intervention of the states by any means. This was inevitably his preference, since his government was a national one, acting on citizens
and therefore by their authority and with their support.

Dislike of the drift of the convention had restrained him from
taking part in the debates. However, "as he meant to support the
plan to be recommended, as better than nothing," he observed
that the revised method of electing the President was an improvement on the former one which made him "a Monster elected for
seven years, and ineligible afterwards." This would have tempted
him to subvert the government in what he would consider his "7
years . . . of lawful plunder." But the present expedient left
much to be desired. Votes of electors would be scattered; appointment would devolve on the Senate. The President would
attach the Senate to his interest "till at length they will . . . act
as one body." (Separation of powers was always an insistence

with him.) Confine the choice of President to electors, on the highest number of ballots, majority or not, and take from the Senate the trial of impeachments. He disagreed with those who demanded that all parts of the report please them. He would "take any system which promises to save America from the dangers with which she is threatened."[74] The efforts of Hamilton and others to keep the selection of President as close as possible to the people, and out of the Senate, resulted in amending the report to give eventual choice, in case of a tie in votes of electors, to the House of Representatives, each state having one vote.[75]

Hamilton was elected one of five on "a Committee . . . to revise the style of and arrange the articles agreed to,"[76] the others being William Samuel Johnson, chairman; Gouverneur Morris, Madison, and King. This committee must have begun its work at once (September 8), for action on its report was to conclude the convention, members were restless to be finished, and some left.[77] However, debates continued through the 10th, and adjournment was taken on the 11th until the Committee on Style was ready to report on the 12th. Thus in less than four days, with minor alterations in convention afterward, the Constitution was given its finished form. The responsibility "for the symmetry and phraseology of the instrument" was greater than Madison[78] or the other members of the committee of style, with the exception of Gouverneur Morris, could have realized at the time. Decisions of the courts were to hang on individual words, their position in clause and sentence, and even on punctuation points. Where every member of the five had unusual talents for the task, it was handed over chiefly to Morris.[79]

However, Hamilton was sufficiently occupied in the closing days of the convention in trying to get general approval among the delegates of a workable Constitution. In debates on the floor and undoubtedly in many conversations he was plying the arts of accommodation. Partly through his efforts at the time, more through reflections of delegates on the whole course of discussions, the instrument as completed approximated to his advocacies, if not to his full wishes.[80] His pleas for agreement, or at least adherence, were the more remarkable because conciliation was not his forte. He had commenced in the convention as an irritant, and was ending as a balm. For some of the delegates the convention had sat overlong; they suffered at the end from cabin fever.[81]   Hamilton, by contrast, had had the benefit of breaks in his attendance, was absent during some of the most stressful contests.   Paradoxically, his moral commitment to a system more centered, national, and consolidated than anyone else held, gave him a practical advantage in urging adjustments between proposals which differed less from each other than they fell below his ideal.   If he could point out a middle ground, this was a recommendation for its acceptance.   So it was that Franklin and Hamilton, the oldest and one of the youngest members of the convention, joined hands as peacemakers.[82]   Others with tolerance and foresight played similarly handsome rôles.

Hardly had the Committee on Style been chosen than Williamson, of North Carolina, moved a reconsideration of the clause governing the number of members of the House, with a view to increasing it.   The new rule, if agreed to, must of course be incorporated in the committee's report.   Madison seconded, but Sherman was opposed as he considered the then provision (65 representatives to begin with, and one for every 40,000 free inhabitants and three-fifths of the slaves thereafter) "amply sufficient."[83]   Hamilton immediately "with great earnestness and anxiety" supported the motion.   He was a friend to a vigorous government, but "held it essential that the popular branch of it should be on a broad foundation."   "The House of Representatives was on so narrow a scale as to be really dangerous, and to warrant a jealousy in the people for their liberties."   As the President would be in position to make common corrupt cause with the Senate, it was the more necessary to have a large representation in the other branch.   This was again Hamilton's mistrust of the states and his insistence on an unmuffled people's voice in the House, though the too frequent impression emphasizes his fondness for the Senate as the security for property.   The motion to reconsider (that is, to enlarge the House) was lost at that time—seemingly the last opportunity—by the vote of 6 to 5, the small states divided.[84]

Much the same question of citizens versus states arose next morning on proposal to reconsider the mode of amending the Constitution.   As it stood, two-thirds of the states could obtain an amending convention, a majority of which, ironically, could change the Union so as to subvert the state constitutions.   Hamilton seconded, but with a different motive from that of Gerry. He did not fear the majority in the nation any more than in a state. The means of amending the Confederation were too arduous; an easier way of correcting defects in the new system should be provided. "The State Legislatures will not apply for alterations but with a view to increase their own powers—The National Legislature will be the first to perceive . . . the necessity of amendments," and should be empowered, two-thirds of each branch concurring, "to call a Convention." Anyhow, the people would finally decide in the case.

The motion to reconsider was overwhelmingly passed. Gerry and Sherman wanted consent of all of the states to an amendment; Wilson lost his proposal of two-thirds, but the convention accepted his concession of three-fourths. Madison substituted, Hamilton seconded, a combination motion—amendments to be initiated by two-thirds of Congress or of the state legislatures, and to stand if ratified by three-fourths of the states. Rutledge secured immunity for the slave trade for twenty years, and with this proviso the amending power was approved as we have it.[85]

The other item that day concerned a grace note. Hamilton supported Gerry in his objection to installing the new Constitution without first obtaining the approval of Congress. The incident has been treated earlier in this chapter as an illustration of his orderly bent, his distaste for a runaway marriage, as it were, when nine states were minded to set up political housekeeping to themselves. Opponents professed to fear that Congress might refuse to submit the Constitution to the states, either from substantive rejection or because Congress had no power to destroy itself. Randolph took this occasion to begin his breast-beating that continued through the remainder of the convention and for months afterward. The states should have opportunity to propose amendments to go to a second general convention with authority to settle the Constitution finally. King and Sherman joined Gerry and Hamilton in asking for courtesy to Congress, adherence or dissent by the states, and an end to the matter. These showed the real respect for the labors of the delegates by declaring that the instrument they had fashioned should stand or fall on its merits, and need not be guarded by any parliamentary maneuver. They were borne down in the voting,[86] but in the event Congress of course approved anyhow, and might as well have been treated with full respect.

The remainder of Hamilton's part in the Constitutional Convention is quickly told. Apparently without his speaking, delegates discussed enlargements of the powers of the general government which were to enter into his policies later.[87] The difficulty of reporting minutely all public expenditures at definite intervals, as pointed out by numerous delegates, must have come back to Hamilton when, several years later, he was suddenly called upon by Congress to rehearse all Treasury operations—and almost immediately if he was to escape public suspicion that amounted to censure.[88] He with others had satisfaction, the very last day, in a quick action increasing representation in the House by allowing one member for every 30,000 inhabitants instead of every 40,000. Hamilton had contended for this in vain before, but now Washington's unique plea was decisive.

On Saturday, September 15, three delegates—Randolph, Mason, and Gerry—had explained with some solemnity why they could not put their names to the Constitution. After adjournment over Sunday, Franklin, Gouverneur Morris, Williamson, Pinckney, Hamilton, and others, hopeful that the objectors would relent, begged for unanimity in presenting the document to the country. "No man's ideas were more remote from the plan," Hamilton said, "than his own were known to be; but is it possible to deliberate between anarchy and Convulsion on one side, and the chance of good to be expected from the plan on the other[?]"[89] He may have had effect on Blount, who when Hamilton sat down said he would sign against his former determination. The obdurate Randolph held himself free to oppose the Constitution. Hamilton in his plea had pointed to the mischief "A few characters of consequence" might work by this attitude. Randolph took the remark to himself, just as Gerry felt personally wounded by Franklin's observations, which were of the kindest. Madison, summing up Hamilton's qualities in long retrospect, singled out his willingness to compromise for the sake of securing an acceptable Constitution. "If his theory of government deviated from the republican standard," wrote his old colleague in 1831, "he had the candour to avow it, and the greater merit of co-operating faithfully in maturing and supporting a system which was not his choice."[90]

As Yates and Lansing had absented themselves for the previous two months as proof of their disagreement, Alexander Hamilton alone signed the Constitution for the State of New York.[91]   Franklin had had the prescience to say that the test of the Constitution would be in the administration of the government of which it was the frame.[92]   His young friend from New York, after exerting himself mightily to secure the acceptance of the paper plan, was to find his greater triumph in making not a constitution, but a country.

25

The Art
of Persuasion

ON the score of popular fame alone, Hamilton's principal part in
The Federalist papers demands full treatment.[1]   The work at once
drew notice above the many other examinations of the Constitution, was five or six times issued in book form during Hamilton's
lifetime, and has since established itself as the historic commentary on the fundamental law of the United States.   Constant
quotation in the courts has made it the companion piece of the
Constitution itself.   Instances of appreciation of *The Federalist*
by statesmen and writers on the American political system could
be multiplied.[2]

Hamilton's public services may be depicted in terms of his
labors for the Constitution.   He repeatedly urged a convention
prior to that at Annapolis which resulted in the call for the Philadelphia gathering; he exerted himself in the latter, in spite of his
own reservations, to counter the inhibitions of others; immediately
afterward he began writing in favor of acceptance of the document.   These newspaper advocacies were preparatory to the
Poughkeepsie meeting where Hamilton's rôle was the most discouraging ever.   Then for half a decade he had daily responsibility for devising and directing instruments to bring the Constitution into operation.   In this sequence of fifteen years of eager
solicitude, *The Federalist* makes an integrating chapter.   If one
could read only a single set of his papers, this might be the choice
as summary of what went before and presage of what he would
accomplish later.

[414]

He did not always get off on the right foot, nor withdraw from a course whose injurious result was deplored by his friends. Of this last his pertinacious public attack on John Adams was the prime example. In the case of *The Federalist* he profited by early error. Hardly was the Constitution offered to the country than Governor Clinton, with the largest political following in New York, began publishing "Cato" against it.[3] Immediately after the first blast, Hamilton answered with his letters of "Caesar."[4] He called Clinton a demagogue, a designing croaker always exclaiming "my friends, your liberty is invaded."[5] But Hamilton soon saw that sarcasm and *argumentum ad hominem* were not what the situation demanded. The "first impressions, made [on the people] by every species of influence and artifice, were too strong to be eradicated" except by a studious effort "to cultivate a favorable disposition in the citizens at large."[6]

The result of second thought was the project of a series of newspaper essays directed "To the People of the State of New-York," in order to secure ratification in their convention. These would discuss calmly the utility of the Union, the insufficiency of the Confederation to preserve it and the necessity of an energetic government such as was provided in the new Constitution. It would be demonstrated that the proposed plan conformed to true republican principles, being analogous, in fact, to the constitution of New York.[7] Hamilton sent a correspondent samples of "Cato's" (Clinton's) attacks on the new Constitution, with the reply by himself ("Caesar"), but added that "On further consideration it was concluded to abandon this personal form and to take up the principles of the whole subject. These [papers] might with advantage be republished in your gazettes."[8]

From the outset it was intended that several authors should contribute over the one signature "Publius." Circumstantial evidence is that Hamilton originated the scheme. He wrote the first essay, an introduction to all that followed, as also, undoubtedly, the preface to the work when it appeared in book form. He wrote about two-thirds of the total number of papers. Madison recorded that the publication "was undertaken last fall [that is, 1787] by Jay, Hamilton, and myself. The proposal came from the two former. The execution was thrown, by the sickness of Jay, mostly on the two others."[9] More participants seem to have been solicited, either at the beginning or when Jay was unable to continue.   Gouverneur Morris, years later, said that he was pressed to help, but declined.[10]   William Duer, according to Madison, was expected to share the burden of authorship; he did prepare three essays in defense of the Constitution, signed "Philo-Publius," but they were not incorporated in *The Federalist* series.[11]

In any event, the work grew under the authors' hands.   Not only did it lengthen beyond first expectation, but after four or five months of steady newspaper publication, it was hoped that the essays, as made available in book form, would persuade readers not only in New York, but in the country generally, especially in the other states yet to ratify.[12]   The first number was in *The Independent Journal: or, The General Advertiser,* New York, October 27, 1787, occupying a column on the second page, the only one without advertisements, and continued another third of a column on page 3.   This was the usual length.   Sometimes two numbers were run the same day.   Advertisements and news items the day of Publius' debut convey the flavor of the town and the times.   Imports of many sorts were prominent in merchants' offerings, from "Swedes Bar-Iron" to Tenneriffe wines in quantity. The Waddingtons would sell (for pot and pearl ashes if necessary) calicoes, Black India Persians, Tammies, Durants and Mock Moreens, and Mohair Shags.   Isaac Hook, from London, made breeches and gloves "in a far superior manner to any yet manufactured in this Country."   Lot Merkel, Hanover Square, said candidly that besides Kitefoot "smoking" tobacco of first quality, he also had "Ditto . . . inferior."   Along with weed for the men he had vile weeds for the women—muffs and tippets of martin throat and real ermine.   If men were jealous, and leaned away from the animal kingdom, they could have, fresh from London, "new invented Vegetable Waistcoat Patterns, Vastly elegant." The news featured violence—a dangerous mob assembled when the King of France exiled the Parliament of Paris; on the Georgia frontier savages shot a girl "in three places" and scalped her, "notwithstanding which it was expected that she would recover." The series continued in *The Independent Journal* three or four essays a week, until April 2, 1788.   Meanwhile, on March 22, the first volume of the collected papers appeared, and on May 28 the second volume, this last containing the final eight numbers, there printed for the first time. Serial publication was resumed in the *Independent Journal* on June 14, 1788, and was completed August 16, three weeks after New York had ratified.[13]

The Federalist papers were written under stress. They must be published quickly if they were to refute the objections of the many opponents[14] and be in time to influence the composition and temper of the New York convention, delayed though that assembly was. John Lamb and Marinus Willett practically revived the Sons of Liberty for "the most thoroughly organized opposition."[15] Henry Knox wrote from New York City to Sullivan of New Hampshire: "The new Constitution! the new Constitution! is the general cry this way. Much paper is spoilt on the subject, and many essays are written, which perhaps are never read by either side. It is a stubborn fact however, that the . . . confederation, has run down. . . . the springs . . . have uetterly lost their tone; and the machine cannot be wound up again. But something must be done speedily, or we shall be involved in . . . the horrors of anarchy. . . ."[16]

Jay dropped out of the collaboration after preparing four numbers, not to contribute again except for a single paper toward the end.[17] Hamilton had his law practice, with attendance on the circuit.[18] Madison had his service in Congress, and must compress his work on the *Federalist* essays in order to leave New York early in March to reach Virginia before the election of delegates to the convention at Richmond.[19] Though both of them were in New York, or mainly so, during four months of the joint enterprise, they had little opportunity for conference to guard against inconsistencies, overlap, repetition, and disproportion. "Though [the publication is] carried on in concert," Madison warned, "the writers are not mutually answerable for all the ideas of each other, there being seldom time for even a perusal of the pieces by any but the writer before they are wanted at the press, and sometimes hardly by the writer himself."[20]

Fortunately, a certain division of labor was obvious: Jay, from his official experience, should treat foreign relations; Madison, having made an extensive inquiry, in preparation for the Philadelphia convention, into the weaknesses of ancient and modern confederacies,[21] should cover that area; fiscal and military matters fell in Hamilton's bailiwick. More important, however, all—Hamilton and Madison especially—were conversant with the whole problem. Madison was the author of the Virginia plan, the basis of the Constitution, and had chronicled every turn of debate at Philadelphia. Hamilton had made his own contribution to debate and document. Added to this knowledge was the mental and moral commitment of both, which had taught them to answer and to anticipate objections to the instrument of union. Thus equipped and prompted, they explored implications with ingenuity. Most would-be guides did not enter beyond the anterooms, while these penetrated to every hall and corridor, cellar to attic, of the proposed political edifice.

The authors of *The Federalist* were careful not to disclose their identities until the work appeared in book form, and then only to a few friends. Madison, in cipher, revealed the partners to Jefferson, and informed Randolph, not very cryptically, that another writer besides himself was a member of the Constitutional Convention.[22] Hamilton had a set specially bound for Washington, and explained, "I presume you have understood that the writers . . . are chiefly Mr. Madison and myself, with some aid from Mr. Jay."[23] Madison was to forward the books, and, evidently a decade later, indicated on the flyleaf the particular numbers by each contributor.[24] The earliest edition to contain the names of the authors was the Paris one of 1792, but long before this their identity was common property.

The authorship of nearly a score of the eighty-five *Federalist* papers has been in intermittent controversy for almost a century and a half. In spite of a sizable literature[25]—partisan and acrimonious, or scholarly and calm—a degree of uncertainty remains. Madison's part in the difference was indirect and terse, as became him, since Hamilton was long dead. The latter's friends and sons, by contrast, were contentious, not to say clamorous. Adair has noticed that[26] the refusal of Hamilton to have authorship of the respective papers ascribed in the Hopkins edition of 1802,[27] and the diffidence of Madison on the same head, was likely because the positions taken by each altered on salient points in the interval since original publication.

We may take the view that the whole was a tempest in a teapot. First, whatever the assignment of disputed pieces, no new light was cast on the opinions of Hamilton or Madison. (Only one of

Jay's contributions was ever in doubt, Number 64; that was early conceded by Hamilton's champions,[28] and soon was proved, by discovery in Jay's autograph, to belong to the latter.) Second, lacking as the controversy was in substantive significance, it rested on little more than Hamilton's carelessness in drawing his own list. The day before his duel with Burr he called at the office of his old friend Judge Egbert Benson; when he found Benson was gone to Massachusetts, he took from the bookcase a copy of Pliny's letters and left in it, in the sight of Robert Benson, the judge's nephew, a slip of paper, a fourth of a note-sized sheet. It was obviously a memorandum of the authors of the different numbers of *The Federalist,* and the elder Benson pasted it with wafers in his copy of that work. Later he kept a copy and presented the original to the New York Society Library, where it was as late as 1818 when William Coleman, seeking to confute Madison's list, invited any doubters to inspect it.[29]

Later this original Hamilton list disappeared, but from the Benson copy Dawson confirmed the report of its brief message:

> "Nos. 2, 3, 4, 5, 54, by J.
> Nos. 10, 14, 37 to 48 inclusive, M.
> Nos. 18, 19, 20, M. & H. jointly.
> All the others by H."

It is improper to attribute any errors in this memorandum to "haste . . . at a most agitating moment,"[30] because it must have been transcribed by Hamilton from the list in his copy of *The Federalist.*[31] The lists by Hamilton and by Madison respectively, as well as those attributed to them in one way and another, are inconsistent within themselves. From a comparison, a dozen numbers are contested, 49 through 58, and 62, 63. Ingenuity has been expended in arguments from external and internal evidence. None is conclusive. On the whole, the guess may be that Hamilton made two slips of the pen in his attribution in the Benson list, assigning 54 instead of 64 to Jay and 37 to 48, instead of 58, inclusive to Madison. On this supposition, his inattention was aided by turning Roman into Arabic numerals, but beside that Hamilton set less store than Madison did by what he had written. If his essays, letters, and reports could contribute to a desired result, that was important, but he did not pride himself upon the papers themselves.[32]   This leaves two numbers for allocation, 62 and 63.   They deal with the utility of the Senate, a favorite topic with Hamilton, and they come in a sequence the earlier numbers in which are admittedly his work.   The tone is less ardent than often, but, taking one thing with another, the choice may be to ascribe them to Hamilton.   If there is any virtue in attempting division, this yields five papers to Jay, twenty-four to Madison, three to Madison (mostly) and Hamilton jointly, and fifty-three to Hamilton.[33]

Thus far, in discussing *The Federalist,* we have dealt with shadow, not substance, spirit, and method of the work.   It was a tract for the times, pitched, in the first instance, to win New York to the Constitution and, at a later stage in the publication, to convince other doubtful states.   Only the calm thoroughness of the treatment gave it a more enduring application than the authors conjectured.   They were making a case in the court of public opinion, not offering a disquisition on republican government except incidentally.   They were not foretelling the far future in the development of American political institutions, save to the extent that eighteenth century writers leaned on "immutable" principles.[34]

Hamilton's tone and method in *The Federalist* papers were superior to his presentation of his own plan of a Constitution in the Philadelphia convention.   In the latter he was extreme and opinionated.   True, he was goaded by Clinton's opposition to the project of reconstructing the government,[35] and was induced by the hostility of Yates and Lansing to declare himself too far in the other direction.   The result was a display of personal preference, in favor of centralized authority, which depended on shock for its effect.   When, later in the meeting, he got down to give-and-take in debate, he was making a more definable contribution to the document that was hammered out.   His final acceptance of the Constitution as the best compromise that could be achieved, and his promise to work for its adoption in spite of his own dissents, launched him into his most useful service in its behalf.   His act of self-abnegation was his real triumph.   Thenceforward he left off arrogance, and took on maturity.

This more modest, but firm and ingenious, espousal of the practicable made his *Federalist* exposition and arguments persuasive.   Of course, his task was now different.   He was addressing not the elect in a closed room, but the voters out of doors.   He must come to particulars, and be patient. He was not proclaiming his own scheme, but was recommending a plan which had weighty composite approval. His plea was more masterful because less so.

If the Constitution itself was subtly devised to protect against popular assault, it is natural that Professor Beard, who elaborated this thesis, should attach the same character to *The Federalist* commentary. ". . . above all," said Beard, "it is to the owners of personalty anxious to find a foil against the attacks of levelling democracy, that the authors of *The Federalist* address their most potent arguments in favor of ratification."[36] Two objections occur. As the essays were pleas for approval by a New York State convention democratically composed, would this be sensible strategy? If the Constitution was disingenuous, should not its design be cloaked, not declared? The second doubt about this interpretation arises from the actual content of *The Federalist* papers. Many are expository, informational, and illustrative rather than argumentative with whatever purpose. It is chiefly Number 10 (by Madison) that is centered upon as betraying the intent of the authors to preserve the advantage of a minority possessing class. "The diversity in the faculties of men, from which the rights of property originate, is . . . an insuperable obstacle to a uniformity of interests. The protection of these faculties is the first object of government." The propertied few must be secured against predations of the politically powerful, but less endowed, many. Hamilton (in Number 9) called over the checks and balances that would prevent this outcome, and (in Number 78) urged the right of federal courts to hold statutes unconstitutional, as a further safeguard.

But the argument of jealousy for the privileged may be turned about. Perhaps the purpose of the *Federalist* writers was to show classes placed in counterpoise to render democracy, or representative government, workable; to protect popular sovereignty against the disruptive effects of passion, whipped up by would-be leaders with more talents than integrity. Plainly, the country was committed to the project of the people's self-government. That was the fact, not to be defeated, but to be furthered by practicable means. A false start had been made under the Confederation. When disaster loomed, the new Constitution was pledged as a rescue not of wealth but of commonwealth. Textual criticism of *The*

Federalist, as of holy writ, can run to lengths, and different quoters serve their different ends.   Just appraisal lies in estimate of the whole.   And not of these papers only, but of antecedent history, the confronting crisis, the opposition to be dissuaded, and the prior and subsequent rôles of the writers in the American scene.   In this light, a broader rather than a narrower interpretation seems proper.   The exertion to promote the Constitution was not covert, for a class, but *pro patria.*   If for no better reason, then because the effort sustained by the three (particularly Hamilton), who took upon themselves the task, was out of proportion to mean rewards for which individuals would volunteer.   We may infer the worthiness of the object from the degree of dedication.   Begin with suspicion of motive, and you may document accusation.   On the other hand, assume a generous purpose, and abundant evidence comes to your support.   The latter approach is here decidedly preferred.

The authors of *The Federalist* were midwives at the birth of modern popular government, not the tutors of youth, and less the counselors of manhood.   Much they did not anticipate.   On the threshold was the prudence of a bill of rights.   Hamilton, especially in the next to the last number (84) urged that such protections to liberty were sufficiently provided in the Constitution as drawn, and that a further specification might, in fact, lead to unexpected invasions of freedom.   Later amendments were more understandably beyond their ken.   Further, they did not envisage several of the by-products of American democracy in the mechanics of party management, such as nominations in conventions, the spoils system, and local boss rule.[37]   But they repelled more errors than they committed.   The President has not become a despot, the Senate an oligarchy; rights and functions of the states have not been lost in "consolidation," nor do the large ones invade the claims of the smaller.[38]   On the other hand, the authors' fear of insufficient strength in the central government, and not enough loyalty to it, proved to be well founded.   Their prescience was demonstrated within a decade in the Kentucky and Virginia Resolutions,[39] fifteen years later in the Hartford convention, after a similar interval in South Carolina nullification, and finally in secession of the Confederacy and civil war.

In parrying blows against and enlisting support for the Consti-

tution, the authors of *The Federalist* did the best job of public relations known to history.   Objectors were not so much repulsed
as refuted.   Honest fears were so far removed as to make the instrument of federal union appear feasible.   Ignorance was supplied with information and illustration of how the new system
might be expected to operate.   Dark examples of the fatal defects
of the Confederation brightened arguments for the substitute
scheme.   The manner was earnest rather than passionate, was
persuasive by a candor that avoided the cocksure.   Hamilton bore
hard on certain irreconcilables whom he knew to be disingenuous,
but these "intemperances of expression" he apologized for.   He
addressed his readers' judgments, and in a spirit of moderation.

His final appeal put all at hazard, as only a master advocate
will do, for the sake of winning all.   He would not pretend that
he felt "an entire confidence in the arguments which recommend
the proposed system to your adoption, and that I am unable to
discern any real force in those by which it has been opposed."
The plan, "not . . . perfect in every part, is, upon the whole, a
good one; is the best that the present views and circumstances of
the country will permit; and . . . promises every species of security which a reasonable people can desire."   That, and the
warning specter of "A nation, without a national government,"
concluded the plea.[40]   The language, always clear, in the last
number grew elementary.   The eloquence was in what critics of
that day called the "pathos" of simple sincerity.   It was not contrived, but sprang from a full heart and anxious mind.   It has
sometimes been said that Hamilton, with fastidious tastes, did not
know how to call forth a sympathetic response from the people,
that is, of all sorts.   It is true that he had no art for this, being
at the other pole from the demagogue.   His dependence was better, was upon his own humility and courage in the face of danger
that threatened all.   Many instances in his life, passages in his
writings, and speeches which, all but the memory, vanished in the
utterance, illustrate this.   The last number of *The Federalist* is an
example, to be read by the skeptical.

Sentences in his reply to "Cato" reveal Hamilton's opinion of
the rôle of the people in constitution-making.   He believed that
the public mind was "wound up to a great pitch of dissatisfaction,
by the inadequacy of powers of the present Congress to the gen-

eral good . . . of the union. . . . that the people were determined and prepared for a *change*." However, he continued, "I
consider them in general as very ill qualified to judge for themselves
what government will best suit. . . . ; nor is this to be wondered
at. . . . men of good education and deep reflection, only, are
judges of the *form* of a government. . . ." How were the people
to profit by their "inherent right" to accept or reject a proposed
constitution? ". . . by a tractable and docile disposition, and by
honest men endeavoring to keep their minds easy, while others, of
. . . genius and learning, are constructing the bark that may . . .
carry them to the port of . . . happiness, if they will embark without diffidence and proceed without mutiny."[41]

Many in the country were concerned to know how the federal
system would work—governments within a government. This was
not readily pictured to one's self or to others. Prospective perils
loomed large. The majority would oppress the minority, or a
minority, under the forms of law, would tyrannize over the majority. A demagogue might rise to despotism. These apprehensions
had to be explained away by *The Federalist* authors. Their task
was harder because most of their readers thought in ideal terms, in
absolutes of freedom or enslavement. The very fact of a written
Constitution invited dogmatism, literal interpretation. Trusting to
the total intention of the document, allowing flexibility for the
future was dangerous.

Hamilton felt less patience with this naïveté than he showed in
his *Federalist* papers. Tugging at his sleeve as he wrote was always the reminder that time would tell, that the proof of the
pudding was in the eating of it. What was needed was an energetic government competent to repair past and present damage and
to open a progressive future. Good administration of the proposed
system would reconcile the most fearful. The constitutional contest was a sham battle; victory or defeat would come on a different
field. This was Hamilton's insight that set him off from the political philosophers. Given a constitution, he knew, we still must
create a country. The mental construct was preliminary only.
The complicated machinery of weight and counterpoise, the contrived checks and balances, the nice equilibrium could be favorable
to the trial, but only successful operation could satisfy hopes. The
people who balked at words would afterward go along with works.

This was Hamilton's Federalist within *The Federalist*. The faith of most was in the letter, which therefore must be hedged. His was in the spirit that could give life. Paradoxically, precept was less ideal than practice. This was a conviction not popular to proclaim to those who considered the Constitution, for better or worse, the law of the Medes and Persians. If Hamilton had said too plainly, the Constitution is tentative, it is an opportunity, he could not have held hearers who demanded a guarantee. But his secret thoughts, betrayed now and then in *The Federalist* papers, were what soon animated his role in the Treasury. If one would read *The Federalist* with a perceiving eye he must run forward to the state papers and policies to which Hamilton gave himself so zestfully. Talk, yes, but his fingers itched to grasp the tools of national fulfillment. Could Galatea—not so perfect, either, as Pygmalion's ivory maiden—come to life? That was Hamilton's burgeoning hope. "Loose construction of the Constitution," some have said, and let it go at that. This short definition may stand if by it we mean that Hamilton admired the deed more than the document.

Hamilton's exertions in *The Federalist* should be viewed in the light of his exceedingly frank estimate of the chances of adoption of the Constitution. Thinking out loud, he listed as forces in its favor the popularity of Washington, the good will of most men of property, the hopes of creditors, and the wish of the people at large for shift from a government that could not preserve the Union and their safety. Against it would be a few important dissenters in the convention, state officers with interested motives, men much in debt, "democratical jealousy . . . of institutions that may seem calculated to place the power of the community in few hands," and some foreign governments. If the Constitution was not adopted, civil war and dismemberment would ensue. If adopted, Washington would be President, and "A good administration will conciliate the confidence and affection of the people, and . . . enable the government to acquire . . . consistency. . . ." The central authority "may then triumph altogether over the State governments, and reduce them to an entire subordination, dividing the larger States into smaller districts."[42] This last is close to what he said in the Philadelphia convention, and went much beyond the arguments in *The Federalist*.

26

Trial of Strength
at Poughkeepsie

FOLLOWING submission of the Constitution to the country, Hamilton was preoccupied with efforts for its ratification by New York, but with a keen concern for favorable results in other states, especially as decisions in these must bear on his own.[1] His Publius (*Federalist*) papers, turned out at the rate of better than two a week, took most of his available time, but his correspondence shows anxious focus on election of delegates to the Poughkeepsie and other conventions. His first optimism for the prospect in New York became doubt, then disappointment, and finally alarm.

Early in October 1787 he thought the outlook "throughout the State" was promising, but later in the month when the conflict was joined, "the artillery of its opponents makes some impression."[2] At the beginning of April 1788 he took comfort in Madison's election to the Virginia convention, and considered the result in New York still moot in spite of endeavors of Federalists in strongholds of the Antis upstate.[3] A month later he had been deep in the elections in New York, and while he awaited returns to resolve doubts lent a hand in Virginia by forwarding bound volumes of *The Federalist* to Governor Randolph.[4] Gouverneur Morris was on the ground in Richmond, working with Federalist leaders, and to him Hamilton wrote (May 19, 1788) his fears that the elections in New York had "gone wrong." He expressed a suspicion, which became a conviction with others of his party, that opponents of the Constitution were really enemies of the Union. "The language is that
[426]

if all the other States adopt, this is to persist in refusing the Constitution." Clinton had privately called the Union unnecessary,
and his stubbornness was a portent.

The people, in spite of falsehoods directed at them, were veering
toward approval of the Constitution. He appended the list of
delegates from New York City, elected "by a majority of nine or
ten to one. . . ."[5] That day he wrote much the same to Madison.
However, it seemed that the poll in Albany County had determined a majority against acceptance. As Clinton was "inflexibly
obstinate" in his authority, Hamilton could "count little on over-
coming opposition by reason. Our only chances will be the
previous ratification by nine States, which may shake the firmness
of his followers," with less hope from a further trend of popular
sentiment toward adoption. Thus action in Virginia would
prove critical. When the two conventions were in session, "It will
be of vast importance that an exact communication should be kept
up between us . . . ; and the moment *any decisive* question is
taken, if favorable, I request you to dispatch an express to me,
with pointed orders to make all possible diligence. . . . All expense
shall be thankfully and liberally paid."[6] He made a similar arrangement with John Sullivan, president of New Hampshire,[7] and
as soon as Sullivan's rider brought news of adoption at Portsmouth,
Hamilton got Schuyler to forward it by express to Madison to aid
the result in Richmond.[8] His eagerness for useful intelligence
spoke in willingness to pay from a slender purse for expresses covering a total of a thousand miles.

Just as Hamilton was in a running exchange with Madison to
ensure that any Federalist advantage in the Richmond convention
should be promptly applied to the deliberations at Poughkeepsie,
so George Mason, among the most influential enemies of the Constitution in the Virginia meeting, offered a correspondence with
Anti-Federalists in New York. Mason, on June 9, sent to John
Lamb, "Chairman of the federal Republican Committee" in New
York City, his proposed amendments, and Lamb passed them on
to the Antis at Poughkeepsie. Robert Yates was at once made
chairman of a committee "appointed by the Members in Opposition to the New System . . . with a special View to continue our
Correspondence on this necessary Subject." Yates found the proposed Virginia amendments congenial to his Poughkeepsie col-

leagues. He recited with satisfaction that the opponents of the Constitution, backed by the yeomanry of the state, had "a Majority of at least two to one" in the convention, and "neither Sophistry Fear or Influence will effect any change in their Sentiments." An opponent called these "a set of ignorant Dutchmen" whom Clinton, Yates, Smith, and Lansing had under "perfect command"; they banished "the most distant prospect that our Convention will adopt the New Constitution."[9]

Yates's confidence in the issue at Poughkeepsie led him to explain to Mason that "We would willingly open a Correspondence with your Convention but [for] the doubtful Chance of your obtaining a Majority, and the Possibility that we will compleat our Determination before we could avail ourselves of your advice. . . ." Mason could "rely on our fixed Determination that we shall not adopt the present Constitution without previous Amendments." Yates added that "We have had no Committee to draft Amendments, we therefore transmit you a Copy of those which many of us have agreed to," though it was possible some of these might be altered and others dropped.[10]

After the form of ratification by Virginia was known at Poughkeepsie, similar language began appearing in the New York convention, though the model may have been in Mason's amendments furnished to Yates and others earlier. In any case the omnibus resolutions introduced by Lansing on July 19 bore unmistakable likeness, not only in substance, but in trick of phrase, to those of Virginia. The appeal "to the Searcher of Hearts for the Purity of our Intentions" at once strikes the eye.

Richard Varick, Recorder, and the aldermen of New York City certified, on May 29, 1788, that "by the greatest number of votes" the delegates to the convention from the city and county of New York were John Jay, Richard Morris, John Sloss Hobart, Alexander Hamilton, Robert R. Livingston, Isaac Roosevelt, James Duane, Richard Harison, Nicholas Low.[11]

When he knew the results of the elections Hamilton was surprised at the size of the Anti-Federal victory—a majority of two-thirds in the convention and, as best he could judge, of four-sevenths in the state at large. But these adverse odds only hardened his resolve to overcome them. Trying to project the strategy of the Clinton forces, he was of two minds. They might make "an effort . . . to precipitate us" into rejecting the Constitution. However, busy inquiries persuaded him that leaders of the Antis in New York City preferred "a *long* adjournment—say, till next spring or summer." His diagnosis was that principal opponents of the Constitution were equally hostile to the Union. But they would not risk a swift veto on the Constitution because that would open a chasm between New York and adopting states, and between the parties within the state which would threaten a separation of the southern portion from the remainder of New York. Therefore a long adjournment would be the artful means to their final purpose. When the new government was organized, necessity of revenue would furnish a topic of declamation to strengthen minorities and perhaps undo the national plan. If the people disappointed this expectation, New York could come into the union at her leisure. In either case—of intended speedy refusal or watchful deferment—it was of prime importance to the result in New York that other states should ratify, else he feared disunion and civil war.[12]

As the sixty-five delegates to the convention assembled at Poughkeepsie, those from New York City and County, Richmond, Kings, and Westchester were solidly Federalist. They were Hamilton's shield and buckler. Contiguous counties were divided—Dutchess 4–2 for the Constitution, and Suffolk 3–1 for, and Queens more in favor. The interior counties, all above Dutchess, were Anti-Federal, with the exception of the towns of Albany and Hudson.[13]

New York City, throughout the sitting of the convention, was noisily for the Constitution, no matter how enervating the prospect at Poughkeepsie. The Federalists of the metropolis kept up a jubilant obbligato, come good news or bad from upriver; on favorable tidings from elsewhere they rang bells, fired cannon whose lanyards seemed ever to hand, and produced a huge civic procession before the destiny of the state was determined. When delegates passed the Battery bound for Poughkeepsie they were saluted by thirteen guns.[14] Governor Clinton and his party arrived by Captain North in twenty-four hours, and Mayor Duane and his company by Captain Mott that same Sunday afternoon. We do not know whether Hamilton came up from New York City or down from Albany, but doubtless he was early on the ground.

With a couple of days of leisure before the convention would
meet on June 17, delegates doubtless read the *Country Journal* of
the young Nicholas Power, especially as his print shop was "next
door to the Tavern of Mr. Thomas Poole, and nearly opposite the
Tavern of Captain Stephen Hendrickson, a few rods South of the
Court-House." As the town was sharply divided on the issue before the delegates, the paper had comfort for both sides. A letter
of "Turtle Dove" to "Mr. Soaring Lark" related, in the best style
of the day, that "The Hawks, Owls, Ravens, Vultures, Kites, & c.
are gathering all the sour, nautious, obscene, and offensive matters
. . . to burn our Phoenix, and out of her ashes is to arise an
enormous big Eagle, that is to prey upon us as long as there is
feather, skin, flesh, muscle, fiber, entrail, & c. left; and then they
are to take our bones to make nests of, to lay in, and to hatch
more of those greedy birds of prey; but let us destroy their eggs
sir. . . ."[15]

Hamilton's leading part in persuading the New York State convention to ratify the Constitution was his foremost political exploit.
His agency in the Annapolis Convention, in turning frustration to
new resolve, was an act of accumulated purpose aptly timed. The
element of surprise assisted him in nerving the disconsolate delegates to demand of Congress that it summon the states to a survey
of the structure of the Union. His work in the Philadelphia Convention contributed to give the Constitution national, as opposed
to federative, features, and strength in the central government
which the plan would have lacked without him. But his influence
and even his attendance was diminished by the dissent of his colleagues from New York.

His *Federalist* papers, aimed at the deliberations to take place
at Poughkeepsie, were ancillary to his achievement there. In this
series he had the major aid of Madison and moral support and
some manuscript, from Jay. While Hamilton wrote his *Federalist*
pieces under pressure of regular business, the problem was one of
exposition and argument where he could choose his own ground.
It was not debate, face to face and extemporaneous.

Some may consider that his reports as Secretary of the Treasury,
the organization of his own department and the power he exercised
in other branches comprise his main political accomplishment, giving sinews to the new government. In office he devised directions

of government as well as modes of administration, but the mixture of economic with political arts was prominent; the critical decision for national competence had been taken and remained to be put into force; Congress was largely innocent of independent program; and Hamilton operated under the sponsorship of George Washington.

But in the New York ratifying convention circumstances that favored his other feats were notably absent. Granted that he had perfectly briefed himself as far as previous thought and experience permitted. However, at Poughkeepsie he met a hostile overwhelming majority ably led. While the convention heard general argument, and points already familiar were reinforced, substantially the evidence was all in. The demand resolved itself into day-to-day, hour-to-hour maneuver to change unwillingness into assent, then and there. Nor was this a national forum where he could in a measure disregard local differences and prejudices. He must now appeal to his own state, which had its peculiar position in the Union and also was divided in sentiment between city and upcountry delegates. Already the prophet not without honor, this slight and fervent young advocate was viewed by most in his home convention with suspicion if not distaste. Hamilton had worthy helpers in men like Chancellor Livingston and John Jay, but he must supply both tenacity and tact, a combination of qualities not natural to him.

In a sense it is meaningless to say that he won the convention to the Constitution by sheer will power, for this is resolvable, as the record shows, into particular words and decisions at particular times in the course of weeks of debate. Yet it is the truth, for his will held not only determination, but readiness to sacrifice much to the main result. Never one to keep back his reserves, at this time more than others he threw himself with all he had into the fateful contest.

The conventions in Virginia and New York were similarly critical. They met simultaneously, late in the season after eight states had accepted the Constitution, and either of these might or might not be the ninth to ratify and so make the new government a reality. No doubt existed about the recalcitrance of Rhode Island toward the Constitution; her enemies were unsparing in their scorn; what friends she had offered for her little in excuse and less in praise. North Carolina was aloof as much as hostile, was recognized to hang upon the action of Virginia, had fewer men of distinction among the leaders, and had not come to anything like her later relative importance. The position of New Hampshire was more in question, she having adjourned her convention to a later decision. But if New Hampshire ratified, and perhaps North Carolina too, the adherence of either Virginia or New York was agreed to be necessary, in fact, to the success of the national project. Probably both were essential, for different reasons. Virginia was the largest, wealthiest, most populous commonwealth, the home of Washington and a corps scarcely inferior; and, despite the claims of South Carolina, Virginia was chatelaine of states below the Potomac. Since Pennsylvania and Massachusetts had already ratified, New York, especially because of the commerce of her metropolis, formed an indispensable link between the two main parts of the country. Both Virginia and New York were supposed to be too capable of economic and political independence for the Union to prosper without them.

Hamilton's problem at Poughkeepsie will be clearer if we contrast the convention at Richmond, which Madison undertook to manage, with that which Hamilton faced. Fewer delegates in Richmond were known, in the beginning, to be committed against the Constitution. The Philadelphia convention had built on the Virginia Plan, more delegates at Richmond had been parties to the construction of the Constitution, and these included the governor, Edmund Randolph. Though Washington was not of the Virginia convention, he was a palpable presence in it, and every delegate knew that to reject the new government was to disavow Washington as its first President. Edmund Pendleton, the presiding officer of the Virginia convention, was a staunch friend of the Constitution, and took active part in the debates. Others of the same persuasion, who were at liberty to speak oftener, were superior in numbers if not in talents to those in New York who stood at Hamilton's side.[16]

In New York Governor George Clinton was president of the convention and, though he spoke little and then only when cornered, was the real leader of the opposition. Unlike Governor Randolph of Virginia, he enjoyed the advantage of having been a general in the Revolution as well as a successful politician. On the other hand, while Randolph's resourceful support of the Constitution at Richmond suffered from his refusal to sign the document at Philadelphia, Clinton's affection for the rights of the state under the old government was diminished as a plea by the failure of New York to meet requisitions during the war.

How did the chief debaters against the Constitution in the two conventions compare? Patrick Henry spoke more than any other man in either assembly. His eloquence has faded in the stenographic report. It is difficult now to see how he could have been convincing when he declaimed for liberty but failed to show how the Constitution would infringe it. To the present-day reader of the debates he was sounding brass, ill equipped in a knowledge of history, and terrifying with possible dangers rather than dealing with the probable operation of the new plan. He reminds us of the Old Bolsheviks of Russia, superlative at revolution but without will or art for operational revision. Most of all, as at other times in his career, his sincerity was in question; his fierce animus toward the Northern states sprang (not very logically) from solicitude for his own holdings of Southwestern lands, and his demand for amendments of the Constitution prior to ratification cloaked his intention to block adoption altogether. Still, there must have been a magic in his manner that was not in his mind, and pride and prejudice accepted him as a champion. Madison, Randolph, Nicholas, Marshall, and Innes countered his echoing periods with calm appraisal. The cause of the Constitution benefited when the convention came to cases and considered the document clause by clause. It was as though night fears had been driven away by daylight.

By contrast, Melancton Smith, who was Hamilton's chief antagonist in the Clinton majority, while he similarly was handicapped by a negative position, was sincere and a reasoner rather than an orator, avoided flourishes, came to grips with particulars, met on their own ground the men who were for the Constitution. He could not be by-passed and left to his laments, as could Henry; he must be confronted and convinced. His integrity and intellect, certainly in the New York setting, made him the more dangerous enemy of the two.

On the other hand, Hamilton, as compared to Madison, in setting himself to win his convention for the Constitution, was ironically aided by the greater likelihood of ratification in Virginia. It was all but taken for granted by the opposition in Richmond that New York would refuse adoption, which encouraged Virginia objection. Contrariwise, New York delegates who were opposed, knowing that the Virginia contest would be close, were more fearful of the consequences of their state being isolated from the Union and open to foreign attack.

A contrast was that Hamilton played for delay at Poughkeepsie until reason could break down party resistance, while Madison feared dragging out of debate at Richmond because this gave time to Patrick Henry and others to confirm Kentucky delegates in their opposition.[17] Under the circumstances of the two conventions, it was probably harder to protract discussion at Poughkeepsie than to provoke decision at Richmond.

These conventions afforded the last instance of fraternal cooperation of Hamilton and Madison in the national cause. In those weeks in the summer of 1788, as one labored in the North, the other in the South, they were the most tried men in America, and they had their triumph together. For three years—in the Annapolis Convention, at Philadelphia, in the assiduous authorship of *The Federalist* papers, and in final ratification—they formed such a team as constitutional history has not seen before or since. During this period they were not so much complementary as they were identical in diagnosis of debility of the Confederation and in design for thorough reconstruction. They were similar in devotion, in knowledge, in habit of reasoning, and in gift of exposition. A temperamental difference there was, and it showed itself in the work of each. Hamilton had a quality of excitement which Madison did not possess, or which lay so deep in his intellectual processes that it rarely needed to be repressed. Both were vintage wine, one effervescent, the other still.

Their mutual assistance, and trust, ended with the second session of the first national Congress, when Madison had qualms about Hamilton's insistence on payment of the domestic debt to the then holders, with no attempt to compensate prior owners for their losses. Madison stood for what he felt to be fair, Hamilton for what he considered feasible. Their break did not come at once and completely. They gradually drew apart as one policy after another had to be whittled out. The national union being established, patriotism for each expressed itself in party. Sectional and local distinctions asserted themselves—Northern and Southern, commercial and agricultural, urban and rural. Madison had been the first of the pair to set in train the events that led directly to the new government. Therefore Hamilton continued on the offensive after Madison slipped back into a defensive role. Further, Hamilton was obliged to devise economic plans that were not in Madison's competence. The severance was melancholy, sympathy that became suspicion. But it could not be otherwise if, as we believe, men are the instruments more than the masters of history.

Our knowledge of the proceedings of the New York State convention that met in the court house at Poughkeepsie, Dutchess County, June 17 to July 26, 1788, is satisfactorily full from numerous sources. Most serviceable is the stenographic report of debates taken, edited, and published by Francis Childs.[18] This is complemented by the printed official journal of the convention, which has no speeches but all of the formal actions and documents.[19] Papers of the convention (certificates of election of delegates, draft resolutions, records of balloting) and a partial report of debates in the hand of John McKesson, one of the secretaries, complete the official accounts.[20] Three members of the convention made notes of debates and outlines of their own speeches. The briefest are Hamilton's, often mere jottings on points made by his opponents, but including plans of two speeches by himself.[21] Gilbert Livingston kept a lengthy record of debates, probably of the whole convention, though what has survived covers only the last third of the meeting.[22] Chancellor Robert R. Livingston left a less orderly account, though supplying deficiencies in Childs's report, and including what might be called the manuscript of his own opening speech.[23] Some of the few speeches of Clinton survive in Bancroft transcripts, though the originals were destroyed by fire.[24] James Kent, then a young attorney in Poughkeepsie, was present daily at the convention as an absorbed spectator and listener, and more than forty years afterward wrote out for Mrs. Hamilton a narrative of her husband's leading part in the assembly.[25] Hamilton's papers in the Library of Congress contain a tolerably full report of debates, in an unidentified contemporary hand; it is not a copy of notes taken by Hamilton or by R. R. Livingston, for each of these is referred to in the third person.[26] Lastly, the *New York Daily Advertiser,* Childs's paper which in the main carried his stenographic report, toward the end of the convention contained shorter and often more revealing descriptions of proceedings that made no pretense to being verbatim.[27]

Poughkeepsie had been in effect the state capital since Kingston was burned by the British in 1777.   The legislature met there most of the time, Governor Clinton lived there (in all probability in the Crannell house), and other state officers remained in the town.   It was a busy river port which doubled its inhabitants in the two decades before the ratifying convention assembled.   Dutchess County, the second in the state, had 32,000 population.   Hamilton, Jay, and other lawyers in the convention were frequently in attendance on the courts, and the bar of the place, headed by Egbert Benson, the attorney-general, included Gilbert Livingston and his young partner James Kent.[28]   The court house was designated in the legislature's call as the meeting place of the convention. The third on the site on the west side of Market Street between Main and Union, it had been completed, at a cost of £4800, only a year before the convention met.   It was of stone, two stories, with a cupola, and an underground vaulted dungeon complete with manacles and iron rings in floor and walls for securing prisoners.   The courtroom was large enough to hold the sixty-five members of the convention, plus a hundred, and occasionally twice as many, visitors.[29]

Kent late in life recorded that the New York convention "formed the most splendid constellation of the sages and patriots of the Revolution which I had ever witnessed, and the intense interest with which the meeting . . . was anticipated and regarded can now scarcely be conceived. . . ."   Of the sixty-five members, "nineteen were Federalists, or in favor of the adoption of the Constitution, and forty-six were Anti-Federalists, or against the adoption of it without previous amendments."[30]   Hamilton and his eight fellow delegates from New York City and County were the corps of the minority in support of approval of the Constitution without conditional amendments, which won to itself a majority.   From Ulster came Governor Clinton and five more; from Albany, Robert Yates and John Lansing, who had been Hamilton's dissenting colleagues in the Philadelphia convention, together with Henry Oathoudt and four others.   Melancton Smith, Jacobus Swartwout, Jonathan Akins, Zephaniah Platt, Ezra Thompson, Gilbert Livingston, and John D'Witt were delegates from Dutchess, the Clinton stronghold.

The familiar question of the hero in history confronts us when we recount the course of the Poughkeepsie convention. It is certain that without able support for the Constitution the large and welded majority against it would have prevented ratification at that time. The method might have been adjournment without action, as Hamilton first surmised, or the Clinton party might have demanded amendments, by a second general convention, as the condition of acceptance by New York. The opposition would not have been deterred from either of these modes of defeat, or delay, by the adherence of the ninth state, New Hampshire, or even the tenth, Virginia. In fact, the result in New Hampshire was already discounted when the Poughkeepsie convention met.

The leaders for ratification overcame the peril of prompt refusal by holding the convention together past the fortnight that Hamilton first thought might close the meeting.[31] The principal means was the agreement, at the outset, to discuss the Constitution clause by clause before a general question on it was taken. Yates betrayed, while he disavowed, misgivings because the Antis, despite their majority, acquiesced in this procedure: "We yeilded [*sic*] to a Proposal made by our Opponents to discuss the Constitution in a Committee of the whole, without putting a Question on any Part, provided that in the Course of the Discussion, we should suggest the Amendments . . . which we deemed necessary. . . . Fully relying on the Steadiness of our Friends we see no Danger in this Mode and we came into it to prevent the Opposition from charging us with Precipitation."[32] The manuscript original of the motion (Number 1) which prevented enemies of the Constitution from using their overwhelming majority to reject the document as it stood begins in the hand of Hamilton and the remainder is in that of Chancellor Livingston. This was early evidence of the cooperation of the two throughout the convention.[33]

But that much said, what then—after more than three weeks of further debate—produced New York's adherence? Was it persuasive argument converting minds to the positive merits of the Constitution, providing an effective union? Or was it mere persistence and parliamentary skill that protracted the meeting until the hazards to New York of remaining outside percolated and

changed a massive majority against to a bare majority for?   In
the end, was victory due to endeavor or to events?

That Hamilton and his talented Federalist colleagues performed
an intellectual and moral feat, rather than simply assisting toward a
foregone verdict, is the correct conclusion.[34]   Not the least evidence of this is that Hamilton's own calculation of the favorable
effect of adoption by other states was long disappointed.

As late as June 27, echoing earlier expressions, he wrote to Madison, laboring in the Virginia convention, that "our chance of
success depends upon you."[35]   R. R. Livingston had directed his
opening speech at the dangers to New York of isolation.   This had
been a common theme with others.   S. B. Webb, in January 1788,
wrote from New York that should Massachusetts reject the Constitution "we are ruined, on them depends every thing, every
Federal Man in this City looks up to your State for our political
salvation, for . . . if Massachusetts, Connecticut & New Hampshire accept it, tolerably unanimous, this state dare not refuse. . . ."
June 26, after New Hampshire ratified, "The question now is,
whether this State are able and choose to remain out of the
Union. . . ."[36]   A Poughkeepsie correspondent, the day after
news of Virginia's adoption was received, said emphatically: "We
fondly (but in vain) expected that the ratification by Virginia would
have a very serious effect on the minds of the antifederal party, and
would have constituted so forcible an appeal to their apprehension,
that it would have compelled them to adopt a system different from
that destructive one they seem intent on pursuing.   We find that
the powers of eloquence and argument are unavailing; we shall
therefore refrain from any further exertions in defense of the Constitution.   We shall close the whole business with a strong pathetic
address to their fears . . . arising from the new position of the
State, if placed out of the Union. . . ."   When Congress acted to
put the government in motion, the majority of delegates (Antis)
would lose confidence of their constituents.   "This probably will
be the foundation of an appeal of the minority to the inhabitants of
the State."[37]

Schuyler, while remaining in Poughkeepsie in hopes of rendering
his country some service, was less optimistic: "The adoption of
the constitution by New Hampshire . . . will be the means of
ultimately bringing this state into the union, . . . yet I have no

reason to conclude that it is attended with such effect as to induce the convention to adopt the constitution otherwise than with previous amendments. Perhaps they may adjourn under pretense of taking the sense of their constituents. . . ."[38] Six days after Virginia's ratification was announced at Poughkeepsie, Hamilton descried nothing better than "some ground of hope,"[39] and casting up the odds a fortnight later, on the very eve of success, could vouchsafe only that "Upon the whole . . . our fears diminish."[40]

After ten states had come in, after the sanction of Virginia portended a new state of Kentucky and that promised the creation of another in Vermont,[41] after New York was left in company of the wavering North Carolina and the utterly wayward Rhode Island, arduous weeks of struggle lay ahead of Hamilton and his friends. The prize at which they aimed was more than New York, as no one realized better than Hamilton. It was the Union, which could not be viable with that central state, its harbor and the Hudson, left out.[42] It was like pounding on a block of granite from which the sledge bounced off with no visible effect, until finally, the inner tensions of the rock destroyed, the whole fell apart. No matter how anxious the effort, Hamilton exulted in it. He was young, believed in his cause and in himself, and was never in his career more resourceful, in completer command of his powers than at Poughkeepsie. A minority was his milieu.[43] Without his reasoning and unwearied refutation of errors dishonest and honest, New York, however nudged into compliance by the example of ten states that ratified, might have chosen to follow the two that were recalcitrant.

From McKesson's minutes it appears that Hamilton was on his feet in the convention fewer times (twenty-six) than either of his chief opponents, Melancton Smith rising forty-five times (often to offer amendments), and Lansing thirty times. However, Hamilton's Federalist colleagues spoke frequently and at length—R. R. Livingston on twelve occasions, Jay on eighteen, Duane eight. Clinton spoke eleven times, Gilbert Livingston seven, Yates only twice. As in most of the state conventions, a few champions were expected to develop the debate, members less prominent and articulate, or perhaps less committed, reserving their testimony for brief deposit at the end.

Hamilton spoke on more than the nine days when he was reported by Childs, as we know from Gilbert Livingston's notes, and as was bound to be the case in the last weeks when the debate became staccato.   Hamilton made his longest speech June 27–28, when the contest enlisted, among others, Chancellor Livingston, Smith, Clinton, Duane, Tredwell, and Lansing.   Heat was engendered, for on Monday, June 30, despite Sunday's intermission, "The personal dispute between Mr. Hamilton and Mr. Lansing was again brought forward, and occupied the attention of the committee [of the whole], for a considerable part of this day."[44]

27

Victory

Against Odds

AFTER organization of the Poughkeepsie convention the first speeches, as was inevitable and useful, ranged over merits and defects of existing and proposed plans of government, and a deal of American and European history besides. The later resolve to consider the Constitution clause by clause was never more than technically observed, for previous and fresh debaters reverted to or were itching to express their general observations. It must have been apparent to everyone that the leaders of both sides were caucusing between sessions, assigning points to be brought forward by each speaker and the juncture at which he would take the floor. Generally Lansing for the *cons* and Chancellor Livingston for the *pros* broached a subject and received the first blows of the other side; Smith and Hamilton came in later to reinforce contentions and later still to clinch the argument. These two were clearly foremost champions. The prepared cooperation of Livingston and Hamilton must have been especially obvious. The chancellor, in addition to his own knowledge and convictions, made good use of Hamilton's briefing, but the superiority of Hamilton's acquaintance both with economic and with political topics, the facility with which he blended detail and principle, and his greater moral earnestness could not have escaped the delegates.

Chancellor Livingston made the opening statement for the Federalists, describing the dangerous weaknesses of the Confederation.

[441]

His exposition and arguments had been planned with Hamilton, as appears from internal evidence and from Hamilton's subsequent defense of Livingston's positions. The chancellor's address was a good keynote for contenders for the Constitution—comprehensive, balanced, reasonable. We may apply what Kent said of him on another occasion, that his "tall and graceful person . . . and his polished wit and classical taste, contributed . . . to deepen the impression . . . from the ingenuity of his argument, the vivacity of his imagination, and the dignity of his station."[1]

Men who were content to put up with demerits of the Confederation were quick to demand that the proposed Constitution contain all the virtues. They would rather bear the ills they had. This line of attack led into denunciation of oppressions with which the new instrument was pregnant. Of these opening gambits of the opposition—depreciation, or what the Constitution would not do, and damning of what it would do—the first was the more dangerous and difficult to counter. Fears could be calmed, but scorn, perched on a pinnacle, was hard to dislodge. Delegates who had not been called upon to construct an improved plan of government, nor been obliged to wrestle with vexations and accept compromises, sat in superior judgment. At Philadelphia, they said, the mountain had labored.

This had been the language of doubters as soon as the text of the Constitution was known, and at many points blocked the path of its friends in the state conventions. Thus Livingston, as he faced the two-to-one opposition, properly commenced with: "I dread lest the chimerical ideas of perfection in government, which gentlemen may have formed, should induce them to reject this, as falling short of their standard."[2] He then reminded of distresses that pointed the necessity of a firmer union. His matter-of-fact allusions were better than detailed indictment: "These topics . . . lie heavy at every patriot heart; they have induced states the most independent . . . to unite . . . to remove them; they operate with peculiar force" on New York. "Our existence as a state depends on a strong and efficient Federal Government."[3] The Confederation possessed, nominally, most of the powers the Constitution conferred on Congress. "But . . . the defect of the system rested in the impossibility of carrying into effect the rights invested in [Congress] by the States."[4]

In sum, "the old confederation was defective in its principle, and impeachable in its execution, as it operated upon States in their political capacity, and not upon individuals; . . . it carried with it the seeds of . . . its own dissolution." Well knowing the proprietary concern of Governor Clinton and his friends in the importance of the State, he concluded with the plea: "As magistrates we may be unwilling to sacrifice any portion of the power of the State—as citizens, we have no interest in advancing the powers of the State at the expence of the Union. . . ."[5]

John Lansing, Jr., followed Livingston. Only a year older than Hamilton, he was the faithful protégé of Clinton, to whom he owed his elevation to a variety of offices. His sincerity and competence in the discharge of these assignments made him a better sort of machine politician. Later in life these qualities, and his occasional independence of Clinton and Yates, justified Hamilton in urging the Federalists to support him for governor against Aaron Burr in 1804, whereby hung a fatal tale. His predilection against the Constitution was plain when, with Yates, he quit the Philadelphia convention after six weeks.[6]

Lansing undertook to answer Livingston and to announce the grounds of the opposition. The modern reader finds his objections lacking. Because the Constitution *was* adopted, the arguments against it now sound hollow, seem to have sprung from self-importance and ill will. In trying to take seats in the audience at Poughkeepsie we may remind ourselves that the wisdom of hindsight obscures the crisis that was then genuine. We know more of what was written and said than any man in that company was possessed of. We have the debates in the Philadelphia convention, which were then in the experience of only a few and in the private notes of fewer. We may examine the reasoning in all of the state conventions, then imperfectly reported or understood. Local and sectional attachments were infinitely stronger than since. Dangers that are for us exploded were for them alive with possibilities. All of the debaters, though they had no shafts that surprised their chief opponents, took as their target the delegates who were wavering, or unapprized of any but a few leading issues. The convention at Poughkeepsie was anything but a sham battle. Furthermore, that was the day of the public platform, now largely usurped by press, radio, and television, when oratorical delivery was expected and enjoyed, when sound, even more than now, could substitute for sense.   The back benches demanded a show, and the front benches would not deny it to them.

Lansing maintained that European confederacies, whose weaknesses Livingston had stigmatized, were not comparable with the more homogeneous American one.   He made no distinction between powers to be lodged with the general and those with the individual sovereignties, "but, as the State Governments will always possess a better representation of . . . the people at large, . . . those powers can be deposited with much greater safety with the State, than the general Government."   Shortcomings of the Confederation were capable of amelioration.   Defect of requisitions might have been remedied "by permitting the United States to legislate on individuals after the requisitions had been made, and not been complied with."   Both sides recognized that if Congress could not supply itself with funds—independently, surely, and swiftly—the whole reform would be nugatory.   Lansing, in the eyes of opponents, did not help his proposal of conditional coercion, by the expedient that "loans of money might be negociated [*sic*] when necessary [because of temporizing by the states], and Congress be authorized to raise money to replace them."[7]

Lansing was persuaded that the languishing condition of commerce could not be attributed to the impotence of Congress.   He neglected a painful history in observing that "all the states, excepting two, has passed laws to enable Congress to regulate commerce. . . ."   He exculpated the Confederation on other scores. No government could have expelled the British from the Western posts while we were defenseless against coastal attack; financial embarrassments flowing from war exhaustion and over-orders from Europe were wrongly laid to want of energy in the system.[8]

Livingston had forecast that New York, if it refused union, would be open to conquest; that at worst, said Lansing, would subject the people to be ruled by those they did not choose—just what the proposed new government would do.   He would risk a possible evil to avoid a certain one, and in the painful event of a dissolution of the Union, New York would doubtless join itself to similarly disposed New England states.   Every amendment to lessen invasion of civil liberty would have his approval.   He rejected Livingston's imputation that state officers opposed the Constitution because it would diminish their autonomy and emoluments; Livingston was himself "possessed of one of the most lucrative offices of the state. . . ."⁹

The chancellor refuted Lansing's "idea . . . that Congress should make requisitions on the states, and on their noncompliance, the compulsory authority should be exercised on individuals." Congress must have its revenue officers; if the states complied, two establishments must be supported, and if they were delinquent, "what an alarming image of disorder is presented to our view! A body of federal officers, in the heart of a state acting in direct opposition to the declared sense of the legislature." A government thus formed for dissension would be forever impracticable.¹⁰

Melancton Smith rose for the opposition. Kent, the best witness, called him "the most prominent and . . . responsible speaker on the Anti-Federal side. . . . There was no person to be compared to him in his powers of acute and logical discussion. He was Mr. Hamilton's most persevering and formidable antagonist. . . . The style . . . of Smith's speaking was dry, plain, and syllogistic, and it behooved his adversary to examine well the ground on which they started, . . . or he would find it . . . embarrassing to extricate himself from a subtle web. . . ."¹¹ He offered rejoinders to the general reasoning of Chancellor Livingston, who, he thought, had overdrawn the perils of the Confederation. "If a war with our neighbors was to be the result of not acceding, there was no use in debating here; we had better receive their dictates, if we were unable to resist them. The defects of the old Confederation needed as little proof as the necessity of an Union: But there was no proof in all this that the proposed Constitution was a good one." He was pleased to hear Livingston candidly admit that the Constitution was no confederacy, but a consolidated government.

On the representation clause, he considered the rule of apportionment unjust because it embraced three-fifths of the slaves who, not being free agents, could have no part in government. The number of representatives ought to be higher—according to an amendment he introduced, one for every 20,000 inhabitants until the total number in the house was 300. Increasing the representation and confining the powers of Congress to national objects only would be essential safeguards.¹²

Hamilton followed Smith this second day.   In his speeches and briefer statements in the convention he was repeating analyses, arguments, and phrases perfected in his efforts of a decade to give the central government new scope and energy.   In the focus of debate his language was terse and more animated than ever.   The verdict of those he addressed was to be decisive, certainly for his own state, probably for the Union.   He had made his compromises and would not grant further concessions.   The Constitution was less than he had first striven for, but he had accepted the practical necessity and become its loyal defender.   He would be conciliatory in manner in order to win over a majority, but he was through with yielding on principles.[13]

Hamilton swiftly rehearsed Livingston's reasoning to support it against the attacks of Lansing and Smith, particularly the attempt of the latter "to cast a light air on this important subject. . . . I will not agree with gentlemen, who trifle with the weaknesses of our country; and suppose, that they are enumerated to answer a party purpose, and to terrify with ideal dangers.   No, I believe these weaknesses to be real, and pregnant with destruction."   It was necessary "to dwell upon the imbecility of our Union; and to consider whether we, as a State, could stand alone."[14]

He repelled the "lurking favorite imagination" that the existing system "with correctness, might become a safe and permanent one. . . . We contend that the radical vice in the old confederation is, that the laws of the Union apply only to States in their corporate capacity. . . . Hence there have ever been thirteen different bodies to judge of the measures of Congress—and the operations of government have been distracted by their taking different courses."   He skillfully appealed to the experience of New Yorkers who when the state was most forlorn in 1779 and 1780 had complied with the requisitions and been "compelled by the delinquency of others, to bear most unusual burdens. . . . Sir, if we have national objects to pursue, we must have national revenues. If you make requisitions, and they are not complied with, what is to be done? . . . to coerce the states is one of the maddest projects that was ever devised.   A failure of compliance will never be confined to a single State. . . . can we suppose it wise to hazard a civil war. . . . Then we are brought to this dilemma—either a federal standing army is to enforce the requisitions, or the Federal

Treasury is left without supplies, and the government without support. What, Sir, is the cure for this great evil? Nothing, but to enable the national laws to operate on individuals, in the same manner as those of the states do."[15]

In this and other allusions to federal taxes conditional upon willingness of the states to respond, Hamilton described military action against a state in terms that would have embarrassed him only six years later when, as Secretary of the Treasury, he urged forceful crushing of the Whisky Insurrection. True, it was not the legislature of Pennsylvania which refused to pay the excise, but only the majority of the people in the western counties, when the national laws were made "to operate on individuals." In the event, because he was aware that the situation approximated the one earlier forecast, he enlisted the reluctant Governor Mifflin and the eastern Pennsylvania militia in putting down the rebellion, and recommended that the disciplinary force contain militia from three neighboring states.

He went on to conclude: "The fundamental principle of the Old Confederation is defective. We must totally eradicate and discard this principle before we can expect an efficient government." During the war common danger prevented full operation of the ruinous weakness, "But since the peace, . . . we have felt the poison of the system in its unmingled purity."[16]

He explained the compromises in the Philadelphia convention, said any future convention—such as opponents proposed—would similarly have to accommodate clashing interests, and defended the apportionment of representatives as convenient and not liable to abuse.[17] His treatment of the last question was a model of persuasion. He appealed to the example of New York, which had sixty-five members in the State Assembly—the same number as would form the first national House—and challenged delegates to give reasons for a better rule than that provided in the Constitution.

Melancton Smith wanted the representation in Congress to be large enough to embrace principally "men in the middling class" rather than members of the "natural aristocracy" of "birth, education, talents and wealth." "To exercise the power of laying taxes . . . with discretion, requires something more than an acquaintance with the abstruse parts of the system of finance. It calls for a knowledge of the circumstances . . . of the people in general," such as is possessed by the yeomanry. A small representation would attract only men of public pretensions and ambition. "This will be a government of oppression."[18]

In answer, Hamilton gave one of the clearest statements of his principles of government. It should be read by those who regard him as striving to engross power for the privileged, excluding the common run of citizens from place and influence. "In my reasonings on the subject of government, I rely more on the interests and opinions of men, than on any speculative parchment provisions whatever." Despotic governments, even, depend in a great degree on opinion. "In free republics, . . . the will of the people makes the essential principle of the government; and the laws which control the community receive their tone and spirit from the public wishes. It is the fortunate situation of our country, that the minds of the people are exceedingly enlightened and refined." In the ancient pure democracies, where the people assembled, "the field of debate presented an ungovernable mob, not only incapable of deliberation, but prepared for every enormity," and "the enemies of the people brought forward their plans of ambition systematically."

But it was not true that popular trust demanded a numerous representation. "The confidence of the people will easily be obtained by a good administration. This is the true touchstone." The information required for regulation of commerce and taxation, in the general government, did not hang upon knowledge of localities, but "is that which is open to every intelligent inquirer; and of which, five men may be as perfectly possessed as fifty. . . . Why . . . are we told so often of an aristocracy? For my part, I hardly know the meaning of this word as it is applied. . . . The image is a phantom. Does the new government render a rich man more eligible than a poor one? No. . . . It is bottomed on the broad and equal principle of your state constitution." And he wanted to know "if the people have it in their option, to elect their most meritorious men; is this to be considered as an objection? . . . It is a harsh doctrine that men grow wicked in proportion as they . . . enlighten their minds. . . . The difference . . . consists, not in the quantity but kind of vices, which are incident to the various classes; and here the advantage of character belongs to the wealthy. Their vices are probably more favorable to the prosperity of the state, than those of the indigent; and partake less of moral depravity. . . . the true principle of a republic is, that the people should choose whom they please to govern them. Representation is imperfect, in proportion as the current of popular favour is checked. This great source of free government, popular election, should be perfectly pure, and the most unbounded liberty allowed."[19]

Here Hamilton bound up in a bundle several of his leading ideas. The body of the people, enjoying free and frequent elections, was the source of all power. The more intelligent and responsible their representatives, the more capable these would be of decision, and the more their interest coincided with the public advantage, the better. This afforded a government at once democratic and serviceable. Excellent administration would enlist popular approval. Freedom had the broadest base in the choice of the citizenry, which at proper intervals would correct or sanction the performance of duties. Democracy would be promoted, not denied, by order and strength in organized society. "I am persuaded," Hamilton said in this speech, "that a firm union is as necessary to perpetuate our liberties, as it is to make us respectable. . . ." Here was nothing of the doctrinaire, but an effort to see the problem of government whole and to find a workable solution. Hamilton was at the opposite pole from the demagogue who would play to and pervert popular rights; neither would he have a designing aristocracy preempt these rights. He distrusted the people's wisdom, not on great and understood issues, but in the day-to-day, often technical, problems of conducting the public business.

The argument continued for several days on the subject of representation, Clinton and Gilbert Livingston chiming in with Melancton Smith and Lansing, and Richard Harison and Richard Morris coming to the support of Hamilton and the chancellor. Kent was struck with the dignity with which Clinton presided and with his "simplicity and unpretending good sense," but came closer to the governor's share in the discussion in referring to his "stern inflexibility of purpose."[20]

We get a glimpse of Smith's confidence of his large majority at that stage when, after the members had been in session less than

a week (June 23), he warned Hamilton that "in the present spirit
of the Convention, to irritate is not the way to conciliate." There
was little occasion for the caution; Hamilton had taken Smith to
task for declamation into which he occasionally fell, and the fact
was that the assemblage was slowly but surely being prepared for
approval of the Constitution. Hamilton and his friends worked
constantly to defeat the extreme conjectures of dangers to individual liberty and state authority which opponents declared lurked
in the new plan. The unlikely chance, rather than the probability
of the case, formed a poor refuge, as Smith, Lansing, and others
found when one after another of their defenses fell to expert probing.

Gilbert Livingston, in a flowery speech signalized by a comical
mixed metaphor ("at which a great laugh in the house") viewed
the Senate with alarm, and introduced an amendment to prevent
any senator from serving more than six years in twelve and subjecting senators to recall by their legislatures. This touched off
the warmest argument to that time. The proposal was designed
to obtrude the states more directly into national decisions, such as
foreign policy, and to enfeeble that branch of Congress intended
to supply superior continuity, wisdom, and stability to the central
government. Lansing seconded, Chancellor Livingston answered
back and forth, and minor figures entered the debate, but Melancton Smith said less than usual.

Not so Hamilton, who made two long speeches that were among
his best efforts in the convention. Sparring was over; it was time
to deliver manful blows. Hamilton was at once unsparing of the
arguments of his leading opponents and at pains to win their followers to him. He urged the dignity and degree of independence
which the Senate must have without belittling the popular house.
His method was patient, forceful explanation, with abundant
pertinent illustration. He made himself one with his hearers,
equally a party to old errors. "In the commencement of a revolution, which received its birth from the usurpations of tyranny . . .
the zeal for liberty became . . . excessive. In forming our confederation, this passion alone seemed to actuate us, and we . . .
had no other view than to secure ourselves from despotism. The
object . . . deserved our utmost attention:[21] But, Sir, there is another object, equally important, and which our enthusiasm ren-

dered us little capable of regarding—I mean a principle of strength and stability in the organization of our government, and vigor in its operations. . . . there should be in every republic, some permanent body to correct the prejudices, check the . . . passions, and regulate the fluctuations of a popular assembly." Infirmities and mutability of the House should be excluded as far as possible from the Senate.[22] If senators were constantly subject to recall at the jealousy or whim of their state, they would put their private interests ahead of public obligation. In this connection Hamilton said briefly what we may believe actuated him in his use of men of means in government: "It is as easy to change human nature, as to oppose the strong current of the selfish passions. A wise legislator will gently divert the channel, and direct it, if possible, to the public good."[23]

On June 24 the convention got news of ratification by New Hampshire, the ninth state, and the next day Chancellor Livingston reminded the delegates that as the Confederation was dissolved, the ground of the debate in New York was shifted from one of principle to that of expediency only. Smith answered that he was not influenced by the fact that the new Union was in effect, for he had long expected the adherence of nine states.[24] He acknowledged himself partly convinced, but clung to the amendment.[25] This strung Hamilton to complete his conquest. He showed that while "The local interests of a state ought, in every case, to give way to the interests of the Union,"[26] the Constitution made the states "essential, component parts of the union; and therefore the idea of sacrificing the former to the latter is totally inadmissible."

The debate took a more crucial turn when John Williams, of the counties of Washington and Clinton, objected that the authority of Congress "to provide for the common defence, and general welfare" implied too great power, especially in the laying of taxes. ". . . Congress will have every source from which money can be drawn," starving the treasuries of the states. He ended by proposing an amendment that was a variant of Mason's insistence in the Virginia convention. He would forbid an excise on any article of the growth or manufacture of the United States; Congress should lay no direct taxes except when proceeds of the impost and excise (the latter on foreign goods) were insufficient, nor then until Congress had first made requisition on the states to collect their shares of revenue as they thought fit.[27]

Melancton Smith urged this restriction because the national government ought to rest on the state governments, and he was sure that, unless Congress was limited in its voracity, "The individual states in time will be allowed to raise no money at all. . . ."[28] Williams returned to the attack; Congress was empowered "to annihilate the state governments," and he challenged the defenders of the Constitution to answer.[29]

Hamilton's hand is evident in the general reply of Chancellor Livingston, followed by his own remonstrance. Reading his speech is like coming to lean meat after fat, or hewing through sapwood to the heart of the timber. Aided by his ardent mien, the delegates must have heard him with admiration of his powers, no matter what their preconceived opinions. It was the eloquence not of words, but of reasoning and purpose, with a touch of impatience and a deal of compassion that was not patronage. Intellect and spirit were merged.

It was easier for the human mind "to calculate the evils, than the advantages of a measure; . . . to apprehend the danger, than to see the necessity of giving powers to our rulers." The Constitution was skillfully designed to ensure free representation and mutual checks. "Now what do gentlemen mean by . . . declaiming against this government? Why do they say we ought to limit its powers, to disable it, and to destroy its capacity of blessing the people? . . . Sir, when you have divided and nicely balanced the departments of government; when you have strongly connected the virtue of your rulers with their interest; when, in short, you have rendered your system as perfect as human forms can be;—you must place confidence; you must give power."[30] Hamilton contrasted the vast responsibilities of the central government with the narrower sphere of the state, and asked "where ought the great resources to be lodged? . . . To what extent shall these resources be possessed? Reason says as far as possible exigencies can require; that is, without limitation." The states needed a concurrent jurisdiction with the central government in the sources of revenue. If Congress was confined in its taxing power, it could not borrow in the emergency of war because it could not command funds to pledge for repayment.[31]

Hamilton here, as at other points in the Poughkeepsie debates, assured his hearers that he was the friend of scope and permanence for the state governments. It could never be the desire of the national legislature to cut off the states. "The blow aimed at the members, must give a fatal wound to the head; and the destruction of the states must be at once a political suicide. Can the national government be guilty of this madness?"[32] He was eager to win for the Constitution men zealous for powers of the state. Besides, he was doubtless convinced of the necessity of preserving "that mutual dependence [between state and central authorities] which forms the essence of union." In the months since the opening of the Philadelphia convention, when he had urged severe subordination of the states, he had thought better of his strictures. The subsequent construction of the Constitution, his review of the subject in preparation of the *Federalist,* and the Poughkeepsie experience had changed his mind. However, his earlier distrust of the states, expressed in terms too trenchant, was soon to rise to plague him, for opponents had good memories.

But Hamilton and his friends got in their licks first by having the secretary read from Governor Clinton's speech to the legislature, and other official New York papers of 1780–1782, lamenting the feebleness of Congress and the burdens which this disability threw upon a state that voluntarily met its revenue obligations. Clinton and Smith expostulated against introduction of these exhibits; Clinton, most embarrassed, said Duane's part in bringing them forward at this juncture was uncandid. Duane and Hamilton answered that the object was to show "that requisitions have been the cause of a principal part of our calamities; that the system is . . . rotten, and ought forever to be banished from our government." Opponents of a liberal federal taxing power were convicted out of their own mouths.

The reading of the record had its effect. Clinton declared himself "a friend to a strong and efficient government," but wanted to be shown that the Constitution was a safe one.[33] Hamilton followed in a long speech in which he took off his gloves. Clinton was an obstructionist, else why did he approve a strong federal government but oppose the Constitution without particular objections or substitute provisions? Why did he say he had favored granting Congress during the war power to lay an import duty when he had in fact disapproved the only practicable mode of collection? Further, the amendment before the committee admitted the need to give Congress unlimited power of taxation. Requisition first, if the state refused, would be worse than useless; better the quiet, equitable mode prescribed in the Constitution. The amendment said that direct taxes should not be imposed till impost and excise had been pressed to the extreme, and that no excise should be laid except on foreign commodities. Men who wanted the interest of New York State would sacrifice it by these provisions. New York, a commercial commonwealth, must relinquish its own import duties to Congress, while neighboring states more destined for manufactures would be relieved of their proportionate part of federal support. The movers of the amendment were shown to have "run blindly against" their own intention.

Hamilton had made two extended speeches, under stress, in successive days. He must have used stronger expressions than were reported, for he apologized if he had hurt the feelings of any opponent. He confessed his vehement nature, which condemned "those indifferent mortals, who either never form opinions, or never make them known." At the same time he rejected insinuations that some in the convention would raise the few upon the ruins of the many. "I declare I know not any set of men who are to derive peculiar advantages from this constitution," and he disclaimed, for himself, ambition that might consign his children to suffer if they belonged—as they might—to the ranks of the oppressed.[34]

While neither opponents nor friends of the Constitution had been palpably checked in their ardors by news that the contested plan was already in effect by the ratification of New Hampshire, the ninth state, frittering debate followed the strenuous exchanges over representation and taxing power. Lansing concluded a speech by recalling that Hamilton, now so sure that the states must be preserved as repositories of the people's liberties, in the Philadelphia convention "argued with much decision and . . . plausibility, that the state governments ought to be subverted. . . ." Hamilton interrupted to deny the charge of inconsistency, and "a warm personal altercation" between the two occupied the remainder of that day and much of the next.[35]

Perhaps Chancellor Livingston thought the fat was in the fire as a consequence of the brush between Hamilton and Lansing, and that he might as well add to the flames with his sarcasm. This was good of its kind but indiscreet. The numerous rejoinders bolstered Melancton Smith to discredit Hamilton's pleas, and to avow himself still a believer in the necessity of amendment. He threw out a challenge—the last that Hamilton wanted to hear—reminding that "Whether the committee have received conviction can easily be settled by a vote."

At half after noon on July 2 Governor Clinton was making one of his few contributions to the discussion, this one on the power of Congress to contract loans. Suddenly the silent respect accorded him changed to "such a buz through the House, that little of his Excellency's Speech was heard." A rider had dismounted before the court house, his bay horse flecked with foam, and delivered his dispatches to Barclay, the doorkeeper, for Hamilton. They were the wished-for letter from Madison and an official certification of Virginia's adherence by Edmund Pendleton, president of the convention there. Federalists in the crowd attracted by arrival of the express were jubilant, were joined by a fife and drum, and marched around the court house several times.[36]

At the close of discussions this day, marked by a sensible appeal for the Constitution by John Jay and a blast against it by Thomas Tredwell, of Suffolk, articles were read in rapid succession and leading opponents as rapidly introduced their amendments. Lansing brought in a bill of rights to be prefixed to the Constitution, and after the lapse of two days when the convention met but did nothing, he submitted a new plan of amendments, some explanatory, some conditional, others by way of recommendation.

Federalists and Antis in the convention dined at different taverns the evening of July 4th, though with friendly visiting back and forth between the two parties.[37]

Debate on the Constitution proceeded clause by clause (in Committee of the Whole) until July 11, when Jay put the general issue with a resolution that the Constitution should be ratified, with the convention's construction of any doubtful parts, and with the recommendation of amendments believed expedient. Debates on this ensued until July 15, when Melancton Smith countered for the Antis with an amendment making ratification conditional.

Until a second general convention should consider amendments, the militia of New York should not be continued in service out of the state for more than six weeks, Congress should not alter the state election procedure, and no direct tax should be levied until the state had failed to meet a requisition.[38]

The crisis of the Poughkeepsie convention is not depicted, except in the barest record, in the journal, nor in Childs's report, nor in any of the private manuscript minutes. It arrived after the Anti-Federalist majority carried the vote for adoption with certain conditions.[39]

This looked like defeat for the friends of ratification, unless qualified approval, with the right of New York to recede from the Union if its amendments were not enacted within a certain period, should be accepted *pro tempore*. Hamilton was not dashed, for Congress would doubtless recommend amendments, these would satisfy the reservations of reasonable Antis, and they would help end the opposition. Hamilton asked Madison's opinion whether contingent approval would be legal. At the same time he declared that "every thing possible will yet be attempted to bring the [Antis'] party from that stand to an unqualified ratification."[40]

Evidently Hamilton was sorely tried, or he would not have entertained hopes that conditional adoption would serve to place New York in the Union. Madison, answering at once from New York (to which he had come when the Virginia convention concluded), was in no doubt. He was sorry that Hamilton was obliged to listen to such a proposition. Madison's opinion was "that a reservation of a right to withdraw, if amendments be not decided on . . . within a certain time, is a *conditional* ratification; that it does not make New-York a member of the new Union, and consequently that she could not be received on that plan. . . . The Constitution requires an adoption *in toto* and *for ever*." He reminded Hamilton that "It has been so adopted by the other States."[41]

Here was a poser, but Hamilton was not beaten. An informal committee was appointed from both parties in the convention to organize proposed amendments "and fix on some accommodating scheme for an adoption." In this committee the Antis offered their budget of amendments as an ultimatum. Jay and Hobart, instructed by Madison's opinion given to Hamilton, said this amounted to a rejection of the Constitution.   Lansing and Smith replied.   Jay repeated that the Federalists "had been insulted by a complete set of propositions presented in a dictatorial manner for their passive acquiescence."

At this point of deadlock, or rather of impending defeat, Hamilton took a hand.   It was now or never.   In "a most argumentative and impassioned address," he "demonstrated that the propositions . . . would be a total rejection of the Constitution."   He referred in an affecting manner to prejudice in the convention against him.   He had been represented as ambitious, insensitive to the interests of the people, "and even his supposed talents had been wrested to his dishonor, and produced as a charge against his integrity and virtue."   He called on the world to witness that he had not departed from public or private duty.   "The pathetic appeal fixed the silent sympathetic gaze of the spectators, and made them all his own."

Having thus prepared his opponents, he hazarded a refusal. The convention had only the power to adopt or reject absolutely. It could recommend alterations, but no more.   Only a body with the authority of the general constitutional convention could change the terms of the plan of government; Congress could not admit New York provisionally; a partial rejection was a total one, and other states would so construe it.   He entreated the committee "to make a solemn pause . . . before they decided on a subject so infinitely important."   The "murmur of admiration and applause" meant that he had won converts.   However, implacables among his antagonists, said the reporter, were jealous of his triumph, and retired more obstinate than ever.   Immediately after adjournment, Governor Clinton made the public declaration that "the advocates of the Constitution are determined to force us to a rejection. . . . If convulsions and a civil war are the consequence, I will go with my party."   (The reporter was possibly Kent, who may have had Clinton's rheumy remark from Gilbert Livingston, a member of the informal committee.)   Now, when Hamilton had persuaded his opponents morally, may have been when Clinton betrayed the struggle in his own unsusceptible breast by leaving his seat to walk for some time up and down the piazza.[42]

Hamilton and twenty-one other pro-Constitution men favored

a motion of Hobart, on July 16, for an adjournment of the convention to permit delegates to discover sentiments of constituents, since the new Union had become a certainty. After prolonged debate the majority, by turning down his proposal 40–22, acknowledged itself in a weak position.[43]

Debate on Smith's motion for conditional ratification was brisk until July 17. Then Duane offered a substitute resolution which preserved explicit adherence to the Constitution (as in Jay's motion), but comprehended Smith's conditions to the extent of a declaration. The convention should express its belief that reserved rights might not be abridged, but that it was better to rely for amendments on the mode prescribed in the Constitution rather than risk dissensions "by pursuing a different course" (that is, invoking a second general convention). Further, the convention had "full confidence" that proposed amendments would be early and maturely considered and that those deemed for the security and advantage of the people would be adopted. Duane appended desired changes (partly a bill of rights), and in order that these constructions should be observed by the federal government, pending possible formal amendment of the Constitution, New York representatives should procure from Congress a declaratory act "in conformity to these presents."[44]

Duane's motion, the first decisive one of a substantive sort to go to a vote, was negatived, 41–20, only the staunchest Federalists, from the lower counties all, voting for it.[45] The Antis returned to the attack. Lansing moved to postpone other propositions before the committee to consider another form of ratification. This was "on the express condition" that a long bill of rights should not be abridged, and "in confidence" that a longer list of amendments should be submitted to another constitutional convention. All was with restrictions on Congress until New York's conditions were complied with.[46] This resolution was accepted, 41–18, the Federalists losing Lewis Morris (Westchester, not voting) and Jones (Queens).[47] If this decision had led to approval of Lansing's form of ratification, and the convention had confirmed this recommendation of the Committee of the Whole, New York would in effect have rejected the Constitution; Hamilton's strenuous efforts of more than a year, so far as his own state was concerned, would have failed. This was July 19, Saturday. Fortunately debate, commencing Monday, July 21, was on Lansing's proposed amendments as such, and while the Federalists were regularly outvoted by the old majority of about two to one,[48] protraction of the discussion gained time in which differences and doubts among opponents[49] began to shake and then to undermine their position.

Smith, on July 23, so far retreated from his antagonism as to move ratification "in confidence," that the recital of rights and amendments "will receive an early . . . consideration. . . ." Verbal shadings made a difference. Smith was approaching the Federalist position. The vote was in the affirmative, 40–19. The alignment was peculiar. For it were the Federalists, and with them Smith, Governor Clinton, Lansing, and Robert Yates of the Antis.[50] Jones, who had wavered before, seized the opportunity to move also (July 23) "that the words *upon condition* [in Lansing's blanket resolution] should be obliterated, and the words *in full confidence* should be substituted in their stead."

The real break in the Clinton forces came on this motion for unconditional ratification. Debate was signalized by Melancton Smith's recantation. He declared that until Virginia came in, he hoped amendments could be had previous to the operation of the government. But now "he was satisfied they could not, and it was equally the dictate of reason and duty to quit his first ground, and advance so far as that they might be received into the Union." He was convinced, as thoroughly as ever, that the Constitution was radically defective. He would pursue his favorite object of amendments, but in the way prescribed by the Constitution. He first thought a new general convention was practicable, "but from the reasonings of gentlemen in opposition to it, and whose opinions alone would deservedly have vast weight in the national councils . . . he was now persuaded the proposition would not be received. . . . The thing must now be abandoned as fallacious, for . . . it would certainly prove in the event, only a dreadful deception to those who were serious for joining the Union. He then placed in a striking light . . . the situation of this State in case we should not be received by Congress. Convulsions in the Southern part, factions and discord in the rest." His own party, anxious to amend the Constitution, would "be dispersed like sheep on a mountain." The best way to serve "the great end of the opposition was to vote against any proposition which would not be received as a ratification of the Constitution."

Lieutenants in his (really Clinton's) cohort were prepared to swing over. Their self-searchings were plain in the speeches of Gilbert Livingston and Judge Zephaniah Platt justifying the votes they would give. "I have had a severe struggle in my mind," declared Livingston, "between *duty* and *prejudice*. I entered this house . . . fully determined on previous amendments. . . . Nothing . . . but a conviction that I am serving the . . . interests of my country, could ever induce me to take another ground, and differ from so many of my friends on this floor." He revealed that some time back the majority of those who opposed the Constitution had determined not to reject it. The only question was how best to ensure a general convention to ingraft amendments. The *"present* situation with respect to our sister states" —that is, the danger of being isolated—seems to have swung him over in the end.[51] A change of front, dictated by reason, was honorable, but especially so when it meant deserting a party leader like Clinton whom they had followed and would follow again. Governor Clinton was adamant. He stood there as a representative of the County of Ulster, and would vote for what he believed was the sense of his constituents—for conditional adoption.

Yates demanded the yeas and nays because he feared the result. The motion passed, 31–29.[52] Yates, Lansing, and Clinton, who had approved Smith's less explicit wording, were now back in the negative, as were six more Antis who had voted with the Federalists just previously.[53]

Next day, Thursday, July 24, successive amendments—concerning militia, elections, excises, and direct taxes—were agreed to, most of them unanimously, since none was a condition of ratification. Then Lansing, still looking for a way to make approval contingent, moved to add that the state reserved the right to withdraw from the Union if after blank years the amendments had not "been submitted to a convention in the mode prescribed in the fifth article of the Constitution."[54]

This revival of conditional ratification brought on the last animated debate of the convention. Hamilton and Jay answered

Lansing that adoption with the right to withdraw could serve no good purpose in itself and implied a distrust of the other states. Hamilton read a letter from a gentleman of high public distinction (Madison) giving the opinion that such a reservation would amount to conditional—that is, no—ratification.[55] Chancellor Livingston and Duane pled for a harmonious decision. This closed debate, and the question was put over to the next day, Friday, July 25.

That morning, still in committee of the whole, Melancton Smith repeated briefly his capitulation of Thursday. Lansing's conditional ratification was voted down, 31–28.[56] An overwhelming majority of two to one against adoption had been transformed, in six strenuous weeks, into a majority of three in favor of outright ratification. A thankful Federalist wrote, "The Constitution has . . . undergone an ordeal torture, and been preserved, as by fire."[57]

The rest was formal. Tredwell introduced changes in the form of ratification—"declaring" rights, expressing "confidence" in early consideration of amendments—to make it consistent with the essential decision just taken. The new wording was approved by the same vote as before, 31–28.[58] The body resolved itself from Committee of the Whole back into convention, when the report—declaration of rights, form of ratification, and explanatory amendments—was adopted, 30–25.[59] Duane, gratuitously as it seems, moved that a circular letter go to the legislatures "pressing in the most earnest manner, the necessity of a general Convention to take into their consideration the amendments . . . proposed by the several State Conventions." This was resolved unanimously, Jay, Lansing, and Smith being elected a drafting committee.[60]

Hamilton, in the Philadelphia convention or afterward, did not call for a bill of rights as a succinct part of the Constitution. The important protections to liberty of the individual, he believed, were sufficiently incorporated in the document, as it stood without amendment. Practically, he felt that debate on the proposition of more express guarantees, unless the Constitution was first adopted and ratified, might delay and endanger the reform of the government which he worked to bring about. His avoidance of such a discussion at Philadelphia did not apply at Poughkeepsie once New York had unconditionally adhered. A second convention, to review the document, had its risks, but possession of the Constitution would prove nine points of the law.   If a circular letter to the states recommending further consideration helped win assent and soothed antagonism, he was willing to compromise in a secondary matter, hence his vote in favor.   It is pertinent to re-member that at this time Madison, later so much the stickler for the letter of the law, was much of Hamilton's mind.   He supposed "further guards to public liberty & individual rights . . . will be added," he told Jefferson, though the opposition to the Constitu-tion was divided on the propriety of it.   While approving a bill of rights, "I have never thought the omission a material defect, nor been anxious to supply it even by *subsequent* amendment, for any other reason than that it is anxiously desired by others."   He had "not viewed it in an important light" because the grant of federal powers was restricted, attempt at definition might in prac-tice limit liberty, and paper protections would hardly avail against strong popular demand for their suspension.[61]

Adjournment was taken to late afternoon, when Jay chanced disharmony by moving to include an amendment restricting to freeholders those eligible to election as President, Vice President, or member of Congress.   It is notable that Hamilton voted with Lansing and others in a mixed group, mostly Anti-Federalists, against this, but Jay's provision was easily carried.[62]

The following morning, Saturday, saw the final act in conven-tion.   The engrossed ratification, with added amendments rec-ommended, was approved, 30–27, and was signed by the president and two secretaries.   Jay's circular letter had unanimous ap-proval.   The convention adjourned sine die.[63]

When all was done, Clinton, from the chair, offered a qualified benediction.   Until a convention was called to consider amend-ments recommended, "the probability was, that the body of the people who are opposed to the constitution, would not be satisfied; he would however . . . endeavour to keep up peace and good order among them . . . ," at which "More than a common pleasantness" appeared in the countenances of delegates and spec-tators.[64]   The New York City members reached home two days later, Monday, Hamilton bringing the signed ratification which he promptly presented to Congress.[65]

The impatience of New York City, with its commercial, industrial, and financial interests, to see the new national government established was proclaimed in early preparations for an elaborate civic procession with varied floats. As soon as the adherence of New Hampshire, the ninth state, was known, making the union certain, tradesmen and mechanics of the city painted the banners they would carry.[66] The parade was put off until after July 4 so as not to interfere with other plans for that holiday "and because our Ship *The Hamilton* will not be ready before."[67] Further postponements were in response to ever grander plans, and in the hope that the convention at Poughkeepsie would ratify.[68] But the patriotic could not be restrained beyond Wednesday, July 23, when "The procession made a very pompous appearance." The ten sections, honoring the ten ratifying states, began forming in the Fields at eight o'clock in the morning, two hours later thirteen guns were fired from the Federal ship "Hamilton" as signal for the grand march to commence. This frigate was the chief feature of the parade, but was only one of numerous displays proclaiming Hamilton's leadership in securing the new national government.[69]

The homage of New York was given him for his loyalty in the Philadelphia Convention, in contrast to desertion by his two up-state colleagues; for his principal share in *The Federalist* papers; and, to top the rest, his determined—though as yet unsuccessful —fight for ratification at Poughkeepsie. These persevering campaigns combined with other efforts, better known to his fellow citizens of New York than to us, to make him the hero of the celebration. Thus the sailmakers, not content with their contribution to the ship "Hamilton," entered their own stage drawn by four horses, bearing their flag, 'in the centre . . . Col. Hamilton, the new constitution in his right hand, and the [Articles of] confederation in his left. Fame with a trumpet and laurels to crown him. . . .'"[70]

The Federalist fashioners of the parade went in for symbolism— a foretaste of the eagles and stars that were soon to plaster inn signs, door knockers, furniture, and clocks. The coopers' display was led by thirteen apprentice boys thirteen years of age. Later in line were more apprentices, "dressed clean, with a green oak branch in their hats. . . ." Workmen on the float, unable to repair a barrel whose ill joined staves stood for the old Confederation, "determined to make a new cask, representing the new constitution, which was

done accordingly while the procession was marching." The "artificial florists" in their gorgeous garland showed three flowers
drooping, "representing the three states that did not sign the constitution." The block- and pump-makers "finished a pump . . .
made 13 blocks, sheaved and pinned compleat, on the stage, during
the procession." Following a band of music, the tailors bore an
oversize banner, "field sky blue, a fine landscape. Adam and Eve
represented naked, excepting fig-leaves for aprons, nearly in full
stature, in a sitting posture—motto, '*And they sewed fig-leaves together.*' " The states, in order of their adoption of the Constitution, were links in a chain, "the sun beaming forth its rays upon
those states that have acceded to federal measures—Rhode-Island
in mourning."

The furriers had a real Indian—or a journeyman got up to look
like one—delivering pelts. The brewers' dray held a 300-gallon
cask of ale, atop it "a *living Bacchus*—a very handsome boy . . .
in flesh coloured silk, sewed tight round from his chin to his toes—
a cap ornamented with hop vines and barley—a silver goblet in his
hand, drinking and huzzaing the whole day with the greatest cheer-
fulness." Silenus, his attendant, sat more soberly on a porter
hogshead labeled "Ale, proper drink for Americans." Hatters,
peruke makers, shipwrights, nailors, paper stainers, upholsterers all
trooped in patriotic holiday.

As the procession moved to acclamation down Broadway,
through Great Dock Street, Hanover Square, and Queen Street,
the "thousands" of spectators could not have missed the proofs
that the Constitution was an omen of prosperity as well as of
union.[71] Amidst the pageants of printers at their presses (and
actually striking off and distributing an ode), blacksmiths fashioning an anchor, and the other urban crafts, the farmers were not
forgotten. A plow drawn by six oxen was "conducted by Nicholas Cruger, Esq., in a farmer's dress, supporting the farmers'
arms," and followed by "A new invented threshing machine
which will thresh and clean 72 bushels of grain in a day."[72]
Cruger, thus ensconced in the celebration, must have felt that he
had sowed good seed when, sixteen years earlier, he sent an orphan
lad from St. Croix to this continent, and that he was in fact now
threshing out an abundant harvest. If Eliza Hamilton and her
four children were then in New York—were not waiting out the

convention with the Schuylers at Albany—they certainly witnessed the procession; the youngest Hamiltons (Alexander, two
years, and James Alexander, three months) could take in nothing,
but neither did Eliza need a parade and a city in cheers to swell
her pride in her husband.[73]

Notes

Chief Symbols and Abbreviations Used in Notes

ADS   (autograph document signed)
ALS   (autograph letter signed)
AM. ARCHIVES   (Peter Force, ed.)
AMH   (Allan McLane Hamilton, *Intimate Life of Alexander Hamilton*)
BURNETT   (*Letters of Members of Continental Congress*)
CHS   (Connecticut Historical Society, Hartford)
CHILDS   (*Debates of Convention of N.Y. at Poughkeepsie*)
DAB   (*Dictionary of American Biography*)
Dan.-Am. Gaz.   (Royal Danish-American Gazette, St. Croix)
FARRAND   (*Records of Federal Convention*)
GW   (Fitzpatrick, ed., *Writings of George Washington*)
H   (J. C. Hamilton, *Life of Alexander Hamilton*)
HEITMAN   (*Officers of Continental Army*)
HLC   (Hamilton Papers, Library of Congress)
JCC   (Journals of Continental Congress)
JCHW   (J. C. Hamilton, ed., *Works of Alexander Hamilton*)
LHW   (H. C. Lodge, ed., *Works of Alexander Hamilton*)
LIHS   (Long Island Historical Society, Brooklyn)
LODGE, H   (*Life of Alexander Hamilton*)
LOLTW   (Gottschalk, ed., *Letters of Lafayette to Washington*)
MHS   (Massachusetts Historical Society, Boston)
NJHS   (New Jersey Historical Society, Newark)
NYHS   (New-York Historical Society, N.Y.C.)
NYPL   (New York Public Library)
NYSL   (New York State Library, Albany)
PHS   (Historical Society of Pennsylvania, Phila.)
PRESBY. HS   (Presbyterian Historical Society, Phila.)
R   (J. C. Hamilton, *History of Republic Traced in Writings of Alexander Hamilton*)
RAMSING   ("Alexander Hamilton og hans mødrene Slaegt")
RD   (Rigsarkivet, i.e., Danish National Archives, Copenhagen)
RIHS   (Rhode Island Historical Society, Providence)
SCHACHNER, H   (*Alexander Hamilton*)
SPARKS   (*Correspondence of American Revolution*)
ST. CR.   (St. Croix)
STOKES   (Iconography of Manhattan Island)
U.S. ARCH.   (United States Archives, Washington, D.C.)

Chief Danish public records, mentioned in early chapters, have following meanings: Kopskatliste, poll tax list; Pantebog, register of mortgages; Skifte, division of inheritances; Skiftebr (Skiftebrevs) protokol, register of deeds of partition; Skifteretsprotokol, register of probate court; Skiftepr. (Skifteprotokol), record of division of inheritances. Matricul, tax list. The rigsdaler was roughly equal to a Spanish piece of eight.

Foreword (Pages ix to xvi)

1. Allan McLane Hamilton, *Intimate Life,* 30.   William Sullivan called him "under middle size, thin in person. . . . " (*Public Characters and . . . Events,* 1834 ed., 235, 260); Brissot de Warville, "not tall" (*New Travels in U.S.,* 135).   "Little Lion" was the nickname given by Robt. H. Harrison, the senior, as Hamilton was the junior, in Washington's military family.

2. Cf. De Warville on his "open and martial" manner (*op. cit.,* 92). Notion that his assertiveness, and desire to excel, if not to command, were psychological compensation for lack of physical size may well be specious; these qualities belonged to the vigor of his mind, from talents which he was bound to exercise.   He was never accused of affectation.

3. Cf. bust by Caracci, portraits (with frequent replicas) by Trumbull, James Sharpless, Charles Willson Peale.   No picture of him, of which we can be sure, was made in years covered by this volume (to the age of 33), or at least none has survived, unless we accept a miniature by Charles Willson Peale (c. 1777?) and an oil portrait by Robert Edge Pine (c. 1786).   On all likenesses, see H. M. Bland and Virginia W. Northcott, in *W&M Quar.,* 3rd ser., XII, No. 2, April, 1955, 187–198, with illustrations.

4. *Op. cit.*

5. One is in a case of Hamilton relics in Museum of City of N.Y., another is in a finger ring in the Hist. Soc. of Penn. Cf. AMH, *Intimate Life,* 29 and n.

6. Sullivan, *op. cit.*

7. Duc de Rochefoucauld-Liancourt, *Voyage dans les États-Unis d'Amérique,* 149.

8. His grandson, a neurologist, said, "He undoubtedly possessed that form of nervous instability common to many active public men and characterized by varying moods, . . . alternating depression on the one hand and gayety on the other" (AMH, *Intimate Life,* 43).   Maclay in 1790 found John Adams pompous, and had no kinder words for Hamilton's "very boyish, giddy manner" (*Diary,* 238).

Chapter 1 (Pages 1 to 14)
Angels Sat on His Tarnished Cradle

1. Biographer is indebted to initial inquiries by Gertrude Atherton which documented her famous novel *The Conqueror* (N.Y., 1902). Her findings were not always accurate, but her fiction was superbly factual. Her artistry re-created H with spirited fidelity. Two generations of readers have admired him in her living portrait. In "The Hunt for Hamilton's Mother" (*N.A. Rev.*, CLXXV, 1902, 229–42), *A Few of Hamilton's Letters* (N.Y., 1903), and *Adventures of a Novelist* (N.Y., 1932), 315–53, she supplemented "the raising from the dead of Alexander Hamilton." After her main work was done, Mrs. Atherton had the important help of Capt. (later Gen.) H. U. Ramsing, though she departed, in respects, from his accurate discoveries (letter to me of Generalinde Julie Ramsing, Aug. 28, 1951). He had been in command of garrison on (then Danish) island of St. Croix where H grew up, and made thorough examination of archives in Copenhagen. His *Alexander Hamilton og hans mødrene Slaegt. Tidsbilleder fra Dansk Vest-Indiens Barndom* (Personal historisk Tidsskrift, 59 de Aargang, 10 Rekke, 6 Bind, 1939), English trans. by Solvejg Vahl, (microfilm in NYPL), is most reliable account of H's origin and early environment. It forms, with additions and minor corrections, main dependence of my recital of H's birth and parentage, for which I cannot be too grateful. Ramsing, in turn, had aid from Harold Larson, drawing on St. Croix records now transferred to U.S. Archives, Washington. Mr. Larson's articles, referred to below, have informed American readers.

2. No documentary evidence for birthplace has been found. His sons accepted Nevis, surely from their father (1 H 1, 1 R 40); Jas. A. H called his home on the Hudson "Nevis" (Columbia Univ., *Nevis* . . .); cf. grandson, AMH 1. Closest to contemporary allusion (1759) is "on an English island" (Skifteretspr. 41 f. Christiansted; Rachael Lewin's skifte, f. 386, U.S. Arch.; see Ramsing, 234, Eng. trans., micro., NYPL, 11; H. Larson, (21 *Am. Genealogist* 161–7).

3. For contemporary maps of Nevis and of Charlestown, see V. L. Oliver, in 2 *Caribbeana* 6; fort shown at southern tip of harbor crescent is now crumbling walls and a single ruined building. John Baskett, *Acts of Assembly . . . of St. Christopher, 1711–1735* (1739); *An Abridgment* [of same] *. . . 1711–40* (1740); and *Acts of Assembly . . . in . . . Leeward Islands, 1690–1730* (1740), pp. 8–10, 73, all in NYPL, throw light on manners and economy that hardly altered by time of H's birth and boyhood there.

4. 1 H 2; spelled here (without given name) Faucette (Common Records, Nevis, 1725–46, p. 429, printed in Atherton, ed., *Few of H's Letters,* 272;

cf. 2 *Caribbeana* 55, 328). Other renderings on Nevis and elsewhere in West Indies about this time are Faucett (Deeds Register, St. Christopher, Bx. X, No. 1, 1755–8, item 5799), Fawsett, Feacey, Faust, Faucet, ffaussett (*ibid.*, 179, 211 221, 267), Fossett (*ibid.*, 80). In contemporary records at St. Christopher are French names, e.g., Perochon, Deschamp, Panton, Guichard, Gilliard, De Brissac, Fieuilleteau, De Laserre, Papillon. Though occupations of men, occasionally of women, were noted in parish register of St. George's, Gingerland, Nevis, none appears for John Fawcett; absence of Dr. before name does not mean he did not practice medicine; cf. at same time and place "Mr. Jacob Andrew Bernhose, Chirurgeon" (*Caribbeana, ibid.*, 267); numbers of intelligent men in isolated communities, self-taught, prescribed for bodily ills.

5. He had a wife, four children, man slave, woman slave, one slave child (3 *Caribbeana* 78; cf. *ibid.*, 80, for John "Fossett," same year and place, with household of different composition).

6. *Ibid.*, 179; March 13, 1707–8.

7. Atherton in *N. Am. Rev., op. cit.*, 234; entry in Common Records of Nevis to which Mrs. Atherton referred, not found.

8. 2 *Caribbeana* 269. Oliver, the genealogist, took this from mss. of Fulham Palace, residence of Bishop of London, as communicated by N. Darnell Davis (3 *ibid.*, 216). L. B. Thomas, rector of St. George's in 1913, reported that "the registers are in very bad order, and . . . indecipherable in places" (3 *ibid.*, 215; cf. Atherton, *op. cit.*, 233). Oliver had transcript of baptismal register, made by Maj. Gen. R. Pemberton from correspondence in muniment room of Fulham; original register afterward disappeared from that place (2 *ibid.*, 266). Oliver found gap in St. George's register between May 24, 1723–24, end of what was sent to Fulham, and April 15, 1730, where register at church began. In 1951 (June 26) Father J. M. Dennington kindly let me see records at rectory, none older that 1828, though continuous since then.

9. May have been applied in her case because she was apparently older sister of "Margaret Uppington, Spinster," who Dec. 26, 1721, married Edward Evans, mason (register of St. George's, Nevis, 2 *Caribbeana* 270; Ramsing [228] thought Evans, who transferred with Jas. Lytton to St. Croix, married Lytton's sister; rather, Mrs. Evans was Mrs. Lytton's aunt; her given name and probable age match with marriage record).

10. Number of families in parish was small, only 73 as reported by Henry Pope, rector at this time, 1716–23 (3 *Caribbeana* 216). Attendance on Sundays was from 50 to 70, other days fewer; sacrament was administered four times a year, with 12 to 20 communicants. Rector said: "We have a good Folio Bible and Common Prayer Book, with 2 chalices and a silver plate for Altar. The Church ruinous and past repair." Richard Morgan gave instruction to a few youths; no parochial library. Parishioners lived on plantations, but variety of callings was represented, including carpenter, mason, fisherman,

"shirurgeon," overseer, planter, merchant, mariner, "taylor," blacksmith, "apothecary late from Britain," and (a woman) mantuamaker (2 *Caribbeana* 269). In floor of church is tomb, about this date, of Dorothy, wife of Thomas Herbert of this island and daughter of Major Henry Lytton of same place, deceased.

11. Pantebog f. St. Cr. 1736–45, p. 48, U.S. Arch.

12. Ramsing, 228, without ref.

13. Dansk. Kirkeb. Landsarkivet of Zealand, Copenhagen, f. St. Cr. 1740–53, RD; cf. 1 H 3, and AMH 203. Jas. Yard, of Phila., but of West Indian family, confused Ann (née Lytton) and her mother, calling her Alexander's aunt (Pickering Papers, Feb. 15, June 29, 1822, MHS; printed in Lodge, *Life of H.*, 289 ff.); for different assumptions, Atherton, *N. Am. Rev., op. cit.*, 230; Lodge, *ibid.*, 292, 294–5; Schachner, H 16.

14. Last seems to have been in existence in 1901 when Mrs. Atherton visited island (*N. Am. Rev., op. cit.*, 234). I am indebted to Miss Eva Wilkins, who lives on "Clayhaugh," an adjoining place, for these particulars. Possibly cane grown on Fawcett plantation was brought to Clayhaugh windmill and boiling house to be turned into muscovado sugar and molasses. These are standing, operated until about 1940. Mill, like all in these islands, is of stone, a great truncated cone, but this in 1951 had boom and interior machinery still in place, though sails that turned in trade winds had been dismantled. Juice, crushed from cane between three sets of iron rollers, ran in trough by gravity to lower boiling house. Here bagasse (crushed cane) was fuel for horizontal furnace or flue over which sat three iron kettles, each six feet across, two feet deep, in which juice was boiled. Then was transferred to barrels set on platform to be drained of molasses.

15. 2 *Caribbeana* 267; probably error of rector for 1719, as same form was used for births of three other children and, with slight variation, for death of one, indicating entries were made at same time.

16. *Ibid.*, 267–70; 3 *ibid.*, 219.

17. 3 *ibid.*, 220; name here spelled Lillingston, as also in Common Records of Nevis, 1754–5, and of St. Kitts, Bk. C, No. 1, 1731–3, item 433.

18. 3 *Caribbeana* 221; name of parents in burial register spelled Faust but is same, as all first names match. No tombstone of any member of Fawcett family was found in graveyard of St. George's, but many inscriptions are indecipherable and more burials went unmarked.

19. Common Records, Nevis, 1725–46, p. 429, printed in Atherton, ed., *Few of H's Letters*, 270–72.

20. Atherton, *Conqueror*, 6, enlarged plausibly on causes for writ.

21. Notarialprotokol f. St. Cr. Nr. 318, f. 15, RD. Protocol is moldering, but the fragment of will is doubtless a piece of f. 15, as there are four

leaves between that and first, where folio number, 20, is preserved. Document following, on f. 16, is dated Christiansted 5 xbr. (Dec.) 1745, so will was entered before that. Will must have been made on Nevis, because Robert Huggins, Jr., a witness with Joseph Burke, was planter there as late as 1754–5 (Common Records, 236 ff.).

22. E.g., 1745 matricul, St. Cr., folio p. 54 (U.S. Arch.); cf. Ramsing, 228.

23. Nor does Rachael's older brother John, if we are correct about him, appear; he may have died.

24. Ramsing, 230, without citation.

25. Edward Evans and wife Margaret bought Golden Rock Plantation, No. 4, Company's Quarter (Pantebog f. St. Cr. 1736–45, pp. 154 ff., RD). Wm. and Elizabeth Huggins, other friends from St. Kitts, in 1742 bought a half and next year a whole plantation in same quarter (*ibid.,* 323, 440). Several times they were sponsors at christenings of Lytton children, and became, with Lytton, guardians of Evans children.

26. 1741 St. Cr. Gen. Ledger, folio p. 12 (U.S. Arch.). He bought stone coal and iron from Danish West India Co. and owed 294 rdl. from previous year. In 1744 he submitted a bill to estate of Edward Evans for clothing and household goods, some items delivered before Evans left Nevis (St. Cr. Byfogedarkiv, skiftepr. 1742–48, No. 3, f. 270, RD).

27. Pantebog f. St. Cr. 1736–45, p. 475 RD; it was later called "Ruby," No. 21, Queen's Quarter.

28. Kopskatliste f. St. Cr. 1744, RD.

29. Pantebog f. St. Cr. 1736–45 (RD, but Ramsing said record, on last page of protocol, crumbled between time he noted it, 1902, and 1936, when he wanted to refer to it again). Lavien paid land tax of 6 rdl. and head tax on three capable slaves (1745 St. Cr. matricul, folio p. 57) and same in 1746 (1746 *ibid.,* folio p. 187, U.S. Arch.).

30. 1745 matricul, St. Cr., folio p. 53 (U.S. Arch.); "Widow (?) Maria Facet" was living on Lindemark plantation, Company's Quarter, near that of James Lytton; beside herself, only her three slaves were noted, though all members of every household were always listed—taxpayer, spouse, children, white servants, slaves, with sex of each. Incidentally, if word "widow" (Enke) is to be translated literally, about which there is some doubt, that of course means John Fawcett had died by this time.

31. At appraisal of his mother's estate in 1768 it was recorded that "Peter Lewine is still living in South Carolina and . . . is about 22 years old" (Ramsing, 245, without ref.). Peter signed personally for his inheritance in Nov. 1769. (Chr'sted Byfogedarkiv, skiftepr. 1766–70 (No. 41), f. 386, Rachael Lewine's skifte, RD).

32. 1 H 2. H's grandson (AMH 8) put him down as "a rich Danish Jew, one John Michael Levine (or Lawein)."

33. AMH 4.

34. Lavin, Lawin, Lawine, Lawien, Lavien, Lewin, Lewien, Lewine, Levin, Lowine, Lovien, Lovine, and Lavion. H, in the two instances we have, wrote it Levine and Lavine. Peter, in the single occurrence of his signature in West Indian papers, spelled it Lavien (Chr'sted Bytogedarkiv, skiftepr. 1766–70, No. 41, Rachel Lewine's Skifte, f. 394, RD). Mary Fawcett had it Lavion (Deeds Register St. Christopher, Bk. X, No. 1, 1755–8, item 5799); this is as given by Atherton in *N. Am. Rev.*, 237, for since she wrote, that bit of the document has disintegrated. Name may be Slavic, possibly deriving from small town of Lowien in western Poland (Ramsing, 237).

35. His first name often occurs as Johan or Johann. He wrote to a Danish-speaking attorney in German; though he spent most of his life on a Danish island, with Danish public clerks, no document of his is in Danish; kept his accounts in English, apparently understood Dutch (Ramsing, *ibid.*)

36. He was at least of age when a merchant on Nevis prior to 1738, which makes him 28 (probably more) when he married 16-year-old Rachael Fawcett in 1745.

37. 1745 St. Cr. Gen. Ledger, folio p. 145; 1747 *ibid.*, 1-6, 1748 *ibid.*, 200 (U.S. Arch.).

38. In June 1750 he sold his half-plantation of cotton, Company's Quarter No. 12, to Merrich Turnbull, and in the same year bought half of (sugar plantation) No. 19, same quarter, from Anna Poul's heirs (Kopskatlister f. Chr'sted 1747 og. 1752, RD; 1752 matricul, St. Cr., folio p. 54, U.S. Arch.). But in 1753 he sold this to moneylenders in Christiansted (Pantebog f. Chr'sted 1752–5, f. 96, RD), and a few months later sold a woman and her child, *ibid.*, f. 123). In 1754–5 he had no land of his own but was on a plantation of the Heiligers (St. Cr. matricul, p. 32); was still working Heiliger land in 1758–9 and in 1760 was on one of von Proeck's plantations (Kopskatlister f. St. Cr., 1753–4, 1758–60, RD; 1760 St. Cr. matricul, folio p. 30, U.S. Arch.). For a year or two he lived in Christiansted (1754–5 St. Cr. matricul, folio p. 48 or latter part, U.S. Arch.), and in 1761 moved to Frederiksted (Ramsing, 235, without ref.). During these years he owned about ten grown slaves, whom, after moving to Frederiksted, he rented out; twice he bought lots, 13 in all, in Prinsensgade.

39. St. Cr. Pantebog 1759, f. 330, U. S. Arch.

40. Fr'sted Byfogedarkiv, skiftepr. 1770–6 (No. 138), f. 7 ff., RD.

41. Lavien owed Evans 20 pistols (Skiftepr. Nr. 3, Byf. f. St. Cr. 1742–8, f. 270, RD).

42. Within a week after the divorce he witnessed will of Charles Hall, was an appraiser of Hall's estate; the widow married Peter Lytton and Lavien witnessed their will (Pantebog f. St. Cr. 1762–5, f. 293, 294–5, RD).

43. No. 19 in same (Company's) quarter; dwelling there now is recent.

44. St. Croix Upper Court Landsting Protokol Vol. A, 1756–72, folio pp. 43–4, U.S. Arch.; Ramsing, 234, cites this as St. Cr. Pantebog 1759, f. 330, U.S. Arch., relying on letter of Harold Larson, Oct. 4, 1937. Larson, 21 *Am. Genealogist,* 161–7 says this and subsequent documents in case were unknown to Dr. Axel Linvald, of Rigsarkivet, or to Ramsing until Larson furnished Danish text to latter, and that the volume was discovered by James A. Bough in 1932. Mr. Bough is a native of St. Croix, was working in island records under direction of Lt. Gov. L. W. Cramer. However, years before that, this old manuscript book, of such singular interest, was rescued from destruction by Rasmus Pedersen, then postmaster of Christiansted. After U.S. bought Danish Virgin Islands in 1917, Danish archivists took to Copenhagen the fullest set of St. Croix records. American military authorities, for their part, clearing out from fort what they considered rubbish, started a bonfire in courtyard. Someone, knowing Mr. Pedersen's solicitude for the records, fetched him in time. Contents of this particular volume took his eye, and he kept book in his office until, after Mr. Bough's survey, most of official papers remaining in island were transferred to Archives in Washington. Incident was recited to me by Mr. Pedersen, 1951. Document is perfectly legible, though folio p. 44, left side, has turned darker than other two.

45. *Dansk Lovbog* (Copenhagen, 1683, 513). Miss Margareth Jorgensen, then of U.S. Arch., identified this statute and translated it for me.

46. James Hendricks, Jemima Gorley, and James William Ash. Ramsing (234) identified them as persons of no special note; they do not otherwise figure in records of Rachael.

47. This estate is directly south of "Contentment" where Rachael first lived with Lavien. Stones of old dwelling have been used for newer buildings; only handsome gateposts of place next it remain to testify to departed architectural pretensions of neighborhood. "Catharine's Rest" is further connected with H's story because it was home of Anna de Nully who became wife of Nicholas Cruger, H's employer in Christiansted.

48. It flanks, on east, waterfront square of Christiansted. Its heavy walls, dry moat, and main battery commanding the harbor were sufficient once for defense, but even then its *place d'armes* was used as much for horse pound as for drills. On one side of this courtyard are the cells (still employed by town police)—dank holes with heavy wooden doors, each with small grating giving mocking view of a magnificent flamboyant tree that dominates enclosure.

49. Kopskatliste f. St. Cr., RD. "The widow Maria Facet" (1746: Faucet) with her 3 slaves is also entered in poll-tax lists for Company's Quarter, 1745–46. She lived by hiring out her slave women and by sewing. She made small purchases of bacon, heavy cotton (for slave clothing?), etc., from cargoes of vessels from Denmark (1745 Gen. Ledger, folio p. 177; *ibid.*, 1747, folio p. 61, U.S. Arch.). In 1745 she was said to "live on James Lytton's land." She was still in the same quarter in 1747, when she was godmother at christening of Elizabeth Lytton (Ramsing, 231, without ref.).

50. Chr'sted Byfogedarkiv, skiftepr. 1766–70 (No. 41), f. 391, RD, where judgment is entered; probate case begins on f. 386. In summons Rachael had been informed that Lavien, if upheld, would be free to remarry, "whereas you are to be further punished if seized in this country according to law. . . ." In 1755 Lavien had a white woman servant living in his household (1754–5 St. Cr. matricul, folio p. 48; cf. Ramsing, 236, for 1758); he remarried, after court gave him the right, for we have this second wife's claim in 1765 against an estate, "To Mrs. Lovien for washing 1 Real 4 Styver" (Fr'sted Bytogedarkiv, 1764–71, f. 175, Thos. Wade's Skifte, RD). He seems to have had by her a son and daughter, who died in infancy (St. Cr. matricul 1766, folio p. 19; U.S. Arch.; Ramsing, *ibid.*, citing poll-tax lists 1758–71). Peter, Rachael's son, had gone to South Carolina by 1765. Lavien's second wife died probably in 1767 (St. Cr. matricul 1767, folio p. 20, U.S. Arch.; cf. *ibid.*, 1768, folio p. 22).

51. Pantebog f. St. Cr. 1749–51, f. 77, 80, RD.

52. St. Cr. Byfogedarkiv, skiftepr. 1747–54, No. 33, p. 542, RD.

53. Common Records, Nevis, 1754–5, p. 74. This was a release, July 23, of Hon. Wm. Maynard of Nevis from any claims she ever had against him.

54. Ramsing, 230, supposed James Hamilton was on St. Kitts as early as 1750, but first certain knowledge of him there or elsewhere is of 1765. JCH (1 H 2, 3; 1 R 41–2) was in error on essentials of family history; e.g., Alexander's whole brother James grew to manhood (Jas. A. Hamilton, *Reminiscences,* 2–3).

55. For his ancestry see Jas. Paterson, 2 *Hist. of Ayrshire,* 201–3; John Anderson, *Memoirs of House of Hamilton,* 254–7; Geo. Robertson, *Topographical Description of Ayshire,* 167 ff.; see Ramsing, 232n. for christening information, etc., obtained from Registrar General of Scotland. AMH, 436, mistakenly gave date of marriage of Alexander Hamilton's paternal grandparents as 1730; 1711 (Ramsing, *ibid.*) is correct. We do not have precise date of James Hamilton's birth, but three older brothers were born in 1712, 1715, and 1717, and James, Walter, and George (last two probably twins) were born before seventh brother, 1721.

56. Jas. A. Hamilton, *Reminiscences,* 302. His brothers remained in Scotland, and two of them and a nephew succeeded to lairdship of Grange

(AMH, 436).   Nevis had many Hamiltons at this time; e.g., for Walter H., see Common Records, March 7–Aug. 15, 1710.   Supposition of Atherton (*N. Am. Rev., op. cit.,* 233, but *Conqueror,* 30, 36), followed by Schachner, H., 7, that Hon. Wm. Hamilton of St. Kitts drew James to the islands is unsupported.

57. 10 LHW 109.

58. 6 *ibid.,* 243.

59. J. A. Hamilton, *op. cit.,* 3.

60. For an appreciation of H's achievement, against handicaps of illegitimacy and poverty, see De Ford, *Love-Children,* 12, 21.

61. He signed a letter to Alexander, from St. Vincent, June 12, 1793, "Your very affectionate father" (19 HLC 2652); only signature, literate but slightly shaky, is in his hand; printed in 5 JCHW 567–8.

62. AMH 7.

63. 5 JCHW 567; 6 *ibid.,* 245–6.

64. AMH 3.

65. 6 JCHW 243.   See exchange of letters, 1797–8, between Alexander H of New York and his first cousin, Laird of Grange, Ayrshire, Scotland (6 JCHW 243–6, 371–3).   H had received laird's brother Robert into his home and recommended him "for the first-lieutenancy of one of the new frigates" (Jas. A. H., *op cit.,* 2–3; cf. AL, W. Pitcairn, Nov. 17, 1827, to JAH, 84 HLC 13653).   JAH, *ibid.,* 302; AMH 19, 438–9.   H called his country home in Harlem "Grange."

66. AMH 3 n.

67. 1 H 2.

68. AMH 9 ff.

69. Smertenko, H, 4–5.

70. Pickering Papers, *op. cit.,* MHS; printed in Lodge, *Life,* 289; cf. 287, 290, 293, and Atherton in *N. Am. Rev., op. cit.,* 234–5.

71. Atherton, *ibid.,* Smertenko, *ibid.*

72. Atherton, *ibid.*

73. Smertenko, *ibid.*

74. *Ibid.*

75. Cf. Buell Gallagher, *Color and Conscience,* 125 n.; M. R. Davie, *Negroes in American Society,* 391.

76. ALS, R. J. Breckenridge to wife, June 9, 1832 (60 Breckenridge Papers, 10701, LC).

77. Larson in *W&M Quar.*, 3rd. Ser., IX, 147 n.

78. In England prior to 1857 only legal separation could be had from courts for adultery or cruelty; neither party could marry again.

79. Evidence in wills in principal families is abundant and unmistakable; e.g., that of John Richardson Herbert, pres. of Nevis, whose niece married Horatio Nelson (1788; 5 *Caribbeana* 224; cf. 2 *ibid.*, 213). Alexander's (much older) cousin and guardian left to a slave mistress and mulatto infant large inheritance, but nothing to his wards, the Hamilton brothers (5 *ibid.*, 37; Ramsing, 248–9, without ref.). For legacies of Hamm, who handled business for Mary Fawcett, see Deeds Register, St. Chris., Z, 6352; cf. register of St. George's, St. Kitts, in 3 *Caribbeana* 352. Knox, clergyman on Saba and St. Croix, lamented illicit sex relations of high proportion of his communicants (see below).

80. As translated from Records of West Indies, Inv. No. 248, Baptismal Register of St. Eustatius 1743–65 (Netherlands Arch., The Hague); this reference was discovered by the ingenuity of Dorothie Bobbé, to whom I am indebted for it.

81. Fol. 386 v., Chr'sted Byfogeds Skifteprotokol 1766 12/4—1770 15/2 (Gl. nr. 41), RD.

82. This last was a slip, intended to mean they were born after Rachael's final separation from Lavien.

83. His family accepted this, e.g., 1 H 1.

84. 6 JCHW 243–4, sketching his life to his cousin in Scotland; cf. File No. 13402 B.L.Wt. 2279–450, Veterans' Rec. Br., U.S. Arch.

85. *Dan.-Am. Gaz.*, Univ. Lib., Copenhagen.

86. Fish Papers, 1822, Columbia Univ.

87. *New Travels in U.S.*, 92. For Geo. Bancroft's doubting reference, 7 *Hist. U.S.*, 79. The (U.S.) National Historical Publications Commn. has adopted 1755 as year of H's birth (Report to President, 1954, p. 54).

88. Award Dec. 14, 1765, payment Jan. 8, 1766 (Pantebog f. St. Cr. 1757–72., f. 116, U.S. Arch.; Pantebog f. Chr'sted 1765–67, f. 118, RD). He collected just in time, for Moir died next month, aged 43 (Register St. John's Ch. Chr'sted, burials).

89. 6 LHW 243.

90. *Dan.-Am. Gaz.*, Jan. 23, 1771; Ramsing, 238, mistakenly puts revolt, and Mr. H, on Grenada.

91. 5 JCHW 567–8, 6 *ibid.*, 245–6.

92. For entry of his burial see Atherton, *Conqueror,* 1902 ed., 544; a line was added, more than five years later, that James H was "Father of General Hamilton in America killed by Col. Baird" (Burr). Mr. Henry D. Baker, sometime U.S. Consul at Trinidad, identified for me a sugar plantation on St. Vincents where he learned that James Hamilton, Sr., worked.

93. 6 JCHW 243.

94. Loves, losses, and lapses of Lytton sons and daughters are given in detail, from original records, by Ramsing, 238 ff.

95. High tide for Lyttons may have been about 1760 when father and two sons had 57 slaves on Grange, No. 9, Company's Quarter, and Peter in addition was operating his wife's plantation, No. 32 in Queen's Quarter, with 42 grown slaves (1760 matricul, St. Cr. VI, folio pp. 26, 31, U.S. Arch.). On Dec. 3, 1764, Lytton sold Grange and its slaves for 60,000 rdl. in large cash payment and security for remainder (Pantebog f. Chr'sted 1765–67, f. 71, RD; *ibid.*, 1762–64, f. 416). Three years later estate was bought at auction by another purchaser for 87,000 rdl., of which more than 26,000 was still owing to Lytton (St. Cr. Upper Ct. Rec., Λ 1756–72, folio p. 156, U.S. Arch.).

96. Poll-tax lists, St. Cr., 1764–66, RD. Indk. Vestind, Br. W. Br. Journ. Lttr. B. No. 486. Gent. Toldk. A. Alexander must have known Grange in one way and another, though his relatives had left it before he came to the island; undoubtedly he was at his mother's burial there. Plantation is two miles sw. of Christiansted, near center of St. Croix. Northeast part of gracious dwelling, two stories, is original.

Chapter 2 (Pages 15 to 28)
Nicholas Cruger's "Young Man"

1. Ramsing, 239.

2. She and her sons appear in tax lists; in 1765 and 1766 she is called Rachael Fatzieth, in next two years Rachael Lewine (Landmaalerens Arbejdspr. pr. 1765–85, f. 64, jf. Arb. pr. f. Chr'sted 1803–34, p. 62, RD). As James Lytton bought for her six walnut chairs on Aug. 1, 1765, she was established here by then (Chr'sted Byfogedarkiv, skiftepr. 1766–70, No. 41, f. 392, RD). As James Hamilton's business for Ingram of St. Kitts was

not completed until four or five months after this, it is evident Rachael had decided, whatever his future plans, to remain on St. Croix. He probably returned to St. Kitts. The house in Company's Lane, no longer standing, was Alexander's first home in Christiansted. Location is on north side of way, next to schoolhouse (now parish hall) of Anglican church.

3. For some months in 1767–68 Rachael moved across street to No. 23, house of Capt. Wm. Eggan. Here she lived with "two white boys" (surely her sons), 3 grown slaves, and 4 slave children under 12 years. Her store continued to be kept as before in Dipnall's (poll-tax list, St. Cr. 1767, jfr. Landm. Arb. pr. 1803–34, 56, RD). Cottage at No. 23, judging from its structural timbers, may be same one Rachael occupied.

4. Common Records, St. Christopher, X (ex), No. 1, 1755–58, item 5799. Atherton, *N. Am. Rev., op. cit.,* 237, found this, but said the page disintegrated while she looked at it. It did not turn to dust; in 1951 Mr. D. S. Brookes, Registrar, helped me put together the remaining dark-brown ginger-smelling scraps, which give, in our arrangement, a somewhat different reading from Mrs. Atherton's. Mary spelled her name both Faucett and Fawcett. Richard Bowrey and John Evans were witnesses when instrument was recorded May 5 before Hon. Richard Wilson, Ct. of King's Bench and Common Pleas. Apparently Mary Fawcett did not appear before judge. She may have been ill, and died soon after. Hamm's will was recorded Nov. 24, 1759 (*ibid.,* Z, item 6352; Bowrey a witness). If Hamm died soon after this, slaves may have been hired by his executors, but they were on St. Croix at Rachael's death in 1768.

5. *Carøe: Den. Danske Laegestand* (The Danish Medical Profession), II 26, contains short biography of Æ. W. Heering.

6. Particulars of Rachael's illness and death are from claims presented to probate court, in Chr'sted Byfogedarkiv, skiftepr. 1766–70, No. 41, f. 386 ff., RD, and from burial register of St. John's Church, Christiansted.

7. When Jas. Lytton sold Grange plantation to John Denn, he reserved possession of burial plot. (Skiftepr. No. 49 f. Chr'sted. James Lytton, Sr's. Skifte f. 660, U.S. Arch.) Lytton himself and others of family were buried there after Rachael's interment. (Cf. Atherton in *N. Am. Rev., op. cit.,* 240; for Mrs. Atherton's disappointed search for Rachael's grave, see *ibid.* and *Adventures,* 333.)

8. Register has "Rachael Levine, Feb. 26, at Mr. Tuite's Plant., by D.O., aged 32." Robt. Tuite probably bought Grange when it was sold at auction in 1776. Entry is in error both as to date of burial and her age. From internal evidence, entries were not made immediately; probate ct. record, made at the time, gives date of burial as Feb. 20. As to mistaken age at death, same church register gives 1746 as year of birth of her son Peter Lavien, which would make her—if we accept her age as 32 in 1768—only 10 when she became a mother. She was, in fact, born about 1729, and

married Levien when 16; Peter was born when she was 17 (cf. Larson in 21 *Am. Genealogist* 161 ff., for full discussion).

9. Poll-tax list, St. Cr., 1768, RD.

10. Commonly held, cf. *Dan.-Am. Gaz.*, Sept. 19, 1772.

11. Cf. St. Cr. Upper Ct., Landsting. Protokol, Vol. A (1758–72), folio pp. 151, 197; Pantebog Bk. K, folio p. 197 left (U.S. Arch.).

12. Chr'sted Byfogedarkiv, skiftepr. 1766–70, No. 41. Peter Lewine's signature is on fol. 394 (U.S. Arch.). Soon after confirmation in St. John's, Christiansted, Peter Lavien was for two years a churchwarden in St. Helena's parish, Beaufort, S.C.; for particulars of his honorable service, see A. S. Salley, Jr., ed., *Minutes of Vestry of St. Helena's . . . 1726–1812*, pp. 139–42. Oct. 12, 1782, H forwarded, through Gen. Greene, then in S.C., an inquiry to Peter's executor (HLC unbnd. box. 1, printed in 2 R 318). Schachner (H 18, 436–7) accused J.C.H. of falsification to cover a family secret. Schachner drew his unworthy suspicions from an ignorant, bastardized copy of H's directions to Greene (4 HLC 477), not having seen original draft. The mystery, thus exploded, has a bearing on other insinuations in Schachner's biography.

13. Chr'sted Byfogedarkiv, skiftepr. 1767–73, No. 49, f. 13, RD, for Peter Lytton, found dead July 16; for James Lytton, St. John's Church register, Chr'sted.

14. Ramsing, 250 ff., set forth in detail vicissitudes which Alexander said reduced and broke them up. Supplements to Ramsing's meticulous account of H's relatives on St. Croix are indicated in my footnotes, mostly from records in U.S. Arch. Minor additional items in latter collection are in St. Croix matriculs as follows: 1743, folio p. 52; 1745, folio p. 54; 1751, Plantation No. 9, Company Quarter; 1753 A, folio p. 27; 1754, folio pp. 21, 54, 73; 1754–55, folio p. 38 of 1755 portion; 1760, VI, folio pp. 26, 31; 1766, folio pp. 31, 58; 1767, folio pp. 3, 5; 1768, folio pp. 9, 44; also St. Croix Hoved Bog (Gen. Ledger), folio pp. 12 (mutilated), 55; 1743, folio p. 129; Vol. A, 1756–72, Upper Ct. Protokol, folio p. 151 (April 5, 1768).

15. Chr'sted Byfogedarkiv, skiftepr. 1769–80, No. 50, f. 638, James Lytton's skifte, RD.

16. Receipts are to Thos. Lillie, dated May 16, 23, 1772, and May 3, 26, and June 3, 1773 (*ibid.*, ff. 324, 325, receipts nos. 965, 994, 1059, 1060 RD). Those for 1773 led Ramsing (252) to suggest that Hamilton left for mainland at least nine months later than others have assumed. However, receipts are merely listed in records of estate of Lillie (died 1776) without place of dating, and receipts themselves are missing (letter from Dr. Axel Linvald, Rigsarkivet, Copenhagen, Jan. 30, 1952). Both Ann and Alexander were on St. Croix in May 1772, and both were probably in N.Y. or vicinity in May–June 1773. Probably Lillie sent drafts to Alexander in America.

Ann was at odds with her husband (*Dan.-Am. Gaz.,* Vol. III, nos. 297–9, May 12–19, 1773), which would explain why he did not act for her. More likely, she was contributing certain sums advanced from her inheritance directly to Alexander, and he retained amounts for which he receipted in her name. Thus document No. 1045 in this series is not a receipt, but is Ann Venton's order on Capt. Lillie, May 3, 1773, in favor of Alexander Hamilton for 15 hhds. sugar from Lytton's estate. Advance to her on March 30, 1773 (for travel expenses to N.Y.?) (Skiftepr. No. 50, *ibid.,* 325), could not have been receipted for by Alexander.

17. Indenture mentioned in list of documents relating to Peter Lytton's estate (Chr'sted Byfogedarkiv, skiftepr. 1767–73, No. 49, f. 14, RD). Thos. McNobeny's skifte (*ibid.,* 1769–80, No. 50, ff. 880–95) contains no allusion to James Hamilton. Except for a letter of Alexander to him, June 1783 (James was in straits and Alexander hoped to settle him on a farm), we hear no more of him. He is not listed on St. Croix for poll tax. Ramsing (249–50) supposes he had died by 1786, when Madame Anna Hamilton (his widow?) was living in Frederiksted; records of division of her estate, Dec. 1787, are lost. (Atherton, *Few of Hamilton's Letters,* 136–8; poll-tax lists St. Cr., 1786–87. Prot. No. 31, gen. rec. of undertaken Skiftepr. St. Cr. 1781–1800. Pantebog f. St. Cr. 1785–88, f. 267, all RD.)

18. Chr'sted Byfogedarkiv, skiftepr. 1761–77, No. 37, ff. 186, 196.; Kopskatliste St. Cr. 1766–70, RD.

19. Geo. Bancroft, 7 *Hist. U.S.* (1866) 79. Lodge, H., 284–5, described a tracing of this signature; neither original nor copy now found.

20. Kopskatlister St. Cr., 1765–68, RD.

21. Both boys were living with Rachael in 1767, but when she died in Feb. 1768, the inventory of her effects showed only one bed in her house; James may have lived with the carpenter to whom he was apprenticed; Alexander may have been in home of James Stevens, family friend. However, it is reasonable to think Alexander began working only after his mother's death, which threw him on own resources. Cruger and Beckman would have known him, as they had sold goods to Rachael for her store; they were ready to assist orphans, for they were appointed guardians for certain minor heirs in the estate of James Lytton, Sr. (Skiftepr. No. 50 f. Chr'sted, ff. 630 ff., RD).

22. 1 JCHW, 1–2; 9 LHW, 37–8; exists in contemporary copy in unknown hand in 1 HLC, 7.

23. 6 JCHW 243.

24. 1 H 3; cf. AMH, 21 n., gratuitous. Ancient Jewish cemetery at Charlestown, Nevis, testifies to size and continuity of Jewish community there; cf. Common Records.

25. AMH, 21.

26. Schoolmasters came and went; cf., for these itinerants and their offerings, *Dan.-Am. Gaz.*, Dec. 15, 1770; Jan. 2, March 9, 20, 1771; Aug. 29, 1772. That Edward Stevens and H were schoolmates on St. Croix is mere assumption; that they were taught by the Rev. Hugh Knox is mistaken (cf. 1 H 4; Atherton, *Conqueror*, 73, 81; Schachner, H, 16–17).

27. 1 H 6.

28. With no pretensions in chemistry, he enjoyed the subject, and recommended it to the curiosity of others; as will appear, he attended lectures in medicine at King's College later.

29. Wrote little reflective pieces on moral topics, a habit in which he indulged sometimes years after for relaxation (H, *ibid.*) Contributions to Christiansted newspaper, echoing his reading, are mentioned below.

30. Felt rewarded by method and facility learned here, "and . . . adverted to it as the most useful part of his education" (1 H 6).

31. Matricul f. St. Cr., 1773, RD. *St. Croixian Pocket Companion* (Copenhagen, 1780, NYPL); Jefferys, *W. I. Atlas,* 1775; Oxholm, Map of St. Croix, 1794, gives estates by name and "quarter" (9 divisions of island) but not by number. Hans West, *Beyträge zur Beschreibung von St. Croix* (trans. from Danish, Copenhagen, 1794, 274 pp. NYPL), covers all features of life of this and neighboring islands only 20 years after H left; some of his friends and associates are mentioned. See also Dr. P. E. Kalmer, *St. Croix . . . as a Sanitary Place of Resort* (St. Croix, 1784, NYPL).

32. See *St. Croixian Pocket Companion,* especially 17 ff., for ordinances governing curfew, militia duty, obligation of whites to answer alarms.

33. Matricul f. St. Cr. 1766, RD; address is No. 8 King's St., belonging to Robt. Mears. John & Henry Cruger Copy Book of Letters (1767), NYHS, has several to Beckman & Cruger of St. Croix; "Mr. Kortrig[h]t" is mentioned (May 1, 1767).

34. Cornelius Durant, chiefly planter, advertised newly imported lumber, staves, hoops, herring, shad (*Dan.-Am. Gaz.,* Aug. 19, 1772; cf. Lillie, July 25; Capt. Larson, Dec. 19, 1770; Capt. Forske, April 27, 1771). General stores (Aug. 22, Sept. 8, 1770; Aug. 1, 1772) offered clothing, household furnishings, plantation supplies. A master might sell from his vessel (cf. Hojer, April 20, 1771). Besides, slaves and mules were put up at auction.

35. Cf. Atherton, *N. Am. Rev., op. cit.,* 239; AMH, photo. facing p. 4 is not of that called now "Alexander Hamilton Hardware Store." Proprietor of latter does not doubt its authenticity, and displays fine engraving of Trumbull portrait of H given, 1929, by Louise Lee Schuyler, great-granddaughter of H.

36. Poll-tax lists f. St. Cr. 1766–70; Landmaalerens Arb. pr. 1765–85, ff. 72, 79; *ibid.,* 1803, p. 6, RD; Public Surveyor's Protokol, Chr'sted, No. 19

(office of Pub. Wks., St. Cr.), p. 95, plat of nos. 7–8 King's St., 173, 195, indicates site was measured and Madame L. Andersen bought property from Cruger's heirs Aug. 2, 1803; descent can be traced to present.

37. Cruger's Wharf figures in old descriptions of N.Y.C., projected from Pearl St. into East River.

38. Chr'sted Byfogedarkiv, skiftepr. 1761–77, No. 37, ff. 186, 196, RD.

39. April 15, 1772 (Dutch Ch. register, St. Cr., 1764–87, Landsarkivet of Zealand, Copenhagen); this was six months before H left Cruger's employ, and reference to marriage is made in Cruger's correspondence in HLC. Cruger's sister-in-law, Mary de Nully, married planter John Rengger, also in 1772. Bertram Peter, eldest son of Nicholas and Anna (de Nully) Cruger was to marry Catharine, daughter of John Barker Church and wife Angelica Schuyler, this young man thus becoming H's nephew by marriage. For particulars of large mortgage debt of Catharine (Heyliger) de Nully, Cruger's mother-in-law, to Dutch bankers after her husband's death, see Protokol 1779, pp. 110 ff., Tax Assessor's office, St. Cr.

40. For Ann (Markoe) Cruger's claims in estate of father, see Landtingsret publicueret følgende Documenter, 1801 ff., 115, St. Cr.; soon after Cruger's death she married Wm. Rodgers (*ibid.*).

41. One of his wards was son of James Lytton, Jr.; this boy was afterward employed in Cruger's business as his cousin Alexander H had been (Ramsing, 268–9, without ref.).

42. Poll-tax lists, St. Cr., 1766–70 RD. From N.Y., he had many of same connections there and in islands as Cruger. He is often in records as guardian of minors.

43. His brother Lawrence was a founder of N.Y. Chamber of Commerce. (Riker, *Harlem,* 563–78, has full Kortright genealogy; Cornelius of St. Croix is No. 23; cf. Banner, *New York,* 697; Stevens, *N.Y. Chamber of Comm.,* 140).

44. *Dan.-Am. Gaz.,* Jan. 26.

45. 1 HLC 38.

46. *Ibid.,* 33.

47. For dissemblance to avoid Danish export laws, cf. ALS, L. Kortright, April 21, 1776, to Thos. Riche, Soc. Autogr. Coll., PHS; for his plantation holdings, St. Croix matricul, 1770, p. 21; Upper Ct. Protokol, G. 1785–88, pp. 15, 16 (U.S. Arch.); for mentions in different connections, *Dan.-Am. Gaz.,* Oct. 17, 1770; Jan. 19, 23; March 23, 1771; Sept. 9, 1772.

48. 1 H 4.

49. 1 HLC 32, N. Cruger to H. Cruger.

50. *Ibid.*, 32, same to same, May 19, June 6, 1772; he could not replace his protested bills "without throwing myself Intirely out of Trade. . . ." About same time earnestly solicited cash owing him, "as my stock in trade is but small" (*ibid.*, 22, Cruger to Rengger, March 11; cf. to T. Cruger, May 25, 1772, *ibid.*, 22, 34).

51. Shortly after, Jan. 1784, Nicholas Cruger gave "a violent beating in the street" to James Rivington, claiming that during the war, when a prisoner in N.Y., he had suffered from the Tory printer's aspersions (Benj. Walker to Steuben, Jan. 12, 1783 [4], 10 Steuben Papers, NYHS; cf. *Ind. Gaz.*, N.Y., Jan. 22, 1784).

52. Pantebog f. Chr. st. 1785–88, f. 168, RD; he gave general power of attorney on St. Croix to Sempill & Co., who also served H in business assignment there.

53. Franks, *N.Y. Directory*, 1786, p. 25. His country place was Rose Hill, land now partly embraced in headquarters of United Nations on East River. On Crugers see DeLancey in *N.Y. Geneal. and Biog. Record*, April 1875; *Ev. Post*, N.Y., Sept. 21, 1901; Hasell, Geneal. Sketches to accompany Cruger Family (ms., *ca.* 1892, NYPL); Sawyer, ed., Wills for N.Y. County, typescript, NYPL); Barber, Index of Deaths from *N.Y. Ev. Post* (typescript, NYPL).

54. 1 HLC 9–45. H of course signed letters to Cruger with own name; others "for Nicholas Cruger, by A. Hamilton," or similarly. H at this time was just turning 17. Nos. 1–20 seem of H's composition. His handwriting, earliest we have except for a reported signature, was as formed and flowing as later. Probably this sheaf of letters is in H papers because Cruger, when H was afterward a famous man, gave them to him as a reminder that he had been faithful in a few things.

55. ALS, H to Teleman (Tileman) Cruger, Nov. 16, 1771, "In behalf of Mr. Nicholas Cruger," 1 HLC 11).

56. Nicholas Fish's notes for a life of H (*ca.* 1823–25) contain query, "Did he receive a letter addressed to Mr. Cruger, when absent, containing a challenge; and as Mr. C's agent offer to *adjust that* as a part of Mr. C's business? & did this chivalrous proposal terminate the dispute happily?" (Columbia Univ.). Nothing is found to substantiate this.

57. Cruger had not arrived in N.Y. when his deputy was already writing him (AL, O[ctober], date torn, 1 HLC 9). Forwarding unanswered letter of Henry Cruger, Jr., of Bristol, Eng., H had forethought to "inclose . . . an abstract . . . of your last letters to him, which perhaps will be requisite in returning an answer." Called attention to erroneous demand of J. H. Cruger and attached memorandum, "a little state of matters between you that you might be able more clearly to convince him of his Mistake."

58. AL, Nov. 4, 1771, 1 HLC 9. This was doubtless one of times that made clergyman-physician friend Hugh Knox remember him as physically frail while on St. Croix (Knox to H, July 28, 1784, 5 HLC 679).

59. *Ibid.,* Nov. 12, 1771, p. 10.

60. 1 HLC 11. This is one of two letters from this correspondence in 1 JCHW 2–3, and only one in 9 LHW 38–9; all deserve printing, as they show how the boy was father to the man. He cautioned Capt. Newton to "be very choice in the quality of your mules, and bring as many as your vessel can conveniently contain—by all means take in a large supply of provender. Remember, you are to make three trips this season, and unless you are . . . diligent you will be too late, as our crops will be early in. Take care to avoid the Guarda Costas." Alexander would have seen references to these last in the Christiansted newspaper, heard reports from captains, etc. Cf. *Dan.-Am. Gaz.,* Dec. 19, 1770; March 4, May 15, 1771; Aug. 12, 1772. Newtons appear often in records. *Thunderbolt,* called by Alexander a sloop, stands in St. Croix Customs Journal, "incoming item" No. 1055 (U.S. Arch.), as "a barque." Her cargo was typical—corn meal, staves, hoops, mahogany dining tables, water-bread, inch and a half boards; total import duty was 45 rds. 72 s. The Journal of course contains all captains, vessels, cargoes mentioned by H—Capt. Wm. Lightbourn in a 50-ton barque; Lowndes in one of 30 tons, Capts. Gibb (variously spelled), Geo. Codwise were all of N.Y. Codwise is in N.Y. records, one connecting him with St. Cr. (Sawyer, Abstracts of Wills of N.Y. County, 29, NYPL). He and H must have been good friends, for we find Alexander Hamilton Codwise, son of Geo. Codwise, dying Oct. 18, 1826, at age of 22; he was born year of namesake's death, 1804 (Barber, Index of Deaths from *N.Y. Ev. Post,* 84, NYPL).

61. 1 HLC 13–14; the capt. required (erased) Joes down; this gave Alexander "high hopes . . . he will be oblig'd to go further, Cash of all kinds being very scarce here—even Danish bits . . . not to be had much less Joes." H was selling staves and provisions for "crop pay."

62. As early as 1716 Bd. of Police and Trade reported to King Frederick IV that St. Thomas must import from countries other than Denmark: "Exceedingly necessary for Sugar mills and plantations: mules from the Spaniards; horses from New York" (Westergaard, *Dan. W. I.,* 314; cf. *Dan.-Am. Gaz.,* March 13, April 6, 1771). New England or "Northward" horses were preferred over native ("Creole") ones (*ibid.,* Dec. 29, 1770; Jan. 5, 1771).

63. Nov. 27, 177 (1, torn) to Walton and J. H. Cruger (1 HLC 13–14).

64. *Ibid.,* to N. Cruger, 15; she had come from N.Y. in less than a month.

65. Jan. 10, 1772, 1 HLC 15. He had Cruger's business under control, down to "rectifying a small error in . . . addition" in account of Willing & Taylor (*ibid.,* 16).

66. AL, Feb. 1, 1771 (in anxiety and haste misdated for 1772), 1 HLC 17. St. Cr. Customs Journal, 1772, incoming item No. 87, U.S. Arch., gives slightly different particulars; mules were valued at 50 rds. each, and with 1,200 staves brought duty to 107 rds. Alexander may have sent half famished mules from *Thunderbolt*'s hold to East End plantation of Edmund Purcell, who advertised "excellent pasture" (*Dan.-Am. Gaz.*, Sept. 23, 1772). More details of argosy of invalids are in reports to owners. Newton took in 48 mules on Spanish Main Jan. 2, but calms, head winds delayed arrival at St. Croix till end of month "with 41 Mere Skeletons." Seven died on passage, eight could hardly stand, "& in spite of the greatest care 4 of them are now in Limbo." He hoped he could pronounce rest out of danger; had sold 17 at 100 pcs. the head (ALS, Feb. 24, 1772, to Walton and J. H. Cruger, 1 HLC 20; to N. Cruger, *ibid.*, 20–22). Worried by employer's absence, tottering mules, calms at sea, and malingering correspondent at Curaçao, young H admonished Capt. Newton against repetition: "Reflect continually on the unfortunate voyage you have just made, and endeavour to make up for the considerable loss . . . accruing to your owners. Lay in at least a Months supply for your Mules" (ALS, Feb. 1, 1771 [1772], 1 HLC 18).

67. Cruger wrote to Boos, a lawyer: "I am glad to find my Clerk in my absence has desired you to take all my affairs in your hands that was in Mr. Hassell's—who . . . has been very negligent in them and triffled away a good deal of money to no purpose" (March 18, 1772, *ibid.*, 23).

68. Indeed, from identity of phrases during and after employer's absence, perhaps some letters with Cruger's signature were composed as well as copied by H. Generally forecasts of business prospects H made were borne out, except that lumber became a "drugg." Cf. H to H. Cruger, Feb. 24, 1772; N. Cruger to same, March 7, 1772, and to Ashburner, May 13, 1772 (1 HLC 18, 22, 31).

69. N. Cruger to J. H. Cruger, March 30, 1772, and to Tileman Cruger, April 26, 1772 (1 HLC 26, 30).

70. "No. 1 to 6 ST," Cruger wrote N.Y. consignees, "are . . . Hhds Clay'd Sugars, that you'll have carted up immediately for fear of a Discovery. . . . have them Enter'd paying the same Duty as Muscovado" (to Walton & Cruger, April 28, 1772, *ibid.*, 28). And a month later: "Rye flour will sell for pcs. 7 a barrel here . . . but the Duty is 25 p C.^{t} however we enter it as corn meal and give the [tide] waiter a fee. . . ." (to Thos. Thomas, May 25, 1772, *ibid.*, 34), draft or copy in H's hand.

71. To Henry Cruger, Jr., N.Y., June 6, 1772, concerning cargo of *Venus* (1 HLC 38; cf. N. Cruger to J. H. Cruger, June 5, 1772, 1 HLC 37): 250 Gold Coast slaves arrived in Danish Guineaman "very indifferent indeed, sickly & thin, they average about 30£," which was less than for mules.

72. In letter of Cruger to Rengger & Co., copied in H's hand, it seems strange to find, "I beg Gentlemen you answer in English—as I don't so well understand the french language. . . ." If Alexander's later full command of French was learned from his mother and grandmother, he must have been able to translate for his employer. Possibly already by this date (July 18, 1772, 1 HLC 45) plans had been made for him to go to the continent. Or Cruger may have had in mind his versatile clerk's temporary absence on errand to St. Eustatia (mentioned in 1 H 6–7 but not in documents).

73. *Dan.-Am. Gaz.*, April 6, 1771.

74. *Ibid.*, April 10, 1771. Alex Bein, *Die Staatsidei Alexander Hamiltons in ihrer Entstehung und Entwicklung* (Munich and Berlin, Oldenbourg, 1927), Beilage B, 173–7, is devoted to influence of Machiavelli on H; Beilage A, 165–72, examines his debt to Hume. H knew both authors well, often cited Hume, a copy of whose *Essays* was in his library (AHM 74).

Chapter 3 (Pages 29 to 43)

To Continent and Career

1. May 27, 1772, to Vincent Lopez (1 HLC 35).

2. Knox, *Discourse on Hurricane*, 16–18 n.; *Dan.-Am. Gaz.*, Sept. 9, 1772 ff., for many reports of damage; H's letter in *ibid.*, Oct. 3, 1772, repeated main particulars.

3. His son (1 H 7) is the earliest authority (1834) attributing Alexander's good fortune to the hurricane letter. In absence of any documentary allusion we suppose he had it from his father or mother. However, his particulars are mistaken in several respects; letter was published in newspaper of St. Croix, not St. Christopher, and produced its impression with "principal persons of the island" before it appeared in print. This is hinted in introductory editorial note; besides, he probably was on his way to Boston by time piece was published.

4. The only known copy of *Gazette* for Oct. 3, 1772 (Vol. III, No. 234), is in the University Library, Copenhagen, but letter is printed in Atherton, *Few of Hamilton's Letters*, 261–7.

5. Knox, *Discourse on Hurricane*. It was delivered in Dutch church before an "audience," not congregation. Knox, recently arrived on St. Croix, had no church edifice as yet; he was chosen as orator before nonsectarian gathering because of his eloquence and public spirit. It was "thought expedient to make [the address] yet more public." It is hard to know whether pamphlet was directed more to conscience of St. Croix or to charity of

creditors elsewhere and to trade lenity of King of Denmark. Knox pictured "the multiplied ruins, the dreadful and almost universal desolation of this lately blooming, fertile, flourishing, but now poor, distressed, miserable, helpless Island. . . ." Cf. wording of title page. Copy in Princeton library was presented by author to Pres. Witherspoon.

6. Incidentally, Alexander's letter in *Gazette* appeared on back of page advertising Knox's pamphlet, "Price 6 Old Bitts," which was printed by publisher of newspaper, Daniel Thibou. With a text from Isaiah, Knox enlarged on wickedness of closing ears to divine warnings. "God spoke to us . . . out of the midst of the whirlwind" on "that awful and terrifick day of the Lord" (26).

7. Ramsing, 263.

8. For more detail see B. Mitchell in 69 *NJHS Proceed.*, 88–114.

9. *Dan.-Am. Gaz.*, Oct. 13, 1790, for date of birth; Miller, *John Rodgers,* had good means of knowing Knox was born in Ireland; O'Brien, *Mulligan,* 44, has Armagh, without ref. Knox said, "I was bred in a very pure district of the Church of Scotland, of which my father was a faithful minister. . . ." (ALS, Saba, Oct. 16, 1766, to Jacob Green, Presby. HS, Phila.).

10. Dr. Hugh Williamson, who had studied under Alison, went to West Indies, 1772, to collect funds for academy, then at New Ark, Del.; he may have seen Knox and his errand may have prompted Knox to suggest that Alexander be sent to mainland for education.

11. *Presby. Ch. in U.S., embracing Minutes of Presby. of Phila., 1706–88,* p. 199.

12. Miller, *Rodgers,* 97; for mean condition of schoolmasters in this district, "hired by the year, by a knot of Families," cf. Holcomb, *Sketch of Early Eccles. Affairs in New Castle, Del., etc.,* 47–8.

13. Miller, 98–110; for Knox's much later allusion to sinful ridicule of sermons cf. his *Transitory Nature . . . of all Sublunary Things,* 53 (Princeton Univ.).

14. Miller, 98–103; Alexander and Carnahan, Notices of Distinguished Graduates of College of N.J. (ms. in Princeton Lib.).

15. Sprague, 3 *Annals of Am. Pulpit* 180; Hugh Knox folder in secretary's office, Princeton Univ.; *N.Y. Mercury,* Sept. 30, 1754, in 1 ser., 19 *N.J. Archives* 418–9.

16. Webster, *Hist. Presby. Ch.,* 659; *Presby. Ch. in U.S.,* 257 ff. Knox's ordination sermon, *Dignity and Importance of Gospel Ministry,* 17, emphasized obligation of pastor to teach from house to house, to "be particularly acquainted with every Person under his Care . . . and to know their principal Weaknesses and Dangers," with special attention to children.

17. Pr. No. 31, gen. reg. of undertaken Skifter, St. Cr., 1781–1800, p. 35, RD; Knox, *Sources of Our Saviour's Tears* . . . *Funeral Sermon for Madam Simmons,* 53–4.

18. ALS, Knox, Saba, Jan. 22, 1772, to the Rev. Jacob Green (PHS, Gratz).

19. Great Britain, Hydrograph. Dept., Admiralty, *West Indies Pilot,* 290, 293–5.

20. Knox's most connected work was *Discourses on* . . . *Truth of Revealed Religion* . . . (London, 1768, 2 vols.). If Knox gave this book of admonitions to young H, as is likely, Alexander may have received from it some of his early piety, his disapproval of slavery, and may even have been bolstered, later, in his policy of excises to diminish consumption of distilled liquors. A figure of speech of Knox (II, 243), "Our duty is written, as it were, with sun beams" (cf. his *Moral* . . . *Miscellany,* vi), may be the origin of celebrated sentences of H in *Farmer Refuted,* 1775: "The sacred rights of mankind are not to be rummaged for among old parchments. . . . They are written, as with a sunbeam, in the whole volume of human nature, by the hand of Divinity itself. . . ." ALsS, Knox, Saba, Oct. 16, 1766; Aug. 29, 1768, to Green (Presby. HS), with others not preserved, became his pamphlet, *Letter to* . . . *Green* . . . *Pointing out Difficulties in* . . . *Calvinistic* . . . *Divinity* (N.Y., 1809, but originally in shorter form, 1770; cf. Webster, 659); Knox preferred deeds to doctrine.

21. ALS, Knox to Green, Jan. 22, 1772.

22. Knox to Green, *ibid.*

23. Ramsing, 262, referring to letters of Larson, and Danske Canc. 4 Departm. open and closed letters, 1771–73, p. 273, RD.

24. Knox, *Discourse on Hurricane,* title page; *St. Croixian Pocket Companion,* 1780, p. 10, listed seven clergymen of congregations on island (one at Frederiksted); "The Revd. Doct. Hugh Knox" was "Minister of the Scotch Presbyterian Church at Christiansted"; the Rev. Henricus Muller was minister of Dutch Reformed Church, same town. Besides these denominations there were two Anglican churches, a Danish Lutheran, a Roman Catholic, and three Moravian churches with a bishop.

25. Longer acquaintance (beginning before Alexander worked for Cruger), in which Knox directed his reading, watched "the unfolding of his mind," was assumed by J. C. Hamilton (1 H 3–4). Atherton was wider of truth, believing Knox baptized Alexander (*Conqueror,* 538–9).

26. 1 *Select Sermons,* iv; writing of "The Value and Importance of a Child," Knox enjoined that one should "instil into [his] tender opening mind the principles of piety, integrity . . . who can conceive the good of which such a child may be made the instrument, or the degrees of happiness and

of glory to which it may be advanced" (*Moral Miscellany,* 279). Knox asked of Green, "When our Lord looked upon the *young man* in the gospel, and *loved him,* can we suppose that he saw nothing in him morally good, which was a motive of his *love?*"

27. Knox was not only a persistent writer of tracts of moral and secular advice, but distributed more; this year offered to dispose of four dozen copies of an "ingenious little Colloquy" of his friend Green (Saba, Jan. 2, 1772, to Green, Presby. HS).

28. Cf. 1 H 3, important because information must have been from H himself. Knox was always urging understanding and education, e.g., ". . . the mind is as much . . . delighted by the discoveries of knowledge and truth, as the body is with animal refreshments. . . ." (1 *Select Sermons* 34–5).

29. H's patriotic pamphlets have style of argumentation reminding of orderly method of Knox's combative pieces, and the language itself is similar.

30. Knox in his writings emphasized that intellect and character must be blended for a useful, happy life, but did not omit to dwell on the need of religious observance as an end in itself. Knox, like numerous clergymen of the time, healed bodies as well as souls. (For his license as physician and apothecary, see *Caroe: Den Danske Laegestand,* I, 71; Danske Canc. Vestind. Sager 1773–86, f. 104; *Dan.-Am. Gaz.,* Aug. 24, 1776; he was designated as D.D. and M.D. in St. Cr. Upper Ct. Protokol, F, 1782–85, folio p. 422, U.S. Arch.). Whether this concern of his mentor prompted Alexander to attend medical lectures his first year at King's is a guess.

31. For proposal that the continent send food to afflicted people of West Indies, see *Boston Gazette,* Oct. 26, 1772.

32. Knox, *Discourse on Hurricane,* Dedication and p. 25.

33. This is son's story, 1 H 7. Whether the governor and other principal persons "made an especial effort to discover" the author of the printed letter "and ultimately traced it to Hamilton" seems doubtful, for letter, as noted above, did not appear in paper until after Alexander, by supposition here, must have been sent off. Instead we know Knox had been showing ms. copy of original for some time. We may be sure he boasted that Alexander had written it, and asked aid for the boy's education.

34. ALS, 5 HLC 679.

35. The shipments to N.Y., probably sugar, which on sale were devoted to H's support, were only two in number, separated by two or three years (Hercules Mulligan, 84 HLC 13695 ff.). Knox, as only teacher in group, would know Alexander must spend some months in preparation, then at least three years in college, the whole costing not less than £400.

36. Statement of his son (1 H 7), "His relations had provided him with ample funds, and had made arrangements for future remittances," was probably misapplied family pride.

37. Cf. De Lancey in *N.Y. Geneal. Record,* April 1875, p. 6; basis not stated but his assumption likely is correct.

38. 1 H 8 n.

39. Ramsing, 267, says he left mid-June 1772 in Capt. Lightbourne's ship and "presumably stayed away . . . for several years."

40. Knox to H, July 28, 1784 (5 HLC 679).

41. 1 H 7 says he arrived in Boston in Oct. Local newspaper had no notice of his departure amidst scant St. Croix items.

42. *Ibid.*

43. Thus *Speed* brig, bound Jamaica to Jamestown, Va., with sugar and £3000 specie to pay for return lading, when just past Bahamas, laid to for vessel thought to be in distress. Suddenly the stranger hoisted French colors, and compelled Capt. Cotton to hand over cash or be sunk (*Mass. Spy,* Oct. 15, 1772); cf. *Mass. Gaz. and Boston News-Letter,* March 25, 1773. Search through 1773 showed no vessel that had been afire.

44. *Mass. Gaz.,* Oct. 22; *Boston Gaz.,* Oct. 26, 1772; *Boston Ev.-Post, ibid.* This is only vessel recorded in newspapers as reaching Boston toward the end of Sept. or in Oct. from St. Croix, though half a dozen more entered from other Caribbean islands. Efforts to trace the name of vessel or anything about Capt. Waters unsuccessful. The ship did not proceed from Boston to N.Y., for *N.Y. Gaz.,* Nov. 23, 1772—first paper that could have mentioned Waters's further movements—had nothing of him.

45. Two of H's close successors in Treasury were similarly of foreign birth, Gallatin the Swiss and Alexander Dallas from Jamaica.

46. His voyage probably took about three weeks. "The Vessels employed in this [West Indies] Traffic are usually of a Construction . . . for fast Sailing & the owners rely much on the . . . frequent returns of their Capitals, by the Expedition of their Voyages. . . ." (Wm. Bingham, Phila., to H as Sec. of Treas., 1789, 10 Wolcott, CHS). Capt. Hodge reached N.Y. in 14 days from St. Croix (*N.Y. Jnl.,* Dec. 16, 1773; cf. *ibid.,* Oct. 1, 1772, April 7, 1774). For the brisk West Indian trade of Boston at this time see *Boston Gaz.,* Sept. 28, 1772 (sloop for sale), many advs. in this paper; Cunningham, ed., *John Rowe,* 209.

47. *Rowe,* April 24, 1770, p. 201.

48. *Ibid.,* Oct. 28, 31, 1772, p. 235.

49. *Boston Gaz.,* Nov. 2, 1772.

50. *Rowe,* 235; *Boston Gaz.,* Nov. 2, 1772.

51. Recollections of two of H's closest friends, recorded years later, were mistaken, in different ways, about his first visit to Boston. Mulligan said he went from St. Croix to Boston (independently confirmed by J. C. H.), but made date Oct. 1773 instead of 1772. Mulligan thought Alexander "wrote two or three political pieces while at Boston which were published in a newspaper there." (84 HLC 13698, ed. Schachner in 3d ser., 4 *W&M Quar.* 209 ff.) No such contributions identified, though some mentioned below may have been his. Troup put arrival prior to 1773, when H entered King's College, but said with a "bias towards the British monarchy, he took a Journey to Boston, soon after the destruction of the East India tea. . . . From Boston he returned to New York . . . an enthusiast for resisting the claims of the British Parliament. . . ." (*W&M Quar., op. cit.,* 213, and 1 H 25). Tea Party was Dec. 16, 1773; unlikely H had occasion, time, or money to break into his first year of college to go to Boston. Later H declared his original monarchist sentiments. Cf. below for political opinions of Boudinot, Livingston, *et al.,* when he was at Elizabethtown.

52. *Boston Gaz.,* Nov. 2, 1772.

53. *Ibid.,* Oct. 19, 1772. His impatient muse took to prose: "The approaches [to slavery] are slow . . . in the beginning. . . . The eyes of the People are at length open, but . . . too late. . . . In the name of God, my countrymen, why this . . . lethargy? . . . Have frequent meetings. Annimate and confirm one another." Alexander may not have lingered in Boston long enough to read conclusion of "Humanity," "founded on the word of God, as well as reason, that Freedom ought to live, whoever dies; and that the Americans would be justified in the sight of Heaven and before all nations . . . in forming an independent government of their own, and cutting off every son of Adam that dared to oppose them by force" (*ibid.,* Nov. 9, 1772). "A British Bostonian" invited subscribers for his libertarian essay, "The AMERICAN ALARM" (*ibid.,* Nov. 30). "Whig Proselyte," after much more, damned "our American Machiavel" (Hutchinson) for his doctrine that "Government is founded in Power. . . ." (*ibid.,* Oct. 5, 1772).

54. Cf. Thwing, *Crooked . . . Streets of Boston,* 109, 136–8.

55. Joseph Ward was advertising his English Grammar School "in a House adjoining to the Treasurer's Office" where, besides elementary subjects, he offered rhetoric, knowledge of globes, history, natural, moral philosophy, and "nature of Civil Government," but Alexander needed, for entrance to college, classical languages, mathematics that Ward omitted (*Boston Gaz.,* Oct. 12, 19, 1772).

56. *Mass. Gaz.,* Oct. 1, 1772; as stage left Boston alternate Mondays, journey must have required better part of week each way.

57. See Mulligan's narrative, *op. cit.;* references here are to *W&M Quar.,* 209–11. Mulligan set down his memories, forty years after events, for J. C.

Hamilton, who leaned on this account in 1 H 7 ff. Nich. Fish, early friend, did not know when H arrived in N.Y. (Fish mss., Columbia Univ.).

58. Mulligan's narrative, 209.

59. Knox (above) said he recommended Alexander to old friends. Rodgers, mentioned by Mulligan, would be first in Knox's mind. Troup recalled Mason (cf. 1 H 7); he and Mulligan spoke of "others" and "other distinguished Presbyterians" to whom Alexander brought introductions from Knox; among these were Elias Boudinot, Wm. Livingston. None of these letters was found.

60. See Miller, *Memoirs of Rodgers*. NYHS has package of Rodgers' ms. sermons, 1755–1806; ALS, Rodgers, Feb. 10, 1779, to Boudinot (NYHS), illustrates friendship between these sponsors of Alexander. Mason, b. Scotland 1734, was minister of Cedar St. Church from 1761, and 20 years later became trustee of Princeton.

61. For an admiring account of this worthy, see Michael O'Brien, Jr., *Hercules Mulligan*. He was one of several Irishmen who came into H's story, always with fervor; others were Barber, Gen. John Sullivan, Wm. Coleman, first editor of *N.Y. Ev. Post* which H patronized; Hugh Knox was born, grew up in Ireland.

62. O'Brien, 16 ff.

63. *Ibid.*, 33–4.

64. Mulligan, *op. cit.*, 210; Mulligan married Elizabeth Sanders, dau. of John Sanders, of N.Y., in Trinity Church, 1773, and between 1774 and 1776 moved home and shop to 23 Queen (now Pearl) St. (O'Brien, 38). If Alexander's income extended to elegance in attire, which later he always contrived to make it do, Mulligan could supply him from his notable stock of finery, as afterward he furnished "resplendent black velvet suit" in which Pres. Washington appeared at levees. Decorative items Mulligan offered included "gold and silver lace, with some half laces for hats," "gold and silver buttons and loops," "gold and silver treble French chain" (*ibid.*, 38–40).

65. O'Brien, 24; "Association of the Sons of Liberty was comprised of a great Number of the principal Gentlemen of the City, Merchants, Lawyers and other inhabitants of all Ranks," perhaps the last predominating, who organized "to testify their Abhorrence of the Diabolical Project of enslaving America" (*N.Y. Jnl.*, Dec. 16, 1773).

66. O'Brien, 115; Freeman, 5 *Washington* 461 ff., 5 Stokes 1173 ff., do not mention.

67. Mulligan recorded afterward that H "evinced his gratitude [through life] for the attentions of my brother & myself by taking one of my sons to study law with him & refusing the least compensation" (*W&M Quar., op. cit.*, 211).

68. Selection of N.Y. area rather than Phila., where Alexander's cousin John Hallwood was sent to school, is another indication Knox, Cruger, and friends had taken over from the Lytton family.

69. E.g., Aaron Burr, a year younger than H, had finished at Nassau Hall a few months before H arrived in this country.

70. Shortest, commonest way was by the ferries, craft of many sorts propelled by sail and oar, from Battery to Elizabethtown Point. John Adams mistakenly supposed young H, from West Indies, "went to Scotland, for education . . . till seventeen years of age; . . . then entered a college at New York. . . ." Adams, in vindictive mood, observed that H's (imaginary) schooling in Scotland helped unfit him to "acquire the opinions, feelings, or principles of the American people." (Letter XII, *Correspondence of . . . President Adams . . . published in Boston Patriot*, 54–5; see correction in Pickering, *A Review of Correspondence between . . . Adams and Cunningham* [Boston, 1824] 157 and Pickering to Nich. Fish, Dec. 5, 1823, Fish Papers, Columbia Univ.).

71. See Peter Kalm's description, a quarter-century before Hamilton knew the village (Pinkerton 13 *Collection of . . . Travels* 389–90), mentioning its two churches, town hall, substantial (mostly frame) dwellings, pleasant gardens, orchards, and salt marshes to south and northeast. More precise is Lt. John Hills's map (Position of British Forces at Elizabeth Town Point . . . June 1780, in Wm. Faden, *Battles of Rev.*), with every building shown, including Presbyterian Church and Academy.

72. Cf. memorial of First Presby. Church to Congress, in Murray, *Notes Concerning Elizabeth-Town*, 106. History of church, religious and political, is in Murray; for year of H's stay, when he undoubtedly attended services there, we have detail in ms. Trustees' Minutes (Princeton Univ.); for physical features, cf. Gugler *et al., Architectural History . . .* ; Hogue, *Public Properties, City of Elizabeth*, with Meyer's map, 1775–83; Wheeler and Halsey, *Inscriptions on Tombstones. . . .* The "fine church with steeple and bells" H knew replaced (1724) original one dating from first settlement. From instructions to sexton, Wm. Woodruff, probably drawn by Boudinot, pres. of Trustees (Minutes, March 24, 1766), we see care for decorum of services. The same worthies who deliberated about maintenance of clock in steeple were soon to regulate weights and springs of province, state, and nation, and in this needed no greater formality in proceedings.

73. 1st ser., 25 *N.J. Archives* 227–8. This was the celebrated Tapping Reeve (1744–1823) who afterward was founder (1775) and for long sole teacher of first law school in America, at Litchfield, Conn. Among thousand graduates were Aaron Burr, Reeve's brother-in-law, and Robert Troup, H's friend (cf. 21 *Princeton Alumni Weekly*, No. 3, and *Connecticut Circle*, Feb. 1939; clipping in Sec'y's office, Princeton Univ.). Control of Academy passed to Church, 1769 (Trustees' Minutes, June 5).

74. Trustees' Minutes, May 22, 1767. This building where Alexander studied was burned by refugees same night as the church, Jan. 25, 1780, when school had been suspended and house was used to store food for army. For it and successors, to present tasteful lecture room, occupying same site, see Murray, *op. cit.*, frontispiece; Gugler *et al.*, 16; Vorhees in *Eliz. Jnl.*, Feb. 16, 1929.

75. Appointed by Church Trustees to inspect school once every quarter, and to hear pupils examined, Visitors during H's year were the Rev. Benj. Hart, John D[e]Hart, Robt. Ogden, Robt. Halstead (Minutes, Nov. 14, 1771), Wm. Livingston, Geo. Ross (*ibid.*, Aug. 12, 1772).

76. Cf. Sedgwick, *Livingston,* 157; 1 H 7–8 has brief, appreciative allusion.

77. *N.Y. Gaz.,* Jan. 6, 1772, in 1st ser., 28 *N.J. Archives* 7–9.

78. For date, about which some doubt, see correspondence of Katharine Hastings *et al.* in Barber folder, Sec'y's office, Princeton; early Princeton records suffered in fires in Nassau Hall.

79. About time of Francis' graduation from college, Patrick and wife Jane (Fraser) moved to Neelytown (then Montgomerytown), N.Y., where he was farmer, judge of general sessions Orange Co., an honest, patriotic man, and exceedingly poor speller, see letters to McKesson, Cross, Duane, (Elias) Dayton, in NYHS and PHS (Gratz), especially last, May 22, 1781, concerning an orderly and horses left with him by sons Francis and William when they set out in Yorktown campaign.

80. *N.Y. Mercury,* Oct. 12, 1767, in 1st ser., 25 *N.J. Archives* 469 ff.; among classmates was Richard Devens, who at once began teaching at Elizabethtown Academy, later was tutor in Princeton, and may have recommended Barber.

81. Wheeler and Halsey, *Inscriptions on Tombstones* . . . , 70; Rivington's *N.Y. Gaz.,* Oct. 14, 1773, in 1st ser., 29 *N.J. Archives* 62.

82. When Barber resumed, the Visitors announced a new plan of guaranteed preparation for college in return for an over-all charge of £45, N.Y. currency, including board in good families. His success in fitting Alexander in short order may have suggested to Barber warranty, for stipulated sum, would be attractive to parents of other pupils from foreign parts (Rivington, March 10, 1774, in *ibid.*, 241). Or scheme may have been patterned after that of Jos. Periam, earlier, at Princeton (*Pa. Jnl.*, Oct. 16, 1766, in 1st ser., 25 *N.J. Archives* 229–32).

83. Heitman, *Officers of Continental Army,* 86. Barber's unit was soon ordered to cross to N.Y. (Stirling to Col. Elias Dayton, March 10, 1776, and *ibid.* to Washington, Wm. Alexander Papers, NYHS).

84. 11 GW 136–7; cf. 163.

85. His ms. orderly book, May 26–Sept. 6, 1779, in NJHS, is printed in the Society's *Proceed.* Vol. 65, p. 61 ff. This is longest continuous record of Barber, for many orders, issued in Sullivan's name, probably were his. Cf. Barber to his (second) wife, July 1, 1779 (PHS, Gratz), when campaign was in prospect.

86. ALS, Benj. Walker to Steuben, Feb. 12, 1783 (NYHS); ALS, Wm. North to Walker, Feb. 16, 1783 (PHS); Elmer, *"Elogy* [sic] *on Francis Barber.* Handsome portrait of Barber by John Herring, engraved by Stephen Comber, is from sketch by fellow officer in field.

87. Since King's was under Church of England auspices, and Wm. Livingston had feuded with its authorities (see below), Alexander's Presbyterian sponsors would not think of its grammar school for him. That of Nassau Hall was "a Nursery for the College" (announcement, Aug. 5, 1768, 1st ser., 26 *N.J. Archives* 269, 384) to which Alexander soon applied for admission. However, Academy at Elizabethtown was directly under Presbyterian control, was taught by Princeton men, had flexible curriculum meeting Alexander's needs; there he could be guest in homes of Boudinot, Livingston.

88. See *N.Y. Jnl.,* Oct. 16, 1766, in 1st ser., 25 *N.J. Archives* 227–8; *N.Y. Mercury,* Dec. 21, 1767, supplement, in *ibid.,* 512.

89. Freshman year was given to Horace, Cicero, Greek Testament, Lucian, Xenophon (Collins, 1 *Witherspoon* 107).

Chapter 4 (Pages 44 to 56)
Elizabethtown and Quest for College

1. Elias Boudinot, ALS to Jos. Reed, Sept. 1, 1775 (Reed Papers, NYHS), praised Washington because he thought a Virginian would moderate rashness of New England men. Witherspoon, of College of N.J., was earlier than local compatriots in advancing from remonstrance to rebellion; however, his demand for independence was latent at time of H's schooling in N.J. (cf. Collins, 1 *Witherspoon* Chap. 2).

2. Narratives of Mulligan and Troup, *op. cit.*

3. See steel engraving of portrait in possession of family, Emmet 4779, NYPL; frontispiece in Sedgwick, *Livingston,* is silhouette supposed made 1773, when H was in Elizabethtown; his thinning hair was curled above high forehead, matching ruffle below his stock. Cf. John Adams' Diary in 2 *Works,* ed. 1856, 361; Thatcher, quoting Alex. McWhorter, in 60 *NJHS Proceed.* 229, and Sedgwick, 444.

4. His grandmother, Sarah Van Brugh, spoiled him to age of 14 in fashion not even a year among Mohawks in company of a missionary could cure.

5. See photostat of indenture in Law Misc., NYPL.

6. Frequently republished in anthologies, e.g., *American Poems, Selected and Original* (Litchfield, Conn., 1793).

7. "The Reflector is determined to proceed . . . fearless of the humble scoundrel and the eminent villain. The cause he is engaged in is [that] of truth and liberty; what he intends to oppose is superstition, bigotry, priestcraft, tyranny, servitude, public mismanagement, and dishonesty in office" (Chap. 11).

8. Always, in the baffling habit of the day, under noms de plume; such were "The Watch Tower," in *Mercury,* 1754–5; "The Sentinel," in *N.Y. Post-Boy,* 1765; "The American Whig," in *N.Y. Gaz.,* 1768–9; "The Watchman," in *N.Y. Jnl.,* 1770; these weekly comments were interspersed with polemical pamphlets.

9. Livingston anticipated Justice O. W. Holmes's "clear and present danger" doctrine, admonishing that "the Civil Power hath no Jurisdiction over the sentiments or opinions of the Subject, till such Opinions break out into Actions prejudicial to the Community, and then it is not the Opinion, but the Action that is the Object of the Punishment" (*Reflector* 24; cf. for excellent summaries of Livingston's principles Thatcher in 56 *NJHS Proceed.,* No. 4; 60, Nos. 2, 4). His opposition to slavery was pronounced; cf. Sedgwick, 399–400.

10. Still, credulousness of the people must "render the establishment of a pure democracy, a thing impracticable" for they were "ever ready to be bewitched, cheated, and enslaved, by a powerful, crafty seducer. . . ." When he spoke of the people as "darlings of Providence" he restricted solicitude to propertied classes; never urged extension of franchise.

11. Immediate result of Livingston's protest was to deprive college of half its intended funds, diverted to a jail and pesthouse (cf. Pine, *King's College* . . . , 6–9, and below).

12. See ms. Livingston Cost Books in Sup. Ct. of N.Y., 1749–72, NYPL.

13. Sedgwick, 155 ff.; this time of completion of new house is borne out by mechanics', tradesmen's accounts in Livingston mss., Bk. A, MHS.

14. Vorhees in *Eliz. Jnl., op. cit.,* assumes contrary and gives description, no less informing on local topography, of Alexander's route in walking from Liberty Hall to Academy. Probably Alexander visited mansion while building. Livingston was devoted gardener, arborculturist; planting at Liberty Hall may have been pleasant recollection to H in developing grounds of his "Grange" country house 30 years later.

15. Sedgwick, 160–6.

16. However, Livingston had a whimsicality and turn for satire that were left out of H's makeup.

17. In Continental Congress he was on comm. that drafted address to people of Great Britain. He stigmatized minority in Congress who fomented the break. "I cannot entertain the most favourable opinion of a man's veracity, who intended to do it [declare independence] when he swore he did not, and when he represented a people who were actually pursuing measures to prevent the necessity of doing it" (Sedgwick, 174). John Adams's slur that Livingston deliberately avoided signing Declaration of Independence was undeserved (to Jefferson, Sept. 17, 1823, Sedgwick, 188). He had been called from Congress to command of N.J. militia (cf. ALS, Camp at Elizabeth Town, Sept. (?) 2, 1776, to son Brockholst, MHS). Livingston's condemnation of weaknesses of Confederation, prompt espousal of Constitution and new government were to prove valuable aids to H.

18. Boudinot's father, also Elias, married, second, Catherine Williams in Antigua; he was silversmith at Princeton, afterward at Elizabethtown (cf. 61 *NJHS Proceed*. 154); *his* parents were born in France. (Boudinot, 1 *Boudinot* 25–6; Boyd, *Boudinot,* 4–6.) Besides his unfailing affection for Alexander, Boudinot aided Alexander's favorite cousin, Ann (Lytton) Mitchell, in his home at Burlington, N.J., when she was aged and needy. Two revealing likenesses of Boudinot are St. Memin's spirited miniature in prime of life, and portrait of patriarch (Am. Bible Soc., variously ascribed), head bald on top, kindly old eyes lighting face of strength and mellow wisdom.

19. Romantic ardors of Elias and Hannah ("Narcissus" and "Eugenia") in youthful courtship threatened to succumb to excessive piety of both, but survived through long and redolent life together.

20. Boudinot, 23–4.

21. Ms. Boudinot Ledger, 1760–1814, NYPL. See *Boudinot Mansion* (Elizabeth, N.J., 1943, hist. notes by Lewis D. Cook) and Mrs. E. M. Field in N.S. 13 *NJHS Proceed*. 393–9.

22. Economy of comfortable household appears in Ledger, *op. cit.*

23. Boudinot Bible, Princeton Univ.

24. His name nowhere occurs in account book, though Boudinot paid £8 to Barber, headmaster of Academy, in 1773 for Thomas Smith, of N.Y., presumably tuition for Smith's son; cf. what Livingston paid for son, John Lawrence, fellow student of Alexander, Aug. 1773 (Livingston MSS., MHS., also 1st ser., 25 N.J. Arch. 227–8). Later, 1781–1804, Boudinot's accounts have many entries for collections, disbursements for orphan children of Caldwell (see below). 1 H 8 speaks of Alexander being in home of Livingston dur-

ing winter, mentions another family (Boudinot not named) in which "he was intimate."

25. See verses in *Dan.-Am. Gaz.*, Oct. 17, 1772, by "Juvenis St. Croix," "The Soul Ascending into Bliss. In humble imitation of Popes.[*sic*] Dying Christian to his Soul." Lines were undoubtedly Alexander's, though dated Oct. 11, perhaps after he left island; Knox probably inserted them.

26. Cf. *Pa. Packet,* Aug. 9, 1773, for formation, by Boudinot, Rodgers, *et al.,* of "American Soc. for Promoting Religious Knowledge among Poor in British Colonies"; anticipated by 42 years Am. Bible Soc. of which Boudinot was first pres. Boudinot Bible is 2 vols., interleaved for extensive commentary. Benj. Bush, who married Boudinot's niece, after a feud, spoke sarcastically of his "uncommon professions of piety" (G. W. Corner, ed., Autobiography of Rush, 374).

27. 84 HLC 13660–1, 13664–5.

28. *Last Will and Testament of Elias Boudinot, LL.D.* (Trenton, 1854).

29. 2d ser., 1 HLC 20; copy, in Mrs. H's hand, and at bottom her note, "Lines Written by Mr. H when residing in New Jersey, preparing for College, on the Death of [crossed out M.^{r} and M.^{rs}?] Boudinots child." Cf. 1 H 8, saying Alexander sat up with corpse, "wrote some consolatory verses. . . ." But date (Boudinot Family Bible) was after H was in King's in N.Y.; must have gone back for funeral, which would show his attachment. On scrap of paper (HLC, *ibid.,* 21, also copy in Mrs. H's hand?) is epigram, probably on this child. His pen was busy if it composed also prologue, epilogue of play performed by officers of British garrison at Elizabethtown (HLC, *ibid.*).

30. See W. R. Dix in N.S. 8 *NJHS Proceed.* 169–85; cf. *ibid.,* 298–310, for other houses nearby which H knew, some still standing, especially oldest in Elizabeth, Hatfield-Bonnell house, which was already turning its first century.

31. Attended there hour every other day (*N.Y. Gaz.,* Jan. 6, 1772, in 1st ser., 28 *N.J. Arch.* 7–9).

32. Murray, *Notes Concerning Elizabeth-town,* ed. 1941, p. 75.

33. ALS to Stirling, n.d., NYPL, Emmet uncalendared.

34. Cf. among many letters illustrating his militancy, ALS to Elias Boudinot, June 11, 1776 (NYPL, Emmet 4762).

35. See ms. "Memorandums" by Chandler (intermittent diary 1775–86), Gen. Theolog. Sem., N.Y.; Frank Gavin, "Chandler in Light of His Diary," in *Church History,* June 1932, 3–19; A. H. Hoyt, Sketch of Chandler in 27 *N. Eng. Hist. and Geneal. Reg.* 227–36; S. A. Clark, *St. John's Church.*

36. 1 H•8. We may even identify gravestones against which Alexander leaned with his book; closest to site of school are those of Stephen Willcock, "died Mch ye 12th An Domini 1770"; Isaac Meeker, 1764; Moses Lyon, 1763. Cf. Trustees' Minutes, April 17, 1772, Feb. 16, 1807, Princeton Univ.

37. *W&M Quar., op. cit.,* 209.

38. One student wrote to P. V. Fithian (Sept. 6, 1773) that loyalist undergraduates were "possessed swine" whom Dr. Witherspoon should "turn off" (Fithian, *Jnl. and Letters,* 42). Witherspoon, at this time on visit to Yale's commencement, was put down by Dr. Stiles as decidedly in colonies' cause as contrasted with cautious Pres. Locke of Harvard (Collins, 1 *Witherspoon* 155).

39. Seems to have lodged with Mulligan on his first arrival in N.Y., boarded in Mulligan's family at some time during attendance at King's.

40. Schachner, *W&M Quar., op. cit.,* 205–6, discounts this.

41. Fithian, *ibid.,* 16.

42. Collins, 1 *Witherspoon* 143; the Rev. Hugh Knox may have been trustees' informant. Cf. *N.Y. Gaz.,* Sept. 24, 1772; Collins *ibid.,* 143.

43. *N.Y. Gaz.,* Nov. 9, 1772.

44. See *N.Y. Gaz.,* Dec. 7, 28, 1772; Jan. 4, 18; Feb. 8, 1773. Alexander was more likely to follow exchange of blows if was rumored (Collins, 1 *Witherspoon* 144–5) Chandler defended King's.

45. *W&M Quar., op. cit.,* 209. House is now residence of dean of college; room where interview took place, then Witherspoon's study, is small one at southeast corner. Probably a few pieces of the mahogany furniture were there in Witherspoon's occupancy. Witherspoon had explained to prospective patrons in West Indies, "The regular course of instruction is in four classes, exactly after the manner and bearing the names of the classes in the English Universities. . . ." (*N.Y. Gaz.,* Nov. 16, 1772). Applicant might be admitted to any class (year) for which qualified; cf. 1st ser., 26 *N.J. Archives* 384; Fithian, *Jnl.,* 7. James Madison received A.B. from Princeton, autumn 1771, after two calendar years on much the program refused to H shortly afterward, by dint of "doubled labour" (Autobiography, ed. Douglass Adair, *W&M Quar.,* 3rd ser., II, 197–8).

46. "He entered King's College in the spring of 75 [misrecollection for, probably, '74] in the Sophomore Class and on the terms he had proposed at Princeton. . . ." (Mulligan's narrative, *W&M Quar., op. cit.,* 210).

47. Letter, Mrs. Charles Matthews, Office of Sec., Nov. 25, 1946.

48. College had royal charter, received at hands of Gov. Belcher, staunch Presbyterian, whose favor was as much act of sect as of state.

49. Charter of King's College, 1754 in 4 Schneider, *Samuel Johnson,* 220.

50. *Ibid.,* 265 ff.

51. See Schneider, *ibid.,* Secker to Johnson, Nov. 4, 1760, p. 71; Aug. 18, 1762 (pp. 82–3); Cooper to Secker, June 23, 1763 (pp. 99–101). He was a prop of plea for American Episcopate; held Whitefield "in most sovereign contempt . . . as a common disturber of the peace of the Church. . . ." (Schneider, *ibid.,* 111).

52. *Friendly Address to All Reasonable Americans, on . . . Our Political Confusions,* 31. More Tory pamphlets were credited to Cooper than he wrote (cf. Chandler's memorial to Royalist Comm. on Loyalist Claims, Ernest Hawkins, *Historical Notices of Church of England in Colonies,* 150 ff., 303–4, 328 ff.) Chandler's diary ("Memorandums," *op. cit.*) shows bosom association of Cooper, Chandler, Samuel Seabury, Isaac Wilkins, Inglis; cf. Bolton, *Church in Westchester County,* 87 ff. *Last Words, Dying Speech, and Confession of J——s R——g—n [James Rivington]* ". . . Supposed . . . written by himself . . . Night preceding . . . his Execution" (in effigy), attributed to Philip Freneau, makes Tory printer exclaim:

> Behold grim Pluto from the infernal plains,
> See how he drags with him my massy chains. . . .
> My reverend friends! O Cooper! where art thou!
> No Seabury, Chandler, to assist me now!

(Broadside, N.Y. ? 1775, NYPL). *American Querist,* by a North American (Cooper), was burned by public executioner in full conclave of Sons of Liberty in N.Y., Sept. 8, 1774 (8 *N.Y. Col. Docs.* 297 n.).

53. Mulligan's narrative, *W&M Quar., op. cit.,* 211.

54. *Independent Reflector,* March 29, 1753, in 4 Schneider 126–7. For his efforts "to baffle the infamous purpose of subjecting [the college] to the sway of a juncto," see Milton M. Klein, *William Livingston: Exponent of Education in New York* (1939), pp. 223, typewritten, CCNY. The Rev. Mr. Chandler, to be Livingston's Elizabethtown neighbor years later, reporting to Archbishop of Canterbury (1753), lamented that "a notable set of young gentlemen . . . in New York have of late set up for writers" in a "pernicious" way in *Independent Reflector,* to antagonize "design of erecting . . . a seminary of the church. . . ." (See 4 Schneider 191–207). Register of King's 1761, 1767, has honorary degrees conferred on Chandler, Inglis, Seabury. Chandler's copies of several Tory pamphlets, including Seabury's *Free Thoughts,* 1774, are in Gen. Theol. Sem.

55. Autobiog. in 1 Schneider 39–40.

56. Oxford, 1751; list of subscribers, mostly members of Queen's, occupies 20 pages. His vivacious portrait is in trustees' room, Columbia Univ.

57. De Witt Clinton, in "Address . . . to Alumni of Columbia College" (Campbell, *Clinton,* 4); though he came a decade later, he had means of knowing.

58. Cooper's "moral character was without any serious reproach, although grave men were occasionally offended by the . . . conviviality of his social habits" (8 *N.Y. Col. Docs.* 298 n.; cf. XIV *Analectic Magazine,* 73; Nath. F. Moore, *Origin and Early Hist. Columbia College,* 25 ff.; Jos. Foster, *Alumni Oxonienses,* Vol. I; De Witt Clinton, *op. cit.,* 13.

59. Reminiscences given to Mason, in *W&M Quar., op. cit.,* 212.

60. In 2d ser., 1 HLC 9–19, are exercises in Homer's *Iliad,* beginning with Book 12; lines in Greek discontinuously numbered, with interlineations in pencil; sometimes lines together are in Latin; back of one sheet has literal translation into English. These exercises may date from King's, or from Barber's Academy. AMH, facsimile facing 24, calls them only "early" exercises; may have been prepared by son Philip at King's, with corrections in H's hand.

61. Ms. "Matricula or Register of . . . King's College" (Columbia Univ.) shows "Samuel Clossy M.D. of Trin. Coll Dublin" was elected Professor of Natural Science? or Philosophy? 1765 (p. 8), two years later was Professor of Anatomy, was named first among six physicians composing faculty of medicine, earliest in America (10); evidently man of vision, organizing capacity; cf. Cooper to Johnson, Aug. 27, 1766, in 4 Schneider 112.

62. Jan. 10, 1774, when H presumably was following the "Anatomical Prelections," second part was in progress, "the Ofteology and Muscling, being completed. On Monday . . . at 11 O'clock . . . the pneumatical optical Lectures will begin and continue, until those Properties of Air and Light are exhibited to View, whereby the primary Use of Respiration, and the visual Operations are wont to be illustrated." Third, fourth, fifth parts would contain "the Distribution of the Arteries, Veins, and Nerves, and the Structure of the Viscera," etc. (*N.Y. Gaz.;* cf. 4 Schneider 254 ff.). H may have gone to other medical lectures also, especially of Dr. Jas. Smith in chemistry, materia medica.

63. King's Matricula, 19.

64. *W&M Quar., op. cit.,* 212; however, in further recollections, 1821, Troup said he and H "were . . . fellow lodgers together in one of the Rooms of the College" when "Liberty Boys" threatened Dr. Cooper, which was in spring 1775 (*ibid.,* 219). At later date Troup must have been reading law with John Jay (*ibid.,* 215), and may have continued to live in college.

65. This was last year of all three; they graduated 1774 (Matricula 19); Stevens and Troup entered in 1770, Sam. Nicoll in 1772; Henry Nicoll's entrance is not recorded. Added in margin of Troup's ms. is "John Nicoll of N. Haven"; he entered in 1772 and "Left the College in his 4th year," i.e., he was only underclassman among H's special friends in H's first year, which was natural considering Alexander's maturity and fact he followed elective, rapid course. Nine were admitted in 1773; H's name is not among them (see below); no one of them comes into H's story.

66. *W&M Quar., op. cit.*, 209 ff. Mulligan was probably confused. No official record of any student entering King's in spring of year. Troup said H at this date shared room with him in college building, and implies when mob came for Cooper (see below) H met them from college (*ibid.*, 219). If H lived with Mulligans, sitting with them in evenings, etc., it was by special permission or in vacations, for statutes required each student must "have an habitation in college . . . in which he shall be obliged to lodge" under penalties; also, he must "dine regularly in the public hall" (4 Schneider 237–8). "Book of Misdemeanours" kept by Pres. (published as "Black Book," 3) shows, in confinements, most or all students lived in college building.

67. Matricula, 18.

68. Others were David Clarkson, (Brandt) Schuyler Lupton, Jacob Shaw, John Gaine, John Whitaker, Samuel Deall, Horatio Smith, Paul Randall, John Brickell, David (*sic*) Moore, Edward Cornwallis Moncrieffe, James Stiles, James Depeyster (*sic*), Tristrim Lowther, Thomas Attwood, and Nicholas Romeyn; three of these—Whittaker, Moncrieffe, and Stiles—"Left College 2.^d Year." This was largest class yet admitted except 18 in 1772. It is only mention of H in record of admissions, graduations to 1777. Black Book, running Jan. 1771–Aug. 4, 1775, does not contain his name, nor does any other original document of college prior to Revolution, except this Matricula.

69. Similarity of ink and quillpoint for several pages together suggest as much. Further, graduations for 1770 overlap admissions for 1771, i.e., list for earlier year was written second; among admissions for 1773, first name of Desauliers not given, and notation after his name, "Staid only 3 Months," suggests, as do others of premature departures, entries were made some time after actual admissions. Given name of Moore, admitted 1774, is down as David though it was Daniel (cf. Black Bk., 13). Schuckburgh (July–Aug. 1772) was confined to college for month "for divers irregularities committed . . . on the afternoon of last Commencement Day" (*ibid.*, 9), and "Mr. Shuckb.^g" was tutored by Prof. Harpur (Acct. Books of Robt. Harpur, Columbia Univ., 54), but he does not appear in Matricula. Peter Ogden was recorded graduating 1776 (*ibid.*, 23) but is not mentioned as having entered.

70. H probably could not have met at this time surprisingly high requirements for admission to the regular medical course (cf. 4 Schneider 241). Not clear at what time of year students were admitted, if all at once. Moncrieffe, listed with H as entered 1774, appears in Black Book, 19, as early as June 20, when Rapalje stole his cotton stockings. Commencement ordinarily in May, but that of 1774 March 29 (Matricula 19); longest "stated vacation" was "one month after commencement" (statutes, in 4 Schneider 238), so admissions may have been in May that year.

71. Ms. Harpur Account Bk., 20 (photostat in Columbia Univ.). Perhaps after meeting regular college tuition charge of 25s. a quarter and 11s. a week for "dieting," for which parents or guardians were required to give bond (4 Schneider 224, 231, 237), he had nothing left for tutor, though miscalculation or neglect seems unlikely; more probably Harpur, after he got to know Alexander, offered to forego his bill, and H acknowledged kindness in small round sum later on when Harpur was in temporarily straitened circumstances (cf. Jnl. and Accts., Columbia Univ., 225). Harpur had private pupils from all classes; among 15 in 1774 were two who matriculated with H; three others of group started with Harpur a little later. Troup was tutored by Harpur for nine months in his freshman year, also in mathematics (*ibid.,* 4); he perhaps recommended Alexander apply for same help. Alexander must have gone to Harpur for advanced instruction in order to overtake classes ahead of him, for he had good knowledge of arithmetic while yet Cruger's clerk, and had further prepared with Barber. We do not know what was studied in mathematics during freshman, sophomore years at King's at this time; for earlier proposed curriculum cf. Schneider, *ibid.,* 65 ff.

72. Born *ca.* 1731. (8 DAB 293).

73. Matricula, 6. Daniel Treadwell, who had held this chair, had died of tuberculosis. Pres. Johnson wrote that "providence has sent us a good teacher of mathematics and experiments from Ireland—bred at Glasgow (he is indeed a Presbyterian, but I think . . . he will do very well) by name Harper [*sic*]. . . ." (to Wm. S. Johnson, Oct. 12, 1761, in 1 Schneider 314; cf. 325, and 4 *ibid.,* 78).

74. Winter before H came, Edward Thomas was ordered before Governors "for abusing, along with many others, Mr Harpur, the Evening before" (Black Bk., 10). Thomas proved his innocence, but soon seven more, including H's later friend Troup, were compelled to ask public pardon "for ill-using Mr. Harpur, by *Calling Names* in the Dark. . . ." (*ibid.*) In July 1774 Geo. Rapalje was suspended "for using Mr Harpur in the most scandalous manner" (*ibid.,* 21). If Harpur resigned as professor in 1767 (cf. DAB, *ibid.,* 293), official roster mentions no change in status; disciplinary record shows he remained in position of authority.

75. Account Books, 12. In May 1775 he took two lads, Luke and John Dewint, "to be lodged & educated by me" (*ibid.*, 22). Harpur did not live, like Pres. Cooper, in all-purpose college building; year before H became private pupil Harpur had married Elizabeth Crygier, and shortly after ceased to dine with "John Badger, Steward," at 8s. a week (*ibid.*, 14). Servant Dina, who lived in, got advances on wages to pay for funeral of (son?) Charley month after H became pupil of her master (*ibid.*, 18); possibly this was child whose body Alexander sat up to watch night before interment, though Mulligan connected incident with death of Boudinot's daughter some weeks earlier (see above).

76. Columbia Univ. Bayard's signature is on it in several places; Harpur's name does not occur, but book was found among his few surviving personal papers and "according to family history . . . was one of several which he wrote and used while teaching mathematics at King's College" (E. M. Johnston, Brooklyn, N.Y., Feb. 3, 1951, to R. H. Logsdon [Columbia Univ.]).

77. P. 1.

78. P. 51.

79. Pp. 157–95; no trigonometry, rules of thumb being used to solve problems involving triangles, circles. Typical examples show what Alexander, perhaps, was doing with Harpur: "Of Fellowship (partnership): Quest. 7. A, B, and C . . . freighted a Ship from the Canaries to England, with 108 Tuns of Wine, of which A had 48^{T}; B 36^{T}; C 24^{T}; but by reason of bad weather they were obliged to cast 45 Tuns over board; how much must each man sustain of the Loss?" (p. 78). Short definition of exchange is given, with tables, then "A Bill of Exchange, viz Leghorn on London. Leghorn, July 31, 1763, for 786 pieces of Eight of Mexico, at 55^{d}, at 3 months. . . . How much Money must be Received in England for this Bill?" (p. 86).

80. Also in Columbia Univ., but not to be confused with his account books in N.Y. State Lib., Albany, of which Columbia has photostats. Under "Lunations," Example 2 (p. 96), is "Req^{d}. the true Time of Full Moon, in May 1762, New Stile?" and he works it out, using "Sun's Mean dist: and true full Moon," "Moons true dist: from the Ascending. Node at the true time of her being in full," etc. Harpur's later career was equally creditable and more varied. He took patriot side in Rev., was member provincial congresses, comm. safety, Assembly, clerk of Council of Appointments which so much irked Gov. Clinton. From 1778–95 Deputy Sec'y. of State, N.Y. After war renewed connection with College as sec'y. of Bd. of Regents which controlled it, then was trustee, serving with H on both bodies (M. H. Thomas, *Columbia Univ. Officers and Alumni*, 11, 62). For business deal involving Cruger, Melancton Smith, Duer, see Acct. Bks., 38, 47–8; Jnl. and Accts. Columbia Univ. has lock of his hair.

Chapter 5 (Pages 57 to 73)

Rebellious Town, Tory Gown

1. They penalized a list of petty offenses such as tardiness and failure to appear in "proper academical habit," but did not think it necessary, as earlier, to condemn fornication, cursing, cock-fighting, or "maiming . . . any person" (4 Schneider 226–7).

2. Troup in 3d ser., 4, *W&M Quar.*, 213; 1 *Boudinot* 165; cf. for half-doubt of his son, 1 H 10; also Adair and Harvey, in 3d. ser., 12, *W&M quar.*, 308–29.

3. 4 Schneider 225 ff.; "Black Bk.," 8, 19, 31.

4. Schneider, *ibid.*, 231.

5. 3d. ser., 4, *W&M Quar.*, 212–3.

6. AL (draft) Fish, Dec. 26, 1823 to Pickering (Fish Papers, Columbia Univ.).

7. Fish, *ibid.*

8. Robt. Harpur was first librarian, though he no longer had this assignment when H was student (Thomas, *op. cit.*, 62). See checklist of books from Boudinot's library in Stimpson Coll., Princeton Univ.

9. Matricula, in Pres. Johnson's hand, therefore prior to 1763 when he resigned.

10. In April 1776 when N.Y. City Comm. of Safety required college building for a hospital for troops, "the Library, apparatus, etc., were deposited in the City Hall" (Matricula, 22). Years later, by accident, the remnant of books was discovered in basement of St. Paul's Chapel, but "philosophical apparatus" had been lost or stolen.

11. Perhaps these were some of "the polemical writers on Religious subjects" that Troup said H had read while yet in college; No. 4 in a vol. of pamphlets is Daniel Featley, *Dippers Dipt; or, The Anabaptists duck'd and plung'd over head and ears*, "at a disputation in Southwark . . ." (London, 1646); others are Edward Chandler, *Defence of Christianity* . . . (2d. ed., London, 1725); Jacques Basnage de Beauval, *History of the Jews* . . . (trans. from French, London 1708), which may have informed H's admiring allusions to Jewish people; and *Letter from Dr. P—— to the Bishop of R——* in vindication of his sermon on Trinity Sunday (London, 1696).

12. This set, like some other remaining books, belonged to Myles Cooper, and was given by him to his firm friend Petrus Stuyvesant, grandson of the governor.

13. He could "mention other excellent writers on . . . the *natural rights* of mankind" (*Farmer Refuted*, 1 LHW 61). We know from exercise assigned in Black Book, 24, that *Spectator* was in library.

14. 1 H 26 n. Fish Papers, Columbia Univ. Cf. *W&M Quar., op. cit.*, 210–11, 214.

15. Troup, *W&M Quar., ibid.*, 213; 1 H 26.

16. See from Boston, *N.Y. Jnl.* Nov. 25; from Charles-Town, S.C., Dec. 9; from Boston again, Dec. 16, then Dec. 23, 1773: "a greater Meeting of the Body than ever" having exhausted all means of returning tea, "a number of People huzza'd in the Street, and in a very little Time, every Ounce of the Teas on board of Capt. Hall, Bruce, and Coffin, was immersed in the Bay. . . ." A few days before, N.Y. Sons of Liberty, John Lamb presiding, had met "with a general No, No, No," message of governor that tea would be protected in fort "till ordered out by Council, King, or Proprietor" (*ibid.*).

17. Cf. "Zeno," *N.Y. Jnl.*, Dec. 23, 1773.

18. Feb. 17, 1774; cf. writer of May 26, 1774, making restrained use of rhetoric and religion that could have been Alexander's at this period; address "To the . . . British Colonies in America" June 19, 1774, the day Boston Port Act was to go into effect, reminds of H in language and thought.

19. Holt had so much material from Boston, he was obliged to leave out even "new Advertisements" (*N.Y. Jnl.* Dec. 23, 1773).

20. *N.Y. Gaz.*, April 25, 1774.

21. *Ibid.*, March 28, 1774; cf. April 11, ode "to the Mercury Packet-Boat occasioned by the embarkation of his Excellency," dated at King's and doubtless by Pres. Cooper.

22. *Ibid.*, March 7, 1774. For the "honest, loyal and prudent" Comm. of 51, eclipsing "the demagogues of a very turbulent faction," ALS, Thos. Young, June 19, 1774, to John Lamb (Lamb Papers, NYHS).

23. Cf. ALS, Paul Revere, March 28, 1774, to Lamb, sharing plans for "one of the greatest strokes that our Enemies have mett with," and a Boston comm., Revere and others, to Lamb, March 1, 1775 (Lamb Papers, NYHS).

24. 4th ser., I *Am. Archives*, 307–8; those for it, besides McDougall, were Peter T. Curtenius, Francis Lewis, Isaac Sears, P. V. B. Livingston, Leonard Lispenard, Jacobus Van Zandt, Abraham Brasher, John Moore, Abraham P. Lott, Thos. Randall, Jos. Hallett, John Broome.

25. *Ibid.*, 309.

26. Evidently by handbill, for there was not time to use newspapers, but no copy occurs in NYPL or NYHS. Advertisement was dated July 5, distributed 6th, a sudden summons. Wording of call is from proceedings of Comm. of 51 (below). Arrival of Capt. Lockyer, of tea ship, "was immediately communicated to the people by a Hand Bill" which crowded the wharf with citizens (*N.Y. Gaz.*, April 25, 1774). Maneuver of popular meeting in Fields must have been encouraged by notices of similar local gatherings resenting Boston Port Bill, approving of Continental Congress to stop trade with Britain; cf. *N.Y. Jnl.*, June 30, 1774. Holt made this paper organ of approaching Congress; beginning June 23, 1774, he replaced royal arms at his masthead by device of snake cut into pieces for colonies and labeled "UNITE OR DIE."

27. 1 H 21–3.

28. 1 R 55 refers to statement of Skaats. He was keeper of Federal (later City) Hall 1789–1802; distinctly Dutch in dress—skirted pea jacket, breeches, square-buckled shoes (see 5 Stokes 1250–1, 1392; at greater length, John Pintard, *N.Y. Mirror,* IX, 154).

29. *N.Y. Jnl.,* July 7; *N.Y. Gaz.,* July 11, 1774.

30. He would not have been so suddenly stirred to put aside reluctance, probably, had he not already marshaled his arguments in newspaper pieces.

31. *N.Y. Gaz.,* July 11; *N.Y. Jnl.,* July 14, 1774. Anonymous call was "conceived in such mystic and ambiguous Terms, that no Person out of the Secret could imagine from whence it could proceed." Maker of reproving motion was surprised to learn one of their number (McDougall) "acted as Chairman to the Promoters" of resolves never submitted to comm. We do not have McDougall's counterblast. For view of Wm. Laight, in conservative majority, cf. to Wm. Livingston, Oct. 3, 1775, 1 Livingston Corr., Ledyard-Griswold deposit, NYPL. In unrepentant minority, besides McDougall and Lispenard, were Lewis, P. V. B. Livingston, Sears, Randall, Curtenius, Lott, Hallet, who, doubtless, had called the meeting in the Fields and drawn the resolves.

32. H, on his title pages, in identifying his opponent, did not precisely follow the Farmer's description of himself. Isaac Wilkins (1742–1830) in *"My Services and Losses in aid of the King's cause . . . ,* said he "Was reputed Author of a Pamphlet under name A. W. Farmer." See Seabury's reference, neither claiming nor denying authorship, in letter of Dec. 29, 1776 (E. Hawkins, *Hist. Notices of Church of Eng. in Colonies,* 328 ff.) P. L. Ford, in note to reprint of above memorial, names pamphlets, 1774, 1775, with titles approximating ones Wilkins acknowledged, but considers Seabury author of Farmer tracts.

33. Cf. Beardsley, *Seabury;* Cross, *Anglican Episcopate and Am. Colonies;* Bolton, *Hist. Westchester;* his episcopal parchments are in Gen. Theol. Sem., N.Y.C.

34. H in *Full Vindication* replied to Seabury's *Free Thoughts* only, neglecting latter's *Congress Canvassed* which had appeared even more recently.

35. Probably Troup boasted of H's authorship; he said Alexander replied to loyalists with "such a fund of information, . . . such maturity, and strength of mind, as to confer the credit . . . upon Mr. Jay. . . . Dr. Cooper . . . insisted that Mr. Jay must be the author of it; it being absurd to imagine that so young a man" as H "could have written it" (*W&M Quar., op. cit.,* 214). Mulligan remarked *Farmer Refuted* was attributed to Wm. Livingston (*ibid.,* 211). Both proud friends misrecalled dates of pamphlets.

36. As originals are rare, refs. here are to Lodge's ed. of *Works;* also in J. C. Hamilton, ed., II, 1–126.

37. Pamphlet controversy between Tories and Whigs prior to Revolution (and afterward by way of l'envoi from loyalist expatriates), in which our items are only the best remembered, was conducted with competence and minimum lapse into mere retort and abuse. Accommodation was sought in both camps; first Continental Congress was willing to adjourn non-intercourse if petitions were successful; Parliament contained opponents of royal obstinacy. Neither set of contenders wanted to burn bridges.

Similar to exchanges between Seabury and Hamilton were Myles Cooper's (?) *Friendly Address . . . on . . . our Political Confusions,* answered by Philip Livingston's *Other Side of the Question,* both 1774; cf. Charles Lee's *Strictures on . . . a Friendly Address,* 1775, and *The General, Attacked by a Subaltern,* n.d. *American Querist,* 1774, attributed to Cooper, enjoyed many editions. *What Think Ye of Congress Now?,* 1775 (Thos. B. Chandler?), fastened on same demerits as Seabury, but ended with a plan of qualified American self-government. Paine's *Common Sense,* 1776, a year after H's passage with Seabury, was not so much a brief as a cry to arms. H's offerings were admired for what they included; Paine's were effective for what they excluded. Inglis's *True Interest of America . . . Stated, in . . . Strictures on . . . Common Sense,* 1776, was no match for Paine's rousing performance.

38. *Free Thoughts,* 1, 3.

39. *Ibid.,* 4–6.

40. *Ibid.,* 6–8.

41. *Ibid.,* 8–18.

42. *Ibid.,* 22.

43. 1 LHW 3–11.

44. *Ibid.,* 12–19. H anticipated own oft-repeated observation, "A vast majority of mankind is entirely biassed by motives of self-interest," which would induce Parliament, unchecked, to "grind the Americans as much as possible."

45. *Ibid.,* 19–34.

46. *Ibid.*, 33 ff.

47. *View of Controversy,* 8–9.

48. *Ibid.*, 34–5; Seabury had no difficulty in citing "Pennsylvania Farmer" (John Dickinson, 2nd letter) on his side: ". . . these provinces . . . are but parts of *a whole* [British Empire]; and . . . a power . . . to . . . preserve the connection in due order . . . is lodged in the parliament. . . ." (*ibid.*, 13).

49. *Ibid.*, 29; Seabury quoted colonial charters to show locally limited authority of taxation.

50. *Ibid.*, 38–9.

51. Cf. Trevelyan, 2 *Am. Revolution* 338 ff.

52. *View of Controversy,* 37.

53. *Ibid.*, 42. H may have been influenced by resolutions of Fairfax Co., Va., Washington presiding (*N.Y. Jnl.*, Aug. 25, 1774). Ninth was "that there is premeditated design . . . pursued by the British ministry, to introduce an arbitrary government into his Majesty's American dominions. . . ."

54. *Ibid.*, 51.

55. *Ibid.*, 57–8.

56. *Ibid.*, 81–2.

57. *Ibid.*, 69.

58. Dated Feb. 5, 1775 (78 pp.), written in little more than one month.

59. 1 LHW 54. Now fairly into the patriot groove, he promised in future he would treat "The destruction of the Tea at Boston,—the act for altering the government of Quebec,—and the Suffolk resolves. . . ." Apparently only second appeared; 1 LHW 181n. mistakenly imputes promise to some piece in *N.Y. Jnl.*

60. Took opportunity to "interweave some strictures" on another pamphlet of Seabury, *Congress Canvassed,* which he had not had time to answer earlier. His use of College library is plain.

61. *Farmer Refuted,* in 1 LHW 61 ff.; cf. 87.

62. 1 LHW 176–7.

63. *Ibid.*, 66–7. "Our title is similar, and equal, to that by which they possess their lands; . . . the king is the legal fountain of both." Cf. *ibid.*, 80, 82.

64. *Ibid.*, 80–81, 90.

65. *Ibid.*, 86, 93 ff.

66. *Ibid.*, 114, 116, 120. H here expressed what became the fighting stand of America. Seabury mistook Dickinson as sanctioning parliamentary power to tax colonies. H adopted Dickinson's distinction between empire duties (permissible) and special duties imposed on American colonies (obnoxious) (*ibid.*, 127).

67. *Ibid.*, 120.

68. *Ibid.*, 71, 122–3, 125.

69. *Ibid.*, 73–4.

70. Cf. Cortland Skinner to Lt. Col. Wm. Skinner, Westburg, Hants, Dec. 1775 (copy, Jos. Reed Papers, NYHS): "They who began . . . feared the Ruin of their Smuggling. . . . others with deeper views took it up & build upon the foundation [,] are attempting a Superstructure [,] a Republic that will deluge the Country in Blood."

71. Inglis instanced (*True Interest of America* . . . , 65) "The King of Denmark's late proclamation . . . that the estate of such of his subjects as shall join the Americans, will be forfeited. . . ."

72. E.g., Billy Chandler, whom he probably knew at Elizabethtown, exactly his age, became captain in British forces.

Chapter 6 (Pages 74 to 84)
Captain of a Spruce Artillery Company

1. For this view, stated not so baldly as above, cf. Parkes, *American Experience*, 109, 116, 137 ff.; Schachner, H, 44.

2. 1 H 48; 1 R 100 referred to Alexander's youthful interposition with "Travis' mob" in behalf of Ralph Thurman, threatened with his fellow merchant Robt. Harding, for sending military supplies to Gage in siege of Boston; see broadside April 13, 1775, calling meeting of inhabitants at Liberty Pole April 15, and Wm. Smith's (ms.) Diary, IV, both NYPL; De-Lancey protected Thurman; no evidence of H traced.

3. Troup (*W&M Quar.*, 3d ser., IV, 219; cf. H, R, *ibid.*) said attempted seizure of Cooper was in consequence of resentment because *Asia* fired on city, but that could not have been because Cooper incident was three months earlier. Troup may have confused mob violence against a humbler loyalist —"one *Tweed,* or *Tweedy,* a Shoe maker"—night before *Asia* affair, Aug. 22, 1775. The complacent newspaper item shows approval that licensed numerous similar acts by Sons of Liberty (*N.Y. Jnl.*, Aug. 24, 1775). For

a case of retaliation against a patriot, if we may call him that, "one Coggeshall [who] turned up his backside towards the bomb brig in the harbour, using some insulting words," see *ibid.,* Nov. 23, 1775, a squib from Newport.

4. 8 *N.Y. Col. Docs.* 297–8, n.; search of N.Y. and Phila. newspapers has not revealed this letter; may have been in a handbill. Colden wrote to Dartmouth, "The odium excited against [Dr. Cooper] is for his warm attachm.^t to Government and his being a supposed author of almost every peice [*sic*] that was published on that side of the Question" (*ibid.,* 581). Mulligan defined him briefly: "Dr. Cooper . . . was a tory and an obnoxious man and the mob went to the Colledge with the intention of tarring & feathering him or riding him upon a rail." (*W&M Quar., op. cit.,* 211.) Troup (and H) feared worse, "that if Dr. Cooper should be taken hold of by the mob his life would be endangered; as he was a most obnoxious Tory" (*ibid.,* 219). As an instance of public denunciation of a Tory, cf. broadside of Wm. Goddard, N.Y., May 2, 1775 (NYPL), stigmatizing one Foxcroft, accused of circulating reflections on Continental Congress. Cf. Freehold, N.J., committee advertising Sam. Osborne as "an enemy to his country. . . ." (*N.Y. Jnl.,* Nov. 30, 1775).

5. Not in a separate dwelling, as in Schachner, H 41; cf. King's "Black Book."

6. *W&M Quar., op. cit.,* 219.

7. 46 *Gentleman's Mag.,* London, 326–7.

8. Troup, who "stood by the side of [H] when he made this harangue" (*W&M Quar., ibid.;* confirmed by Mulligan, *ibid.,* 211).

9. Paraphrased in 1 H 48, 1 R 100, but not found.

10. *N.Y. Col. Docs., ibid.,* 297–8, n.; Colden to Dartmouth, June 7, 1775 (month after the event, *ibid.,* 581); Cooper himself in *Gentleman's Mag., op. cit.,* just a year later; N.Y. and Phila. newspapers had no account of episode, except for one indirect allusion noticed below.

11. Cooper memorialized his deliverance in anniversary "Stanzas written on the Evening of the 10th of May, 1776. By an Exile from America" (*Gentleman's Mag., op. cit.*). The mob was at the gate

> When straight, a heaven-directed youth,
> Whom oft my lessons led to truth,
>   And honour's sacred shrine,
> Advancing quick before the rest,
> With trembling tongue my ear addrest,
>   Yet sure in voice divine.
>
> "Awake! awake! the storm is nigh,—
> This instant rouse,—this instant fly,—
>   The next may be too late. . . ."

The heaven-directed pupil who so improved Cooper's moral precepts is not further identified in the verses.

Colden related Cooper "escaped, only half dressed, over the College fence; reached the shore of the river, and found shelter in the house of Mr. Stuyvesant" (*N.Y. Col. Docs., ibid.*) Cooper himself told how he worked his way along banks of Hudson, "My faithful pupil by my side," by morning reached "The good Palemon's cot," and thence next night boarded "Kingfisher,—Capt. James Montagu." There were two Stuyvesant houses at the time, neither one a "cot"; cf. Stokes 4 *Iconography Manhattan* 786 and 3 *ibid.*, Landmark map 952. As Cooper was friendly with Peter Stuyvesant, he and Alexander doubtless went to the upper, near present First Ave. and Fifteenth St. Cooper, with Rivington and Dr. Chandler, also "proscribed for their Loyalty," dropped down in *Kingfisher* to Sandy Hook May 19; Cooper and Chandler sailed May 25 for Bristol (Chandler, "Memorandums," Gen. Theol. Sem., these dates).

12. *Pa. Jnl.*, May 17, 1775.

13. *Rivington's N.Y. Gazetteer*, May 4, 1775; cf. Isaac Wilkins's card to public day before, May 3 (*ibid.*, May 11, 1775); he was embarking for England because he could neither raise his hand against his sovereign nor draw his sword against his country.

14. Colden to Dartmouth, June 7, 1775 (8 *N.Y. Col. Docs.* 581). Ten days later Rivington was still aboard the *Kingfisher* (Chandler, *op. cit.*, May 20). Other N.Y. editors took no notice of assault on their colleague, but cf. *Pa. Jnl.*, May 17, 24, 1775. Rivington's paper continued to appear. Colden stigmatized the mob that menaced Cooper and Rivington and rejected claim of N.Y. Association that it deserved praise for keeping order. For Colden's measures against mobs, *N.Y. Col. Docs., ibid.*, 584, 586–7, and 4 *Am. Arch.* II, 636–7.

15. For avowals of Westchester loyalists that angered heated N.Y.C. patriots, see *N.Y. Jnl.*, April 6, 20, 1775, and Lewis Morris's comment, *ibid.*, May 18, *Rivington's Gaz.*, May 11, 18, 1775.

16. *Pa. Jnl.*, Dec. 6, 1775; for reports, overdrawn and hysterical, of Connect. men threatening to prod patriotism of N.Y.C., cf. 8 *N.Y. Col. Docs.* 579 ff., *N.Y. Jnl.*, April 27, 1775.

17. *Pa. Jnl., ibid.* Sears and his men were received at New Haven with cannon salute and feast. Seabury was imprisoned 5 weeks until his spirited memorials to Connect. legislature, Gen. Commtee. of N.Y.C., and Provincial Congress secured his release (Dawson, *Westchester . . . during Am. Rev.*, 136–9; 4 *Am. Arch.* III, 1626; *ibid.*, IV, 185–8, 402; 8 *N.Y. Col. Docs.* 646; *New Eng. Chronicle*, Dec. 7, 1775; Manhattan Com. Coun. [1868] 813–27.)

18. He said H "went to the place [,] addressed the people . . . and offered if any others would join him to prevent these intruders from taking the types

away" (*W&M Quar., op. cit.,* 211). Cf. 1 H 49; less inaccurate, 1 R 101. Troup in recollections made no allusion to the Rivington episode, but mentioned H burlesqued in doggerel antagonists of Whig printer, Holt (*W&M Quar., op. cit.,* 214).

19. He forgot Rivington had published his pamphlets against the Farmer.

20. H misc., NYPL.; printed in AMH 24–7. Jay and City Comm. chose to act through N.Y. Provincial Congress rather than enlisting the uncertain power of the Continental convention. Before he could have received H's plea he wrote Nath. Woodhull, pres. of Provincial body, "I think [raid on Rivington] neither argues . . . wisdom nor . . . bravery; . . . if it was to have been done, I wish our own people, and not strangers, had taken the liberty of doing it" (Nov. 26, 1775, 1 *Jnl. N.Y. Prov. Cong.* 218). H wrote Jay month later he suspected Tories would use confusion of times to capture new Assembly. He had already "thrown out a hand bill or two to give the . . . alarm, and shall second them by others" (Dec. 31, 1775, in Johnston, 1 *Correspondence of Jay* 41; none of his handbills has been found).

21. Lt.-Gov. Colden wanted a N.Y. militia controlled by government, not "by election of the People. . . ." (to Dartmouth, April 4, 1775, 8 *N.Y. Col. Docs.* 564–5). Militia regulations that lapsed May 1, 1774, required that every man from 16 to 50 must enlist with his local company, be armed and equipped to exercise twice a year. Officers were appointed by Gov. "and the whole Militia is under his command. . . ." (*ibid.,* 450–1). However, May 2, 1775 N.Y. Gen. Comm. unanimously recommended every inhabitant "perfect himself in Military Discipline and be provided with Arms," etc. (*Rivington's N.Y. Gaz.,* May 11, 1775). John Anderson, Beekman's Slip, advertised he sold "The Manual Exercise, Evolutions, Manoeuvers, &c. For the Militia of the Province of New-York." (*N.Y. Gaz.,* May 8, 1775); cf. promise of a former officer in King of Prussia's army "to teach, in a very short time, the most . . . necessary manoeuvres, especially quick Firing, even without a Rammer. . . ." (*Pa. Gaz.,* May 21, 1775).

22. *W&M Quar., op. cit.,* 218–9; Mulligan, as to time, said only that H joined this "volunteer uniform company . . . while in Colledge" (*ibid.,* 210). Nich. Fish was more precise: ". . . in . . . 1775 immediately after the Battle of Lexington [Hamilton] attached himself to one of the uniform Companies of Militia then forming . . . under the command of Captain Fleming in which he devoted much time . . . and zeal. . . ." (AL, to Pickering, Dec. 26, 1823, Columbia Univ.). Colden wrote Dartmouth, June 7, 1775, "The Spirit of arming, and military Parade still runs high in the City [.] Several companies are . . . well armed and cloathed in uniform. . . ." (*N.Y. Col. Docs., ibid.,* 580). St. George's Chapel of Ease, Trinity Parish, built 1748–52, notable for its high steeple, stood on n.w. cor. Beekman and Cliff sts. (4 Stokes 633–4, and Landmark ref. key, III, 933). Enthusiasm was sufficient to permit selective recruiting; cf. Drake's company of foot (*N.Y. Jnl.,* May 4, 1775), and broadside, N.Y., 1775, to "All those

gentlemen who are forming themselves into companies in defense of their country . . ." (photostat, NYPL).

23. 1 H 47, 1 R 99. He added a song of this title was favorite during Revolution. *N.Y. Jnl.,* Aug. 18, 1774, had verses of "a new song, The Glorious Seventy-four," to tune of Hearts of Oak.

24. Neither Troup nor Mulligan (*W&M Quar., ibid.*) mentioned H's company by title "Hearts of Oak."

25. A list of "Officers belonging to a Battalion of Independent Foot Companies in New-York City," presumably 1775, said "The Corsicans" wore "short Green Coats, Small round Hats Cock [*sic*] on one side. A Red Heart of Tin with the words, *God and our Right.* round the Crown *Liberty or Death.*" "The Bold Foresters" also stepped out in "Short Green Coats small round Hats, one side up [,] the word Freedom on a Brass plate on Front [.] Hatchetts on their Backs," which armament seems close to oaken hearts; Marinus Willett was lt. (8 *N.Y. Col. Docs.* 601–2). Incidentally, "Bold Forrester" was name of stallion standing in Morris Co., N.J. (*N.Y. Gaz.,* May 8, 1775). Cf. Schachner, H, 40 and n. for surmise "Corsicans" may have changed title to "Hearts of Oak." Fleming was lt. col. of battalion as well as capt. of "Corsicans." He was a member of the Gen. Comm. for City and Co. of N.Y. (8 *N.Y. Col. Docs.* 601), was col. and dept. adj. gen. N.Y. Dept., Aug. 28, 1775; resigned June 15, 1776, from ill-health after service under Montgomery in Canada (15 *ibid.,* 538, and Heitman, 177).

26. 15 *N.Y. Col. Docs.* 5, 7–8, 11–12. Lasher's battalion was specifically included in militia system (*N.Y. Gaz.,* Aug. 28, 1775).

27. Colden Papers, 413; cf. Colden to Dartmouth, June 7, 1775, *ibid.,* 581–2. "When Congresses and Committees," Colden explained, "had taken the entire direction of the Government, it was extremely disagreeable to Me to remain as Spectator of the . . . confusions in Town, when ·I had it not in my Power to prevent; I therefore retired to this Place" (his country retreat at Flushing).

28. Tryon, Sept. 5, 1775 to Dartmouth (*ibid.,* 631).

29. Vanderput to Mayor Whitehead Hicks, Aug. 24, 1775 (*N.Y. Gaz.,* Aug. 28, 1775).

30. Ezra Stiles, 1 Diary 601; earlier, by order of Cong., more than 100 ship cannon belonging to merchants had been taken inland (*N.Y. Col. Docs., ibid.,* 580).

31. *N.Y. Gaz.,* Aug. 28, 1775.

32. Colden to Dartmouth, June 7, 1775 (*N.Y. Col. Docs., ibid.,* 582–3, 592, 599.

33. Accounts are numerous. Boudinot was present, reported volunteer soldiers "regarded the Shot, but little more than if they had been stones

thrown by Boys, and never desisted till they got every mounted Cannon away" (to Jos. Reed, Sept. 1, 1775, Reed Papers, NYHS). ALS, Holt to *ibid.*, Aug. 24, 1775, went into detail, remarked on "a very general Conversion, from Tory to Whig principles. . . ." (*ibid.*). *N.Y. Jnl.*, Aug. 24; *N.Y. Gaz.*, Aug. 28; *Pa. Jnl.*, Aug. 30, 1775, last with two letters of Aug. 24 from eyewitnesses; Mulligan's story (*W&M Quar., op. cit.*, 210), written 35 or 40 years later, had date, by mistake, Aug. 28 for 23.

34. Mulligan, *ibid.* (*W&M Quar., op. cit.*, 219). 1 H 48 mistaken in saying one of Alexander's companions was killed at his side. No American was killed; "one lost the calf of his leg," two had slighter wounds (*Pa. Jnl.*, Aug. 30, 1775). J. C. H. was confused by later incident recited by Mulligan; Capt. H was firing his piece of artillery from Battery at *Phoenix* and *Rose* passing up North River, "When his Cannon burst and killed two of his men who I . . . recollect were buried in the Bowling Green" (*ibid.*, 210).

35. One of roofs penetrated by 18-pound ball was that of Fraunces' tavern, still standing; (see *Rivington's Gaz.*, Aug. 31, 1775; 4 *Am. Arch.* III, 259; *Pa. Jnl., ibid.*, and *Poems of Philip Freneau* (1786), 312. For extent of firing from *Asia*, cf. *N.Y. Jnl.*, Aug. 24, 1775 and *Pa. Jnl., ibid.* Next evening Tryon heard of capture of guns and that he too would have been dragged off if found, but came to town morning of 25th, begged all of congressmen, committeemen he could reach to reestablish order; (see Tryon to Dartmouth, Sept. 5, 1775, 8 *N.Y. Col. Docs.* 631–2; cf. *Pa. Jnl.*, Aug. 30, 1775). Battery exploit gave New Yorkers much-wanted cannon and accoutrements. However, seven months later, when H was helping prepare city's defenses, Capt. Badlam reported to Prov. Cong. that the 220 cannon available in N.Y. lacked almost all articles to equip them (15 *N.Y. Col. Docs.* 88–9).

36. 1 R 121 said H had instruction from a British bombardier. Fish, companion of H's earliest military training, doubted whether he could have prepared himself "in the course of two or three weeks" for successful examination in gunnery. (Fish mss., Columbia Univ.)

37. 1 *Jnl. N.Y. Prov. Cong.* (Comm. of Safety), 239.

38. *Ibid.*, 321, also *N.Y. Col. Docs., ibid.*, 72. Jas. Moore, already lt. in "Bold Forresters," was nominated for capt.-lt., and Johnson, "who was in service last year & who was lately appointed by the Committee of Safety [,] for First Lieut." Identity of Johnson is uncertain; see (*N.Y. Gaz.*, Oct. 5, 1776, and Pay Book, 1776–7, HLC, separate vols.

39. *W&M Quar., op. cit.*, 214; Troup thought H's Whig pamphlets introduced him to Jay, but their friendship must have dated from three years before in home of Livingston.

40. 1 *Jnl. N.Y. Prov. Cong.* 359. McDougall was to see that H's company was paid. No other commission than this record has been found; many years later, applying for his pension, Elizabeth H said he "served in a military

capacity" from that date (File No. W 13402 B. L. Wt 2279–450, Veterans' Record Branch, U.S. Arch.). 1 R 121, referring to *Am. Arch.*, said Mc-Dougall was present at H's examination by Badlam, but this has not been traced. Badlam afterward certified others for artillery commissions (15 *N.Y. Col. Docs.* 93). At same time Jas. Gilleland was commissioned 2nd lt., Jas. Moore was commissioned earlier, as that day Col. Drake was authorized to transfer from his regt. four men "inlisted with Capt. Lieut. *James Moore* in his Artillery Company. . . ." (*ibid.*, 84).

41. E.g., Maj. Sebastian Beauman (*sic*) March 30, 1776, was appointed capt. of "the Continental Company of Artillery ordered to be raised in this Colony. . . ." (*ibid.*, 92). H's was not only provincial artillery co., as John Grinnell was capt. of another (*ibid.*, 85).

42. *W&M Quar., op. cit.*, 210. Mulligan put date of commission four months later, "About the 10 or 12 July 1776," and minutes of Prov. Cong. do not make it conditional on enlistments, but Mulligan would hardly have been mistaken. Commissions to officers in N.Y. companies to be employed in Continental service were conditional on recruiting 72 men accepted by muster master; until then warrants for recruiting, not commissions, were issued (15 *N.Y. Col. Docs.* 11–12; cf. 18, 94); cf. Alex. Graydon, *Memoirs,* 117–8. For superior qualifications demanded in artillerymen, cf. Capt. John Lamb, in Continental service July 17, 1775, to N.Y. Comm. of Safety (*ibid.*, 20; copy of minute, Aug. 2, 1775, 1 Lamb Papers, NYHS; cf. Lamb's commission as "Captain of the Company of Artillery in the New York Department in the Army of the United Colonies," signed by John Hancock June 30, 1775, in *ibid.*).

43. Elisha Boudinot wrote Stirling: "On my brother's return from New York he informed me that Mr. H had already accepted the Company of Artillery, therefore was deprived of the pleasure of attending your Lordships Persons as Brigade Major"; he recommended Capt. Harry G. Livingston, who was given the place (ALS, Newark, March 10, 1776, Alexander Papers, NYHS, garbled in Duer, *Alexander,* 136). H admired Stirling, whom he had known as brother-in-law of Livingston and father of "Lady Kitty." Elias Boudinot recommended other young Jerseymen to favor of Col. Jos. Reed, then at Cambridge as sec. to Washington, among them Aaron Burr, Matthias Ogden (ALS, July 24, 1775, Reed Papers; cf. *ibid.*, Sept. 1, 1775, and Elisha Boudinot, ALS, March 1776, Alexander Papers, both NYHS).

44. Mulligan, *W&M Quar., op. cit.*, 201; 1 H 52, 1 R 121 added, misquoting Mulligan, that H used for this purpose the remnant of his second and last remittance from St. Croix. Cont. Congress recommended, May 26, 1775, Prov. Congress "allow no Bounties or Cloathing" (15 *N.Y. Col. Docs.* 3), but soon N.Y. assured officers that "Troops raised by this Colony will be placed precisely upon the same footing, as to pay, Cloathing &c. with other the Continental Troops. . . ." (1 *Jnl. Prov. Cong.* 114–6 and *N.Y. Mercury,* Sept. 4, 1775); this still left provincial troops naked. For what N.Y. Con-

tinentals were to receive, see orders for Billing's co., March 30, 1776, including frocks, hats, shoes, blankets (*Jnl., ibid.,* 92).

45. *N.Y. Col. Docs., ibid.,* 20; for deduction of cost of blue coats from men's pay, 79; later, facings of artillerymen's uniforms were red. Hunts' bills (2 ser. 1 HLC 23) were paid promptly except for balance of £6.8.7 not receipted for till March 9, 1785; cf. Pay Bk., 141, 154. For Curtenius' acct., N.Y. Office of State Comptroller, 2 *N.Y. in Rev.* 72 and AMH 204.

46. 1 *Jnl. N.Y. Prov. Cong.* 396. Comm. of Safety was "fully informed that Capt. Alexander Hamilton's Company of Artillery raised for this Colony now consists of so many men that they may safely & easily perform that Duty." Substitution of Provincial guards (Lasher's "City Battalion of Independents") was extended week later by order of Stirling; records were lodged at house of Nich. Bayard (*ibid.,* 93). See Orderly Book, N.Y. City, June 28–July 28, 1776, NYHS, June 29 and July 1, concerning guard duty at City Hall.

47. Stirling told N.Y. Comm. of Safety, March 18, 1776, that "all the Cannon below Six pounders are in want of every article and would take up more time than we can spare at present to Complete them" (Stirling Papers, NYHS). In 1775 state of N.Y. loaned Continent six brass field pieces (6-pounders) which were delivered to Captains H and Bauman; after much correspondence, were restored (cf. Washington to Gov. Clinton, June 13, 1779, 15 GW 276; also N.Y. Office of Comptroller, 2 *New York in Rev.* 53).

48. May 26, 9 LHW 40–1; 1 *Jnl. Prov. Cong.,* 462; for Bauman's appointment, March 30, 1776, *ibid.,* 92. Possibly because H suggested two months earlier enlistment in provincial regt. would be encouraged if those already enrolled "could be uniformed with Frocks," it was ordered Commissary Curtenius "do not deliver out any Frocks" to Continental companies until further notice (*ibid.,* 93).

49. Pay Book preserved runs from Aug. 31, 1776, to end of H's command March 1, 1777; later entries to May 23, 1777, are merely soldier's receipts

"in full of all demands on Co. Hamilton," as witnessed by Capt. Lt. Thompson. Accounts are carried forward from previous book or books. Ninety-eight officers and men are listed, with one crossed out, but at any one time there were not more than 68, judging from returns on three Fridays in Oct., 1776. Most were paid as "Motrosses."

50. E.g., Patrick Kelly, Matthew O Harro (*sic*).

51. E.g., Hugh Cameron and H's own name.

52. Wm. Van Tile, M. Van Winkle.

53. Next in order of listing were bombardiers, gunners, drummers, fifers, matrosses.

54. *N.Y. Gaz.*, Oct. 5, 1776; advertisements for deserters soon after battle of L.I. were numerous, cf. *ibid.*, Sept. 21, 1776.

55. Mulligan, *W&M Quar.*, *op. cit.*, 214–5; Troup, *ibid.*, 210 (*Regulations for the . . . Troops of the U.S.*, Part I, 1779, pp. 138, 140; cf. Steuben on neglect of company commanders, in Cronau, *Army of American Revolution and its Organization*, 16). However, John Little of H's Company was sentenced by Court-martial to receive 39 lashes for abusing and striking Adjt. Henly (6 GW 37, Sept. 8, 1776).

56. Cf. Ord. Bk., Scott's Brigade, *op. cit.*; general orders for July 18, 1776, recommending "the Evolutions" in spite of "the Greate Fatigue duty of this army," cf. July 13. Scott's brigade, to which H's co. soon belonged, was one often ordered to contribute to working parties of 800 or 900; they were to report for tools, instructions at 5 in morning and labor until sunset (Scott's Ord. Bk., July 1, 3, 1776). Those not working on fortifications were to parade every morning at 6; Gen. Scott's orders must have owed something to soldierly demands of brigade major Fish, H's old friend of volunteers in St. George's churchyard.

57. 9 LHW 42; most soldiers were issued 1½ pounds of meat a day, but begged to have vegetables in lieu of part of this.

58. 1 *Jnl. Prov. Cong.*, 497, 564. Lamb's artillery was similarly embraced in N.Y. quota Aug. 29, 1775, (Lamb Papers NYHS). Scott had been appointed Brig. Gen. of the 3,000 militia of colony June 9 (*ibid.*, 112). For ref. to H, Scott's Ord. Bk.

59. Aug. 12, 1776, 1 *Jnl. N.Y. Prov. Cong.*, 573; from remarks later he had little help from two officers in recruiting and training, hence his commendation of first sgt.

60. *Ibid.* (Aug. 14, 1776).

61. *Ibid.*, 574 (Aug. 15, 1776); for former method of promoting, by election, 30; Gilleland does not appear further in records of Prov. Cong. nor in Heitman; six months later H described Bean to Congress as "so incurably addicted to a *certain failing*" that he could not be favored (9 LHW 45); one Adam Bean (*sic*) was 2d lt. in 1st (later 2d co.) of 6th Regt.

62. LHW, *ibid.*, 44–5.

63. See Heitman, 398.

64. True, as H told Cong., Thompson had seen service in Germany, and artillery officers were scarce (LHW, *ibid.*, 42–3).

Chapter 7 (Pages 85 to 99)
New Jersey Retreat and Retaliation

1. 5 GW 402; two guns at Ft. George were also to fire.

2. *Ibid.*, 442–3. Almost four years later, when H asked Washington if he might lead troops in an intended attack on N.Y.C., his "primary idea" was "to attempt with my detachment Bayard's Hill. . . . I should prefer it to any thing else, both for the brilliancy of the attempt in itself, and the decisive consequence of which its success would be productive." He knew the ground of Bayard's Hill (Nov. 22, 1780, 9 LHW 227–8).

3. An accurate map of the time is Ratzen, "Plan of City of N.Y.," conveniently found in 1 Stokes, Pt. 2, Pl. 41; John Hills, "Plan of N.Y. and Environs" (survey of 1782), in Valentine, *Manual of Corp. of City of N.Y.* for 1857, is best for fortifications; see also Bancker, "Plan of . . . Fort [George]," 1774, NYPL. Contemporary drawings show topographical features not appearing in maps, e.g., Des Barres, pub., five views of N.Y. harbor, probably shortly before 1773 (Stokes Coll.), and St. Memin, "N.Y. from L.I.," 1796, all in NYPL.

4. Bayard's Hill redoubt was also known as Independent battery, Montgomery's, and Bunker's Hill (cf. 5 GW 443; Fish to Varick, April 9, 1776, 2d ser., 5 *Hist. Mag.* 203). See map by Samuel Holland, 1757, showing "Bayard's Hill commanding over all the high grounds" (1 Stokes, plate 36-C).

5. Fish to Varick, *ibid.*

6. 5 GW 50; however, on later dates pick-and-shovel parties were assigned there, perhaps completing defenses of general hospital nearby, also constructed by Lasher's troops.

7. Return of March 24, 1776 (4th ser., V *Am. Arch.* 480); later it had eight 9-pounders, four 3-pounders, six royal and Cohorn mortars (Johnston, *Campaign of 1776*, 8). A letter from N.Y., April 12, 1776, said: "You remember Bayard's Mount covered with cedars? It commanded a prospect exceedingly extensive! The top of it is so cut away, that there is room enough for a house and garden; a fortification is there erected as well as round the *Hospital*. . . ." (Johnston, *ibid.*, docs., 132–3).

8. 1 H 54, after describing battle and Washington's withdrawal across East River, says H "brought up the rear, having lost his baggage and a field-piece"; 1 R 126 is more emphatic. This misreads Mulligan's reference to abandonment of city more than fortnight later. Mulligan wrote: "When

the enemy came in the City on Sunday at 8 o'clock Capt. H. commanded a post on Bunker's [Bayard's] Hill . . . and in retiring he lost as he afterwards told me his baggage and one of his Cannon which broke down" (*W&M Quar., op. cit.,* 211). Troup spoke of H's army service immediately before and soon after, but made no mention of his being in L.I. action, in which Troup, on lookout, was captured, to damage of the day (see 2 *Jnl. N.Y. Prov. Cong.* 410; Sir Henry Clinton, *American Rebellion,* 41–3; Sabine's *Loyalists,* 367, doc. 38; 1 R 125–6, quoting Sullivan; Johnston, 176 ff.). H's pay bk. begins early enough, Aug. 31, 1776, to reveal that his battery had been in the action, but first identifying memos. relate to Harlem Hts., King's Ferry, and places falling later.

9. Washington was clear New York must be protected by whatever means; cf. to Lee, Jan. 8, 1776 (4 GW 221–2; to Sullivan, March 14, 1776, *ibid.,* 395). However, see Lee's dissent (to Washington, Feb. 19, 1776, quoted in Johnston, 54).

10. *W&M Quar., op. cit.,* 210–11; Fish queried, "What share had he in the measures for evacuating L.I. and N.Y.?" (Fish Papers, Columbia Univ.).

11. See 6 Ezra Stiles's Diary, Sept. 11, 1776, transcript in LIHS.

12. 5 GW 495–6. He underrated extent of British success, until the last; e.g., *ibid.,* 494, 496–7. See Sir Henry Clinton, *American Rebellion,* 44, in praise of Washington's management of withdrawal.

13. Council of general officers on island, late on 29th agreed "under all Circumstances it is . . . eligible to leave Long Island . . . & remove to New York" (facsimile of opinion in 5 GW facing 496; cf. *ibid.,* 508–9). Boats were hastily collected from Sound, Spuyten Duyvil Creek, reached ferry after dark (Hugh Hughes's memoir in Leake, *Lamb,* 361; cf. Washington to Hughes, Aug. 22, 1784, 27 GW 461).

14. Washington, Aug. 30, informed N.Y. legislature of unanimous advice of council of war "to give up Long Island; and not, by dividing our force, be unable to resist the Enemy in any one point of attack" (5 GW 498–9, 502, 506–8).

15. To Washington, Sept. 5, 1776 (1 Greene's *Greene,* 210–11). Congress wanted no damage done to N.Y. by Washington's troops if they quitted it, believing town could be recovered (5 JCC 733).

16. ". . . we should on all occasions avoid a general action. . . ." Washington to Congress, Sept. 8, 1776 (6 GW 27 ff.).

17. Though H's company was not separately noted, general returns of Aug. 3 (5th ser., I *Amer. Arch.* 763) indicate all of Lasher's battalion was so brigaded; however, by Sept. 8 a soldier sentenced by a court martial was identified in G.O. as "of Col [.] Knox's Regt of Artillery, Cap. Hamilton's Company" (6 GW 37) and return of Sept. 21 of troops at Kingsbridge showed Lasher had lost half his companies (5th ser., II *Am. Arch.* 450–1).

18. *W&M Quar., op. cit.,* 211; cf. Drake's *Knox,* 30.

19. Foot of present 34th St.

20. 6 GW 54.

21. To Cong. Sept. 16, 1776 (6 GW 58); cf. Wm. Smallwood, Oct. 12, 1776, to Md. Conv. (5th ser., II *Am. Arch.,* 1012 13).

22. Humphreys, *Putnam,* 133–6.

23. Drake, *Knox,* 30, with no ref.; he adds Burr led them, unlikely since H. and Knox knew roads. Schachner H, 50–52, fancifully lengthens encounter, supposing it the first between Burr and H (though both had been in army in N.Y. for months, for fortnight in same division).

24. Livingston, *Putnam,* 311, gives route probably more accurately than marked on Faden, "Plan of N.Y. Island," London, 1776, NYPL.; see also for retreat Humphreys, *Putnam,* 120–1.

25. 6 GW 58.

26. *Ibid.,* 59.

27. See *ibid.,* 64–5, 67–9; part of fighting took place on farm of Kortright, members of whose family had been H's benefactors.

28. 1 H 56 ascribed this to (Egbert) Benson, N.Y. patriot, lifelong friend of H; Benson lived until 1833, may have related incident to H's son; not found in Benson's mss. or few printed papers.

29. See 6 GW 184–5, 197, 202–3, 243; Johnston, *op. cit.,* 266 ff.

30. 6 GW 214–5, n.

31. See Haslet to Rodney, Nov. 12, 1776, in Ryden, ed., *Letters to and from Rodney,* 142–3; Heath's *Memoirs,* Wilson, ed., 86 ff.

32. Heath, *ibid.,* 89; Haslet, *ibid.* For two days enemy lay inactive; when Washington withdrew to stronger heights across Croton River to North Castle, Howe shifted his forces to Dobbs Ferry and Kingsbridge.

33. His pay book shows in incidental references company was at King's Ferry, N[orth] Castle, Pickskill (*sic*), and we may safely suppose at White Plains. His close military associate Fish thought he was "With the Army at white Plains" (Fish Papers, Columbia Univ.). J. C. H. (1 H 56) said merely that at "the battle of White Plains . . . his conduct was remarked," but later in 1 R. 132–4 offered questionable detail. 1 Morse 24, though he had given imaginary account of H in battle of L.I., ventured only that he "was in the engagement at White Plains." Shea, 411–2, Schachner, H., 52–3, followed JCH with added touches. Hufeland, *Westchester During Rev.,* 138, thought guns were H's, but were "commanded by some subordinate officer whose name has not been recorded."

34. Haslet to Rodney, *ibid.*, 143, made no mention of other gun firing at all, but Heath, who viewed action from mile north, said "the cannonade was brisk on both sides" (*op. cit.*, 88).

35. Pay bk. shows that Cpl. Martin Johnson and Robt. Burrage, "Motroess," got shoes at "Picks Kill" (14, 158). 1 H 56 had it that immediately after White Plains H was "detached to cover a post in the neighbourhood of Fort Washington," and only after fall of that stronghold rejoined army on west side of Hudson; perhaps misled by dispatch of Lasher, King's Bridge, to Heath, Oct. 26, 1776 (5th ser., II *Am. Arch.*, 1250); corrected in 1 R 136.

36. 6 GW 263–6.

37. *Ibid.*, 275–8.

38. *Ibid.*, 271–3, 279–83.

39. A few citations are conclusive; see Washington to Greene, Nov. 8, 1776 (6 GW 257–8) and Greene's reassurance same date, *ibid.*, 258 n.; Washington to Congress Nov. 16 (*ibid.*, 285; cf. on 19th to John Augustine Washington, *ibid.*, 245). Greene's formal responsibility for decision was ended when Washington reached Ft. Lee Nov. 13 (Washington to Congress Nov. 14, 1776, *ibid.*, 279, and Greene to Knox, Nov. [17, 1776], Johnston, *op. cit.*, Pt. II, 100–1).

40. 1 H 56; story omitted, impliedly disclaimed in later 1 R 136, but 1 Morse 24 repeated fiction.

41. Washington to Congress, Nov. 21, 1776, 6 GW 295–6.

42. *Ibid.*, 297–9.

43. 9 LHW 37–8.

44. 5th ser., III *Am. Arch.*, 925, 1058.

45. Washington, Hackensack, Nov. 21, 1776 to Lee, (6 GW 298).

46. Washington, Brunswic (*sic*) to Heath, *ibid.*, 311; to Gov. Livingston, Nov. 30, 1776, *ibid.*, 312–3.

47. Washington, HQ, Bucks Co., Dec. 15, 1776, to Pa. Council of Safety, *ibid.*, 376. Lee's dissemblance in Nov.–Dec. 1776, then unknown to H in any detail, must have strengthened his blame of Lee during Conway cabal and later. Commander in chief's distress was sharpened by accidental discovery Adj. Gen. Jos. Reed disparaged him to laggard Lee. Washington's note to Reed wrapped up perfect reproof in half-dozen words (Brunswick, Nov. 30, 1776, *ibid.*, 313). H's skill with pen was afterward many times availed of, but that Washington needed no one to give him lessons in this department is plain in this searing apology.

48. Washington to Livingston, Dec. 1; to John Augustine Washington, Dec. 18, 1776, 320–21, (*ibid.*, 397–8).

49. To Cong. Dec. 1, 1776 (6 GW 318–20; cf. Greene to Gov. Cooke, *ibid.*, 318 n.).

50. *Ibid.*, 321–2.

51. Every field piece would be called on; while Washington took 18 to attack on Trenton, some of these would have come from White Plains; at New Brunswick he probably had not so many (Knox to wife, Dec. 28, 1776, MHS, and Stryker, *Trenton and Princeton*, 371–2). New Brunswick is mentioned in pay bk. of H's battery.

52. Custis, *Recollections of Washington*, Lossing ed., 344–5; Wilkinson, 1 *Memoirs*, 119.

53. To Congress, Dec. 3, 1776 (6 GW 325; 1 H 137, Stryker, *op. cit.*, 15, and others followed Custis). (For location of bridge, cf. Benedict, *New Brunswick*, 39, 57, using local records.) Marker on campus of Rutgers Univ. supposedly locates H's battery.

54. Irving, 3 *Washington* 88; 1 R 137 quoted "a friend" of H: "Well do I recollect the day when Hamilton's company marched into Princeton. It was a model of discipline; at their head was a boy, and I wondered at his youth; but what was my surprise when . . . he was pointed out to me as that Hamilton of whom we had already heard so much."

55. Cf. 6 GW 347, 366, 372, 373.

56. Only documentary evidence of H's presence at Trenton is incidental reference in his pay book. Given this, his part in attack, and location of his guns, may be assumed, though particulars offered by subsequent writers are questionable. Years later H spoke of victories at Trenton, Princeton as "the dawnings of that bright day which afterwards broke forth with such . . . lustre" (eulogy on Greene, 1789, 8 LHW 67). Fish, years later, apropos H's artillery company, queried, "Was he in any severe action while at their head?" (Fish mss., Columbia Univ.)

57. Stryker, *Trenton and Princeton*, 142, without citation; Washington's order Christmas morning for embarkation, march on Trenton (*ibid.*, 113–15) also without source, is so reprinted in 6 GW 438–9 n. Stryker, 308–9, listing units of American army in campaign of 1776–7, puts H's artillery Co. in Reazin Beall's brigade, which was not in order of march for Trenton, Dec. 25.

58. Cadwalader, Dec. 27, 1776, 38 Papers GW, 27, LC, printed in Stryker, *op. cit.*, 241.

59. To Cadwalader, Dec. 27, 1776 (6 GW 446–7).

60. John Howland, 71.

61. Cf. Jnl. of Sam'l. Shaw, in Stryker, *op. cit.,* 482; Stephen Olney in Williams, *Biog. Rev. Heroes,* 193–4.

62. Cf. Thos. Rodney, *Diary,* 1776–7, 32; Knox to wife, Jan. 7, 1777, in Stryker, 449–52; Lambert Cadwalader, same date, to Mrs. Sam'l. Meredith, *ibid.,* 448–9.

63. Letter from an officer, Pluckemin, Jan. 5, 1777, in Stryker, 446. He had remained behind at Brunswick, but that was to cover a real retreat, not to mask an advance.

64. *Ibid.*

65. Rodney, in *ibid.,* 439.

66. Knox, above, 450; picture of Mawhood, on brown pony, with pet spaniels bounding ahead (Stryker, 280, without ref.), was suddenly wiped from slate.

67. Rodney, above, 439–40; Knox, *ibid.,* 450; "officer of distinction," *ibid.,* 447–8. Freeman, 4 *Washington* 352 finds two pair of field pieces, one belonging to Capt. Daniel Neil of N.J., abandoned when Neil was killed.

68. Wilkinson, 1 *Memoirs* 144–5, said "there was but one gun fired at the college, and this from a six pounder, by an officer who was not advised the enemy had abandoned it; the ball recoiled, and very nearly killed my horse as I passed in rear of the building." Rodney (Stryker above, 440) mentioned building as principal one in town, but nothing further. Significantly, Wertenbaker's scholarly *Battle of Princeton,* 109–11 makes no mention of H. Cf. letter of A. Cuthbert, son of officer in Moulder's battery, in Haven, *Thirty Days in New Jersey* . . . 44–5; Sgt. Jos. White's narration, Stryker, 480. Bill, *Campaign of Princeton,* 112–3, says, without citation, H fired two shots at Nassau Hall; Stryker, 290 is similar; Woodhull, *Battle of Princeton,* 20, lays H's shots ("at the south face of the college") to tradition.

69. Wertenbaker, *ibid.,* 111.

70. Pluckemin, Jan. 5, 1777, to Congress (6 GW 470).

Chapter 8 (Pages 100 to 124)
Aide-de-Camp to Washington

1. Lt. Thompson witnessed the men's receipts in which they renounced any further claims against "Coll." Hamilton, showing that he had already joined Washington's staff, and been promoted, when these entries were made. March 17, 1777 Provincial Congress permitted artillery company

lately commanded by Capt. H to enlist in service of Continent; Mr. Morris was to inform H (1 Jnl. Prov. Cong., 838). For some reason John Jay dissented. H suffered a considerable spell of sickness at Morristown, prior to March 1, 1776, which may have given him his only chance for this sort of study (letter to N.Y. Provincial Congress, March 6, 1777, 9 LHW 44).

2. Malachy Postlethwayt, *The Universal Dictionary of Trade and Commerce*, "translated from the French of Monsieur [Jacques] Savary [des Brulons] . . . with large additions and improvements . . . " (London, 1751 [Vol. I, pp. 1017], 1755 [Vol. II, pp. 856], both vols. with tables, maps). Three more editions appeared before H used the work, 1766, 1767, and 1774.

3. H's condensations of Postlethwayt are readily identified in original; e.g., Sir Walter Raleigh's estimate of ships and seamen in Dutch herring fisheries is on p. 228 of Pay Book and Vol. I, 783–4 of Postlethwayt; H (Pay Book, 234) refers specifically to Postlethwayt's "articles Cash [Vol. I, 461] & Circulation" [*ibid.*, 498].

4. Pay Book, 232.

5. *Ibid.*, 234; in 1 Postlethwayt, 464, 499.

6. Pay Book, 243. "The par between land and labour is twice the quantity of land whose product will maintain the labourer—in France one acre and a half will maintain one[,] in England three owing to the difference in the manner of living."

7. *Ibid.*, 245.

8. *Ibid.*, 278–9.

9. *Ibid.*, 280; H may have met this kind of problem in mathematical exercises under Harpur at King's.

10. *Ibid.*, 251.

11. *Ibid.*, 284.

12. For example, *Britain's Commercial Interest Explained and Improved* . . . (London, 1757, 2 vols.); *Great-Britain's True System* . . . (London, 1757); and, earlier, *The African Trade* . . . (London, 1745).

13. However, Cantillon's *Essai sur la Nature du Commerce* was not current until published in France in 1755, and Quesnay's *Tableau Économique* appeared only in 1758, while Postlethwayt was an established writer earlier.

14. ". . . Rivalship . . . between the Commodities of the Nation's own produce, and foreign Commodities . . . ought . . . to be proscribed," but "home Rivalship is Emulation in Work between the Subjects. . . . The more numerous [industry's] Productions are, the cheaper they will be, *and that Cheapness will obtain the Preference at foreign Markets.*" As a result of inflow of money, all parts of a state "act and communicate . . . Motion to each other: it then enjoys all the Strength and Vigor it is susceptible of."

(*Great-Britain's True System,* 235–7). He praises Colbert's program of bringing in foreign artisans (*ibid.,* 250–51). "All Diminution of Security, in a State, suspends the Effects of . . . *Circulation,* and destroys Trade itself. . . . the more quick . . . the Circulation . . . the more Wealth and Prosperity we must enjoy" (*ibid.,* 362; cf. *Britain's Commercial Interest,* II, 259). In colonial policy he was an orthodox mercantilist (cf. *ibid.,* 427). H must have noticed the treatment of "Various schemes for the payment of the national debts, but none comparable to that . . . of a sinking fund. . . ." Postlethwayt berated its alienation from its original purpose (*Dictionary,* ix).

15. Pay Book, 252.

16. "Camillus" was to be signature to one of H's notable series of public letters.

17. *Ibid.,* 258 ff. When H calls senate, composed of older men, "a wise institution," we think of his arguments for such a body in American Constitution.

18. *Ibid.,* 250.

19. G. W. Greene, 1 *Nathanael Greene* 193; did not say Greene recommended H for Washington's staff, remarked only that "Hamilton's entrance into Washington's family added materially to the pleasure of [Greene's] intercourse at head-quarters" (310, 333–4). Pickering believed Greene was sponsor, but took this from Johnson's *Greene.*

20. We have little from H's pen for period of military service until he joined Washington's staff, so must depend on indirect news of him. Perhaps letters of these months, and also of college and school days, were once collected and then were lost, in a batch.

21. 6 GW 444, 483–5; to Harrison, Jan. 20, 1777 (7 GW 38). "Captn. Hamilton" is identified by Fitzpatrick (*ibid.,* 519) as Alexander. We wonder where H was; obviously not with Harrison, for enclosure was to be forwarded. Shortly before entering military family H was ill, (Morristown, March 6, 1777, to N.Y. Prov. Cong., 9 LHW 44), but army had been two months at Morristown, so his absence in late Jan. was from another cause. Geo. Johnston joined family Jan. 20 but only replaced S. B. Webb (7 GW 37, 41, 120–1, 523; 6 *ibid.,* 488, 499).

22. 7 GW 218; see AMH, facing p. 36, for facsimile of certificate of appointment as aide. A supposed miniature on ivory of H at just this time, by Charles Willson Peale, is reproduced in *W&M Quar.,* 3d ser., XII, No. 2, April 1955, facing 196; Bland and Northcott (*ibid.,* 188–9) give plausible reasons for thinking it genuine. The face is handsome, sensitive, but above all, youthful. Richard K. Meade ("Friend Dick" as Washington addressed him), who was coupled with H because they joined staff almost together, was announced as aide March 12 (GW *ibid.,* 280).

23. Pickering rode to Morristown from Bound Brook with Gen. Lincoln, "and then I received the impression (I suppose from Lincoln) that Hamilton was a very extraordinary young man" (47 Pickering papers 70–71, MHS). Similarly, Tilghman received appointment some time after he commenced duties Aug. 8, 1776 (6 GW 65; cf. Washington to Sullivan, May 11, 1781, 22 GW 70–71).

24. *Washington and His Aides.*

25. For Harrison, G. T. Ness, Jr., "A Lost Man of Maryland," 35 *Md. Hist. Mag.* 315–36; cf. to H, March 26, 1781, 1 JCHW 215–7, and H, Nov. 27, 1789, 9 LHW 464–5. For Tilghman, O. Tilghman, *Memoir . . .* has letters, journal extracts; additional particulars in Homer Bast in 42 *Md. Hist. Mag.* 71–94; see honorific portrait by Trumbull in group with Washington and Lafayette.

26. To R. H. Harrison, Jan. 9, 1777 (6 GW 487).

27. 4 GW 269. On information from HQ, Washington to Gov. Patrick Henry, Feb. 24, 1777 (7 GW 199–200). For Tilghman's correspondence with N.Y. comm., to and from Duer, Sept. 22–Oct. 21, 1776, clippings from *N.Y. Times,* 1895, NYPL. For Washington's distresses, which cast light on help H soon gave him, see to Pres. of Cong., in own hand after midnight, Sept. 24, 1776 (6 GW 106–16).

28. Tilghman, *op. cit.,* 147; cf. 134–5.

29. P. L. Ford, *True George Washington,* 66.

30. July 25, 1776 (5 GW 337–8).

31. See, for his practice, Washington to Tilghman, July 14, 1785 (O. Tilghman, *op. cit.,* 115–6), and illustrative case in ALS H to Knox, Oct. 17, 1791 (29 Knox Papers 149, MHS).

32. 47 Pickering commonplace book p. 87, MHS; cf. autograph excerpt, letter to C. Gore, Jan. 31, 1827; 16 *ibid.,* 178. Cf. draft ALS Jan. 8, 1801, to Foster, 14 *ibid.,* 2; draft AL, Jan. 16, 1827 to Jas. A. Hamilton, 16 *ibid.,* 176.

33. 1 R 176–7; cf. below, p. 224. H drafted Washington's letters to Rochambeau and was frequently present at their conferences. ". . . I could never too highly praise the solidity of his judgment and the amenity of his style," said the French commander (1 *Memoirs* 248). Cf., with more particulars, Chastellux, 1 *Travels in N. America* 372. In 2 R iii–vi J. C. Hamilton denied he detracted from Washington's fame by pointing out H's contribution to conception as well as phraseology of hundreds of his chief's public letters.

34. Rests on local tradition (Weig and Craig, *Morristown,* 5); no contemporary identification of building used for HQ has been found. Wash-

ington did not occupy mansion of Col. Jacob Ford until second encampment at Morristown more than two years later.

35. Cf. ALS, Janet Montgomery, n.d., n.p. [to R. R. Livingston], Livingston misc. ms., NYHS.

36. April 23, 1776 (4 GW 506–7; cf. H for Washington, on qualifications of aides, 10 *ibid.*, 377–8).

37. 11 NYHS *Collections,* 435.

38. Aug. 18, 1776, in O. Tilghman, *op. cit.,* 131–2. ". . . you cannot conceive what a constant Scene of Business we are engaged in" (Aug. 15, *ibid.,* cf. to same, Oct. 31, 1777, p. 147).

39. Cf. ALS, April 12, 1777, to comm. N.Y. Conv. (R. R. Livingston misc. mss., NYHS, printed 9 LHW 54); April 5, 1777 (LHW *ibid.,* 53).

40. Aide must have been often besought by friends to secure general's consent to personal requests; see, e.g., ALS, H, to Webb, Feb. 22, March 2, 1781 (Webb Papers, Yale Univ.).
Again, he was glad to be able to soften the general's understandable asperity; cf. H, as A.D.C., on back of ALS, Washington, March 14, 1777, to Col. Andrew Ward (Yale Univ.), and H's draft, Washington, March 13, 1777, to Maj. Gen. Stephen Chatham (Emmet 9284, NYPL).

41. Nov. 5, 1777; Jan. 3, 1778; Mil. Corr., typescript, LIHS.

42. At first he wrote fewer letters than Harrison, Tilghman, or Johnston (7 GW 515, 519–20, 523, 549).

43. See, e.g., to comm. N.Y. Conv., March 20, 1777 (9 LHW 46 and successive dates to May 7 in *ibid.,* 48, 50, 54, 66, 67).

44. Cf. to Patrick Henry, Feb. 24, 1777 (7 GW 199–200).

45. Capt. Johann Ewald's suspicion that Cols. Hamilton and (Wm. S.?) Schmidt came to his post near New Brunswick at opening of campaign in 1777, ostensibly to deliver letters from captured officers, but really to reconnoitre his camp, is without support. Ewald dismissed his visitors with speed. (3 *Belehrungen* 339; cf. Edward J. Lowell, *Hessians and Other German Auxiliaries . . . in Rev.,* 112–3).

46. Cf. H, April 20, 1777, to comm. N.Y. Conv. (9 LHW 56–7), "meddle with none but those whose crimes . . . are of a pretty deep dye." And to Gov. Livingston that "His Excellency desires to avoid . . . the least encroachments either upon the rights of the citizens or of the magistrate" (April 1777, *ibid.,* 59–61; cf. May 12, *ibid.,* 68–9). On suppression of Tories and spies by N.Y. Conv. at this time see 1 *Jnls.* 856, 857, and G. Morris to H, 1 JCHW 28, 29.

47. *Memoirs,* 275–7. For H offering toasts after supper at HQ, Nov., 1780, Chastellux, *Travels in N. America,* 67–8.

48. To Henry Laurens, Nov. 26, 1777; Feb. 9, 17, 24, March 9, 1778 (H. Laurens Papers, LIHS); cf. Henry to John L., Sept. 30, Nov. 30, 1777, *ibid.*

49. May 12, 1777, in 51 NJHS Proceed. 152 (mispaged for 252); describes Morristown, H's fellow aides, agreeable society of camp.

50. Pickering Papers, MHS.

51. *Memoirs of Washington,* 345–6.

52. H dissuaded Washington from an enterprise to make Sir Henry Clinton prisoner, because this might be only to put in his place an abler British commander of unfamiliar ways (related in 1 R 527–8).

53. Referring to a subsequent period, John Marshall, like Pickering, was astonished H could write so much outside of his stated commitments. These *obiter* efforts, they agreed, are evidences of "a mighty *mind*" (46 Pickering Papers 359–61, MHS; cf. AL, Marshall, March 9, 1822, to Jas. A. Hamilton, 84 HLC 13643).

54. Comm. was G. Morris (who usually wrote to H), R. R. Livingston, Wm. Allison. For resolution of N.Y. Conv. authorizing employment of suitable person at HQ to send intelligence, 1 *Jnls.* 835 (March 13, 1777); acceptance of invitation by Archibald (*sic*) H was noted March 24 (*ibid.,* 847). Doubtless Morris was responsible for H's selection; he had handled H's recommendations about the military company at this time, and had just been added to comm. (*ibid.,* 835, 838; comm. to H, March 17, and Livingston to same, March 29, 1777, 1 JCHW 12, 14). The pay for Hamilton's letters was not stipulated; Conv. voted Tilghman for similar services earlier a present to cost not exceeding £80 (*Jnls. ibid.,* 851). For further letters, comm. to H, see JCHW, *ibid.,* 19–21, 22, 27–9. Legislators were concerned principally for safety of their state from southward march of Burgoyne and expectation Howe would move northward to join him.

55. March 20, 22, 1777 (9 LHW 45–6, 49).

56. E.g., April 5, 1777, "As to . . . an attempt up the North River, . . . you may discard any uneasiness on that score. . . . It is almost . . . a certainty, that the . . . views of the enemy, in the ensuing campaign, will be directed towards . . . Philadelphia. . . ." (9 LHW 51–2). A month later he was obliged to revise this judgment (*ibid.,* 67, 69).

57. ALS, June 28, 1777, R. R. Livingston Papers, NYHS, printed 9 LHW 79–82; cf. to Hugh Knox [July 1777], *ibid.,* 85: ". . . our hopes are . . . in preserving a good army . . . to take advantage of favorable opportunities, and waste and defeat the enemy by piecemeal." H's reports to N.Y.

comm. furnish running account of military operations spring and early summer 1777, when, especially from Middle Brook, Washington confined and harassed enemy; see to G. Morris, July 6, 1777 (9 LHW 88).

58. May 7, 1777, to G. Morris (9 LHW 65–6). Most active members of comm. to draw constitution were R. R. Livingston, G. Morris, Jay (Jay to Livingston and Morris, April 29, 1777, Johnston, ed., 1 Jay Papers 128–36). Duane reported draft to Conv. March 12, 1777; interspersed debate on it continued until adoption April 20 (1 *Jnls.* 833, 892).

59. To Morris, April 28, May 7, 1777 (9 LHW 59, 65). Conv. ordered 500 copies speedily struck off (*Jnls., ibid.,* 898); Constitution was not submitted to people for ratification.

60. To H, May 16, 1777 (1 JCHW 27). Contrary to Morris's advocacy, naming civil and military officers was lodged not with gov., but (Jay's suggestion) in a Council of Appointment; veto power, better entrusted to gov., was vested in a Council of Revision (cf. debates in *Jnls.,* and Jay to Livingston and Morris, above).

61. ALS, HQ, Morristown, May 19, 1777, R. R. Livingston Papers, NYHS, printed with typographical changes in LHW *ibid.,* 71–3; Robt. Harper (Harpur), H's old tutor at King's, now in N.Y. Conv., in debates on the constitution, wanted manhood suffrage (*Jnls., ibid.,* 843). Morris, congenial to H's ideas, made valiant effort, in this first constitution of N.Y., to abolish slavery as soon as a future legislature thought public safety would permit. Jay helped but recommendation was lost at instance of Livingston (*Jnls. ibid.,* 887).

62. Correspondent at this time for comm.

63. July 6, 22, 29, 1777 (9 LHW 86–95); cf. Sir Henry Clinton, *American Rebellion,* 61–2.

64. He referred to N.Y. as "your State," not as his own. An accurate description of H is title he gave to a series of polemical letters, "The Continentalist." Though later N.Y. was his home—domestic, professional, political—H remained, to extent shared by few contemporaries, an American. He never referred, as others did familiarly, to "my country," meaning "my state."

65. Morgan's men were so deadly that care must be taken to avoid jealousy of them among Northern troops. (ALS, Aug. 18, 1777, R. R. Livingston Papers, NYHS, printed in 9 LHW 95–8).

66. Sept. 1, 1777 (9 LHW 99–100).

67. H's awareness of handicap of enemy is documented in Edward E. Curtis, *Organization of British Army in American Revolution,* which goes far

to correct tempting contrast between pipe-clayed professional and tattered continental. Former was transplanted, the latter had roots in native soil. Gage, Howe, Clinton, Cornwallis often suffered from limitations in men and means.

68. Cf. to G. Morris, July 22, 1777: "Should [Howe] be satisfied with the splendor of his acquisition, and shut himself up in Philadelphia, we can ruin him by confinement. . . . the foremost [disagreeable consequence] is the *depreciation of our currency,* which, from the importance in which Philadelphia is held, cannot fail to ensue" (9 LHW 90–1; cf. to Hugh Knox [July 1777], *ibid.,* 84–5).

69. Sept. 1, 1777, R. R. Livingston Papers, NYHS; 9 LHW 99–100 has it to G. Morris, as does 1 R 269–70, though here without date, and place is mistakenly given as Chad's Ford.

70. *Ibid.*

71. HQ, Wilmington, Aug. 29, 1777, to Gates for Washington, who was busy reconnoitering (Gates Papers, Box 7, NYHS).

72. To Livingston, *ibid.*

73. To Sullivan, Oct. 24, 1777 (9 GW 425–6).

74. R. H. Harrison to Pres. of Congress, Sept. 11, 1777 (9 GW 206–7).

75. 9 GW 230–1.

76. H to Hancock, Sept. 18, 1777, and *ibid.,* 9 LHW 101–2; Lee, 1 *War in Southern Dept.* 19.

77. 8 JCC 754, Sept. 18, 1778.

78. Charles Francis Adams, 1 *Life of John Adams* 267; John Adams, 2 *Diary* 439. Lamenting "the . . . timorous, defensive part, which has involved us in so many disasters," he exclaimed "O, Heavens! grant us one great soul! One leading mind would extricate the best cause from . . . ruin which seems to await it. . . ." He was too bent on his own diligent skirting of scene of conflict to offer as the "one active, masterly capacity" that he prayed should "bring order out of this confusion, and save this country."

79. Sept. 22, 1777, 9 GW 248–9, also (draft by Meade) *ibid.,* 249–50; cf. H to Pres. of Congress, Sept. 22, 1777, 9 LHW 102.

80. He evidently spoke of this, with some pride, to his son (1 R 284), who, however, could not find text of public appeal; not in any Phila. newspaper or preserved handbill.

81. Marshall, 1 *Life of Washington* 163.

82. *Ibid.*

83. He could not have reached there before the night of Sept. 21 (to Pres. of Congress, above), and British approach two days later (9 GW 263) hampered his efforts to collect supplies (Washington to Gerry, Sept. 27, 1777; *ibid.*, 275).

84. Sept. 22, 1777 (9 GW 249–50).

85. Sept. 22, 1777 (9 LHW 102–3).

86. Sept. 23, 1777 (9 GW p. 259).

87. In directions prepared for Washington's signature, H tried vehemently to keep Delaware blocked (cf. 9 GW 370). His instructions to Col. Christopher Greene, sent late in night of Oct. 15, 1777, is illustration (facsimile in 1 R 298, printed in 9 GW 375–6). General had gone to bed, so H signed it as aide-de-camp. His urgent injunctions for vigilance remind of his admonition, in boyhood, to captain of Cruger's sloop bound for Spanish Main.

88. Enoch Anderson, "Personal Recollections" (26 *Papers Hist. Soc. Del.*, 44).

89. Lee, 1 *War in Southern Department* 29–30. Lee was there with dragoons as guard to commander in chief; in his account did not conceal his disagreement with Knox and Washington. Pickering, years later (1828), referred Lafayette to this recital, and amplified arguments he and H had used (draft ALS, Salem, Mass., July 23, 1828; 16 Pickering Papers 310 ff., MHS).

90. Anderson, *ibid.*, 45.

91. ALS, Camp at White Marsh, Nov. 21, 1777, to Gates (Gates Papers, NYHS). Cf. *ibid.*, Camp near Pawling Mill, Oct. 6, 1777, to wife (Charles J. Stillé, *Wayne and Pennsylvania Line* . . . 95–6); cf. Gen. John Armstrong's description of "ill judged delay" at "Mr Chews Germantown House" (ALS, Oct. 9, 1777, to Gates, Gates Papers, NYHS). Walter Stewart exaggerated British strength in Chew's to "four field Peices & 500 Men. . . ." (ALS, Oct. 12, 1777, to Gates, *ibid.*).

92. It was one of severest tours of duty during Revolution—40 miles of marching, more than two hours of fighting, with nothing to eat, only water to drink (Anderson, *op. cit.*, 45).

93. Oct. 7, 1777 (9 GW 319–23). H must have taken peculiar pleasure in wording recommendation of McDougall, his old friend of the Fields, in N.Y., for promotion to major general.

94. 1 *War in Southern Department* 28–9. Knox did not admit his fault at Chew's; cf. to Artemas Ward (from Perkeomy [*sic*] Creek, Oct. 7, 1777; Drake's *Knox*, 52–3; to wife, *ibid.*, 53).

Chapter 9 (Pages 125 to 142)
Success of a Delicate Mission

1. Schuyler to Washington (July 1777, 1 R 232–3); ALS, Pierre Van Cortlandt, July 17, 1777, to N.Y. delegates in Congress (Duane Papers, NYHS).

2. For a remarkably impartial review of this tilt between New England Yankees and Schuyler the Yorker, see 1 R 225 ff. Cf. Lafayette in 84 HLC 13722–3.

3. 8 GW 456–60. That this was H's own opinion is plain in his private letters at the time. See H Papers, NYPL, first p. missing, but undoubtedly July 1777 to Dr. Hugh Knox, of St. Croix, as in 9 LHW 82–6; to G. Morris, July 22, 29, and to R. R. Livingston, Aug. 18, 1777 (*ibid.*, 89–98).

4. 8 GW 456–60, 462–3.

5. Cf. Van Cortlandt to Gov. Trumbull, of Conn., 1 R 249–50.

6. Aug. 4, 1777 (9 GW 13).

7. H had particulars of Gates's defeat of Aug. 16, 1780, from Otho H. Williams (from Hillsborough, N.C., Aug. 30, 1780, 1 JCHW 148–50), who dealt charitably with the general's long-distance scamper, 180 miles in 3½ days. H commented: "It does admirable credit to the activity of a man at his time of life. But it disgraces the General and the soldier. I always believed him to be far short of a Hector. . . ." (Sept. 6, 1780, to Duane, *ibid.*, 170–1, and not, as in 2 R 123, to Williams; cf. to Eliz. Schuyler, same date, 1 JCHW 169–70.)

8. 9 GW 461–4, with facsimile.

9. *Ibid.*, 478–9.

10. Oct. 30, 1777; LS., Gates Papers, NYHS. Letter sent is in R. H. Harrison's hand; 1 GW 452 says draft also. Gates relied on Pres. of Congress to relay messages to Washington (ALS, draft, Gates to Hancock, Albany, Nov. 15, 1777, Gates Papers, NYHS). This was not most expeditious or dutiful means of sending momentous military news to commander in chief, who had forbidden such indirection (to Gates, copy, May 15, 1777, *ibid.*). In this instance Gates's courier, his aide Wilkinson, arrived at York, Pa., tardily, owing to illness and loitering.

11. Oct. 30, 1777 (9 GW 466–8). 1 R 339 says "Hamilton departed under instructions drawn by himself," but 9 GW 468 n. says draft is in hand of Tilghman.

12. Cf. Washington to Putnam, Oct. 30, 1777, to be delivered by H (9 GW 464–5); also LS, Putnam, Fishkill, Oct. 31, 1777, to Gates enclosing decision of council of war; also ALsS, Geo. Clinton, Fishkill, to Gates, Oct. 30, 1777, and Malcolm, New Windsor, *ibid.* (For return of Morgan's riflemen to Washington's army, 9 GW 264–5, 466 n.)

13. H to Washington, Fishkill, Nov. 2, 1777 (1 JCHW 39).

14. See table of distances, in unknown hand, undoubtedly prepared for H's journey, "From Gen.¹ Washington's Camp, at the 15 Mile Stone— Octo.ʳ 30, 1777," to Albany; way was by Correyll's Ferry, Morris Town, Ringwood, New Windsor, Fish Kill, Rienbeck, and Kinderhook (Gates Papers, Box 8, NYHS).

15. H's report to Washington (9 LHW 106–9) is dated only Nov. 1777, but letter to Gates, written at Albany a few hours after first interview, is dated Nov. 5 (*ibid.,* 109–10).

16. To Pres. of Congress, Aug. 3, 1777 (8 GW 8–9).

17. (Above) 9 LHW, 103–105.

18. H to Washington, Albany, Nov. 1777 (9 LHW 106–8).

19. Cf. ALsS, to Artemas Ward, Aug. 25, 1777, to Arnold (copy) Aug. 26, 1777; to Lincoln, *ibid.;* to Stark, Sept. 10, 1777 (Gates Papers, NYHS).

20. Behmus's (*sic*) Heights, Oct. 5, 1777, copy, Gates Papers, NYHS.

21. Gates scrupulously preserved every item (see below); all is now in NYHS.

22. 9 GW 468 n.

23. ALS, Camp Stilwater [*sic*], Oct. 1, 1777 (Gates Papers, NYHS).

24. LS, Jer: (?) Powell, Boston, Oct. 2; Wm. Gordon, Jamaica P[lain], Oct. 3; ALS, Thos. Cushing, Boston, Oct. 4, 1777 (Gates Papers, NYHS).

25. LS, John Hancock, York-Town [Pa.], Oct. 4, 1777, in *ibid.*

26. ALS, York Town, Oct. 5, 1777, *ibid.;* probably Lovell, ". . . this Army will be totally lost unless you come down & collect the virtuous Band, who wish to fight under your Banner, & with their Aid save the Southern Hemisphere" (Reading, Nov. 17, 1777, to Gates; copy made 1816 in *ibid.,* NYHS).

27. Letters of Oct. 7 from Hugh Hughes, [Continental] Village, and Geo. Clinton, New Windsor, were followed by that from Putnam at Fishkill next day (NYHS). Putnam reported Clinton's belief British troops would proceed upriver in their ships, "therefore prepare for the worst."

28. LS, Geo. Clinton, New Windsor, Oct. 11, 1777, with copy of short message of Oct. 8 found when bullet was unscrewed; cf. H. Hughes, Fishkill, Oct. 10, 1777, to Gates (Gates Papers, NYHS). Cf. Sir Henry Clinton, *American Rebellion,* 79–80, 83.

29. See letters of John Armstrong, Oct. 9, 12, 1777; two from Gen. Wayne, Nov. 10, 21, 1777, reached Gates too late to affect his treatment of Washington's request for reinforcements (NYHS).

30. For effusive congratulations, cf. ALS, Samuel Hodgdon, Albany, Oct. 10, and Capt. Duncan, Oct. 11, 1777; Jonathan Trumbull, Albany, Oct. 11. Jer: Powell, Oct. 13, and Lafayette, Oct. 14, 1777, were more restrained (all in Gates Papers, NYHS).

31. On peril and destruction of Kingston, as Gates learned of it, cf. ALsS, Pierre Van Cortlandt, Kingston, Oct. 15; Geo. Clinton, *ibid.,* Oct. 16, 17, 21, 1777, and Oct. 15 to Van Courtlandt (Gates Papers, NYHS).

32. Proposals and counterproposals are mostly in hand of Wilkinson, whose aid in arranging the capitulation Gates later proclaimed. Gates's original terms were also harsher than would be expected were Gates's position as weak as Wilkinson described to Congress; cf. LS, Wilkinson, Nov. 2, 1777 (Gates Papers, NYHS).

33. LS, Robt. (?) Rensselaer and Robt. Yates, Oct. 17, 1777, to Gates. Cf. ALS, G. V. Schaick, same date; Peter H. Livingston, Dirck Jansen (?), and Peter Wynkoop, Jr., Oct. 18, 1777, to Comm. of Albany (Gates Papers, NYHS).

34. ALS, Head Quarters 17 Miles from Philad.^{a} Oct. 30, 1777, in *ibid.*

35. ALS, Camp White Marsh, Nov. 10, 1777, in *ibid.* "You well know . . . that no Aspiring Genius . . . or shining Military Character can expect to pass with Impunity here" (*ibid.*).

36. ALS, Nov. 21, 1777; cf. ALS, St. Clair, same place, date; ALS, Mifflin, Nov. 17, 1777; ALS, Lovell, York, Nov. 27, 1777 (NYHS).

37. ALS, Camp, Nov. 11, 1777 (NYHS).

38. *Ibid.,* Nov. 12 (NYHS).

39. ALsS, Moses Hazen, Bethlehem, Oct. 26; Wm. Gordon, Jamaica Plain, Oct. 27; Henry Babcock, Stonington, Oct. 28, 1777, copy; this last voices strong New England distaste for Schuyler, who "tho' a polite man, is no Soldier, and would have made a much better Figure as an Assistant Dep.^{y} to Gen. Mifflin in his Q.^{r} Master Gen-^{ls} Department than in the exalted Rank the Congress mistakenly gave" him (all in Gates Papers, NYHS).

40. MSD, signed by John Laurens, Pres., Nov. 1, 1777 (Gates Papers, NYHS).

41. MSD, signed by Chas. Thomson, Sec., Nov. 4, 1777, in *ibid.*

42. ALS, H, Albany, Nov. 5, 1777, to Gates, Gates Papers, NYHS; printed 1 JCHW 43–4, and 9 LHW 109–10.

43. Gates Papers, NYHS.

44. At Oct. 17 return, Patterson's, 732 Continentals; Glover's, 1,362 total.

45. It must have been a conversation, for no letter of H to Gates, in interval, is in Gates Papers. These were scrupulously kept by Gates. See to Mifflin, copy, Dec. 4, 1777, Gates Papers, NYHS.

46. H wrote Washington from New Windsor, Nov. 10, 1777, where he had arrived night before from Albany: "Having given General Gates a little time to recollect himself, I renewed my remonstrances on the necessity . . . of sending you more than one brigade . . . and finally prevailed upon him. . . ." (9 LHW 111).

47. AL, unfinished (probably first) draft, Gates, Nov. 7, 1777, to Washington (Gates Papers, NYHS).

48. Another p. must be missing, though endorsement is on back of this one.

49. *Ibid.;* second draft not in Gates's hand.

50. AL, draft, Gates, Nov. 8, 1777, to Gov. Trumbull (Gates Papers, NYHS), asking for 50 ox teams, 200 draft horses with drivers for this purpose; destinations were Westbury and Springfield (AL, draft, Nov. 10, 1777, to Pres. of Congress [?]).

51. *Ibid.*

52. H, New Windsor, Nov. 10, 1777 (9 LHW 111–114).

53. Gates knew of mutiny as soon as H did, on 10th sending to Congress Scammell's letter describing it. Gates was ordering paymaster down to take care of arrears to last of August (Gates to Pres. of Congress above; cf. ALS, Laurens, Nov. 14, 1777, to Gates, Gates Papers, NYHS). Gates's aide, Hughes, wrote him of mutiny from Fishkill, Nov. 5, 1777 (ALS, *ibid.*). On arrival he had found Col. H on his way to Gates, and it was order H transmitted, for Poor's brigade to march next day to southern army, that provoked the disobedience.

54. Putnam had written to Gates, from Fishkill, Oct. 13, 1777, that enemy, strengthened by 5,000, intended to push up to Albany. Should Putnam come up and reinforce Gates? However, "Dislodging [the enemy] at N York, is certainly an Object worth our attention, & if they realey do approach I Ought to Immediately Proceed Down to N:York." He had at Fishkill 2,500 troops, chiefly militia. But Gates was emphatic to Putnam: "As to any Attack upon N York I utterly disapprove of it. . . ." (AL, draft,

Albany, Nov. 2, 1777; cf. same to same, copy, Sept. [Oct.?] 15, 1777.) Geo. Clinton tactfully disparaged idea of attack on N.Y. (ALS, Fishkill, Oct. 30, 1777, NYHS).

55. H, New Windsor, Nov. 12, 1777, to Washington (9 LHW 116).

56. *Ibid.;* ALS, Geo. Clinton, New Windsor, Nov. 13, 1777, to Gates, and ALS, H, Fishkill, Nov. 13, 1777, to Gates, both in Gates Papers; 9 LHW 115–18 dates these letters Nov. 12, probably from drafts.

57. 9 LHW 115. Dated from New Windsor, Nov. 12, 1777.

58. *Ibid.,* 114. Gen. Putnam did not know until much later he had been relieved of his post and ordered to join main army at White Marsh as per ms. extract from minutes of Congress, Nov. 5, 1777, signed by Chas. Thomson. Cf. ALS, Lovell, York Town, same date, to Gates: "I wish good old Putt may not think hard of the proposals of congress sent you at this Time." Cf. LS, Putnam, White Plains, Dec. 12, 1777, to Gates; ALS, Hugh Hughes, Fishkill, Dec. 13, 1777, to Gates. Maj. Jas. M. Hughes, while not knowing of Putnam's recall, lamented that "all Hopes of taking New York are entirely blasted, as General Washington has order'd almost all the Continental Troops in this Department to join him. . . ." (ALS, Fishkill, Nov. 19, 1777, to Gates, all in Gates Papers, NYHS).

59. 1 R 348–50; date incorrectly given in 9 LHW 120–22 as Dec.

60. 9 LHW 115, 119.

61. Jones to Clinton (2 *Public Papers of Clinton* 541–2).

62. I. Gibbs, Peekskill, Nov. 29, to Clinton (*ibid.* 556). Laurens had taken over H's duties at HQ, and was distressed (after H was actually on his feet again) to report he "lies dangerously ill on the road" (to H. Laurens, Dec. 3, 1777, Army Corr. of John Laurens, 92–3, LIHS). My colleague, Edward Hurtado, M.D., reviewing the known facts, suggests H perhaps had attack of acute rheumatic fever.

63. ALS, H. Hughes, Fishkill, Dec. 5, 1777, to Gates (Gates Papers).

64. H to Washington, New Windsor, Nov. 12, 1777 (9 LHW 115); cf. ALS, Jas. M. Hughes, Fishkill, Nov. 5, 1777, to Gates, NYHS. In a postscript to his wife at York, Gates cautioned: "The Bearer has got the Itch, don't let Bob *lay* with him" (AL, Albany, Nov. 17, 1777, *ibid.*).

65. From "Mr. Kennedy's House," in 9 LHW 119–20. In spite of H's remonstrance to Putnam Nov. 9 (above), Hugh Hughes wrote Nov. 27 Putnam still had Parsons and Warner near him, though latter's brigade would soon be replaced by Conn. militia (ALS, Fishkill, to Gates, *ibid.*).

66. HQ, Nov. 15, 1777 (1 JCHW 52). Letters of H to Washington must have gone by expresses; that of 12th was received by 15th, though Washing-

ton's reply of that date was first H had from HQ since he left more than two weeks before.

67. ALS, Wayne, Nov. 21, 1777, to Gates, *ibid.*

68. ALS, [Maj. Gen.] John Armstrong, Nov. 20, 1777, *ibid.* Walter Stewart wrote Gates from White Marsh, Nov. 12, 1777, that Washington's force had "lain very Inactive for a long time past, waiting . . . for a reinforcement from you. . . ." (ALS, Gates Papers, NYHS). However, two days later Mifflin notified: "The Northern Army is expected to join us to morrow or next Day. [torn] said One Brigade was at Prince town Yesterday on their Way to Red Bank" (ALS, Nov. 14, 1777, to Gates, *ibid.*).

69. ALS, *ibid.,* Nov. 21, 1777, to Gates, *ibid.*

70. LS, Washington, Dec. 2, 1777, to Gates, *ibid.*

71. ALS, draft, Albany, in Gates Papers; cf. Gates, AL, draft, Nov. 15, 1777, to Col. (Timothy) Bedel, directing him on secret attack on St. John's, in *ibid.* ALS, Thos. Chittenden, Bennington, reported to Gates that Ethan Allen with 50 Green Mountain Rangers was successful in "Harising the Enemies rear" in their retreat from Ticonderoga, took 47 prisoners. Maj. (Jason) Wait found nothing left by British at Mt. Independence except boats sunk, 40 cannon spiked, barracks and bridges burned (Gates Papers).

72. ALS, Laurens, Pres. of Congress, Nov. 28, 1777, notifying Gates of his appointment (Gates Papers, NYHS). Lovell wrote Gates with unconcealed disparagement of Washington: "We want you most near Germantown. Good God! What a Situation are we in! . . . Come to the Board of War if only for a Short Season." Lovell spoke derisively of the name "grand army" (ALS, York, Nov. 27, 1777, in *ibid.*).

Chapter 10 (Pages 143 to 157)
Winter of Our Discontent

1. Lafayette, 84 HLC 13722.

2. 11 GW 309.

3. LS to Elizabeth H, March 21, 1822 (84 HLC 13645 ff.).

4. The prospect of French companions in arms demanded fresh exertions by America (1 R 456–8, and in part in 11 GW 351).

5. Cf. S. W. Patterson, *Horatio Gates,* and, more objective, Bernhard Knollenberg, *Washington and the Revolution: A Reappraisal.*

6. To Geo. Clinton, Feb. 13, 1777 (9 LHW 126–7). Lafayette thought intrigue to displace Washington with Gates was genuine. Gates, flattered, was receptive, but "Conway . . . was a principal mischievous intriguer." However, chief command, in event of a shift, "would probably have devolved on Gen. Lee. . . ." (84 HLC 13720 ff.). Washington knew he had scheming enemies; cf. on Gates, to Lafayette, Dec. 31, 1777 (10 GW 236–7); on Conway, to Gates, Jan. 4, 1778 (*ibid.*, 265). He complained of "a malignant faction . . . for sometime forming to my prejudice" (to H. Laurens, Jan. 31, 1778, *ibid.*, 410), and more pointedly to Patrick Henry, that "General Gates was to be exalted, on the ruin of my reputation and influence" (March 28, 1778, 11 *ibid.*, 164). Cf. Beveridge, 1 *Marshall*, 121; Trevelyan, *Am. Rev.*, Pt. III, 307 ff.

7. Washington to Laurens, above.

8. To Pres. of Congress, Dec. 23, 1777 (10 GW 192); cf. numerous others, especially in Dec., Jan.

9. Cf., e.g., report of comm. on letter of Commissary Gen., Nov. 21, 1777 (9 JCC 960–3).

10. Gates was nominated president on "warm Sollicitude" of Mifflin "from a Conviction that his Military Skill would suggest Reformations in the different Departments of the Army essential to good Discipline, Order and Oeconomy, and that his Character and Popularity in the Army would facilitate the execution of such Reformations when adopted by Congress. . . ." (9 JCC 959 ff.). The backhanded slap at Washington is not to be missed.

11. Feb. 13, 1778 (9 LHW 122–7). He approved of N.Y. representatives, Duane, Morris, Duer, but wished Jay, R. R. Livingston, and Schuyler were there also.

12. [Nov. 9, 1777], 10 GW 29.

13. To Stirling, Feb. 4, 1778 (1 *Memoirs* 383–4); cf. Washington to Gates, Jan. 4, 1778 (10 GW 263).

14. Wilkinson to Stirling, Feb. 4, 1778 (1 *Memoirs* 383–4).

15. Washington to Gates, Jan. 4, 1778 (10 GW 263–5).

16. AL (signed JM), Nov. 28, 1777, Gates Papers, NYPL, printed in Wilkinson, *ibid.*, 374.

17. Dec. 3, 1777, in Wilkinson, *ibid.*, 375–6. Gates's alarm prevented him from catching Mifflin's meaning, that Wilkinson had blabbed at Reading.

18. Wilkinson, *ibid.*, 372–3. See Troup's illuminating, terse account, years after, of this contretemps. Gates's "disposition was open, and communicative," so his favorite, Wilkinson, "became acquainted with the correspondence, passing between General Conway, and General Gates, to the prejudice

of General Washington's military character." Wilkinson conceived that he could plausibly put blame for disclosure on Troup, who tipped off H. What more likely, as these two had slept in the same bed at college, and were constantly in each other's company during H's recent visit to Albany? Gates seized this insinuation against H who, "tho then very young, had, by his extraordinary talents . . . acquired a standing at Head Quarters that kindled the jealousy of some officers who were inclined to think unfavorably of General Washington" (DS, Oct. 26, 1827, 84 HLC 13649–51).

19. Dec. 8, 1777 (1 *Memoirs* 395).

20. Jan. 4, 1778 (10 GW 263–5).

21. Jan. 23, 1778, Wilkinson, *ibid.*, 398–401. This was sharp retraction of previous appreciation. When sending his adjutant, Oct. 18, 1777, to announce his victory, Gates's puff was, ". . . from the beginning of this Contest, I have not met with a more promising Military Genious than Col. Wilkinson, . . . whose Services have been of the last importance to this Army" (to Hancock, copy, Gates Papers, NYHS).

22. Feb. 9, 1778 (10 GW 437–41).

23. *Ibid.*, 508–9.

24. 1 *Memoirs* 387–9.

25. See letters between them, March 18, 1778, in *ibid.*, 391–2, and Washington to Stirling, March 21, 1778 (11 GW 125; cf. Duer's *Stirling*, 190 n.). On Wilkinson's embarrassed interview with Washington, see 1 *Memoirs* 394–5. Wilkinson resigned ill-deserved commission as brig. gen., and appointment as sec. of Bd. of War (*ibid.*, 390–1).

26. Appropriately, medallions of last two appear on Steuben statue in Lafayette Sq., Washington; he adopted them as his sons.

27. 9 JCC 1026.

28. 10 *ibid.*, 399.

29. See his claim to contrary to Charles Carroll of Carrollton, Nov. 14, 1777, 52 Sparks Transcripts 131 ff., Houghton Lib., and others here, to Congress, as examples of what H called "impudent importunity and vain boasting of foreign pretenders" (to Geo. Clinton, Feb. 13, 1778, 9 LHW 123). H described Conway as "one of the vermin bred in the entrails of this chimera dire, and there does not exist a more villainous calumniator and incendiary" (*ibid.*, 127).

30. Washington countenanced Conway in latter's official character only (Washington to Pres. of Congress, Jan. 2, 1778, 10 GW 249–50; cf. 252–3, n.).

31. To Duer, June 18, 1778 (9 LHW 132).

32. Congress in accepting his services, Jan. 14, 1778, and ordering him to report to Gen. Washington (10 JCC 50).

33. He was sure recognition would follow from substantial services rendered (Jan. 27, 1790, Kapp's *Steuben,* 73).

34. The 33 original sheets of Hamilton (in 1 HLC 99 ff.) comprise two versions, one 11, the other 22 pp., but it is difficult to say which was drawn first, as both have corrections and parts in skeletal form; half of one sheet is in Washington's hand. Neither contains considerable material in final draft (10 GW 362–403), which was not available when 2 JCHW 139–52 printed from H's incomplete worksheets.

35. Cf. H to Duer, June 18, 1778 (9 LHW 134–6).

36. 10 GW 362–82.

37. Early instance of H's insistence on large governmental foreign borrowing to carry on the war.

38. *Ibid.,* 382–96. H doubtless had pleasure in recording Washington's approval of conduct of Boudinot as Commissary of Prisoners.

39. *Ibid.,* 403.

40. Kapp's *Steuben,* 113–118.

41. G.O., March 17, 1778 (11 GW 98); corps was ordered to parade two days later (*ibid.,* 107).

42. March 28, 1778 (11 GW 163). Cf. to Barber, March 24, 1778 (*ibid.,* 136–7); G.O., May 4, 1778 (11 GW 346–7). For H's concern for morale in inspector gen's. dept. see to Steuben, Dec. 4, and Barber to Steuben, May 9, 1780 (Steuben Papers, NYHS).

43. 11 GW 328–31. Cf. scheme for office of inspector gen., draft by H, May 5, 1778, 2 JCHW 153–5, there said to have been submitted by Washington to Cong., but not in GW. Probably informed Washington's letter to Cong. (above) and G.O. of June 15, 1778 (below). Nothing came of proposal that H's old drillmaster of college days, Col. Fleming, be added to Steuben's staff.

44. H to Wm. Duer, June 18, 1778 (9 LHW 133).

45. June 15, 1778 (12 GW 66–8). Cf. Steuben Papers, xiii, NYHS; Kapp, 139–40, and to Washington, May 27, 1778, Steuben Papers, Kapp, 144.

46. Washington to Steuben, and to Pres. of Congress, June 18, 1778 (GW *ibid.,* 78–9, 81–2).

47. June 18, 1778 (9 LHW 132–6).

48. Part I. Phila., Styner and Cist, 1779, 154 pp., 8 plates.

49. G.O., May 4, 1778. Though Steuben, with the aid of Fleury and Walker, completed the rules, in Philadelphia in the winter of 1778–9, and Congress approved them March 29, 1779, delays in printing necessitated ms. copies for some months later; certificate of Pres. John Jay in *Regulations,* above; Steuben to Washington, March 17, 1779 (Steuben Papers, NYHS and Kapp, 215–6; Pickering to Steuben, June 19, 1779; *ibid.,* I, and Kapp, 217–8). Similarities suggest H contributed to insistence on responsibility of commanders for welfare, training of troops, record keeping (e.g., *Regulations,* 138, and Hamilton to Duer, June 18, 1778, 9 LHW 134–5).

50. Same was manifest throughout remainder of war, including storming of Yorktown redoubt, under H's leadership (Rudolf Cronau, *Army of Am. Rev. and Its Organizer,* 120).

51. Cf. H to Steuben, Dec. 19, 1778 (9 LHW 156).

52. July 26, 1778 (9 LHW 147–9). For further instance of H's solicitude to keep Steuben active but off others' toes, see H to him, 9 LHW 199–200, and ALS same to same, June 30, 1780 (Steuben Papers).

53. Doubtless more of these ghostings have vanished than have survived in his mss. Besides those for important persons, there are reports of committees of which he was not chairman, but draftsman.

54. Photostat in H Papers, NYPL, not dated, presented to Congress Feb. 11, 1785 (28 JCC 60 n.).

55. Nov. 23, 1785 (9 LHW 413).

56. Oct. 30, 1787 (9 LHW 425–7); with Steuben's printed pamphlet of claims, he enclosed first number of *Federalist.*

Chapter 11 (Pages 158 to 181)
Brand from the Burning

1. ". . . the American arms," said H week after battle, "might have gained much more signal . . . success . . . had not the finest opportunity America ever possessed been fooled away by . . . Gen. Lee. . . ." (ALS, to Boudinot, July 5, 1778, PHS; for defective printed versions of this spirited account of the day see below.)

2. Instructions to Mease, June 18, 1778 (12 GW, 89); cf. Washington to Arnold, June 19, 1778 (*ibid.,* 94–5).

3. *Ibid.,* 75–8.

4. Washington to Col. Daniel Morgan, June 18, 1778 (*ibid.,* 88).

5. Emmet, 9295, NYPL. Cf. Stryker-Myers, *Monmouth,* 68, putting Washington's marquee near Fell's house, HQ at Dr. Sherman's (in G.O. of that day "Shennons," in HQ Expense Acct., "Shannons," 12 GW 93 and n.). H was occupied part of that evening in writing for the gen. to Arnold (*ibid.,* 94–5).

6. McHenry, *ibid.* Diary, entries not dated, was probably posted tardily, which accounts for omitting camp of that rainy afternoon, night at Buckingham, "within Ten Miles of Coryel's ferry [New Hope-Lambertville] (Washington to Congress, *ibid.,* 97); the gen. ordered a gill of spirits to every man that afternoon (*ibid.,* 98), as again on 21st (*ibid.,* 104).

7. *Op. cit.*

8. 12 GW 104

9. See Washington to Gov. Livingston, *ibid.,* 100, and to Gen. Dickinson, 103 (Clinton, *American Rebellion,* 90).

10. Cf. Freeman, 5 *Washington* 13–14.

11. Now Columbus, N.J.; Philemon Dickinson to Washington, June 23, 1778 (78 Papers of Washington 10, LC).

12. William B. Reed, *Life . . . of Joseph Reed,* I, 368.

13. 1 HLC 119, draft in H's hand, dated Hopewell, etc., June 23, 1778, quarter past one o'clock, endorsed with Washington's autograph signature. No address given, but 1 JCHW 193 and I R 465–6 say to Cadwalader; not in Fitzpatrick's GW. Cf. Washington to Council of War, June 24, 1778 (12 GW 116), and to Pres. of Congress, July 1, 1778 (*ibid.,* 140).

14. R. H. Harrison drafted propositions for council's deliberation (*ibid.,* 115–17).

15. ALS H to Boudinot, July 5, 1778, PHS, and 2 *Penn. Mag.* 140; 9 LHW 140–42 took text from 1 R 468, 478–9, with unfortunate omissions, typographical error, but with correct date. Council-of-war decision is in 78 Papers of Washington, 33, LC.

16. Lafayette, *Memoirs,* ed. 1837, I, 50; LOLTW 46–7.

17. Lee's prestige had not suffered appreciably by his laggard response to Washington's calls in retreat across N.J. in 1776, nor by his ignominious capture at Basking Ridge. Boudinot, Comm'ry. of Prisoners, suspected Lee's duplicity with Gen. Howe, but his misgivings had no bearing at this juncture. See incident of Dr. David Griffith's warning to Washington concerning Lee night before battle, given (without citation) in Custis, *Recollections . . . of Washington,* 290–91.

18. LOLTW 46–7; Wayne in R. Hughes, *Washington,* 348; Greene in 78 Papers of Washington 35, LC.

19. 1 R 467 and 1 H 194; no authority is offered, and scene in Washington's "tent" is at variance with fact his HQ were in a house, either John Hunt's (Freeman, 5 *Washington* 15 n.) or Joseph Stout's (Stryker-Myers, *Monmouth,* 75–6, n.). Argument sounds like Greene's letter to Washington, above: "If we suffer the enemy to pass . . . without attacking, . . . we shall ever regret it. . . . People expect something from us and our strength demands it."

20. "Eulogium on Major-General Greene," delivered before Society of Cincinnati, July 4, 1789 in 8 LHW 68.

21. H penned order (12 GW 114); cf. H to Boudinot, *op. cit.;* several regiments of Continentals in Scott's command (cf. Stryker-Myers, *Monmouth,* 78) were to behave well in the battle. Maxwell was to aid Scott against left flank (GW, *ibid.,* 113–4).

22. To Dickinson, GW, *ibid.,* 113.

23. To Morgan, *ibid.,* 115.

24. *Ibid.,* 140.

25. *Ibid.,* 117; this order gave subcommand to Poor, but Washington in reporting to Congress (*ibid.,* 140) corrected it to Wayne, also named by H in his account (2 Lee Papers 467).

26. 12 GW 140. "The project was," said H, "that this advanced corps should take the first opportunity to attack the enemy's rear on the march, to be supported . . . by the whole army" (Lee Papers, *ibid.*).

27. 1 R 468. On Lee's claim to command, which was in contrast to his earlier opposition to any attack, see his letter, Kingston, 25 June, 1778, to Washington (2 Lee Papers 417–18). See Washington, Cranbury, June 26, 1778, to Lafayette (12 GW 119), same to Lee (*ibid.,* 120), and Lafayette [Hightstown], June 26, to Washington completely accepting the compromise (Lee Papers, *ibid.,* 418–19); also Lafayette, 84 HLC 13722.

28. Copy, H to Lafayette, from Dr. Stiles's House, Cranbury Town, 9 o'clock [P.M. June 25, 1778] (1 HLC 120; printed in 9 LHW 137).

29. Present open countryside, with paved highways that span streams and erstwhile bogs, allows little notion of troubles of transport and communication in same area at that time, when bodies of hundreds or thousands of troops might be lost to each other. Landmarks remain, especially unusual number of old houses.

30. To Lafayette, June 25, 1778, above.

31. H [to Washington] from Robin's Tavern, twelve o'clock, June 26 [1778], (copy in 1 HLC 121, printed in 9 LHW 138–9).

32. 2 *Lee Papers* 418–9.

33. 12 GW 121–2.

34. Copy, H to Washington, 1 HLC 122, wrongly dated June 28, as in 9 LHW 139–40; 12 GW 123 n. misdates it 27th. H's scouting of enemy withdrawal across N.J. overcame "perplexed conjectures" which Major André believed British had produced "by the secrecy . . . respecting our route and the false movements made to deceive" Americans (2 *Journal*, 1777–8, p. 16). Indeed, it is difficult to know how a column eight or ten miles long could have proved elusive. On placement of élite troops cf. Clinton, *American Rebellion*, 91.

35. 12 GW 122–3 repeated an order of two hours before which has not survived.

36. Wm. Alexander Smith Coll., NYPL; 12 GW 124 n. says it is in Metropolitan Museum, N.Y.C.

37. Half past 10 P.M. [26], June 1778 (2 *Lee Papers* 425–6).

38. Changes have been made, a few in terrain itself; cf. Freeman's description, 5 *Washington*, reverse of p. 29.

39. H to Boudinot, July 5, 1778, *op. cit.*

40. Letters of Wayne and Scott to Washington June 30, 1778 (2 *Lee Papers* 438–40).

41. *Proceedings of a General Court Martial . . . for Trial of Major-General Lee*, 1778, p. 66, H's testimony; 1 R 473 says H had gone forward with Lafayette "before break of day," but this does not seem to be supported by evidence.

42. Tilghman in *Court Martial*, 91–2.

43. H to Boudinot, July 5, 1778 (2 *Lee Papers* 467 ff.); Hamilton's contrast was with Gates at Saratoga. H thought Boudinot drew on his description of battle for letter in *Penn. Packet* (July 26, 1778, extracted in N.J. Arch., 2d ser., II, 303–6), and deplored Boudinot's remark, "even the Secretaries caught the general contagion and by putting themselves in places of danger, shared some of the honors of the day." Unintentionally, this sounded derogatory; Harrison and Tilghman were hurt (autographed "A H" evidently to Boudinot, endorsed July 26, 1778, PHS). Incident showed H's jealousy for rights of staff officers on battlefield. Actually, Boudinot's backhanded compliment to secretaries was almost verbatim from McHenry's account (ALS, HQ, near New Brunswick, July 2, 1778, to Boudinot, Emmet 9394, NYPL).

44. 84 HLC 13722.

45. *Court Martial*, 69, 71–2, H's testimony, and Olney's, 146.

46. New Brunswick, July 2, 1778 (Emmet, 9394, NYPL). Spirited description of Americans' retreat, resistance, counterattack is in Wayne, ALS, Spottswood [N.J.], July 1, 1778, to wife (4 Wayne Papers 57, PHS). See also McHenry's Journal, Emmet 9295, stressing Lee's retreat and Washington's rally; Samuel Adams, a Mass. army surgeon, ms. "Private Miscellaneous Diary Ann: Dom: 1778 (NYPL); Boudinot, to wife (ALS, June 30, 1778, uncalendared Emmet, NYPL). Strangely, John Taylor, writing as ADC "In behalf" of Washington, said flatly Lee "had a severe engagement with the Enemy . . . But maintained his ground with a much greater loss on the side of the Enemy. . . ." He pictured Washington as changing firm resistance to spirited attack (ALS, monday morning [June 29, 1778], to Col. Jno. Neilson, Rutgers Univ.).

47. Withdrawing northward, army celebrated anniversary of independence at New Brunswick. HQ was at Ross Hall, handsome house in Dutch style, yet standing despite neglect. On route to Paramus, Washington and his family stopped for picnic lunch at "the falls of Passaic"; this was H's first view of site where he and friends of Society for Useful Manufactures founded city of Paterson (McHenry, Jnl.).

48. Correspondence conveniently found in Stryker-Myers, *op. cit.*, Appendix IV, 282–4.

49. Court sat also at North Castle, gave its judgment and sentence at Peekskill Aug. 12. Shortly after his second testimony H was dispatched (July 18) to Black Point, N.J., to concert measures with Count d'Estaing, and was delayed by several causes from returning to HQ before July 26 (to Washington, July 20, 23, 1778, 9 LHW 145–7). Because of this distraction, or because trial was in progress, H made no allusion to Lee's conduct in any surviving letter of these weeks save to Boudinot, July 5, ending: "What think you now of General Lee? Whatever a court martial may decide, I shall continue to believe and say,—his conduct was monstrous and unpardonable" (PHS).

50. *Court Martial* 22.

51. *Ibid.,* 12–13.

52. *Ibid.,* 13; testimony of Lafayette, Forman, Laurens, *et al., ibid.,* 19 ff., confirmed H's evidence that Washington designed an attack which Lee did not make.

53. *Ibid.,* 66, 69–70, 72; cf. 87, Boudinot, *Jnl. of Rev.,* 81, and Lee, *ibid.,* 229–30. H himself, day following his evidence, reinforced what he had said (ALS, draft, 1 HLC 123; no date [July 14 surely] or address [to Stirling as pres. of court-martial?] printed in 9 LHW 142–4).

54. *Court Martial,* 229–30; cf. Mercer's testimony, *ibid.,* 131. Custis, whose memory played him tricks, and who did not consult court-martial

record, said H made his sententious declaration not to Lee but to Washington (*Recollections*, 219).

55. Evidence is reviewed in Stryker-Myers, *Monmouth*, 188–92; cf. 11 DAB 574–5, under Mary McCauley.

56. *Court Martial*, 68. Lee told court that when he expected "congratulation and applause," Washington accosted him "with the most disgraceful reproach" (*ibid.*, 219, 233; cf. 2 *Lee Papers* 435). Lafayette and Scott years later are said to have described abusive terms used by Washington to Lee (Stryker-Myers, *op. cit.*, 180–81), but see Lafayette, 84 HLC 13722. For Hamilton's denial, 1 R 476 n., no citation. Custis, though not present, had means of knowing, called it "a warm conversation" (*op. cit.*, 219). Evidence as to whether Lee, after meeting Washington, busied himself with reversing retreat is conflicting.

57. *Court Martial*, 238.

58. See, e.g., Henry Lee, *War in Southern Department*, 38. Congress upheld sentence (Dec. 5, 1778, 4 JCC 1195), later dismissed Lee from army permanently (Jan. 10, 1780, 16 *ibid.*, 33). Lee's plea was he sought to draw enemy through ravines toward vantage ground on heights where Washington launched attack (cf. *Court Martial*, 234; *Pa. Packet*, Dec. 3, 1778). Years later H said Lee's retreating troops obeyed "the commands of a leader who meditated their disgrace" (8 LHW 68; cf. H Laurens, Phila., July 6, 1778, to J. Laurens, 2 *Lee Papers* 472–3). Sir Henry Clinton, unconscious of any bias, approved Lee's retreat (*American Rebellion* 96). Lee told Lafayette "that very morning" American troops could not "resist the first onset of British Genadiers," and this "extravagant idea . . . did . . . cramp his meneuvers. . . ." (84 HLC 13722 ff.). On Lee's "partial lunacy," cf. Boudinot, *Jnl. of Rev.*, 81.

59. 2 *Lee Papers* 430.

60. 3 *ibid.*, 273.

61. See Lee to Laurens, accepting challenge (Dec. 22, 1778, *ibid.*, 283). For joint statement of H and Edwards, Dec. 24, 1778 (2 HLC 137–8, printed in 9 LHW 156–9). Maj. John S. Eustace, formerly aide to Lee, more than a year after Monmouth publicly impugned H's "veracity on the Tryall" and sought a duel with him (3 *Lee Papers* 363, 381–2, 393–4). Apparently nothing came of this. That Col. Eleazer Oswald, who testified for Lee at court-martial, decade later challenged H, but that matter was composed, is given, without citation, in Alden, *Lee*, 301). For H's moral support to his friend Steuben in the baron's challenge to Lee, see H's letter of Dec. 19, 1778 (9 LHW 155–6; cf. Steuben to Lee, 3 *Lee Papers* 253). For Wayne's resentment of Lee's disparagement of *his* military conduct, which barely missed coming to a duel, *ibid.*, 291–2.

62. 13 GW 454 ff., 14 *ibid.*, 1–68 n., show many letters in H's hand.

63. Jan. 8, 1779 (13 GW 485–9), with different order of paragraphs and verbal variations from H's draft; cf. Washington to Jay, April 14, 1779 (14 *ibid.*, 381); H wrote this long letter at Washington's direction. Cf., on ability of badly depreciated currency "to draw out the resources of the country a good while longer" in absence of major fighting, H to unknown, Nov. 8, 1778 (9 LHW 155).

64. Washington to Conference Committee Jan. 13, 1779 (14 GW 10–11, H's draft).

65. Cf. JCC. Cf. AL, Duane, March 31, 1779, to N.Y. legislature (Duane Papers, NYHS), Boudinot to Hamilton, July 8, 1778 (PHS); Washington to Schuyler, July 22, 1778 (12 GW 200–1).

66. March 6, 1779 (14 GW 198–201). Washington would have chosen Schuyler except latter was uncertain of continuing in army (to Jay, April 14, 1779, *ibid.*, 384).

67. Informing John Laurens of this refusal, H said Gates "has lately given a fresh proof of his impudence, his folly, and his rascality" (ALS, no place nor date, 2 HLC 209, printed in part in 1 JCHW 109–11, completely in 9 LHW 184–8 but misdated Dec. 1779; context shows it should be about April). This had been an ungenerous comment of Gates on Washington and Schuyler. H, for Washington, told Jay that Gates's "conduct . . . is continually giving me fresh proofs of malevolence and opposition" (April 14, 1779, 14 GW 385).

68. March 6, 1779 (14 GW 201–2). Later, however, H was obliged to write long letters for Washington to Congress (Aug. 15, 21, 1779, 16 GW 98–108, 140–2) defending commander in chief against complaints of Sullivan that HQ preparations for expedition had been mismanaged. For Washington's efforts to assist Sullivan on march, see letters drafted by H to Sullivan July 5, 1779 (15 GW 370–2); to Reed and Pa. Council (*ibid.*, 376–8).

69. H had seen D'Estaing off from N.Y.; see H to Washington, July 20, 23, 1778 (1 HLC 124–5, second printed in 9 LHW 146–7).

70. Aug. 28, 1778 (12 GW 367).

71. Cf. Greene to Washington on Sullivan's "absolute censure" of D'Estaing, 12 GW 368 n.

72. Sept. 1, 1778 (12 GW 385; cf. Sept. 2, 1778, to D'Estaing, *ibid.*, 389).

73. Lafayette to H, Sept. 1, 1778 (1 JCHW 68–9).

74. Endorsed Sept. 8, 1778 (PHS, printed in part in 9 LHW 149–52). Far from censuring Sullivan, Congress thanked him and his army, declared D'Estaing and his officers "fully entitled to the regards of the friends of America" (4 JCC, 1800 ed., 378, 434).

75. 1 R 498.

76. See Washington to Schuyler, Jan. 18, 1779, and after (14 GW 18 ff., especially one of Feb. 11, 1779, *ibid.,* 94–8). Cf. copy, Charles Stewart, Jan. 3, 1779, to Sullivan, giving stages for march, Easton to Chenise [*sic*] Castle, and cumulative table of distances, 280 miles; includes opportunities for grass, water, features of terrain that made for safety or danger (1 Edward Hand Papers 92–3, PHS; also Washington to Pres. Reed, Feb. 27, 1779, 14 GW 159–60).

77. Feb. 24, 1779 (*ibid.,* 142–3); March 2, 1779 (*ibid.,* 176–8).

78. Jan. 31, Feb. 15, 1779 (*ibid.,* 58–62, 114–8).

79. May 31, 1779 (15 GW 189–93). Cf. this date in orderly book of Francis Barber, adj. gen. for Western army (NJHS, printed in *Proceed.,* 1948), also letters of Barber to wife, NJHS and PHS, Gratz and Canarroe colls., and campaign notes of Capt. John Weidman (typescript), PHS.

80. May 8, 1779 (15 GW 23–6). Cf. to John Jay two days later H's draft with emphasis by Washington (15 GW 38–9), deploring vulnerable state of both morals and money. Duane to wife: "It would be for every Man's Interest to give one half of [the paper money] to the Flames. . . ." (ALS May 26, June 12, 1779, Duane Papers, NYHS); cf. Geo. Clinton to Mason, Feb. 27, 1779 (Clinton Papers, NYHS). Thos. Anburey, at Charlottesville, Va. (May 1779), found 500 paper dollars exchanging for one guinea (2 *Travels* . . . 230–1).

81. May 11, 1779 (15 GW 42–3); Lamb's letter (endorsed Feb. [?] 3, 1779) 2 HLC 153.

82. 15 GW 13–15.

83. To Washington, May 8, 1779, with Washington's letter to Maxwell, May 10 (Papers of Continental Congress, U.S. Arch.).

84. To Maxwell, May 10, 1779 (15 GW 32–3); officers withdrew memorial, legislature voted sum demanded, regiments marched.

85. He sent this to Jas. Duane (9 LHW 172), eager for information of expedition, e.g., to H, Sept. 16, 23, 1779 (1 JCHW 89–91).

86. Oct. 26, 1776 (5 *S.C. Hist. Mag.* 205–6).

87. Same to same, HQ, Jan. 14, 1778 (LIHS, typescript).

88. H. to J. Laurens, Aug. 14, 1776 (10 *S.C. Hist. Mag.* 49–50); Wallace's *Laurens,* 446.

89. Same to same, Feb. 18, 1778 (H. Laurens Papers, LIHS, typescript).

90. To H. Laurens, Feb. 15, 1778 (Army Correspondence of J. Laurens . . . 1777–8, LIHS, typescript).

91. See Lowndes, Feb. 3, 1779, to H Laurens (Laurens Correspondence of Rev., LIHS, typescript); efforts at reform of militia were slow "when the Enemy are at our door."

92. This preliminary was successful, for Congress recommended S.C., Ga. raise 3,000 Negro troops under white officers; Continent would recompense masters for slaves thus serving and freed at war's end (13 JCC 387–8).

93. Cf. ALS, J. M. Mitchell, DQMG, Phila., Nov. 10, 1779, tersely informing H of battle of Savannah (2 HLC 203).

94. March 14, 1779 (9 LHW 159–62). Washington's tentative reaction to proposal was unfavorable (14 GW 267, and J. Laurens to Washington, Feb. 2, 1778, Army Corr., LIHS). Laurens shared his son's enthusiasm, on military grounds (March 16, 1779, 14 GW 267 n.).

95. To H from Charles Town [S.C.], July 14, 1779 (2 HLC 142), with incomplete date in 1 JCHW 114–5; a couple of years later, having "resumed the black project," he still found his arguments opposed by "avarice, prejudice, and pusillanimity" (1 JCHW [1781] 214–5; cf. Wallace, *H. Laurens,* 450).

96. 1 LHW 199–209, the first dated Oct. 19, 1778; I R 515–6 implies they were written month or so later. Chase is identified in corr. of H with McHenry (see note, below), as also in letter of W. C. Ford in *N.Y. Ev. Post,* Nov. 1, 1886, cited in LHW, *ibid.,* 201 n. and in E. S. Corwin, 4 DAB 34 ff., but search in *Post* failed to reveal item. JCC does not mention malfeasance of Chase, but 12 *ibid.,* 974 ff. (Oct. 2, 1778, and later) has resolution condemning "the wicked arts of speculators. . . ."

97. 1 LHW 206. Washington to Reed, Dec. 12, 1778 (13 GW 383). ALsS McHenry to Giles, Jan. 19, 21, 1782 (3 HLC 404–5); H to McHenry, Feb. 26, 1782 (*ibid.,* 406).

98. *Ibid.,* 206–7.

99. *Ibid.,* 203, 204. In the two following years Md. legislature did not return Chase to Congress.

100. Cf. H to [John] Auldjo, N.Y., July 26, 1787 (9 LHW 421); acting as friend to Auldjo, challenged by Maj. Peirce, H helped compose difference. Auldjo was client of H in "dispute with Mr. Rhinelander," (Samuel?) Jones being latter's counsel. (ALS, Auldjo to H, 1 HLC, 2d ser., 70). Neither Auldjo nor Rhinelander appears in Franks' *N.Y. Directory,* 1786.

101. From Newark, N.J., July 23, 1778, one o'clock, after concerting arrangements with D'Estaing for projected attack on R.I., begged Washington's indulgence; he would not "make all the dispatch back, which a case of emergency would require" out of "attention to my frail constitution" (1 HLC 124, printed in 9 LHW 146–7).

102. J. C. H. took no notice of the episode in *Life, Hist. of Republic,* or his ed. of *Works.*

103. H, West Point, Aug. 6, 1779, to Brooks (9 LHW 168), Sept. 11, 1779, to J. Laurens (*ibid.*, 174–5).

104. H to Henley, July 12, 1779 (2 HLC 141, printed in 9 LHW 167).

105. To Brooks, Laurens, above; Dana, July 25, 1779, to H; Dana said H had disabused his mind of Dr. Gordon's charge (2 HLC 143).

106. AL (draft) to Gordon, Aug. 10, 1779, "No. 8" (2 HLC 147, printed in 9 LHW 169). H asked Brooks to furnish "the names of all the gentlemen that composed the company before which I had the honor of being exhibited. . . ." (Sept. 10, 1779, "No. 12," 2 HLC 157, printed in 9 LHW 172–3).

107. To Laurens, *ibid.*

108. H to Gordon, Dec. 10 [1779], No. 11 in calumny series (2 HLC 204, printed in 9 LHW 188–9).

109. See Washington to H, May 2; to Gordon, May 3, 1780 (18 GW 320, 322); and ALS, H to Washington, Morristown, May 2, 1780 (2 HLC 232, printed with a verbal error in 9 LHW 189–91).

Chapter 12 (Pages 182 to 208)
Affairs of State and Morristown Romance

1. Nov. 24, 1778 (McDougall Papers, NYHS, printed in 13 GW 320–2).

2. June 9, 1779 (15 GW 242–3). For efforts to seal off Stony Point against British operations inland, cf. Washington to Gen. St. Clair at Galloways, in H's hand, June 6, 1779 (Wm. Irvine Papers, II, 30, PHS, printed in 15 GW 237–8).

3. July 1, 1779 (*ibid.*, 354–5).

4. *Ibid.*, 355–6.

5. July 9, 1779 (*ibid.*, 386).

6. July 4, 1779 (Wayne Papers, VII, 10, PHS, printed in 15 GW 367).

7. Cf. Washington to Wayne, McDougall, July 14, 1779 (15 GW 423–4).

8. ALS, n.d., but from context July 15, 1779, HLC unbnd. Box 1; cf. Washington to Maj. Henry Lee (H's draft), July 12, 1779 (15 GW 411–12).

9. ALS July 17, 1779 (Allan McLane Papers, I, No. 99, NYHS).

10. July 21, 25, 1779 (15 GW, 452, 486–7). Apparently H preferred to H. Laurens Fleury's request to be given captured flag, but Congress refused (H. Laurens to Hamilton, July 29, 1779, 1 JCHW 80–1).

11. Washington to Howe, McDougall, July 16, 1779 (15 GW 428–9), and to Congress, July 21, 1779 (*ibid.*, 447–53), in which H reviewed, at Washington's direction, whole undertaking, in motives and results.

12. May 8, 1780 (18 GW 341).

13. May 11, 1780 (*ibid.*, 347–8).

14. May 13, 1780, to Pres. of Congress (*ibid.*, 351–2).

15. May 14, 1780 (*ibid.*, 356–8). Former letter in Washington's hand, draft of latter in H's. That to Duane probably written first, and Washington followed it in addressing Jones.

16. In other letter he wished, besides, for Duane, R. R. Livingston, John Mathews.

17. May 14, 1780 (9 LHW 192–4). Congress elected comm., Schuyler, Mathews, Nathaniel Peabody (16 JCC 362, April 13, 1780). He sought same end of prompt mobilization by trying to compose differences of Q.M. Gen. Greene with Bd. of Treas. (See 2 Greene's *Greene* 287; 2 R 39–42, a reference incorrect in 9 LHW 195 n.)

18. 18 GW 341, letters of May 15, 16, 18, 1780 (*ibid.*, 360ff.).

19. May 16, 1780 (*ibid.*, 369–73).

20. May 18, 1780 (*ibid.*, 383–4).

21. May 26, 1780, *ibid.*, 425–6; cf., more fully, to Pres. of Congress, May 27, 1780, *ibid.*, 428–31.

22. To Comm. of Cooperation, May 25, 1780 (18 GW 416–7).

23. May 28, 1780 (*ibid.*, 434–40). Douglas Freeman, after years of work on his *Washington,* called this "one of the greatest, if not the very greatest, letter I yet have found in the entire Revolutionary period. The Hamilton of 1790 is anticipated in this" (letter of Jan. 10, 1951). Washington made only three brief amendments to Hamilton's words, to emphasize meaning. Incidentally, Washington's former disappointment in Reed, for disloyal doubts at Valley Forge, seemed now to matter not at all.

24. This view of Britain throws H's postwar program for America into bold relief. Would summon potential wealth of country to rescue public credit. So far from trampling Constitution, would enormously strengthen it. Wanted sufficient central governmental authority to produce solvency and safeguard popular sovereignty.

25. Cf. H, July 13, 1780, for Washington to Comm. of Congress (19 GW 166).

26. Legislature conferred all but dictatorial power on Pres. Reed and directed immediate supplies to army. For applause by Madison, with caveat on "the risk of the precedent," see to Jefferson, June 2, 1780 (18 GW 439 n.).

27. Washington to Bowdoin, Aug. 28, 1780 (H's drafts, 19 GW 453–5).

28. For a convenient summary of conventions, 2 R 79 ff.

29. Aug. 28, 1780 (19 GW 453).

30. Schuyler's active interest in these efforts (cf. R 110–11 and Schuyler to H, 1 JCHW 169, 182–3) helped stir H's endeavors. Cf. Lossing, 2 *Schuyler* 431 ff., Curtis, 1 *Hist. of Const.* 415.

31. 3 HLC 311–21; 3 LHW 319–41; 1 JCHW 116–32.

32. For newspaper demands spring and summer 1779, for stop to printing-press money, cf. Burnett, *Continental Congress,* 410–11.

33. Cf. *ibid.,* 409.

34. 1 R 570 places this draft letter in late 1779 or early 1780, as also 1 JCHW 116. 3 LHW 319 dates it 1780 but says mistakenly Morris had just become Financier. Sumner, *Hamilton,* 107–8 makes it probably Nov. 1779.

35. Cf. Stan. V. Henkels, *Confidential Correspondence of Robert Morris* (Cat. No. 1183, Phila., 1917[?], 208 pp.).

36. Refs. here to 3 LHW, above being p. 341.

37. Sumner, 108, depreciated H's acquaintance with standard economic writings; cf., however, C. F. Dunbar, "Some Precedents Followed by . . . Hamilton," in *Economic Essays,* ed. O. M. W. Sprague.

38. 3 LHW 320–24. Cited external loans of European countries.

39. *Ibid.,* 324–32.

40. *Ibid.,* 332–3.

41. *Ibid.,* 333–36. Sumner, frequently lofty, pronounced "the scheme . . . crude in the extreme. It is not a plan for a bank, but for a trading company, in which . . . government and . . . rich men were to be jointly interested" (Sumner, *op. cit.,* 110–11). More generous concerning H's project "of a real bank" given to Morris April 1781, but complained (his own misapprehension) H confused wealth (revenue) and money (medium of exchange) (*ibid.,* 113).

42. 2 HLC 251–70; 1 JCHW 150–68; 1 LHW 213–39. Complying with Duane's request may have emboldened H to volunteer recommendations to Morris. For environs of Liberty Pole at this time, see ALS, Capts. Thos.

Blauch and John Huyler, May 27, 1780, to Gov. Wm. Livingston (1 bound Livingston corr., Ledyard-Griswold deposit, NYPL).

43. 1 R 555 says when visiting Congress with Washington, winter of 1779–80, that H formed his "particular acquaintance with Duane," but that they were friends, correspondents before this; cf. H to him, Aug. 28, Sept. 7, 1779 (9 LHW 169–70, 171–2, 192–4).

44. In a covering letter (Sept. 6, 1780, 9 LHW 204–5) he alluded to Gates's defeat at Camden as "a . . . comment on the necessity of changing our system," particularly its reliance on state militia, which he elsewhere called "the mimicry of soldiership" (to Greene, 2 R 33, more fully for Washington to Pres. of Congress, 20 GW 14–15). Same day, his mind still on reforms he was urging on Duane, he told fiancée he was not worse dashed by Camden disaster "because I think our safety depends on a total change of system, and this . . . will only be produced by misfortune" (to E. Schuyler, above).

45. 1 LHW 213–15.

46. May be said to announce historic division between adherents of liberal ("loose") and strict construction of Constitution, advocates of central authority and partisans of local powers, nationalism and states' rights.

47. *Ibid.,* 215–16.

48. 1 LHW 217–220. Cf. N. Greene: "There is a parcel of little politicians at the head of the treasury board. Their plans have led our currency to death's door" (July 15, 1779, Johnson, 1 *Greene* 186–7; cf. H to Greene, May 1780[?] HLC unbnd. Box 1). Pelatiah Webster (*Third Essay on . . . Finance,* Phila., 1780, in *Essays on Money, Public Finances,* 1791, p. 72) proposed, months before H, a single financier whose "one mind" should control Treasury operations; cf. 90–1, 162 ff. Webster may have influenced H's advocacy, though they differed on other important points.

49. Referred to commander in chief's recent letter to Congress; left date blank (was Oct. 11, 1780; 20 GW 157 ff.) and is in writing of H. Soon after, occurred mutinies in Pa. and N.J. lines.

50. 1 LHW 223–26. Only for Trade (anticipation of Commerce Dept., not established until 1903), did he recommend a board, which he took, surely, from Postlethwayt.

51. *Ibid.,* 226–29. A permanent, "considerable body of troops" would give Congress "a solid basis of authority. . . ." In suppressing Whisky Insurrection 14 years later, militia proved adequate, though some were called out with difficulty.

52. Idea that to make a creditor was to make an ally figured in his proposal, decade later, for national assumption of war debts of states.

53. *Ibid.*, 229–37.

54. *Ibid.*, 237–9.

55. H to Duane (Oct. 18, 9 LHW 225). Washington's efforts at this juncture, partly through Duane, to get Congress to draft "army for the war" (II writing letters), also met with objections, and only qualified success; cf. Washington to Duane, Oct. 4, 1780 (20 GW 117–8).

56. 3 HLC 352–74; 1 JCHW 223–257; 3 LHW 342–87; refs. here to last.

57. See H to Washington, De Peyster's Point, April 27, May 2, 1781 (9 *ibid.*, 238–42).

58. 3 LHW 343.

59. Cited Hume's *Essay on Balance of Trade* (1752) and statement of Richard Price, 1775.

60. *Ibid.*, 345–60.

61. Prosperity consisted in industry, commerce, not "mines [which] have had great influence in banishing industry from Spain, and sinking it in real wealth and importance" (*ibid.*, 361). Spoke of "that spirit of enterprise and competition on which the prosperity of commerce depends," but approved of large trading companies with public participation, "for private adventurers are not a match for the . . . obstacles resulting from the present posture of affairs" (*ibid.*, 340–41).

62. A favorite conviction, encouraged by Postlethwayt, and echoed by H's followers in American national school of economic writers, e.g., the Careys and Stephen Colwell, who set regulated paper currency above specie.

63. *Ibid.*, 361–66.

64. *Ibid.*, 387.

65. Reformed Church, Albany, register of marriages, photostat in NYPL; under date is "Colonel Alex Hamilton & Elisabeth Schuyler," the "Alex" in lighter ink, evidently later, in a space left for it, indicating groom was not well known to that minister or clerk. Copy of letter, H, Albany, Dec. 9, 1780 (3 HLC 306, and so dated in 1 JCHW 201 and 9 LHW 229), adding "Mrs. Hamilton presents her respectful compliments," should be 19th; Washington's reply, ALS, New Windsor, Dec. 27, 1780 (3 HLC 307, 1 JCHW 202), referred to H's of 19th, brought "by the Doctor," i.e., McHenry who was present at ceremony. This correction removes "doubt about the date of the marriage" (cf. AMH 135). In 17 marriages in register that year many names were Dutch; same day with Alex and Betsey were married Richard Smith and Lyntje (?) Fonda.

66. She was born Aug. 9, 1757; her father entered in family Bible after her name, "Lord do according to thy will with her" (Mary G. Humphreys,

Catherine Schuyler, 52). Schuylers had eleven children; three died in infancy; five girls grew up.

67. AMH 129–30; instructions to H. *et. al.*, March 8, 1780 (18 GW 87–9). Schuyler's letter to H, cordially approving "the connection you have made with my family," is dated April 18, 1780 (2 HLC 228–31); first part in AMH 125, and only remainder, on other matters, in 1 JCHW 135–6. H to Mrs. Schuyler, entreating her "to accept the assurances of my gratitude for your kind compliance with my wishes to be united to your amiable daughter," is dated April 14 (AMH 125–6).

68. See Schuyler to Steuben, (Humphreys 178). On possible earlier acquaintance, 9 LHW 202 n.; Humphreys 179; O. Tilghman 90 ff.; H to Mrs. Schuyler, AMH 126; H to Miss Livingston, Mar. 18, 1779 (Sedgwick, *Livingston* 320). However, Kitty Livingston, May 13, 1779 asked Betsey to give her love to Dr. and Mrs. Cochran, which may connect Betsey with Morristown that early (AMH 99).

69. Gen. Heath, in command at West Pt., sent an asst. quartermaster to aid them when they crossed ferry on a November morning (Humphreys, *ibid.*).

70. *Ibid.*, 178–9.

71. O. Tilghman, *op. cit.*, 90 ff.

72. 1780, AMH 97–9. Forwarding letter from Betsey to her sister whom he did not know, apparently not to Angelica, as here supposed. Betsey's lack of affectation won her friends, also, among girls of own age; cf. letters from Catherine and Gertrude Livingston (*ibid.*, 99–103).

73. Tilghman's *Tilghman*, 173.

74. See W. Jay Mills, *Historic Houses of New Jersey*, 209 ff.; G. W. Schuyler, *Colonial New York, Philip Schuyler and His Family*, II, 242–3, 251–2, 283. Schuyler to Jas. Duane, June 5, 1780 (Duane Papers, NYHS); Mrs. Schuyler joined husband at Morristown in spring (see same to same, March 6, 1780, *ibid.*).

75. ALS (draft), H to Lt. Col. Laurens, no place, no date, 2 HLC 209; penciled note, "I must not publish," must be by J. C. Hamilton, for in 1 JCHW 109–11, with filial self-consciousness, he omitted all of what H called his "Jeu *de folie.*" 9 LHW 184–88 first printed whole, but misdated Dec. 1779. H's prescription for wife was given Laurens shortly after latter left Congress on way to S.C. to raise battalions of slaves, for at same time H acknowledged his friend's letters from Phila. and Chester; allusion to Sullivan coming to take "the Indian command" further fixes date as spring 1779, not Dec.

76. ALS, no place nor date, but from camp at Morristown to Elizabeth at Albany, and endorsed, apparently by her, "received the beginning of

Sep.^r"; in possession Mrs. John C. Hamilton, Elmsford, N.Y., to whom I am indebted for its use. Contrast ALS, Fleury, Oct. 20, 1780, to H, congratulating on engagement because would ensure influence, financial ease (3 HLC 292).

77. ALS, Phila., April 8, 1780 (2 HLC 228–31).

78. Oct. 18, 1780.

79. 2 R 176.

80. Humphreys, *Catherine Schuyler* 194–6, 202–4.

81. April 8, 1780, *op. cit.*

82. He did not make drafts or copies; perhaps she withheld originals when she placed bulk of H's papers in hands of successive intending biographers, and by this scruple they were lost. Most we have are printed in AMH 127 ff. Hers to him, probably fewer by fashion of day, have disappeared.

83. These couplets, says her grandson, were "found in a tiny bag hanging from his wife's neck after her death, and which she had evidently always worn. . . ." They were "written upon a piece of torn and yellow paper, fragments of which had been sewn together. . . ." (AMH 126).

84. *Ibid.,* 127.

85. July 2, 1780 (AMH 127–8). Three days before he had written to John Laurens: ". . . I am on the point of becoming a benedict. . . . Next fall . . . I give up my liberty to Miss Schuyler. She is a good hearted girl who I am sure will never play the termagant—though not a genius she has good sense enough to be agreeable and though not a beauty, she has fine black eyes[,] is rather handsome and has every other requisite of the exterior to make a lover happy. And believe me, I am lover in earnest. . . ." (June 30, 1780, HLC unbnd. Box 1).

86. Oct. 5, 1780 (*ibid.,* 133–34).

87. Those to Elizabeth, which we have, are of Sept. 25 (from Robinson's[?] immediately after event, and Oct. 2, from Tappan, day of André's death (1 JCHW 186–87; 9 LHW 206–9). That to Laurens, in JCHW *ibid.,* 172–82, is dated Sept., while LHW *ibid.,* 209–23, dated it Oct., with note that earlier date "is an obvious error, as André was not executed until Oct. 2, and this letter describes his execution." Possibly both dates correct, since H in postscript to Elizabeth, Oct. 5, said: "I promised you a particular account of André. I am writing one of the whole affair of which I will send you a copy" (AMH 134).

88. See H to Washington, Nov. 22, 1780 (1 JCHW 195–6; 9 LHW 226–28).

89. Cf. H to J. Laurens, June 30, 1780 (HLC unbnd. Box 1), and Schuyler to Duane, May 13, 1780 (Duane Papers, NYHS).

90. House built 1760–62 (statement of Miss Elizabeth Halahan, of Rochester, N.Y., who established much about house from Schuyler Papers, NYPL, for restoration. See ms. report of Ralph Isham (N.Y. State Lib.); Philip Schuyler (1836–1906), in *Quarterly Journal*, N.Y. Hist. Assn., 1929, typescript in Schuyler Papers, NYPL; J. J. Vrooman, *Historic Sites of N.Y. State*, N.Y. State Education Dept., 15–23, with pictures and particulars of Schuyler mansion, and of Ft. Crailo, Rensselaer seat across Hudson. Noble house of orange brick tops hill overlooking river, was originally surrounded by ample yard, appurtenant buildings, and home farm of 90 acres. Style is Georgian, marking departure from Dutch type which had been characteristic of Albany, just as Schuylers themselves, brought up in the older tradition, were in most respects Anglicized. For pleasant life in Schuyler mansion, see Baroness Riedesel, *Letters and Journals Relating to American Revolution* . . . .134–6; Maj. Gen. Riedesel, *Memoirs, etc., During Residence in America,* I, 171, 211, 214; Chastellux, *Travels in N. America,* 371 ff.

91. AMH 137–9; in the verses the best man gave advice, in which prudence tempered passion.

92. H wrote from there Dec. 19 to Washington, and Washington wrote him there Dec. 27, 1780 (above); cf. ALS, R. R. Livingston to Schuyler, Jan. 1 (Schuyler Papers, NYPL), ALS Greene to H, Jan. 10, 1781 (3 HLC 327).

93. H to Washington, *ibid.* Maybe Eliz. tarried briefly at Fishkill while H pressed on to HQ (ALS, H to Capt. Fisher, Jan. 5[?] 1781, H Papers, NYPL).

94. Chastellux, 379 ff.

95. Schuyler Papers, NYPL, particularly Box 35, containing abundant evidence of his consequence as landholder, leader in his region; antecedents of Philip and Catherine Schuyler elaborately given in G. W. Schuyler, *Colonial N.Y. etc.,* 2 vols., 1885.

96. See Tuckerman, *Life of Schuyler,* 253.

Chapter 13 (Pages 209 to 221)
Witness to Treason

1. H knew his private letters about the treason would become public record; see his note, on retained copy of that of —— Oct., 1780, to Laurens (3 HLC 279–87; printed in 9 LHW 209–23; 1 JCHW 172 ff., misdated Sept.)

directing order in which paragraphs should be read. This long, celebrated letter was written on, more probably finished by, Oct. 2, 1780, for he enclosed in one of that date to Elizabeth Schuyler "my account of Arnold's affair" (9 LHW 208). Earliest newspaper appearance may have been in *Pa. Packet,* Oct. 14, 17, 1780; see below for British use of it. Cf. Lafayette: H's "narrative of the events, and a portraiture of . . . André, . . . is a masterpiece of . . . amiable sensibility" (84 HLC 13725).

2. For vivid illustrations see [John Becker] *The Sexagenary, or Reminiscences of American Revolution* (Albany, 1833), 12–13, 97–100.

3. 19 GW 412.

4. See H's two letters ridiculing Gates's scamper to safety, exceeding John Gilpin's breakneck ride, to E. Schuyler and to Duane, Sept. 6, 1780 (9 LHW 202–5). H admitted he wrote in recollection of Gates's "unjust and unprovoked attacks upon my character," but he exposed bad generalship in battle as well as swift exit from it. In Steuben's papers (NYHS) is the extract of a journal of Col. Scrift (?) concerning "Battle near Cambden," which doubtless the baron shared with Hamilton. It tries in vain to put good face on Gates's flight.

5. He owned the house opposite West Point which was Arnold's headquarters; became an officer of Royal Americans.

6. H, describing this episode (to Laurens, Oct. 1780, 9 LHW 211–2), mistakenly put date Sept. 20, when Washington was in fact at Hartford.

7. *Ibid.,* Col. John Lamb, stationed at West Pt., had given Arnold same advice (Dawson, ed., *Record of Trial of Joshua Hett Smith,* 104). Robinson's letter to Arnold is in Freeman, 5 *Washington* 191.

8. To Laurens, *ibid.,* 212.

9. Testimony of Robt. H. Harrison and H, *Trial of Smith, ibid.,* 20, 26. Both officers were repeating what Smith had related when examined by Washington who wanted to know how a man brought from British warship, and to be returned there, could be considered a friend to U.S. Even Smith's boatmen, the brothers Cahoon, or Colquhoun, demurred at such an errand under cover of night, with muffled oars (*Trial of Smith,* 6 ff., 12).

10. See 20 GW 76–80, two papers covering conference; one gives, translated into English from Lafayette's French, Washington's answers to questions by Rochambeau and De Ternay, other H's summary of their conversation, exclusive of above, endorsed by Washington, Tilghman. Chief point was "That of all the enterprises which may be undertaken, the most . . . decisive is the reduction of New York. . . ."

11. Hay's testimony, *Trial of Smith,* 80.

12. Washington to Heath, Sept. 26, 1780 (20 GW 88–9).

13. [Jas. McHenry] Robinson's House, Sept. 26, 1780, in *Pa. Packet,* Oct. 3, 1780. For photograph of Robinson's house (Arnold's headquarters), on east bank of river and slightly below West Pt., see *Proceedings of . . . Trial of . . . André, and Letters pertaining to . . . Treason of . . . Arnold.* Photographed from originals, 1908 (no place of pub., 52 pp., NYPL) p. 3.

14. *Varick Court of Inquiry to Investigate Implication . . . in Arnold Treason,* A. B. Hart, ed. (Boston, 1907), Franks' testimony, 129. Varick had been sick in bed for several days, but dressed long enough to welcome Washington (Varick to sister Jane, in *ibid.,* 190).

15. *Varick Inquiry, ibid.* Franks' testimony.

16. Varick to Jane, *ibid.,* 191–2.

17. Dr. Wm. Eustis' testimony, *Varick Inquiry, op. cit.,* 42–3.

18. Lamb's testimony, *ibid.,* 151–2, and Varick's, 180–81. Their conjecture they were afraid "to lisp . . . to any creature living, lest [it prove] untrue. . . ." Eustis' testimony, *ibid.,* 142.

19. Franks in *ibid.,* 129. McHenry, already arrived, "observed an embarrassment [in Arnold] which I could not at that time account for" (*Pa. Packet,* Oct. 3, 1780).

20. H to Laurens, *op. cit.,* 214.

21. McHenry, *op. cit.*

22. H, *ibid.*

23. Inferred, since he did not instantly take alarming contents to Washington. Lafayette, years later, implied H read papers when received and on Washington's return from West Point "had to give him the unexpected tidings" (84 HLC 13725).

24. See "Remarks on Works at West Point," by Arnold, Sept. 1780, in *Minutes of Court of Inquiry upon Case of André* (Albany, 1865), 42–3, and other disclosures given by Arnold to André, below.

25. H to Laurens, *op. cit.,* 214; for these papers, which Tilghman testified were in Arnold's hand, see *André Ct. Minutes,* 37 ff.

26. Mentioned by H, *ibid.,* but not now found.

27. Sept. 24, 1780, *André Ct. Minutes,* 11–13; for H's summary, to Laurens, 216–7; he did not list André's letter with other documents; may have come by express separately (cf. Freeman, 5 *Washington* 200 n.)

28. That H knew main facts is plain from his short letters to Washington and Greene from Verplanck's, both Sept. 25, 1780 (9 LHW 205–6); Arnold's letter to Washington, which he enclosed, declared his guilt (see below).

29. [McHenry] in *Pa. Packet,* Oct. 3, 1780; H to E. Schuyler, Sept. 25, 1780 (9 LHW 206–7), and to Laurens, *ibid.,* 215. Washington, Sept. 26, 1780, to Heath (20 GW 88–9; to Pres. of Congress 912). Ride probably required an hour.

30. To E. Schuyler, 9 LHW 206–7.

31. Washington to Heath, 20 GW 88–9. Arnold passed Verplanck's with a flag and gained *Vulture* few miles below. Ironically, the 8 bargemen who rowed traitor to safety had been permitted by Washington, on Arnold's application, to remain at his service (to Arnold, Sept. 14, 1780, 20 GW 48), countermanding order for them to rejoin their regiment under Putnam (*ibid.,* Sept. 7, 1780).

32. Sept. 25, 1780 (9 LHW 205–6, facsimile in *Proceed. of Trial of André,* 35) shows his haste; to Greene, same date, 206, added only necessary news of treason.

33. For Arnold to Washington, Sparks, 7 *Washington* 533; Robinson to Washington, *Proceed. of Bd. of Gen. Officers . . . Respecting . . . André,* 8–9; Arnold to Peggy, sent to her by Washington unopened, is not found.

34. To Laurens, *op. cit.,* 221–3.

35. Varick to Jane, *op. cit.,* 192.

36. *Ibid.;* Franks in *Varick Ct. of Inquiry,* 131–2, and Lamb, *ibid.,* 151; Freeman, 5 *Washington* 201–2, puts visit to Peggy after dinner, at variance with Varick, and has H present, which is unlikely.

37. 20 GW 84–85; for the bustle at Tappan caused by orders to Greene, see Wm. North ms. (1823), Yale Univ.

38. GW *ibid.,* 85.

39. *Ibid.,* 86–87.

40. Dawson, ed., *Trial of Smith,* testimony of Knox, 71–2.

41. *Smith Trial, ibid.;* for picture of Smith, bold features under curly, unpowdered wig, see *Proceed. of Trial of André, op. cit.;* for photograph of his large square house near Haverstraw, *ibid.,* 29.

42. *Smith Trial,* 31.

43. To Congress, Sept. 26, 1780 (20 GW 92–3).

44. To Gov. Clinton, *ibid.,* 94.

45. *Smith Trial,* 26 ff.

46. *Narrative of Death of Major André* (London, 1808), 133; however, this apologia of Smith offers strong indication of his complicity.

47. *Smith Trial*, 30–1.

48. *Ibid.*, 106.

49. To Laurens, Oct. 1780 (9 LHW 215–6).

50. To E. Schuyler, Sept. 25, 1780 (*ibid.*, 207). Cf. to Laurens, above.

51. To Laurens, above, 216.

52. *Proceed. of Trial of André*, 43.

53. Arnold, in letter from *Vulture*, Sept. 25, 1780, enclosed by H in own dispatch late that day from Verplanck's (9 LHW 205), at once protesting his high motives and admitting his debasement, asked Washington's protection "for Mrs. Arnold from . . . a mistaken vengeance. . . . It ought to fall only on me[.] She is as good, and as Inocent as an Angel, and is [*Ignorant,* crossed out] Incapable of doing wrong." (See facsimile in *Proceed. of Trial of André, op. cit.,* 22.)

54. See her father, Edward Shippen, Oct. 5, 1780, to Vice Pres. Moore, quoting Washington's pass to her to Phila. (facsimile in *Proceed. of Trial of André,* 43). Years later his grandson, of same name, trying to dissuade Wm. Gilmore Simms from intended insinuations against Peggy, called H's letter to Betsey "a . . . complete refutation of an idea . . . that Mrs. Arnold had a previous knowledge of the . . . treason." Mrs. H herself had recently assured him "that Mrs. A was a lady of the highest . . . virtues & attached warmly to the American Cause. . . ." (ALS, March 11, 1853, to Baird, Carey Gardiner Coll., No. 173, PHS).

55. Carl Van Doren, *Secret History of Am. Rev.,* 346–7; Flexner, *The Traitor and the Spy,* 253–9, 307 ff. Something is made of the story that Peggy, stopping at Paramus, N.J., en route to Philadelphia, confessed to Mrs. Prevost, widow of a British officer, that she had persuaded Arnold to treat with enemy (Van Doren, 350; Flexner, 378, with full acceptance). The tale, from Matthew L. Davis, *Aaron Burr* (1852), 219, derived at third hand from Burr, who later married Mrs. Prevost; plainly erroneous particulars cast whole in doubt (cf. *Varick Ct. of Inquiry* 42).

56. André himself, in first letter to Washington following capture, tried to exculpate himself on these grounds (see Egbert Benson, *Vindication of Captors of André,* 32–5; cf., at greater length, Sir Henry Clinton, Sept. 26, 1780, to Washington (*Proceed. of Bd. of General Officers . . . Respecting André . . .* Printed by Order of Congress, 1780, p. 9); cf. Clinton's *American Rebellion,* 217; Beverly Robinson, *Vulture,* off Sinsinck [*sic*], Sept. 25, 1780, to Washington (*ibid.,* 8–9); Arnold, N.Y., Sept. 26, 1780, to Sir Henry Clinton (*ibid.*); Jas. Robertson, *Greyhound* schooner, flag of truce, Dobbs Ferry, Oct. 2, 1780, to Washington (*ibid.,* 13–14). H called excuse "frivolous." Had every formality been observed, not violated as was the fact, "it would be an abuse of language to say that the sanction of a flag

for corrupting an officer to betray his trust, ought to be respected" (to Laurens, *op. cit.*, 221–2).

57. *Ibid.*, 216, 220–21.

58. *Ibid.*, 219–20. H's son, however, century later warned sentimentality should not obscure André's guilt (A.J.H., *Letter to Mr. Henry Whittemore, of Rockland Historical Society* . . . N.Y., 1885, 7 pp.).

59. Inn that became his prison for week before execution Oct. 2, 1780, is standing. Like others composing village (Washington's HQ also an example), is in Dutch style; see Albert H. Heusser, *The '76 Stone House, Tappan* . . . (reprint. from *In Footsteps of Washington*). n.p., n.d., 15 pp.).

60. H to Laurens, *op. cit.*, 217; André, Tappan, Sept. 29, 1780, to Sir Henry Clinton (*Proceed. of Bd. of Gen. Officers . . . Respecting . . . André*, 10); cf. Washington to Greene, Sept. 27, 1780 (20 GW 97–8).

61. Hamilton to Laurens, *op. cit.*, 217–8, and André in *Proceed.*, *ibid.* As Lafayette remembered it, "Col. Hamilton . . . was one of those who daily were searching for some way to save him," and reluctantly accepted the impossibility (84 HLC 13725).

62. Of Elizabethtown, N.J., for several years asst. teacher in Barber's Academy which H attended.

63. Perhaps slip of memory, as Washington had HQ in a brick dwelling.

64. Autobiography (written 1833), in *NJHS Proceed.*, 2d ser., XII, 1892–3, pp. 23–4.

65. John G. Simcoe, *History of Operations of . . . Queen's Rangers . . . During . . . Am. Rev.*, 393, letter from Lee, Oct. 2, 1780.

66. *Ibid.*, 152.

67. Autograph Memoirs, Vol. 6, Oct. 1, 1780, NYPL.; cf. for plans for mission, Sept. 30 (entered Oct. 3), 1780.

68. Facsimile in Van Doren, *Secret History*, facing 376.

69. In Clinton Papers, Clements Lib. Comparing facsimile with examples of H's autograph about same date, Mr. Edward Morrison, MSS. Division, NYPL, was not satisfied to say they were from same pen (May 17, 1954). Bottom lines run uphill, as often in H's mss., but some capitals are structurally different, and grave accent on Andrè (thus) would be contrary to H's knowledge.

70. 9 LHW 222.

71. "I . . . had the weakness to value the esteem of a dying man, because I revered his merit" (*ibid.*, 209). Van Doren, *op. cit.*, 366, thought it "fairly certain" H wrote "AB" letter, especially since language and argu-

ment are similar to those used to Laurens. However, unnecessary introduction, citing André's capture, was not H's method, and Van Doren overlooked his distaste for project, as told to Betsey (cf. Flexner, *op. cit.,* 389–90; Freeman, 5 *Washington* 217 n. doubted H proposed it). If H's letter, it is the only one of his in disguised hand, or stealthily delivered.

72. Facsimile in *Proceed. of Trial of André,* 9.

73. Facsimile in *ibid.,* 37.

74. H to Laurens, *op. cit.,* 218–9; André's mortification when he first glimpsed gallows figures in all accounts, including H's (9 LHW 219).

75. H to Laurens, *op. cit.,* 218.

76. "When . . . present resentment is over," he added, "the refusing him the privilege of choosing the manner of his death will be branded with too much obstinacy" (To E. Schuyler, Tappen, Oct. 2, 1780, 9 LHW 208–9). Fate of Nathan Hale, hanged by British, figured with many as unavoidable precedent.

77. Thacher, *Military Diary,* 58 ff.

78. See, e.g., letter, Tappan, Sept. 28, 1780 (*Pa. Packet,* Oct. 3, 1780), assuming "the most cursed plot . . . for the seizing of the person of . . . General Washington, with his family, on their return from the eastward, which would have taken place on the night of the 25th instant." Beverly Robinson was to have led picked party from *Vulture* to his own house (Arnold's HQ) to capture commanders before West Point was attacked.

79. Sept. 15, 1780, in code: "General Washington will be at King's Ferry Sunday Evening next on his way to Hartford . . . and will lodge at Peaks Kill" (facsimile in Van Doren, *Secret History,* facing 314).

80. Wm. Smith, 6 *Memoirs,* Sept. 28, 1780 (NYPL); Clinton gave particulars of planned assault with 5,000 troops and like number in reserve; of course, notion Rochambeau was at West Point was mistaken.

81. To Laurens, *op. cit.,* 215.

82. See *Royal Gazette,* Extraordinary, n.d., probably end of Oct., 1780, in Smith, *Memoirs, ibid.,* with other letters from Greene and group of New England officers, from Ezekiel Cornell, and Richd. Langdon; cf. *ibid.,* Nov. 2, 9, 1780.

83. *Case of Major John André, . . . put to Death by Rebels . . .* (N.Y., 1780, photostat in NYPL), 21–2. Also H's letter to Laurens, circulated in newspapers, was called stratagem to promote Washington's seizure of dictatorial authority (22 ff.). Had British known of H's letter to Duane, Oct. 18 (9 LHW 225), they would have discovered grounds for suspicion in his lament for "the absolute insufficiency of our present system to our safety

. . . ;" they would have been more delighted with sentences in his note to Betsey Oct. 2: "Poor André suffers to-day. Every thing that is amiable . . . pleads for him; but hard-hearted policy calls for a Sacrifice. He must die—." (9 LHW 208.)

Chapter 14 (Pages 222 to 248)
Hasty Words and Quitting of Headquarters

1. His position was preferable to that of McHenry, who "as a *Secretary* to commander in chief . . . has . . . no military existence properly speaking, no rank." McHenry wanted "to quit a station which among foreigners is not viewed in a very reputable light," so H asked Duane, in Congress, to get McHenry made a major, with which rank he would become aide to Lafayette (copy of ALS, HQ, Morristown, endorsed July 22, 1780, Duane Papers, NYHS). Washington had recommended giving "Commissions of the usual form" to those who had served, though perhaps without rank, in staff appointments (to Bd. of War, Jan. 15, 1780, 17 GW 403–4).

2. To Washington, Oct. 30, 1780, in 7 Sparks 558.

3. Oct. 30, 1780 (20 GW 266–7).

4. Nov. 20, 1780 ff., to Pickering, Gouvion, *et al.* (20 GW 379 ff., 424–34). Eleven months before (Jan. 1780) H had crossed to Staten Island on ice with Stirling and 2,500 troops. But the enemy made a fort of a stone house against which Hamilton had warned, where they would quickly be relieved from New York, and Americans were obliged to return to mainland without result (2 R 5, quoting a letter of H to Washington; Duer's *Stirling,* 206).

5. Lafayette to H, Nov. 22, 1780 (1 JCHW 194).

6. 9 LHW 226–8. H's contention that he was eligible for field command was fully supported by position Washington had taken. The general replied to Bd. of War concerning aides de camp: "it is clearly my opinion, that those appointed before the 27th. May 1778 and now in service as Aids, and who are not admissible into any State line, are eligible to commands. . . ." Otherwise, "the Rank given these Officers would be a mere sound . . ." and mockery of their services (Jan. 15, 1780, 17 GW 402–4).

7. Nov. 24, 1780, to Moylan and others (20 GW 395–7).

8. Greene's letter of Nov. 19, 1780, said he was persuaded the "appointment [of H] will be received with great gratitude . . . from what he said to me before I left camp" (20 GW 470 n.).

9. Dec. 13, 1780 (20 GW 470–1), cf. to Pres. of Congress, Nov. 28, 1780 (*ibid.,* 419–20).

10. LOLTW 130–1.

11. 1 JCHW 196–7.

12. Dec. 9, 1780 (3 HLC 302–5, partially printed in 1 JCHW 199–200). H was at Albany, about to be married, and Lafayette said that only a matter of military preferment warranted "interrupting your amorous occupations."

13. 2 R 144. Hamilton would have been affected by Laurens's "desire of gaining Fame, [which] leads me to wish for the command of men" (to H. Laurens, March 9, 1778, Mil. Corr., LIHS). Congress had confidence in John Laurens for several reasons: he had been field commander as well as aide to Washington, spoke French, possessed charm of manner, was son of Pres. Henry Laurens.

14. It has been objected (see 2 R iii–vii) that Washington would not copy what his aide had composed. But what is obviously first draft is in H's hand (Jan. 15, 1781, 21 GW 105–10), and differences, as they appear in 4 *Diplomatic Corr.* (Wharton) 318–20 are of mere editorial rearrangement, shortening. Cf. on Washington's part in this letter, Humphreys to Pickering, same date, 21 GW 98, 105 n. Pickering mentioned to Fish, "You told me that you knew, that some letters written for Washington were copied by him & signed as his own" (ALS, July 30, 1822, Fish Papers, Columbia Univ.).

15. Two years later, when Washington was consulted concerning H's fitness for the post of Superintendent of Finance, to which Robt. Morris was named, he replied in cordial endorsement of former aide's talents but said he was not informed how far H had cultivated fiscal subjects (Washington to Sullivan, Feb. 4, 1781, 21 GW 181).

16. ALS, Ramapough, June 30, 1780 (HLC unbnd. Box 1). Cf. Schuyler to Duane, Morristown, May 13, 1780: Lafayette's news of French help on the way made it "Incumbent on us to strain every nerve for a spirited co-operation, the country is far, very far, from being destitute of the necessary supplies, the means to draw them forth are also within our reach," but states paid no attention to the merely recommendatory powers of Congress; commander in chief, alone or with small committee of Congress, should be given dictatorial powers (Duane Papers, NYHS; cf. ms. letter, unsigned, Jan. 14, 1780, to Duane, *ibid.*). This had undoubtedly been subject of conversation between Schuyler and H at headquarters.

17. Unoccupied spaces had only latent value. "Paper credit cannot be supported without pecuniary funds" (mutilated letter, Feb. 7, 1781, 9 LHW 231).

18. 2 R 78.

19. Jan. 15, 1781 (21 GW 105–10); J. Laurens, Versailles, April 9 [17], 1781, to Congress (Mil. Corr. LIHS). H wrote for Washington to Franklin, resident minister at Paris, explaining Laurens joined him as military witness to our needs (21 GW 100–1). Bancroft considered Laurens less fitted than H for mission to France (5 *Hist. U.S.* 452). Wallace antagonized this (*Henry Laurens,* 479).

20. HQ, New Windsor, Feb. 18, 1781 (9 LHW 232–7; with serious omissions in 1 JCHW 211–14).

21. HQ house at New Windsor in which this occurred long since disappeared. In 1831 it was standing a few yards back from south dock, "a low house with three dormant [*sic*] windows"; land rose behind it (R. J. Vandewater, *The Tourist, or Pocket Manual for Travellers on Hudson River,* 22). Like house occupied by Knox, yet standing, belonged to member of Ellison family, was of Dutch design. Painting, apparently from tradition, is in Washington Headquarters museum, Newburgh. If as compact as other dwellings of this type, with open stairwell, anyone in lower hall could hear angry exchanges between general and aide.

22. Henry Lee (*War in Southern Department,* 501 n.) related incident, with inaccuracies.

23. Stirling was one; other may have been Greene.

24. H wrote similarly to McHenry (n.d., photostat, 2d ser., I McHenry Papers, LC): "The Great man and I have come to [torn] rupture. Proposals of accommodation have been made on his part and rejected. I pledge my honor to you that he will find me inflexible. He shall for once at least repent his ill humour. . . . I wait till more help arrives. . . . Except to a very few friends our differences will be a secret, therefore be silent." H's characterization of Washington, cold because offered in heat, contrasts with that of Rendon, Spanish representative; "to his . . . perfections, [the American people] are most justly indebted, for his constancy and love of his country . . . are incomparable" (Oct. 8, 1780, in 100 Sparks Transcripts 129–30, Houghton Lib., Harvard).

25. Cf. H's description of prevailing disorder in *Continentalist,* 1 LHW 255.

26. Washington to Rochambeau, Feb. 24, 1781 (21 GW 285). See H's review of situation, from HQ, Feb. 7, 1781 (9 LHW 230–1).

27. H, ALS to Pickering, QMG, who endorsed it "rec'd at midnight" (H Papers, NYPL). Press of business next day, with only two aides at HQ, was mentioned by H to Schuyler (above).

28. Lafayette's answers to queries concerning H, no date, copy in another hand, 84 HLC 13718. He added "That nothing very blamable is to be ascribed to either party, their own character and subsequent mutual con-

nexions sufficiently assert." Lafayette confirmed what we know otherwise, that, though aide had formally left family, Washington "in several circumstances friendly asked . . . the advice of hamilton." Implication that the marquis tried at once to compose difference is at variance with his exchange of letters with Washington shortly afterward (see below). As to Washington's irritability, we may remember that some weeks later he lost usual firm grip on himself in letters complaining of Rochambeau, Destouches (above).

29. 9 LHW 237; also he was already thinking of "studies relative to my future career in life."

30. 2 R 176–7. Cornelis De Witt, foreigner who thoroughly appreciated Washington, yet remarked, "The hardships of the revolutionary struggle, . . . had shaken the masterly control Washington had gained over his passions; and the officers of his staff . . . had to suffer, not unfrequently, from the irritable temper and punctilious susceptibility of their commander" (*Histoire de Washington et de la Fondation de la République des États-Unis*, 75). Washington Irving, (4 *Life of Washington* 230 ff.), properly judged H "in the wrong," but failed to note reasons of aide for not obeying instantly general's summons.

31. 9 LHW 232 n.

32. Webster's inquiry, ALS, N.Y., July 14, and Washington's answer, ALS, Mt. Vernon, July 31, 1788, are in Morgan Lib.; privately printed in limited ed., *1781 Yorktown. Letter from Noah Webster to . . . Washington . . .* (Brooklyn, N.Y., 1881). See for Webster's use of Washington's reply, [Jedidiah Morse] *History of America . . .* Phila. 1790, p. 253. Showing expectation N.Y. was Washington's object, see MsDS, Pres. Thos. McKean to Gov. Trumbull (circular), July 25 (Houghton Lib.), ALS, Greene to Pickens, July 30, 1781 (Morgan Lib.).

33. Cf. Freeman, 5 *Washington* 284 ff., especially 287, 288, 290, 297, 298, 304, 305, 307; Ward, 2 *Revolution* 879 ff.

34. 2 *Diaries of Washington* 217–8; cf. June 28, 231 ff., July 18, 237 ff.

35. *Ibid.*, 248–9. Knox was now asked to "make every necessary arrangement" for southern concentration "in his own mind, estimating the ordnance and Stores which would be wanting. . . ."

36. 2 R 258–9, without citation.

37. Ms. Journal of Jean C.L.I.F., Baron von Closen, LC; von Closen returned with Washington, H, and Tilghman to Newport. I am indebted to Miss Evelyn M. Acomb, of Poughkeepsie, N.Y., for these entries. Cf. Doniol, 5 *Hist. de la Participation de France . . .* 423, and 1 JCHW 215.

38. Washington to Lafayette, March 1, 1781 (21 GW 322–3).

39. 21 GW 328, 329; cf. to Lafayette, March 8, 1781 (*ibid.*, 331).

40. To Gordon, March 9, 1781 (*ibid.*, 332).

41. "I shall be obliged to you for the answer to the address as soon as it is convenient to you" (ALS Washington, to H [Newport, March 7, 1781], signed "affectly," 3 HLC 337. JCH (2 R 183 and n.) mistakenly thought H did not go with Washington to Newport.

42. To comm. of Newport, Christopher Ellery, *et al.*, March 8, 1781 (21 GW 330–1).

43. Washington to H, above; to Lafayette, March 8, 1781, 10 P.M. (GW *ibid.*, 331).

44. To Weare, March 10, 1781 (*ibid.*, 334–5), to Gordon, above.

45. To Gen. Wm. Heath, March 21, 1781 (*ibid.*, 342).

46. *Ibid.*, 400 n., 434 n.

47. Harrison, New Windsor, March 26, 1781, to H (1 JCHW 215–17). In affectionate letter justified own departure from army (to be Chief Justice of Md. Sup. Ct.), without reflection on H's break with general, of which he had just learned.

48. 2 R 183 says H went direct from HQ to Phila. to obtain commission in line. Unlikely, for authorization by Congress not until May 25 (20 JCC 541); H's appointment was not announced until July 31, 1781 (22 GW 438); see below. *Jnls.* of Congress at this interval mention no request by H.

49. Cf. Washington to Pres. of Congress, April 16 [–19], 1781, with amusing reason for exchanging Burgoyne *in absentia* (21 GW 474–5).

50. April 21, 1781 (*ibid.*, 488–9); cf. to Greene, April 22, 1781 (*ibid.*, 492–3), seeking employment for meritorious Maj. MacPherson.

51. April 10, 1781 (3 HLC 341–2; also, with altered spelling, in 1 JCHW 217–9); he suggested commands for four of H's special friends. Letter of Laurens to H, trusting he would not quit public life, in 1 JCHW 214 and 2 R 190, dated 1781 belongs to 1782, probably July, for it refers to events just preceding—birth of H's son (cf. H. to Meade, March 1782, 9 LHW 253–5) etc.; H answered Aug. 15, 1782 (9 LHW 280–1).

52. April 15, 1781, from Susquehana [*sic*] Ferry by hand of Gouvion (LOLTW 184).

53. 21 GW 489–91; H mentioned to Schuyler some of his friends were "privy to the affair" (Feb. 18, 1781, 9 LHW 236).

54. 2 R 187–8, with above date; 9 LHW 237–8 dates it Feb., which from context is too early.

55. 3 HLC 340.

56. April 16, 1781, Box 1, HLC. Allusion to Mrs. Cuyler's cutlery is incidental evidence H, after Washington's Newport conferences, went to Albany. (Cf. Schuyler, Albany, Feb. 5, 1781, 3 HLC 335, to H, saying Wadsworth and friend, at H's recommendation, had been entertained in his home; this part omitted in 1 JCHW 210.) More conclusively, Fleury, writing from Newport (above), where he had doubtless seen H, wanted to know "are you come back from Albany, with your Sweetheart?"

57. ALS, Stewart & Totten, Phila. April 13, 23, 1781, to H at HQ, had not been able dispose of his bill, but were sending by Col. [Udny] Hay 16 guineas (2d ser., 1 HLC 24; cf. from same, May 5, 1781, and H's note on back, 3 HLC 377).

58. April 21, 1781 (21 GW 488–9).

59. April 22, 1781 (*ibid.,* 493–6).

60. 21 GW 386.

61. One, to Benj. Harrison, gave frank revelation of military plans discussed with Rochambeau (*ibid.,* 380–3, in Tilghman's hand).

62. April 4, 1781.

63. April 15, 1781 (LOLTW 183–4). Cf. Lafayette to H, same day: "You . . . certainly can explain to me what is the matter that . . . while the French are coming, I am going" (1 JCHW 219).

64. Letter of April 26, 1781 (172 Papers of GW 25, LC, and with editing in Sparks, 8 *Writings G. W.* 28 n.).

65. April 30, 1781 (22 GW 16–17); cf. Washington, ALS, to Lafayette, April 22, 1781 (21 *ibid.,* 489–91), in similar tenor. Rivington's quotation was in fact accurate, which best served enemy purpose. Washington had written similarly to other friends; cf. March 23, to Schuyler (*ibid.,* 360–1), March 24 to Jones (*ibid.,* 372–3), March 25 to Fitzhugh (*ibid.,* 376); Schuyler's commiserating answer, April 3, 1781, is in 3 Sparks, *op. cit.,* 281.

66. Letter of May 5, 1781, in 173 Papers of G. W. 19, LC.

67. Feb. 3, 1781 (21 GW 178–80).

68. To Sec. at War, June 5, 1782 (24 GW 319–20).

69. June 7, 1782 (9 LHW 256–8).

70. 23 JCC 845–6; cf. Knox to H, 2 R 286; Washington to Duane, Sept. 30, 1782 (25 GW 222–3); David Humphreys, *Conduct of Washington Respecting Asgill.*

71. 100 Sparks Trans., 129, Houghton Lib. H and Harrison going at once left Washington shorthanded at HQ. Varick two months later was appointed to copy general's war papers (2 GW 112, 113–15); Jonathan Trum-

bull, Jr., became military secretary (*ibid.*, 81), and soon entered as aides David Cobb, Peregrine Fitzhugh, and Wm. S. Smith (*ibid.*, 216, 323, 333).

72. Name must have been in familiar local use, but did not find way to maps or gazetteers of period. Point is now called Denning's, directly across river from New Windsor at present Beacon, N.Y. Abraham De Peyster, N.Y.C. merchant, bought 300 acres, with grist mill, wharf, from Widow Catharine Brett, 1743, at mouth of Vis Kil (Fish Creek), where built ample Dutch-style dwelling, brick and stone. He died 1775 and "Mill Farm," at time of the Hamilton's sojourn, was in hands of Isaac De Peyster and wife Alice (Schenck). With altered roof, stairs, minus original front doorway, and sadly hemmed in by railroad, factory, and brickyard, house stood until 1953, when was taken down. (See Helen W. Reynolds, *Dutch Houses in Hudson Valley* . . . 335–8, and Plate 115; *ibid., Dutchess County Door Ways* . . . 84–6 and Plates 5, 6, 54, 101, 102, 194.) Door, with bull's eyes in lights, is now built into Gillet house, 263 Wolcott Ave., Beacon (letter of Edwin R. Corwin, Historian of Beacon, Jan. 21, 1955, to whom I am indebted for other particulars). This was scene of Alexander and Betsey's first housekeeping.

73. HLC.

74. Tilghman wrote from HQ April 27, 1781, as though the "gulf" had separated them some time; he would not attempt "walking upon the waters," but would "go over" to see Hamiltons soon (1 JCHW 219–20). That H was still in close touch with HQ appears from letter from Schuyler, Saratoga, April 29, 1781 (*ibid.*, 222–3).

75. Feb. 18, 1781 (9 LHW 236–7). He might take place of Lt. Col. [Thomas] Forrest, who wished to retire, but drawbacks on score of late-dated commission and renewed artillery studies gave light infantry superior appeal. Lafayette had beckoned him southward for field service (April 10, 15, 1781, 1 JCHW 218, 219). See ALS, Carter (Church) to H, May 18 (3 HLC 381), and ALS, Schuyler to same, May 30, 1781 (*ibid.*, 386).

76. De Peyster's Point, April 27, 1781 (9 LHW 238–9).

77. When Maj. Macpherson, holding a brevet commission, was appointed to command Pa. troops in light infantry, Aug. 1, 1780, line officers of that state instantly protested to Washington against injury to their rank, threatening resign (G.O., 19 GW 299). Ten days later in long letter to Brig. Gens. Wayne and Irvine over Washington's signature, H justified assignment in every view. He had own claims in mind when wrote: "Military rank and an eligibility to military command . . . cannot be separated" (Aug. 11, 1780, *ibid.*, 353–8). Macpherson's assignment at time appointment to command gave umbrage does not appear from Heitman, 281.

78. Immediately after return from Newport (when H was not at HQ) Washington had to quiet the dissatisfaction of Lt. Col. Jas. Mellen and six

other field officers who "were hurt at the appointment of Colo. Gemat and Majr. Galvan to commands in the detachment which marched. . . ." Even Heath was ruffled because not he but Lafayette was sent south at head of 800-man detachment (21 GW 342-4).

79. Commissions in line for aides were at this time under consideration by Washington and Congress (see general's letter of Dec. 20, 1780, 20 GW 501-5 and his "Remarks on Report of a Committee of Congress" on this letter, April 3, 1781, 21 *ibid.*, 403-10). Comm. report on Washington's revisions was passed May 25 (20 JCC 541). Pertinent provision was: ". . . officers not annexed to any line, serving . . . as aids-de-camps with . . . general officers, retain the rank they now hold, and shall be eligible to command upon detachments. . . ." Tilghman was commissioned in the line as lt. col. to rank from April 1, 1777; McHenry was made major "in the army of the United States" from Oct. 30, 1780. Not clear how H received commission making him specifically eligible for line duty prior to May 25, 1781, as he claimed in application to Washington of April 27, 1781.

80. 22 GW 2-3.

81. 9 LHW 240-2.

82. In postscript he distinguished between brevet, as Congress appeared to understand it, and his own "regular commission." Cf. to Laurens earlier (probably April 1780): "By your appointment as aide-de-camp to the commander-in-chief, you had as much the rank of lieutenant-colonel as any officer in the line" (9 LHW 185; truncated, and apparently out of sequence, in 1 JCHW 109-11).

83. See pp. 195-6.

84. In copy in 3 HLC 352-74 his hand does not begin until p. 18 and continues for 20 pp.; remainder is in several hands, especially that of Mrs. H. Work on it at places supposed fits his explanation to Morris that he had lacked materials and leisure for accurate calculations (1 JCHW 224-5).

85. 2 JCHW 171-5.

86. He was purchasing agent for French forces.

87. 3 HLC 381; personal allusions, not printed in 1 JCHW 261-2, imply he was not at Albany. Cf. Noailles, May 10, 1781, wishing be remembered to Washington (1 JCHW 261). Certainly not there May 30, 1781, when Schuyler wrote him from home, expected find H at Fishkill ten days later (*ibid.*, 265-6).

88. 1 H 374, omitting mention of Wethersfield conference, attributed results of it to earlier one at Newport.

89. May 30, 1781 (1 JCHW 265-6); cf. same to same, Sept. 16, 1781.

90. Only three days after, financier sent famous entreaty to Schuyler, as famously answered. Morris, hardly entered on office, found "an empty Treasury and a totally exhausted Credit," but "Gen. Washington is distressed for want of an immediate supply of Flour. . . . I request that you will take the most speedy . . . measures to deliver to . . . His Excy . . . One Thousand Barrells. . . . you can upon your own credit . . . either borrow the money . . . or . . . make the purchases on . . . credits . . . , and for your reimbursm. you may either take me as a Public or a private man for I pledge myself to repay you. . . ." (ALS, Phila., May 29, 1781, Schuyler Papers, NYPL).

91. May 26, 1781 (1 JCHW 264–5).

92. 2 R 231, though here visit placed slightly earlier.

93. John Carter (Church) to H, May 18, 1781, *op. cit.*

94. These papers appeared in Loudon's *N.Y. Packet,* published, during the British occupation, at Fishkill. Prefatory note to printer dated Fishkill, July 12, 1781, four days after he had in fact gone to camp at Dobbs Ferry (to Mrs. H, July 10, 1781, 1 JCHW 266). He spoke of submitting then only first number; possible, but unlikely, succeeding ones, through fourth, were prepared in camp. These came out promptly, July 12, 19, Aug. 9, 30, 1781, and two last not until April 18, July 4, 1782. (All are in 1 LHW 243–87.) None of ms. now in HLC except outside sheet, marked by him "No. 1 . . . July 12, 1781."

95. 1 LHW 238.

96. Earlier he had called adoption of Articles of Confederation "a happy event if it does not make people believe that the Confederacy gives Congress power enough and prevent their acquiring more" (Feb. 7, 1781, 9 LHW 230).

97. 1 LHW 286–7.

98. *Ibid.,* 244–60 n.

99. *Ibid.,* 261–7.

100. *Ibid.,* 267–77.

101. This became the inspiration of American nationalist school of economists typified in Mathew and Henry C. Carey. Further, these writers picked up H's emphasis on peculiar situation of America which rendered improper analogies with other societies in other climes and times. "There is a total dissimilarity in . . . circumstances . . . among us, and it is as ridiculous to seek for models in the small ages of Greece and Rome, as . . . to go in quest of them among the Hottentots and Laplanders" (*ibid.,* 282).

102. *Ibid.,* 279–87. Was evidently influenced by Hobbes's approval of making all mines of precious metals absolutely property of government.

Chapter 15 (Pages 249 to 261)
Capture of the Last Redoubt

1. July 10, 1781 (9 LHW 243). He quartered with Gen. Lincoln, at latter's invitation, and met courtesies in both armies.

2. 22 GW 438.

3. Cf. H to wife, 2 R 257.

4. Aug. 7, 1781 (1 JCHW 267–8). True, the men had received £30 each in bounty, but it was spent and the state would leave them barefoot.

5. 22 GW 484–5.

6. 2 *Diaries* 24. Lafayette, day before, had written Washington, "Should a French Fleet now come in Hampton Road the British Army would . . . be ours" (July 31, 1781, LOLTW 213; cf. same to same, Aug. 6, 1781, *ibid.*, 216).

7. LOLTW 215–17; 23 GW 12.

8. 9 LHW 244–5. Letter is without date, and previous one, and another to Schuyler for purpose of gradually intimating to her the disagreeable truth, are not preserved. Dr. Thacher, Aug. 15, preparing to cross into N.J., rather thought Washington intended attacking N.Y. City (*Mil. Jnl.*, 268–9).

9. General orders, Aug. 19, 1781 (23 GW 19; cf. Fish, LS March 21, 1822, to Mrs. H, 84 HLC 13645). Washington (2 *Diaries* 255), describing light infantry that were to form van of American force, mentioned these Conn. companies to be joined with two of N.Y.; lack of punctuation leaves doubt whether H thus received a net addition to his command, or whether Conn. men replaced light companies of First and Second N.Y. Regts., which may not have arrived.

10. Washington, *ibid.*, 256. All Americans were across the 21st, French not till 25th (Cromot du Bourg in 4 *Mag. Am. Hist.* 376).

11. Washington, *ibid.*

12. *Ibid.*, 257.

13. Dr. Thacher recorded of Laurens, "We have the pleasing information that he has brought with him from France a large sum of specie for the United States" (Aug. 31, 1781, *Mil. Jnl.*, 269).

14. See *ibid.*, 271 ff., for particulars of crossing the Delaware, being pulled over "a small river at Shammany's rope ferry," and Phila. procession.

15. See Freeman, 5 *Washington* 318–21 for account of commander in chief's anxiety.

16. Washington, 2 *Diaries* 258–9.

17. 9 LHW 246; arrival of De Grasse was announced in G.O. Sept. 6, 1781 (23 GW 93–4).

18. Thacher, sailing Sept. 11 from Head of Elk, was more than a night in 18-mile stretch to Bay and, with detention at Annapolis, reached Jamestown, on opposite side of peninsula from Yorktown, only after 12 days. (*Mil. Jnl.,* 271, 275).

19. 2 R 260, original not found.

20. Letters of Barber, to wife and to Col. Elias Dayton, punctuating months of maneuvers that made him thin "& something of the colour of an Indian," are in PHS and Morgan Lib.; requisition for his light infantry, Williamsburg, Sept. 25, 1781, is in NYPL, Emmet 4769.

21. Sept. 16, 1781 (3 HLC 391); these personal matters, omitted in 1 JCHW 270, concerned the absent soldier more immediately than could Schuyler's forecast that friends in the legislature, to meet in a fortnight, would propose H for Congress.

22. 23 GW 134.

23. Sept. 25, 1781, Morgan Lib. and 23 GW 136–9, and n. Lafayette was to deliver this, with an appeal from Rochambeau. No confirmation found of report (2 R 262) H accompanied marquis.

24. *Correspondence of . . . Washington and . . . De Grasse . . . Aug. 17–Nov. 4, 1781,* 51–2.

25. Elias Dayton Papers, 9 NJHS Proceed. (1864) 187 n.

26. William Feltman, *Journal . . . 1781–2* (PHS 1853, pp. 48, 15).

27. Feltman, *Jnl.*

28. Cornwallis, Portsmouth in Va., July 27, 1781, to Sir Henry Clinton (*Campaign in Virginia, 1781,* B. F. Stevens, compiler, II, 108, and returns, 197, 198), and Clinton, *American Rebellion,* 328 ff.

29. Feltman, *ibid.,* 16; 1 Pickering 303, MHS, among others, reported that "It was barbarously done; for, after two dragoons had him their prisoner, a third came up and shot him through the side. Of this wound he died the 6th . . . at Williamsburg. . . ."

30. Sept. 30, 1781 (LOLTW 233). It is not clear whether this was done, for by G.O., Oct. 8, Laurens was to command half the troops lately Scammell's (23 GW 199).

31. Feltman, *ibid.*, 19. G.O. Oct. 10 (23 GW 204–5); Knox, Camp before York, Oct. 21, 1781, to John Adams (Morgan Lib.).

32. Thacher, *op. cit.*, 283–4.

33. Excellent contemporary maps of the siege, containing, in legends as well as locations, much not to be gathered from narratives, are those of Sebastian Bauman, Phila., 1782; Jean-Baptiste Gouvion, Washington, 1952, U.S. Arch., Facsimile No. 21; John Hills, London, 1785; Fage, London, 1782.

34. This was done the night of the 11th–12th. Lt. Feltman (*op. cit.*, 19) was there with another officer in charge of a detail of 82 Pennsylvanians. Every second man, in addition to an entrenching tool, carried out a fascine. They had themselves covered in an hour. But as we know, both assault parties were to start at the same signal and to arrive at the forts at the same time. From what is known of assaults on Redoubts 9 and 10, epaulement must have been about 500 yards east and slightly north of where Freeman conjectured (5 *Washington* 366 and n.).

35. Feltman, 19.

36. Could not be seen in flight in daylight, made little noise in descent (Feltman, 20).

37. 2 Washington *Diaries* 266–7; 23 GW 229; anon. diary in 7 *Mag. Am. Hist.* 223.

38. Sept. 30, 1781 (LOLTW 234–5).

39. Rochambeau's rept., in Henri Doniol, *Histoire de la Participation de la France à L'Établissement des États-Unis* . . . V, 578–9. Rochambeau designated Major General Vioménil, who placed under him Lt. Col. Guillaume de Deux-Ponts and, second, Lt. Col. L'Estrade.

40. Lafayette's report to Washington, Oct. 16, 1781 (LOLTW 235–6); H's report to Lafayette, Oct. 15, 1781 (copy in 3 HLC 393–4, printed 9 LHW 247). Lafayette's answers to queries concerning H., n.d., copy, 84 HLC 13718; 2 R 268, citing a letter of Fish, not found, had it that precedence was first given, by Washington, to Lt. Col. Barber, who had made Virginia campaign with Lafayette; Fish shared H's tent and mess during siege (LS, Fish to Mrs. H, March 21, 1822, 84 HLC 13645–6). C. J. McCarthy, "Lieut. Col. Francis Barber of Elizabethtown," in 50 NJHS Proceed. 273–84, an account full of errors, adopted story it was Barber who was supplanted. Henry Lee (*op. cit.*, 501 n.), reporting conversation with H at Yorktown, did not differ essentially from Lafayette; cf. R, above, misreading Galvan, in Lee's story, for Gimat, and Freeman, 5 *Washington* 369, putting H's claim over Gimat on prior date of commission.

41. Lafayette to Washington and H to Lafayette, above (LOLTW 235–6, 9 LHW 247).

42. Feltman, 20.

43. Time recorded varied; Washington noted 6:30 (2 *Diaries* 266–7); Cromot du Bourg, aide to Rochambeau (4 *Mag. Am. Hist.* 447) and Thacher, (*op. cit.,* 283–4) said eight o'clock; Lee, (*op. cit.,* 500) "as soon as it was dark."

44. Wm. de Deux-Ponts, *My Campaigns in America,* Samuel A. Green, trans. and ed., 143.

45. Tarleton, *History of Campaigns of 1780 and 1781* . . . , 385, said Hamilton's force assaulted "from the American works," and that of Vioménil "proceeded from the French trenches." Gaspard de Gallatin (*Journal of Siege of Yorktown,* 11) mentioned that French troops "issued by the right flank of the American battery," which seems to have been from extreme right of second parallel. Lee (*op. cit.,* 501) had simply from "their respective posts."

46. In this Lafayette and H rejected advice of Vioménil, who urged on them an elaborate maneuver (Lafayette, 84 HLC 13718).

47. First-hand accounts are H's report to Lafayette, and Lafayette's to Washington, above; Dr. Thacher (*Mil. Jnl.,* 285) was called to wounded in redoubt "even before the balls had ceased whistling about my ears. . . ." Washington, dismounted, in exposed place awaiting result (*ibid.*) described assaults on both redoubts (2 *Diaries* 266–7); Knox witnessed scene with Washington, related it briefly, Oct. 21 to John Adams (ALS, Morgan Lib.); Lamb (Leake, *op. cit.,* 279) got his particulars at siege. Rochambeau's rep't to Washington (5 Doniol 578–9), Vioménil's to Rochambeau (Deux-Ponts, *op. cit.,* 157, mistakenly dated 1783), and Deux-Ponts' own (*ibid.,* 142 ff.), all allude to progress of American attack. British commander was doubtless Maj. Patrick Campbell, 44th Regt., whose commission dated from 1772, though a capt. of same name and unit was commissioned 1768 (W. C. Ford, comp., *British Officers* . . . *in the Am. Rev.*). Lamb offered incident of H reaching parapet from shoulder of one of his men (Leake, *op. cit.,* 279 and n.; not in 1 H 382 but picked up in 2 R 269), but his information was remote; referred to picture, suggested by a law pupil of H.

48. *History of Rise, Progress, Establishment of Independence of U.S.* . . . III, 257–8. Thacher, *op. cit.,* 284–5, had variant account. Lafayette and Washington did not figure, nor did New London massacre of prisoners by Arnold's men; in redoubt a capt., of N. Hampshire, threatened to kill Maj. Campbell to avenge death of his friend Col. Scammell, but H interposed; cf. Lee, *op. cit.,* 501, with substitution of McPherson for Campbell. J.C.H. credited this (1 H 384; 2 R 270), and H himself seemed to do so (rep't to Lafayette, above, and in *N.Y. Ev. Post,* Aug. 10, 1802, below).

49. Letter to ed. *N.Y. Ev. Post,* Aug. 10, 1802; also in 2 R 271; *Mag. Am. Hist.,* 363.

50. To H, March 31, 1803. He told another friend he had seen the "atrocious absurdity" in Berlin newspaper, but added, frankly, that Dr. Gordon misconstrued remark of his own that troops would be merciful, notwithstanding their generals had spoken of reprisals (to M. de Archenholz, Sept. 20, 1804, both in *Mag. Am. Hist., ibid.,* 363–7); see later allusion by Lafayette, 84 HLC 13718.

51. Detailed accounts are in the French reports above, especially those of Deux-Ponts, Gallatin; cf. Washington, 2 *Diaries* 266–7.

52. *Diaries, ibid.* Cf. G.O., Oct. 15, 1781 (23 GW 223), congratulating Allied army and adding, "The General reflects with the highest degree of pleasure on the Confidence which the Troops of the two Nations must hereafter have in each other."

53. Lee, *op. cit.,* 503, Oct. 16, 1781 (23 GW 231); Cornwallis, Oct. 15, 1781, in cipher (*Campaign in Va., 1781,* 188); Tarleton, *Hist. Campaigns 1780 and 1781,* 387; H to wife, 9 LHW 250; Washington to Schuyler, Oct. 27, 1781, (23 GW 280), and Laurens to Meade, below.

54. LS, Cornwallis, Morgan Lib.

55. *Journal,* 37–8.

56. J. Laurens, near York[town], Oct. 22, 1781, to R. K. Meade (copy, 3 HLC 396–7), summarizing negotiations and articles of surrender. 2 R 273, on authority of Fish, said Washington consulted H on subject.

57. ALS, J. Laurens, camp before York, Oct. 19, 1781, Morgan Lib. [to one of British commissioners], "I am instructed to inform you that the Generals of the Allied Army will be at the Redout on the right of our second parallel at 9 o'Clock this morning—when they expect to receive Ld Cornwallis's definitive Answer and sign the capitulation." Site has been mostly destroyed by falling in of bluff, but companion fort, No. 9, has been reconstructed, with other earthworks of siege, by U.S. Govt.

58. 2 *Pictorial Field Book* 318–20. G.O., Oct. 18, 1781 (23 GW 238), contain nothing concerning surrender ceremony. On O'Hara, see Jonathan Trumbull's *Minutes,* 337. Currier print (1852) of Trumbull's painting of surrender shows H in group with Fish, Stewart, Laurens, all in low beavers, with egrets. Colored steel engraving of J. F. Reneult's (partly fanciful) rendering has H, in a good likeness, between Washington and Rochambeau. Spirited black-and-white engraving, by Fontaine, of Couder's painting, has Rochambeau and Washington "donnent derniers ordres pour l'Attaque," with H, presumably, in foreground, Deux-Ponts farther off (all in Morgan Lib.).

59. Washington, Oct. 27, 1781, to Schuyler (23 GW 280); H had left camp before Washington could send letter by him.

60. Schuyler to Duane (whom H was sorry not to stop to seeJ, Dec. 6, 1781 (Duane Papers, NYHS). However, Hamilton's friend Fleury wrote Duane about victory (York[town], Oct. 31, 1781): "we shall I hope by this last blow, get the better, of the british obstinacy, to enslave america. . . ." And in postscript, "I Din'd yesterday with Lord Cornwallys & o'hara. I was so bold as to inquire of the last, why they took so many nigros. by god, said he, we had no other allieds Left in this Country. you forget did I answer, your faithfull friends the indians" (ALS, Duane Papers, NYHS).

61. Cf. G.O. Dec. 27, 1777 (10 GW 215); Trevelyan, 3 *Am. Rev.* 328–9.

62. An official and a personal letter, March 1, 1782 (9 LHW 251–3). Cf. to Meade, March 1782, *ibid.*, 253–5, in which he said more plainly his difficulty in securing a command last campaign deterred him from applying again. Magnanimous renunciation of any further payment for his past services raised difficulties for his widow years later.

63. *Journal*, 38.

Chapter 16 (Pages 262 to 276)
Apprenticeship with Robert Morris

1. For list of those serving during H's incumbency, see U.S. Supt. of Finance, *Statement of Accounts of U.S.*, Feb. 20, 1781 to Nov. 1, 1784; cf. Oberholtzer, *Robert Morris*, 141–3.

2. Sept. 3 1780, (1 JCHW 163). Morris gave cogent reasons for avoiding dependence on the clamorous loan officers: they were delinquent in settling their accounts, many were unfit, and funds in their hands, before they could reach Congress for immediate war purposes, would be raided by security holders demanding interest (12 *Diplomatic Correspondence of Am. Rev.*, Sparks ed., 253–4, n.).

31. Cf. R. Benson to Duane (July 23, 1782, Duane Papers, NYHS). tion of H's letter on finance, by which he had profited (*ibid.*, 265); H had preferred Morris for post of Supt. (*ibid.*, 159, 224), and Morris must have known that the younger man had himself been mentioned for the national office.

4. *Ibid.*, 278–9; invitation was at friendly instance of Col. Charles Stewart, late Commissary General of Issue; a mezzotint of him is in Myers 558, NYPL.

5. May 18, 1782 (1 JCHW 279–80); cf. Abr. Yates, Jr., draft AL to Duane and L'Hommedieu, Oct. 19, 1782 (Yates Papers, NYPL).

6. June 4, 1782 (1 JCHW 280). H had not misinterpreted offer of "one fourth per cent. on the moneys you receive"; Morris in second letter contradictorily said his intention had been for larger sum, twice what H had calculated.

7. *Ibid.*, 281–2. Four months later, when about to resign the office, he told Abr. Yates, Jr., he "would have [accept?] no pay for what he had Done" (Yates, to Duane, L'Hommedieu, above).

8. June 17, 1782 (1 JCHW 281–2). He at once sought estimates from Duer and Sands of disbursements for army supplies in N.Y.; see to Sands, June 22, 1782 (*ibid.*, 282–3); Duer, ALS, Albany, Aug. 16, 1782 (4 HLC 451).

9. Morris said "what remains of the war [is] only a war of finance" (1 JCHW 285).

10. To R. Morris, July 13, 1782 (*ibid.*, 286).

11. 2 *Votes and Proceed., N.Y. Senate*, 80; a quorum was not present until July 11 (p. 79).

12. *Ibid.*, 37 ff. From Feb. 23 to May 14, 1782, legislature heard complaint of unpaid N.Y. infantry regiments (41), public purchasing agents pursued by creditors (*ibid.*), districts demanding their taxes be reduced or remitted (48, 50, 54, 57). An act did give a monopoly in N.Y. to Bank of N. Am. (51). Legislators found specie to pay own salaries (66).

13. 1 JCHW 286.

14. July 16, 1782 (*ibid.*, 287).

15. *Votes and Proceed., ibid.*, 84.

16. Gov. thought tax laws were "founded in Justice," yet arrearages were so great, "there must be some Defect in our System," and he recommended revision of mode of collection. (*Votes and Proceed., ibid.*, 80; cf. 82).

17. Cf. *ibid.*, 86.

18. Cf. *ibid.*, 84.

19. *Ibid.*, 88.

20. Malcolm, J. Lawrence, Stagg, Bachelor, Hopkins, from Assembly; Schuyler, Yates, Paine from Senate (*Votes and Proceed., ibid.*, 92).

21. Sept. 7, 1782 (Duane Papers, NYPL).

22. ALS, Sept. 15, 1782 (Abr. Yates Papers, NYPL).

23. Letters of Yates of Oct. 19, Nov. 1, 4, and L'Hommedieu, Oct. 28, 1782 (Yates Papers, NYPL).

24. 12 *Dipl. Corr. Am. Rev.* 253 n.

25. ALS, Albany, Aug. 13, 1782 (HLC unbnd. Box 1).

26. "A Freeholder," 1786, Yates Papers, NYPL; cf. draft ALS Yates to Howell, of R.I., July 12, Aug. 29, 1785. A mezzotint of Yates (round face, with glasses, powdered hair, and tricorn) is in Myers 591, NYPL.

27. *Votes and Proceed., ibid.,* 89.

28. *Ibid.,* 91–2; cf. ALS, Clinton, Poughkeepsie, Aug. 5, 1782, to Duane at Phila. (Duane Papers NYHS), reporting with apparent approval joint resolution "for amending the Confederation by giving the Government of the American Empire more Energy. . . ."

29. 1 JCHW 287–9; date given as May, for July 22, 1789; correct in 9 LHW 264–6; reports H's representations to legislature to time he left it, two days before adjournment. Surely he and Schuyler had induced agreement of both houses that Cong. should readjust quota of N.Y. as Morris recommended (*Votes and Proceed., ibid.,* 90, 93).

30. *Ibid.,* 91.

31. Cf. R. Benson to Duane (July 23, 1782, Duane Papers, NYHS).

32. His son's account (1 H 398), probably had from Mrs. H. Troup was himself a fledgling; he was admitted by Sup. Ct. of Judicature to practice as attorney April 23, 1782 (Minute Bk., July 31, 1781 to Nov. 1, 1783, p. 145; in Record Rm., N.Y. County Clerk).

33. Troup, 3d ser., 2 *W&M Quar.,* 215. Troup was confused, writing 30 years later, about time of his tutorial residence with H, which he placed in spring, 1783, after H left Congress, instead of year earlier. J.C.H. (1 H 398 n.) said men were living who had copied manual as a guide; quarter-century later (1858, 2 R 282 n.) he learned such a transcript was in existence. A dozen pp. of notes in H's hand, seemingly concerning Schuyler's landholdings, probably belong to period of legal study at Albany (Hamilton Papers, NYPL). Apparently he talked with tenants and jotted down their information about boundaries, perhaps to supplement vagueness of Indian deed, of March 24, 1668, here included.

34. In Assn. of Bar of City of N.Y. Judging from signatures on flyleaves, this copy was used by Abraham Van Vechten (1762–1837, admitted to practice 1785), H. J. Bleecker, another with initials "H.B.H.," one or more of whom may have been in law school of Peter Van Schaack, commenced at Kinderhook in 1786. See B. Mitchell in *Record* of Bar Assn., vol. 11, No. 4, 210–11.

35. He referred to Burrows, various English statutes. English handbooks he consulted might be those of Robt. Richardson, John Impey, Geoffrey Gilbert, Wm. Style, John Lilly. Appearance of Wm. Wyche's *Treatise on*

Practice of Sup. Ct. of Judicature of N.Y. in Civil Actions (1794) must have superseded use of H's work. Whether H had benefited from two earlier American works—Jas. Parker's *Conductor Generalis* (1764) and *Young Clerk's Vade Mecum* (1776)—is doubtful. Cf. for H's study, P. M. Hamlin, *Legal Education in Colonial N.Y.* (1939).

36. Minute Bk., Sup. Ct. of Judicature, July 31, 1781 to Nov. 1, 1783, April 26, 1782, p. 151. Mr. Chief Justice Morris and Mr. Justice Hobart presided.

37. See certification of P. W. Yates and Troup in his behalf, Min. Bk., *ibid.*, 365.

38. This is from parchment "Roll of Attornies of . . . Sup. Ct. of . . . N.Y., 1754–95" (Record Rm., N.Y. Co. Clerk); no session of ct. recorded between April 27 and July 31, 1782, and no notation of his admission as attorney found in later minutes.

39. To Meade, Aug. 27, 1782 (9 LHW 284).

40. Min. Bk., *op. cit.*, 245, 289. His mentor, Troup, admitted attorney before him, was not made counselor until six months after, April 15, 1783 (p. 360–1); directly afterward ordered no one be admitted counselor who had not practiced in state two years as attorney (367).

41. To Morris, July 22, 1782 (9 LHW 266).

42. 9 LHW 266–8; Morris's circular in 11 *Diplomatic Corr.* (Sparks) 400–405.

43. 1 JCHW 290. Clinton's empty response (Aug. 13, 1782, *ibid.*, 295–6) showed H's apprehensions were well founded.

44. Aug. 5, 1782, *ibid.*, 292–3.

45. To Benson, Aug. 18, 1782, unbnd. Box 1, HLC; hearing nothing, three weeks later sent Benson a duplicate (4 HLC 463).

46. July 31, 1782 (4 HLC 433).

47. July 22, 1782 (9 LHW 266).

48. Aug. 13, 1782 (*ibid.*, 269–73).

49. *Ibid.*, 273–6.

50. *Ibid.*, 276–7. H said only that letter of Morris, referred to, was written in previous winter or spring. Morris (to H, Aug. 28, 1782; Sparks, 12 *Dip. Corr.* 249) supposed it was to Clinton, Dec. 11, 1781 (*ibid.*, 63–6), saying legislature must substitute taxes for commodity supplies; another possibility, though Morris did not name it, was circular to all governors, May 16, 1782 (*ibid.*, 151–3), declaring states had been "deaf to the calls of

Congress, to the clamors of the public creditors, to the just demands of a suffering army. . . ."; cf. H to Morris, Sept. 28, 1782 (9 JCHW 293); see complaints that Financier underrated efforts of N.Y. (ALS, Duane, April 7, 1782, to Washington, and ALS, Schuyler May 30, 1782, to Duane, Duane Papers, NYHS).

51. 9 LHW 277–80. He closed by observing army contractor in that quarter (Duer) gave satisfaction; cf. Duer, Aug. 2, 1782, to Willett (Willett Papers, NYPL).

52. This most private part of letter, dozen pp., omitted, with much else, in I JCHW 293–5, with no indication of excision; similarly 9 LHW 269–80. Neither editor had more than an autograph portion, now in 4 HLC 447–8. Mrs. Nixon, Morris's daughter, in 1844 scrupled to give Mrs. H full original (Henkels, [auction] Catalogue No. 1183, *Confidential Corr. of Robert Morris,* Phila., 1917, pp. 189–90, 112–3). Henkels printed letter complete "for the first time," n.p., n.d., 8 pp., copies in H Papers, NYPL. Original, entire, is in HLC unbnd. Box 1; Morris's endorsement has catchword "Characters." Seems was purchased by Dr. Allan McLane H for $2,000 (ms. note beside Item 251, Henkels, *ibid.*).

53. See below, p. 273.

54. Morris, Aug. 28, 1782 (4 HLC 457–8), thanked H warmly for "Descriptions of . . . Characters, Sentiments and Opinions. . . ."

55. Aug. 20, 1782 (1 JCHW 296–7). H replied (*ibid.,* 306) he was unable then to comply.

56. Aug. 25, 1782 (9 LHW 282).

57. 9 LHW 281: cf. Clinton to H, 1 JCHW 303. Statement of Bancker of taxes ordered and monies paid into N.Y. treasury, March 28, 1778 to March 6, 1780, has on back H's notation, "Estimating . . . average depreciation of [17] 79 at 25 to one . . . at 58 for one in [17] 80. . . ." (3 HLC 380).

58. LS, Morris to H, Sept. 6, 1782 (4 HLC 462).

59. 9 LHW 285–6; cf. H to Clinton, ALS, Aug. 25, 1782 (4 HLC 456).

60. Aug. 1, 1782 (4 HLC 434), Aug. 31, 1782 (9 LHW 284–5); Sept. 7, 14, 21, 1782 (*ibid.,* 284 ff.); Morris's comprehensive request was July 25, 1781 (11 *Dip. Corr.* [Sparks], 400–405); by time H could answer, rates of depreciation Morris wanted reported were academic, for "the circulation has now totally ceased." Cf. H to Morris, July 22, 1782 (9 LHW 266).

61. Sept. 21, 1782 (9 JCHW 290–2); cf. to Morris, Oct. 9, 1782 (9 LHW 295–6). Duer, who surely talked with H at Albany, had been writing Morris with same plea (Morris to H, Oct. 5, 1782, 1 JCHW 312–3). Few weeks earlier H noted on his copy of a letter to Financier: "The ability of a

people to pay taxes is in a compound ratio to the q[uantity? torn] of the property in a place and to the quickness of the circulation of property" (Oct. 13, 1782, 4 HLC 446).

62. To Morris, Sept. 14, 1782 (9 LHW 288–9).

63. To H, Aug. 28, 1782 (12 *Dip. Corr.* [Sparks] 248–52; in part in 1 JCHW 299–302).

64. ALS, Oct. 28, 1782 (4 HLC 489), acknowledging report of H not found. Cf. Morris's circular to governors, Oct. 21, 1782 (*Dipl. Corr., ibid.,* 286–91).

65. To Morris, Oct. 26, 1782 (9 LHW 302).

66. To H, Aug. 28, 1782 (1 JCHW 299). H's proposal of a prominent N.Y. citizen for Commr. of Accts. for state (July 22, 1782, 9 LHW 266) was not in line with Morris's policy of outsiders for this assignment. Financier accepted his nominations of Malcolm, Lawrence for R.I. and N.H., but both declined.

67. Sept. 28, 1782 (9 LHW 293; copy in 4 HLC 471 is in Mrs. H's hand), but later (Oct. 9, 1782) he promised to send address adopted (*ibid.,* 296).

68. Cf. 2 R 315.

69. This anticipated his later conspicuous refusal to allow a distinction between original holders and subsequent purchasers of the debt.

70. 2 R 309–12.

71. *Ibid.,* 313–14.

72. Cf. H to Noailles [1782] (9 LHW 300). Whether Morris saw funded debt as basis of circulation, in his letter to H (Aug. 28, 1782, 12 *Dip. Corr.* (Sparks) 251), is doubtful.

73. After, as evidenced by his letters to Morris at this time.

74. Rough correspondence of conclusions of comm. (H to Morris, Oct. 5, 1782, 9 JCHW 294–5) with H's scheme indicates as much.

75. Cf. Morris to Pres. of Congress, Feb. 27, July 29 (12 *Dip. Corr.* [Sparks] 226 ff.), Oct. 5, 1782 (22 JCC 429 ff.); H's appreciation, 9 LHW 293.

76. His conjectures about quantities of property of different kinds, division of population by employments, and consumption habits, furnish informed opinion on economy of N.Y. at the time.

77. A bank, to be incorporated on condition of furnishing one-eighth of its income to loan office, was merely mentioned.

78. He calculated taxes, exclusive of import duties, would yield some £51,000; we may assume he thought imports would produce, for state treasury, £20,000 to £30,000.

79. 4 HLC 487–512, partially printed in 2 JCHW 204–11. If H also drew up at this time plan of a lottery (2 R 304), it has not been found.

80. Aug. 13, 1782 (9 LHW 279).

81. Sept. 28, 1782 (*ibid.*, 293).

82. July 29, 1782, 12 *Dip. Corr.* (Sparks) 226 ff., Morris urged low single rate would compel monopolizers to relinquish land to govt. or otherwise pass it "into the hands of those who would use it for the benefit of society,"—a remarkable anticipation of Henry George's expedient a century later.

83. To Morris, Oct. 5 (9 LHW 294–5).

84. ALS, Sands, Livingston & Co. to H, Sept. 25, 1782 (4 HLC 470), and H to Morris, Oct. 9, 1782 (9 LHW 295–6).

85. Albany, Oct. 26, 1782 (9 LHW 302–3); most of retained copy (4 HLC 479) is in Mrs. H's hand. See list of papers, relating to Receiver's office, receipted for by Tillotson, n.d. (*ibid.*, 486). For last quarter of 1782, H received in taxes in N.Y. $5,209 8/90 and paid into Treasury $6,250. H not mentioned in Morris's *Statement of Accts. of U.S., 1781–4,* after first quarter of 1783. For difficulties of any N.Y. receiver, Morris to Tillotson, Oct. 15, 1783 (Bancroft Trans., 2 Rev. Papers 467, NYPL).

86. Albany, Nov. 3, 1782 (9 LHW 304); cf. to De Noailles, about this time (*ibid.*, 296–300), somewhat more hopefully.

Chapter 17 (Pages 277 to 294)

"We Must Pledge an Ascertained Fund. . . ."

1. 23 JCC 750–51; the certificate, Oct. 25, was attested by Robert Harpur as Depy. Sec., the same who had been H's tutor at King's. All but H's were reelections.

2. *Ibid.*, and Madison to Randolph, Nov. 26, 1782, in Burnett, 6 *Letters of Members of Continental Congress* 549. Duane, eager for leave, expected H and Floyd would arrive "pretty early in the . . . month," but had to stretch both his patience and his purse (to Gov. of N.Y., Oct. 9, 1782, *ibid.*, 502).

3. 23 JCC 754, 755.

4. For the reflections of N.Y. members preceding arrival of H and Floyd, see Scott, Duane, and L'Hommedieu in 6 Burnett, 327–8, 365, 386, 490–1, 521–2, 531, 540–2.

5. 9 LHW 303–4.

6. Aug. 15, 1782; 9 LHW 280–81, and n.

7. Williams called Laurens "That sensible, gallant, elegant fellow." H to Greene, Oct. 12, 1782 (9 LHW 301).

8. H to Greene, *ibid.;* anticipating entering Congress H told Meade, "I shall endeavor to do all the good I can" (Aug. 27, 1782, *ibid.,* 284).

9. July 25, 1783 (9 LHW 382).

10. See, e.g., Jensen, *The New Nation, A History of . . . U.S. During . . . Confederation. . . .*

11. To Jay, July 25, 1783 (9 LHW 381–2).

12. Complaint was not so much of those who came to Congress as of those who, duly elected, absented themselves, e.g., Chase of Md., Rodney of Del.

13. To Randolph, Nov. 19, 1782, in 6 Burnett 545–6; cf. 549.

14. 23 JCC 757–8.

15. *Ibid.,* 758–62.

16. *Ibid.,* 765–9, H and Floyd to gov. of N.Y. Dec. 9, 1782 (6 Burnett 557–8); cf. L'Hommedieu [Nov.] and Duane to same, Nov. 15, 1782 (*ibid.,* 540–41).

17. 23 JCC 770 ff. Madison in notes on debates of this day (*ibid.,* 863–4) said Pa. would resume appropriating herself (from proceeds of requisitions she raised) for the satisfaction of her citizens unless Congress made effectual provision. This spurred H to press R.I. Cf. R.I. delegates to gov., Dec. 7, 1782 (6 Burnett 556), also Va. delegates to gov., probably Dec. 10, 1782 (*ibid.,* 558–9), exhorting to fuller compliance with impost, and Madison, same date, to Randolph (*ibid.,* 559–60).

18. 23 JCC 863–4, Madison's notes; cf. Howell, Oct. 16, to Carter, Oct. 18, 1782, to Greene (6 Burnett 510–12), supporting letters to gov. of R.I., Oct. 13 and 15, damning impost in all its parts, and calling on legislature to reject it (*ibid.,* 502–7).

19. Thus, "Congress have demanded of you an immediate answer in regard to the Impost. . . . After Congress shall have obtained a . . . permanent revenue at their disposal, will it not be a Temptation . . . to vote themselves Perpetual. . . ." (6 Burnett 503–7).

20. 23 JCC 788–90.

21. 23 JCC 799–800.

22. 23 JCC 798 ff.

23. *Ibid.*, 867, Madison's notes for Dec. 16, 1782. Madison must have postdated his letter of Dec. 17 to Randolph (6 Burnett 564); cf. Arnold, Jan. 8, 1783 (7 Burnett 7–10).

24. Howell had been granted leave of absence Dec. 12, and John Collins had arrived in his place, but, as Arnold explained to gov., Dec. 18, "Mr. Howell is still here, . . . Congress having taken measures . . . relative to his public Conduct, which renders his stay of absolute necessity" (6 Burnett 565–6).

25. 23 JCC 812 and n.; cf. 1 *Secret Jnls. C.C.* 246 ff.

26. JCC, *ibid.*, 811–2.

27. *Ibid.*, 868, Madison's notes.

28. 23 JCC 867–8, Madison's notes. Naturally Howell's colleague, Arnold, put a different face on this (6 Burnett 565–6, cf. *ibid.*, 555–6; for lengthier review of incident, 7 *ibid.*, 7–10).

29. 24 JCC 45–6. When this history was ordered sent to R.I. executive, Arnold, fearing "the Constructions . . . and Colourings" of majority, wanted summary of "the Letters and papers themselves" transmitted (to gov. of R.I., above). Wolcott moved a preamble stigmatizing R.I. delegates. H composed the difficulty with justice (24 JCC 32, 35–6, 45–6; 23 *ibid.*, 822).

30. Osgood to Lincoln, Jan. 1 (7 Burnett 1); Wharton to Del. Council, Jan. 6 (*ibid.*, 3), Madison to gov. of Va., and to Randolph, Jan. 7, 1783 (*ibid.*, 6, 7).

31. Madison to Randolph, Dec. 24, 1782 (6 Burnett 568). Recession of Va. "by disarming [the deputation] of their most pointed argument . . . produced great hesitation." Cf. same to same, Dec. 30, 1783 (*ibid.*, 570).

32. 23 JCC 871–2, Madison's notes.

33. Madison to Randolph, above; Va. delegates to gov., *ibid.*, 570–71; official notice of Va.'s retraction was Jan. 27, 1783 (24 JCC 96).

34. 23 JCC 871–2, Madison's notes. Madison and his Va. colleagues besought Randolph and gov. to "be circumstantial . . . as to the parties and motives which led to the repeal. . . ." (Madison to Randolph, above, and Jan. 22, 1783; 7 Burnett 3). Unless Va. renewed the law "the example of a repeal may be followed by other States" and rob Congress of its best plea

to R.I. (Va. delegates to gov., above). But Gov. Harrison had "never heard a word of it till the Bill was laid on my table after the rising of the Assembly." He felt mortified to be obliged to acquiesce (7 Burnett 20 n.). Randolph observed that some of the proffered reasons sounded like echoes from R.I. (to Madison, Feb. 7, 1783, *ibid.*, 21 n.). Wharton of Del. was for dispatching deputations to R.I. *and* Va. (to Del. Council, Jan. 6, 1783, *ibid.*, 3). For assumption impost was in part unworthily inspired, see Jensen, *New Nation* . . . 63–7; for summaries not similarly suspicious, cf. Burnett, *Continental Congress*, 530–35, and *Letters*, xvi–xviii.

35. See 23 JCC 831–2 and n. for proceedings of Dec. 24, 1782, and postponements; cf. Madison to Randolph, Dec. 3, 1782, in 7 Burnett 550–55, for explanation of various solutions.

36. White to pres. of N.H., May 13, 1783 (7 Burnett 161).

37. White to Bartlett, Jan. 9, 1783 (*ibid.*, 13); 40 to 1 had been Robt. Morris's recommendation "in rigid adherence to his maxims of public faith" (Madison to Randolph, above).

38. 24 JCC 39–42.

39. Boudinot to Pintard, Dec. 24, 1782 (6 Burnett 567); H to Clinton (9 LHW 308–9); cf. Wolcott to wife (Burnett, *ibid.*, 569).

40. "Deranged", term in use then, might have been taken in the emotional sense to define state of forces under Washington at Newburgh. Three months earlier the commander in chief had written to the Sec. of War of discontent owing to "the total want of Money . . . and the prospect of poverty and Misery before them" (Oct. 2, 1782, 25 GW 226). In mid-Dec., 1782, he gave advance notice of what deputation of officers would present. "The dissatisfactions of the Army had risen to . . . alarming height," but "by some address . . . their resolutions have been converted into the form in which they will now appear before Congress" (to Jones, *ibid.*, 430).

41. Samuel Wharton forecast entreaty for "a settlement of . . . Accounts, an advance of the Amount of Them, and a satisfactory Assurance of half Pay." This renewed demand of creditors increased chagrin that R.I. had balked import duty (to Del. Council, Jan. 6, 1783, 7 Burnett 2). Immediately petition was presented, Madison felt similarly robbed of any reply (to Gov. of Va., Jan. 7, 1783, *ibid.*, 6).

42. See 24 JCC 291–3, and n.

43. 23 JCC 831, and n.

44. Jan. 12, 1783 (9 LHW 309). This was echoed by the knowing Abner Nash: "The truth is, the fault is in the constitution of Congress; and if these distresses should . . . point out a remedy . . . we shall by and by say . . . all is for the best" (to Iredell, 7 Burnett 19).

Chapter 18 (Pages 295 to 314)
". . . A Fatal Opposition to Continental Views"

1. Tortured progress of application in Congress is detailed in letter of McDougall and Ogden to Knox, Feb. 8, 1783 (7 Burnett 35–6, n.). Since all of this was *sub rosa*, the formal *Jnl.* intimates nothing; above is from Madison's notes (25 JCC 847–9).

2. 24 JCC 43–44, Jan. 10, 1783, proceedings from 1 *Secret Journals*, 252–3.

3. See references in letters at this juncture of White, Hamilton, Virginia delegates, and Wolcott, in 7 Burnett 13–20.

4. 25 JCC 852–3, Madison's notes.

5. *Ibid.*, 853; cf. 850–51.

6. 24 JCC 93–5. See res. of Comm. of Whole, Jan. 29 (*ibid.*, 97), adopted by Congress Feb. 12, 1783 (*ibid.*, 126–7), to this effect; in hand of Boudinot, sounds as though H guided his pen.

7. *Ibid.*, 112–13.

8. *Ibid.*, 114–16.

9. *Ibid.*, 114 n.; cf. H to Clinton, Jan. 12, 1783 (9 LHW 309), and 25 JCC 853–5, Madison's notes.

10. 24 JCC 135 ff. Lee and Madison, in Va. delegation, also voted No.

11. Use made of H's concept of national wealth by the Careys, Raymond, List, Rae, and more is indicated elsewhere. Sismondi and members of historical school of economists, though later, embraced same principle independently. Unified program of Tennessee Valley Authority, developing reciprocally all physical, mental, moral, and political abilities of region, and plans of United Nations for bringing forward poor countries are examples of same awareness.

12. Feb. 24, 1783 (9 LHW 313–322). He had introduced res. that in final adjustment of accounts allowances be made to states, like N.Y., parts of which had been in hands of enemy; lost 8 to 1, March 4, 1783 (24 JCC 163).

13. 24 JCC 170 ff.

14. *Ibid.*, 188 ff. Largest quota assigned was Va.'s, $256,487, smallest Georgia's, $16,030.

15. 25 JCC 928–45.

16. *Ibid.*, 929, Madison's notes.

17. *Ibid.*, 932–3, Madison's notes. He said candidly of Jay "that altho' . . . a man of profound sagacity & pure integrity, yet he was of a suspicious temper, & . . . this trait might explain the extraordinary jealousies which he professed."

18. 24 JCC 193–4.

19. *Ibid.*, 936, Madison's notes.

20. *Ibid.*, 940.

21. *Ibid.*, 942.

22. 24 JCC 210–11.

23. 25 *Ibid.*, 943–5, Madison's notes.

24. 7 Burnett 27–8.   Madison wrote Randolph (Feb. 11, 1783) that "after all the projects and discussions [over means to revenue] . . . we . . . have gone round in a circle to the point at which we set out. . . . The deputation from the army is waiting the upshot of all these delays and dilemmas" (*ibid.*, 40–41).   Two days later he confided in painful cipher his fear that "the arms which have secured the liberties of this country will not be laid down until justice is secured to those who have wielded them and that dangerous convulsions would be hazarded by orders for that purpose" (*ibid.*, 44).

25. 26 GW 185 n. gives date of H's letter as Feb. 13 or 17, as H wrote it over; 9 LHW 310 gives Feb. 7.   As Washington did not reply until March 4, latest date probably correct, and ms. seems to bear this out.

26. 9 LHW 310–13.   H's estimate of Washington, a few days later, in a caucus of friends of established revenue, is exactly pertinent here.   The resolve was hardening not to lay down arms until pay was in prospect, and leading characters in camp wanted to displace Washington for another who would advance their design.   "Mr. Hamilton said that he knew Gen. Washington intimately & perfectly, that his extreme reserve, mixed sometimes with a degree of asperity of temper, both of which were said to have increased of late, had contributed to the decline of his popularity; but that his virtue his patriotism and his firmness would . . . never yield to any dishonorable or disloyal plans . . . ; that he would sooner suffer himself to be cut into pieces; that . . . Mr. Hamilton . . . wished him to be the conductor of the army in their plans for redress. . . ." (25 JCC 906–7, Madison's notes).

27. Newburgh, March 4, 1783 (26 GW 185 ff.).

28. ". . . unless Congress have powers competent to all *general* purposes, . . . the blood we have spilt . . . will avail us nothing."

29. 26 GW 216–7; 24 JCC 296–7 (April 29, 1783). As early as Feb. 20 H had confided to close friends news of such agitation at Newburgh (25 JCC 906, Madison's notes).

30. GW *ibid.,* 217–8, 237 n.; 7 Burnett 71.

31. 9 LHW 323–6. H and others in Congress must have talked like Gouverneur Morris, who wrote to Gen. Knox (Feb. 7, 1783): ". . . the only wise Mode is for the army to connect themselves with the public Creditors of every Kind . . . to urge . . . general permanent Funds. . . . The army may now influence the Legislatures and if you will permit me a Metaphor from your own Profession after you have carried the Post the public Creditors will garison it for you" (7 Burnett 34–5, n.; 11 Knox Papers, 109, MHS).

32. 24 JCC 93 ff. H wrote the report presented Jan. 25, 1783.

33. This passed, nine states agreeing, March 22, 1783 (*ibid.,* 209–10); H approved with no benefit to himself, for he had renounced "all claim to the compensation attached to my military station during the war or after it. . . ." (cf. 183). Congress' action was announced to Washington same day by Bland (7 Burnett 92–3) and the next day by Boudinot (*ibid.,* 93–4) as joyful accomplishment. For earlier history of the legislation, cf. McDougall, Ogden to Knox, in *ibid.,* 34–5, n.

34. Washington to Pres. of Congress, March 16, 18, 1783 (26 GW 228 ff.; 24 JCC 300 ff.). H drew res. of Congress thanking commander in chief for his "prudence and . . . attachment to the welfare of the community" in resisting the attempts to create disturbances in army, and praising officers for their patriotism (24 JCC 306 n.). Officers' meeting was occasion of Washington's famous remark, in adjusting his glasses, that he had not only grown gray but blind in service of the army. Incident is ascribed by P. L. Ford (*Washington,* 56–7) to Col. David Cobb; "This little address, with the mode . . . of delivering it, drew tears from [many] of the officers." Story is told in ALS, Pickering, Nov. 12, 1825, to Fish (Fish Papers, Columbia Univ.); he denied that Washington read or alluded to letter said by John Armstrong (*U.S. Mag.,* Jan. 1823) to have come to him from Col. (John) Harvie, of Va., accusing H and Robt. and G. Morris of plot at seat of govt. to displace Washington. Cf. other Pickering-Fish corr., *ibid.,* and Johnson, 2 *Greene* 394 ff. In preparation for meeting with officers, Washington two days before (March 13) in G.O. made public res. of Congress of Jan. 25, which H helped frame, promising provision would be made for pay of army (26 GW 221–2). Cf. letters of Washington, *ibid.,* 229, 232, 245–6, which must have owed some of their vigor to H's suggestions.

35. 24 JCC 151, 268, 283–4. Morris had sent his letter of resignation Jan. 24, 1783, to take effect end of May unless proper provision was made (*ibid.,* 92 n.). "This letter," Madison recorded, "made a deep & solemn impression on Congress. It was considered . . . as ruinous . . . to do-

mestic & foreign credit; & as producing a vacancy which no one knew how
to fill, & which no fit man w.^d venture to accept." Wilson desponded, "since
the known firmness of Mr. Morris . . . w.^d render all attempts to dissuade
him fruitless. . . ." (25 *ibid.*, 862, Madison's notes). Feb. 26 Morris asked
his resignation be no longer kept secret, saying those who had trusted him
rather than govt. had right to know. Congress granted request (24 *ibid.*,
151) in "lengthy & warm debates" on a proposal to defer action. Bland
and Lee disparaged administration of Morris, threw oblique censure on his
character. "On the other side Mr. Wilson & Mr. Hamilton went into a
copious defence & Panegyric of Mr. Morris," and danger from his departure.
Most, fearing single financier might be supplanted by a board, of fateful
memory, postponed by referring Morris's resignation to still another committee (25 *ibid.*, 919–20; 24 *ibid.*, 165–8). For Washington's concern over
Morris's resignation, see letter of March 8, 1783 (26 GW 200–1).

36. Cadiz, Feb. 5, 1783, to Pres. of Congress is in 6 Wharton, *Rev. Dipl.
Corr.*, 237; cf. Boudinot to Washington, March 23, 1783, in 7 Burnett 93–4;
1 HLC 325–7. Congress gave thanks to Lafayette April 10, 1783, in res.
drafted by Peters, perhaps at H's suggestion (24 JCC 234).

37. March 24, 1783; 7 Burnett 94–5 gives verbatim; 9 LHW 327 edits
punctuation.

38. Newburgh, March 31, 1783 (26 GW 276–7).

39. 24 JCC 195 ff. Time limit was to remove fear that collections were
to service a perpetual debt. Jealousy of states was recognized in provision
collectors be inhabitants of states concerned—nominated by Congress, appointed by states, removable by Congress.

40. April 1, 1783; *ibid.*, 214–16, 224. Device of three-fifths of slaves was
to have worrisome future.

41. March 25, 1783 (9 LHW 328–30); comm. consisted of Osgood, Bland,
H, Wolcott, Peters (24 JCC 305–6, n.).

42. 9 LHW 330–31.

43. Bland, as well as H, had inquired of Washington whether army could
be disbanded without settlement (7 Burnett 106–8). Washington's reply
showed influence of H's recommendations: "We have now a National character to establish . . . let justice . . . be one of its characteristics, and
gratitude another" (26 GW 293–6).

44. April 4, 1783 (26 GW 291–3).

45. H mentioned, as main movers, Arthur Lee, whose accusations against
Silas Deane for profiteering in negotiations in France had been repelled by
Morris, and another who may have been Stephen Higginson; cf. Higginson to
Parsons, April 7(?), 1783 (7 Burnett, 122–4).

46. 9 LHW 331-7; letter undated, but from internal evidence was written April 9, 1783.

47. 24 JCC 210-11; cf. 3 *Secret Jnls.* 355-8.

48. April 9, 1783 (9 LHW 337-8). Others of committee, H said, were Madison, Osgood, Wilson, Ellsworth, but its appointment not in Jnl. April 7 H, as chm. of comm. (with Peters, Gorham) "to consider the means of reducing expenditures in the military department," presented his report; resulting resolution directed Secretary at War to settle a plan with commander in chief (*ibid.*, 230 and n.).

49. JCC *ibid.*, 242.

50. *Ibid.*, 242-3.

51. *Ibid.*, 252; cf. 3 *Secret Jnls.* 328-9, 354-5.

52. Phila. April 15, 1783 (9 LHW 338-9). Apparently H did not have Peters's idea (see to Steuben, same day, 7 Burnett 139) that British captives, "*set at liberty*," in accordance with provisional articles, be not delivered to enemy but be allowed to become citizens if states chose to make them such. H's objection to expelling loyalists and his later efforts to induce immigration would seem to make discharged prisoners welcome addition, in his eyes, to American population. Cf. R. R. Livingston to Washington, also April 15, in *ibid.*, 141 n.

53. 24 JCC 256-61. Jos. Jones, of Va., called it result of "the most difficult and perplexing discussion . . . we were obliged to take a middle course . . . or hazard . . . loss of the measure" (to Washington, May 6, 1783, 7 Burnett 159; cf. Bland, *ibid.*, 143-4).

54. Other members were Gorham, chm.; Madison, FitzSimmons, John Rutledge (cf. 24 JCC 188).

55. At one point "Mr. Hamilton . . . wished the valuation of land to be taken up in order that its . . . futility might become manifest. The motion passed in the affirmative. . . ." (25 JCC 888, Madison's notes).

56. Madison's full notes on the searching debate on general revenue measure (*ibid.*, 847-962) illumine terser official record. Disabilities of Confederation, fiscal and political, are portrayed. H was "strenuous" against "every plan that made but partial provision for the public debts." He wanted federal levy, and tax collectors "deriving their emoluments from & consequently interested in supporting the power of Congress." Madison regretted this "imprudent & injurious" remark, while Bland and Lee, in private conversation, exulted that H had "let out the secret" of his design (*ibid.*, 872; cf. H's contrast between ostensible and true grounds of opposition of R.I. and Va. to impost, *ibid.*, 902; also Madison's analysis of motives of each state, *ibid.*, 913-15, notes).

57. May 9, 1783 (7 Burnett 160–161; 24 JCC 335); address is in Madison's hand.

58. For text of address, 24 JCC 277–83; accompanying exhibits in *ibid.,* 285–311; all show complete financial embarrassment of Cong., with no prospect of relief unless states comply with recommendations now made.

59. Higginson, of Mass., Collins and Arnold, of R.I., all declared foes of the scheme, or of essential parts of it, were the others (*ibid.,* 261).

60. May 14, 1783 (9 LHW 339–42).

61. April 22, 1783; 24 JCC 268; see rept. of same persons, on another committee, *ibid.,* 269–71.

62. April 28, 1783; 24 JCC 283–5; cf. 311 and n. and 342–4. H's desire for further application to France was in spite of positive refusal of such aid in letter of Luzerne which Congress received six weeks before (cf. *ibid.,* 288–90). Peters, with dry wit, wrote to Steuben: "The Difficulty which heretofore oppress'd was how to raise an Army. The one which now embarrasses is how to dissolve it. . . . But an empty Purse is a Bar to . . . the best Intentions." And he added: "We have just under Consideration a Plan for establishing a Mint. All we want . . . is the *necessary Metal.* . . . Justice to our Creditors and Alacrity in paying Taxes are the best Mines we can spring. But . . . we have not yet found the Vein in which these precious ores are lodged" (April 23, 1783, 7 Burnett 150; cf. 24 JCC 273).

63. 24 JCC 266.

64. *Ibid.,* 313–315, H seconding Wilson's motion.

65. *Ibid.,* 275–6; ironically, some of Pa. troops arrived from S.C. by water in time to be involved in mutiny that expelled Congress in spite of H's efforts to quell disturbances (see *Pa. Packet,* June 24, 1783, No. 1058).

66. JCC *ibid.,* 320–321.

67. JCC *ibid.,* 321–2.

68. *Ibid.,* 323–4. H's motion, May 2, 1783, for additional advance on French loan was seconded by Wilson (*ibid.,* 325–6). At next session, May 5, Bland and Mercer moved expunge res. for further application to France as unconstitutional since it did not secure assent of nine states, but action stood, with only three individual votes against (*ibid.,* 328–9).

69. See draft LS, Livingston to comm. of Congress, May 9, 1783 (R. R. Livingston coll., NYHS); 24 JCC 336–7; Madison to Randolph, Feb. 11, 1783 (7 Burnett 41); Congress could not find the money, many members were disinclined anyhow, and Livingston left; H drafted unanimous thanks for his services (JCC *ibid.,* 382 June 4); cf. letters of Thomson, Higginson, Madison at this time (Burnett, *ibid.,* 179–86).

70. JCC *ibid.*, 334–5. Pres. of Congress, Boudinot, temporarily took over duties of Sec. of Foreign Affairs (to Franklin, June 18, 1783, Burnett, *ibid.*, 192). In debate two weeks later, May 23, 1783, some opposed a diplomatic corps as costly and corrupting; H must have been with those who thought our young Republic would profit by established interchange that might avoid collisions (25 JCC 967, Madison notes).

71. Thus Higginson to Sam. Adams (May 20, 1783, 7 Burnett 167): "There are those also among us who wish to keep up a large force, to have large Garrisons, to increase the navy, to have a large diplomatic Corps, to give large Sallaries to all Our Servants. Their professed view is to strengthen the hands of Government, to make us respectable in Europe, and I believe . . . to divide among Themselves and their Friends, every place of honour and of proffit. but . . . Congress . . . is not yet prepared for such Systems."

72. 26 GW 374–98.

73. 24 JCC 337–9.

74. JCC *ibid.*, 348–357; cf. 3 *Secret Jnls.*, 344 ff. "Armed neutrality of the North" was formed by Russia, Sweden, Denmark, later joined by other powers, to resist British depredations on shipping. Rodney's naval victory over De Grasse in West Indian waters, spring of 1782, put a term to this undertaking. H may have antagonized American entry into league because, our independence won, he wanted to restore commercial relations with Britain. Madison noted Congress "generally concurred in" fear that formal commitment to armed neutrality would too far involve us, at that juncture, in European politics (25 JCC 966). New England and So. Car. were for commercial treaty with Russia; former wanted iron, hemp for shipbuilding, latter hoped to find Russian market for rice (*ibid.*).

75. 24 JCC 358–61; 25 *ibid.*, 965–6, Madison's notes. Five weeks earlier, April 15, 1783, H doubted we should add to British strength by restoring prisoners (cf. to Washington, 9 LHW 339).

76. 24 JCC 348; 25 *ibid.*, 966, Madison's equally laconic note. H's motion (in his hand in *Papers of Continental Congress*, No. 69, II, folio 443) may have been suggested by Madison's, just before, that definitive treaty protect rights of Canadians who had suffered confiscations for engaging in service of U. S.

77. 24 JCC 372–6.

78. See 25 JCC 968, Madison's notes for Monday, June 9, 1783: "Not States enough assembled to make a Congress." Apparently same was true Friday, June 6 (*ibid.*, and 24 JCC 386 n.).

79. Form of certificate was specified in motion H drafted, but date of res. of Congress, characteristically, had to be left blank (*ibid.*, 383, and n.).

80. *Ibid.*, 384–6.

81. 25 JCC 968–9, Madison's notes; 7 Burnett 187, Madison to Randolph. Jnl. makes no allusion to debate under June 10, nor did Congress meet the following Monday, when vote was to be taken, and thereafter mutiny at Phila. intervened and postponed final action for ten months, when Congress accepted Va's. new, unrestricted cession of Old Northwest.

Chapter 19 (Pages 315 to 328)
Champion of Congress Against Mutineers

1. Washington's letter is in 26 GW 478–9.

2. May 26, 1783 (24 JCC 364).

3. May 2, 1783 (*ibid.*, 325–6).

4. Madison recorded this "mutinous memorial from the Sergeants" was read in Congress June 13 (1 *Writings* 477); Boudinot said 15th (1 *Diplomatic Corr. 1783–9*, p. 9), probably mistaken, as that was a Sunday; *Jnl.* has no mention. For demand of mutineers on Congress, Madison to Randolph, June 17, 1783, in 7 Burnett 189. John Armstrong, Jr., who had written Newburgh Addresses, was in Phila. nursing army discontents; see to Gates, June 16 (ALS, Emmet 4816, NYPL).

5. Report of Dickinson to Assembly, Phila., Aug. 18, 1783, in 4th ser., 3 *Pa. Archives* 905; Boudinot, *Diplomatic Corr.*, 1783–9, above, p. 9, mistakenly said Congress received letters June 18; *Jnl.*, June 19, makes no mention of alarming news, though that day Congress adopted resolve of comm. of H, Madison, Bland that states be sent letter of Washington, June 7, describing discontents of troops at HQ and be exhorted "to facilitate the punctual payment of the notes issued to the army. . . ." (24 JCC 402–403; cf. Pres. of Congress to states, June 20, 1783, in 7 Burnett 192–3).

6. William Henry, Lancaster, June 17, 1783 to Pres. Dickinson, in *Diplomatic Corr.* above, 14–15.

7. *Diplomatic Corr., ibid.*, 15–17.

8. *Ibid.*, 18.

9. This is noted for June 19 in Committee Book, No. 186 (24 JCC, 405 n.), but does not otherwise appear in transactions of that day; nothing in *Jnl.* for June 20. New charge was given comm. Sat., June 21, when State House was surrounded by rebellious troops (JCC, *ibid.*, 410), but action of comm. from June 19 forward not recorded in *Jnl.* until July 1,

when Congress was settled at Princeton (*ibid.*, 413 ff.). When alarm was greatest Peters was dropped from negotiators for Congress, perhaps because a Philadelphian (JCC 416).

10. H understood his rôle: ". . . it happened to be my lot, as chairman, principally to conduct the conferences on the part of the committee." (AL, undated and unaddressed, 5 HLC 613–23, certainly to Dickinson subsequent to Aug. 18 when Dickinson had reported to his Assembly; cf. 9 LHW 350, correcting 1 JCHW 374).

11. Written report ordered entered on *Jnl.* July 1 (see 24 JCC 413 ff.).

12. Dickinson said H's comm. at this first interview was divided on wisdom of calling out militia. (*Pa. Archives, op. cit.*, 905.) Peters may have been in doubt; chief reluctance belonged to Dickinson and Council.

13. 24 JCC 415–6; *Diplomatic Corr., op. cit.*, 20–21; instructions to Jackson, though penned under stress, were admirably prudent.

14. Boudinot mistakenly said June 19 (*Diplomatic Corr., op. cit.*, 10, also 2 R 562); H's first written report to Congress, only hours afterward, was on 20th.

15. Boudinot, *Diplomatic Corr., ibid.*

16. For this chief demonstration of mutineers: Boudinot to Washington, June 21, 1783, 4 P.M., and another to same, 11 P.M. (7 Burnett 193–4); Proclamation (Phila., June 24, 1783, *ibid.*, 195–6); Boudinot to U.S. ministers at Paris, July 15, 1783 (*Diplomatic Corr., op. cit.*, 8 ff.); Dickinson, Report to Assembly, Aug. 18, 1783 (*Pa. Archives, op. cit.*, 905 ff.); 24 JCC 410, 416 ff.

17. Boudinot, in *Diplomatic Corr., op. cit.*, 35; also in *Pa. Archives, op. cit.*, 906.

18. 24 JCC 410. H demanded that St. Clair and Exec. Council of Pa. "take order for terminating mutiny" (Madison, 1 *Writings* 483).

19. JCC, *ibid.*

20. Report of H and Ellsworth, JCC, *ibid.*, 416–7.

21. *Pa. Archives, op. cit.*, 908–10.

22. H to Dickinson, 9 LHW 358–61.

23. H to Dickinson, June 23, 1783 (24 JCC 421).

24. *Ibid.*, 417–20.

25. *Pa. Archives, op. cit.*, 911–18.

26. 9 LHW 352 ff.

27. JCC, *ibid.*, 417, 429–30, 432–3; cf. FitzSimmons and Montgomery to Pres. of Pa., Princeton, July 9, 1783 (NYPL Misc. MSS.) FitzSimmons, printed in 7 Burnett 219.

28. James Bennett to Capt. James Chrystie, Phila. Barracks, June 23, 1783, in *Diplomatic Corr., op. cit.,* 36. Not until next day did Chrystie notify Dickinson sergeants had withdrawn death threat, "confessed their conduct on the 21st . . . disorderly," and promised to moderate their demands (*ibid.*, 35–6). H observed comm. of commissioned officers were reluctant to inform St. Clair of their proceedings.

29. 24 JCC 420–21.

30. *Diplomatic Corr., op. cit.,* 33–4; copy of original broadside is displayed in Boudinot house, Elizabeth, N.J.

31. Dickinson to Assembly, *Pa. Archives, op. cit.,* 918–22; retraction and plea for pardon of sergeants and soldiers are in *Diplomatic Corr., op. cit.,* 24–5, as also Lt. John Sullivan's confession, on flight to England (*ibid.*, 37–8). Washington, instantly he received request, ordered 1,500 troops under Maj. Gen. Howe toward Phila. (Washington to Pres. of Cong., Newburgh, June 24, and instructions to Howe, June 25, 1783, in 27 GW 32–6; for his later part, JCC, *ibid.*, 411–12).

32. See *Pa. Gaz.,* June 25, July 2, 1783 (Nos. 2767–8). It required a correspondent to point out that "mischief *was intended,* or why did the two officers abscond as soon as they found that their secret designs were discovered." Delay in calling militia was "a plain declaration that the laws of the State do not provide sufficient security" (*ibid.*, July 9, No. 2769). *Phila. Packet,* June 26, 1783 (No. 1059), printed Boudinot's proclamation; July 8 (No. 1064), the object of Howe, with infantry and artillery, not mentioned; however, July 10 (No. 1065), resolutions of Cong., June 21, and H's long report of July 1 printed in full; cf. *Independent Gazetteer.* Rush, Phila., July 4, 1783, to Montgomery (7 Burnett 205–6, n.); Armstrong, June 26, 1783, to Gates (Emmet 1050, NYPL).

33. H to Madison, June 29, 1783 (9 LHW 377–8; he renewed application July 6; cf. *ibid.*, 379–80).

34. 24 JCC 420.

35. June 23, 1783 (7 Burnett 195; cf. McComb to Pres. Van Dyke of Del., June 27, 1783, *ibid.*, 202–3).

36. Cf. 24 JCC, 423–5; Pres. Boudinot, July 24, 1783, to Wm. Burnet of New-Ark [Newark], N.J. (7 Burnett 232).

37. Cf. res., Gen. Ass. Pa., chastened and cordial, Aug. 13, 29, 1783, in *Diplomatic Corr., op. cit.,* 45–7; see revealing exchange of letters between Montgomery, in Congress at Princeton, July 8, 1783, who was more correct

in sentiments than in spelling, and Rush, in Phila., July 12, whose defect was other way, in Burnett, *ibid.*, 215–217, and 217 n.

38. 24 JCC 424–5 (July 2, 1783).

39. Printed in 2 JCHW 269–275 and 1 LHW 305–314 as *Resolutions for a General Convention.*

40. 24 JCC 411–12, and n. They included H's motion directing Howe's march, H's appointment as chm. of comm. to confer with Howe, in pursuance of motion (JCC, *ibid.*, 412–13). Among letters communicated this day, one from Howe announcing approach, two from Washington, three from Dickinson, and others pertaining to mutiny (JCC, *ibid.*, 412 n.). H himself must have been unusually busy because his earlier reports on mutiny, written and oral, were then recommitted to be consolidated for presentation July 1 (JCC, *ibid.*, 415 n.).

41. "We were not able to make a House until Monday . . . ; we have now only seven states on the Floor; so that we must have unanimity, which is hardly ever to be expected, or we can do nothing" (Ellsworth to Reed, Princeton, July 1, 1783; 7 Burnett, *ibid.*, 209; cf. Montgomery to Rush, June 30, 1783, *ibid.*, 206). H and Madison moved, July 2, as public business was suffering from underrepresentation in Congress, states not present should send forward their delegations (24 JCC 422; cf. McComb to Pres. of Del., June 27, 1783, in 7 Burnett 203; Rutledge to Read [June 26, 1783], NYPL, Misc. MSS., Rutledge; and Burnett, *ibid.*, 200–201).

42. Ellsworth to Reed, above.

43. Whole of H's remonstrance to Dickinson (9 LHW 350 ff.), reviewing mutiny, had undertone in this vexed problem; cf. especially p. 370: "The insult was not to Congress personally; it was to the government, to public authority in general. . . ."

44. 1 LHW 305 ff. Greene was among those closest to H in stigmatizing faults of Confederation and pointing to correction; see to R. Morris, May 16, 1783, and to G. Morris (2 Johnson's *Greene* 441–2, 445–6). Cf. similar proposal in *Phila. Packet* at this time, July 3, 1783 (No. 1063).

45. Phila., March 24, 1783 (9 LHW 327).

46. 9 LHW 385–6; Washington's circular, Newburgh, June 8, 1783 (26 GW 483–96). Cf. H to Jay, Phila., July 25, 1783 (9 LHW 381–2): "We have now . . . concluded the great work of independence, but much remains . . . to reap the fruits of it. . . . Every day proves the inefficiency of the present Confederation; yet the common danger being moved, we are receding instead of advancing in a disposition to amend its defects. . . . It is to be hoped that when prejudice and folly have run themselves out of breath, we may return to reason and correct our errors." Madison said he accepted seat in Congress, 1782–3, to plead "the cause of reform in our

federal system, then in the paroxism of its infirmities, and filling every well informed patriot with the most acute anxieties" (Autobiography, *W&M Quar.*, 3d ser., II, 200).

47. 1 LHW 327–331. Lodge in ftn. says JCH thought remainder of *Vindication* lost, yet made further quotations. Lodge confused this paper with H's refutation of Dickinson in his letter of 1783 (9 LHW 350 ff.; cf. above), from which numerous quotations were given.

48. Phila., May 14, 1783 (7 Burnett 165–6); he renewed application to Clinton June 1 (*ibid.*, 176). His colleague Wm. Floyd had been longer out of patience, even more out of pocket; see April 16, 1783, to Clinton (*ibid.*, 142, and to Udny Hay, March 24, 1783, Burnett, *ibid.*, 94 n., referring to Henkels, Cat. No. 1074, item 10).

49. See to Clinton, Princeton, July 27, 1783 (7 Burnett 237–8); he intended to take leave of Congress "in a day or two," and closed with acknowledgments to legislature for his appointment. Floyd must have left immediately after April 24, day of his last recorded vote (24 JCC 275). Thereafter H voted alone for N.Y. until June 20, when no vote for state was recorded (*ibid.*, 407), he being absent, trying to forestall mutiny. H took part in proceedings during July (*ibid.*, 422, 424, 438 n., 440, 441 n., 477 n.); he was of comm. for proclamation of treaty with Sweden, but had gone when rept. was accepted Sept. 25, 1783 (3 *Secret Jnls.* 394–5).

50. Institution, in final form, adopted three days later, May 13, at Verplanck mansion, Fishkill, Steuben's quarters; first formal meeting held, Steuben again in chair, June 19, 1783 (see E. E. Hume, ed., *Washington's Corr. Concerning Cincinnati*, 108).

51. He received from Mrs. Washington "order" of Society, gold eagle surrounded by sprays of diamonds and emeralds, given to Washington by French officers (Winslow Warren, *Society of Cincinnati, A History* . . . p. 11).

52. *Institution of Society of Cincinnati . . . with List of Members of New-York State Society, 1851*, pp. 50, 75. H doubtless sat *in corps* with members of Cincinnati when Congress attended Princeton commencement, 1783. H was among many N.Y. members delinquent in dues; ms. list, no date, but near formation, in possession (Nov. 1953) F. G. Sweet, Battle Creek, Mich.

53. Mirabeau, Honoré, *Considerations on Order of Cincinnatus*, tr. from French, London, 1785.

54. Cassius, *Society or Order of Cincinnati . . . Creates . . . Hereditary Patricians* (Phila., 1783).

55. Brackenridge, 1 *Modern Chivalry* 140–41. For amusing anecdotes of Burke, including his seconding of Burr in latter's duel with H's brother-in-

law, Church, see Hume, in 33 *Americana* (quar. of Am. Hist. Soc.) 597–638, especially p. 11; also Beatty, *Assaults on Society of Cincinnati.*

56. *Op. cit.;* an elaboration on Burke's pamphlet, published in French, English, German.

57. C. F. Adams, ed., 5 *Works* (1851) 488–9; Cincinnati was "founded on no principle of morals . . . or our . . . constitution."

58. To G. Morris, Feb. 10, 1784 (H. P. Johnston, ed., 3 *Jay Papers* 111–12).

59. April 8, 1784 (Hume, *Washington's Corr. Concerning Cincinnati,* 130–31). Washington inquired similarly of Benj. Walker (March 24, 1784, *ibid.*, 124); Lafayette, Knox, Greene, and more offered views and reports (*ibid.*, 107–9, 132, 139–40, 142–3).

60. April 16, 1784 (*ibid.*, 135–9).

61. *Ibid.*, 152–63.

62. Dec. 11, 1785 (Hume, *ibid.*, 241).

63. *Institution of Society of Cincinnati* . . . , 51 ff. On H's comm. were Richard Morris, D[avid] Brooks, E[dward] Dunscomb, and Robt. Troup. Cf. AD (Nov. 1, 1786) in H's hand, signed by him, Duane, Duer as comm. of N.Y. Society, and addressed to Va. Society, soliciting unity in upholding original principles of Institution (Wetmore Coll., Yale Univ.).

Chapter 20 (Pages 329 to 345)

Devil's Advocate

1. ALS, HLC unbnd. Box 1; cf. Oct. 1, 1783, *ibid.* A month after H's gloomy verdict, when Congress was perched at Princeton, Ellsworth put the case similarly to Gov. Trumbull: ". . . it will soon be of very little consequence where Congress go; if they are not made respectable, as well as responsible; which can never be done without giving them the power to perform engagements as well as make them" (July 10, 1783, Ellsworth Papers, transcripts, NYPL). Other friends stigmatized crippling of Congress; cf. Schuyler to H, ALS May 4, 1783 (2d ser., 1 HLC 25–6); J. M. Scott, ALS, Aug. 6 to Duane (Duane Papers, NYHS); also H to Clinton, July 12, 1783 (Sparks Trans., 3 Misc. Papers, Rev. 372–3, Houghton Lib.); Robt. Livingston, ALS, to Duane, Jan. 30, 1784 (Duane Papers, NYHS).

2. July 23, 1783, H wrote from Princeton, "We have been for some time in point of representation at sixes and sevens; when we get to nine" states

on the floor any proposal out of the ordinary would still be hazardous (to R. R. Livingston, Livingston Papers, NYHS); see H, ALS, N.Y. City, Aug. 5, 1783, to Duane at Princeton (Duane Papers, NYHS); Duane, draft ALS, Phila., Nov. 25, 1783, to Gov. Clinton, drawing for expenses which covered a servant and two horses (*ibid.*).

3. ALS, Schuyler to H, May 4, 1783, *op. cit.*

4. ALS, H to wife, July 22, 1783 (5 HLC 586); printed in 1 JCHW 396 and 9 LHW 380, with terms of endearment, showing his impatience, omitted. "The members of Congress are very pressing with me not to go away at this time, as the House is thin, and as the definitive treaty is momently expected." Cf. ALS, H to Livingston, July 23, 1783 (R. R. Livingston Coll., NYHS) and Peters to FitzSimmons, July 26, "We do no Business. . . . The Absence of one Member breaks us up" (7 Burnett 233).

5. July 27, 1783 (1 JCHW 397-8), written at Princeton, sent from Albany.

6. ALS to Duane, Aug. 5, 1783 (Duane Papers, NYHS).

7. ALS (Albany), to R. R. Livingston (Livingston Papers, NYHS). H was doubtless familiar with appeals of or on behalf of Tories to Schuyler, e.g., March 5, 1783 (Colden); April 22, June 27, 1784 (St. Leger), July 13, 1785, all in Schuyler Papers, NYPL. H may have received some Tory clients through Schuyler.

8. Duane Papers, NYHS.

9. To Livingston, Aug. 13, 1783 (R. R. Livingston Papers, NYHS).

10. Fragment, 4 pp., in 5 HLC 635-6; cf. 2 JCHW 287 and 1 LHW 331 n.; 2 R 566 seems to quote from otherwise lost residue.

11. ALS, Sept. 30 (1783, HLC unbnd. Box 1).

12. ALS, fragment, Sedgwick Papers, Box 5, MHS.

13. AMH 190.

14. ALS, Aug. 4, 1783 (2d ser., 1 HLC 27).

15. Sept. 29, 1783 (AMH, *ibid.*). This may have been "Petition of Alexander Hamilton, Esq." read in Assembly Feb. 4, 1784, referred to comm. of which his old tutor Robt. Harpur was chm. (*Votes and Proceed.,* 7th sess., Jan. 21 to May 12, 1784, p. 27.)

16. ALS, Oct. 8, 1783, to Henry Livingston (Duane Papers, NYHS). Robt. Livingston swore to defeat trespass with all his resources. H tried to calm crusty client, warning "the very act [of pulling down the mills] would have an appearance of passion which might raise prepossessions against his right." An action of trespass *quare clausam fugit* was more prudent (autograph opinion, 5½ pp., Nov. 3, 1783, *ibid.*).

17. Jacob Cuyler, ALS, Dec. 11, 1783, to Philip Schuyler: "Col: Hamilton & Mrs. Hamilton were well & also Master Phil: they had Just moved into their house; I left New York . . . the 20.th Nov.^{r}" (Schuyler Papers, Box 35, No. 423, NYPL); cf. solicitous AL, H, Albany, addressed to wife at No. 57 Wall St., not 58 as listed in Hodge, Allen and Campbell, *N.Y. Directory . . . for 1789*. Philip, only child at this time, was nearly two; Angelica not born until nearly year later. Perhaps his office was at different address; cf. Comfort Sands to H, 1795: "If . . . possible I will engage a room for you for an office. It will be difficult to get one" (AMH, 162).

18. Pp. 62–5. Refs. are to Patterson's reprint, 1874. Among addenda, H's trusted lawyer friend Richard Harison, who was restored to practice after having been loyalist. Wm. Popham, who appears in several friendly connections in H's story, was down as notary public. Complete roster of officers, employees of Bank of N.Y., H a director, with hours and rules of business are here. H's name not among 175 members N.Y. Society of Cincinnati, but he is listed in St. Andrew's Society with many other Scots, including Troup, the Rev. John Mason (*ibid.*, 65–6, 75).

19. AMH, 155 and n.

20. H frequently appears in ms. "Mayor's Court Register" of Troup (NYPL), usually for defendant. In case running Sept. 20, 1784, to June 20, 1786, he defended Jas. De[s]brosses against Troup's plaintiff, Howell (p. 55). Amounts involved were small; H was instrumental in settling several cases out of court, e.g., p. 89, Barclay *vs.* Francis.

21. H's cash book, in AMH, 190–1.

22. See power of atty., March 27, 1784, to H from Charles & Hugh Smith and Co., merchants, London, authorizing him to sue, accept composition, etc.; probably typical claim of British creditors, this one for £7,400 due from John Wilkes (H Papers, NYPL).

23. Minute Book, Jan. 18 to Nov. 5, 1785, Record Rm., N.Y., County Clerk. First record of his cases in this court, but as they are so numerous he doubtless had many earlier, Nov. 1783 to Jan. 1785, for which vols. are missing in N.Y.C. and not at Albany (letter of R. J. Cannon, clerk, Albany, June 8, 1955).

24. Cf. Minute Bk., July 25 to Oct. 28, 1786, pp. 5, 15; Jan. 15 to Nov. 1, 1788, p. 104.

25. AMH, *ibid.*, 189–91, cases of Johnathan Jackson, Stephen Delancey (£20, "your cause being . . . critical . . . and having succeeded"), executors of Desbross (*sic*).

26. Declined retainer from Gouverneur because he had uttered "an unjustifiable reflection on the profession to which I belong. . . ."; in another

case retainer of $1,000 endorsed "Returned as being more than is proper" (AMH, *ibid.*, 169 n., 189).

27. AMH, *op. cit.*, 190–1.

28. Many times H acted for Church as business agent (and as friend, relative) rather than as lawyer (cf. ALS, John Chaloner, Jan. 25, 1784, to H, 2d ser., 1 HLC 29; ALS, Church to Hamilton, Paris, Feb. 7, 1784, 5 HLC 637).

29. Receipt for retainer, April 19, 1786 (Knollenberg Coll., Yale Lib.)

30. ALS, Pickering to H, Sept. 30, 1784 (5 HLC 684).

31. AMH, *op. cit.*, 190.

32. Pickering, *ibid.*

33. AMH, *ibid.*, 192.

34. Among many instances, see ms. constitution of Bank of N.Y., March 15, 1784, and directors' application to legislature for charter, Oct. 8, 1784 (Bank of N.Y. Coll.); AMH, *ibid.*, 190.

35. References in his brief in error in De Riemer *vs.* Verrion (1784) include Williams's Reports, Viner on Fraud, Coke, Littleton, Blackstone.

36. See below re Waddington, and AMH, *op. cit.*, 196.

37. AMH, *ibid.*; when he acquired "the standard folios, many . . . printed in Latin" does not appear.

38. AMH, *op. cit.*, 159–60.

39. AMH 160.

40. *Ibid.*

41. H's autograph certificate in Record Rm., N.Y. Co. Clerk.

42. *Address before Law Assn. of City of N.Y.*, 1836.

43. E.g., Jay, R. R. Livingston, G. Morris, Geo. Clinton; for full list of those admitted before Rev., see parchment "Roll of . . . Attornies of . . . Supreme Court of . . . New York" (1754–95), Record Rm., N.Y. Co. Clerk. Among exceptions were Samuel Jones, Richard Harison, Egbert Benson; *ibid.*, 17–18.

44. *Ibid.*, 16, 19 ff. Kent cited H's appearance in early cases, one in Sup. Ct. of N.Y., pitted against Chancellor Livingston. H upheld Mansfield's approval of right of court to award new trials; this discretion, H maintained, did not subvert jury system; prevented it, on occasion, from exciting disgust. Kent's address (25 ff.) applies to H's later practice, as also Kent's *Commentaries on American Law*, 3d ed., 1836, I, 62–4, and III, 20;

cf. Duer, *Old Yorker,* 1867 ed., 23 ff. for estimate of H and brethren at bar, patterned after Kent. For proof of rush of litigation after war, and promptness with which H and others, immediately on admission, received large numbers of clients, see Minute Bk., Sup. Ct. of Judicature, 1781. Cf. Oct. 26, 1782, ct., by special ruling, expedited clearing docket.

45. To Mason, March 22, 1810, in *W&M. Quar.,* 3d ser., IV, 215–6.

46. March 21 (9 LHW 402).

47. April 7, 1784 (*ibid.,* 403).

48. To G. Morris, March 21, 1784, above; was resigned to reflection "it is in vain to attempt to kick against the pricks" (to same, April 7, 1784, above).

49. For expert exposition, see Spaulding, *New York in Critical Period, 1783–1789;* cf. D. T. Lynch, "The Growth of Political Parties, 1777–1828," in N.Y. State Hist. Assn., 6 *Hist. of State of N.Y.* 37 ff. Alexander, 1 *Political Hist. N.Y.* 26–7. H elaborately reviewed Clinton's rôle in "Letters of H—— G——" in *N.Y. Daily Adv.,* March 10, 1789 ff.

50. Prohibited articles of growth, produce of U.S. being carried to British West Indies in any but vessels British built, owned, navigated.

51. C. XXV (Oct. 22, 1779), *Laws of State of New-York,* . . . Poughkeepsie . . . John Holt, 1782, p. 85.

52. 3d sess., c. LI (March 10, 1780), *ibid.,* 116; 4th sess., c. XIII (Oct. 7, 1780), 159–60; 4th sess. (March 31, 1781), 192–5; 5th sess. (April 14, 1782) 250; 8th sess. (April 5, 1785), c. LIX, 50.

53. 6th sess. (July 12, 1782), c. I, *ibid.,* 257; cf. 8th sess. (Nov. 24, 1784), c. XII.

54. 7th sess. (May 12, 1784), c. LXVI, 125–7.

55. 7th sess. (April 6, 1784), c. XX, 26; 8th sess. (March 31, 1785), c. XLIX, 42–3; 9th sess. (May 1, 1786), c. LVIII, 106.

56. 6th sess. (July 12, 1782), c. I, 257.

57. 2d sess. (June 30, 1778), c. XLVII, 43.

58. 3d sess. (Oct. 9, 1779), c. XII; cf. *Ass. Jnl.,* 54. On all such discriminations see *Laws of . . . Legislature of . . . New York, in force against Loyalists* . . . London, H. Reynell, 1786, pp. 186, NYPL.

59. *N.Y. Assembly Jnl.,* 7th sess., Jan. 21 to May 12, 1784, p. 27, petitions of Colden, H. and D. Van Schaack, Harison, "praying to be relieved of banishment, and to be admitted free Citizens of the State," and similar ones pp. 19, 29, 30, 34, 38, etc.

60. *Ibid.,* 26, 44.

61. *Ibid.,* 75, 145–6; also Council of Revision consented to act for immediate sale of certain forfeited estates, *ibid.,* 88.

62. Phila., June 1, 1783, to Gov. Clinton (9 LHW 342–9). Five months later, on behalf of clients suffering under confiscation laws, he applied to Pres. of Congress for exemplification of definitive treaty, without which N.Y. courts and legislature would not stop prosecutions (Dec. 8, 1783, *ibid.,* 394–5).

63. *Sen. Jnl.* 1st meet., 7th sess., begun Dec. 6, 1784, p. 14 (Jan. 14, 1784).

64. *Ibid.,* 75 (March 30, 1784). Under Clinton's leadership N.Y. went its separate way in other respects at this juncture. Consent to 5 per cent impost by Congress, with national collectors, given March 19, 1781 (*Laws of N.Y.,* 4th sess., 177, c. XXXI), was retracted two years later, March 15, 1783 (6th sess., 279–80, c. XXVII); schedule of duties allowed to stand, if other states uniformly concurred, but in any event collectors to be "under the Authority of this State." Legislature established customs houses, enacted detailed tariff, tonnage duties (8th sess., Nov. 18, 1784, pp. 7, 10, c. VI, VII; 8th sess., 1785, pp. 5, 61; 9th sess., 1786, p. 7, etc.). Concerning frontier garrisons, 9 LHW 349–50, 384, 388–94.

65. *A Letter from Phocion* . . . , 3d ed., N.Y., Samuel Loudon, 20 pp., and *A Second Letter . . . Containing Remarks on Mentor's Reply,* 40 pp., both 1784 (NYPL). First provoked numerous retorts, chief being *Mentor's Reply . . . with Some Observations on Trade . . .* (N.Y., 1784, Evans 18555, NYPL, supposed to be by Isaac Ledyard, leading Clinton supporter). Cf. Leake's *Lamb,* Appendix F, 389 ff., attributing to H selfish political purposes, since those defended would "attach themselves with devotion, to the man who was stemming the torrent of a just . . . prejudice. . . ." Leake went on to typical charge H "fought for independence of the Mother Country, rather than for an alteration of its form of government."

66. 4 LHW 288–9.

67. *Ibid.,* 244–6, 286.

68. Provisional treaty had been received by Congress four days earlier.

69. *Laws of N.Y. Passed at Kingston, in 2d Meeting, 6th Sess. of Legislature,* c. xxxi.

70. Owner-tenant relations between widow and Waddington were not improved when brewery burned with loss of £4000 in equipment to late British occupier; premises had been used to store pitch, turpentine, etc. (*N.Y. Packet,* Nov. 24, 1783; Van Krafft's Journal, 199; 5 Stokes 1173), AMH 152–3. For other particulars, Howdell-Canot s.w. view of N.Y.C. (*circa* 1763), map by S. Holland, 1757 (1 Stokes, plates 37, 36b), and Stokes, *ibid.,* 1090; also *N.Y. Jnl.,* May 18, 1775, No. 1689. Waddington occupied

two other Rutgers breweries not in this proceeding (*Arguments and Judg-ment of . . . Mayor's Court . . . in a Cause between . . . Rutgers and Waddington*, 1784, p. 6); adv. of B. Waddington is in *Royal Gazette*, Oct. 4, 1780, No. 419.

71. *Arguments and Judgment of Mayor's Court*, 3. See in H's hand memo. of cases in "New York Mayor's Court Dogget" for 24th Feb. 1784, H attorney, led by "Waddington Adsn Elizabeth Rutgers. I appear for de-fendant" (Hamilton misc. ms., NYHS), Plea, 10 pp., signed, but not in his hand except for few corrections, endorsed "Filed April 21st 1784." De-murrer and joinder in demurrer, slightly over page in his autograph; notes for argument, 19 closely written foolscap pages (AMH 153, printed in Ap-pendix H., 457–68).

72. Cf. ALS, R. Livingston, Jan. 30, 1784, to Duane (Duane Papers, NYHS); Constable, ALS, Phila., Feb. 3, 1784, to Carson (Constable Letter-book, NYPL). Hamilton's cases for loyalists accumulated rapidly even be-fore Rutgers *vs.* Waddington advertised his zeal in their behalf. See memo of eleven suits pending in mayor's court May 11, 1784, after most of which, "I appear for Defendant" (H misc. mss., NYHS); Oasthy (?) *vs.* Gardiner, in Troup's Mayor's Ct. Register, May 21, 1784 ff. (NYPL); 16-page plea as attorney in Thompson *vs.* Tucker, few words in H's hand, signed, (HLC unbnd. Box 1) is on identical principles with Rutgers case; ALS, Ezek For-man (?) Phila., July 4, 1784, re status nonresident whose estates were for-feited (5 HLC 668); ALS, N. P. Skene, Aug. 10, 1785, aimed at restoration confiscated property, relied on "the Report of your . . . readiness upon the fairest principles to take in Hand the Cause of the unfortunate." (6 HLC 713–4; cf. A. P. Skene, Quebec, Nov. 24, 1785, to Schuyler, Schuyler Papers, NYPL; cf. ALS, Stephen J. De Lancey, Sept. 12, 1785, to H, *ibid.*, 2 ser., 1 HLC 60, and others, 67–9, 71–2).

73. To G. Morris, March 21, 1784 (9 LHW 399). Eighteen months later he explained that apparent inattention to a particular client was "owing to the continual hurry in which my engagements, for a long time past, have kept me. . . ." Most of two months had been "out of town on indispensable business. In the intervals I have been occupied about objects of immediate and absolute necessity, which could not have been delayed without letting my business run into utter confusion" (Nov. 8, 1785 to Wilkes, *ibid.*, 410).

74. Robt. Livingston was putting this idea to Duane. Trade regulations "should be general through all the States . . . I trust [they] will soon be convinced of the Necessaty of giving [Congress] powers" (Jan. 30, 1784, Duane Papers, NYHS).

75. 5 HLC 299; cf. autograph notes, 2 pp., "Things remarkable in the Confiscation act" (6 *ibid.*, 692), and his legal opinion (*ibid.*, 699), dealing

with validity of decisions, executions of British courts in America subsequent to time when, by treaty, Western posts should be surrendered.

76. 5 HLC 629, autograph notes, some missing, on 3 foolscap sheets, half of each page left blank for elaborations.

77. Notes for Argument in Trespass Case, AMH 461–2. Foregoing is severe condensation from *ibid.*, from *Arguments and Judgment of Mayor's Court* . . . , *op. cit.*, and *Address from Committee* . . . *to People of State of N.Y.* (N.Y., 1784, also in *New-York Gazetteer*, Oct. 26, 1784, No. 110, no vol.); cf. 3 R 13 ff. for reconstruction of argument from H's "Notes" (above).

78. *Address from the Committee, op. cit.*

79. *Arguments and Judgment, op. cit.*, "Advertisement."

80. *Ibid.*, 4.

81. Waddington & Co. held not liable for occupancy for three years under authority British commander of city, but liable for year and half earlier when admitted to property by commissary-gen. (*ibid.*, 36).

82. Aug. 13, 1784. Wm. Vandewater is in Franks' *N.Y. Directory*, 1787 (p. 39), keeping tavern "opposite Brick-Meeting."

83. *N.Y. Gazetteer*, Oct. 26, 1784; cf. in same issue, "A Citizen" questioning sanctions of writers on international law hitherto unknown to ordinary people. Urge to appeal case to higher court, mentioned here and in decision itself, was dropped; statute itself precluded it.

84. *Assembly Jnl.*, 1st meet., 8th sess., Oct. 12 to Nov. 29, 1784 (NYPL, no title page, 22).

85. *Ibid.*, 23, 29, 32–3.

86. *Ibid.*, 33. Admonition to Council of Appointments to choose different court officers voted down, but proposal for court for trial of impeachments and correction of errors approved unanimously (*ibid.* 34). Further meeting of legislature upheld Trespass Act in spite of court ruling.

Chapter 21 (Pages 346 to 355)

A "Money Bank" for New York

1. Cf. the official narratives, Henry W. Domett, *History of Bank of New York, 1784–1884*, and Allan Nevins, *History of Bank of New York and Trust Company, 1784 to 1934*, both privately printed; *Catalogue of Mural*

Paintings in Bank of New York (pub. by Bank, n.p.), describing Panel No. 2, H the principal figure, and much incidental publicity material.

2. Cf. Domett, *ibid.*, 9–10.

3. Church to H, Paris, Feb. 7, 1784 (ALS, 5 HLC 637); cf. ALS, John Chaloner, Jan. 21, Feb. 2, 1784 to H (4 *ibid.*, 514, 513); ALS, H, Feb. 21, 1784, to G. Morris (more printed in 9 LHW 399–402 than is now in 5 HLC 639), and *ibid.*, April 7, 1784 (LHW *ibid.*, 402–3).

4. See R. R. Livingston Papers, NYHS, "Thoughts on the Establishment of a Bank," 8 ms. pp., n.d., probably 1784.

5. Cf. prospectus in *The Independent Gazette: or the New-York Journal Revived,* Feb. 12, 1784, No. XVIII. After disarming introduction declaring benefit of banks to commerce, scheme for this establishment was outlined with no notion of danger of assets preponderantly nonliquid. Subscriptions to 750 shares of $1,000 each would be taken by Stephen Sayre and John Stevens at No. 6 Wall St. 5 Stokes 1184, referring to newspaper notices, confuses land- and money-bank schemes.

6. *N.Y. Journal of Assembly,* 7th sess., 1784, p. 47 (Feb. 21); Isaac Sears brought in bill.

7. Livingston, "Thoughts on Bank," above.

8. *Ibid.*, p. 27, Feb. 4, 1784. His protest was referred to comm. of Harpur (his old tutor at King's), Lamb, Jacob Ford.

9. Among H's papers (5 HLC 641–8), dated N.Y., Feb. 23, 1784, but not in his hand, is "Plan of a State Bank & Loan Office." Author was sensible of utility of bank circulation beyond hard money that must form its capital, wanted to join government and private investors in bank ownership, was sure "nothing can be more dangerous and incompatible with the nature of Banks, than where Lands become part of their funds." But at variance with H and Church by demanding no stockholder, "however large his quantity of . . . shares may be, shall have any other than one vote. . . ." This was just in a popular govt., would prevent monopoly, protect "the honest and industrious young Trader."

10. First notice was in *Packet,* Feb. 23.

11. Books also opened by John Alsop, Broadway; Robt. Bowne, Queen St., Nich. Low, Water St. (*Independent Journal,* N.Y., April 7, 1784, No. 37, adv. of Wm. Seton, cashier, dated March 18, 1784).

12. They wanted to participate in a bank on a large scale, were taking "measures to vest our Property in America. . . ." (to H, 5 HLC 637, Feb. 7, 1784; cf. same, London, July 24, 1784, *ibid.*, 669).

13. Doubtless Feb. 26, 1784 (*N.Y. Packet,* March 1, 1784).

14. *N.Y. Packet* March 15, 18, 1784. H gave this result to Church in his letter of March 10, 1784 (9 LHW 396–8), but he held it open to include news of first formal meeting, and constitution. Other directors were Samuel Franklin, Robt. Bowne, Comfort Sands, Joshua Waddington (whom H was defending against suit of Widow Rutgers), Thos. Randall, Wm. Maxwell, Nicholas Low, Dan'l. McCormick, Isaac Roosevelt, John Vanderbilt, Thos. B. Stoughton; Wm. Seton was chosen cashier.

15. Church was agreeable, writing H from London, May 2, 1784, "I should be glad to be interested in the Shares of that Bank if they are not disposed of," and he was instructing Chaloner to use monies in his hands in this way (5 HLC 659–60). However, cautioned later, "if the Bank is not Solidly established I do not wish to be concerned in it" (*ibid.*, 669). H was writing Church constantly, as appears from acknowledgments, but most of H's letters, which would fill gaps, not now found. H's part in formation of Bank of N.Y., where not otherwise indicated, is taken from his letter to Church, March 10, 1784, *op. cit.* (1 JCHW 414 ff. and 9 LHW 396 ff. with omissions).

16. These partners subscribed for 20 half-shares ($5,000) July 31 and for 23 full shares ($11,500) Aug. 10, and were still stockholders (Wadsworth $10,500, Church $6,000) in June 1786, year after ending of their partnership (Bank of N.Y. Ledger 1784–6, f. 13). (For these particulars I am indebted to researches of Prof. James O. Wettereau, letter of Feb. 24, 1948, to Landon M. Townsend of Bank of N.Y., Bank's hist. coll.). Bank may have been more attracted to Wadsworth than vice versa, as he was largest subscriber to stock of Bank of N.A., in Phila. (104 of 1,000 shares).

17. Nevins, *op. cit.*, iii.

18. Fair copy, in a clerk's hand, is in 6 HLC 695–7, printed in 2 JCHW 330–3.

19. H to Church, March 10, 1784 (9 LHW 398).

20. Art. 16, 2 JCHW 332. One subscriber, though wishing Bank well, refused pay in his installments, as called for June 1, unless charter was obtained. The constitution stipulated that no subscriber should be liable for more than his stock, which presupposed grant of a charter (*Journal and State Gazette*, N.Y. n.d., Bank N.Y. hist. coll.).

21. 6 HLC 698; *Journal N.Y. Assembly*, 7th sess., p. 27 (Feb. 4, 1784), notes petition by H alone, for this was before promoters of the Bank of N.Y., as such, had taken any action. Petition died in committee.

22. "One Fifth of the Actual Stock of the Bank to be always let out on landed Security to the Several Counties of the State, according to such Quotas . . . as the Legislature shall appoint"; however, "the Sums lent to be paid by Installments in four years with lawful Interest. . . ."

23. Scotsman, merchant, and shipping agent, precise but agreeable; his choice to remain in the city under British occupation did not militate against him in bank, but would have been offset by election as president of Mc-Dougall, formerly famous in Liberty Boys. Cf. ALS, Elizabeth Seton, July 13, 1784, to Seton (Bank N.Y. hist. coll.).

24. To FitzSimmons, March 21, 1784 (9 LHW 399), and identical one to Morris, 5 HLC 651.

25. April 7, 1784 (9 LHW 403); ALS, Jefferson to H, April 26, 1784 (5 HLC 658).

26. ALS, Jan. 21, 1784 (4 HLC 514). Ten days later Chaloner informed progress of new Bank of Pa. was rapid; 715 shares subscribed, soon directors would be chosen (*ibid.*, 513).

27. March 21, 1781 (9 LHW 399).

28. 9 LHW 400–1.

29. March 27, 1784 (1 JCHW 416–8); cf. Chaloner, May 26, 1784, to H (5 HLC 662); though discounting was resumed, prospect of bank remained gloomy.

30. April 7, 1784 (9 LHW 402–3). Before knew from Seton of serious-ness of situation, H mentioned to Church that Bank of N.A. had stopped discounts, but he had "no apprehension that there is any thing more . . . than temporary embarrassment from having a little overshot their mark in their issues of paper. . . ." (March 10, 1784, 1 JCHW 415–6).

31. *N.Y. Jnl.*, May 6, 1784.

32. *N.Y. Packet*, June 7, 1784. House also known as 156 Queen St., later as 326 Pearl St.; in 1787 bank moved to Hanover Sq., in 1796 pur-chased house and lot at n.e. corner William and Wall sts., that had been Wm. Constable's; following year this house was replaced by building shown in early pictures (cf. 5 Stokes, *Iconography*, plate 72*b*, 1: 458).

33. See Mathew Carey, ed., *Debates and Proceedings of General Assem-bly of Pennsylvania on Repeal or Suspension of Law annulling Charter of Bank.* Phila., 1786; A Citizen of Philadelphia [Pelatiah Webster], *An Essay on Credit, In Which . . . some Remarks are made on present State of Bank of North-America.* Phila., 1786, 42 pp.; [James Wilson], *Considera-tions on Bank of North-America.* Phila., 1785, 35 pp.; Thomas Paine, *Dissertation on Government, Affairs of Bank and Paper Money,* 1786, espe-cially 23.

34. Bank of N.Y. hist. coll., signed by Pres. McDougall and 11 directors including H (Thos. Randall omitted); dated Oct. 8, 1784, endorsed as read in Senate Nov. 13th "& Ordered that M.ʳ McDougall bring in a Bill." Bank was organized in expectation of charter, "a Measure essential to the com-

plete success of the Institution," and this was second address of memorial-
ists to legislature on subject. At last meeting no decision had been reached.

35. The day of administrative, not to speak of policy-making assistants in
govt. service, was only beginning, though of course Washington used Cabinet
in this way. Gallatin was student before and while minister of state, but
those who followed him in Treasury were not similarly self-briefing.

36. Bank of N.Y. hist. coll. Dated Feb. 15, endorsed as submitted in
Senate Feb. 26.

37. *Assembly Jnl.*, 8th sess., 2d meeting, 14–15, Feb. 4, 1785.

38. *Ibid.*, 53–4, Feb. 25, 1785.

39. *Ibid.*, 55–6, Feb. 26, 1785.

40. *Ibid.*, 62–3.

41. *Ibid.*, 119, March 26, 1785.

42. *Assembly Jnl.*, 8th sess., 2d meeting, 77–8, March 9, 1785.

43. Contradiction of arguments betrayed general hostility to incorporation. Chartered society of mechanics would antagonize immigration, but
month later urged that organization to invite Germans "will be productive
of . . . fatal evils to the State" by introducing "a great number of Foreigners, differing from the old citizens in language and manners. . . ."
(*ibid.*, 73, April 7, 1785). Council of Revision had to be overridden to
incorporate City of Hudson (*ibid.*, 175, April 22, 1785).

44. *Senate Jnl.*, *ibid.*, 79, April 9, 1785. In comm. enacting clause of bill
negatived, 10-5, minority of friends of bank being McDougall, its pres.;
Roosevelt, director; Duane, Floyd, Townsend. No roll-call vote is given on
rejection of bill as whole, and *Jnl.* of Assembly shows no action on it.

45. Cf. his reference (Nov. 8, 1785, to John Wilkes, 9 LHW 410) to
"continual hurry in . . . my engagements." Incidentally, the Wilkes with
whom H had exchange of letters was John, as shown by signature to complaining one of Nov. 8, apologetic one of Nov. 9, 1785 (6 HLC 721–3).
Lodge (9 LHW 406–9, n.), ignorant of these originals, attempted to correct
1 JCHW 424–7 to make H's correspondent Israel Wilkes, "eldest brother of
the agitator." For John Wilkes, and his presence in N.Y., ALS, Eliz. Seton,
July 13, 1784, to Wm. Seton, *op. cit.*

46. *Senate Jnl.*, 13th sess., 2d meeting, 22–3.

47. Bank had ready-made friends to vote for it—Schuyler, Duane,
L'Hommedieu, John Vanderbilt, Ph. Livingston, Micheau, Van Cortlandt,
Lewis Morris, John Lawrence (*ibid.*).

48. To Jas. Watson, Jan. 18, 1791 (Bank N.Y. hist. coll.).

49. *Assembly Jnl.,* 14th sess., 53, 91, 94, 98, 99, 109, 110, 111, 113, 120. Council of Revision raised no objection.

Chapter 22 (Pages 356 to 369)
Curtain Raiser for Constitutional Convention

1. To Jefferson, July 3, 1784 (2 *Writings,* Hunt. ed., 57–8).

2. Dec. 25, 28, 1784 (*ibid.,* 99–100).

3. To Jefferson, April 27, 1785 (*ibid.,* 137).

4. To Washington, Dec. 9, 1785 (*ibid.,* 198); Madison's allusion to action at Mt. Vernon is conclusive; also see Marshall, 5 *Washington* 90. For Washington's desire for power in Congress over commerce, cf. to McHenry, Aug. 22 (28 GW 227–30), and to Madison, Nov. 30, 1785 (*ibid.,* 335–8). See Madison's notes for speech in Va. House of Del., Nov. 1785, which, with apt illustrations of evils, furthered his scheme for "a general regulation of . . . Commerce. . . ." (*ibid.,* 194–6). In 1835, recalling antecedents of Constitutional Convention, Madison said complaint of N.J. against anarchy in foreign and domestic commerce promoted acceptance of resolve of Va. legislature (Jan. 21, 1786) for "a meeting of Deputies from all the States" to achieve harmony (*ibid.,* 395 ff.; cf. Madison to Jefferson, Jan. 22, 1786, *ibid.,* 214 ff.). In interval before Annapolis gathering, public sentiment matured, so "the Convention . . . did not scruple to decline the limited task assigned to it and to recommend . . . a Convention with powers adequate to the occasion" (*ibid.,* 398).

5. *N.Y. Daily Adv.,* July 24, 1787, Vol. III, No. 753.

6. March 18, 1786 (2 *Writings* 228; Monroe had early been of same opinion, as cf. to unnamed correspondent, Feb. 20, 1780, item 470, catalogue of Am. Art Assn., Nov. 24, 1925, clipping in Monroe Papers, NYPL).

7. 2 *Writings* 395.

8. *Ibid.,* 218.

9. Madison denounced "immediate augmentation of property and wealth" as political ambition of an antisocial "interest" (to Monroe, Oct. 5, 1786, 2 *Writings* 272–3).

10. Emmet 11167 ff., NYPL.

11. ALS, April 21, 1786 (6 HLC 789); cf. on need for uniform plan of meeting debts to British merchants, ALS, Jefferson, Paris, May 10, 1786, to Monroe (Monroe Papers, NYPL).

12. N.Y. act passed May 4, 1786. Washington understated this obstruction (May 10, 1786, to Lafayette, 28 GW 421–2). Cf. ALS, Noah Webster, April 25, 1786, to Messrs. Hudson & Goodwin (Webster Papers, NYPL).

13. 31 JCC 555, Aug. 23, 1786.

14. *Jnl. N.Y. Assembly*, 10th sess., 7 ff.

15. Washington noted that "it is regretted by many, that more objects were not embraced by the meeting. A General Convention is talked of by many for . . . revising and correcting the defects of the foederal government; but . . . this . . . is the dread of others from an opinion that matters are not yet sufficiently ripe for such an event" (to Lafayette, above). Cf. to Jay, May 18, 1786 (*ibid.*, 431).

16. Aug. 12, 1786 (2 *Writings* 262).

17. To Monroe, Sept. 11, 1786 (*ibid.*, 271).

18. *N.Y. Assembly Jnl.*, 1st meeting, 9th sess., p. 83.

19. *Ibid.*, 85–6; Gerard Bancker was spokesman of comm.

20. *Ibid.*, 149–50.

21. May 5, 1786 (*ibid.*, 175–6).

22. Madison to Jefferson, March 18, May 12, 1786 (2 *Writings* 227; cf. 398). For omission of New England states to send delegates to Annapolis, Knox to Washington, Jan. 14, 1781 (Sparks, 9 *Writings of Washington* 513); however, Jabez Bowen, Providence, Aug. 18, 1786, wrote Pres. Sullivan of N.H. that coming Annapolis meeting "is an offer that we of New England ought not to let pass unnoticed if we can secure the Carrying trade of the Southern States. . . ." (ALS, Emmet 9339, NYPL).

23. Rosamond R. Beirne and Edith R. Bevan, *Hammond-Harwood House*. Annapolis, 1941, 22–3. Madison's bill for Sept. 5–15, for himself, servant, horses, was £14. 7. 2, receipted by Mann; lodging and breakfast was 3/9, dinner same, wine and porter extra; four nights Madison was charged for club, H doubtless making one of company (Madison, 2 *Writings* 271–2, n.). Madison on arrival found only two commissioners there; others trickled in with discouraging slowness (to Ambrose Madison, Sept. 8, 1786, *ibid.*, 269–70). More modest inn was Reynolds's Tavern (photo. in Ruby R. Duval, *Guide to Historical Annapolis*, 17).

24. O. Tilghman, *Annapolis* . . . , 17.

25. No. 2070; no report appeared in the next issue, Sept. 21. This assemblage marked end of Annapolis' early distinction, for rise of Baltimore

left town little except its monumental mansions (cf. W. O. Stevens, *Annapolis . . .*, 154–5, and "Freeman" to Samuel Chase, in *Md. Gazette*, Aug. 31, 1786, No. 2068).

26. Emmet 9328, NYPL., above; cf. 9360.

27. Autobiography, in *W&M Quar.*, 3d ser., II, 202.

28. To N. Webster, Oct. 12, 1804 (7 *Writings* 164–5).

29. MS. bill, Emmet 9354, NYPL.

30. 2 *Writings* 399.

31. Morse, 1 *Hamilton* 167, without ref.; passage has not been found in Benson's published or unpublished papers. Morse also offered Troup's assurance (again no ref.) that H from beginning "had not any partiality for a commercial convention, otherwise than as a stepping-stone to a general convention to form a general constitution." Troup, Duer, Malcolm, in legislature, at H's urging, bent efforts to have N.Y. send delegates to Annapolis, H one of them (*ibid.*, 165–6). Thomas A. Emmet (*Annapolis Convention*, extra-illus. vol. NYPL) mistaken in saying Dickinson, who signed address, also drafted it.

32. No. XI, Letters of H. G., March 4, 1789 (2 LHW 157–8).

33. See Emmet, *ibid.*, 9427, 9367–8, 9376, 9374, 9358, 9342, 9344. For H at this time, Bland and Northcott, *W&M Quar.*, 3d. ser., XII, 187 ff., portrait by R. E. Pine.

34. Bound in Emmet, *ibid.*, 9398–9. Emmet describes accidental discovery of Benson's Minutes in 1893.

35. Copy, in clerk's hand, with Dickinson's signature, and covering letter, from Annapolis, Sept. 14, 1786, sent to gov. of Mass., in Emmet 9401 ff.

36. Madison planned "to ride back as far as Philad.ᵃ before I proceed to Virg.ᵃ" (Annapolis, Sept. 11, 1786, to Monroe, 2 *Writings* 271); his letter of Oct. 5, 1786, to same was from Phila. We do not know H's exact movements, but he would go that way. Tench Coxe, later H's associate in Treasury, was doubtless in company. Coxe submitted his report of convention to Exec. Council of Pa. Sept. 20; his bill was £14. 12. 6 ([*Records of Pa.*], Minutes of Council XV, 5, 86, 135).

37. Madison, 2 *Writings* 395, 400–2, n.

38. Cf. Madison to N. Webster, Oct. 12, 1804; Madison "pressed him to step over the difficulty. It is very probable that he might consult . . . particularly with Mr. Hamilton and that . . . his exhortations . . . may have contributed more than mine to [Washington's] final determination"; cf. to Thos. J. Wharton, Aug. 1827 (9 *ibid.*, 289–91).

39. No. XI, Letters of H. G., March 4, 1789 (2 LHW 158–9). Clinton's opposition "was the first thing that gave me a decisive impression of the insincerity of his . . . former conduct." He had maintained Old Congress "was not fit to be trusted with power" to collect an impost, but now "it was not expedient to *constitute them differently.*"

40. 31 JCC 674 ff.; the papers are here printed. As happened, same day were presented letter of Gen. Knox listing stores in Springfield arsenal and his plea to Gov. Bowdoin for protection of arsenal against Shaysites.

41. *Ibid.,* 770.

42. 32 JCC 42–3, n.

43. *Ibid.,* 66.

44. *Ibid.,* 71ff. 4 No—N.J., Pa., N.C., S.C., plus single-member representation of Del. and Md.; 3 Aye—Mass., N.Y., Va.; Conn., Ga. divided.

45. *Ibid.,* 73–4. Recited that Articles of Confed. provided for alterations and "several of the states and particularly . . . New York by express instructions to their delegates . . . have suggested a Convention. . . ." Congress did not initiate, but at least formally called Constitutional Convention.

Chapter 23 (Pages 370 to 388)
From State Vexation to National Solution

1. Assembly had enough members in their seats Jan. 12 to proceed to business, when Varick was elected speaker (N.Y. *Assembly Jnl.,* 10th sess. 1787, p. 3).

2. Jan. 13, 1787 (*ibid.,* 6–7).

3. *Ibid.,* 7, 16–17. Two years later H reviewed this episode in No. IV of *Letters to H.G.* (2 LHW 151–5) as evidence of Clinton's "enmity to the Union" and treatment of Cong. "in a contemptuous manner."

4. *Assembly Jnl., ibid.,* 51–53.

5. *Ibid.,* 20, 91.

6. *Ibid.,* 94, 138–9. He was in majority against motion for disabling former Tories from holding state office (*ibid.,* 27); cf. his vote permitting a man attainted by law of N.Y. to return to state (*ibid.,* 72, 130).

7. *Ibid.,* 24–5; in Assembly Schuyler had received only one vote, that of Peter Vrooman.

8. *Ibid.,* 20.

9. *Ibid.,* 55.

10. Feb. 26, 1787 (*ibid.,* 68).

11. *Ibid.,* 71.

12. *Senate Jnl.,* 10th sess., 1787, pp. 44–5.

13. *Assembly Jnl.,* 82–4; Melancton Smith, later H's chief opponent in ratifying convention, got but one nomination as delegate to Phila., that of Jones.

14. *Ibid.,* 84; they must follow set procedure of report and ratification.

15. *Ibid.,* 53, 130.

16. *Ibid.,* 70, 88.

17. *Ibid.,* 62.

18. *Ibid.,* 124.

19. *Ibid.,* 65, 69, 95.

20. *Ibid.,* 125; cf. *Senate Jnl.,* 10th sess., 69–70.

21. *Assembly Jnl.,* 10th sess. (March 14), 1787, p. 97. O'Callaghan, 4 *Doc. Hist. N.Y.* 331–618, prints original materials of dispute.

22. See *N.Y. Daily Adv.,* March 16, 1787, Vol. III, No. 641; unnamed correspondent, regretting that illness of editor deprived public of verbatim speech of "that zealous patriot Col. Hamilton," supplied it as best he could, in more than a column; conveniently found in E. P. Walton, ed., 3 *Records of Gov. and Council of Vt.* 423–4.

23. *Ibid.,* April 3, 1787, Vol. III, No. 657, giving Harison's speech in four columns; cf. for petition to be heard, *ibid.,* March 26, 1787, Vol. III, No. 650. Harison's speech also in 3 *Records of . . . Vt.* 424–30.

24. 8 LHW 42–4. Entire speech, filling seven solid columns, was printed in *N.Y. Daily Adv.,* April 5, 1787, Vol. III, No. 659, evidence of intense public interest in policy to be adopted; also in 3 *Records of . . . Vt.* 430–8.

25. Documentation of H's suspicions was available later; see 3 *Records of . . . Vt.* 395 ff. and W. H. Crockett, 2 *Vermont* 313–44.

26. 8 LHW 45–58.

27. *Ibid.,* 58–62.

28. *Assembly Jnl.,* 10th sess., 153–4 (April 11, 1787).

29. Sent to Comm. of Whole, April 13, 1787 (*Senate Jnl.,* 10th sess., 85).

30. 33 JCC 617 ff. Mass. projected would have run, on north, roughly through present Amsterdam, Syracuse, across top of Finger Lakes, to Batavia, Tonawanda, and struck Lake Erie north of Buffalo; on south Mass. line would have passed through Saugerties, Binghamton, Elmira, Olean, Jamestown.

31. 31 *ibid.*, 693. For his leading rôle in controversy, see *Memoir of Jas. Duane,* in O'Callaghan, *op. cit.,* 652.

32. 32 JCC 231; 33 *ibid.,* 483, 617 ff.

33. *Ibid.,* 617 ff. Accepted by Congress (Oct. 6, 1787).

34. *Assembly Jnl.,* 10th sess., 6. Clinton, not belligerent for once, thanked Divine Goodness that "the animosities . . . to which we have been exposed by a controverted jurisdiction, are at length decisively terminated"; public tranquillity was secured while trial costs were avoided. H reported for a comm. cordial response to message on this head (*ibid.,* 17).

35. Apparently commrs. assembled at Hartford Nov. 13, reached agreement Dec. 16, 1786 (33 JCC 617 ff.).

36. Duane Papers, NYHS. The 17 foolscap pages are drawn with marginal notes; among authorities cited are Grotius, (Thos. R.) Rutherford (*Institutes of Natural Law*), Barbey (Jean Barbeyrac), Blackstone, Vatel, (Wm.) Robertson's History of South [*sic*] America, Prince's Chronology (*History of New England*), Hume's *History of England,* (Hakluyt's) Collection of Voyages and Travels, *Purchas, his Pilgrim,* Lahontan's *Voyages,* Hutchinson's *History of Massachusetts,* "Dutch Records Lib G [,] Stuyvesant's Letter to the General Court of Massachusetts 20 April 1660," "A Relation of the Discovery of N E published by Council of Plymouth Phi. Lib. N° 951," and "Trumball."

37. Certificate of Curtenius, State Auditor, and Gerard Bancker, Treasurer, N.Y., April 7, 1789, that £112 is due H, and H's receipt, April 14, 1789; he charged for "35 days Service." (photostat in H Papers, misc., NYHS).

38. April and Aug., 1785, Duane Papers, NYHS; here also, undated, is a memorandum of services of M[elancton] Smith and Robt. Yates, each 25 days at Hartford, and of Duane, 23 days at Trenton.

39. 3 *Records of . . . Vt.* 441–2.

40. *Ibid.,* 442–3; Daniel Chipman, *Life of Nathaniel Chipman . . . with Selections from his . . . Papers,* 70 ff. Daniel, the messenger, receiving H's answering letter of July 22, asked what he should report in N.Y.C. when asked for prospect of ratification at Poughkeepsie. H, in deep anxiety, replied: " 'God only knows. Several votes have been taken in the convention, and it appears that there are about two to one against us.' " Chipman was about to leave, when H added, "in a most emphatic manner,

'Tell them that the convention shall never rise until the constitution is adopted.' " Chipman's letter in 1 JCHW 466–7, H's in *ibid.*, 467–8.

41. Chipman, *ibid.*, 81 ff.; see H to N. Chipman, Sept. or Oct. 1788, in 3 *Records of . . . Vt.* 445–6.

42. *Assembly Jnl.*, 1st meet., 13th sess., 19; *N.Y. Senate Jnl., ibid.*, 14, 18.

43. 3 *Records of . . . Vt.* 461.

44. *Ibid.*, 459–60.

45. Speech is given in *ibid.*, 468–72.

46. Ellsworth assigned a principal role to H in drawing Constitution (3 Farrand 396–7). Gouv. Morris said "Hamilton . . . had little share in forming the Constitution. He disliked it, believing all republican government to be radically defective" (Anne C. Morris, ed., 2 *Diary and Letters of Gouverneur Morris* 523).

47. From H's outline of his principal speech in Constitutional Convention; cf. Farrand, 1 *Records of Federal Convention* 308.

48. 3 R 339–40, 665; cf. Mason in 5 *Doc. Hist. Const.* 246–7. Wilson, almost at end of sessions (Sept. 10), objecting to H's motion to submit Constitution first for agreement of Cong., "expressed in strong terms his disapprobation of . . . suspending the plan of the Convention on the approbation of Congress. He declared it to be worse than folly to rely on the concurrence of . . . Rhode Island. . . . Maryland had voted . . . for requiring the unanimous assent of the 13 States. . . . N—— York had not been represented for a long time past in the Convention." (Madison's votes, in 2 Farrand 562.)

49. Cf. 1 Farrand 282, 294.

50. A dozen men in convention led discussion and contributed disproportionate part of it. Besides Wilson and Madison, these were Randolph, Mason, Gerry, Dickinson, Charles Pinckney, Sherman, Ellsworth, Gouv. Morris, Paterson, Brearly, Williamson; at times, Franklin got his Pa. colleague Wilson to read remarks that carried peculiar weight with delegates.

51. 3 Farrand 89.

52. 2 *Diary, Letters of Gouv. Morris,* 525–6. By this perversity he "promoted the views of his opponents, who, with the fondness for wealth and power which he had not, affected a love for the people which he had and . . . they had not."

53. Luzerne was quoted as calling him, in 1780, "homme d'esprit, d'une médiocre probité," and Otto, soon after Phila. convention, made epigram, "Il a un peu trop de prètentions et trop peu de prudence" (Farrand, *ibid.*, 234).

54. *Ibid.*, 89.

55. While Madison—and not only for success of Va. plan—is rightly called architect of Constitution, careful reading of debates may convince that James Wilson was master workman in building of it.

56. 1 Farrand 126, from Madison's notes; King quoted Read more baldly: "We must come to a consolidation—The State Govts must be swept away— We had better speak out. . . . The State Magistrates may disagree but the people are with us" (*ibid.*, 143). Read was similarly emphatic at other times.

57. Farrand, *ibid.*, 552–3 (Madison's notes).

58. *Ibid.*, 471 (Yates's notes). McClurg, of Va.; Gouv. Morris, of Pa.; Broome, of Del., at one point (July 17) favored chief executive during good behavior (2 *ibid.*, 33). Dickinson was quoted as remarking, fortnight before H spoke, "No Government can produce such good consequences as a limited monarchy, especially such as the English constitution" (Pierce's notes, 1 Farrand 92).

59. 2 Farrand 479; this was Aug. 31. King "never could sign the Constitution if Rho: Island is to be allowed two members . . ." (*ibid.*, 623–4). Among other instances, refusal of Randolph to sign (cf. *ibid.*, 561, 631), though Franklin sought to mollify him (*ibid.*, 646); later Randolph regained his balance, strongly supported ratification by Va.

60. *Ibid.*, I, 500–501 (Yates's notes).

61. *An Economic Interpretation of the Constitution* . . . 1935 ed., 149; cf. 188. His diligent researches revealed that of the 55 men who attended, 40 were on records of Treasury as owners of sums from a few dollars to more than $100,000; 14 had invested in lands for speculation; 24 had money on loan; 11 had invested in mercantile and manufacturing ventures; 7 in shipping; 15 had personalty in slaves.

62. *Ibid.*, 17–18; however, he entered caveat, "It may be that some larger world process is working through each series of historical events, but ultimate causes lie beyond our horizon."

63. Irving Brant alludes scornfully to "those who . . . fought desperately (and still do) to perpetuate what Beard destroyed forever—the myth of a Constitution written by moral supermen in an economic vacuum" (*James Madison, Father of Constitution,* 60).

64. After dozen pp. probing H's affairs and connections, and his conduct after Constitution was adopted, Beard was forced to say: "That he was swayed throughout the period of the formation of the Constitution by large policies of government—not by any of the personal interests so often ascribed to him—must . . . be admitted" (*op. cit.,* 100 ff.; 114). Parring-

ton, *Main Currents in American Thought*, I, 292 ff., though he draws harsh picture of H as reactionary, callously materialistic in his policies, grounds these in "temperament and experience," not in personal economic incentive.

65. Madison devoted himself "to political pursuits rather than commercial or economic interests of any kind. He does not appear to have been a holder of public securities. . . ." (Beard, *op. cit.*, 125). Morris "declared in the Convention that he did not hold any public securities, and the records seem to bear out his assertion. . . ." (*ibid.*, 133). Nor could Beard make much of Rufus King's property stake in Constitution (*ibid.*, 118–20).

66. Mason had enormous Western land tracts (*ibid.*, 127–8); Lansing, "immediately after the establishment of the new financial system . . . appeared at the New York loan office with paper to fund to the amount of over seven thousand dollars," and his whole family followed his example (*ibid.*, 123); Gerry was considerable speculator in government securities shortly before convention (*ibid.*, 95 ff.). For Beard's effort to explain away recalcitrance of these wealthy ones, cf. *ibid.*, 151 n.

67. Thus Beard: "It may be that 'the critical period' [as expounded, e.g., by John Fiske] was not such a critical period after all; but a phantom of the imagination produced by some undoubted evils which could have been remedied without a political revolution" (*ibid.*, 48). Beard's notion that convention made political revolution was echoed in Burgess' implication that framers, disregarding prescribed mode of amendment, were guilty of a *coup d'état* (*Pol. Sci. and Comp. Constitutional Law*, I, 105). For a later effort at resuscitation of reputation of Old Congress, cf. Jensen, *The New Nation; a history of U.S. during Confederation, 1781–1789.*

68. *Federalist*, X; Locke constantly identified liberty in one's person with security of his property: "Man . . . hath by nature a power, not only to preserve his property, that is, his life, liberty and estate, against the injuries . . . of other men; but to judge and punish the breaches of that law in others. . . ." Cf. *Essay Concerning True Original Extent and End of Civil Government* . . . Boston, reprinted 1773, NYPL (45): ". . . every man has a *property* in his own *person*. . . . Whatsoever then he removes out of the state that nature . . . left it in he hath mixed his *labour* with, . . . and thereby makes it his property" (15). "The great and *chief end* . . . of men's . . . putting themselves under government, *is the preservation of their property*. . . ." (51). Madison often echoed this; ". . . as a man is said to have a right to his property, he may be equally said to have a property in his rights" (6 *Writings* 101; Chap. 103). See Parrington, *op. cit.*, 270, 282 for brief analysis.

69. "He saw that by identifying their interests with those of the new government, the latter would be secure; they would not desert the ship in which they were all afloat" (*op. cit.*, 101; cf. Parrington, *op. cit.*, 303 ff. to same effect).

70. *Leviathan* (Everyman's ed.), 94.

71. "Now in Monarchy, the private interest is the same with the publique. The riches, power, and honour of a Monarch arise onely from the riches, strength and reputation of his Subjects" (*ibid.*, 98).

72. Cf. *ibid.*, 177.

73. *Ibid.*, 184–5. Possible, not likely, H read *Leviathan* in Chandler's library, Elizabethtown (see *Catalogue of Books for sale by Mrs. Chandler,* 1790, photostat NYPL.

Chapter 24 (Pages 389 to 413)

"No Man's Ideas . . . More Remote from the Plan. . . ."

1. Washington, 3 *Diaries* (Fitzpatrick ed.) 216.

2. Washington, *ibid.*, 217; *Penn. Jnl. and Weekly Adv.,* May 19, 1787, which lists also Lansing from New York, but journal of convention shows he first took seat June 2 (1 Farrand, *op. cit.,* 76).

3. Manasseh Cutler spent the evening of July 13 with H, in the "Hall" which delegates had to themselves, others in the company being Strong, Gorham, Gerry of Mass.; Madison, Mason and his son, of Va.; Martin, Williamson, of N.C.; and Rutledge, Pinckney of S.C. The tavern was described as "kept in an elegant style. . . ." For hospitality of Indian Queen delegates to citizens of Phila., doubtless in return for similar courtesies, cf. dinner invitation to Judge McKean (PHS). Mason found living at the "old *Indian Queen*" cheap; he hoped to defray his expenses from his public allowance. We do not know what H was paid for attendance on convention; Randolph received $6 a day, including travel time (to Beverley Randolph, June 6, 1787; 3 Farrand 36).

4. 3 Farrand 18, 24, 28, 65; I, xii, n., 32 n.

5. 1 Farrand 7–17. On motion of Pierce Butler Rules Comm. included provision for secrecy of convention proceedings; H thought this necessary to prevent premature, misconceived public debate; for Jefferson's objection to "so abominable a precedent" see from Paris, Aug. 30, 1787, to John Adams (4 *Doc. Hist. Const.* 266, also in 3 Farrand 76). Another rule from Butler was that no member interrupt the representation of his state by absence, without leave; H was unable to vote for N.Y. after Yates and Lansing departed early in July, but no indication in journal they secured permission.

6. 1 Farrand 35.

7. Cf. *ibid.*, 94, on veto power of executive.

8. 6 HLC 784–795.

9. See W. C. Ford's revised printing in *Am. Hist. Rev.*, Oct., 1904, X, 97–109. Most apply to dates shortly before and after his own chief speech, June 18. H did not note votes or other actions of Comm. of Whole or convention.

10. June 6, printed in 1 Farrand 146–147.

11. *Ibid.*, 249–280.

12. Rumor that H had moved a govt. of king, lords, and commons, sped on its way by Commodore Nicholson on authority of Abraham Baldwin, in 1803 (5 *Doc. Hist. Const.* 249–50) probably contributed to a near duel between H and Nicholson two years later (see the correspondence through seconds, in Fish papers, Columbia Univ., and see M. H. Thomas in *Penn. Mag. Hist. and Biog.*, LXXVIII, No. 3, July 1954, pp. 342–52). Cf. Pickering to H, April 5; H's reply, Sept. 16; Pickering's acknowledgment, Oct. 18, 1803, in 3 Farrand 397–99, and Jno. W. Eppes to Madison, Nov. 1, 1810, in 5 *Doc. Hist.* 294. These defenses and detractions took wide latitude because proceedings of convention were not published until 15 years after H's death. Much written since about H's role in making of Constitution, whether viewing him as constructive contributor or as extremist with nuisance value, has turned on that one thrust.

13. 2 H 489; for hours of meeting, 2 Farrand 322. Johnson noted cruel heat, and that H's address signaled the date (3 *ibid.*, 552–3). For Martin's infliction, 2 *ibid.*, 438, 439.

14. 2 H 490; quotation has not been traced.

15. 1 Farrand 363 (Yates's notes); this was June 21, three days after H's speech.

16. *Ibid.*, 463 (Madison's notes); Yates quoted Read that Va. scheme was not sufficiently national; "The plan of the gentleman from New-York is certainly the best—but the great evil is the unjust appropriation of the public lands" (*ibid.*, 471). And H in his notes of a speech of Lansing, two days after his own, reported his colleague "Would like my system if it could be established—System without example." (6 HLC 784–95 and 1 Farrand 351.)

17. 7 HLC 832–8. See 2 H, 481–9; 2 JCHW 409–416; 1 LHW 370–378; 1 Farrand 304–311. J. C. H, printing outline for first time, rearranged in places and gave more revealing later portion not now found in H mss.

18. Unused draft "Preface to Debates in the Convention of 1787," in 3 Farrand 551. J. C. H. (2 H 490–92, n.) objected "it is not possible to

give credence to his [Madison's] statement," because Madison's report does not agree with H's outline, contains misstatements of fact which H would have corrected, omits (with intent to deceive) essential explanations such as Yates gives. It is hard to impugn Madison's accuracy, not to say good faith; he devoted more space to H's speech than to any other, and labored over it. Perhaps this was one of J. C. H's "hits at . . . Madison" which his brother thought "adroit & well sustained" (Jas. A. H., ALS, June 3, 1859, to Gen. Webb, NYPL).

19. 1 Farrand 281.   Indeed, the convention must have been ready for H's offering, as all states voted for Dickinson's motion except Pa., divided.

20. Madison's phrasing (*ibid.*, 282–3).   Yates reported H's "great doubts whether a national government on the Virginia plan can be made effectual" (*ibid.*, 294).   H's own outline notes under practicability of "a new government . . . with complete sovereignty," as first difficulty, "Immense extent unfavourable to representation" (*ibid.*, 305).

21. *Ibid.*, 308, 309, 310.

22. H to Pickering, Sept. 16, 1803 (3 Farrand 398).

23. 1 *ibid.*, 291 (Madison).

24. 3 *ibid.*, 396.

25. 1 *ibid.*, 299, Yates's report.   Though fearful republican government could not be established over so great territory as ours, "He was sensible at the same time that it would be unwise to propose one of any other form" (*ibid.*, 288; from Madison).

26. 1 Farrand 291.

27. *Ibid.*, 283 (Madison); here H was putting to use in the Constitutional Convention the words he had employed in the report of the Annapolis commissioners.   King in his notes of H's speech (*ibid.*, 301) was blunt: "Our powers have this object—the Freedom & Happiness of our Country—we must go all lengths to accomplish this Object—if the Legislatures have no powers to ratify because thereby they diminish their own Sovereignty the people may come in on revolution Principles—"

28. 1 Farrand 284 (Madison).

29. *Ibid.*, 306 (H's outline).

30. *Ibid.*, 296 (Madison).

31. *Ibid.*, 287 (Madison).

32. *Ibid.*, 308–9 (H's outline).

33. *Ibid.*, 309.

34. *Ibid.,* 290 (Madison).

35. *Ibid.,* 288–9 (Madison).

36. *Ibid.,* 303–4 (King).

37. *Ibid.,* 289, 291 (Madison).

38. *Ibid.,* 299.

39. 3 *ibid.,* 398, but H declined "to impeach the purity of Mr. Maddison's motives" (396). Cf. Luther Martin in approval of H's proposals as purely republican (3 R 341–3).

40. Cf. 2 H 490–1; 1 LHW 327–31, n. Yates's notes, reporting H's explanation of plan, prove was short version he then offered, e.g., without vice pres. (1 Farrand 300). See Jameson, "The Text of Hamilton's Plan," in *Studies in Hist. Fed. Conv.,* 143–50, for comparison of original with copies taken by delegates, concluding H "retouched" his ms. to conform to his later preferences. Madison and J. Q. Adams agreed (3 Farrand 433, 434). H's longer draft (NYPL) is that Madison referred to as "a paper Communicated to J. M. by Col. Hamilton, about the close of the Convention . . . which he said delineated the Constitution which he would have wished to be proposed. . . ." (3 Farrand 619). It is that H described as "the plan of a Constitution, which I drew up while the convention was sitting, and . . . communicated to Mr. Madison about the close of it, perhaps a day or two after," which expressed his "final opinion" as contrasted with his "experimental propositions" (to Pickering, Sept. 16, 1803, *ibid.,* 397–8). For history of this ms., sent to Jefferson and once feared lost, see Madison, 6 *Writings* 151; 5 *Doc. Hist.* 294. Bound with it is an accurate memo. by W. R. Leech and mistaken one by G. H. Moore. Soiled, worn cover sheet, with jottings from debates, indicates H carried ms. in pocket, worked on it from time to time. It was not a first draft, for crossed-out matter at top of first sheet suggests he discarded four earlier pp. H was in error in saying, much later, his detailed plan confined president to "a moderate term of years. . . ." (3 R 341–3, followed in 2 H 539); cf. Madison to Paulding, April 1831 (3 Farrand 500–1), pointing to this "decisive" case of fallibility of H's memory.

41. Story of Jonathan Dayton, unreliably reported long afterward that when Franklin urged prayers to calm dissension, H opposed "calling in foreign aid" (3 Farrand 471–2), not supported by Madison's notes of that day (June 28, 1787, in 1 *ibid.,* 452 and n.).

42. H, Sept. 16, 1803, to Pickering, in 3 Farrand, *op. cit.,* 397–8.

43. See 1 Farrand 291–93; 2 JCHW, 393–5; 1 LHW 347–50.

44. In H's ms., designation of chief executive was at two removes from people, by electors chosen by electors voted for by people.

45. In H's ms. the twelve judges of Sup. Ct. were included.

46. 1 Farrand 293; Madison noted that H did not find leisure to write out the explanations for him as promised, but that Yates included them with his account of speech (Gilpin, 2 *Papers of Madison* 892–3). If H approved Madison's version of speech, without observations on sketch of a constitution, latter must have introduced little new matter.

47. 1 Farrand 16; 2 *ibid.*, 98.

48. H, Sept. 16, 1803, to Pickering, 3 Farrand 398. This was always his emphasis—liberty through strength, not weakness, of govt. Seven years before, acknowledging for Washington a proposed constitution for Mass. sent by Gov. Bowdoin, he thought it "judicious" because it had "all the requisites towards securing the liberty and happiness of individuals, and at the same time giving energy to the administration. This last . . . is essential to the former, though in some of our constitutions it has not been sufficiently consulted" (April 26, 1780, 18 GW 298).

49. This summary follows H's original ms. (NYPL) which differs slightly in capitalization and punctuation from Madison's copy as given, e.g., in 3 Farrand 619–630. 1 JCHW 395–409 printed his father's version as also 1 LHW 350–369.

50. Perhaps not quite all, as H nearly at close of sessions (Sept. 10) wanted to require approval of Congress for proposed Constitution before it was submitted to states—this for decorum and orderly procedure. Supported by Gerry, Williamson, Sherman, who were not his usual adherents, and opposed by his friends Wilson, Clymer, King. H's motion lost, 10 to 1. (2 Farrand 559–563). Perhaps he did not include this provision in his draft because toward last he was conforming it to sense of convention where he could, was satisfied with covering letter merely submitting document to Congress (*ibid.*, 582–4).

51. See G. Turner to Webb, June 30, 1787 (Webb, 3 *Corr. and Jnls.*, 81): Madison noted H's absence for a period after this date (1 Farrand 465 and n.). Yates and Lansing remained through July 10, after which no votes recorded for N.Y. (1 Farrand 563 ff.).

52. 1 Farrand 463 (Madison's notes).

53. 6 HLC 801; 9 LHW 417–18; 1 JCHW 435–6. Pierce, describing fellow delegates, said H's language was "sometimes didactic like Bolingbroke's. . . ." (3 Farrand 89); true of present letter; H earnestly spoke his thoughts, not finding it necessary to subordinate his youth to wisdom of older correspondent, and Washington encouraged this candor.

54. Yates, Lansing to Clinton (3 Farrand 244–7); cf. Luther Martin, Baltimore, Jan. 27, 1788, to T. C. Deye (*ibid.*, 269–70). Lansing, finding Yates's notes ended with July 5, wrote they quit convention "At this period"

(*ibid.*, I, 536), but as N.Y.'s vote was recorded through July 10, later date must be correct.

55. 1 JCHW 437.

56. 1 Farrand 567.

57. Before Md. House of Rep., Nov. 29, 1787, in 3 *ibid.*, 154.

58. Cutler, *Life, Jnls., of M. Cutler*, 253.

59. Cutler probably mistaken, for July 11 Rufus King spoke of H as well absent (to Henry Knox, 4 Farrand 68).

60. 1 Farrand 604.

61. Cf. applause of H for exposure of "the Anti-federal dogmas of a great personage in your State" (Humphreys to H, 1 JCHW 443), and confidence in Convention (*N.Y. Daily Adv.*, Aug. 14, 1787). Just about this date (July 21, 1787), French chargé d'affaires wrote his govt.: "Les partisans de la réforme . . . ont soin en attendant, d'attaquer publiquement les plus redoubtables de leurs antagonistes. Leurs traits sont principalement dirigés contre le Gouverneur de New York, l'ennemi le plus actif et le plus dangereux de la puissance du Congrès. Son intérêt personel le porte à ne sacrifier aucune de ses prérogatives et à conserver à son Etat tous les droits de la souveraineté" (Otto to Montmorin, N. Y., July 25, 1787, in 3 Farrand 63).

62. 2 JCHW 422–6. H said Clinton possessed *"consummate talents* for popularity." Right of citizens, within legal bounds, to oppose magistrate might have risen to plague H seven years later when he urged Pres. Washington to condemn "democratical societies" which, by their influence, hampered collection of federal excise. Alien and Sedition Acts revived question more acutely. A little later, with same polemic in mind, Otto wrote of H as "Partisan zélé et même outré de la nouvelle Constitution et ennemi déclare du gouv. Clinton, qu'il a eu le courage d'attaquer publiquement dans les Gazettes, sans aucune provocation" (same to same, 1788, *ibid.*, 234).

63. 1 JCHW 444–5; 9 LHW 423–5 dates it Oct. 1787, probably correctly. Washington regretted political dispute between H and Clinton, for both of whom he had highest regard, but explicitly contradicted any report that H had joined his staff by contrivance or been dismissed from it (Oct. 18, 1787, 1 JCHW 447; for H's thanks, Oct. 30, 1787, *ibid.*, 448).

64. "Cato" in *N.Y. Jnl.*, Sept. 27, 1787 to Jan. 3, 1788, and "Caesar" in *Daily Adv.*, Oct. 1, 17, 1787, conveniently found in P. L. Ford, *Essays on Const.*, 245 ff.

65. Hamilton to ———— (Peirce's second?), N.Y., July, 1787(?); to Peirce, 1787; to Auldjo, N.Y., July 26, 1787 (6 HLC 804–6, and 9 LHW

419–421). H composed quarrel, saying (what applied to his fruitless efforts with Burr) he was unwilling "to see extremities take place if it be in his power to prevent them, or until they become an absolutely necessary sacrifice to public opinion."

66. 2 Farrand 265, 267, 268–9, 271–2. Mason made thrust which, few years later during controversy over Jay Treaty, would have been seen as directed at H. In formative stage of govt., "If persons among us attached to G—— B. should work themselves into our Councils, a turn might be given to our affairs & particularly to our Commercial regulations which might have pernicious consequences." Wilson, on other hand, pointed out three of Pa. delegates in convention were not natives—R. Morris, Fitz-Simmons, and himself.

67. H to King, Aug. 20, 1787 (9 LHW 422).

68. Same to same, Aug. 28, 1787 (*ibid.*, 423).

69. Alex. Martin, of N.C., promptly scouted idea (to Gov. Caswell, 3 Farrand 73), evidently got *Pa. Jnl.* (Aug. 22, in *ibid.*, 74) to repeat denial. Three weeks later, however, Sydney, reporting to Ld. Dorchester, took suggestion seriously, advised counterintrigue lest Bourbon influence in America be strengthened through a Hanoverian king (*ibid.*, 81). Sydney was worse posted than French diplomat Otto, who earlier told his home minister any project of Cincinnati to give Washington kingly powers was too extravagant to merit discussion (*ibid.*, 43).

70. HLC. 9 LHW 422–3, and 1 JCHW 440 give Reynolds's name, but J. C. H. in 2 H 534 omits, substituting "a person in this city." Perhaps son's preference not to identify Reynolds was that this is first mention in H's annals of schemer who, with unhappy help from H, later produced personal embarrassment and political intrigue. Reply of Wadsworth developed only that Wetmore (H was mistaken in Whitmore) was friend of good govt., and that letter was calculated to prepare Anti-federalists "to comply with the doings of the Convention, lest worse befell them. . . ." (1 JCHW 440–441; cf. D. Humphreys to H, New Haven, Sept. 16, 1787, *ibid.*, 442–3). From tone of H's inquiry, he had never heard of proposal before. Had he been inclined to monarchy as feasible system for U.S., would not have treated purported project as hostile to work of convention; cf. Morgan Lewis's statement that H in interview soon after convention "explicitly denied" "the monarchic proposition" (2 H 550).

71. 2 H 537. He would not have returned from circuit until Sept. 1 (to King, above), then expected to go for probable "termination" of convention.

72. 2 Farrand 493 ff.

73. Cf. *ibid.*, 501 (Pinckney); 511 (Williamson, Rutledge); 512 (Mason); 513 (Madison, Randolph, Dickinson); 522 (Wilson).

74. Blend of notes of Madison (2 Farrand 524–5), McHenry (*ibid.*, 530–31).

75. *Ibid.*, 521.

76. Journal, in 2 Farrand 547; cf. opposition of N.C. delegates, 526.

77. 3 *Diary of Ezra Stiles* 295, in *ibid.*, 170.

78. Madison to Sparks, April 8, 1831 (Sparks, 1 *Life of Gouv. Morris* 284–6, and 3 Farrand 499).

79. "The *finish* given to the style and arrangement of the Constitution fairly belongs to the pen of Mr. Morris. . . ." (Madison, *ibid.*) A generation later, Morris answered inquiry of Pickering: ". . . what can a history of the Constitution avail towards interpreting its provisions. [?] This must be done by comparing the plain import of the words, with the general tenor and object of the instrument. That instrument was written by the fingers, which write this letter" (Dec. 22, 1814; 3 Farrand 420). Morris was sharpening his quill whole of days before report, for he does not appear in convention proceedings, though H, King, Madison were present (2 *ibid.*, 555–64).

80. H's son attributed too much to father's part in comm. of revisal (2 H 537 ff.), but quoted Johnson in just estimate: "If the constitution did not succeed on trial, Hamilton was less responsible . . . than any other member, for he . . . pointed out to the convention . . . the infirmities to which it was liable."

81. Cf. "Landholder" (Ellsworth) in open letter to Gerry, in *Conn. Courant*, Dec. 24, 1787, reprinted P. L. Ford, *Essays on Constitution*, 172–175, and in 3 Farrand, *op. cit.*, 170–72; Gerry is pictured as turning to "intemperate opposition to the whole system he had formerly praised." Gerry's reply was given in *Mass. Centinel*, Jan. 5, 1788, reprinted Ford, *ibid.*, 127–8, and Farrand, *ibid.*, 239–240.

82. Most dramatic touch in Howard Chandler Christy's painting of signing of Constitution, hanging in National Capitol, is friendly exchange going on, in center of picture, between relaxed philosopher and his yeasty junior.

83. Williamson, Madison, Sherman had been prominent in earlier debates on this question, crucial because of division between Northern, Southern, and future Western states with distinct economic interests. For H's history of treatment of this issue in the Constitutional Convention, see his reply to Lansing in N.Y. ratifying convention (Elliot, 2 *Debates* 272–4, also 3 Farrand 335–7).

84. 2 Farrand 553–4.

85. *Ibid.*, 557–9.

86. *Ibid.*, 559–63.

87. *Ibid.,* 615–6.

88. *Ibid.,* 618–19.

89. 2 Farrand 645–6.

90. 4 *Writings* 176.

91. Technically, N.Y. was not one of "States present," as two delegates of the three were necessary to permit vote. In resolution laying Constitution before Congress, etc., eleven states are listed, with "Mr. Hamilton from New York" (2 Farrand 664–5).

92. *Ibid.,* 642.

Chapter 25 (Pages 414 to 425)

The Art of Persuasion

1. Yet no attempt is made here to present in any detail arguments he used in defense of Constitution in the two-thirds of whole number of essays believed to be his. H's constitutional reasoning elsewhere is given because documents in these cases are less accessible than *The Federalist,* which, in special fashion, speaks for itself.

2. As examples at different periods: H's young friend James Kent (later Chancellor of N.Y.) wrote as early as Dec. 22, 1787, "You may praise whom you please, and I will presume to say that I think 'Publius' is a more admirable writer and wields the sword of party dispute with justice, energy and inconceivable dexterity. The author must be Alexander Hamilton, who, . . . in genius and political research, is not inferior to Gibbon, Hume and Montesquieu" (to N. Lawrence, quoted in catalogue No. 18, Bodley Book Shop, tearsheet in Kent Papers, NYPL). Guizot, French foreign minister: "in the application of elementary principles of government to practical administration, it was the greatest work known to him." (said to Richd. Rush, Paris 1849; Dawson ed. of *Federalist,* 1863, p. xliv; cf. *Corr. between Jay, Dawson, etc. . . . Concerning . . . Federalist*). And Beard: "In my opinion it is the most instructive work on political science ever written in the United States; and, owing to its practical character, it ranks first in the world's literature" of that subject. (*Enduring Federalist,* vi.)

3. These papers appeared, Nos. I–VII, in *N.Y. Jnl.,* Sept. 27, 1787 to Jan. 3, 1788; conveniently found in P. L. Ford, *Essays on Constitution,* 245–78.

4. *N.Y. Daily Adv.,* Oct. 1, 1787, No. 812; Oct. 17, 1787, No. 826 (Vol. III), and Ford, *ibid.*

5. *N.Y. Daily Adv.*, Oct. 17, 1787. All Cato could say against new Constitution "has been already disseminated in a neighbouring State, by the glorious defenders of *Shayism*. I shall . . . leave Cato to the wicked influences of his own heart. . . ." Clinton's mood may be gathered from remark to his daughter, though his precise reference is lacking: "Learn . . . to compassionate the Folly of the Faction. . . . They are . . . below Contempt & their Conduct ought not to give you a Moments Pain" (ALS, Feb. 29, 1788, Clinton Papers, NYPL). Apparently at first H did not identify Clinton as "Cato," for he wrote to Washington in Oct., 1787, "the Governor has not publicly declared himself. . . ." (9 LHW 425).

6. To Madison, N.Y., May 19, 1788 (9 LHW 430–1).

7. From first number, written by H (11 LHW 8; this vol. and 12 contain *Federalist,* and references are to this ed.).

8. This letter came into hands of Lamb, who copied, sent it to Clinton, his political chief. (Ford, ed., *Essays on Constitution, op. cit.,* 245; letter was then in Clinton ms., NYSL.) This was doubtless basis of note in *N.Y. Jnl.* that on failure of attempt to frighten off "Cato," "*Caesar* retreated and disappeared; and since that a publication under the signature of Publius . . . has appeared. . . ." The two ran along together for a while. Though H left off replying to Clinton, others entered against him, especially "Curtius" (*N.Y. Daily Adv.,* Oct. 18, Nov. 3; supplement, Nov. 7, 1787).

9. Aug. 10, 1788, to Jefferson (5 *Writings* 246).

10. Sparks, 3 *Life of G. Morris* 339.

11. Adair, Douglass, "The Authorship of the Disputed Federalist Papers," *W&M Quar.,* 3d. ser., I, 245. They appeared as apocrypha in appendix of J. C. H's ed. of *Federalist;* Dawson in his ed., xxi, conjectured H hoped to draw in Schuyler and Duane.

12. Hamilton in preface to vol. 1: "It is supposed that a collection of the papers which have made their appearance in the Gazettes of this City, under the Title of the Federalist, may not be without effect in assisting the public judgment on the momentous question of the Constitution for the United States, now under the consideration of the people of America. . . . The great wish is that it may . . . lead to a right judgment of the interests of the community" (N.Y., M'Lean, 1788). Madison, shortly before his death, noted "The [*Federalist*] papers were first meant for the important and doubtful state of New York and signed a 'Citizen of New York' — afterwards meant for all the States under 'Publius' " (Adair, ed., J. Madison's Autobiography, *W&M Quar.,* 3d ser., II, 202). Madison's recollection was at fault about a change of pseudonym; "Publius" was signed to all of the essays in newspapers; no authorship attributed in first ed., 1788, though announcement of forthcoming volume (only one then contemplated,

Daily Adv., Jan. 8, 1788, Vol. IV, No. 893) spoke of essays as "By a Citizen of New-York." Cf. notice week before (*ibid.,* Jan. 1, 1788); "The numbers already published will make more than 200 pages, and the author does not seem to be nigh a close."

13. *The Independent Journal,* published every Wednesday, Saturday by J. M'Lean & Co., 41 Hanover Sq., was only N.Y. paper to carry whole of *Federalist;* M'Lean also first published in book form. *N.Y. Packet* (S. and J. Loudon) reprinted, from the *Ind. Jnl.,* nos. I–LXXVI, Oct. 30, 1787 to April 4, 1788, but no more. *Daily Advertiser* (Childs, who reported Poughkeepsie proceedings) carried nos. I–L, Oct. 30, 1787 to Feb. 11, 1788; *N.Y. Jnl.* (Greenleaf) contained essays for few weeks Dec.–Jan.; see ed. note Dec. 18, 1787, introducing No. XXIII. *Country Jnl. and Poughkeepsie Adv.* (Power) began *Federalist* with No. 15 (Supplement, Jan. 18, 1788, No. 128), and seems to have printed only through No. 20 (Supplement, Feb. 5, 1788, No. 131). When the last number was written, by H, concluding Vol. II (May 28, 1788), he noted "the hold we now have . . . upon seven out of the thirteen States"; those in which *Federalist* could still plead for ratification were N.Y., Va., N.H., S.C., N.C., with no immediate hope in R.I., which had refused to call a convention (12 LHW 345). First edition was *The Federalist: A Collection of Essays, written in favour of the New Constitution,* as agreed upon by the federal convention, September 17, 1787, in two volumes. New-York: Printed and Sold by J. and A. M'Lean . . . M, DCC, LXXXVIII. 12 mo., pp. vi, 227, vi, 384; long primer, 10 pt. Constitution appended to Vol. II. Most copies of first ed. on ordinary paper, few on heavy, former in boards, latter calf (referred to by H as "the common copies and . . . the finer ones" (to Madison, May 19, 1788, 9 LHW 431). The 2 vols., plain paper, sold, even to new subscribers, at 8s. (*Ind. Jnl.,* May 28, 1788), but first ed., especially in de luxe form, is rare; for more particulars, Sabin 21127. NYPL has fragment, pp. 11–18 (Richmond or Alexandria, Va., 1787–8?), embracing all of No. 2, parts of nos. 1 and 3; P. L. Ford, ms. insert, said taken from a coll. Va. pamphlets, thought it theretofore unknown edition, issued in parts by newspaper in which Washington procured its publication (No. 42, Ford's *Bibliography of Constitution,* not in Evans). The second, or, if we accept above, third ed. was *Le Fédéraliste, ou Collection de quelque Écrits en faveur de la Constitution* . . . "par MM. Hamilton, Madisson et Gay, Citoyens . . . de New-York."
A Paris, Chez Buisson, Libraire, rue Hautefeuille, n., 20 1792, 2 vols., pp. 366, 511; const. at front Vol. 1. (Ford, *Bibliotheca Hamiltoniana,* 18; Sabine 23993); ms. note in NYPL copy says trans., introduction (18 pp.) and few notes by Trudaine de la Sabliére; this ed. reissued same year, introduction omitted. Second French ed. 1795, with Jay's name spelled correctly. Next ed. Tiebout, N.Y., 1799, reprint of first (M'Lean) ed. Last ed. in H's lifetime, Hopkins, N.Y., 1802, 2. vols., with verbal revisions, probably (11 LHW xxxiv–xxxv) by Wm. Coleman. For fuller bibliography, Ford, *ibid.*

14. Among attackers were Cato, Brutus, Brutus, Jr., Centinel, Cincinnatus, Son of Liberty, Observer, Officer of Continental Army, Medium, Countryman, Citizen, Old Whig, One of Common People.

15. *Federalist,* Dawson ed., 1863, xiii–xiv.

16. Bancroft Trans., 2 Rev. Pap. 507–9, NYPL.

17. However, Jay published *An Address to the People of the State of New York;* was on all fours with *Federalist,* in last number of which H commended it (12 LHW 341); H's copy is in 6 HLC 811 ff.

18. April 3, 1788, H sent Madison numbers "to the conclusion of the commentary on the Executive Branch," but was "too much engaged to make a rapid progress in what remains. The Court of Chancery and a Circuit Court are now sitting" (9 LHW 427–8).

19. Cf. Madison, 5 *Writings* 107 n., and Madison to Pendleton, Washington, Randolph, March 3, 1788 (*ibid.,* 110–14); Adair (*W&M Quar.,* 3d. ser., Vol. I, 254): "If Madison was not writing as 'Publius' during February his delay in leaving New York [for Orange, Va., March 4] is inexplicable." (Cf. *ibid.,* ed., Madison's Autobiography, *op. cit.*)

20. Aug. 10, 1788, to Jefferson, 5 *Writings* 246. "In the early stage the papers were shown by the writers to each other before going to press," but this was dropped for want of time (cf. Madison's Autobiography, *op. cit.*). In preface to first ed. H apologized for imperfections of structure, but comforted himself that accidental iteration might serve good purpose. For an effort to avoid internal contradiction, see H to Madison, April 3, 1788, 9 LHW 427. Madison had at hand material supplied by H for nos. 18, 19, and 20, though these went to printer from Madison's pen, were based mainly on his own notes (*Federalist,* Gideon ed., note to No. 18).

21. Cf. Autobiography, *op. cit.*

22. To Jefferson, Aug. 10, 1788 (5 *Writings* 246); to Randolph, Dec. 2, 1787 (*ibid.,* 61). Friends made mistaken guesses about authorship when papers first appeared. Jefferson took for granted that Madison wrote most; Kent paid this compliment to H (above). John Jay (1864) found in grandfather's papers drafts of his numbers (*Corr. between Jay and Dawson . . . Concerning . . . Federalist* 19).

23. To Washington, Aug. 13, 1788 (9 LHW 441).

24. This copy is now in U.S. Arch.; it was an item in "Freedom Train" exhibit of U.S. Govt., 1950. Lodge (11 LHW xxi) referred to memo. as "in Washington's well-known handwriting," but apparently did not see actual page. Washington's signature in each vol., and binding, mark this as set presented by H. In memo. H given title of "Gen.," which did not have until July 1798. Supposition is Madison wrote list, for Washington or another, after this time.

25. Earliest ed. of *Federalist* to append an author's name to each paper that of John Wells, friend of H (N.Y., 1810). Gideon ed. (Washington, 1818) gave Madison's assignment of authorship. Earliest with full critical apparatus, Dawson (N.Y., 1863, 1 vol. of intended 2). E. G. Bourne, in *An. Rept. Am. Hist. Assn.*, I, 226, approving Gideon's list, answered by P. L. Ford, in *Am. Hist. Rev.*, II, 675–82 (July 1897). Briefer is S. A. Bailey, in *Case and Comment*, Rochester, N.Y., XXII, 674–5 (Jan. 1916). Latest (and possibly final) examination is Douglass Adair in *W&M Quar.*, 3d ser., I, No. 2 (April 1944), 97–122; No. 3 (July 1944), 235–64.

26. *Ibid.*, 100–1; cf. 106–9.

27. J. C. Hamilton, ed., *Federalist* (1888), cii–civ.

28. For Wm. Coleman's admission see Dawson, ed., *ibid.*, xlvii; cf. 11 LHW xviii, xx.

29. Dawson, *op. cit.*, xxvi, got the story from Egbert Benson, brother of Robert.

30. 11 LHW xxvii–xxviii.

31. See *Port Folio*, Phila., Nov. 14, 1807 (new ser., IV, No. 20), letter, supposed to be by Kent, quoting memo. from this book, given to N.Y. Soc. Lib. by H's executors, 1807; cf. Dawson, ed., *op. cit.*, xxvii. Search has confirmed reports century ago H's copy of *Federalist*, with his notation of authors, and list he gave Benson, are not there. Library had first ed. (*Catalogue*, 1813 . . . p. 100), but only Vol. 2 remains; on ordinary paper, leather bound, lacks back flyleaf, has nothing to show H ever owned it. Possibly was his, and Vol. 1 was taken because it had his name and list. This was larger of two "public" (subscription) libraries in N.Y.C.

32. Cf. Adair, 3d ser., 1, *W&M Quar.*, 99–100 n.

33. For doubt of "propriety or utility of . . . an altercation," Gideon ed., Prefatory, 3.

34. They did not present themselves as prophets, but as "the censors of present evils" (Bryce, "Predictions of Hamilton and De Tocqueville," in *Johns Hopkins Studies*, 5th ser., IX, 344).

35. Cf. unsigned article in *N.Y. Adv.*, July 21, 1787 (Vol. III, No. 751).

36. *Economic Interpretation of Constitution*, 1935 ed., 153–4; softened in *Enduring Federalist*, and in *The Republic*.

37. Cf. Bryce, above, and Tench Coxe in 2 *Am. Museum* (1787) 389.

38. Bryce, *ibid.*, 17, serial p. 341.

39. With irony for Madison.

40. 12 LHW 339, 340, 345. H remonstrated with Gov. Clinton ("Cato") just before beginning the *Federalist:* The wisdom of America had been "drawn into a focus," and the Constitution was proffered with remarkable unanimity. ". . . shall we now wrangle and find fault with the *excellent whole,* because . . . some of its parts might have been more perfect?" Rather, we should "take it as it is and be thankful." (Ford, ed., *Essays on Constitution,* 284).

41. Ford ed., *ibid.,* 286–7.

42. 2 JCHW 419–21, there called "Impressions as to the New Constitution," 1787.

Chapter 26 (Pages 426 to 440)
Trial of Strength at Poughkeepsie

1. H's second service in Continental Congress, 1788, is not treated here. Meetings were mostly frittering and tentative, for this body would expire if new Constitution replaced Articles of Confederation, as seemed week by week more likely. Nor did H have time or desire for any but desultory attendance between late Feb. and early Oct. When Congress awoke briefly, after Constitution had become a certainty, contest was over seat of new national govt. But this rightly belongs to H's next phase, as member of Washington's administration.

2. To Washington, n.d. [Oct. 1787], and *ibid.,* Oct. 30, 1787 (9 LHW 423–5); he took pains to bolster his political credit against insinuations of Anti-Federalists (cf. *ibid.,* 424–5, and 1 JCHW 447).

3. To Madison, April 3, 1788 (9 LHW 428). Madison at first demurred from offering for election from Orange County to his state convention, but abandoned this delicacy when he saw that others who had been in the national convention thought this no bar to acting on ratification locally (ALS to Ambrose Madison, Nov. 8, 1787, Madison Papers, NYPL); Hamilton, with no such inhibitions, probably influenced Madison's change of intention: cf. ALS, Andrew Shepherd, Orange [Va.], Dec. 22, 1787, to Madison (Madison Papers, *ibid.,* and Randolph, Jan. 3, 1788, to same (Emmet 9537, NYPL), urging that Madison return home for the canvass. As illustrations of Federalist electioneering in Albany Co., N.Y., see letter, badly torn, from Schuyler(?), Albany, March 9, 1788, to Duane, and ALS, Robt. McClellen, chm. of Federal Comm., Albany, March 12, 1788, to same (Duane Papers, NYHS).

4. 9 LHW 428.

5. *Ibid.,* 428–30. Unscrupulous misrepresentations of Antis, mentioned by H, soon became theme with his friends. Witness G. L. Turberville, who had failed of election as advocate of Constitution in Va., to Madison (ALS, April 16, 1788, Madison Papers, NYPL): "What has not been done [by Anti-foederal declaimers] . . . by cunning, Interest, and Address to blast and blacken this Production? [Constitution]." Delegates from Ky. had been targets of "Clamour upon ye passions." Barrell, of Boston, comforted that if honor should finally win, the "remorse & Shagreen" of "the wretched Antis . . . will be a sufficient punishment for all their Vilainy" (3 *Corr. and Jnls. of Webb* 101).

6. *Ibid.,* 430–1; three weeks later, June 8, he reported injunction with more urgency (*ibid.,* 434).

7. June 6, 1788 (*ibid.,* 432). Five weeks later Sullivan paid Capt. Roche, his express rider, in cash and was drawing on H for amount; "Laming a horse was unfortunate but could not be avoided" (July 10, 1788, 3 *Letters . . . of Sullivan* 591). Sum must have been considerable, as Sullivan had hoped bills might be bought by N.H. treasurer for supply of state's delegates in Congress (Sullivan to Gilman, July 10, 1788, *ibid.,* 592–3). Capt. Roche not in Heitman. Rufus King, in Boston, arranged for an express to take (presumably favorable) result in N.H. to Springfield, Mass., whence Knox had engaged conveyance to H at Poughkeepsie, but no record of arrival of this second messenger (King to H, June 12, 1788, 1 JCHW 456).

8. 9 LHW 436; Madison did not get the express from New Hampshire via Poughkeepsie till June 31, (so dated), after Va. ratified (Madison to H, 1 JCHW 463).

9. Webb, July 1, 1788 (3 *Corr. and Jnls.,* 108–9).

10. ALS, Yates, Poughkeepsie, June 21, 1788, to Mason (Emmet 9528, NYPL). H the same day told Madison "The object of the [opposition] party at present is undoubtedly conditional amendments" (1 JCHW 460). Madison warned H Antis were cooperating for rejection by Va. and N.Y. together. June 9 said Col. (Eleazer) Oswald, of Phila., "has closet interviews with the leaders of the opposition," and week later was confident "delay is on foot between the opposition here and with you. . . . the policy is to spin out the session . . . to weary the members into an adjournment, without taking any decision." However, they did not despair of preferable tactic of carrying previous amendments. Henry Lee, n.d., notified H of efforts of "malcontents of P. and N.Y." through Oswald, "but I believe we are still safe. . . ." (1 JCHW 456–8). McKesson Papers, NYHS, give 29 pp. of proposed amendments, as handed up to table.

11. Misc. mss., N.Y.C., Box 14, item 32, NYHS. Webb (May 11, 1788), enclosing political handbill said to be by H, wrote that of 2,900 or 3,000 votes in N.Y.C., Antis could muster less than 400 (3 *Corr. and Jnls., ibid.,* 102–3).

12. To Sullivan, June 6, to Madison June 8, 1788 (9 LHW 432–4). Low, shortly before N.Y. Conv. met, reported friends of Const. could count on only 19 members. His correspondent estimated Va. would adopt, else "The Worst Consequences will follow" (ALS, Robt. Gilmore & Co. to N. Low, June 20, 1788, Low misc., NYHS).

13. Orin G. Libby, "Geographical Distribution of Vote . . . on . . . Federal Constitution. . . ," in *Univ. of Wis. Bull.*, I, No. 1, 18 ff. Libby surmised Hudson Valley, unlike Conn. Valley, was for state's rights because "extravagant grants" of land, unsurveyed, expelled freeholders to N.J. and elsewhere; this left homogeneous group of landgraves who knew that in abolishing state impost, Constitution would shift the cost of govt. to land tax. In Federalist counties small farmers predominated over land monopolists (*ibid.*, 21 ff.; cf. Plate 1 showing distribution of vote in all states).

14. *N.Y. Daily Adv.*, June 16, 1788, No. 1035.

15. June 17, 1788, No. 150. Editor was charged by another correspondent with being "inlisted in the service of one particular party" in "the present dispute about forms of government," which he untruthfully denied, for all his notices from Va. and other states put approval of Constitution in brightest light. However, he declared accurately: "Upon this honorable body *thousands* cast their eyes, and perhaps no TEN of the *thousands* are divested of a *party* prejudice."

16. For composition of Va. convention see Madison to Jefferson, April 22, 1788 (5 *Writings* 120–22): ". . . it seems probable . . . that a majority of the members elect are friends of the Constitution. The superiority of abilities . . . seems to lie on that side." However, "Mr. H[enr]y is supposed to aim at disunion," and "Col. M[aso]n will probably in the end be thrown by the violence of his passions into the politics of Mr. H——y."

17. Madison, June 13, 1788, to Washington: "Our progress is slow and every advantage is taken of the delay, to work on the local prejudices of particular sets of members. . . . the event may depend on the Kentucky members; who seem to lean . . . agst . . . the Constitution. The business is in the most ticklish state. . . ." (5 *ibid.*, 179; cf. same to same, June 5, 1788: "Kentucky has been extremely tainted. . . ." *ibid.*, 124 n.).

18. *Debates and Proceedings of . . . Convention of . . . New York, assembled at Poughkeepsie, . . . 17th of June, 1788. . . .* "Taken in Short Hand. New-York: Francis Childs. M,DCC,LXXXVIII, pp. ii, 144" (Evans 21310; facsimile reprint, Poughkeepsie, Vassar Brothers Inst., 1905). Childs explained (ii) substance was justly reported, but apologized to gentlemen "for the imperfect dress in which their arguments are given to the public," as he was "not long accustomed to the business" and could not persuade speakers to revise his text of their remarks. Beginning July 4 Childs reports main motions, with no speeches; even so, his is best single record. Elliot's *Debates in State Conventions . . .*, Vol. 1, incorporated Childs's account.

19. *Journal of . . . Convention of . . . New-York: Held at Poughkeep-sie, . . .* 17th of June, 1788, Poughkeepsie, Nicholas Power, p. 86. (Evans 21313).

20. "Proceedings of New York Ratifying Convention," McKesson Papers, NYHS. Jnl. of debates, in one hand, 75 sheets, 141 sides, covering June 17 to July 4, a sheet without date, then July 6(?)–7, 10, 12 and 15, with nothing on debates after that. Certificates of 23 counties to election of delegates. Amendments, in different hands, as drawn by proposers; other fragments. These are official records of convention as left in McKesson's keeping. John McKesson (1734–96), clerk of N.Y. Assembly, was natural choice as secretary of convention; cf. Mary H. McKesson, photostat ALS, June 15, 1939, "Data gathered from family papers" (NYHS). McKesson's notes, unlike G. Livingston's, cover most of convention, were not influenced by writer's own sentiments; not published.

21. 6 HLC 796–7; 7 *ibid.*, 924–8, contain autograph notes for two of his speeches; 2 JCHW 463 ff. gives roughly half of first.

22. Ms. notes of debates in N.Y. convention (NYPL), 64 pp. covering July 14–26; all sheets 4-p. folios numbered 37–52; some 144 pp. of ms. missing. Also notes of speech of his, and fragments. Reports debates in much of later period which Childs recorded sketchily, but notes, made in convention for own use, are jerky, at times incomprehensible.

23. R. R. Livingston Papers, NYHS, "Notes on Poughkeepsie Convention," 50 sheets; own speech, June 19, is 13 foolscap pp. These notes may be related to individual days of debate, and report speeches of Jones (June 25), H, Harison and Jones (June 26), M. Smith, G. Livingston (July 4), H, Lansing, Williams, Clinton, M. Smith (July 17), omitted by Childs.

24. Remarks of Clinton in N.Y. conv. on power to levy taxes as granted to Congress by new Constitution, Bancroft Trans., 5976, pp. 35, NYPL.

25. Wm. Kent, *Memoirs . . . of James Kent*, Appendix, 303–12. Kent, in reminiscences for Mrs. H, 1832, used Childs's published report for detail of H's chief speeches, though gave valuable personal impressions too. Incidentally, Childs wrote out shorthand notes in evenings at Kent's house (*ibid.*, 300). Kent, H's confidential friend, had met him few months before conv., at Schuyler's house, Albany. Kent despaired of making abridgment of *Federalist* essays for "small and humble" *Poughkeepsie Journal*, but received first 36 nos. in collected form; he and Benson distributed them at Dutchess Co. meeting for nomination of delegates (*ibid.*, 302).

26. 7 HLC 867–86; seems to be original paper, with material corrections, doodling.

27. Following complaint of "A Citizen," June 28, 1788, No. 1046 that N.Y.C. readers were entitled to account besides Childs's own, paper began shorter reports with July 4, 1788, misnumbered 1046 for 1049 (NYPL).

28. Many residents of Poughkeepsie had Dutch names; for the kind of Dutch they spoke, or wrote, cf. Trintie (Van Kleeck) Crannell, Sept. 3, 1785, to daughter Catherine, wife of G. Livingston (*Dutchess Co. H.S. Yr. Bk.*, 1938, p. 72).

29. See map of Poughkeepsie, 1790, from survey of 1788, in Edmund Platt, *Eagle's Hist. Poughkeepsie*, 65, and map of Dutchess Turnpike, 1804, in *ibid.*, 78; Helen W. Reynolds, comp. and ed., "The Court House of Dutchess County . . ." in *Dutchess Co. H.S. Yr. Bk.*, 1938, pp. 74 ff.

30. *Memoirs*, 303.

31. To Morison, June 21, 1788 (9 LHW 435).

32. Yates to Mason, June 21, 1788 (Emmet 9528, NYPL); cf. Jnl. Conv., does not note.

33. McKesson Papers, NYHS.

34. Cf. Elihu Root: "For more than a month with undivided leadership on the floor of the convention, with splendid courage and persistency . . . he incessantly assaulted this solid and sullen phalanx. He broke the phalanx by convincing the judgment of the most logical and able of his antagonists . . . and won the majority . . . to the adoption of the Constitution." (Address at Hamilton College, *N.Y. Sun*, June 17, 1918; cf. Lodge, H, 69 ff; Oliver, H, 176 ff.).

35. 9 LHW 436.

36. To Barrell, 3 *Corr. and Jnls.* 89–91, 107–8.

37. *N.Y. Daily Adv.*, July 7, 1788, No. 1053. Cf. Nich. Gilman, N.Y., to Sullivan, March 23, 1788 (2 Bancroft Trans., NYPL, p. 510½). "A Pennsylvanian" (Tench Coxe?) warned convention against putting the people, especially merchants of N.Y., "on the footing of foreigners," and a North Carolinian declared his convention would "never be so mad as to *vote themselves out of the Union*. . . ." (*N.Y. Daily Adv.*, June 17, 18, 1788.)

38. To J. B. Schuyler, June 26, 1788 (2 Bancroft Trans., NYPL, 511–13); he praised eloquence of all friends of Constitution, but proudly observed of H: "his sentiments are so true, his judgment so correct, his elocution so pleasing . . . and yet so [forcible?] . . . that he reaches the heart . . . where every avenue of conviction is [not] shut up. Alas! . . . too many . . . labor under the prejudice."

39. To Madison, July 8, 1788 (9 LHW 436).

40. To same, July 22, 1788 (*ibid.*, 440).

41. N. Chipman, July 14, Sept. 6, 1788, to H (1 JCHW 466–7, 472–3), and H to same, July 22 and (Sept. ?) 1788 (*ibid.*, 467–9, 477–9).

42. He several times reverted to ambition of Gov. "to establish Clintonism on the basis of Anti-federalism" (to Madison, June 1788, *ibid.*, 435).

43. Cf. 3 R 522–3.

44. Childs, 123.

Chapter 27 (Pages 441 to 464)
Victory Against Odds

1. Kent, *Memoirs*, 294. His fluency ran a little to the oratorical, though he did not fall into strained interpretations nor indulge in declamation that smote ears of delegates at Richmond.

2. Childs, 7.

3. *Ibid.*, 8.

4. *Ibid.*, 9–10.

5. *Ibid.*, 10–11. Kent, describing to Troup the opening of the convention, registered Federalist feeling at that juncture: "I look forward to [the result] with anxious uncertainty. I do not abandon hope. I think the opposition discover great embarrassment. . . . Some of them . . . have said that they will not vote against it" (June 10, 1788; Kent, *op. cit.*, 30).

6. They wrote to Gov. Clinton in explanation: ". . . we were of opinion that the leading features of every amendment ought to be the preservation of the individual states in their uncontrolled constitutional rights . . . before we left the Convention, . . . no alteration was to be expected, to conform it to our ideas of expediency and safety" (Elliot, 1 *Debates* 481). Lansing outlived Hamilton by 25 years; on a late December afternoon in 1829 he left his home to post a letter on the Albany boat, and was never seen again; see for brief particulars of Lansing's career, Joseph R. Strayer, ed., *The Delegate from New York . . .* , 2–6.

7. Childs, 11–12.

8. *Ibid.*, 12–13.

9. *Ibid.*, 14.

10. *Ibid.*, 15.

11. Kent, *op. cit.*, 305, 306; he spoke further of "the metaphysical mind, prepossessing plainness, and embarrassing subtleties of Smith" (*ibid.*, 304). See a pencil drawing of Smith, about this date, signed by him (Emmet 9411,

NYPL); he had large head, irregular features, curly hair reaching down back of his strong neck.

12. Childs, 16–20.

13. Kent recorded that he "spoke with . . . energy and with considerable gesture. His language was clear, nervous. . . . He . . . brought to the debate a mind filled with all the learning and precedents applicable to the subject. . . . His candor was magnanimous. . . . His temper was spirited but courteous, . . . and he frequently made pathetic and powerful appeals to the moral sense and patriotism, the fears and hopes of the assembly. . . ." (Kent, *op. cit.*, 305–6).

14. Childs, 21. Many expressions H used, such as "imbecility" of confederation and need for powers in central government equal to "exigencies" of Union, have become identified with him, but were frequent if not common language of advocates of his persuasion.

15. *Ibid.*, 21–3.

16. *Ibid.*, 23–5.

17. *Ibid.*, 25–27.

18. *Ibid.*, 31–3.

19. *Ibid.*, 35–40.

20. Kent, *op. cit.*, 304, 306.

21. Lansing had offered negative definition of govt.: ". . . its object is to restrain and punish vice; . . . to deter the governed from crime, and the governors from tyranny" (Childs, 67).

22. *Ibid.*, 71.

23. *Ibid.*, 84.

24. Childs, 85, 86. Tidings from N.H. did not pull carpet from under opponents or relieve advocates from arguing merits.

25. *Ibid.*, 89.

26. *Ibid.*, 72.

27. *Ibid.*, 91–2.

28. *Ibid.*, 93.

29. *Ibid.*, 96–8.

30. *Ibid.*, 103–4.

31. *Ibid.,* 105. He observed that "sound policy condemns the practice of accumulating debts. A government, to act with energy, should have the possession of all its revenues to answer present purposes" (*ibid.,* 106). This was not inconsistent with his emphasis, elsewhere, on utility of public debt, for latter was not to be "accumulating," was not regarded as Treasury policy but as basis for credit and currency in preparatory stage of national economy.

32. *Ibid.,* 107.

33. June 28, 1788; Childs, 109–12.

34. Childs, 118–9.

35. *Ibid.,* 122–3.

36. Before sunset Nicholas Power had struck off an "extra" of his *Country Journal* (broadside 7 × 10 in.) giving the form of Va.'s ratification. That night Federalists pounded news into ears of Antis with 10 guns, lit bonfire. Express rider was Col. Wm. S. Livingston; he covered 82 miles of rough road from N.Y.C. in less than ten hours, changing horses only twice. (*Country Jnl. and Poughkeepsie Adv.,* July 5, No. 154; *N.Y. Daily Adv.,* July 8, 1788, No. 1054; B. J. Lossing in *Poughkeepsie Daily Eagle,* Feb. 18, 1888, reported interview with witness of scene almost century earlier; reproduction of Power's broadside is in Platt, *Eagle's Hist. Poughkeepsie,* 60.) The letters from Richmond were brought to N.Y.C. about 2:30 A.M., July 2, by Madison's express, Col. David Henly, week after Va.'s action June 25. City's bells began ringing at dawn, salute from ten 24-pounders was fired at sunrise (S. B. Webb, July 1[2], 1788, 4 A.M., to Barrell, same day to Miss Hogeboom, 3 *Corr. and Jnls.* 108–10; *N.Y. Daily Adv.,* July 2, 1788, No. 1046 [*sic*], said news brought not by express but "By a passenger of veracity, who came in the stage from Philadelphia"; cf. *ibid.,* July 3, 1788, No. 1050). However, Madison's letter to H, from Richmond, June 27, 1788, announcing ratification by Va., went by post, for is so stamped; was addressed to H in Cong., had to be forwarded. H wrote Madison by express same day, notifying him of adoption by N.H. (7 HLC 863).

37. Wm. Duer was Cincinnati orator at St. Pauls, N.Y.C.; Steuben was elected pres. of society, H vice pres. One of toasts "drank" at dinner was "Wisdom to our Convention, and may they pursue the true interest of our Country." (*Country Jnl.,* July 8, 1788; cf. curses called down on heads of Antis at July 4 dinner of 13 Federalists at Dawson's Tavern, Brooklyn [*sic*], *N.Y. Daily Adv.,* July 4, 1788, No. 1051.)

38. *Jnl.,* 43–4. Madison, in N.Y.C. for the meeting of Congress, sent Randolph "the latest intelligence from Poughkeepsie. . . . Some of the most sanguine calculate on a ratification. The best informed apprehend some clog that will amount to a condition." He wanted state to come in, but began to wonder whether that would not fix first national Congress in N.Y.C. to the prejudice of a Va. location of capital. (5 *Writings* 236, Hunt ed.)

39. Smith's motion of July 15 was sustained, against Duane's effort at rejection, and July 19 Lansing carried his more elaborate motion for approval contingent on prior amendments (*Journal*, 43–58; Childs, 142).

40. Poughkeepsie, Saturday, July 5 (?), 1788 (9 LHW 437–8).

41. Sunday evening [July (13?) 1788] (1 JCHW 465). He added, "The idea of reserving a right to withdraw was started at Richmond, and considered as . . . worse than a rejection." Clinton spoke twice on issue of acceptance of Constitution contingent on amendments, or outright in expectation of alterations later. His was states' rights position, earnestly but dogmatically declared. States formed compact of govt.; as they "are the creative principle, the power of the confederacy, must originate from and operate upon them, and not upon the individuals, who compose them. . . ." Some days later (probably July 17) he renewed his entreaties for conditional adoption. The other states would receive New York on these terms. To put the question of outright ratification was to defeat it. This would be taken as rejection of Constitution, and state would be internally divided (Clinton Papers, NYPL).

42. N.Y. *Daily Adv.*, July 16, 1788, No. 1061; cf. Kent, *Address before Law Assn.*, 27 ff.; Jas. A. H, *Reminiscences*, 10.

43. *Jnl.*, 37–9.

44. *Ibid.*, 44–6.

45. *Ibid.*, 48–9; July 18, 1788.

46. *Jnl.*, 49–58.

47. *Ibid.*, 58; see H to Madison, July 19 (8 LHW 191); Madison to Washington, July 21 (5 *Writings* 237).

48. *Ibid.*, 58 ff. One of first of Lansing's amendments passed forbade Congress to impose excise on any article of domestic growth or manufacture, save ardent spirits.

49. Echoing earlier intimations, H reported to Madison: "There is so great a diversity in the views of our opponents that it is impossible to predict any thing. Upon the whole, however, our fears diminish" (Poughkeepsie, July 22, 1788, 9 LHW 440).

50. *Jnl.*, 67.

51. N.Y. *Daily Adv.*, ibid., *Country Jnl.*, July 29, 1788, 156.

52. *Jnl.*, 68; Childs, 143. On sacrifice of Antis' pride, Madison to Randolph, July 22, 1788 (5 *Writings* 239). Having secured immediate entry of N.Y. into the Union, H and his friends were glad save antagonists' faces by amendments merely recommended.

53. *Jnl.*, 68. The 6 Antis who, besides Clinton, Yates, Lansing, scurried back to negative, were Ten Eyck (Albany), Cantine, Clark (Ulster), Haring, Woodhull, Wisner (Orange). However, Federalists retrieved Lewis Morris. For H's condemnation of Clinton's obdurance, even after 9 states ratified, "H—— G——" in *N.Y. Daily Adv.*, March 19, 1789.

54. *Jnl.*, 69–70.

55. *N.Y. Daily Adv.*, July 28, 1788, No. 1071.

56. *Jnl.*, 70.

57. *N.Y. Daily Adv.*, July 28, 1788, No. 1071. For wise words of Madison on N.Y.'s recommended alterations, see to Jefferson, July 26 P.S. to letter of July 24, 1788 (5 *Writings* 243); to same, Aug. 10 (*ibid.*, 244); to Pendleton, Aug. 22, 1788 (*ibid.*, 252).

58. *Jnl.*, 71 ff.

59. *Ibid.*, 76.

60. *Jnl.*, 76–7.

61. 5 *Writings* 271–5; cf. Oct. 8, 1788, to Philip Mazzei, *ibid.*, 267–8. G. Morris, in 1811, called amendments "Mere Verbiage. . . . the original Constitution contained those guards which form the apparent object of the amendments" (2 *Diary* 529–30).

62. *Jnl.*, 77–8.

63. *Ibid.*, 83 ff. "Several articles in [Constitution] appear so exceptionable to a majority of us," read circular, "that nothing but the fullest confidence of obtaining a revision . . . by a General Convention, and an invincible reluctance to separating from our sister States, could have prevailed upon a sufficient number to ratify it, without stipulating for previous amendments" (*ibid.*, 84). Madison laid the unanimous vote of the Federalists for the letter to determination to secure ratification at any price rather than see congress leave New York City (to Washington, Aug. 24, 1788, 5 *Writings* 256). Earlier, H feared "too general a concurrence in some very injudicious recommendations" (to Madison, 9 LHW 436–7). Both were mistaken, as turned out.

64. *Country Jnl.*, July 29, 1788, No. 156.

65. City had received news from Poughkeepsie earlier, by post; for joyous reception of delegates, *N.Y. Daily Adv.*, July 29, 1788, No. 1072 and S. B. Webb to Miss Hogeboom, July 27, 1788 (3 *Corr. and Jnls.* 111–12).

66. *Country Jnl.*, June 31 (*sic*), 1788, No. 152, letters from N.Y.C.

67. Webb, July 1, to Barrell, July 2, 1788, to Miss Hogeboom. (3 *Corr. and Jnls.* 108–10.)

68. *Country Jnl.*, Aug. 5, 1788, No. 157; *N.Y. Daily Adv.*, Aug. 2, 1788, No. 1076.

69. She was 27 feet in the keel, 10 ft. beam, 32 guns, manned by 30 seamen and marines commanded by Commodore James Nicholson, and drawn by 10 horses. A carving of Hamilton was the figurehead (see *Country Jnl.*, July 26, 1788, No. 156). Nicholson's piloting Federal ship was ironic, for he was to become conspicuous Republican (Jeffersonian) supporter, and all but engaged in shooting duel with H over political difference.

70. *Country Jnl.*, Aug. 19, 1788, No. 159. Flag of tallow chandlers had figure of Washington at one end, of H at other (*ibid.*, Sept. 2, 1788, No. 161). Carters had standard with, inter alia, "the Federal Ship Hamilton," and on reverse:

> "Behold the federal ship of fame,
> The Hamilton we call her name;
> To every craft she gives employ,
> Sure Cartmen have their share of joy."

(*ibid.*, Aug. 26, 1788, No. 160). In Newburgh celebration, by time No. 4 toast was "drank," thankful excitement was high enough to salute "The whole gradation of Heroes and Benefactors of mankind, from the first of human race to the immortal Washington, and all the sons of wisdom, from Solon to the invincible Hamilton" (*ibid.*, Aug. 12, 19, 1788).

71. Bakers carried mammoth federal loaf and "A flag, representing the declension of trade under the old confederation," and promising brisk business under new régime (*ibid.*, Aug. 12).

72. *Ibid.*, Aug. 5, No. 157.

73. Procession wound up in Fields; here Maj. L'Enfant had supervised erection of pavilions; here members of Congress, etc., were served at 10 tables from two bullocks and mutton roasted whole "for their regale." Federal ship came to anchor beside Bowling Green, saluted by "different orders" as they dispersed (*Country Jnl.*, Aug. 26, 1788, No. 160; *N.Y. Daily Adv.*, July 25, 1788, No. 1069). Even unfortunate citizens confined in Castle Percy (though dining on bread and water?) lifted glasses to new Constitution, added, "May Virtue flourish and Vice decay" (*ibid.*). Silk banner carried by pewterers, much repaired, is preserved in museum of NYHS. See ALS Richard Platt, chm. of comm., to city delegates, July 23, 1788 (Duane Papers, NYHS). Detailed account of parade, which appeared for days in papers of N.Y., prepared by Noah Webster (see anon. letter to him, July 31, 1788, N. Webster Papers, NYPL); Duer took from this in *Old Yorker*, 1867 ed., 50–67.

Bibliography

CHIEF MANUSCRIPT SOURCES

Clerk New York County, record room, Hall of Records, New York City: Minutes Supreme Court of Judicature

Columbia University, New York City: Nicholas Fish; Robert Harpur; King's College Matricula and Book of Misdemeanors

Connecticut Historical Society, Hartford: Jeremiah Wadsworth; Oliver Wolcott, Jr.

General Theological Seminary, New York City: Thomas B. Chandler; Samuel Seabury

Historical Society of Pennsylvania, Philadelphia: Mathew Carey; William Hand Irvine; Hugh Knox; Kortright family; Robert Morris; Edward Stevens; Anthony Wayne

Houghton Library, Harvard: Sparks Transcripts

John Carter Brown Library, Providence: Elias Boudinot Journal; Nathanael Greene

Library of Congress: Hamilton

Long Island Historical Society, Brooklyn: Henry and John Laurens

Massachusetts Historical Society, Boston: Hamilton; Henry Knox; William Livingston; Timothy Pickering; Theodore Sedgwick

Morgan Library, New York City: Yorktown Campaign collection

Nevis, British West Indies: Register's Office, Charles Town, Common Records

New Jersey Historical Society, Newark: Francis Barber

New York Historical Society, New York City: William Alexander (Lord Stirling); John and Henry Cruger, Copy Book of letters; James Duane; William Duer; Horatio Gates; Rufus King; John Lamb; Robert Livingston; R. R. Livingston; Nich. Low; Alexander McDougall; John McKesson; Allan McLane; Misc. mss., New York City; Joseph Reed; F. W. von Steuben.

New York Public Library: Bancroft Transcripts; Elias Boudinot; George Clinton; William Constable; Emmet collection; Hamilton; Thomas Jefferson; James Kent; Gilbert Livingston; William Livingston; Nicholas Low; James Madison; James McHenry; James Monroe; Robert Morris;

Philip Schuyler; William Smith Diary; Robert Troup; Noah Webster; Marinus Willett; Abraham Yates

Princeton University: Elias Boudinot; Minutes First Presbyterian Church, Elizabethtown

Presbyterian Historical Society, Philadelphia: Hugh Knox

Rhode Island Historical Society, Providence: Nathanael Greene

St. Christopher, British West Indies: Basseterre, Register's Office, Common Records.

St. Croix, United States Virgin Islands: Christiansted, Tax Assessor's Office, deeds; Department Public Works, real property surveys; St. John's Church, register

Yale University: Hamilton

United States Archives, Washington, D.C.: Virgin Islands records; Military records

PRINTED SOURCES

WRITINGS

Adams, John, *Works of* . . . , *with a Life of the Author,* . . . by Charles Francis Adams (Boston, Little, Brown, 1850–56. 10 vols.).

————, *Correspondence of the Late President Adams. Originally Published in the Boston Patriot* (Boston, Everett & Munroe, 1809).

————, *Correspondence between* . . . *John Adams* . . . *and the late Wm. Cunningham* . . . , *1803–12* (Boston, E. M. Cunningham, 1823). See, in connection, Timothy Pickering, *A Review of the Correspondence between* . . . *Adams* . . . *and Cunningham* (Salem, Mass., Joshua & J. D. Cushing, 1824).

Burnett, E. C., ed., *Letters of the Members of the Continental Congress, 1774–1789* (Washington, Carnegie Institution of Washington, 1921–36, 8 vols.).

Burr, Aaron, *Memoirs of, with* . . . *Selections from His Correspondence,* ed. M. L. David, (New York, Harper, 1836–38, 2 vols.).

Clinton, George, *Public Papers,* Hugh Hastings, compiler (New York and Albany, published by State of New York, 1899–1914, 10 vols.).

Colden, Cadwalader, *Letters and Papers of* . . . , *1711–1775* (New York, NYHS, 1918–37, 9 vols.).

Cutler, Manasseh, *Life, Journals, and Correspondence* (Cincinnati, R. Clarke & Co., 1888).

Dayton, Elias, "Papers," in 1st. ser., Vol. 9, *NJHS Proceed.,* 175–94.

Fithian, P. V., *Journal and Letters, 1767–74.* Vol. 1 ed. J. R. Williams; Vol. 2 by R. G. Albion and L. Dodson (Princeton, Princeton University Press, 1904–34, 2 vols.).

Hamilton, Alexander, *Works,* ed. J. C. Hamilton (New York, J. F. Trow, 1850–51, 7 vols.).

—————, *Works,* ed. H. C. Lodge (New York and London, Putnam, Federal Edition, 1904, 12 vols.).

Jay, John, *Correspondence and Public Papers,* ed. H. P. Johnston (New York, Putnam, 1890–93, 4 vols.).

Lafayette, Marquis de, *Letters . . . to Washington, 1777–1799,* ed. Louis Gottschalk (New York, privately printed by Helen F. Hubbard, 1944).

—————, *Memoirs, Correspondence, and Manuscripts,* published by his family (London, Saunders & Otley, 1837, 3 vols.).

Lee, Charles, *The Lee Papers, 1754–1811* (New York, NYHS Collections, vols. 4, 5, 6, 7, 1871–74).

Maclay, William, *Journal,* ed. E. S. Maclay (New York, Appleton, 1890).

Madison, James, *Writings,* ed. Gaillard Hunt (New York, Putnam, 1900–10, 9 vols.).

Morris, Gouverneur, *Diary and Letters,* ed. Anne C. Morris, (New York, Scribner, 1888, 2 vols.).

Morris, Robert, *Confidential Correspondence,* (Philadelphia, S. V. Henkels, 1917?).

Rodney, Caesar, *Letters to and from Caesar Rodney, 1756–84* (Philadelphia, University of Pennsylvania Press, 1933).

Rowe, John, *Letters and Diary,* ed. Anne R. Cunningham (Boston, W. B. Clarke Co., 1930).

Sparks, Jared, *Correspondence of the American Revolution; being Letters of Eminent Men to . . . Washington* (Boston, Little, Brown, 1853, 4 vols.).

Stiles, Ezra, *Literary Diary,* ed. F. B. Dexter (New York, Scribner, 1901).

Sullivan, John, *Letters and Papers,* ed. O. G. Hammond, (Concord, *New Hampshire Historical Society Collections,* vols. 13, 14, 15; 1930–39).

Washington, George, *Correspondence Concerning the Society of the Cincinnati,* ed. E. E. Hume (Baltimore, Johns Hopkins Press, 1941).

—————, *Correspondence of . . . and Comte De Grasse, Aug. 17–Nov. 4, 1781* (Institut français de Washington, Washington, Government Printing Office, 1931).

—————, *Diaries,* ed. John C. Fitzpatrick (Boston, Houghton Mifflin, 1925, 4 vols.).

—————, *Writings,* ed. John C. Fitzpatrick (Washington, Government Printing Office, Bicentennial Edition, 1931–44, 39 vols.).

—————, *Writings,* ed. W. C. Ford (New York, Putnam, 1889–93, 14 vols.).

—————, *Writings,* ed. Jared Sparks (Boston, American Stationers' Co., 1834–37, 12 vols.).

Webb, Samuel B., *Correspondence and Journals,* ed. W. C. Ford (New York, Wickersham Press, 1893–4, 3 vols.).

RECORDS AND PROCEEDINGS, OFFICIAL AND SEMIOFFICIAL

American Archives: . . . A Collection of Authentic Records, State Papers, . . . forming a Documentary History of . . . Origin and Progress of the North American Colonies (Washington, M. St. Clair Clarke & Peter Force, 1836–46, 4 vols.; often referred to as Force).

Carey, Mathew, ed., *Debates and Proceedings of General Assembly of Pennsylvania on Repeal or Suspension of Law Annulling Charter of Bank* (Philadelphia, Carey & Co., 1786).

Dickinson, John, Report to Assembly, in 4th ser., 3 *Pennsylvania Archives* 905 ff.

Elliot, Jonathan, ed. *Debates in . . . State Conventions on Adoption of Federal Constitution* (Washington, printed by editor, 1836–45, 5 vols.).

Farrand, Max, ed., *Records of the Federal Convention of 1787* (New Haven, Yale University Press, 1911, 3 vols.).

New York, *Debates and Proceedings of . . . Convention of . . . State of New York assembled at Poughkeepsie, . . . 17th June, 1788. . . . Taken in Short Hand* (New York, F. Childs, 1788).

New York, *Documents Illustrative of Colonial History of* (Albany, various publishers, 1853–87; see especially Vol. 15).

New York, *Journal of Assembly of State of* (also called *Votes and Proceedings*), seventh sess., Jan. 1784 through eleventh sess., Jan. 1788; publisher and place vary).

New York, *Journal of . . . Convention of . . . State of New-York: Held at Poughkeepsie, 17th June, 1788* (Poughkeepsie, Nicholas Power, 1788). This is the bare record of motions, votes, etc., but supplements *Debates and Proceedings* of Childs, above.

New York, *Journal of the Provincial Congress, Provincial Convention, Committee of Safety, etc., 1775–1776–1777* (Albany, Thurlow Weed, 1842).

New York, *Journal of Senate of State of* (same dates as New York, *Journal of Assembly of State of*).

New York, *Laws of . . . Legislature of . . . New York, in force against Loyalists* (London, H. Reynell, 1786).

New York, *Laws of State of* (Poughkeepsie, John Holt, 1782, 1783; New York, Elizabeth Holt, 1784; S. Loudon, 1785; S. & J. Loudon, 1786, 1787).

New York, Office of State Comptroller, *New York in the Revolution as Colony and State,* J. A. Roberts, compiler (Albany, Brandow Print Co., 1898).

New York City, *Minutes of Common Council, 1675–1776* (New York, Dodd, Mead, 1905; same, 1784–1831, published by City of New York, 1917; see analytical index by D. M. Matteson [New York, M. B. Brown, 1930, 2 vols.]).

Records of Pennsylvania, *Minutes of Executive Council* (Harrisburg, Theodore Penn & Co., 1853).

United States Continental Congress, *Journals, 1774–1789* (Washington, Government Printing Office, 1904–37, 34 vols.).

———, *Secret Journals of the Acts and Proceedings of* (Boston, Thomas B. Wait, 1820–21, 4 vols.).

United States Bureau of Rolls and Library, *Documentary History of the Constitution* (Washington, Department of State, 1894, 3 vols.).

United States Department of State, *Diplomatic Correspondence of the American Revolution,* ed. Jared Sparks (Boston, N. Hale, Gray & Bowen; New York, Carvill, 1829–30, 12 vols.).

United States House of Representatives, *Revolutionary Diplomatic Correspondence of the United States,* ed. Francis Wharton (Washington, Government Printing Office, 1889, 6 vols.).

United States Inspector General [Steuben, F. W. von], *Regulations for . . . the Order and Discipline of the Troops of the United States,* Part I (Philadelphia, Stymer and Cist, 1779).

United States Superintendent of Finance [Robert Morris], *Statement of Accounts of United States, Feb. 20, 1781, to Nov. 1, 1784* (Philadelphia, R. Aitken, 1785).

Valentine, D. T., *Manual of the Corporation of the City of New York* (New York, 1842–70).

Vermont, *Records of Governor and Council,* ed. E. P. Walton (Montpelier, J. & J. M. Poland, 1873–80, 8 vols.; see especially Vol. 3).

PAMPHLETS, CHIEFLY POLEMICAL

"Cassius" (AEdanus Burke), *Considerations on the Society or Order of Cincinnati, Proving that it Creates . . . Hereditary Patricians* (Philadelphia, Robert Bell, 1783).

Cooper, Myles, *A Friendly Address to All Reasonable Americans, on . . . Our Political Confusions* (New York, James Rivington, 1774).

[Dickinson, John] *Letters from a Farmer in Pennsylvania* (Philadelphia, Hall & Sellers, 1768).

Ford, P. L., ed., *Essays on the Constitution . . . Published during its Discussion by the People* (Brooklyn, New York Historical Printing Club, 1892).

———, *Pamphlets on the Constitution* (Brooklyn, 1788).

Goddard, William, *To Friends of Freedom in City of New York* (New York, May 2, 1775, broadside in NYPL).

Hamilton, Alexander, *The Farmer Refuted: or, A more Impartial and Comprehensive View of the Dispute between Great-Britain and the Colonies* (New York, James Rivington, 1775).

——, *A Full Vindication of the Measures of the Congress* (New York, James Rivington, 1774).

Jay, John, *An Address to the People of the State of New York* (New York, S. & J. Loudon, 1788).

[Ledyard, Isaac] *Mentor's Reply . . . with some Observations on Trade* (New York, Sheppard Kollock, 1784.)

Lee, Charles, *Strictures on a Pamphlet, entitled a "Friendly Address . . . "* (Philadelphia, W. & T. Bradford, 1774).

Livingston, William, *The Independent Reflector* (New York, J. Parker, 1753).

——, "The American Whig," in *New York Gazette,* 1768–9.

——, "The Sentinel," in *New York Post-Boy,* 1765.

——, "The Watch Tower," in *New York Mercury,* 1754–55.

——, "The Watchman," in *New York Journal,* 1770.

Mirabeau, H. G. R., Comte de, *Considérations sur l'ordre de Cincinnatus* (London, J. Johnson, 1784; English trans., same, 1785).

"North-American" [Myles Cooper], *American Querist* (New York, James Rivington, 1774).

Paine, Thomas, *Dissertations on Government Affairs of Bank and Paper Money* (Philadelphia, Charles Cist, 1786).

"A. W. Farmer" [Samuel Seabury], *A View of the Controversy between Great Britain and her Colonies* (New York, James Rivington, 1774).

——, *The Congress Canvassed: or, an Examination into the Conduct of the . . . Grand Convention . . . held in Philadelphia, 1774* (New York, James Rivington, 1774).

"A Farmer" [Samuel Seabury], *Free Thoughts on Proceedings of the Continental Congress* (New York, James Rivington, 1774).

"A Citizen of Philadelphia" [Pelatiah Webster], *An Essay on Credit, in which . . . some Remarks are made on present State of Bank of North-America* (Philadelphia, E. Oswald, 1786).

Webster, Pelatiah, *Political Essays on . . . Money, Public Finance* (Philadelphia, J. Crukshank, 1791).

[Wilson, James], *Considerations on Bank of North-America* (Philadelphia, Hall & Sellers, 1785).

AUTOBIOGRAPHY, RECOLLECTIONS

Duer, William A., *Reminiscences of an Old Yorker* (New York, W. L. Andrews, 1867).

Graydon, Alexander, *Memoirs of His Own Times* (Harrisburgh, John Wyeth, 1811; Phila., Lindsay and Blackiston, 1846).

Hamilton, James A., *Reminiscences* (New York, Scribner, 1869).

Kent, James, *Memoirs and Letters,* ed. Wm. Kent (Boston, Little, Brown, 1898).

Madison, James, *Autobiography,* ed. Douglass Adair, in 3d ser., 2 *William and Mary Quarterly,* 191–209).

Ogden, Aaron, *Autobiography,* annotated by Wm. Nelson (Paterson, N.J., Press Printing Co., 1893).

Rush, Benjamin, *Autobiography,* ed. G. W. Corner (Princeton, Princeton University Press, 1948).

Wilkins, Isaac, *My Services and Losses in Aid of the King's Cause during the American Revolution* (Brooklyn, Historical Printing Club, 1890).

Wilkinson, James, *Memoirs of My Own Times* (Philadelphia, A. Small, 1816, 3 vols.).

WAR DIARIES, LETTERS

Anderson, Enoch, "Personal Recollections of an Officer in the Delaware Regiments in the Revolutionary War," in 16 *Historical and Biographical Papers of Delaware* (Wilmington, Historical Society of Delaware, 1896).

André, John, *André's Journal. An Authentic Record of the Movements . . . of the British Army in America, June 1777 to Nov. 1778* (Boston, H. O. Houghton & Co., 1903).

Boudinot, Elias, *Journal or Historical Recollections of American Events during the Revolutionary War* (Philadelphia, F. Bourquin, 1894).

Bourg, Cromot du, "Diary" in 4 *Magazine of American History,* 205 ff.; Vol. 7, 283 ff.

Clinton, Sir Henry, *The American Rebellion,* ed. W. Willcox (New Haven, Yale University Press, 1954).

Deux-Ponts, W. de, *My Campaigns in America,* trans., ed. S. A. Green (Boston, J. K. Wiggin and W. P. Lunt, 1868).

Ewald, J. von, *Belehrungen über den Krieg* (Schleswig, 1798).

Feltman, William, *Journal . . . 1781–82, including the Siege of Yorktown* (Philadelphia, H. C. Baird, 1853).

Gallatin, Gaspard de, *Journal of Siege of York-Town* (Washington, Government Printing Office, 1931).

Haven, C. C., *Thirty Days in New Jersey Ninety Years Ago* (Trenton, State Gazette Office, 1867).

Heath, William, *Memoirs of the American War,* ed. R. R. Wilson (New York, A. Wessels Co., 1904).

Krafft, J. C. von, "Hessian Military Journal, May 1776–Jan. 1784," in 15 *NYHS Collections,* 1–200.

Laurens, John, *Army Correspondence. . . , 1777–78,* ed. with memoir by William Gilmore Simms (New York, Bradford Club, 1867).

Lee, Henry, *Memoirs of the War in the Southern Department of the United States* (New York, University Publishing Co., 1869).

Riedesel, Baroness von, *Letters and Journals Relating to the War of American Independence* (New York, G. & C. Carvill, 1827).

Riedesel, Major General, *Memoirs during Residence in America*. W. L. Stone, trans. (Albany, J. Munsell, 1868, 2 vols.).

Rochambeau, Comte de, *Mémoires militaires, historiques et politiques* (Paris, Fain, 1809, 2 vols.).

Rodney, Thomas, *Diary of . . . , Dec. 1776–Jan. 1777*, ed. Caesar A. Rodney (Wilmington, Historical Society of Delaware, 1888).

Simcoe, J. G., *A Journal of Operations of . . . the Queen's Rangers* (Exeter, privately printed, 1787).

Stevens, B. F., compiler, *The Campaign in Virginia* (London, 1888, 2 vols.).

Tarleton, Banastre, *A History of the Campaign of 1780 and 1781 in the Southern Provinces of North America* (London, T. Cadell, 1787).

Thacher, James, *A Military Journal during the American Revolutionary War* (Boston, Richardson & Lord, 1825).

Trumbull, Jonathan, Jr., "Minutes of Occurrences Respecting the Siege and Capture of York in Virginia. . . ." in ser. 1, Vol. 14 *MHS Proceed.*, 331–38.

TRAVELS

Anburey, Thomas, *Travels through . . . Interior Parts of North America* (London, W. Lane, 1791, 2 vols.).

Brissot de Warville, J. P., *New Travels in the United States* (New York, T. and J. Swords, 1792).

Chastellux, François Jean, Marquis de, *Travels in North America, 1780–82* (London, G. G. J. & J. Robinson, 1787, 2 vols.).

Kalm, Peter, *The America of 1750; Peter Kalm's Travels,* in John Pinkerton, 13 *Collection of Travels* 374–700 (London, Longman, Hurst, Rees and Orme, 1808–14).

Rochefoucauld-Liancourt, F. A. F., Duc de, *Voyage dans les États-Unis d'Amérique, 1795–97* (Paris, Du Pont, 1799, 8 vols.).

SECONDARY MATERIALS

BIOGRAPHICAL

Atherton, Gertrude, *Adventures of a Novelist* (New York, Liveright, 1932).

———, *The Conqueror* (New York, Macmillan, 1902).

———, *A Few of Hamilton's Letters* (New York, Macmillan, 1903).

———, "The Hunt for Hamilton's Mother," in 175 *North American Review* (1902), 229–42. (Mrs. Atherton's contributions, with errors of fact, throw light on H's childhood and youth in West Indies.)

Bast, Homer, "Tench Tilghman—Maryland Patriot," in 42 *Maryland Historical Magazine,* 71–94.

Beardsley, E. E., *Life and Correspondence of Samuel Seabury* (Boston, Houghton Mifflin, 1881).

Beveridge, A. J., *Life of John Marshall* (Boston and New York, Houghton Mifflin, 1916–19, 4 vols.).

Boudinot, J. J., *Life of Elias Boudinot* (Boston and New York, Houghton Mifflin, 1896, 2 vols.).

Boyd, G. A., *Elias Boudinot* (Princeton, Princeton University Press, 1952).

Brant, Irving, *James Madison, Father of the Constitution, 1787–1800.* This volume (3) of Brant's detailed biography (Indianapolis, Bobbs-Merrill, 1941+) is pertinent for this period of H's career.

Chipman, Daniel, *Life of . . . Nathaniel Chipman . . . with Selections from his . . . Papers* (Boston, C. C. Little & J. Brown, 1846).

Collins, V. L., *President Witherspoon: A Biography* (Princeton, Princeton University Press, 1925, 2 vols.).

Cross, A. L., *The Anglican Episcopate and the American Colonies* (New York, Longmans, Green, 1902).

Custis, G. W. P., *Recollections and Private Memoirs of Washington* (Philadelphia, J. W. Bradley, 1861).

Drake, F. S., *Life and Correspondence of Henry Knox* (Boston, S. G. Drake, 1873).

Duer, W. A., *Life of William Alexander, Earl of Stirling* (New York, Wiley & Putnam, 1847).

Ford, P. L., *The True George Washington* (Philadelphia, J. B. Lippincott, 1896).

Foster, J., ed. *Alumni Oxoniensis* (Oxford and London, Parker, 1891, 4 vols.).

Freeman, D. S., *George Washington, a Biography* (New York, Scribner, 1948–54, 6 vols.).

Gavin, Frank, "Chandler in Light of His Diary," in *Church History,* June 1932, 3–19.

Greene, G. W., *The Life of Nathanael Greene* (New York, Putnam, 1867–71, 3 vols.).

Hamilton, Allan McLane, *Intimate Life of Alexander Hamilton* (New York, Scribner, 1910).

Hamilton, J. C., *Life of Alexander Hamilton* (Vol. 1, New York, Halsted & Voorhies, 1834; Vol. 2, Philadelphia, Appleton, 1840. No more published).

———, *History of the Republic of the United States . . . as Traced in the Writings of Alexander Hamilton* (New York, Appleton, 1857–64, 7 vols.).

Hoyt, A. H., Sketch of T. B. Chandler in 27 *New England Historical and Genealogical Register,* 227–36.

Humphreys, David, *Life of . . . Israel Putnam* (Philadelphia, W. Mc-Carthy, 1811).

————, *Conduct of Washington Respecting Asgill* (New York, Holland Club, 1859).

Humphreys, Mary G., *Catherine Schuyler* (New York, Scribner, 1897).

Irving, Washington, *Life of George Washington* (New York, Putnam, 1856–59, 5 vols.).

Johnson, W., *Sketches of the Life and Correspondence of Nathanael Greene* (Charleston, privately printed, 1822).

Kapp, Friedrich, *Life of Frederick William von Steuben* (New York, Mason Brothers, 1859).

Klein, M. M., *William Livingston: Exponent of Education in New York* (typescript, College of City of New York, 223 pp.).

Leake, Isaac Q., *Memoir of the Life and Times of . . . John Lamb* (Albany, J. Munsell, 1850).

Livingston, W. F., *Israel Putnam* (New York and London, Putnam, 1901).

Lodge, H. C., *Alexander Hamilton* (Boston and New York, Houghton Mifflin, 1909).

Lossing, B. J., *Life and Times of Philip Schuyler* (New York, Sheldon & Co., 1873, 2 vols.).

McCarthy, E. J., "Lieut. Col. Francis Barber of Elizabethtown," in 50 *NJHS Proceed.* 273–84.

Marshall, John, *Life of George Washington* (Philadelphia, C. P. Wayne, 1804–07, 5 vols.).

Miller, Samuel, *Memoir of the Rev. John Rodgers* (New York, Whiting & Watson, 1813).

Morse, J. T., *Life of Alexander Hamilton* (Boston, Little, Brown, 1876, 2 vols.).

Ness, G. T., Jr., "A Lost Man of Maryland," in 35 *Maryland Historical Magazine,* 315–36.

Oberholtzer, E. P., *Robert Morris* (New York, Macmillan, 1903).

O'Brien, Michael, Jr., *Hercules Mulligan* (New York, P. J. Kenedy, 1937).

Oliver, F. S., *Alexander Hamilton: An Essay on American Union* (London, Constable, 1915).

Patterson, S. W., *Horatio Gates* (New York, Columbia University Press, 1941).

Ramsing, H. U., "Alexander Hamilton og hans mødrene Slaegt. Tidsbilleder fra Dansk Vest-Indiens Barndom," in *Personalhistorisk Tidsskrift,* 59 de Aargang, 10 Rekke, 6 Bind, 1939.

Reed, W. B., *Life and Correspondence of Joseph Reed* (Philadelphia, Lindsay & Blackiston, 1847, 2 vols.).

Schachner, Nathan, *Alexander Hamilton* (New York, Appleton-Century, 1946).

———, ed. "Alexander Hamilton Viewed by His Friends. The Narratives of Robert Troup and Hercules Mulligan," in 3d. scr., 4 *William and Mary Quarterly*, 203–25).

Schneider, H. and C., eds. *Samuel Johnson, President of King's College* (New York, Columbia University Press, 1929, 4 vols.).

Schuyler, G. W., *Colonial New York, Philip Schuyler and His Family* (New York, Scribner, 1885, 2 vols.).

Sedgwick, Theodore, Jr., *Life of William Livingston* (New York, J. & J. Harper, 1833).

Shea, George, *Life and Epoch of Alexander Hamilton* (Boston, Houghton, Osgood, 1879).

"Sketch of the Life and Literary Character of the late President Cooper," in 14 *Analectic Magazine*, 73–6 (Philadelphia, M. Thomas, 1813+).

Smertenko, J. J., *Alexander Hamilton* (New York, Greenberg, 1932).

Sparks, Jared, *Life of Gouverneur Morris* (Boston, Gray & Bowen, 1832).

Spaulding, E. W., *His Excellency George Clinton, Critic of the Constitution* (New York, Macmillan, 1938).

Sullivan, William, *Familiar Letters on Public Characters and Public Events . . . 1783–1815* (Boston, Russell, Odiorne, & Metcalf, 1834).

Tilghman, Oswald, *Memoir of Lieutenant Colonel Tench Tilghman* (Albany, J. Munsell, 1876).

Tuckerman, Bayard, *Life of . . . Philip Schuyler, 1733–1804* (New York, Dodd, Mead, 1903).

Wallace, D. P., *Life of Henry Laurens, with a Sketch of the Life of . . . John Laurens* (New York, Putnam, 1915).

WAR HISTORIES

Bill, A. H., *The Campaign of Princeton, 1776–1777* (Princeton, Princeton University Press, 1948).

Cronau, Rudolf, *The Army of the American Revolution and Its Organization* (New York, R. Cronau, 1923).

DeWitt, Cornelis, *Histoire de Washington et de la fondation de la République des États-Unis* (Paris, E. Perrin, 1884).

Doniol, Henri, *Histoire de la participation de la France . . . a l'établissement des États-Unis* (Paris, Libraire des Archives et de la Société de L'École des Chartes, 1886–92, 5 vols.).

Gordon, William, *History of the Rise, Progress, and Establishment of the Independence of the United States* (London, privately printed, 1788, 4 vols.; New York, Hodge, Allen, & Campbell, 1789, 3 vols.).

Heusser, A. H., *In the Footsteps of Washington* (Paterson, N.J., privately printed, 1921).

Johnston, H. P., *The Campaign of 1776 around New York and Brooklyn* (Long Island Hist. Soc., *Memoirs,* Vol. 3, Brooklyn, 1878).

Knollenberg, Bernhard, *Washington and the Revolution: A Reappraisal* (New York, Macmillan, 1940).

Lossing, B. J., *Pictorial Field Book of the American Revolution* (New York, Harper, 1850–51, 2 vols.).

Lowell, E. J., *The Hessians and Other German Auxiliaries . . . in the Revolutionary War* (New York, Harper, 1884).

Sabine, Lorenzo. *The American Loyalists.* (Boston, C. C. Little & J. Brown, 1847).

Stillé, C. J., *Wayne and the Pennsylvania Line* (Philadelphia, Lippincott, 1893).

Stryker, W. S., *The Battle of Monmouth,* W. S. Myers, ed. (Princeton, Princeton University Press, 1927).

———, *The Battles of Trenton and Princeton* (Boston and New York, Houghton Mifflin, 1898).

Trevelyan, G. O., *The American Revolution* (New York and London, Longmans, Green, 1926–29, 4 vols., extends only to 1778, is continued in his *George the Third and Charles Fox,* same pub., 1921–27, 2 vols.).

Wertenbaker, T. J., "The Battle of Princeton," in *The Princeton Battle Monument* (Princeton, Princeton University Press, 1922).

Whiteley, Emily S., *Washington and His Aides-de-Camp* (New York, Macmillan, 1936).

Woodhull, A. A., *The Battle of Princeton* (Princeton, W. C. Sinclair, 1913).

ANDRÉ-ARNOLD

André, John (1751–80), Defendant, *Minutes of Court of Inquiry upon Case of . . . André, with . . . Documents* (Albany, J. Munsell, 1865).

———, *Proceedings of a Board of General Officers . . . Respecting Major John André, Sept. 29, 1780* (Philadelphia, F. Bailey, 1780).

———, *Proceedings of . . . Trial of . . . André, and Letters Pertaining to . . . Treason of . . . Arnold* (photographed from originals, no place of pub., 1908; copy in NYPL).

Benson, Egbert, *Vindication of . . . Captors of André* (New York, F. S. Hoffman, 1865).

Dawson, H. R., ed. *Record of Trial of Joshua Hett Smith . . . for alleged complicity in . . . Treason of . . . Arnold* (Morrisania, 1866).

Flexner, James T., *The Traitor and the Spy* (New York, Harcourt, Brace, 1953).

Hart, A. B., ed. *The Varick Court of Inquiry* (Boston, Bibliophile Society, 1907).

Inglis, Charles, *The Case of Major John André, . . . who was put to Death by the Rebels* (New York, James Rivington, 1780).

Smith, Joshua Hett, *An Authentic Narrative of . . . Death of Major André* (London, Mathews & Leigh, 1808; New York, E. Duyckinck, 1809).

Van Doren, C. C., *Secret History of the American Revolution* (New York, Viking, 1941).

FEDERALIST

Adair, Douglass, "The Authorship of the Disputed Federalist Papers," in 3d ser., 1 *William and Mary Quarterly*, 97–122.

Beard, C. A., ed. *The Enduring Federalist* (New York, Doubleday, 1948).

Dawson, H. B., ed. *The Foederalist* (New York, Scribner, 1863, Vol. 1 only).

The Federalist: a Collection of Essays written in Favour of the New Constitution (New York, J. and A. M'Lean, 1788, 2 vols.; this is the first edition).

Ford, P. L., and E. G. Bourne, *The Authorship of The Federalist* (Brooklyn, Historical Printing Co., 1897; reprinted from Vol. 2, No. 4, *Am. Hist. Rev.*, 675–87).

Gideon, Jacob, Jr., ed. *The Federalist* (Washington, Gideon, 1818).

Hamilton, J. C., ed. *The Federalist* (Philadelphia, Lippincott, 1864, 2 vols.).

Jay, John (1817–94), *Correspondence between John Jay and Henry B. Dawson, and between James A. Hamilton and . . . Dawson, concerning the Federalist* (New York, J. M. Bradstreet & Son, 1864).

LOCAL HISTORY

Adams, S. A., *The Episcopal Church in the American Colonies. The History of St. John's Church, Elizabethtown, N.J., 1703–* (Philadelphia, Lippincott; New York, T. N. Stanford, 1857).

Alexander and Carnahan, Notices of Distinguished Graduates of College of New Jersey (MS., Princeton University).

Anderson, John, *Memoirs of House of Hamilton* (Edinburgh, J. Anderson, Jr., 1825).

Barber, Gertrude A., Index of Deaths from *New York Evening Post* (typescript, NYPL).

Benedict, W. H., *New Brunswick in History* (New Brunswick, privately printed, 1925).

Bolton, Robert, *History of County of Westchester* (New York, Alexander S. Gould, 1848, 2 vols.).

Caribbeana; "being miscellaneous papers relating to the history . . . , genealogy, topography and antiquities of the British West Indies," ed. V. L. Oliver (London, Mitchell, Hughes and Clarke, vols. 1–6, Jan. 1909–Oct. 1919; no more published).

Carøe, Kristian Frederik, *Den Danske Laegestand,* II, 26 (København and Kristiania, 1906).

Chamber of Commerce of State of New York, *The Charter and By-laws, with a History of the Chamber,* by Charles King (New York, The Chamber, 1855).

————, *Colonial Records of the New York Chamber of Commerce, 1768–1784* (New York, J. F. Trow & Co., 1867).

————, *Catalogue of Portraits in the Chamber of Commerce* (New York, 1924).

Clinton, DeWitt, "Address . . . to Alumni of Columbia College," in W. W. Campbell, *Life and Writings of DeWitt Clinton* (New York, Baker and Scribner, 1849).

Columbia University, *Columbia University Officers and Alumni 1754–1857,* M. H. Thomas, compiler (New York, Columbia University Press, 1936).

Cook, Lewis D., *The Boudinot Mansion* (Elizabeth, N.J., for New Jersey Commission on Historic Sites, 1943).

Dansk Lovbog (Copenhagen, 1683).

De Lancey, E. F., "Original Family Records, Cruger," in 6 *New York Genealogical and Biographical Record,* 74–80.

Dix, W. R., "Old Houses of Elizabethtown," in new series, 8 *NJHS Proceed.,* 169–85.

Domett, H. W., *A History of the Bank of New York, 1784–1884* (Cambridge, Riverside Press, 1902).

Duval, Ruby R., *Guide to Historic Annapolis* (Baltimore, Norman, Remington, 1926).

First Presbyterian Church, Elizabeth, N.J., *Record Book of the Sextons . . . , 1766–1800* (Elizabeth, 1891?).

Franks, David C., *The New-York Directory* (New York, Kollock, 1786).

Gugler *et al., Architectural History of First Presbyterian Church, Elizabeth* (First Presbyterian Church Building Fund, 1947).

Hague, J. T., *Parks and Other Public Properties of the City of Elizabeth* (City of Elizabeth, 1921).

Hasell, B. D., The Cruger Family in America (MS., 1892, in NYPL).

Hatfield, E. F., *History of Elizabeth, New Jersey* (New York, Carlton & Lanahan, 1868).

Holcomb, Thomas, *Sketch of Early Ecclesiastical Affairs in New Castle, Delaware* (Wilmington, Delaware Printing Co., 1890).

Hufeland, Otto, *Westchester County During the . . . Revolution* (New York, Knickerbocker Press, 1926).

Kalmer, P., *The Island of St. Croix as a Winter Residence for Invalids* (St. Croix, C. Dahl, 1871).

Kelley, F. B., compiler; W. R. Dix, ed. *Historic Elizabeth, 1664–1914* (Elizabeth Daily Journal, ca. 1914).

King's College "Matricula or Register" (MS., Columbia University).

———, "Book of Misdemeanours" in King's College, 1771–75, MS., published as *Black Book . . . in King's College* (Columbia University Press, 1931).

Moore, C. C., *The Early History of Columbia College,* ed. M. H. Thomas (New York, Columbia University Press, 1940).

Murray, Nicholas, *Notes, Historical and Biographical, Concerning Elizabethtown* (New York, Columbia University Press, 1941, reprint from ed. of 1844).

Nevins, Allan, *History of Bank of New York and Trust Company, 1784 to 1934* (New York, privately printed, 1934).

New-York Directory and Register, 1789–96 (New York, printed for Hodge, Allen, and Campbell; after 1796 publisher varies).

Paterson, James, *History of the Counties of Ayr and Wigton* (Edinburgh, J. Stillie, 1863–66, 3 vols.).

Pine, J. B., *King's College and the Early Days of Columbia College* (New York, Columbia University Printing Office, 1917).

Platt, Edmund, *The Eagle's History of Poughkeepsie . . . , 1683 to 1905* (Poughkeepsie, Platt & Platt, 1905).

Reynolds, Helen W., *Dutch Houses in the Hudson Valley . . . before 1776* (New York, Payson and Clarke, 1929).

———, *Dutchess County Doorways* (New York, W. F. Payson, 1931).

Riker, James, *Harlem, Its Origin and Early Annals* (New York, privately printed, 1881).

Robertson, George, *A Genealogical Account of the Principal Families in Ayrshire* (Irvine, Cunninghame Press, 1923–25; 3 vols.).

———, *Topographical Description of Ayrshire* (Irvine, Cunninghame Press, 1820).

St. Christopher, *Acts of Assembly . . . of St. Christopher, 1711–1735* (London, J. Baskett, 1739–40). See also abridgment of same, 1711–40, and *Acts of Assembly in . . . Leeward Islands, 1690–1730* (same publisher, 1740).

The St. Croixian Pocket Companion (Copenhagen, privately printed, 1780).

Salley, A. S., Jr., ed. *Minutes of the Vestry of St. Helena's Parish, South Carolina* . . . , *1726–1812* (Columbia, S.C., The State Co., 1919).

Sawyer, R. C., ed. Wills for New York County (typescript, NYPL).

[Schuyler, Georgina] *The Schuyler Mansion at Albany* (New York, De-Vinne Press, 1911).

Smith, Elias D., *The School Interests of Elizabeth, 1664–1910* (Elizabeth, N.J., 1911).

Society of the Cincinnati, *Institution of,* with List of Members of New-York State Society (New York, J. M. Elliott, 1851).

Stevens, W. O., *Annapolis* (New York, Dodd, Mead, 1927).

Stokes, I. N. Phelps, *Iconography of Manhattan Island* (New York, R. H. Dodd, 1915–28, 6 vols.).

Tilghman, Oswald, *Annapolis* [Annapolis, 1925?].

Vandewater, R. J., *The Tourist, or Pocket Manual for Travellers on the Hudson River* (New York, Harper, 1841).

Vrooman, J. J., *Historic Sites of New York State* (Albany, New York State Education Department, 1949).

West, Hans, *Beyträge zur Beschreibung von St. Croix* (trans. from Danish, Copenhagen, C. G. Proft Sohn und Co., 1794).

Westergaard, Waldemar C., *The Danish West Indies under Company Rule (1671–1754), with a Supplementary Chapter, 1755–1917* (New York, Macmillan, 1917).

Wheeler, W. O., and E. D. Halsey, *Inscriptions on Tombstones and Monuments in Burying grounds of* . . . *First Presbyterian Church and St. John's Church at Elizabeth, N.J., 1664–1892* (New Haven, Tuttle, More-house, & Taylor, 1892).

MISCELLANEOUS

Alexander, D. S., *Political History of New York* (New York, Henry Holt, 1906–09, 3 vols.; continued in *Four Famous New Yorkers,* same pub., 1925).

Alexander, S. D., *The Presbytery of New York, 1738–1788* (New York, A. D. F. Randolph & Co., 1888).

Arguments and Judgment of . . . *Mayor's Court* . . . *in a Cause between* . . . *Rutgers and Waddington* (New York, S. Loudon, 1784; see also H. B. Dawson's reprint with historical introduction, Morrisania, N.Y., 1866).

Bancroft, George, *History of the United States* (New York, Appleton, 1888, 6 vols.).

Beard, Charles A., *An Economic Interpretation of the Constitution* (New York, Macmillan, 1935 ed.).

———, *The Republic; Conversations on Fundamentals* (New York, Viking, 1943).

Bein, Alex, *Die Staatsidei Alexander Hamilton in ihrer Entstehung und Entwicklung* (Munich and Berlin, Oldenbourg, 1927).

Bryce, James, *The American Commonwealth* (London, Macmillan, 1888, 2 vols.).

————, *The Predictions of Hamilton and De Tocqueville* (Baltimore, Johns Hopkins University, 1887).

Burgess, J. W., *Political Science and Comparative Constitutional Law* (Boston and London, Ginn, 1902, 2 vols.).

Burnett, Edmund C., *The Continental Congress* (New York, Macmillan, 1941).

Cooper, Myles, *Poems on Several Occasions* (Oxford, W. Jackson, 1761).

———— ("An Exile from America"), stanzas in 46 *Gentleman's Magazine* (London), 326–27.

Davie, M. R., *Negroes in American Society* (New York, Whittlesey House, 1949).

De Ford, Miriam A., *Love-Children; A Book of Illustrious Illegitimates* (New York, Dial Press, 1931).

Dunbar, C. F., "Some Precedents Followed by Hamilton," in his *Economic Essays,* ed. O. M. W. Sprague (New York, Macmillan, 1904).

Evans, Charles, *American Bibliography* (Chicago, 1903–55, printer varies, 13 vols.).

Fiske, John, *The Critical Period of American History, 1783–1789* (Boston, Houghton Mifflin, 1888).

Ford, P. L., *Bibliography . . . Relating to the Adoption of the Constitution* (Brooklyn, no pub., 1896).

————, *Bibliotheca Hamiltoniana* (New York, Knickerbocker Press, 1886).

Ford, W. C., "Alexander Hamilton's Notes in the Federal Convention of 1787," in 10 *American Historical Review,* 97–109.

Freneau, Philip, *Poems . . . Written chiefly during the late War* (Philadelphia, F. Bailey, 1786).

Gallagher, B. G., *Color and Conscience* (New York, Harper, 1946).

Hawkins, Ernest, *Historical Notices of Missions of Church of England in the North American Colonies* (London, B. Fellowes, 1845).

Heitman, F. B., *Historical Register of Officers of the Continental Army . . . 1775–83* (Washington, Rare Book Shop Publishing Co., revised ed., 1914).

Hobbes, Thomas, *Leviathan* (London, Dent, Everyman's library, 1914).

Hume, David, *Essays, Moral and Political* (London, A. Millar, 1748).

————, *History of England* (London, A. Millar, 1754–62, 6 vols.).

Hume, Edgar E., "Early Opposition to the Cincinnati," in 30 *Americana*, 597–638.

Jameson, J. F., *Studies in the History of the Federal Convention of 1787* (Washington, Government Printing Office, 1903).

Jansen, Merrill, *The New Nation: A History of the United States During the Confederation, 1781–89* (New York, Knopf, 1950).

Kent, James, *An Address . . . before the Law Association of the City of New-York* (New York, G. & C. Carvill, 1836).

———, *Commentaries on American Law* (New York, Halsted, 1826–30, 4 vols.).

Knox, Hugh, *The Dignity and Importance of the Gospel Ministry* (New York, Hugh Gaine, 1755).

———, *Discourses on the Truth of Revealed Religion* (London, T. Cadell, 1768, 2 vols.).

———, *A Discourse . . . on Occasion of the Hurricane* (St. Croix, Daniel Thibou, 1772).

———, *Letter to Rev. Jacob Green* (New York, T. & J. Swords, 1809).

———, *Moral and Religious Miscellany* (New York, Hooge & Shober, 1775).

———, *The Probable Sources of Our Saviour's Tears* (no place or publisher, 1765?).

———, *Select Sermons* (Glasgow, R. & A. Foulis, 1782).

———, *Transitory Nature . . . of all Sublunary Things* (Glasgow, A. Foulis, 1782).

Larson, Harold, "Alexander Hamilton; the Fact and Fiction of His Early Years," in 3d. ser., 9 *William and Mary Quarterly* 139–51.

———, "The Birth and Parentage of Alexander Hamilton," in 21 *American Genealogist*, 161–67.)

Locke, John, *An Essay Concerning the True Origin Extent and End of Civil Government* (Boston, reprinted by Edes & Gill, 1773).

Lynch, D. T., "The Growth of Political Parties, 1777–1828," in New York State Historical Association, 6 *History of State of New York*, 37 ff.

Machiavelli, Niccolò, *The Prince,* trans. W. K. Marriott (London, Dent, 1908).

Mitchell, Broadus, "The Man Who Discovered Hamilton," in 69 *NJHS Proceed.,* 88–114.

———, "Practical Proceedings in the Supreme Court of . . . New York," in 11 *Record of Association of Bar of City of New York,* 210–11.

Montesquieu, C. L., *De L'Esprit des Loix* (Leyde, Les Libraires Associés, 1749).

New Jersey Historical Society, *Archives of the State of New Jersey* (Newark, 1900+).

————, *Proceedings* (Newark, 1847+).

New York Society Library, *Catalogue of Books Belonging to the Society, 1813, with Supplement* (New York, C. S. Van Winkle, 1825).

Parkes, H. B., *The American Experience* (New York, Knopf, 1947).

Parrington, V. L., *Main Currents in American Thought* (New York, Harcourt, Brace, 1927–30, 3 vols.).

Postlethwayt, Malachy, *Britain's Commercial Interest Explained and Improved* (London, D. Browne, 1757, 2 vols.).

————, *Great-Britain's True System* (London, A. Millar, 1757).

————, *The Universal Dictionary of Trade and Commerce,* translated from French of [Jacques] Savary [des Brulons] (London, 1751, 1755, 2 vols.).

Presbyterian Church in the United States, General Assembly, *Records of the Presbyterian Church . . . , embracing the Minutes of the Presbytery of Philadelphia, 1706–1788* (Philadelphia, Presbyterian Board of Publication, 1841).

Pufendorf, Samuel von, *Of the Law of Nature and Nations* (London, J. Walthoe, R. Wilkin, 1729).

Root, Elihu, "Address at Hamilton College," *New York Sun,* June 17, 1918.

Sabin, Joseph, *Bibliotheca Americana* (New York, Bibliographical Society of America, 1868–1936, 29 vols., ed., pub. vary).

Spaulding, E. W., *New York in the Critical Period, 1783–1789* (New York, Columbia University Press, 1932).

Strayer, J. R., ed. *The Delegate from New York, or Proceedings of the Federal Convention . . . from the Notes of John Lansing, Jr.* (Princeton, Princeton University Press, 1939).

United States, *Proceedings of a General Court Martial . . . for Trial of Major-General Lee, July 4, 1778* (Philadelphia, J. Dunlap, 1778).

Vattel, Emmerich de, *Le Droit des Gens* (Londres, 1758; another edition Neuchâtel, Societé Typographique, 1773).

Warren, Winslow, *The Society of the Cincinnati, A History* (Boston, Massachusetts Society of Cincinnati, 1929).

Webster, Richard, *A History of the Presbyterian Church in America* (Philadelphia, J. M. Wilson, 1857).

William and Mary Quarterly, 3d ser., Vol. 12, No. 2 (April 1955, Bicentennial Number), *Alexander Hamilton, 1755–1804.*

JOURNALS AND NEWSPAPERS

American Museum (Philadelphia, Mathew Carey, ed. and pub., 1787–92).

Boston Evening Post and General Advertiser (1781+).

Boston Gazette (Edes & Gill, then Benj. Edes & Sons, 1756–93).

Boston News-Letter and New England Chronicle (1762+).

Country Journal, and the *Poughkeepsie Advertiser* (Nicholas Power, 1785+).

Independent Gazetteer (Philadelphia, Eleazer Oswald, 1782–96).

Maryland Gazette (Annapolis, F. and S. Green, 1745+).

New York Daily Advertiser (Francis Childs, 1785+).

New York Evening Post (Wm. Coleman, 1801+).

New York Gazette and Weekly Mercury (Hugh Gaine, 1768–83).

New York Journal, or the General Advertiser (John Holt, 1766+).

New York Packet (Samuel Loudon, 1784+).

Pennsylvania Gazette, and *Weekly Advertiser* (Philadelphia, Hall & Sellers, 1779+).

Pennsylvania Journal and Weekly Advertiser (Philadelphia, Thomas Bradford, 1742–93).

Pennsylvania Packet (Philadelphia, John Dunlap, 1771–90).

Rivington's New York Gazetteer (James Rivington, 1773, and as *Royal Gazette,* 1777–83).

Royal Danish-American Gazette (Christiansted, St. Croix, Daniel Thibou).

MAPS, ETC.

Bauman, Sebastian, "Siege of Yorktown" (Philadelphia, 1782).

Gouvion, J.–B., "Siege of Yorktown" (U.S. Archives, Facsimile No. 21, 1952).

Great Britain, Hydrographic Office, Admiralty, *The West India Pilot* (London, Eyre & Spottiswoode, 1866, 3 vols. Vol. II, pp. 177–83, has sailing directions for St. Croix).

Hills, John, "Siege of Yorktown" (London, Page, 1782).

Jefferys, Thomas, *The West India Atlas* (London, R. Sawyer and J. Bennett, 1775).

Oxholm, Peter L., *Plan of the Island of St. Croix from an Actual Survey, 1794–9* (London, W. Faden, 1809; also New York, Baker, 1839, and Geoffrey Owen, 1948).

Index